The Age of Paradox

THE AGE OF PARADOX

A BIOGRAPHY OF ENGLAND 1841–1851

John W. Dodds

GREENWOOD PRESS, PUBLISHERS
WESTPORT, CONNECTICUT

For Marjorie—companion on
the voyage through strange seas of thought.

Contents

Page

Introductory Note   XV

PART ONE

1841–1844: GROWING PAINS

Chapter

1 1841: Birth of a Decade   3
2 1842: The Year of the Locust   58
3 1843: "To Amuse and Instruct"   102
4 1844: England's Green and Pleasant Land   149

PART TWO

1845–1848: CRISIS

5 1845: Steam; Smoke; Speed   197
6 1846: Political Crisis. England and the Arts. Advertisements.   238
7 1847: Food and Famine   286
8 1848: Revolution and Escape   317

PART THREE

1849–1851: THIS BRAVE NEW WORLD

9   1849: Authorship and the Reading Public   355
10 1850: Metropolis   395
11 1851: The Crystal Palace: Utopia Around the Corner   443
12 1841–1851: Panorama   482

Notes   489

Index   495

List of Illustrations

CHAPTER ONE

Figure   Page

1. Torchlight view of Smithfield Cattle Market   4
2. John Henry Newman   32
3. The *President* steamship   35

4–19. Hill and Fox Talbot photos   38–44
4. The chess players   38
5. Handyside Ritchie and William Henning   39
6. Unknown gentleman   40
7. Elizabeth Johnstone   40
8. Master Miller   40
9. Fisherman and boys at Newhaven   40
10. The birdcage   41
11. Mrs. Webster   41
12. George Combe   41
13. Miss Wilhelmina Fillans   41
14. Conversation   42
15. Newhaven fishwives at St. Andrews   42
16. Garden harvest   43
17. The Finlay children   43
18. James Fairbairn, D.D., and fishwives   44
19. Fox Talbot's printing works   44
20. Rachel as Marie Stuart   48
21. An early pun of *Punch*   51
22. Fireworks at Vauxhall Gardens   51
23. Samuel Warren   55

CHAPTER TWO

24. A ballad broadside   66
25. Prince Albert   70
26. Queen Victoria   70
27. Mrs. Caroline Norton   75
28. Lady Blessington   75
29. Count D'Orsay   76
30. William Harrison Ainsworth   76
31. The waltz *à deux temps*   78
32. Fashions in 1841   79
33. Fashions in 1851   79

34. Lord Ashley (Shaftesbury)   91
35. Child "hurriers" at work in a mine   93
36. Girl dragging coal tubs   93
37. Hewing coal in 1842   93
38. The Monument, Fish Street Hill   96
39. Apsley House, Hyde Park Corner   97
40. The Glaciarium   98
41. Madame Tussaud's exhibition of waxworks   99

CHAPTER THREE

42. Mudie's Lending Library   105
43. Excitement for all the family   114
44. "Travels in the East" for penny readers   123
45. Illustration from Reynolds: *The Mysteries of London*   125
46. Playbill for Browning's *A Blot in the 'Scutcheon*   137
47. Going to the Derby   139
48. The Duke of Wellington   141
49. Trafalgar Square   147

CHAPTER FOUR

50. "General" Tom Thumb, "the American Dwarf"   151
51. A gin palace   164
52. The slums of Smithfield   165
53. Chatsworth, Derbyshire   173
54. Disraeli as a young author   184
55. Announcement by the *Times* of a royal birth   185
56. The new Royal Exchange   187
57. Robert Chambers   188
58. A November fog   192

CHAPTER FIVE

59. Sir Robert Peel   203
60. Viaduct on the Sheffield and Manchester Railway   215
61. London and Northwestern Railway Station   218
62. Croydon's "Gothic" engine house   220
63. "The Excursion Train Galop"   222
64. Map: Railroads of Great Britain, 1841   224
65. Map: Railroads of Great Britain, 1851   225
66. John Leech: "The Railway Juggernaut of 1845"   226
67. George Hudson, "the man wot knows how to get up the steam,"
      by HB   229
68. The *Great Western* steamship   232
69. The *Great Britain* steamship   232
70. Henson's "Ariel" in supposed flight   235

CHAPTER SIX

71. Richard Doyle: "The Land of Liberty"   248
72. The Ethiopian serenaders   252
73. Haydon's "The Banishment of Aristides"   253
74. Exhibition of the Royal Academy   255
75. C. R. Leslie: "Sancho and the Duchess"   257

76. Daniel Maclise: "Malvolio"   257
77. William Etty: "Bathers Surprised"   258
78. William Etty: "The Penitent"   258
79. J. M. W. Turner: "Peace: Burial at Sea"   260
80. Wyatt's colossal statue of Wellington   262
81. The Quadrant, and part of Regent Street   263
82. St. George's Hall, Liverpool   264
83. The Athenaeum Club, Pall Mall   265
84. Villa in the "cottage" style   267
85. The Birmingham Musical Festival   269
86. The perambulating hat   277
87. Beauty by the bottle   278
88 and 89. Cures for everything   280

CHAPTER SEVEN

90. One of the first ether inhalers   289
91. Alexis Soyer   297
92. Jenny Lind   305
93. George Cruikshank   308
94. From Cruikshank's *The Bottle* (Plate VI)   310
95. From *The Drunkard's Children* (Plate I)   310
96. Albert Smith's perilous balloon ascent   314

CHAPTER EIGHT

97. Louis Philippe   321
98. John Leech's comment on the abdication   321
99. Lord Palmerston   325
100. A special constable   329
101. The battle of Widow McCormack's Cabbage Patch   334
102. London drinking water   338
103. Thomas Babington Macaulay   343
104. William Ewart Gladstone   343
105. Lord Brougham   343
106. Michael Faraday   343
107. Exhibition of the electric light in Trafalgar Square   344
108. The sea serpent   345
109. The grocer's shop at Christmas   351

CHAPTER NINE

110. "San Francisco in 1851, with Yerba Buena Island"   358
111. An English gold-rush song   359
112. Charles Dickens in the early forties   366
113. W. M. Thackeray in 1848   366
114. Dickens reading to his friends from his own writings   367
115. Alfred Tennyson   370
116. Robert Browning in the late thirties   370
117. Thomas Carlyle in 1841   370
118. John Ruskin in 1843   370
119. Martin Tupper   372
120. The British Museum on a holiday   376
121. The British Museum reading room   376

122. Dante Gabriel Rossetti: "The Girlhood of Mary Virgin"   383
123. The Astor House riot in New York   384
124. The Mannings, drawn by Robert Cruikshank   388
125. View of the kitchen where O'Connor's body was found   388
126. An execution at Newgate   391
127 and 128. Richard Doyle, in *Punch*   393

CHAPTER TEN

129. Great Protectionist meeting in Drury Lane Theatre   397
130. Hyde Park   401
131. The soirée   401
132. General view of London from the Southwark side   403
133. Hyde Park Corner and Apsley House   404
134. Belgrave Square   404
135. A new shop in Regent Street   408
136. The street stationer   412
137. The street seller of crockery ware   412
138. The London coffee stall   412
139. The baked-potato man   412
140. The London dustman   413
141. The London costermonger   413
142. Long-song seller   413
143. Song illustrations   413
144 and 145. Street "cocks" and ballads   414
146. A "life, trial, and execution" broadside   416
147. Haymarket Theatre   418
148. Covent Garden Theatre   418
149. Burlington Arcade   419
150. Egyptian Hall, with Tom Thumb's carriage   419
151. Drury Lane Theatre: wrestling scene in *As You Like It*   421
152. Astley's Amphitheatre   421
153. Macready delivering his farewell address   425
154. The Cider Cellars, by Doyle   426
155. Cross section of Wyld's model of the globe   429
156. The Gothic Aviary at the Colosseum   430
157. Bell's patent "locomotive" balloon   431
158. The Crystal Palace in its early stages of construction   433
159. John Everett Millais: "Christ in the House of His Parents"   435
160. Cardinal Wiseman   439

CHAPTER ELEVEN

161. The Crystal Palace   445
162. Joseph Paxton   448
163. Going to the Exhibition   448
164. Opening of the Great Exhibition   450
165. South transept   450
166. Interior of transept   451
167. Main avenue, looking east   451
168. Main avenue, looking west   452
169. Kiss's "Amazon"   452
170. Power's "Greek Slave"   453
171. E. Davis's "Venus and Cupid"   453

172. Statuary in the main avenue — 453
173. Ornamental chimney piece — 454
174. Fireplace — 454
175. Cabinet — 455
176. Four-foot vase in silver electroplate — 455
177. Group of plate — 455
178. Mahogany sideboard — 456
179. Walnut chairs — 456
180. The "dreamer's" chair — 457
181. Ridgway and Co.'s cabinet water-closet — 457
182. Copper bath — 457
183. Portable steam engine, threshing machine, and grain drill — 458
184. Crompton's "Folkstone" locomotive — 458
185. Applegarth's vertical printing press — 459
186. McCormick's reaper — 460
187. Model of floating Seaman's Church at Philadelphia — 460
188. The yacht *America* — 465
189. Prince Albert's model lodginghouse — 474
190. Louis Kossuth — 476
191. Louis Napoleon — 479
192. *Punch* on "Bloomerism" — 480

STRICTLY interpreted, no historical period has a life of its own apart from the past of which it is the projection and the future to which it leads. Yet in a sense each day has its own biography. It is born, reaches high noon, lives on into its turbulent or passive afternoon, and dies into night. To plunge, therefore, into a decade in mid-nineteenth-century England, to feel its pulse beat, to establish its rhythms, to catch the ebb and flow of its passions, delights, miseries, and even its boredoms, to observe its confusions and its glorious affirmations and certainties—this is to get a sense of life lived. There is an essential biographical integrity for every such spot in time.

More than most decades the 1840's were an age of paradox—and this beyond the paradoxes which are inherent in the human dilemma or the more specialized ones which some people like to think are uniquely English. Even the English themselves saw that the mid-century was full of contradictions. It could be called, with equal truth, an Age of Bewilderment, an Age of Hope, an Age of Anxiety, an Age of Accomplishment, an Age of Enthusiasm, an Age of Desperation. In religion, in manners, in economic theory and practice, in the whole complex and delicate scale of social, political, and industrial adjustments the age stood rooted in the past—from even the debris of which it had no desire to be detached by cataclysm. But at the same time it kept a hopeful eye cocked toward the New Jerusalem.

The main drift of the 1840's is easy to identify. It is much more difficult to determine the contribution that the tributaries and even the eddies made to that current. Some of that which we are able to see, a hundred years afterward, as subtly important, did not seem so to the early Victorians. And much which excited them day by day has been lost in the inconsequential backwash of time. Yet everything which happened to them *was* important—in terms of the intellectual and emotional temper of the age. Sibthorp was of less moment than Palmerston, Martin Tupper than Browning. But Sibthorp meant much to the constituency which returned him to the Commons time after time, and Tupper was adored where Browning was unread. It is the task of this book to sift out from the solid mass which is history (which properly includes much more of the everyday than of the catastrophic) the particular combination of trivia, curiosa, and the significant event which gives shadow and highlight to a portrait of a people. Attitudes meant much, and attitudes are more difficult to define than ministerial crises or diplomatic victories.

This is not, therefore, a history of the great books, or great ideas, or even the great people and events of a decade—except as those ideas, personalities, and events engaged the interest and attention of the ordinary sensual Englishman. Frequently these momentous things did impinge upon his consciousness. But not infrequently the seminal ideas or the creative acts which molded the future were buried under waves of custom or indifference. Occasionally, under the impact of high circumstance, the Englishman became aware that he was making history, or at least participating in it. It was more likely, however, that as he got out of bed each morning he felt much as the reader of these notes feels at this moment: a spectator of large events, one who was important chiefly to himself and to a small circle around him; grateful for small blessings; a little harried and sometimes a little desperate; with fleeting aches and pains, with hungers and desires and little vanities; but for the most part busy and hopeful, as human beings are, in the span that separates their light from the darkness.

The present volume is meant to rescue, insofar as it can be caught, what the decade of the 1840's meant to this Englishman—the immediacy of it, the whole welter of seemingly non-sequential events in the midst of which he lived, from the Irish famine to the latest addition to the royal nursery to the Rowland's Macassar Oil with which he groomed his locks. Behind the event lies the matrix of the culture which gave it form and pattern, and over it the perspective which to all omniscient biographers is their right for having been born a century later.

A NOTE ON SOURCES

There is no bibliography appended to this book; for beyond indicating the obvious standard historical and biographical sources, it would be bootless to recount in detail the hundreds of volumes of minor memoirs, letters, pamphlets, parliamentary investigations, critical and descriptive books, novels, magazines, and newspapers, as well as the wide variety of ephemera, which lay across the trail of this particular exploration. Some of that which illuminates the folkways of a people a century ago emerges from the driest of statistical reports. Much of the non-statistical (and still more important) evidence is very difficult to come by nowadays. Obviously of no long-run significance, it was not the sort of stuff to which crowded libraries wanted to give shelf space. What at the time would have been the cheapest and commonest record of the tastes and interests of the period has become, not expensive, but extraordinarily difficult to find. One wonders what library today is making the definitive collection of the so-called "comic" books which historians of American culture a hundred years from now will hear of as an important social phenomenon, but which will have completely disappeared by then.

Not the least of the pleasant surprises for the explorer in this field is the way in which, grubbing amid all sorts of unconsidered trifles, he comes across material of high relevance for social portraiture. One example of this, among many, would be records of the actual circulation of newspapers and magazines, and of the sale of books—important cultural data which have been too little studied and which pop up in the most unexpected places.

As a whole, however, the recollection which remains does not concern the difficulty of finding materials sufficient to reveal the continuum of a decade, but the difficulty of determining what to leave out! The result, of course, is that this "biography," like any history, is merely one man's reading of the character of an age.

The illustrations included here are gathered from a wide range of strictly contemporary sources—catalogues, pamphlets, broadsides, books, magazines, and newspapers. Some of the photographs I owe to the courtesy of the Science Museum and the Victoria and Albert Museum. A number of the Hill and Fox Talbot photographs were generously made for me by the Royal Photographic Society from copies in its possession.

For the release of time which made possible the writing of this book I am indebted to generous fellowships from the Wenner-Gren Foundation and the Guggenheim Memorial Foundation.

JOHN W. DODDS

Stanford University
May, 1952.

PART ONE

1841 - 1844

* * *

GROWING

PAINS

CHAPTER ONE

1841 * Birth of a Decade

FRIDAY, JANUARY 1ST.
SUNRISE: 8:08; SUNSET: 4:00. TEMPERATURE AT LONDON, 9 A.M.: 37.8°.
SKY OVERCAST. BRISK WEST WIND THROUGHOUT THE DAY AND INTO THE
EVENING.

ACROSS all England the New Year had been "let in" at midnight. Church bells had rung the length of the land—in Middlesex and Lincolnshire, in Staffordshire and Devon, in Dorset and Yorkshire. Carols had been sung, and there was dancing in the streets. In hundreds of churches the pious had watched the old year out with religious services. Crockford's gambling club in St. James's Street was ablaze with lights, but at midnight old Crockford had made his farewell speech announcing his retirement. It was the end as well as the beginning of an era.

The noise of the merrymakers died away, and London was for the most part quiet. But down in Billingsgate the market was an island of seaweedy smell and activity, brilliantly lighted by streaming flares of gaslights. It was market morning, too, at Smithfield. All night by Whitechapel Road and through Highgate Archway drovers had been

[3]

Figure 1. Torchlight view of Smithfield Cattle Market

herding thousands of cattle, sheep, and pigs into central London. By 2 A.M. the confusion at Smithfield had reached its height—a lurid scene of milling oxen and sheep and barking dogs, the darkness broken by scores of smoking torches. In surrounding streets the rows of silent shops were punctuated by the occasional lighted windows of a coffee shop serving early breakfast to workmen. Soon in the morning twilight apprentices and clerks would be taking down shutters, and the hum of a great city's activity would begin.

Dawn came slowly out of the North Sea. It crept up the Thames, past the Isle of Dogs, lighting the crowded masts of the ships at anchor in the docks. It caught the top of the Monument and the dome of St. Paul's. It rolled over the quiet houses in the West End squares and over the fetid courts and alleys of St. Giles and Saffron Hill. It touched Apsley House on the edge of Hyde Park, where the great duke lay asleep behind iron shutters. Down Constitution Hill the gray mass of Buckingham Palace began to take shape—innocent of royalty, however, which lay on youthful pillows at Windsor. Slowly the gaping foundations for the new Royal Exchange emerged from the dusk—as did the scaffolding of the new Houses of Parliament, the boarded fence at the top of the stairs leading down to the steamboat station at the north end of Waterloo Bridge, the enclosure hiding the construction of the Nelson Monument in Trafalgar Square.

The dawn rolled west across far fields and villages, over moors and into towns, through congested manufacturing districts and seaports and on into the Irish Sea. A new year, and a new decade, was born. It was a particular moment in history.

This new decade did not yet quite feel that it was "Victorian." More than most times it was full of paradoxes and anachronisms, and of some of them its people were painfully aware. Their certainties were mingled with confusions, their hearts with their heads, their hopes with a quivering uncertainty. The virtues which were later to become self-conscious were still tentative. The deep-rooted national disbelief in profound and sudden changes was being challenged by a new specter of equalitarianism. Yet foreigners still noticed the British complacency (particularly as far as their attitude toward the foreigners themselves was concerned), and even the more fervid of the equalitarians would have argued the general superiority of British culture and institutions. A Daniel O'Connell could whip a vast audience into a fervor of anathema against the Government, and in the same speech raise roars of affectionate concern for the dear young Queen who needed to be protected against her evil ministers. The skeptical foreigner was unaware that what seemed like hypocrisy was only the Englishman's ability to wake up each morning and believe the impossible. To believe, for example, that there were economic laws supporting predatory individualism so completely that it would be futile to question them (no one would think of repealing the law of supply and demand, would he?) and yet to spend his time formulating legislation to neutralize those economic commandments. For the Englishman to emerge safely from the troubled forties into the later glow of what we call Victorianism was to require a godlike indifference to consistency. Nowhere is the record easier to read than in this decade with its prophets and its false prophets, its gloom and its confidence, its retreats and its consolidations, its panaceas and its despairs.

The cynicism of the Regency days in matters of public and private morality was dying out, yet there were still overtones of the old coarseness and brutality. Dueling was forbidden by law, but Lord Cardigan, caught in a particularly flagrant violation, could be acquitted in 1841 by his peers in the House of Lords on a most absurd technicality. The same Cardigan ordered the flogging of a man in the Eleventh Hussars; whereupon his commanding officer issued a general order, condemning such conduct only because it took place on a Sunday, during divine

service.* Public executions with their attendant grossness aroused the
horror of such people as Dickens and Thackeray, but continued until
1868.† Prostitutes frequented the theaters openly, yet decent public
sentiment was on the side of Macready when he tried to banish them
from Drury Lane. Hoodlumism among some of the wilder sprigs of
the aristocracy was not uncommon: Lord Waldegrave assaulted policemen, and Henry, the Marquess of Waterford, led gangs who out of
mere high spirits went around stealing door knockers.

In journalism particularly the confusion between the old looseness
and the encroaching morality was evident. Obscene ballads were no
longer hawked on the streets, and there was an increasing emphasis
upon the purity and "moral influence" of books and magazines to be
admitted to the family circle. The scandal sheets which throve in the
heyday of Theodore Hook's *John Bull* and Westmacott's *Age* were
commonly frowned upon now, though Renton Nicholson with his
Town and Barnard Gregory with the *Satirist* made low journalism,
scandalmongering, and obscenity pay. Journalism could be, by modern
standards, bitterly vindictive and insulting, but there was growing agreement that the seamier side of Victorian delinquencies should not appear
in the public prints. Yet no one seemed to comment on the coarseness
of the advertising which ran side by side with the purified columns
of the newspapers and magazines. On January 8, 1841, the sedate *Times*
ran an advertisement for Wray's Balsamic Pills, "a certain cure for
gonorrhea," and about the same time announced the following books:

A Practical Essay on the Debilities of the Generative System.
Manhood: the cause of its Premature Decline with Plain Directions
   for its perfect Restoration.
The Aegis of Life: a comprehensive physiological history of manhood
   and its decay owing to the progress of self-abuse, intemperance, or
   debility.
The Syphilist for "those suffering from an invidious complaint, so frequently resulting from indiscretion or gaiety."

The age which eventually became hypersensitized to the blush on a
maiden's cheek took this in its stride in 1841, as also the advertisement
in the *Times* of January 7th extolling the genial benefits of Dr. Scott's
Aperitive Fountain which "is so convenient that it may be used by a

---

* The even-tempered *Spectator* said on this occasion: "Lord Cardigan seems
to be like pitch—he defiles every man who handles him."
† England was less medieval than her neighbors, however. Early in January,
in Prussia, the murderer of the Bishop of Ermeland was executed publicly on
the wheel, "being broken from below upwards."

child, and so portable and well closed that (containing a pint of liquid) it may be put into the pocket. By its means a little water acts upon the bowels as effectively as a dose of opening medicines . . ." Squeamishness did not come in immediate access to the early Victorians.

It was a decade, too, from which enthusiasm and color had not disappeared. It was romantic—romantic in religion, whether medievalism or muscular Christianity; romantic in architecture, in literature, in art, in love of household ornament, in dress. Drab uniformity had not yet taken hold of men's fashions. Beau Brummell had died as recently as 1840, and the age of Victorian dandies was not past. D'Orsay's waistcoats and cravats were the wonder of the fashionable world. The young Disraeli had risen to deliver his maiden address in the Commons with hair carefully curled, wearing a bottle-green coat and a white waistcoat covered with gold chains. Bulwer affected a dandyism; even young Matthew Arnold, nineteen years of age in 1841, put on French airs and dressed grandly. Men could and did wear clothes of almost every color. Short frock coats with deep velvet collars; white or black stocks; shirt cuffs turned back over coat sleeves; low-cut waistcoats of wildly daring patterns; gray or white top hats—this was the dress of the gentleman of fashion or of him who wanted to be thought such. Standardization in dress and in character was stealing in but was not yet universal.

In 1841 those who were to be remembered by later generations as bearded patriarch were, for the most part, young men. This is important to keep in mind. Carlyle, fresh from *Heroes and Hero-Worship*, was forty-six. Pusey, Macaulay, and Chadwick were forty-one. Newman had just turned forty, as had Lord Ashley. Tennyson was thirty-two; Browning, twenty-nine; Thackeray, thirty; Dickens, twenty-nine. Bulwer and George Borrow were thirty-eight; Disraeli and Cobden, thirty-seven; John Bright, thirty. John Stuart Mill was thirty-five and Gladstone thirty-two—as was also Charles Darwin. David Livingstone, who this year arrived in Africa and made his first journey into the interior, was only twenty-eight. Charlotte Brontë was twenty-five; George Eliot, twenty-two. John Ruskin and Charles Kingsley were youngsters of twenty-two. These people had already begun to shape the ideas and feelings of the Victorian age. Their energy was that of young men and women coming into the prime of life. And on the throne there was a young woman of twenty-two, with a husband the same age.

But most of the Englishmen who picked up their copies of the *Times* or read *Lloyd's Weekly Newspaper* in the coffee shop on January 1st

were unaware that they were making history. Through all the multiple
and complex gradations of English society—including those members
of the aristocracy who were quietly satisfied that they *were* history
—the feeling, as in all ages, was that of spectatorship rather than participation. No narrative such as this can make that obvious fact too
clear. The real concerns of life in the many Englands coexisting (city,
country, town; castle and hovel), were sleep, food, the begetting of
offspring, the winter fogs, that gnawing toothache, the children's head
colds, the maid who was leaving Saturday next; and, above all, the daily
task that consumed most of the waking hours in the house in Chelsea,
the shop in Regent Street, the field in Devon, or the mill in Manchester.

The later recorder cannot penetrate far into this complex, which is
the life of any age and the real stuff of history. Routine is not news.
Yet certain rhythms may be established, and identifications made of
those aspects of the current scene, trivial or important, which held the
common interest of all. Much of that which seemed important to the
average Englishman is forgotten. Much that is remembered seemed at
the time of slight importance to him. What, in this first week of the
new year, was discussed across the breakfast table, from the state of
trade to the capture of the forlorn escaped eagle in Regent's Park; from
railway accidents to the announcement that Madame Tussaud & Sons
had added a full-length model of the late Signor Paganini to their collection, and that the flea show at 209 Regent Street was now displaying ropedancers, blacksmiths, and duelists? Let us begin with a
panorama.

Stilton cheese is advertised at 1s. per pound, rich and ripe. Hams,
7½d. and 9d.; Hampshire bacon, 7d.; Dorset butter, 1s.*

There were faraway wars in Afghanistan and China, reports of which
were trickling through five weeks after leaving Bombay and three
months after leaving China. Tensions were also mounting with the
United States over the latter's arrest of a British subject.

At the London theaters, Mme. Vestris was playing Oberon in *A Midsummer Night's Dream* at Covent Garden. *Venice Preserved* was at the
Royal Victoria. But it was the accompanying Christmas pantomimes
which were filling the houses nightly. *Tom Thumb* at the Haymarket;
The Castle of Otranto, or, Harlequin and the Giant Helmet at Covent

---

* It must be remembered that the purchasing power of the pound sterling in
the 1840's was the equivalent of £1, 15s. in 1937, and the equivalent of—what at
the time this note catches the reader's eye? Some £3 in 1952.

Garden ("the moonlit ruins and the Castle of Otranto at sunset are fine pictures"). In the harlequinade of the performance one of the scenes showed the Temple of the Drama shored up by Melodrama and Spectacle—a parable of the times! *Harlequin and the Enchanted Fish,* from the *Arabian Nights,* was at the Adelphi; *Goosey Gander* at the Surrey. The promenade concerts at Drury Lane languished amid such competition.

Across the Channel, the French were indulging in some ostentatious saber-rattling. The French press was screaming against England and supporting M. Thiers, who was heading a committee to throw up fortifications around Paris. All this had grown out of the strained international relations accompanying English participation in a brief foray against Mehemet Ali of Egypt, who had seized control of Syria from the Turks. In a glorious naval action "to maintain the integrity and independence of the Ottoman empire," which aroused great enthusiasm in England, the allied fleet on November 3d, under command of Admiral Stopford, had bombarded and captured St. Jean d'Acre. (British losses: 22 killed; Egyptians killed, 2,000.) As concerned France, there was hope that the new ministry of M. Guizot, "the recognized friend of peace," might quiet the Gallic breastbeating. The apprehensions of the people may be judged, however, by an event accompanying a violent thunderstorm which visited London early on the morning of Sunday, the third. The storm damaged Spitalfields Church, and was particularly severe over Woolwich where, the *Times* reported, "from the distant noise of the thunder appearing like the noise made by a park of artillery when marching, many persons jumped out of their beds in the firm belief that the French had landed, and were engaged in deadly contest with our troops."

Item: "the Royal Cheese is ready for presentation to Her Majesty. Made by the farmers and yeomanry of West Pennard, in Somersetshire, it is three-feet-one-inch across and twenty-two inches high, ornamented with the Royal Arms and at present on exhibit at Egyptian Hall, Piccadilly. A song has been composed by Mr. T. Williams, and inscribed to the farmers of the West of England. The song has been sent to the Royal Palace, and approved by the Queen and the Royal Consort."

The sufferings of the poor were currently aggravated by the cold weather, which by Thursday the seventh sent the thermometer to 10°. Yorkshire had snow of six to twenty inches. In Kensington Gardens the attendance of skaters was most numerous, said the *Times,* "and of great respectability." On the Serpentine the skaters were estimated at 14,000 to 16,000; in St. James's Park, at 10,000. Few of them came from

Bethnal Green or Spitalfields, however, where the London Committee for Nightly Shelter to the Houseless announced that it had given 5,626 nightly lodgings and distributed 13,347 rations. The Association for the Relief of the Poor of the City of London had delivered 2,300 bushels of coal and 27,600 pounds of potatoes to poor applicants. In Bethnal Green destitution and starvation were spread over the parish to an alarming degree. Of the 70,000 inhabitants of the parish, most of them weavers, the majority were suffering extreme hardship.

England was in the midst of a trade depression. The *Nottingham Review* might report that "the drawers and pantaloon trade is still in good condition," but wages had been low ever since the commercial crisis of 1837. The condition of the hand-loom weavers was notoriously bad. Many mills were idle, and crowds of workers were destitute in Manchester, Stockport, Birmingham, and Liverpool. In Leeds there were 19,936 people with only 11¼d. per head a week to live on.[1]* Wheat was 60s. per quarter, with a duty on foreign wheat of 27s. 8d.

This was fertile soil for the Chartists, who were gathering their forces again after the debacle which followed the widespread riots of 1839. In November of that year a mob at Newport, Monmouthshire, led by John Frost and Zephaniah Williams, had been subdued only after the soldiery had fired upon it. Frost and Williams had been transported for life. And in 1840 Feargus O'Connor, another Chartist leader, had been sentenced to eighteen months' imprisonment in York Castle for libel. As 1841 opened, itinerant agitators were holding new mass meetings. On Christmas Day 5,000 assembled at Merthyr Tydfil, the center of the large ironworks of Monmouthshire, to petition for the release of Frost and his companions. On January 4th thousands of the London Chartists met on Clerkenwell Green, in freezing weather. Fifteen hundred of them repaired to an assembly room where they sang with great gusto the *Marseillaise:*

> March on, march on,
> All hearts resound
> To Liberty or death.

On the same day, at Newport, in a field adjoining the Salutation Inn, a thousand inhabitants of the town gathered also to protest the transportation of the Chartist leaders. On January 4th the *Times* reported the meeting in great detail.

The time was rapidly approaching when British "hearts of oak"

---

* Arabic figures refer to notes at the end of the book.

could not afford to shrug off this sort of thing. Yet there were hopes on the part of many that sweet reasonableness would win, or at least that argument could convince. A typical example of this occurred at Norwich at a meeting of the Society for the Propagation of the Gospel in Foreign Parts. The Chartists consistently followed a plan whereby they attended meetings called for other purposes and tried to take over the proceedings. According to custom, the Chartists disturbed this meeting, which had to adjourn. The scene is made very clear by a reporter: A Chartist took the chair, with cheers from his party. But one of the several members of the original meeting gave him into the custody of a policeman, who removed him from the hall. Increasing confusion. Some of the members of the Society tried to argue with the crowd. By this time most of the ladies had left the hall, as had many of the supporters of the original meeting. (Cries of "We want more bread and less Bibles, more pigs and less parsons.") The hall gradually emptied, but a Mr. Crofts still stood his ground, arguing with the Chartists. "You complain of the rich, but you could not live without them." (Cries of "Oh, yes, we could; give us the land and we will try.") A Chartist leaped to his feet to compare the favorable conditions of the slaves in the West Indies with the degradation of English workmen. "I am a slave to the classes above me . . . I work hard, and cannot get food for myself and children . . . I am whipped in the belly, while the black slave was only beaten on his fat back." The meeting was adjourned, but the report was not comfortable reading for the New Year's breakfast table.

Currently, too, the *Times* was carrying on a campaign against the New Poor Law, a Whig measure, which many members of all classes combined to condemn as an aggravation of the prevailing discontent. According to the provisions of this law passed in 1834 no more outdoor relief was to be given except to invalids and the aged. All those physically able to work, and their families, were, if destitute, forced into the large union workhouses. Husbands and wives were separated, and conditions were made as uncomfortable as possible on the assumption that loafers would therefore stay off relief. There was reason behind the Act itself: heretofore poor relief had been counted on by farmers, particularly in the south of England, to eke out the miserable wages they paid to laborers. The result of this policy was that wages were depressed, the poor rates excessive, and the people pauperized. But the new law brought an equal train of injustice in its wake, and its administration seems to have been unsatisfactory. The *Times* liked to point out dreary, unfeeling aspects of the new law—that 292 ounces of food were allotted weekly to a convicted felon in the penitentiary and 145 ounces to an able-bodied man in a union workhouse.

During those days the *Times* ran many columns from special correspondents reporting the violent ill-treatment and flogging of four pauper girls in the Hoo Union-Workhouse, and accounts of similar abuses at the Eton Workhouse.

Panaceas for this "condition-of-England question" abounded. Many well-intentioned people believed that a reduction of drunkenness on the part of the laboring classes would set everything right. Public houses and beer shops dotted the streets in every town.* It was small wonder that desperate and hungry operatives tried to stupefy their misery with gin. Nevertheless, the cause of temperance seemed to make some headway, particularly with the Irish under the leadership of Father Theobald Mathew, who had organized huge temperance demonstrations all over Ireland. Sometimes the crush of people was so great at his assemblies that the cavalry called out to preserve order were swept off the ground. Thousands were eager even to touch Father Mathew's coat. At Nenagh 20,000 persons took the pledge in one day, and 100,000 in Galway in two days. The next year he was to visit Scotland and distribute his temperance pledge to masses of people in Edinburgh, Glasgow, and other cities. In the meantime, in Glasgow, 10,000 of the Irish population had taken the pledge. On January 2d 3,000 of these paraded through the streets of the city—led by a band and several people carrying flags. All wore medals and white ribbons and carried flags on which were portraits of Father Mathew. When the priest later came to London he was met by a crowd of 20,000 on Blackheath, where the publicans ineffectually attempted an opposition display. All this was at least a finger in the social dyke.

Other temperance meetings were held too. On the last day of the old year in Dublin, Daniel O'Connell, the Irish "liberator," addressed a large crowd in the Rotunda. "A few respectable ladies graced the platform," wrote the *Times* reporter, "and Mr. O'Connell took the chair at half-past 7 o'clock. . . . It was four months, he said, since he had become a teetotaller, and he solemnly assured the company that he was never in better health in his life. . . . As for stuffs and cordials,

---

* In Manchester alone, excluding Salford, in 1850, there were 475 public houses and 1,143 beer houses—one for every eighty men of twenty years of age and upwards. In Edinburgh the number of persons found so drunk in the streets as to make it necessary to take them to the police office for protection increased from ,225 in 1842 to 7,575 in 1846. (Letter from Wm. Kerr, police officer, Edinburgh. ee *A Plea on Behalf of Drunkards and Against Drunkenness*, by Thomas Guthrie, dinburgh, 1851.)

he hated them; and he sincerely recommended his fellow-countrymen to avoid all those rascally bowel cordials (Laughter)."*

About the same time O'Connell, the most popular leader in the agitation for repeal of the Union, had things to say about another measure being urged as a palliative for the current social distress: emigrat on. As reported in the *Times* of January 6th, O'Connell "again took occasion to allude to the subject of emigration, which he said required their utmost vigilance, as attempts were being made to get the people to emigrate to Texas, Jamaica, and other pestilential places. If any were determined to emigrate let them go to the Canadas, Australia, the Northern States of America, etc., but let them not go into the destructive miasmata of Texas or Jamaica, thereby risking their own immediate death."

> Item: Court Circular. Windsor, Thursday. "Her Majesty and his Royal Highness Prince Albert walked for some time this morning on the terrace of the Castle."
> Item: Court Circular. "Her Majesty and Prince Albert fell through the ice at Frogmore on Tuesday last, he skating, and she following him around in her sledge. But they were extricated with only a slight inconvenience from the cold water."

There was little political talk in this first week of the new year. Parliament would not reassemble for three weeks, and people were waiting to see whether the prophecies of the precarious position of the Whig majority would prove to be true. In lieu of political excitement there were a number of mildly exciting fires, notably the total destruction of the sugar house of Messrs. J. Goodhart and Sons in Ratcliffe Highway, with an estimated loss of £16,000. At Dundee, Scotland, on the morning of the third, a violent fire destroyed a group of 700-year-old churches.

The police courts in London handled cases of drunken driving, theft of a Bible, rape, assault and battery, and a series of commitments of enthusiastic celebrators of the holiday season. At the head police office

---

* At the same time, however, the proportion per head of spirits (not beer or wine) consumed in the United Kingdom rose steadily from .80 gallons in 1841 to .99 gallons in 1846. The actual number of gallons charged with duty for home consumption in the United Kingdom in 1842 was 18,841,890; in 1851, 23,076,000. This increase of 22 per cent occurred while the population of England and Wales was increasing 13 per cent. In Ireland the increase of consumption of liquor was even sharper. In spite of a loss of population there of 1,659,330, or 20 per cent, between 1841 and 1851, more liquor was drunk in 1851 than in 1841: 7,550,000 gallons as against 6,485,000 gallons. (*Journal of the London Statistical Society,* December, 1852, p. 363.)

on Sunday morning forty were charged with drunkenness, twenty with "tippling." A John Chivers, "a pale-faced man, with a long beard, a baker by trade, but who calls himself a preaching prophet, was charged with assaulting the police in the execution of their duty. Rowland, a police constable, stated that the prisoner, who had predicted that the world would cease to exist in 1842, occupied a house in Mile-end-road, at the rent of 4s. a week, and had got 7l. in debt to his landlord. Five men could hardly secure him and take him into custody. . . ."

At Mansion House, reported the *Times* for January 2d, "Matilda Stratford, a woman of great strength of body, was brought before the Lord Mayor, charged with having beaten a man, and also with having, upon being taken into custody, whopped some policemen, and broken several panes of glass.

"The prisoner, who was said to have fought several men at different times, swaggered up to the bar as if she feared no man, and displayed an awful clenched fist. The complainant said that, without receiving the slightest provocation, the virago attacked him. 'Mind your eye, old fellow,' said she, and in an instant gave him a straight-forward pelt between the eyes. She then tore his coat and shirt, and when the policemen were called to his assistance she turned upon them and fastened upon them like a tiger.

"The policeman said that the woman had been frequently charged with having assaulted men, women, and children. When she was tipsy she did not care how many were opposed to her.

"The Lord Mayor.—Why, Matilda, this is a very bad account that I hear of you.

"Prisoner.—It is, indeed, my Lord.

"The Lord Mayor.—What can you say for yourself?

"Prisoner.—I'm blest if I remember anything about it.

"The Lord Mayor.—What! you were so much intoxicated that you forget what happened?

"Prisoner.—Just so, please your Lordship. Wasn't I precious lumpy! But it is all the fault of the new year.

"The Lord Mayor.—Well, you shall begin the new year at the tread-mill.

"Inspector Woodruff said that wherever she appeared she excited terror, and that her knack of breaking windows from long experience was such that some publicans thought it safer to let her have drink for nothing than, by refusal, hazard their taproom windows.

"The prisoner, who laughed at the recital of her qualifications, was then committed to prison."

Not a few new books were advertised in the newspapers for this first week. Obtainable at the bookshops and the lending libraries were the following:

The Second Funeral of Napoleon, by Michael Angelo Titmarsh. Thackeray's ironic account of ceremonials with which the French brought Napoleon's body from St. Helena and reinterred it at Paris.

The Thirst for Gold, a novel in 3 vols. by Miss Burdon.

Tippoo Sultaun, an Historical Romance, 3 vols., by Capt Meadows Taylor, author of *Confessions of a Thug.*

Principles of Geology, by Charles Lyell, sixth edition, revised, with 250 illustrations, 3 vols.

Important Truths in Simple Verse, Being a collection of Original Poems on Religious and Miscellaneous Subjects, for the Use of Young Persons.

The Palace Martyrs: a Satire, by the Hon . . ., author of *The Princess Royal.*

Britain Betrayed, or, The French Bubble Burst. "A brief but spirited poetical effusion" [ran the blurb]. "The author deals some hard blows at the French."

The Gardeners' Chronicle, first issue (weekly).

The Ecclesiastical Almanac for the Year of Our Lord 1841.

The Book of Popery, by Ingram Robbin, M.A., a fifth edition.

Light in Darkness, or, The Records of a Village Rectory.

The Scriptural Character of the English Church Considered in a Series of Sermons, with copious notes and illustrations, by the Rev. Derwent Coleridge, M.A.

The Secretary of Macchiavelli, or, The Siege of Florence, by Daniel MacCarthy, 3 vols.

Gregory VII, a Tragedy, with an Essay on Tragic Influence, by R. H. Horne. "A Magnificent Tragedy," *Westminster Review.*

The Comic Almanack. Illustrated by Cruikshank.

Etiquette for the Ladies: 80 Maxims on Dress, Manners, & Accomplishments, nineteenth edition.

Etiquette for Gentlemen: with Hints on the Art of Conversation, thirteenth edition.

Elements of Natural Philosophy, by Golding Bird, M.W., F.L.S., F.G.S.

The Premier Dissected, or Comments on the Public Life and Character of Lord Melbourne.

The Cook's Oracle. A new edition.

Sermons. By the Rev. John C. Miller, M.A.

Tour to the Sepulchres of Ancient Etruria in 1839, by Mrs. Hamilton Gray.

Christian Charity, Its Obligations and Objects, by John Bird Sumner, D.D.

And always the newspaper advertisements, where so much is to be learned of the habits and life of a people. Advertisements for governesses: "Five children, 6–14, £20 per year. The usual branches of a finished English education, pianoforte, singing, the rudiments of the harp, Italian, etc." People wanting cooks, valets, footmen, housemaids, tutors, etc., with the refrain "no Irish need apply." Bankrupt businesses for sale. Business opportunities. Public auctions.

Shipping advertisements. Passage in sailing barques and brigs of small tonnage for Bombay, Madras, Calcutta, Mauritius, Chusan, Canton, Van Diemen's Land, Sydney, New York.

The British and American Steam Navigation Company announces sailing dates for their steamships:

"The President, 2,366 tons, 600 h.p."
"The British Queen, 2,016 tons, 500 h.p."

NOSTRUMS:

"Pectoral Cough Lozenges, patronized by His Majesty the King of Prussia, and recommended by some of the most Eminent Medical Men. By allaying the tickling and irritation of the Throat, promoting a gentle and easy expectoration," etc.

Messrs. Rowland and Son (without whose notices no journal of the decade was complete), in their "annual address," express their "proud and high satisfaction that they are the authors of productions which have obtained so large a share of the patronage of a polished and enlightened age as have the *Kalydor* and *Macassar Oil*." They acknowledge the "favours they have enjoyed for a long series of years from the nobility and gentry, not only of England, but of the whole civilized world."

A NEW INVENTION:

"S. Jones's Thermo-Crepida, or Patent Shoe Warmer. Altogether apropos to this cold weather." A pair of tin pantoufles, which are filled with warm water and then placed in the footgear.

PATHETIC LAST-OF-THE-YEAR ITEM:

An angry letter to the *Times* from Mr. C. Appleby, written at midnight, December 24th, from the Bell Inn, Gloucester. Mr. Appleby, trying to get home for Christmas Eve, had missed a train connection by three minutes, and the notepaper sizzles as he anathematizes the Brighton and Gloucester and the Derby and Birmingham Railway Companies for not keeping the promises of their timetables. He ran up to the manager, waving one of the railroad's own bills in his face, and demanded to be carried on by special train. He didn't get it.

Thus the trivial and the important jostle each other in the newspapers during this first week of 1841. A complex nation was entering a very complex period of its history.

China and Afghanistan seemed very far away in 1841—as indeed they were—and most people had only a vague idea of what was happening in those distant parts of the world. The idea of empire as it was later to be celebrated had not yet occurred to the early Victorian Englishman. The colonies were there, yes, and were becoming increasingly important to the accelerating industrialization of Britain. If you were going to be the workshop of the world it would be just as well to have a few indisputably certain markets abroad. But they could be embarrassing at times, too, requiring all sorts of niggling little wars to control; and even where there were no wars there did not always seem to be identity of interest. A decade later even Disraeli could complain of "those wretched colonies" that "they are a millstone round our necks." The religious exaltation of the white man's burden was a later growth. Nevertheless, there the colonies were, and English feet were planted in most of the corners of the globe. Sometimes the native populations seemed curiously slow to understand the blessings of the commerce which Britain insisted they should enjoy. That frequently meant punitive campaigns; and lo, before one knew it, there was another native state to police. Yet in these early years politicians were as likely to complain about the cost of expeditionary armies as to rejoice over another victory of British arms in Asia. It must be remembered, too, that the total army in 1840 was only 120,000.

Thus the first Afghan war and the first China war.

As early as 1837, Captain Alexander Burnes had arrived at Kabul, in northern Afghanistan, his purpose being to enter into commercial relations with Dost Mahomed, the ruler of Kabul. Contrary to Burnes's advice, the British Government decided to treat Dost Mahomed as an enemy, made a series of alliances with hostile princes, and dethroned him. Insurrection arose, and eventually Dost Mahomed's son, Akbar Khan, moved in and became the real ruler. Burnes was murdered. Akbar Khan demanded unconditional surrender from Sir W. Macnaghton, the civil authority, and from General Elphinstone, the superannuated and feeble military commander. Macnaghton was murdered next. Then, in midwinter (January 6th), began the evacuation of the British garrison and the long trip over the treacherous mountain passes —4,500 fighting troops and about 12,000 native troops, together with women and children. They were ambushed along the way, and of the whole number only one man, a Dr. Brydon, reached Jelalabad—this on January 13, 1842. The India mail carrying word of the disaster did not reach England until early in March. Seldom had British prestige known such a series of humiliations. Never had there been such a series of official stupidities making the disaster possible. Wiser heads knew that the British should never have been there in the first place; now, of course, they would have to stay and re-establish their authority.

The story of the Chinese or Opium War is even less savory. The fault here was not that of mismanagement, but of calculated greed.

Under the East India Company England had developed the opium traffic in China. It proved an admirable outlet for the Indian supply of the drug. As early as 1796 the Chinese Government had forbidden the importation of opium, to no effect, for with every possible kind of bribery and corruption the smuggling continued. In 1839, every appeal having failed, the Chinese dumped and burned smuggled opium worth millions of pounds. This was clearly an attack upon British prestige and commerce, so Britain declared war. It was no great trick to overwhelm the meager Chinese resistance. The Island of Chusan fell July 5, 1840. On January 7, 1841, the Bogue forts were taken, and Chinese resistance seemed to be at an end.

Captain Elliot demanded that Hong Kong be given to the British Crown, that an indemnity of $6,000,000 be paid, and that the trade of the port of Canton be re-opened. Not a word was said about the opium traffic—the source of all the difficulties. When it appeared to the English that the Chinese did not intend to fulfill their agreements, Hong Kong was finally taken possession of in Her Majesty's name. And on March 18th, after reducing the Chinese forts, the English forced their way to Canton. The Chinese called for a truce. This time British troops were to remain in position until the whole indemnity had been paid. In this action fifteen British troops were killed.

In August Amoy fell without resistance to the British forces. The war dragged on into the next year, however, the British taking seaport after seaport after slight resistance. Late in August, 1842, with the squadron before Nanking, the Chinese finally asked for peace on any terms, and the treaty of Nanking, involving the indemnity, the cession of Hong Kong, and the opening of five major ports to British trade, including opium, was signed.

In due course of months, word of the final success got back to England, and on February 14, 1843, the Duke of Wellington, hero of Waterloo, moved the thanks of the House of Lords to the fleet and army engaged in the China service. Shortly afterward missionaries began to carry Christian teachings to the heathen Chinese.

It is of interest to note the reactions on the home front to this inglorious and predatory little war. Lord Ashley, the Evangelical statesman, made a three-hour speech in the Commons on April 4, 1843, in which he declared that Britain was smearing her honor and crucifying her soul for gold, that honorable commerce was being submerged by the rising tide of opium. The young Gladstone spoke out heavily against the war and against the trade. But Palmerston had earlier spoken cynically to ask if anyone really believed that the motive of the Chinese Government was the promotion of the growth of moral habits; this was an exportation-of-bullion question. Arguments were advanced in the Commons to the effect that opium smoking was really less harmful than the consumption of alcoholic beverages. The real solution was for the Emperor of China to legalize the trade! Sir Robert Peel, for his part, could not see beyond the loss of income that would come with the abolition of the trade.

The *Times,* on the other hand, commended Ashley warmly and had earlier spoken ironically of the "laudable endeavors" of the British dealers in opium "to force a poisonous trade upon the territories of an unwilling Power." As late as 1847 the *Colonial Intelligencer; or, the Aborigine's Friend,* the organ of the Aborigine's Protective Society (a typical Victorian institution), had this to say in general about colonization: "The history of discovery and colonization is a history of crime, fraud, and blood-guiltiness. Wherever civilized races have penetrated amongst aboriginal populations, the result has been the gradual extinction of the owners of the soil . . . it is partly effected by violence and rapine, partly by ardent spirits. We inoculate them with our vices, enfeeble their frames, sap their rude virtues, rob them of their lands, and finally extirpate them."

The High Morality of colonial and commercial endeavor took time to develop. It is doubtful if at this time many Englishmen lost sleep over the reluctance of yellow pagans to accept the refinements of civilized trade. Indeed most of them couldn't have told what it was all about.

The Americans were another story, and they were to come in for a good deal of attention during the 1840's. Travelers had brought back strange tales from this far country on whose cotton England was so dependent but whose people puzzled her greatly. She had reason to feel morally superior to this primitive land, still clinging to the institution of slavery which she had abolished in her colonies eight years earlier. The United States was obviously a nation of bumptious people, loud, truculent, "republicans," murderous, given to threatening war on slight provocation, coarse in manners, boisterous in humor. There was a kind of primitive fascination about the country, of course, which the average Englishman took to be reflected correctly, as of 1841, in the *Leatherstocking Tales* of Cooper, very popular in England. Frances Trollope had penetrated as far as Cincinnati, and out of her unhappy experiences there in trying to launch a "bazaar," had in her *Domestic Manners of the Americans* shown that they had no manners. All Americans chewed tobacco, the English knew, and expectorated on the floor.

In September, 1841, the *Quarterly Review* discussed at length two new books on the United States: James Silk Buckingham's *America— Historical, Statistic, and Descriptive;* and George Combe's *Notes on the United States of America, During a Phrenological Visit in 1838– 39–40.* "We have had of late no scarcity of books on the United States," said the reviewer. "Soldiers, sailors, divines, dandies, apothecaries, attorneys, Methodists, infidels, Quakers, actors and ambassadors, projectors and bankrupts—wives, widows, and spinsters:—we thought we had had something from almost every possible class and calling. . . ." If not openly hostile, the reviewer was at least consistently contemptuous of everything about the United States. His method is to excerpt from the index of Combe's book, and to comment on, such items as these: "Americans—peculiarly sensitive to the censures of foreigners, especially English; deplorably indifferent to sanguinary outrages; too much characterized by an inordinate love of gain and mania for speculation; amusing specimen of their inflated language; their reading of a light and trifling character;* have a nasal tone; instances of violence and coarseness in their manners; their excessive national vanity," etc.

The *Times* of January 1st had devoted the better part of two closely printed columns to a review (with long excerpts) of the

---

* No one later seems able to account, however, for the fact that in such a backward country there were more than three times as many newspapers and periodicals as in the United Kingdom; and that the state of New York alone had more than two thirds as many as England, Scotland, and Wales and Ireland. The figures for 1839 were: United States, 1,555; Great Britain and Ireland, 493. By 1850 these had risen to 2,800 and 593 respectively. In 1839 the number of newspapers in the United States was, in proportion to the population, five times as great as in the British Isles. The total United States annual circulation was 100,000,000; United Kingdom, 58,516,000. But, says P. L. Simmonds, reporting this (*Journal of the London Statistical Society,* July, 1841, pp. 120–22), "the American style of writing is florid to excess. . . . An American writer cannot describe the simplest affair without a flourish of trumpets; and their periodical press is almost without exception characterized by redundancy of expression, turgidity of diction, and an extravagance of style and sentiment."

Playfair Papers, or Brother Jonathan, the Smartest Nation in All Creation. This was a grotesque burlesque of the crude, ungrammatical American. Said the reviewer: "These three volumes, with their pictures of American society in all its various phases and aspects, look at least like broad caricatures, though we are assured by some who have travelled in 'Uncle Sam's country' that they are but little, if at all exaggerated."

The primitive condition of the country, the real extent of which was a mystery to most Britons, was underlined by a news item of the very next day: "The packet-ship *Independence*, which sailed from New York December 10th, arrived yesterday (January 1st) at Liverpool. She has not brought a copy of the Message of the President to the Congress. The state of the roads from the fall of snow had prevented the arrival of a sufficient number of members at Washington the 7th to constitute the houses."

Of the crudity and vulgar boastfulness of backward America in 1841 as an English traveler saw it there could be little doubt. Diplomatically, too, Brother Jonathan was proving difficult this year, even to the verge of possible war. The northeast boundary situation was a problem but was subject to negotiation. The M'Leod case, however, caused much angry feeling, and almost precipitated a conflict. In 1837 the American steamer *Caroline* had been carrying arms to the rebels in the then-current Canadian civil war. Canadian loyalists boarded her while she was lying within the jurisdiction of New York, set her on fire, and floated her over Niagara Falls. One American citizen was killed. In January, 1841, a British subject named Alexander M'Leod was arrested in New York, charged with having been concerned in the destruction of the *Caroline*. This led to ministerial altercation between the two countries and a good deal of inflated language in Congress. The issue turned chiefly on territorial jurisdiction. Fortunately for international relations, M'Leod was acquitted by a New York State jury in October.

When Heine visited England he had noted the drab monotony of middle-class London and what seemed to him the English "troubled spirit even in pleasure itself."[2] Obviously he mistook a stiff taciturnity for moroseness. The Englishman of the 1840's did not relish his pleasures sadly, whether they were "beer and fun" at one end of the social scale or horse racing and grouse-shooting at the other. Witness the turbulent conduct of the shilling spectators crowded under the roof at the Olympic watching a melodrama. Witness the public's demand for sentiment, sensationalism, and romance in its fiction; the extravagant admiration of popular leaders and the equally extravagant abuse of such leaders. Its lusty enjoyment of everything from flea circuses to railroads to hour-long sermons and three-hour political harangues. Its tolerance of every man's right to be prejudiced, affected, or eccentric; its approval of "characters." And a broadness in its humor quite at odds with the later conventional conception of English understatement as the essence of wit. The English laughed heartily and wept gustily.

A kind of boiling energy is the clue to the reading of English character and life during these early Victorian years—in the mill, the countinghouse, the shop, on the hustings, or on the farm. An example of the strenuosity of a practical farmer is given by a Rev. Mr. Robinson of Cambridge in a letter to a friend.

> Rose at three o'clock. . . . Rang the great bell, and roused the girls to milking, went up to the farm, roused the horsekeeper, fed the horses while he was getting up; called the boy to suckle the calves and clean out the cow-house; lighted the pipe, walked round the garden to see what was wanted there; went up to the paddock to see if the weaning calves were well; went down to the ferry to see if the boy had scooped and cleaned the boat; returned to the farm, examined the shoulders, heels, traces, chaff and corn of eight horses going to plough, mended the acre-staff, cut some thongs, whip-corded the plough-boys' whips, pumped the troughs full, saw the hogs fed, examined the swill-tubs, and then the cellar; ordered a quarter of malt, for the hogs want grains, and the men want beer; filled the pipe again, returned to the river, and brought a lighter of turf for dairy fires, and another of sedge for ovens; hunted out the wheelbarrows, and set them a trundling; returned to the farm, called the men to breakfast, and cut the boys' bread and cheese, and saw the wooden bottles filled; sent one plough to the three roods, another to the three half-acres, and so on; shut the gates, and the clock struck five; breakfast; set two men to ditch the fire roods, two men to chop sods, and spread about the land, two more to throw up manure in the yard, and three men and six women to weed wheat; set on the carpenter to repair cow-cribs, and set them up till winter; the wheeler, to mend the old carts, cart-ladders, rakes, etc., preparatory to hay-time and harvest; walked to the six-acres, found hogs in the grass, went back and set a man to hedge and thorn; sold the butcher a fat calf and the suckler a lean one—The clock strikes nine. . . .[3]

And then, perhaps, he rested. Howitt, who quotes the letter, remarks mildly enough that the reverend gentleman was fond of farming.

Much of this kind of energy, in the mushrooming new towns, was poured into a tacit glorification of an expanding commerce and industry: Carlyle preached a gospel of work to a nation with its sleeves already rolled up. Those who defended the dominant economic and social philosophies of the day—individualism, free competition, free trade, *laissez-faire*—were no more energetic than the prophets or politicians who set themselves against these currents. This endemic strenuosity took moral as well as material form. It was reflected in manners and attitudes, and the history of the decade is that of a progressively consolidating moral earnestness in almost every aspect of human activity. The process did not begin, of course, in 1841, nor had it reached by 1851 the crystallization of conduct and attitude which some social historians have oversimplified as the pattern of High Victorianism. These were formative years, however, and almost any portion of the human record which one touches has a reference of emerging ethical fervor.

Thomas Arnold had set this tone in public-school education, where earnestness in work, play, and conduct had laid its solemn hand upon generations of Rugby youths. It enters the whole vast business of Victorian philanthropy and social reform, from Chartism to Christian Socialism to the Societies for the Diffusion of Useful Knowledge. Utopians such as Owen, who violated many of the current canons, were motivated by the highest of principles. Even the Co-operative Movement, which seemed superficially to be merely a means of lowering the cost of living for the poor consumer, gathers its forces in an aura of missionary zeal. The distribution of millions of pious tracts for the poor as well as the production of "improving" literature for the home and fireside becomes a major industry. A Ruskin *preaches* art as well as industrial and economic morality. Dickens is much concerned with the moral effect of his writing. Even a Thackeray can think of a novelist as a "weekday preacher."

Religion, then, in its broader as well as its narrower sense, is a dominant clue to an understanding of the time. Books of sermons had an incredible popularity. It is no accident that of 45,000 books listed in the *London Catalogue* between 1816 and 1851, 10,300 were works on divinity; or that in the lists of new books appearing in the *Athenaeum* for a single month in 1841 sermons, works on theology and church history, volumes of "pious thoughts," children's hymnals, and pictorial Bibles were greater in number than all the histories, novels, biographies, and books of travel put together. Of these new works a shilling pamphlet entitled *Tracts for the Times, No. 90*, was one, and Newman's bombshell brings us to one of the crucial intellectual events of the decade.

First, however, what was the religious temper of England in 1841? The Established Church, of course, was dominant in power, prestige, and wealth. Writers to the *Times* kept insisting that it was the "church for the poor," as indeed it was for vast areas of the population, particularly in the country districts, where Dissent had been slow in establishing itself.* The official leadership of the Establishment, consistently Tory, was more concerned with the distribution of livings than with the spiritual life of its constituency. The poorly paid parish clergy frequently achieved through good works the affection of its parishioners; it christened and buried and gave in marriage; but it was not expected to show, nor did it show, much sign of spiritual activity. This was not so true of the Evangelical wing of the Church, which, during the mid-part of the century, reached the height of its influence. The Evangelicals stood between the so-called Orthodox (later High Church) party and the Broad Church party, members of which, like Thomas Arnold or Charles Kingsley, were more interested in the historical, ethical, and social implications of Christianity than in its dogma. Holding closely to a few central doctrines such as salvation by faith in the atonement of Christ and the literal interpretation of the Bible, the Evangelicals brought a crusading enthusiasm and zeal (vastly suspect in influential quarters) into the Anglican Church. As Gladstone later said, they "aimed at bringing back . . . the Cross . . . both into the teaching of the clergy and into the lives as well of the clergy as of the laity." They developed the use of hymns in divine service and introduced the second sermon on Sunday. Like their Nonconformist brethren they abhorred the theater, dancing, and cardplaying, and above all the use of Sunday for anything except strictly religious purposes. They were likely to be addicted to the close interpretation of prophecy, like the Rev. Mr. William Marsh ("Millennial Marsh") of Birmingham, who, in 1845, believed that in about twenty-five years the Antichrist would be revealed.

The Evangelicals, like the Dissenters, took literally the command "go thou into all the world." The early part of the century had seen the birth of the great missionary and evangelizing societies: The Society

---

* It is interesting to note that a committee of the Statistical Society of London, in surveying the living conditions of the laboring classes of St. George's in the east, found that of 1,954 heads of families 1,328 professed adherence to the Church of England, only 64 to the Wesleyan Methodists, and 177 to other denominations of Dissenters. The committee reasonably expressed doubt, however, that many of the Anglican group had much more than an inherited or sentimental affiliation. Like Hardy's peasant commenting on Chapel folk: "I bain't such a fool as to pretend that we who stick to the Church have the same chance as they, because we know we haven't. But I hate a feller who'll change his old ancient doctrines for the sake of getting to heaven."

for the Propagation of the Gospel in Foreign Parts; the London Missionary Society; the Religious Tract Society; the Society for the Promotion of Christian Knowledge; the Society for Promoting Christianity among the Jews; the British and Foreign Bible Society. Many of these were undenominational, combining Evangelicals and Dissenters. The last of these societies at its May meeting in 1841 reported the distribution during the preceding year of 900,000 Bibles and Testaments, and the grand total of 22,000,000 since its establishment in 1804. From the presses of all, tracts and pamphlets rained like dew. In 1850 the Religious Tract Society advertised a "present annual circulation of the Society's works of about 24 millions," receipts of £60,000, and a total distribution since its founding of about 524,000,000 copies.*

One wonders what the net influence of this paper warfare against sin was. Some have attributed England's escape from the revolutions which swept the Continent later in the decade to the influence exerted by these energetic religions. Certainly the social philosophy behind these endeavors was that of teaching "the industrious classes" (a euphemism supposed to take away the sting of poverty, but reflecting strongly upon the working habits of the upper classes!) to be happy with their lot. It was a part of religion to accept without question the condition into which you had been born. To be poor was not a crime, although the current treatment of the poor would seem to say so. It was an estate marked out by divine providence, and if you were hungry and ill-housed, you should remember that life is short. As William Wilberforce, who labored valiantly to free the black slave, put it in his *Practical View of the System of Christianity:*[4] "The more lowly path of the poor has been allotted to them by the hand of God; . . . it is their part faithfully to discharge its duties and contentedly to bear its inconveniences; . . . if their superiors enjoy more abundant comforts, they are also exposed to many temptations from which the inferior classes are happily exempted."

It is important to remember that this was not hypocrisy but an honestly mistaken and narrow religious humanitarianism. The measure

---

* May was the month of the annual meetings of religious societies in Exeter Hall. In 1841 the Sunday School Union announced a total of 481 of its Sunday schools within fifteen miles of London, in which were 86,000 children. The British and Foreign School Society, with Lord John Russell in the chair, reported a total of 51,696 children on their books. The Home Missionary Society employed 149 agents, whose labors extended over 500 towns, villages, and hamlets of England and Wales. Its 168 Sunday schools gave gratuitous instruction to 9,500 children. More than 4,000 copies of scripture and 250,000 tracts had been distributed within the year.

of the growth in wisdom of the nineteenth century is the extent to
which Evangelicals such as Shaftesbury devoted their lives to releasing
the laborer from his slavery, making it possible for him to enjoy at
least a few minor temptations.

All that has been said about the Evangelicals applies also to the Nonconformist sects, whose growth and influence are one of the great
phenomena of the first half of the century. In 1800 the Wesleyan
Methodist Church had 90,000 members; in 1850, 358,277 in Great
Britain alone. In 1812 the Primitive Methodists (who broke off from
the parent stock) had 200 members; in 1850, 104,762. In 1850 one out
of every thirty-four people in the nation was a Methodist.[5] In 1851 the
number of Methodist meetinghouses in the country was 11,000; Independents (Congregationalists), 3,244; Baptists, 2,789; Primitive Methodists, 2,871; Established Church, 14,077.* Dissent then outweighed
Conformity. Yet socially it was still *déclassé*. Dissenters could not
receive degrees at Oxford or Cambridge, and the Established Church
still levied a tax for ecclesiastical purposes from parishioners of all
denominations. She still had the power to read her burial service at
the graveside of Dissenters.†

Dissent was ignored, if not scorned, by the upper classes, but it
nevertheless included some of the important people of the day. John
Bright, who entered the Commons as a member for Durham in 1842,
was a Quaker. Mrs. Gaskell was the wife of a Unitarian minister in Manchester. Michael Faraday attended a little Sandemanian meetinghouse.
The Brownings were Nonconformists, as was John Ruskin. More and

---

* The following list of Dissenting meetinghouses in Central London, from a
guidebook of 1848, gives an idea of the current diversity of sects: Arian, 2; Baptist,
53; General Baptist, 2; Particular Baptist, 7; Calvinist, 50; Calvinistic Methodist,
2; Freethinkers, 2; Huntingdonian, 1; Independent, 60; Followers of Irving, 1;
Followers of Joanna Southcott, 1; Lady Huntingdon, 4; Moravian, 1; New Jerusalem Church, 1; Presbyterian, 3; Scotch Calvinist, 11; Scotch Church, 1; Scotch
Secession, 2; Sandemanian, 3; Socialist, 1; Unitarian, 11; Wesleyan Methodist, 22;
Whitfield Methodist, 7; Welch [sic], 2. Roman Catholic chapels, 21; Jewish
synagogues, 8; Quaker meetinghouses, 5.

† A contemporary controversy over "lay baptism" is reported in a 300-page
octavo volume published in 1841 by W. C. Curteis, L.L.A.: *A Full Report of the
Case of Martin J. Escott, clerk, for refusing to bury an infant baptized by a
Wesleyan Minister, containing all the arguments on both sides* . . . Escott pleaded
that he had acted in obedience to and conformity with his obligations to the
Church of England; that since the Wesleyan Methodist minister was unordained
(in the Church of England, of course) any rite or form of baptism performed
by him was null and void. The judge ruled that lay baptism is valid under the
laws of the Church of England: "It has not been shown to my satisfaction that
a Wesleyan minister is a schismatic or a heretic."

more Nonconformity was making its way among the middle classes; the Independents or Congregationalists in particular drew heavily from them.[6] It has been said that in Leeds, to take one example, the "best people" in mid-century were Methodists.[7] The real strength of Dissent was in the manufacturing towns, and in the mines and collieries. There it brought to families almost destitute of hope a ray of equalitarian sunshine. In the chapel there were few rented pews as yet, and all were equal before God. And if chapel did not teach you the way to improve your condition in this vale of tears, at least it helped you to bear your lot without complaining. The Mine Commissioners reported in 1842 on the effects of religion in the South Staffordshire mines. Said one of the men: "There are pits in which there are prayer meetings every day after dinner, and all are obliged to attend, as the butties and the men will not work with any who do not. We have had preaching down in the pits." This, one would gather from other sections of the report, did not describe the moral climate of all mines. But it is easy to understand why the masters approved, and why some insisted on the men having prayers and reading the Scriptures in the dinner hour!

This, then, is the kind of religion—Evangelical and Nonconformist— which was one of the real forces of the age. It was narrow and in many ways unlovely. John Ruskin, in *Praeterita*,[8] describes a chapel attended by the families of small shopkeepers in the Walworth Road: "An oblong, flat-ceiled barn, lighted by windows with semi-circular heads. brick-arched, filled by small-paned glass held by iron bars . . . galleries propped on iron pipes, up both sides; pews . . . filling the barn floor, all but its two lateral, straw-matted passages; pulpit, sublimely isolated, central from sides, and clear of altar-rails at ends. . . ." It must have been some such chapel as this that Browning had in mind when he described the services on Christmas Eve in "Zion." But this religion did give to many a kind of inner warmth which the Established Church lacked, and a sense of community—even though community under hardship—which made it possible to bear the travail of each day's degradation.

One of the results, however, of Evangelical and Dissenting fervor was that unique institution, the British Sunday, the gloom and depression of which must have gone far to rob it of its spiritual relief. All through the forties the more enlightened kept pointing out that by closing libraries, parks, art galleries, museums, and zoological gardens you drove the proletariat to the one source of pleasure which was not legislated against—the gin mill and the beer shop! But the Sabbatarians were in control; the Lord's Day Observance Society and the Working Men's Lord's Day Rest Association never rested, even on the seventh day.

Sunday manners in certain areas had not improved in the forties, however, much beyond the description given in 1833 by Cruikshank in his fourteen illustrations for the book *Sunday in London*. This was a racy if somewhat oversimplified analysis of the way the various classes of British society defaced the Sunday.

> And in that grey of the Sunday morning, at the sound of the matin bell, the gin temples open wide their portals to all comers. . . . The 'Lower Orders' begin to shake off the beery slumbers of the mid-night pay-table, and wander forth in maudlin, unwashed multitudes to the temples of the Great Spirit, Gin . . . crowding and jostling like so many maggots in a grease-pot.
>
> Meanwhile the butchers, the fishmongers, the gardeners, and the huxters, are spreading out their wares for the Sunday markets, no attention being paid to the law against Sunday trading.
>
> A great mass of the Middle Orders 'observe the Sabbath' by a cleaner shave, a cleaner shirt, an extra pudd'n, a leisurely tooth-pick, a 'sporting Sunday paper,' and a country jaunt. [Others, good folk, went their way to church], but the nearer they approach thereto, they find their olfactory nerves offended by the fish offal and refuse of the Sunday market, their feet slipping on pavements covered with the frequent vomit, and flooded with that which shall be nameless; their ears assail'd with oaths, imprecations, and obscenity; and at the church-gates they have to elbow their way through whole squads of drunken fighting men and women. [The author buttresses his point here by quotations from the Report of a Select Committee of the House of Commons.]
>
> What delectabilities distinguish the afternoon and the evening of the Sunday in London? For the Higher Orders there are Hyde Park and Kensington Gardens, where they collect, exhibiting their taste in turnouts—a melée of equestrians, pedestrians, and charioteers; Dukes and Duchesses, horses and carriages, Lords, ladies, grooms, pimps, panders, and black-legs. . . . Thus the Higher Orders observe this portion of the Lord's Day by . . . extra gallivanting, gambling, gourmandery, and other such dulcet diseases, and making their 'servants and their cattle', both within and without their gates, *work* ten times harder than they do on any 'working day' in the whole week!
>
> For the Middle Classes on the 'Lord's Day afternoon' there are the omnibi—the ever-rolling omnibi!—each omnibus 'huge and unwieldy lumbering along' . . . average number in each, two dozen. . . . They bear the worshipped 'Middle Orders' to *their* Sunday 'recreations, viz., imbibing beer, blue ruin, fresh air, and tea, amid clouds of dust and tobacco-smoke in the suburb *tea* gardens.

One curious item needs to be added to the picture of Dissident sects. Even before the new Mormon community was established at Nauvoo, Illinois, two Mormon missionaries had landed at Liverpool. They worked first at Preston, and before long half-a-dozen counties had heard the word. In 1840 the Church reported 4,019 Saints (or members) in England. In 1851 the Mormons, or Latter-Day Saints, had 602 churches and 50,389 baptized Saints in England and Scotland.[9] In 1840, while Brigham Young was in England, a periodical, *The Latter-Day Saints Millennial Star*, was started, and by 1851 had a circulation of 22,000. The first European edition of the Book of Mormon was published in Liverpool in 1841. Before Brigham Young left England in 1841 he arranged for copies of the Book of Mormon to be bound richly for presentation to Her Majesty and the Prince Consort. The presentation was made in 1842, and it must have been one of the more curious spectacles of the Court. It is not recorded that Victoria ever read the book.

It is certain, however, that the activities of the missionaries caused a fluttering in clerical dovecotes. The working clergy saw conversions taking place under their noses, and although they charged the missionaries with heresy and blasphemy they seemed to be able to do little to impede the Mormon progress. Sermons were preached against the strange visitors. Pamphlets were printed: "Mormonism or the Bible? A Question for the Times"; "Friendly Warnings on the Subject of Mormonism," etc.

In a period of economic depression it was easier for the missionaries in the towns and villages to stimulate the newly baptized to emigrate to the new religious colony in America. The first company of forty hardy souls sailed from Liverpool in 1840. The report of a Mormon Conference of June, 1851, showed that up to that time nearly 17,000 of those baptized in England "had emigrated from her shore to Zion."[10] These emigrants were farmers and mechanics of a superior class from Wales, Lancashire, Yorkshire, Staffordshire, and the southern counties of Scotland.

The whole episode is a strange footnote to mid-nineteenth-century religious history. In spite of the incredible abracadabra which accompanied it, and in spite of the notorious overtones of bigamy, it is difficult to bracket the movement with the wilder religious phenomena of the Irvingites and the Followers of Joanna Southcott, for the Mormon converts appear for the most part to have been solid citizenry, their conduct exemplary, and their success in the new world reputable.

Into this complex of British religion, early in the year, fell *Tract 90*. Oxford, the Anglican hierarchy, and all breeds of Evangelicals and Dissenters were soon in full cry. The controversy, or distortions of it, quickly reached the intelligent laity. As Newman wrote later: "In every part of the country and every class of society, through every organ and occasion of opinion, in newspapers, in periodicals, at meetings, in pulpits, at dinner tables, in coffee rooms, in railway carriages, I was denounced as a traitor who had laid his train and was detected in the very act of firing it against the time-honored establishment." Yet it is to be doubted that most of the public followed the subtleties of the arguments, beyond the obvious cry of "Popery." Later, with the No-Popery agitation of 1850, mobs were violently to besiege churches in Knightsbridge and Pimlico—mobs to whom the surplice, lighted candles, an Eastward position, and a processional cross were synonymous with an invasion of England by the Roman Church.

In 1841 the reaction was strong and bitter. Lord Ashley, who mobbed no churches, yet spoke of Pusey, his first cousin, in inflammatory terms. "All the realms of Pusey are vomiting out essays," he wrote.[11] At the same time the jovial and worldly Palmerston, also Ashley's relative by marriage, showed no signs of knowing what the dispute was about. Ashley said in 1845, "Why, it was only a short time ago that he heard, for the first time, of the grand heresy of Puseyites and Tractarians!"[12] Yet the battle had shaken the Church of England, and in so doing was modifying the intellectual and religious life of the century.

The story of the outward events is a simple one. They stemmed from the quiet cloisters of Oxford, and were essentially an attempt on the part of a few devoted and articulate leaders to reinvigorate the Estab-lished Church by turning her back to medievalism. The fight of the reformers is a clue, in a larger frame of reference, to the deep national forces which were shaping the age, and to the extent that it was a lost cause, with many of its leaders fleeing Romeward, it was a seeming defeat by the forces of a Liberalism which was penetrating the political and economic, and inevitably the religious, texture of the time.

The beginning of the Oxford Movement is usually dated by Keble's Assize Sermon at St. Mary's in 1833 on "National Apostasy." John Keble, like Newman, was a Fellow of Oriel. His tender sacred poems, *The Christian Year*, were a standard part of the library of every religious Anglican family. He himself was a gentle and simple person, remarkably sweet and humble where the intensity of his religious convictions was not concerned. But, like his famous colleagues, he felt that the Estab-lishment was spiritually complacent and moribund and hence ineffectual in combating the encroachment of the state upon church freedom and authority. She needed a new vitality, which, it seemed, could come only by reclaiming for the Established Church its place as the True

Church in the Apostolic Succession and by reviving the vital doctrines of the church fathers which had been forgotten or neglected.

Keble was joined by others, notably, in the beginning, by Richard Hurrell Froude and John Henry Newman. Froude, whose *Remains* show him to have been a morbidly intense and devout young man, died in 1836 at the age of thirty-three. Some time after the new crusade was under way Dr. Edward Pusey joined the others, giving it, as Newman said, "a position and a name." From 1840 on "Puseyism" rather than "Newmanism" was the popular name of the Movement. Pusey was a professor and canon of Christ Church, remarkably learned and awe-inspiring, remote and not a little heavy in his scholarship. A little later W. G. Ward, voluble and impetuous, joined forces with the others. Ward was an indomitable logician who wielded arguments like clubs. He was marked for Rome from the beginning; unlike Keble and Pusey, he went ultimately with Newman into the Catholic Church. Newman's early efforts had been bent quixotically toward bringing Roman Catholicism closer to the principles of the English Church. Ward, on the other hand, "felt bound to retain his external communion with the English Church" only "because he believed that he was bringing many of its members toward Rome."[13]

Of all these, John Henry Newman was the real leader and the greatest mind. His influence had early been felt in the sermons he preached on Sunday afternoons as vicar of St. Mary's. Gladstone spoke of "the solemn music and sweetness in his tone." Matthew Arnold, long after, remarked on that "religious music, subtle, sweet and mournful." Lean and ascetic, compound of mystic and logician; subtle and persuasive, giving through his mastery of English prose apparent simplicity to the most difficult subject; charming and gracious; sensitive and other-worldly; a tragic figure, indeed, in the internal conflict which drove him, weary of arguing and disputing, out of the Church which he had tried to save and away from the friends to whom he was devoted, into the arms of the only creed in which his restless spirit could find peace—Newman, both in achievement and in influence, was a giant among his contemporaries. It is easy to forget, however, how much his storm-tossed mind was representative of the spiritual uncertainties of an age which was pre-Darwin but which yet seemed terribly confused to earnest seekers after truth and certainty. Carlyle, like Newman, turned back to the Middle Ages for an entirely untheological solution to present miseries. John Stuart Mill, in quite another intellectual world, was early frustrated and despairing in his quest for something to give him satisfaction. Arthur Hugh Clough wandered between his two spiritual

Figure 2. John Henry Newman, after a portrait by Richmond, 1845

worlds. John Sterling was beset by doubts, and died with them un-
resolved. Later, John Ruskin and William Morris, each in his own way
discouraged with his generation, were to turn to the distant past for a
model for Utopia. The early Victorian air was a chilling one for many
sensitive spirits.

On September 9, 1833, Newman published the first of the *Tracts for
the Times*, of which he was ultimately to write twenty-nine—including *90* as well as *1*. These tracts were intended to startle the clergy
into an awareness of their spiritual responsibilities. From the first they
emphasized the dogmatic element in English orthodoxy, the Apostolic
Succession, and the dangers of Latitudinarianism. It should be noted
that the atmosphere of austerity and holiness which marked the Movement from the beginning did not, as was popularly assumed, depend
upon ritual and formalism in the church service. It did have a strong
strain of mysticism and poetry within its intensity, and it was perhaps
romantic in its flight from the present to the past. But the *via media*
which Newman hoped to recover for the Church of England depended
not at all upon the surplice or smoky ceremonials.

Tract 90 appeared in February. Its title was "Remarks on Certain
Passages in the Thirty-nine Articles," and it was an attempt to show

that the Articles of the Church of England were as capable of a Catholic as of an Anglican interpretation. Newman was careful to make clear that he was thinking of the Catholicity of the Primitive Church and not necessarily of the Roman Church. This seemed, however, like Jesuitry to a clergy progressively more and more sensitized by the preceding tracts, which to them smelled of Rome. The storm broke. On March 15th the Hebdomadal Board of the University condemned the tract as "inconsistent with the statutes of the University, which require subscription to the articles and the instruction of Students in them." Newman immediately acknowledged his authorship. The Bishop of Oxford asked Newman to stop the issue of further tracts. Newman complied. "Our business," he said, "is with ourselves—let the Church of Rome make itself (as we should try to make ourselves) more holy, more self-denying, more primitive,—it will come *nearer to us. . . .*"

Pamphlets began to fall like autumn leaves. Several score were published in Oxford in March—some in defense of, some violently attacking, *Tract 90*. In September Pusey had to write a letter clearing himself of the charge of having attended Roman Catholic ceremonies, as well as the charge of "professing to adore the Eucharistic sacrifice as identical with that which was offered on the Cross." Thomas Arnold had earlier published an article in the *Edinburgh Review* called "The Oxford Malignants."* In London the conservative press refused to get excited. The *Morning Post* (March 18th) said: "We believe that upon the whole the Tracts for the Times have had great success in the achievement of these objects [to awaken thought], and have therefore done great good." The *Times*, in two leaders (March 4th and 6th), said: "We think it will be difficult for any man to show that . . . their doctrine or practice (whether erroneous or not) contradicts any oaths which they have sworn. . . . Fair play and no favour is all that any man engaged in controversy can reasonably desire; and it is all that we shall ever undertake to give."

But the noise of battle still lingered in the Oxford quadrangles and the bishops' palaces. Newman, tired of controversy, went up to Littlemore in the summer. Even there the mounting denunciations of the bishops followed him. "Already are the foundations of apostasy laid," wrote one. "If we once admit another gospel, Antichrist is at the door." The year went out in that religious atmosphere.

---

* Newman and Arnold met only once, in 1842, shortly before Arnold's death, at dinner in the Common-Room at Oriel. Newman remembered later that they talked about the productions of North Africa, as a fruitful and harmless subject. (J. L. May: *The Oxford Movement*, 1933, p. 36.)

Eighteen forty-one had begun very quietly in political circles. The Queen had opened Parliament on Tuesday, January 26th, and "never within our experience," said the *Spectator*, "has the opening of Parliament excited so little attention, so little manifestation of hope or fear." The great deal of congratulation over the success of the small Syrian venture indicates how really little there was to worry about in international affairs. Commodore Napier, commander of the expedition, was attaining all the honors which it was the custom of the time to bestow on popular heroes. On coming home he had been shouted after and feasted. "No doubt," continued the *Spectator*, "he is booked for the third stage of popularity, that of standing godfather to boots and coats, haberdashery warehouses and coffee-shops, suburban streets, and colonial cities."

The great party struggle of the session was over the ministerial measure for reforming the registration of voters in Ireland. The Government lost, and the episode won attention chiefly as an illustration of the ministerial weakness and as an indication of the probable approaching downfall of Melbourne and the Whig administration.

Items: In January occurred the "singular and melancholy" death of Samuel Scott, the American diver. Scott had for some time been making leaps from the top of Waterloo Bridge into the Thames. On the 11th he gathered a crowd of 10,000 persons to witness his plunge. Before taking off from his scaffolding he put his head into a noose to simulate hanging. The rope slipped, and before anyone could cut him down he was dead.

On March 4, General W. H. Harrison was installed as President of the United States, succeeding Martin Van Buren. On April 4th he died after an attack of pleurisy, and the following day the oath was administered to John Tyler, the vice-president.

April 9. The *President* steamship, sailing from New York and overdue at Liverpool, had not yet been heard from. It was speculated that she might have put back to New York or run to Bermuda.

April 17. No word yet from the *President*. She had 27 passengers aboard, one of them Tyrone Power, the comedian. A guess was that the machinery might have been damaged and that she was slowly making her way to England under canvas.

July 3. Still no word, despite many false rumors. She had been seen, however, laboring in tremendous seas on March 12, pitching heavily. It was supposed that she went down with all passengers. She was never heard from again. "It was, we believe," said the *British Almanac*, "the largest steamship ever built. It measured 268 feet in length, 42 feet in breadth within the paddle-boxes."

Alexis Soyer, the famous French chef, took possession of the finest kitchens in London—the Reform Club—on March 1st.

Figure 3. The *President* steamship, 2,360 tons; length, 268 feet; horsepower, 540 (nominal)
British Crown Copyright. Science Museum, London.

On May 7, Thomas Barnes, longtime editor of the *Times*, died, and was replaced by John T. Delane.

On June 1st, Sir David Wilkie, the famous painter, died on board the *Oriental* steamship, on his way home from Egypt.

June 12. Franz Liszt's London concert was enthusiastically reviewed in the *Athenaeum*. "He came among us as a wonder, and some of the graver musicians, repelled by such reputation, set themselves, in the first instance, to magnify his individualities and eccentricities. . . . But the extent of his skill and genius is almost universally accepted now."

The Queen prorogued Parliament in person on June 22d. In order to test the waning popularity of the Melbourne ministry, Sir Robert Peel moved a vote of no confidence against it. On June 4th the vote had been carried by one against the Government. But the Whigs decided to go to the country rather than resign, and the whole question of Free Trade versus Protection was laid before the voters during the summer.

The new invention of photography was exciting the English in the

early forties—known variously as sun drawing, sun pictures, the helio-
graphic art, or photographic drawings.* On June 10th Henry Fox
Talbot read a paper before the Royal Society in which he described his
new process of photography, called "Calotype." But the process with
which most people were familiar was the daguerreotype, announced
by Daguerre in France in 1839. As is often the case where similar inventions are developed along independent lines by men far apart, there
was an unedifying dispute concerning priority. In point of fact, however, the two methods were quite different.

In January, 1839, in Paris, Daguerre had described his process of
fixing images by means of exposing silver iodide on a plate of copper
to the scene projected on the plate by a camera lens.† The daguerreotype
produced a single opaque picture which could not be reproduced. It
involved a complicated process of preparing the plate, exposing it to
the vapors of iodine, and then, after exposure, developing the image
by bathing the plate in mercury vapor. In spite of the fact that with
the early lenses an exposure of from five to ten minutes in full sunlight
was required, the invention gained immediate popularity. Even after
improved lenses were developed in 1841, several minutes were necessary. "The sitters, without wincing, stared fixedly into the direction of
the mysterious machine. Coming back again after a time, one would
find the same person still sitting in the same position, pinned down to
the chair, motionless, speechless, as if asleep with open eyes. . . . And
the same with the photographer, always on the same spot, by the mysterious apparatus, a watch in his hand. . . . Everybody was able to understand that there was a secret relation between the young man, the box
with the short, cannonlike brass tube, and the sitter. . . ."[14] One wonders
if much of the grimness we read into the faces of the early Victorians
was not superimposed there by the necessity of sitting unblinking in
a chair, head held by a fixed clamp, while the minutes were counted.
The daguerreotype was a work of art, however, with a fineness of
detail and a silver delicacy of light and shade which have not yet been
surpassed.

* It seems to have been Sir John Herschel who first used the word "photography"; certainly it was he who introduced the terms "negative" and "positive,"
and suggested the use of hyposulfites as fixing agents—a recommendation adopted
by both Daguerre and Talbot. (Robert Taft: *Photography and the American
Scene*, N. Y., 1938, pp. 104-5.)

† Talbot, hearing the first announcement of Daguerre's success, had, in January,
1839, sent a description of his own accomplishments to the Royal Society.

Daguerre had investigated the possibilities of international patent, but convinced that anyone who knew the process could duplicate it, he decided to "give it freely to the world," at the same time petitioning the French Government for a pension. Talbot did patent his invention, which may account for the fact that while daguerreotype studios were springing up in every street (some studios in London had daily returns of approximately £60 in 1841), Talbot's more flexible invention was relatively unknown and little used.

Talbot's calotypes involved the use of a paper negative, coated with table salt and sensitized with silver chloride, from which an infinite number of positive prints could be made. Talbot, therefore, anticipated the modern technique of photography. He reduced the time of exposure, too, to about three minutes. His effects were not as delicate as those of the daguerreotype, but the grain of the paper itself gave a softness to the outline of the picture and resulted in a broad, pictorial kind of treatment which in portraiture expressed very real characterization. Even today one can learn as much about the Victorian personality from some of the early photographs as from pages of letterpress.

The other great name in English photography of the 1840's is that of David Octavius Hill, a Scottish painter of ordinary talent who accepted a commission to do a vast group study (500 likenesses on a surface of 57 square feet) of the first General Assembly of the Free Church of Scotland in 1843. As preparation for his work Hill, collaborating with Robert Adamson, a young chemist, made a series of calotype photographs of his subjects. Hill's paintings are forgotten, but his photographic portraits are still superb examples of camera art. He composed his portraits like a painter, emphasizing face and hands, and achieving a naturalness—an unposed quality—remarkable in view of the primitive techniques which he had to use. All his photography—some 1,000 portraits—was done between the years 1843 and 1848. When Adamson died in 1848, Hill deserted the camera for his painting.

By the end of the decade the basis had been laid for the next important advance in photography. Guncotton was discovered in 1846, and in 1851 Frederic Scott Archer "found that a certain kind of this substance, if dissolved in ether—collodion—was not only suitable for carrying the sensitive chemicals, but also that glass could be coated with it evenly and permanently."[15] Thus was created the basis of the wet-plate process, which was to remain the method for several decades.

Photography in the 1840's was more than an exciting new toy; it was an adventure both for him who took and him who was taken.

Figure 4. The chess players *(left)*
   British Crown Copyright. Science Museum, London. (Fox Talbot Collection)
Figure 5. Handyside Ritchie and William Henning

Figure 6. Unknown gentleman

Figure 7. Elizabeth Johnstone, the beauty of Newhaven

Figure 8. Master Miller

Figure 9. Fisherman and boys at Newhaven

Figure 10. The birdcage (Hill and Adamson)

Figure 11. Mrs. Webster*

Figure 12. George Combe, the phrenologist*

Figure 13. Miss Wilhelmina Fillans

*Victoria and Albert Museum. Crown Copyright

Figure 14. Conversation
  British Crown Copyright. Science Museum, London. (Fox Talbot Collection)

Figure 15. Newhaven fishwives at St. Andrews (Fox Talbot)

Figure 16. Garden harvest
  British Crown Copyright. Science Museum, London. (Fox Talbot Collection)

Figure 17. The Finlay children

Figure 18. James Fairbairn, D.D., and group of Newhaven fishwives

Figure 19. Fox Talbot's printing works at Reading

The General Election was held in July. "Notwithstanding the party spirit that had been much excited upon some points," said the *Annual Register*, "and that much excitement prevailed among the partisans of rival candidates, the public peace was in few instances broken." Yet at Blackburn the declaration that the Liberal candidate had been defeated so enraged the mob that they made a furious attack on the Bull Inn, the headquarters of the Conservatives. Paving stones were thrown, windows smashed, and some of the rioters threw the furniture out into the street, nearly gutting the house. Not until the magistrates had read the Riot Act and the soldiers had been called out did the mob disperse. In Liverpool a crowd of some 600 Irishmen, armed with brickbats, bludgeons, and pokers, fought for two hours with a police force of 130. The crowd in St. James's Street numbered 20,000 persons. In Grafton Street thousands of Tory rioters and Irish clashed, until finally dispersed by the police. At Ashton-under-Lyne the nomination was the scene of another riot. Women took a vigorous share in the hooting and hissing in the marketplace, and a volley of stones made the persons on the hustings retire. The mayor sent to Manchester for a military force. There were also serious riots at Carlisle, with the military called out to restore order. "The public peace," if not broken, was certainly badly bent.

As was expected, the election was a severe defeat for the Liberals or Whigs. The Conservatives made a net gain of forty seats; it could therefore be only a short time until the present ministry would fall.* Disraeli, who had spoken in favor of the Chartist petition of 1839 and was yet a strenuous supporter of the Corn Laws, was returned as Conservative member for Shrewsbury. He was longing for a cabinet post which the new ministry would be unable or unwilling to give him. The flamboyant young man, however useful in opposition, was still suspect in the inner circles. Richard Cobden, a well-to-do Manchester calico manufacturer, was returned as member for Stockport—his first seat in Parliament. He was a man to watch, for he was the leading figure in the Anti-Corn-Law League, and the tormented question of the Corn Laws was to become the great political issue of the administration.

Until the Napoleonic Wars Britain had normally been, on a small scale, a corn (cereal grain)-exporting country. In 1815 the first effective law for the restriction of corn imports had prohibited the release of foreign wheat from bond unless the price of wheat on the home market

---

* The newspapers of the period use the terms Whig and Liberal, Tory and Conservative, interchangeably. Before long the transition would be complete, and Liberal-Conservative the accepted designation.

exceeded 80 shillings a quarter. But now that England was shifting to a manufacturing economy, legislation for the protection of the farmer seemed to great masses of the people merely a device for increasing the price of food. The fact that by this time the farmer's rents were so high that he needed large profits on his crops, and that the landlords, in turn, demanded high rentals from the farmers in order to pay increased taxes to support the poor, brought a vicious wheel full circle and complicated an intricately confused national picture.

Already the Anti-Corn-Law League was very active. No item recurs more frequently in the newspapers of the period than a note about some meeting, somewhere, of the "Leaguers." The cause had enlisted the support of the manufacturers, to whom were pointed out the glories of free trade and the interference that the Corn Laws were making with the growth of trade. The people were told that their miseries came chiefly through the artificially high price at which bread was kept because of the protective Corn Laws. Great sums of money had been poured into the agitation. Up to the autumn of 1841 the League had spent only £10,000; by the autumn of 1842 it had expended £90,000. In 1843 it collected £50,000; in 1844, £100,000; and in 1845, £250,000 for support of its campaign.[16] But Peel's ministry was returned in 1841 pledged to the support of the Corn Laws. The great battle was building up slowly.

Parliament reassembled on August 19th. The first division resulted in the defeat of the Government, which, under Lord Melbourne's ministry, had been in power since 1834. The Queen (with obvious reluctance, for she had become devoted to Melbourne and did not like the cold, awkward Peel) invited Sir Robert Peel to form a new ministry. Peel was the First Lord of the Treasury, and of course Prime Minister; Sir James Graham became Home Secretary. Lord Stanley became Colonial Secretary. The young William Ewart Gladstone accepted the vice-presidency of the Board of Trade. The Duke of Wellington agreed to serve in the Cabinet without office. Thus was drawn the new political front.

The publisher Moxon was found guilty of blasphemous libel in the printing of Shelley's *Queen Mab.* . . . In the meantime the summer had worn on. Prince Albert had performed his princely office, and had laid the first stone of the Infant Orphan Asylum near Wamstead. . . . The new penny postage, introduced in 1840, was proving tremendously successful, and this year the first adhesive postage stamps were used. . . . Telegraph wires were strung along the railways as far as Glasgow. . . . Wood pavements were being introduced on London streets (they proved very slippery). . . . Fifty-one persons were killed by the overturning of a barge during its launching at Rotherham in Yorkshire. . . . The London and Brighton and the Great Western Railways were opened—the latter all the way from London to Bristol—with great ceremony. . . . The London Library, which Carlyle had been instrumental in organizing, set up business in two rooms of a house at 49 Pall Mall. . . . Palmerston, the relentless nationalist, was still in Parliament, but out of office in spite of his diplomatic triumph over the French and of the military success in Egypt. Melbourne, tired, absent-minded, made his last tender farewells to the Queen.

At the theaters, Macready, the new lessee of Drury Lane, was performing in Bulwer's *Money* and *The Lady of Lyons;* at Covent Garden a new play, *London Assurance,* was produced as the work of a twenty-one-year-old actor Mr. Lee Moreton (really Dion Boucicault). Mme. Vestris played the heroine, and the first-night audience acclaimed it uproariously a success. Great excitement was caused a little later (November) by Adelaide Kemble's return from Italy and her appearance for the first time on an English stage. She sang Bellini's *Norma,* and succeeded in reminding the critics of both her father and her mother—the Charles Kembles. "Her singing," they said, "is full of passion and energy," and her acting "superb."

The great theatrical event of the year, however, was the first appearance in England of the young French actress Rachel, "the Siddons of the *Théâtre Français.*" The highest rank and fashion turned out to hear her—even the Queen. She appeared first in Racine's *Andromaque,* and the public capitulated completely to her charm and her acting genius. The critics excitedly expressed their rapture. "She has much that distinguished Mrs. Siddons in her day," said the *Sunday Times* of May 16th. "She has much that distinguished the celebrated Edmund Kean . . . his intensity, the intensity of genius." "She gesticulates little," wrote another critic, "and the distinguishing characteristic of her manner is calm, determined self-possession. . . . Her voice is full, sweet-toned, and melodious. . . . The applause elicited by her performance throughout and at the close was fervent to a pitch of rapture." Fanny Kemble wrote concerning her: "Everyone here is now raving about her. . . . Her appearance is very striking. . . . Her voice is the most remarkable of her qualifications for her vocation, being the deepest and most sonorous voice I ever heard from a woman's lips . . . and expresses admirably the passions in the delineation of which she excels—

Figure 20. Rachel as Marie Stuart

scorn, hatred, revenge, vitrolic irony, seething jealousy, and a fierce love. . . . She is completely the rage in London now; all the fine ladies and gentlemen crazy after her; the Queen throwing her roses on the stage out of her own bouquet, and viscountesses and marchionesses driving her about, *à l'envie l'une de l'autre*, to show her all the lions of the town."[17]

On June 8th Astley's Amphitheatre, at the foot of Westminster Bridge, burned to the ground—"one of the most extensive and disastrous fires," reported the *Times*, "since the destruction of the Royal Exchange in 1838." This huge theater, with a capacity of 3,000, had been the home of equestrian performances—plus tumbling, Egyptian pyramids, slack-rope vaulting, tricks on chairs, etc. Most of the stable of fifty horses was saved, but a servant perished in the flames. The loss to Ducrow, the manager, was £30,000. He went insane, and died shortly after.

Another kind of farewell was being said in July to still another famous place of entertainment: Vauxhall Gardens. The glory of the "lustrous long arcades" which had been enjoyed by Englishmen for a century was dimmed; the Gardens had fallen upon evil financial days and were for sale to the highest bidder. They covered eleven acres, and in their prime had been a sort of magic Arabian Nights for thousands. Colonnades three hundred feet long, with an arched Gothic roof; a blaze of radiance from dazzling festoons of lamps—as many as 20,000 on nights of gala illumination; magnificent chandeliers and colored lights; the Hall of Mirrors; the Rotunda, with its stage for ballets and the pit for displays of horsemanship; its groves and its fountains and its statues; its William Tell cottage and its hermit's cave—its balloon ascensions, with Mr. Green and his Nassau balloon daring the law of gravity and, indeed, coming near disaster on the night of July 12th, when his valve wouldn't work, and he rose to a height of six or seven thousand feet before he got it under control—all this was disappearing, to the sentimental regret of those who had enjoyed the festivities. Even the attenuated chicken sandwiches in their winding sheets of ham were remembered fondly.

The Gardens was bought in for £20,000, and among the effects at the sale in October were half-a-dozen pictures said, traditionally, to have been painted by Hogarth. "A Drunken Man" brought four guineas, and the original of a scene later used in "A Rake's Progress," five pounds.*

The publishing event of midsummer was announced in the magazines and by hand bills as follows:

"Too-to-tooit-tooit. On Saturday, July 17, 1841, will be Published, Price Threepence (size of the 'Athenaeum') No. 1 of a New Weekly Work of Wit and Whim, Cuts and Caricatures, to be called 'Punch; or the London Charivari.' This Guffawgraph will be a refuge for destitute wit; an asylum for the thousands of orphan jokes which are now wandering about . . . and will contain original humorous and satirical articles by all the funny dogs with comic tales."

Thus was set loose what was to become an institution as British as roast beef—the one spot where, through the years, not merely the humor but also the aspirations, prejudices, blind insularities, and generous humanities of the English middle classes found adequate expression. At this distance it becomes a "social document" for one who would discover the temper of life in the forties.

In its early stages the humor of Punch was startlingly broad and elementary. It was at its best in satire. Its humor, accurately indicated in the beginning at least by the tone of its announcement, was of the same

* Vauxhall, however, was resuscitated under other management. The day of its brilliant success was over, but it lingered on as a place of entertainment until it finally closed in 1859.

broad school that one finds in *Cruikshank's Omnibus*, edited by Laman Blanchard; in the *Comic Almanack*, also illustrated by Cruikshank; in *Hood's Magazine and Comic Miscellany* and his *Comic Annual*, which, appearing in November, 1841, contained his famous "Miss Kilmansegg," a minor classic; in Albert Smith's *Man in the Moon*, and in half-a-dozen lesser boisterous effusions of the period. It lived on a diet of terrible, egregious, and unrelenting puns—in both pictures and letterpress. It found humorous the most extravagant dialect stories—which the maligned United States could not have exceeded in banality. It was touchy and savage when foreigners criticized England. It was unfair to Prince Albert. But it was essentially and healthily sane—and not, at its best, unfunny!

Punch made great capital of the political vagaries of the time, and its cuts told—even sifted through the favorite awkward device of putting semi-serious drawings of the heads of Peel and Russell on the bodies of dogs and asses. Colonel Sibthorp, the member for Lincoln and the comic relief of the House of Commons, was a staple subject for humor throughout the decade. Sibthorp, Toryism incarnate, opposed everything that smacked of progress, and his speeches were usually greeted with roars of laughter from his colleagues.* But *Punch* was at its best when it turned a calculating eye on the social absurdities of the day and pilloried all forms of pretension, affectation, and folly. It punctured bladders of self-esteem and hit heads of stupidity wherever it saw them.

The real clue to *Punch* is that it took itself seriously. Mark Lemon, its first editor, Henry Mayhew, Douglas Jerrold, Gilbert à Beckett, Thackeray, when he joined the staff in 1842—all were men with social consciences, champions of the underdog, burningly earnest in their humanitarianism. It branded as "a heartless insult thrown in the idle teeth of famishing thousands" the Duke of Wellington's statement in 1841 that England is "the only country in which the poor man, if only sober and industrious, was quite certain of acquiring a competency." It published in the Christmas number of 1843 Tom Hood's "Song of the Shirt," which had an electrifying impact. Cruel legal treatment of

---

* "He is a fine-looking, hearty man, with a jovial countenance; is a great racer, gambler, and wine-drinker. He makes short speeches, full of odd ideas and humorous arguments. He is one of the aristocracy—a kind of pet of theirs. He often crows like a cock in the House when he is tired of the speech of a fellow-member, or will interrupt him in other ways. . . . He is a notorious libertine, and we were told by excellent authority that upon the death of a favorite mistress an English bishop condoled with him upon his loss." (D. V. G. Bartlett: *London by Day and Night*, N. Y., 1852.)

A HANDSOME LEG-I-SEE (LEGACY).

Figure 21. An early pun of *Punch*

Figure 22. Fireworks at Vauxhall Gardens. Joel il Diavolo descending on a single wire from the top of the Campanile

destitution as a crime; harsh sentences for juvenile delinquents; flogging in boys' schools or in the army—these all came under *Punch's* own lash. The comic and the crusading shoulder each other in its pages. It carries more of the real form and pressure of its time than one would have any right to expect from such a journal.

Summer grew into autumn. The weather had been even more temperamental than usual. There was much concern about the coming harvest: late July and early August had been "deplorable"—rainy, foggy, and cold by turns. In October more rain fell than in any other October for a quarter of a century. The winds were bleak and gusty; floods swept over many districts, and on an extraordinary tide the Thames overflowed into London and its neighborhood. At Dover storms carried away an immense quantity of beach. The price of grain rose to 72s. 8d. per quarter, and there were rumors of a partial failure of the potato crop in Ireland. As it turned out, the final wheat and oat crop was one third below normal. The suffering in town and countryside grew more severe. In Leeds a committee was established to examine the condition of the unemployed poor. Some 1,946 families had no visible means of subsistence whatever.

On the last day of October a great fire broke out in the Tower, destroying the Grand Storehouse, the Clock Tower, and the Round Tower, and threatening the Jewel Tower, from which the heroic efforts of the warders rescued the crown jewels. But a stand of 280,000 arms was destroyed, as well as a vast quantity of ancient military trophies. There was general surprise that the jewels, the records, the powder, etc., should have been kept in such combustible places. Immense public excitement was aroused by the calamity, and the Tower was besieged by hordes of sight-seers.

The Duke of Wellington, pursued early in November by a committee seeking relief for the poverty-stricken hand-loom weavers of Paisley, and refusing audience on the strange grounds that he "is not in the Queen's political service . . . and exercises no power or authority," admitted that he had come up to London "in order to attend at Buckingham House, where Her Majesty will be confined."*

On November 9th the following bulletin was posted outside Buck-

---

* This was a rather cavalier excuse on the part of the great national hero, a member of the Cabinet without portfolio, whose influence in high circles was incalculably great. The *Spectator*, in commenting on the event, said, "It now appears he is in the Queen's obstetrical service."

ingham Palace: "The Queen was safely delivered of a Prince this morning at 48 minutes past 10 o'clock. Her Majesty and the infant Prince are perfectly well." The *London Gazette* revealed that present on the occasion were Prince Albert, the Duchess of Kent, and, according to old tradition, the officers of state—among others, the Duke of Wellington, the Bishop of London, Sir Robert Peel, the Earl of Aberdeen, and Sir James Graham. Immediately after birth the royal infant was carried by the nurse into the adjoining room and shown to the illustrious personages in waiting. The Cabinet ministers were attired in Windsor uniform.

Ballads were written and hawked for the occasion, guns were fired, crowds gathered shouting in the streets. It was Lord Mayor's Day, and the birth occurred just as the gala procession was starting from the City for Westminster. "In memory of the happy coincidence," the Lord Mayor for the year, Mr. Pirie, was created Sir John Pirie, Baronet. Greville in his memoirs noted another curious point. "It has been the custom for the officer on guard at St. James's Palace to be promoted to a majority when a Royal Child is born. The guard is relieved at forty-five minutes after ten. At that hour the new guard marched into the Palace Yard, and at forty-eight minutes after ten the child was born. The question arises which officer is entitled to the promotion. The case is before Lord Hill for his decision."[18] History records that the old guard won.

On January 25th, at Windsor, amid great pomp and circumstance, the infant Prince of Wales was christened Albert Edward. Ambassadors and foreign ministers were there in full dress, the Knights of the Garter in full regalia, all the royalty and princes in uniform. The Duke of Wellington bore the Sword of State. The King of Prussia stood sponsor, and the Hallelujah Chorus was sung by full choir. The baby prince, later to become King Edward VII, by proxy renounced the lusts of the flesh. He did not cry once, said reporters of the occasion, "he only winced a little at the holy water." No one at the time saw any future significance in that, however.

As the year ran out, new books were coming from the presses. The printed form of Carlyle's lectures of the previous year, *Heroes and Hero-Worship*, found respectful acceptance in intelligent circles and were met by reviewers with a combination of respect for the ideas and of irritation with the style in which they were imbedded. The *Athenaeum* greeted Browning's *Pippa Passes* with the comment that because the poet has an apparent disposition to *think*, "we have taken more than ordinary pains to understand [him], more than it may turn out that he is worth. Our faith in him, however, is not yet extinct—but our patience *is*. . . . These 'Dramatical Pieces' are produced in cheap form . . . to meet and help the large demand . . . which Mr. Browning anticipates for them! Stillborn, itself, it [*Pippa Passes*] is also, no doubt, the last of its race—that is, if their being maintained by the public is a positive condition of their being begotten."

Thackeray, better known to his public as M. A. Titmarsh, published *The Great Hoggarty Diamond* and *Comic Tales and Sketches*, and was writing steadily for *Fraser's Magazine*. Dickens published for the first time in separate editions *The Old Curiosity Shop* and *Barnaby Rudge*, both of which had appeared serially in *Master Humphrey's Clock*.

The "popular" novelists were turning out their annual or semi-annual works of fiction. G. P. R. James (still several novels ahead of his publishers) produced *The Jacquerie*; Mrs. Gore, *Cecil, the Adventures of a Coxcomb*, and *Cecil, the Peer*; William Harrison Ainsworth (just resigned from the editorship of *Bentley's Magazine*), *Old St. Paul's*; Charles Lever, *Charles O'Malley*; Frederick Marryat, *Masterman Ready* and *Joseph Rushbrook*. But of all the novels the one which aroused the widest popular interest was Samuel Warren's *Ten Thousand a Year*, which had been appearing anonymously in *Blackwood's Magazine*— anonymously, it was said, so that the author might ask everyone what he thought of the new novel. It had enormous sales, going through several editions, was translated into French and Russian, and was dramatized by R. P. Peake at the Adelphi—timed to appear almost simultaneously with its publication in three volumes. Warren was the author of the successful *Diary of a Late Physician* (which *Punch* called *The Diarrhoea of a Late Physician*); yet *Ten Thousand a Year* surpassed all possible expectations. The reviews were "mixed"; nevertheless the trade sold it by the hundreds.

Here is a book completely forgotten, and it is instructive to try to discover its contemporary appeal. Some of the reviewers attributed its popularity to the fact that it eulogized the Tories and satirized the Whigs. It is to be doubted, however, that its sale depended upon party implications, though it is true, as one reviewer put it, that all the Liberals are "described as unprincipled scoundrels, whether dupes or knaves, and most of them ill-looking, low-bred persons, with vulgar names; the Tories, on the contrary, pictured as paragons of virtue, talent, and propriety, high-minded, dignified, and handsome, with euphonious names—models of human perfection." Its humor was of

Figure 23. Samuel Warren

the kind likely to appeal to popular taste—broad and farcical—in spite of the author's claim that he was trying to exhibit, "in a course of natural events, and by the agency of natural characters, the aspect, professionally, politically, and religiously, of English society in the nineteenth century." This statement bears about as much resemblance to the finished work as Gainsborough does to Cruikshank.

It is a politico-legal novel, the hero of which is a haberdasher's shop-man, Tittlebat Titmouse—a brainless little coxcomb. For a time it is supposed that he inherits a large estate, and his adventures in the toils of the law as well as his naïve delight with his new-found wealth furnish the staple of the story. At this distance, however, and at that level, there is a kind of triumphant vigor about the story and the characters, a clear, rapid forcefulness of style, and an accumulation of little details that gives it liveliness, if not verisimilitude. Its proper fate, to be sure, would have been to be reviewed in the United States as "reflecting accurately the tastes and activities of a large section of the English public." Yet as a study in what was read and liked in the

1840's, *Ten Thousand a Year* is more useful than many a better book.

Another readable and popular work was Charles Mackay's *Memoirs of Extraordinary Popular Delusions,* in two volumes. Mackay gave accounts of the Mississippi Scheme, the South Sea Bubble, the Tulipomania, the Witch Maniac, the Slow Poisoner, etc.*

One book of 1841 received polite though not extended attention—one among several volumes published between 1839 and 1842 entitled *Zoology of the Voyage of the Beagle,* by a man of thirty-two—Charles Darwin.

Eighteen forty-one was census year, and the Victorians, who loved statistics, were much interested in what the figures showed about the state of the country as it entered the new decade.

The total population of Great Britain was over eighteen and a half million, as follows:

England:	14,995,508
Wales:	911,321
Scotland:	2,620,610

The population of Ireland 8,175,124.

This represented a total growth since the census of 1831 of 14 per cent for England and Wales, 11 per cent for Scotland, and 5 per cent for Ireland—an over-all average of 11 per cent. Although the rapid growth of the manufacturing towns had slowed somewhat (there were only five towns, besides London, of more than 100,000 population), the movement from the agricultural districts to the towns was still marked. In 1831, 28 per cent of those employed in productive labor were engaged in agriculture, 42 per cent in trade and manufacture. But in 1841 there were twice as many engaged in trade and manufacture as in agriculture. The increase of population in the great manufacturing districts—most rapid in Lancashire, Lanarkshire, and Forfarshire—was 30 per cent, the decrease in the agricultural districts, 2½ per cent.

London reported a population of 1,948,417,† an increase of 293,423.

---

* This book, reprinted in New York in 1932, with a preface by Bernard M. Baruch, went through five editions by 1950.

† As defined within the area of the London weekly tables of mortality, being parts of the counties of Middlesex, Surrey, and Kent. In 1831 the figure was 1,654,994. Manchester and Salford townships had grown from 182,812 to 217,056; Liverpool from 165,175 to 223,003; Birmingham from 110,914 to 138,215; the parish of Leeds from 123,393 to 152,054.

Trade had boomed fantastically. The official value of exports in 1841 was £101,750,000—a growth of 70 per cent in the ten-year period; of imports, £62,750,000—a growth of 30 per cent.

Bradshaw's first railway guide was published in December, 1841, and it reflected a steady increase in the number of lines open for service. The total number in operation, using steam locomotives, up to the beginning of the year, was sixty-six. The longest of these was the Great Western: 117½ miles; twenty-three were eight miles or under in length. In 1841 four new lines were partially opened, and of twelve in progress in 1840, two were completed and opened in 1841.

A total of 1,000,000 domestic servants was reported for England and Wales alone.

Behind these figures in the statistical tables lies the human story in this birth of a decade—the story of a nation that was old and yet new, where land and its proprietors still carried traditional authority and prestige, and yet where the balance of power was in process of shifting from the great estates to the industrial towns. Every time a railway was opened across the park of a protesting aristocrat, every time a Cobden or a Bright was elected to Parliament, every time a new factory in Birmingham sent up its stacks, the old order changed slightly. The economic and agricultural distresses of the moment could not hide the fact that a new kind of civilization was boiling and bubbling beneath the ancient way of life. There were still too many anachronisms and suddenly acquired dislocations for Progress to be much more than a gleam in the eye of a Macaulay or a Manchester mill owner. But in the first year of its life the new decade was on its way—where, no one was quite sure.

In the last days of the old year a deputation of the unemployed weavers of Spitalfields waited upon the Lord Mayor at the Mansion-house; the Duke of Northumberland forwarded £100 to the fund for the relief of the distressed operatives in Paisley; a great Anti-Corn-Law meeting was held in Dublin and a Chartist tea party in the town hall of Birmingham. But at the theaters the Christmas pantomimes flourished. The postmen, the dustmen, the brewers' draymen, the greengrocers' and bakers' boys all expected their Christmas boxes, and got them. Charles Dickens was preparing to sail in the *Britannia*, from Liverpool, for the United States. There was a private meeting of the Royal Buck-hounds at Windsor, with Prince Albert "sporting the scarlet." On the Castle Terrace the Queen took walking exercises.

The weather was cold, and there was skating again on the Serpentine.

CHAPTER TWO

1842 * The Year of the Locust

THE critical year of 1842 began quietly enough. Most busy Londoners were more concerned with grumbling about the yellow fogs through which they had to grope their way, and about the raw weather compounded of alternate freezing and thawing, than with the rumblings from the provinces about growing distress in the manufacturing districts. Ever since the financial crisis of 1837 trade had been bad, and in the early forties the depression reached critical proportions. Disturbing items kept creeping into the newspapers. In January the Spitalfields silk weavers held a meeting at the Crown and Anchor, Bethnal Green, to receive a report which indicated that fully one half the looms were unused, while those at work were only partially busy. About the same time the *Carlisle Journal* reported the meeting of a committee of inquiry into the state of the town: "It shows that the fourth of our population is living in a state bordering on absolute starvation. The number of families . . . without any means of subsistence beyond a dependence on casual charity was found to be 309. . . . The number of persons whose weekly means of maintenance do not exceed one shilling per head (per week) is 1,465. . . . We have 5,561 individuals, in a population of 22,000, reduced to such a state of suf-

[58]

fering that immediate relief has become necessary to save them from actual famine." Of 1,120 paper mills throughout the kingdom only 120 were in operation. On January 5th a meeting was held at the White Hart Hotel, in Bath, to consider the distressed state of the manufacturing districts of the west of England. Mr. E. Edwards, Junior, reported that of nineteen broadcloth manufacturers in Bradford, only two remained, the others having failed or having shut down for want of trade. Of 462 looms, only eleven were in full operation. The same tales were told of other places—Chalford, Stroud, Ulley, Wotton, Frome, Trowbridge, etc. The meeting joined in demanding free trade as the solution of the difficulties. On the fourteenth an Anti-Corn-Law banquet was held at Glasgow, with 2,000 present, as part of a two-day demonstration against depressed weaving and spinning conditions. To be sure, the assemblage broke up at 11 P.M. with three cheers for the Queen and Prince Albert. The following Monday a meeting of 3,000 was held at Derby to petition for the total and immediate removal of the Corn Laws.

But there was much else to distract attention at the moment. There was the railway accident on the Great Western at Sunning in which eight lost their lives and seventeen were injured. . . . William Harrison Ainsworth announced his new *Ainsworth's Magazine*. . . . Charles Knight published the first volume of his twelve-volume edition of Shakespeare (using the folio of 1623 as the foundation of the text); and John Payne Collier announced his competing edition, which proposed to collate all existing quarto copies and the second folio of 1632. Shakespearean scholars, and the more learned journals, maintained an attitude of watchful expectancy.

The King of Prussia, Frederick William IV, at Court for the christening of the Prince of Wales, visited the Zoological Gardens, Newgate Prison, and the learned societies at Somerset House. He received addresses from the Bishop and the clergy of London, the Society for Promoting Christianity among the Jews, the Bible Society, and the Imperial Continental Gas Co. On his way to the steamer he witnessed a review of the Royal Artillery at Woolwich, and caught a cold in the head.

Splendid rites attended the laying of the cornerstone of the New Royal Exchange by Prince Albert on Monday the seventeenth. A canvas pavilion to hold 1,450 persons had been erected on the site; the floor was covered with crimson cloth—and for that one day the sun shone. The workmanlike dexterity with which the prince took the trowel and spread the mortar seemed to astonish the company, "who gave vent to their feelings in a round of cheers." A medal had been struck to commemorate the event. That night a grand banquet was held at the Mansionhouse, which was fitted up in gorgeous splendor; the hall glittered with gold and silver plate, and the entire company appeared in court dress.

A redecorated Drury Lane Theatre* was opened with a performance of *The Merchant of Venice,* with the new manager, Macready, as Shylock. Macready was generally recognized as the greatest of living actors, and long before the doors were opened, every entrance was besieged by eager crowds. Hundreds were unable to gain admission. Macready's first appearance "was like a spark to a mine—the pent-up enthusiasm burst forth in a succession of explosions, accompanied by waving of hats and handkerchiefs, which continued until the shouters were fairly tired out." For the first time in the English theater the seats in the pit as well as the boxes were numbered, and some were divided into stalls—the signs of the approaching change by which the pit was to become both more comfortable and less disreputable.

Not a little enthusiasm was shown, too, by the respectable middle classes over the efforts of Macready to purify the saloon-lounge of its notorious reputation as an assignation ground for prostitutes.

Thus January. On February 3d the Queen opened Parliament in person.

The Government was facing a deficit, and much of the session was taken up with Sir Robert Peel's budget proposals, which he introduced in a speech of three hours and forty minutes, "acknowledged by everybody," said the diarist Greville, "to have been a masterpiece of financial statement. The success was complete; he took the House by storm. . . . It is really remarkable to see the attitude Peel has taken in this Parliament, his complete mastery over both his friends and his foes."[1] The chief measure by which Peel succeeded in turning the budget deficit into a surplus was the imposition of a tax of 7d. in the

---

* In this connection, the *Spectator* (March 5th) has a recommendation concerning stage lighting which seems curiously modern, though it was not generally adopted for many years to come. "It was suggested some time ago, that in lieu of the foot-lamps, which are prejudicial to personal appearance and expression of the face by casting shadows upward, a strong illumination might be thrown from above: The Bude light offers facilities for adopting that suggestion; its rays being not only more powerful, but warmer than gas or the Drummond light. [The Bude light was a light obtained by directing a stream of oxyhydrogen gas on a quantity of pounded eggshells.] A lamp placed in front of the gallery might be so contrived as to throw a stream of light upon the stage . . . and by using gauze screens of various colours and densities, the effects of moonlight, twilight, midnight, and fire, might be imitated almost to illusion."

pound on all incomes over £150 a year. This measure, it was piously hoped, would not be needed after an initial three-year period. At the same time Peel got through the Commons a measure reducing the tariff on 750 out of a total of 1,200 dutiable articles—in addition to a reduction of duty on imports of coffee and timber. Parliament was moving faster than it knew toward complete free trade.

The Corn Laws, however, were another matter. Everyone was aware of inconsistencies in the old sliding scale of duties, but only a minority were ready for complete repeal. Mr. Villiers made his annual motion to repeal the laws entirely and was, as usual, overwhelmingly defeated in spite of Cobden's vehement speech against the principle of the Corn Laws. Lord John Russell, for the Liberals, wanted to impose a fixed duty. Peel, instead, introduced a new sliding scale which, it was hoped, would remove some of the inequities. It was noted that his "manner was anxious—uneasy; we never saw him address the House with so little confidence." He had notable support from young Mr. Gladstone, and the House passed the bill. It aroused little enthusiasm in any quarter —it was not enough to please the Anti-Corn-Law Leaguers, who would be satisfied only with total repeal, yet it was enough seriously to disturb the agricultural Protectionists, who quaked when any free-trade foot was put in the door. Farmers and aristocratic agriculturalists in the Reading district held a public meeting to make a demonstration against the Government measure. Mr. J. Haslam, who was unanimously voted to the chair, spoke in this strain—"Should it be said that Sir Robert and his colleagues had the country with them? ('Hear!' and cries of 'No, no!') Were they satisfied with the measures proposed? ('No, no!') If they had felt hitherto that they had not been sufficiently protected, did they believe it likely that they should be protected now? ('No, no!')" Meetings were held at Manchester, Birmingham, Bradford, Bolton, and the other great manufacturing towns. Peel was burned in effigy during a riot in Northampton.

One other question presumably of national concern with which the Commons concerned itself during this session was the introduction of a bill to legalize marriage between a widower and his deceased wife's sister—at the time forbidden by law, although marriage of first cousins was considered quite respectable, indeed, had royal sanction. Lord Ashley (later Lord Shaftesbury) said that the clergy and the women were opposed to the measure, presumably because "such a connection might create domestic dissensions and embitter the wife's feelings during her lifetime with harassing anticipations and suspicions regarding her sister." It was further suggested that a measure of this kind "would diminish to some extent the sanctity now supposed to invest . . . the character of the sister of a wife." Appeal was made to the revealed Word of God and the motion to bring in the bill was defeated 123 to 100.

In the meantime, up at Edinburgh, people crowded the Zoological Gardens to see a rattlesnake ("generally in a torpid condition," but now evidently ready for its semi-annual feeding) swallow a mouse. The process occupied half an hour. And on March 16th London passed one of its major crises. For some time a report had been floating in certain circles that the capital was to be swallowed by an earthquake on the sixteenth. The rumor was based on two metrical prophecies, dated A.D. 1203 and 1598, said to be in the British Museum. These were printed and circulated in a penny pamphlet during the early part of the year. According to this publication, the first prophecy ran:

> In eighteen hundred and forty-two
> Four things the sun shall view:
> London's rich and famous town,
> Hungry earth shall swallow down;
> Storm and rain in France shall be
> Till every river runs a sea!
> Spain shall be rent in twain,
> And famine waste the land again,
> So say I, the Monk of Dree,
> In the twelve hundredth year and three.

The other, purportedly by Dr. Dee, the sixteenth-century astrologer:

> The Lord have mercy on you all,
> Prepare yourselves for dreadful fall
> Of house and land and human soul—
> The measure of your sins are full!

> In the year one eight and forty two
> Of the year that is so new;
> In the third month, of that sixteen,
> It may be a day or two between.

> Perhaps you'll soon be stiff and cold,
> Dear Christian be not stout and bold;
> The mighty kingly proud will see
> This come to pass as my name's Dee.

To confirm these scholarly predictions was added the testimony of a Russian monk, more extensive in his scope, who said that the whole of England in 1842 "would disappear from the Globe by an Earth-quake." And thus many timid persons (including numbers of Irish) "removed eastward of Stepney Old Church, on the supposition that the earthquake is not to extend beyond that venerable edifice." The *Times* of March 17th reported:

> The frantic cries, the incessant appeals to Heaven for deliverance, the invocations to the Virgin and the Saints for mediation, the heart-rending supplications for assistance, heard on every side during the day, sufficiently evidenced the power with which this popular delusion had seized the mind of these superstitious people. . . . Long before the hour appointed for the starting of steamboats from London Bridge Wharf, Hungerford Market, and other places, the shore was thronged by crowds of decently attired people of both sexes . . . About 11 o'clock the *Planet* came alongside the London Bridge Wharf, and the rush to get on board of her was tremendous, and, in a few minutes, there was scarcely standing room on board. The trains on the various railways were, during the whole of Tuesday and yesterday morning, unusually busy in conveying passengers without the proscribed limits of the metropolitan disaster. . . . From an early hour in the morning, the humbler classes from the east end of the Metropolis sought refuge in the fields beyond the purlieus of Stepney . . . and Primrose Hill, also, was selected as a famous spot for viewing the demolition of the leviathan city. The darkness of the day and the thickness of the atmosphere, how-ever, prevented it being seen.

Numbers of the middle and upper classes went to Brighton to avoid the earthquake. On the night of the fifteenth nearly twenty carriages arrived there—more than since the opening of the London and Brighton Railway. Only a skeptical journalist could speculate as to whether the convulsion was to be coextensive with the twopenny or threepenny post district.

On the seventeenth, it can now be revealed, the fearful ones were able to return to an unshaken city.

Shades of the eighteenth century returned briefly in this month of March with the announcement of the sale of Strawberry Hill and its objects of art—Horace Walpole's Gothic castle at Twickenham. The place had been neglected for fifty years, rarely visited, and the generation which went to see the collection broken up had only a distant curiosity as to what it had meant in the old days. The sale took place —with the famous George Robins as auctioneer—in a temporary shed erected on the grounds. The prized books, the drawings and manuscripts, the miniatures, the old china, the grotesque fragments of Gothic carving, the armor, the paintings and enamels and glass—all were sold between April 25th and May 21st. The sum obtained was £33,450, 11s. 9d.

More exciting news than this was discussed in April in coffee shops and at dinner tables. Not for some time had the London public had a chance to read the details of a really first-class murder, including sex, dismemberment, and all the relevant gory details. The *Times* presented just as lengthy descriptions as did the sensational *Weekly Dispatch* or *Bell's Sporting Life.*

Daniel Good, a middle-aged Irishman and coachman to Mr. Quelaz Shiel, an East Indian merchant, lived at the stables about a quarter of a mile from Mr. Shiel's house. Good had been suspected of stealing a pair of black breeches, but when a policeman, William Gardiner, searched the stable, the coachman exhibited great uneasiness. At last, beneath some hay, Gardiner discovered what he supposed to be a dead goose. He exclaimed, "My God! what's this?" whereupon Good rushed from the stable and locked the door after him.

The object in the hay proved to be the trunk of a woman's body, shorn of its head and limbs, and ripped open in front. In the meantime Good had escaped. A surgeon's assistant discovered upon examination that the flesh of the body had been separated with "a sharp instrument," and the bones broken or sawed through. The female had been about twenty-five years of age. During the course of this examination an overpowering stench came from the harness room, and there in the fireplace was found the burned remains of a human head and limbs. A large ax was also discovered, and a saw, both covered with blood.

It developed that Good, after he had fled, left his house at No. 18 South Street, Manchester Square, and took a cab, telling the man to drive as fast as possible to the Birmingham Railway. He was so ghastly pale that the cabman asked him if he were ill.

The inquest on the remains of the body brought out the fact that Good had been living with a Jane Jones, known as Mrs. Good.

Another woman, Lydia Susannah Butcher, testified that Good had been courting her, and that she had expected to be married to him in about a fortnight.

Dr. Benjamin Ridge of Putney, who had examined the remains found in the stable, said that he did not think the woman had ever had a child, but he was of the opinion that she would have had one in about four or five months. Small pieces of clothing found in the room and marked with blood were identified as belonging to Mrs. Good. The coroner's jury gave the verdict that Jane Jones, otherwise Jane Good, had been wilfully murdered by Daniel Good.

Good eluded pursuit for nearly a fortnight, but was at last found working as a bricklayer's helper at Tunbridge. On the sixteenth he was discovered by Thomas Rose, who had formerly been a policeman at Wandsworth. The fugitive was seized and carried before the magistrates. While denying his identity to them, he took out a comb, and with it turned back the hair from his forehead, as if to hide a bald place on his head—a gesture which had been mentioned in the police description as a habit with him. On the evening of the seventeenth he was removed to Bow Street police station. He was then committed to Newgate for trial on the charge of murder.

The trial took place in the Central Criminal Court. The place was crowded, with women and young ladies present. Good pleaded "Not Guilty," but within half an hour after its retirement the jury returned with a verdict of "Guilty."

Good burst into a passionate declaration of his innocence, protesting that Susan Butcher was the cause of it all, and that Jones had cut her own throat, after which a man of whom Good occasionally bought matches cut up the body and burned some of it.

The crowd outside the prison greeted the verdict with tumultous cheers.

On the Sunday before the execution there was a large crowd, including the lady mayoress and other ladies, in Newgate Chapel to hear the "condemned sermon" preached at Good. The prisoner was executed on Monday morning, persisting in his story to the last. The crowd assembled to witness his execution "was greater than any since the execution of Fauntleroy. . . . A brief and violent struggle terminated his life. Dr. Elliotson afterward took a cast of the convict's head, in the presence of several medical and scientific gentlemen."[2]

According to Henry Mayhew,[3] 1,650,000 copies of broadsheets containing ballads on the crime and execution were sold at the time. One of these sets of verses ran, in part, as follows:

Of all the wild deeds upon murder's black list,
Sure none is so barbarous and cruel as this,
Which in these few lines unto you I'll unfold,
The recital's enough to turn your blood cold.

In the great town of London, near Manchester Square,
Jane Jones kept a mangle in South Street we hear,
A gentleman's coachman oft visiting came,
A cold-blooded monster, Dan Good was his name.

As a single man unto her he made love,
And in course of time she pregnant did prove,
Then with false pretences he took her from home,
To murder his victim and the babe in her womb.

To his master's stables in Putney Park Lane,
They went, but she never returned again:
Prepare for your end then the monster did cry,
Your time it is come for this night you must die.

Then with a sharp hatchet her head did cleave,
She begged for mercy, but none would he give,
Have mercy dear Daniel my wretched life spare
For the sake of your own child which you know I bear.

. . . .

And when she was dead this sad deed to hide,
The limbs from her body he straight did divide,
Her bowels ript open and dripping with gore,
The child from the womb this black monster he tore.

He made a large fire in the harness room,
Her head, arms, and legs in the fire did consume,
But e'er his intentions were fulfilled quite,
This dark deed by Providence was brought to light.

. . . .

He soon was found guilty and sentenced to die,
The death of a murderer on the gallows high,
The blood of the murdered must not cry in vain,
And we hope that his like we shall ne'er see again.[4]

Thus ended the *cause célèbre* of 1842.

Figure 24. A ballad broadside

May came, and with it the London "season." On May 12th the Queen gave a fancy-dress ball in the Throne Room of Buckingham Palace, to the great interest both of those who were able to attend and those who were not. The press spent columns of type on the description of the elaborate costumes—the Queen appearing as Queen Philippa and Prince Albert as Edward III. Lady Caroline Fox Strangways wrote a description of the occasion to Lady Harriot Frampton:[5] "The Queen . . . and her Court sat upon a raised throne, upon which a great light was thrown by a Bude light, and behind them were hangings of silk embroidered with coats-of-arms, etc.; above, quite high up, was one of the bands, also dressed up. Everybody came into this room and passed by her to make their bows, beginning with the quadrilles. It was rather formidable. . . . It was a beautiful sight, but I was very glad when it was over to get rid of my dress which was hot and stiff. The Queen's dress was not becoming, and she looked hot and oppressed. It was a heavy crown with gold things coming down on each side of her face. Prince Albert's dress was very magnificent, and very becoming. He was, I think, the best dressed person there. . . ."

About half-past six on the evening of May 30th the Queen was returning from her usual drive, with Prince Albert at her side. As they came down Constitution Hill toward the Palace, a man who had been leaning against the wall of the Palace garden advanced close to the low open carriage, drew a pistol, and before anyone could prevent him, fired at the Queen. The smoke from the pistol covered the face of Colonel Wylde, who rode beside the coach, but the Queen was untouched. The man, John Francis, was seized; the carriage continued at a rapid rate into the Palace grounds. The Duchess of Kent met her daughter and dissolved in a flood of tears, while the Queen reassured her with cheerful words.

Parliament adjourned amid great agitation, and nearly fifty Privy Councilors met hastily at the office. But in the evening the Queen courageously attended the opera, where she was enthusiastically cheered.

Francis, the would-be assassin, was tried and found guilty of high treason, but the sentence was commuted to transportation for life. This was the second attempt upon the Queen's life; in 1840 a young lad named Oxford, later judged insane, had fired at her from almost the same spot. And later on in this same year—July 3d—when the Queen was driving from Buckingham Palace to the Chapel Royal, St. James's, a deformed young man named Bean drew a pistol at her. There was no explosion and it was not certain that he meant to fire. Nevertheless, these events—and Victoria's brave facing of them—aroused a great wave of public concern and devotion.

"The Queen and People," wrote one reporter,[6] "were drawn into more intimate communion. Compassion for the woman—young, a mother, and present to the view in all the most engaging relations of life—thus exposed to senseless perils, from which no general loyalty, no guards, and scarcely any precautions might be able to shield her . . . all these considerations prompted a display of popular feeling that had a deeper seat than mere 'loyalty' or attachment to the office of the Sovereign."

It is important, in assessing the 1840's, to understand the position that the Court held in public estimation during these years. It is sometimes difficult to detach the deeper attitude of the British public toward the Crown from the delight it takes and the enthusiasm it shows for all that hedges the throne—the display, the mummery, the affectionate and excited clinging to the medieval trappings and exercises of royalty. At its simplest the throne is the symbol of national unity, not a bit the less emotionally impressive because you have spent a number of centuries carefully delimiting the power of that throne.

Victoria had not yet become what she was to be in her widowed old age: the object of reverent worship, of an adulation the more complete because she seemed withdrawn and far away. Yet in these early years of her reign she gave something that the English needed even more. She was young and impulsive, to be sure, given to strong affections and equally strong dislikes; and for some years her ministers stood in uncertain expectation of her whims. She could be stubborn, too, and she could make mistakes. But she brought to the throne a graciousness which it had not known for a long time. In these early years can be seen the growth of what is perhaps strongest in the relationship of the English and their sovereign: a sense of *familyhood*— a comfortable awareness that there behind the palace gates was a wife and mother, with her growing brood around her knees, subject to the same endearments and family follies as the rest of us: the epitome of the household virtue which was the blessing of the English fireside. Victoria had married for love; the children who were the fruits of that love were beginning to arrive with dependable regularity; and love and the glowing sense of youthful moral domesticity were things which England had not had a chance to admire in its sovereigns within the memory of living man. Small wonder that its enthusiasm was more than that of subject for so-called ruler. A husband and wife who sang Mozart in the evening and went to bed at half-past ten! No more gambling at Windsor! What an example!

With Prince Albert the case was somewhat different. He, too, was young and good-looking. What his influence would be in his somewhat anomalous position was a matter of dubiety to many. After all, he was a foreigner, and he had to win his way more slowly; "Saxe-Coburg" and "Consort" did not go well together. He was not popular at first—his interest in the arts seemed a little strange, and his fetish for designing new uniforms for the army was the subject of some amusement. He appeared a little shyly distant—and strange, though amiable. But he went unostentatiously about his business, opening orphans' homes and laying cornerstones and reviewing troops with commendable assiduity. The papers made a point of reporting that, during the first year of his marriage, he spent much time, under tutelage, in studying the English Constitution. Before the decade was out he was accepted as more than an ornament—a hard and conscientious and intelligent worker, a worthy consort.

At the end of the summer Victoria and Albert made their first visit to Scotland. The Queen, proud of her Scottish blood, was enchanted by all that she saw; she gave her heart to the Highlands. All the pageantry of a royal procession hovered about the royal heads. There was a little confusion at first, for the time of the Queen's landing and her approach to Edinburgh was not properly signaled to the waiting dignitaries. All night long the civic authorities had sat up, in full costume, awaiting the hour; and now they had to trail ineffectually after the royal party, missing it at every turn. Pride was hurt, but the Queen subdued injured feelings by re-entering Edinburgh the next day, and the city keys were tendered according to plan. It was a busy fortnight, a succession of receptions, dinners, and levees, with fireworks and bands, and enthusiastic crowds of subjects standing undaunted in heavy rain to catch a glimpse of royalty. Albert, whose conception of sport had always been that of the amateur and who was unable to understand the British absorption in hunting and shooting, nevertheless found that deerstalking could be fun. One hundred and five men rounded up the game for him. He was the only person allowed to fire, and he killed nineteen deer, "beside several brace of grouse and other game." The royal couple became thus a part of the British family.

The attitude toward the Queen opens the still larger question of English domesticity in general, and particularly woman's place in the early Victorian scene. Like everything else in this complex generation it is easy to oversimplify. Certainly at this stage the new morality touched the aristocracy but lightly; the gayer titled nobility kept its women with impunity, if not quite so openly as in the old days. In this

Figure 25. Prince Albert   Figure 26. Queen Victoria

very year Lord Frankfort dragged one such relationship into the courts when he sued a former mistress for the possession of certain jewels which she had secured under his "protection." It is to be noted here, however, that Frankfort was generally condemned in the public prints. The girl was freed by a jury, and appeared to full houses, amid great excitement, at the City of London Theatre. This public appearance was also censured by the newspapers, but sympathy was obviously on the side of the erring girl.

Yet the middle classes and the respectable part of the laboring classes, feeling the dignity of a newly-to-be-consolidated position in society, influenced in part by royal example and more pervasively by the morality taught both by Dissent and Evangelicalism, were establishing new standards of private and public conduct. Nor were these held hypocritically; the tribute paid to family was not lip service. If there was some spiritual ugliness and a good deal of inflated sentimentalizing about womanhood in the pattern of Victorian life, they were aided and abetted by the victims of the compromise.

Tennyson gave poetic authority to accepted doctrines in 1847:

> Man for the field and woman for the hearth:
> Man for the sword and for the needle she:
> Man with the head and woman with the heart:
> Man to command and woman to obey:
> All else confusion.*

---

* The next line of *The Princess* is not often quoted: "Thus [spake] the hard old king." But the sentiment as it stood found sympathetic listeners in Victorian society.

In *The Young Bride's Book; being hints for regulating the conduct of Married Women* (1839), Arthur Freeling wrote concerning "the general duties of a Wife Towards her Husband":

"Nature, reason, and religion declare that men should be vested with the controlling power. When two persons differ upon a subject which must be decided, one *must* give way. You have in your marriage vow sworn to 'obey'; this is a difficult lesson for a proud spirit to learn, but when learned, is the most active principle in the production of a woman's happiness. It is useless to attempt an evasion of this duty, by assuming to yourself abilities superior to those of your husband."

This was a man writing. A still more authentic voice is that of Mrs. Sarah Ellis, who poured out during the early forties *The Women of England*, which reached a seventeenth edition in 1842, *The Wives of England*, and *The Mothers of England*. Writing avowedly to and about the middle classes, "the pillar of our nation's strength," she mingles common-sense moralizations with evangelistic fervor. Her initial premise is that "the women of England are deteriorating in their moral character, and that false notions of refinement are rendering them less influential, less useful, and less happy than they were. . . . By far the greater portion of the young ladies (for they are no longer *women*) of the present day are distinguished by a morbid listlessness of mind and body, except when under the influence of stimulus, a constant pining for excitement, and an eagerness to escape from everything like practical and individual duty." She believed that women's education did not fit them for the duties they must assume immediately after leaving school. (When she wants to say that governesses should be paid more, she writes: "Nothing can more clearly indicate a low state of public morals than the vulgar disrespect and parsimonious remuneration with which the agents employed in education are sometimes requited.") "The number of languid, listless and inert young ladies who now recline upon our sofas, murmuring and repining at every claim upon their personal exertions, is to me a truly melancholy spectacle." She is not without her own contradictions, however—unless one is to assume a startling metamorphosis between girl and mother. "Oh! but the mothers of England are too busy in the present day. There is really so much to be done for the public good, so many subscriptions to be raised, so many charities to be attended to, so many public meetings, committees, and societies of every description to be kept up, that in large towns, especially, the mother has literally no time—absolutely none—to attend to the instruction of her own children."

Mrs. Ellis's ruling theme as she addresses the wives of England is that the wife is distinctly the weaker vessel, the lesser creature, whose chief job is to make her lord and master happy. Let her state this in her own buxom periods:

> One important truth . . . is the superiority of your husband simply as man. It is quite possible you may have more talent, with higher attainments, and you may also have been more generally admired; but this has nothing whatever to do with your position as a woman, which is, and must be, inferior to him as a man. . . . In the character of a noble, enlightened, and truly good man, there is a power and a sublimity, so nearly approaching what we believe to be the nature and capacity of angels, that as no feeling can exceed, so no language can describe the degree of admiration and respect which the contemplation of such a character must excite. To be permitted to dwell within the influence of such a man, must be a privilege of the highest order; to listen to his conversation must be a perpetual feast; but to be admitted to his heart—to share his counsels, and to be the chosen companion of his joys and sorrows!—it is difficult to say whether humility or gratitude should preponderate in the feelings of the woman thus distinguished and thus blest. . . . And after all, what is it that man seeks in the companionship of woman?—An influence like the gentle dew, and the cheering light, more felt throughout the whole of his existence. . . .

In the midst of this apostrophizing good sense sometimes breaks in, and in the midst of ecstasy a subtle grim realization of reality. " 'What!' exclaims the young enthusiast, 'shall we not even hope to be happy?' Yes. Let us hope as long as we can; but let it be in subservience to reason and to truth." And in a moment when her guard is down, she speaks of the "married state as one of the trial of principle, rather than of the fruition of hope."

This sentimental, devotional attitude, with its emphasis on *feeling* (feeling without passion), was the convention. The patronizing attitude of the male was typified by *Punch*, in whose pages females, if not harridans in the Mrs. Caudle manner, were always simpering, vacuous creatures, demure and kittenish. Much is to be learned, too, from a study of the books of etiquette which were flooding the forties—in themselves a symptom of social uncertainty and of the desire of a class rapidly improving itself financially to keep its feet firmly on the social ladder. Etiquette was described in the forties as "the barrier which Society draws around itself, a shield against the intrusion of the impertinent, the improper and vulgar." Women, as Mrs. Ellis pointed out, were in process of becoming ladies.

One must avoid the temptation, however, to describe as universal that which various pieces of evidence would indicate to be merely a dominant tendency. Not all Americans of the mid-twentieth century subsist on "comic" books—whatever archaeologists a thousand years from now may try to prove to the contrary—and it is more than probable that many of those who read Mrs. Ellis did not subscribe to her sentiments. The general mood or atmosphere of an age is always being controverted by notable exceptions. The supposed subjection of women did not mean that many women, operating within the conventions, did not subtly get what they wanted; or that many others, thumbing a Victorian nose at Mrs. Ellis, did not dominate their households by sheer matriarchal affrontery. Thackeray's Campaigner in *The Newcomes* had her originals.

Then, too, there is the formidable list of women who won public reputations for themselves in the forties. The writing sorority, of all kinds and abilities: Mrs. Ellis herself; Mrs. Jameson, who first became famous in 1842 with her *Companion to the Public Picture-Galleries of London* and went on from there to write very successful travel books and books of religious legends; the Brontë sisters; Harriet Martineau, who began as a writer on religious subjects but became better known by popularizing economic and social subjects in a series of stories, who wrote stories for children, translated Comte, worked as an active journalist for the *Daily News*, contributed propaganda on behalf of mesmerism, and wrote a *History of the Thirty Years' Peace, 1815–45;* Maria Edgeworth, who lived until 1849; Eliza Cook, indefatigable poet and editor; Elizabeth Barrett; Mrs. Gore, the author of some seventy fashionable novels and plays; Lady Charlotte Bury, a lesser writer of worse novels, as well as poet, romancer, and compiler of cookbooks; Mrs. S. C. Hall, wife of the editor, and a novelist of Irish life; Miss Agnes Strickland, whose *Lives of the Queens of England*, published throughout the forties, won great recognition; Mary Howitt, who translated Hans Andersen and in collaboration with her husband lived an active journalistic life. There were scores of others, unknown to later generations, who had their little day in the annuals, wrote books of travel, and occasionally found their names in the lists of "esteemed" authors.

The stage, of course, had the brilliant Fanny Kemble and her sister Adelaide, accepted socially beyond the usual limits of their guild. Others, like Mrs. Grote (wife of George Grote the banker, M.P., and historian of Greece) shone in intellectual and political society. She was the female center of the Radical party in politics, "had a dictatorial style of expressing her conversational powers, and sometimes threw her modest and refined husband into the shade in general society." According to Fanny Kemble, she was one of the cleverest and most eccentric women in London society, who was defeated, however, in her gigantic attempt to "make an honest woman" of Fanny Ellsler, the popular dancer, and to introduce her into London society.

Among the best known of these women who obviously were not mere household doves were Mrs. Caroline Norton and Lady Blessington, appreciated not merely for their occasional literary productions, but because they were beautiful and unconventional hostesses and centers of attraction for the literary, artistic, and political figures of the day. In the case of each, an incredibly tangled domestic career lent an aura of polite notoriety—which each surmounted, at least as far as the men of the time were concerned, by sheer brilliance of personality.

Caroline Norton, gifted, impetuous, recklessly generous, was the granddaughter of Richard Brinsley Sheridan. After a series of quarrels she separated from her brutal and suspicious husband, George Norton, who, in bringing civil action, named as co-respondent the Whig Prime Minister, Lord Melbourne. The jury pronounced for the defense without leaving the box, but Norton succeeded in keeping possession of the children until, partly through his wife's efforts, the Infant Custody Bill was passed in 1839.

Between 1846 and 1849 she was editor of *Fisher's Drawing-Room Scrap-Book*, writing most of the contributions herself. She published collections of songs and long poems one of which, *The Child of the Islands* (1845), Abraham Hayward in the *Edinburgh Review* called "true poetry, great poetry." So difficult was it to disentangle her modest versifying ability from the charm of her personality that when Hartley Coleridge reviewed her *Dream* in the *Quarterly Review* he placed Mrs. Norton first among ten other British poetesses. Miss Barrett was second on the list![7]

Her freedom of manner and the curiously dubious household of which she was the center—as well as her ability to charm all males who came within her range—were enough to keep the fashionable ladies away from Lady Blessington and Gore House, Kensington. But thither flocked the literary and political lights of the day, for she captivated them all. Bulwer, Thackeray, Landor, Dickens, Forster, Macready, Louis Bonaparte, Wellington, Disraeli dined there; and many of them were assessed for contributions to the annuals which she edited in a brave and desperate attempt to stave off the financial ruin which finally descended upon her ménage.

The Countess of Blessington had married the first Earl of Blessington upon the death of her first husband, Captain Farmer, from whom she had separated after three months of savage treatment. They lived on

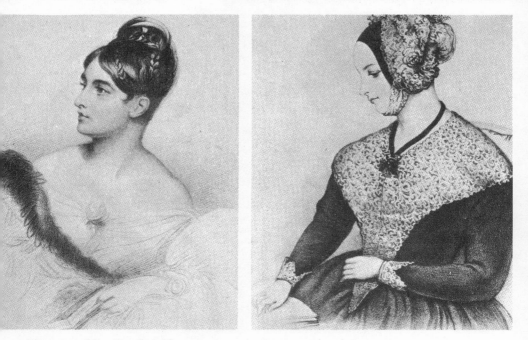

Figure 27. Mrs. Caroline Norton
Figure 28. Lady Blessington, after a lithograph of a drawing by D'Orsay

the Continent, where Count d'Orsay became part of the household, eventually marrying Blessington's daughter. The earl died in 1829, and in 1831 Lady Blessington, d'Orsay, and his wife came to London. In 1836 she took a lease on Gore House, in Kensington Road, which was to become one of the great social centers of London. Before long d'Orsay and his wife separated, but he stayed on with Lady Blessington, in a relationship the true nature of which is at this distance unclear. At the time the worst was generally believed.

Nothing is more remarkable than the courage, tact, and patience shown by this great lady, tied by association and whatever other intangible bonds to the charming and handsome d'Orsay, "the last of the dandies"—an amateur in art, liked by all, but beyond his graceful accomplishments an idler, a gambler, and congenital clubman, devotedly maintaining his fashionable life and dress at the expense of all financial integrity. Between 1841 and 1849 he dared not emerge from the grounds of Gore House between sunrise and sunset on weekdays, lest the bailiffs should seize him. The tragedy of the warmhearted, witty, and hospitable Blessington, who never complained to her friends, and went down to ultimate catastrophe with her head high, is one of the human documents of the time.

Her literary abilities, of which she made the most, were mediocre. Her *Conversations with Lord Byron* sold well, her journals of her

Figure 29. Count D'Orsay, self-portrait
Figure 30. William Harrison Ainsworth, after a drawing by D'Orsay

tours in France and Italy had considerable success, but her novels were slight and ineffectual. Her greatest success came with the annuals which she edited: *The Book of Beauty*, 1834–47, and *The Keepsake*, 1841–49. These and the other annuals* were "gorgeous inanities," as Greville described them, produced each year for the Christmas trade. Clad in the most handsome of watered silk or velvet, illustrated lavishly with beautifully engraved steel plates representing cow-eyed beauties and romantic landscapes, with poems and sketches extracted by the importunities of the editors from the literary celebrities of the day or willingly given by unknowns and by aristocratic pretenders—these volumes embalm little except vapid mediocrity. That they should have been sold by the thousands, to lie upon drawing-room tables, is a comment upon both household décor and the contemporary literary taste. By the end of the decade, however, their popularity was waning.

This hunger for elegance is underlined by the contemporary courtesy books. From the *Ladies' Pocket-Book of Etiquette* (1838) we learn, partly by implication, the temptations and restrictions of the time. "Abjure that unblushing exposure of the bust which is now so

---

* In 1842 at least nine were announced: *The Picturesque Annual, The Gift,* Montgomery's *Sacred Gift, The Forget Me Not, Friendship's Offering, The Keepsake, The Book of Beauty, The Drawing-Room Scrap-Book,* and the *Juvenile Scrap-Book.*

fashionable. . . . Ladies do not wear gloves during dinner. . . . Fish must be divided with a silver fork; in most respectable houses they have silver forks. . . . Servants should wait at table in white gloves; servants are not always very particular in having their hands clean; and nothing would annoy you more than to see a dirty thumb protruding into the plate of your friend" (or your own plate!) The author launches into a seven-page anathema against the waltz: "Among the most obvious proofs of the laxity of the regulations of etiquette is the fact that *waltzing* is permitted. . . . Ask the father, before the movings of ambition have calcined his heart, and directed his eyes only to the graces it displays, and the probable consequences of this display—a good match for his daughter, by which his ambition, either of purse or station, may be gratified, probably at the expense of that daughter's happiness—ask him if he would commit the innocence of his child to the pollution of the waltz? Ask the mother, before the demon of fashion has taken possession of her feelings," etc.

On the other hand, the more sophisticated "Cellarius," writing his *Drawing Room Dances* in 1847, approved of the waltz as rectifying the complaint against the young people of the present day "who are so often accused of walking instead of dancing," and waxes lyrical, not over the *waltz à trois temps,* which is in process of abandonment, but over the *waltz à deux temps:* "the waltz of the day—the dance in which they spring with that fascinating vivacity . . . relaxing or quickening their pace at will, promenading their partner in every way . . . varying their pace with every step, and arriving at that sort of giddiness, which I may venture to call intoxication."

Manners for would-be gentlemen were also becoming important. The eleventh edition of the *Gentleman's Pocket-Book of Etiquette*[8] urges its readers "Never convey food to your mouth with your knife—it is only to be used as a divider. . . . In taking soup, be careful not to make any disagreeable noise, by strongly inhaling your breath. . . . Do not pick your teeth at table, unless from absolute necessity." One's attitude toward servants should be that of "condescension without familiarity . . ." and "if, in the course of a walk in company with a friend, you happen to meet, or are joined by, an acquaintance, do not commit the common, but most flagrant error, of introducing such persons to one another."

Above all "always seek the society of those above yourself. . . . The man who is content to seek associates in his own grade (unless his station be very exalted) will always be in danger of retrograding. What is good company? becomes an important question. It is composed of

Figure 31. The waltz *à deux temps*

persons of birth, rank, fashion, and respectability. . . . If you cannot, from your station, obtain entrance to the best company, aim as near to it as your opportunities will permit."

Small wonder that in this emerging society, an amount of snobbishness became endemic, or that Thackeray, with his clinical eye for affectations, had such scope to display "The Snobs of England" in *Punch*.

The feminine dress of the period contributed to the ornamental rather than the practical aspect of womanhood. There was little change in fashion throughout the forties, though the skirts were fuller toward the end of the decade, moving toward the crinoline of the fifties. Pointed stays emphasized a long waist;* the bodice was form-fitting,

---

* Common sense made little progress here. In the *Ladies' Cabinet*, a fashion magazine of 1846, an article on stays quotes a conversation "attributed to a late eminent surgeon, whose strong sense and great love of truth frequently carried him beyond the bounds of politeness, even with the female sex. A lady of high rank complained to him of certain internal pains and disagreeable sensations she could not in any way account for. 'Madam,' he replied, 'it is your d——— stays; we are just like bladders half-filled with wind and water; if we press too hard upon one part, the contents must overflow another. Leave off your stays and take my pills,—you'll soon be better, if you mind what I say!'"

The fashion magazines of the forties, such as *The Belle Assemblée*, *The World of Fashion*, *The Court Magazine*, etc., are instructive in matters other than dress. They also give a clue to the kind of reading best liked in the boudoir: sweet and sentimental poems, romantic or Gothic stories by the most esteemed female

Figure 32. Fashions in 1841. Morning dress; public promenade dress. Half-figures: carriage, evening dress, evening headdress and cloak
Figure 33. Fashions in 1851. Morning promenade costume. Evening costumes

and held the arms in such a position that it was impossible to raise them. The skirt, over its six petticoats, was so full that a double skirt of three flounces required fifteen yards of material thirty-six inches wide. Thus was the female figure distorted and hidden. Nor did the advertisements of the time make any secret of the aids to fashion and beauty: artificial busts, paddings, "patent merino drawers," paint, powder, dyes, artificial ringlets, eyebrow thickeners, breath-sweeteners, and depilatories.

Bonnets rode on hair either swept back straight from the face or allowed to dangle in tubular curls over the ears. In general, comfort

writers, "The Last Trial of Fidelity," "The Dwarf Lover, a Tale of the Rhine" (continued), "The Gondola," "The Maniac Boy," "The Spectre Bride, or, Mysteries of Life and Love" (by the Baroness d'Alzel), "The Italian Bandits," "The Fatal Marriage"—in general a diet of banditti, pirates, and dark foreigners, of dukes, earls, barons, and lords; the fashionable novel at its worst. Occasional articles would punctuate these stories, such as "Courting in Andalusia," or departments of "Gossip and Gaieties of High Life." Here is the evidence which supports the traditional complaint of the social satirists of the time that wealth was too often seeking to marry title, or vice versa. From *The World of Fashion*, March, 1850: "The marriage of Lord Robert Montagu, second son of the Duke of Manchester, and Miss Cromie, only daughter and heiress of Mr. John Cromie. . . . The marriage of the Hon. Charles Augustus Murray, second son of the late Earl of Dunoore, and nephew of the Duke of Hamilton, with Miss Elizabeth Wadsworth, of Genesee, New York. . . . The bride possesses a very large fortune."

and hygiene—and certainly ease of locomotion—were disregarded. The well-dressed woman glided past furniture, through doors, and into carriages with a sort of preoccupied demure helplessness. Encased as she was, it was no wonder she needed lessons to faint advantageously.

As far as dress materials were concerned, the lady of the forties had a wide range of choice. Beautiful silks, ribbons, and brocades were imported from France. English mills were turning out quantities of superb cloths—shot, marbled, clouded—crepe, gauze, muslin, organdie, tarlatan, in all sorts of intense or subdued colors. As one looks through old books of samples he is pleased by the delicacy and loveliness of the woven and printed materials of the time.*

Fashions for men were moving slowly toward the darker colors which marked the middle and later years of the reign. Dandies and men of high fashion, however, still wore brilliant low-cut waistcoats, with tight trousers strapped under their boots. Those who wore loose trousers frequently indulged in wild tartan checks and stripes. The top hat was worn universally, by policeman and banker. Swallow-tailed coats were still in evidence, though short frock coats were more common. Overcoats had deep fur or velvet collars. The black or white stock was conventional. The hair was frequently worn long. Most men were clean-shaven, though side whiskers were beginning to appear.

All this, both male and female, applied chiefly to the metropolis and the fashionable centers of the larger towns. In the provinces one could still come across bewigged Georgians, and the fashions for women lagged several years behind those of the cities. Smocks were still the traditional uniform of the farmer, and many men lived and died in their local parishes without ever becoming aware that London, for example, really existed as more than a legend. The age of universal transportation was just making its beginnings; England was in some respects still many countries.

June came and went. A few weeks earlier England had been shocked by the news of a terrible railway accident in France—the worst in the history of railways. A Paris train, returning from the celebration of the King's fete at Versailles, was wrecked by a broken axle on the leading locomotive. The carriages caught fire, and fifty-three passengers,

---

* Such samples, pasted onto the pages, are the chief interest of the now-rare *Journal of Design and Manufactures*, issued between 1849 and 1852. It also includes samples of wallpaper, some of which seem very modern and some of which, the flock deep reds, particularly, reinforce the conception of Victorian stuffiness.

locked in according to railway rules, were burned to death. In England the Board of Trade immediately ordered the Great Western Railway to stop locking its carriages.

Thomas Arnold died suddenly on June 12th. . . . Macready sued the *Weekly Dispatch* for libel, and won. . . . Mr. Hullah held the first great choral meeting of his musical classes at Exeter Hall, which was filled by 1,500 of those who had taken his course of instruction in singing. Prince Albert, Wellington, and the Bishops of Canterbury and York, who were in attendance, expressed themselves as well pleased. . . . Dickens returned from his six months' visit to the United States and began immediately to write his *American Notes*.

The *American Notes* was a disappointment to Dickens's friends. There were certain passages of whipped-up liveliness, particularly the section dealing with his stormy voyage across the Atlantic; but for the most part it was a dull and routine record of his visits to public institutions—jails, insane asylums, and reformatories—and a comparison of them with similar English institutions. In spite of his determination to be pleasant he revealed a more or less insular reaction to strange sights and customs. The white wooden houses of Boston, so unlike good dull English brick, hurt his eyes; the prairie disappointed him; the Mississippi was just an enormous ditch running liquid mud at six miles an hour; he discovered that Americans still spat.

It had been in truth a tempestuous visit, socially speaking. He had started with a round of visits, speeches, banquets, receptions, cheering crowds, and assiduous autograph seekers. Dickens always had a rather high level of tolerance for public admiration, but when he found he was almost mobbed on the streets and was pointed at in trains even he grew weary and wanted to be left alone. He was puzzled, too, by the oppressive silence which greeted him when, in dinner speech after dinner speech, he attacked the Americans for their piracy of English books and urged the necessity of an international copyright law. The American press he found mean, paltry, silly, and disgraceful. When his book was read in the United States, and shrieks of anger came across the Atlantic from his former but nationally hypersensitive hero-worshipers, he retreated momentarily into a hurt seclusion as far as America was concerned—except for a foreword to new editions of his book declaring his affection for the people of the United States. His feelings were somewhat assuaged by the £1,000 which the book brought him before the year was out. Dickens had no ill will toward the United States, which was indeed, beyond New England borders, a primitive and pioneer country. It was just a case of mutual incompatibility. The

Edinburgh Review considered his reserve and self-control in avoiding offensive topics in *American Notes* "scarcely less than heroical."

By the end of June sinister reports began to come in from the manufacturing and mining districts. Distress was growing, and increasingly numerous riots were the reflection of a dangerous discontent on the part of the operatives. Foreign trade had shrunk until the manufacturers were beginning to reduce wages, already severely low.

As early as April operatives in Worcestershire, upon announcement of the wage cut, had dragged their masters by force to a meeting with a deputation of workers; and the affair issued in a general riot at Rowley Regis, quelled only when troops arrived from Birmingham. By July the Commons had to spend three nights discussing resolutions which declared the country to be in a state of distress. Nothing was done about it, although Cobden pointed out that inflammatory placards headed "Murder" were being distributed in Manchester. In Bolton the average wages of a thousand families did not average more than 10d. per head per week. A foreign visitor remarked on the dignity and moral courage with which these people endured unparalleled privations.[9] But starvation was another matter. In January the Poor-Law Commission had reported twenty-one manufacturers bankrupt and 5,000 hands currently thrown out of employment; 30 per cent of the manufactories were closed. Of 7,000 dwelling houses in a town of 50,000, 1,632 were unoccupied. In three years the Bolton poor rate increased 300 per cent.

The real disturbances, however, began in the Staffordshire Potteries, where a 7d. per week reduction in every man's wages brought on riots. Some thousands of men who had deserted their work visited the collieries, ironworks, and potteries, and inflicted violence upon those who were still at work at the reduced wages. The Third Dragoons came in from Birmingham.

These disorders grew steadily more alarming throughout the summer, spreading to Manchester, and reaching a peak during the second week in August. The *Manchester Guardian* reported that a mob collected and stopped all the mills in Stalybridge and Ashton, compelling the workmen to turn out and join them. The next day 10,000 of them marched on Manchester, armed with sticks. They were met and turned aside peaceably, but the crowd grew to 30,000 men, women, and children, crying that the wages of 1840 in the textile industry must be restored. Crowds wandered the streets demanding bread. The *Times* reported that on Wednesday, the tenth, a mob of 5,000 pelted the police with stones. Trade was totally suspended, every shop closed. Large parties went over to Salford to turn out the hands in the factories there. The Riot Act was read three times during the day, and 300 special constables were sworn in. The mob attacked the cavalry barracks at Hulme and razed the prison at Newton. On Thursday 15,000 persons met at Granby Row, with the defensive forces—dragoons, rifles, infantry, artillery, and armed police—drawn up before them, blocking all the outlets from the meeting. Both parties remained in position until eleven o'clock at night.

In the Midlands the crisis continued to mount. On Wednesday a party of 14,000 marched through Dudley; by the time it reached Wednesbury it had grown to 25,000. There they were joined by a number of Scottish miners, also turned out. They did nothing, however, beyond passing resolutions resisting the reduction of wages.

In the Home Office accounts were received from Major T. Stranger from Macclesfield that "several thousands of men and boys armed with bludgeons are on their way from Stockport. They succeeded in stopping every factory in the town, turning out the hands and putting out the engine fires." Hence the name "Plug Plot" given to these riots. It was significant that instead of smashing machinery, as the earlier Luddites had done, these strikers merely knocked the plugs out of the boilers, thus extinguishing the fires. The Congleton mayor informed the Home Office that the town was invaded by 10,000 individuals armed with bludgeons. At Huddersfield thousands of men were said to be putting an end to work wherever they went. At Skipton the military charged the mob. Sixty prisoners were taken at Bradford.[10]

In this way the riots spread beyond Staffordshire and Lancashire, cutting into Cheshire and Yorkshire and extending finally to the manufacturing towns of Scotland and the collieries of Wales.

At Preston the mob was fired upon by the police, and four people killed. Thirty-eight prisoners were taken at Walton. Another crowd was fired upon and five persons wounded at the Adelphi Works at Salford. At Blackburn on August 15th the military shot into the crowd, wounding several and killing a girl. Fifty-four persons were arrested at Halifax.

The scores of persons arrested by police, together with the large turnout of troops and a proclamation by the Queen against the offenders, finally gave a check to the rioters, and as time went on the operatives drifted back to work. But the "Condition-of-England Question" had been thrown directly into the lap of the nation. As late as November Greville could write in his diary:

Lord Wharncliffe and Kay Shuttleworth, who are both come from the north, have given me an account of the state of the country and of the people which is perfectly appalling. There is an immense and continually increasing population, deep distress and privation, no adequate demand for labour, no demand for anything, no confidence, but a universal alarm, disquietude, and discontent. . . . Certainly I have never seen, in the course of my life, so serious a state of things as that which now stares us in the face; and this, after thirty years of uninterrupted peace, and the most ample scope afforded for the development of all our resources . . . and being, according to our own ideas, not only the most free and powerful, but the most moral and the wisest people in the world. One remarkable feature in the present condition of affairs is that nobody can account for it, and nobody pretends to be able to point out any remedy.[11]

It was during this autumn that Carlyle planned his *Past and Present*, which was written at white heat in the first seven weeks of 1843. "Of these successful skilful workers," he wrote, "some two millions,* it is now counted, sit in Workhouses, Poor-law Prisons; or have 'outdoor relief' flung over the wall to them—the workhouse Bastille being filled to bursting, and the strong Poor-law broken asunder by a stronger. . . .† These poor Manchester operatives . . . put their huge, inarticulate question, 'What do you mean to do with us?' in a manner audible to every reflective soul in this kingdom; exciting deep pity in all good men, deep anxiety in all men whatever . . . England will answer it; or, on the whole, England will perish. . . ."[12]

The strikes ended, but the distress continued; England was lucky that worse revolution had not come out of the August riots. In the meantime Parliament debated taxes, but was helpless in getting at the root of the national troubles.

It is not surprising that crime reached an all-time high in 1842, with 19.4 criminals to every 10,000 people. A total of 31,309 persons were committed—3,500 more than in the previous year, and 50 per cent more than in 1839. Emigration rose, too, from 90,743 in 1840, to 118,592 in 1841, to 128,592 in 1842.[13]

The state of the operatives in 1842 calls attention to the general attitude of contemporary England toward poverty and to the vast business of philanthropy which had grown up about it. There was a widespread feeling that since "the poor we have always with us," the so-called "deserving" poor were in a state of nature from which it was impossible to be redeemed in this world, though it might be ameliorated

---

* The return of paupers at Lady Day, 1842, was actually 1,429,089.

† The fact is that the Poor Law of 1834 had never been put into force in many of the manufacturing districts, notably in Lancashire.

somewhat by charity. This feeling was complicated, however, by an irritated belief of some members of society, to whom God had allotted a more comfortable way of life, that poverty was by and large the result of laziness or shiftlessness or dissolute habits and that it was therefore a crime to be poor—an attitude epitomized by Wellington's famous remark that he never knew an industrious laborer who could not get a competence.* There was a tradition that no one starved in England, and so you created poor laws under which the bodies and souls of paupers might be kept together. What really had happened, as became more evident in a time of crisis such as this, was that the Manchester economic theory which was the bible of the new capitalists simply did not take into account the rapidity with which the industrial and therefore social and economic texture of the country was being transformed.

Orthodox political economy was being shaken to its roots in the 1840's. Such of its proponents as Nassau Senior, who voted consistently against factory bills to alleviate working conditions, still liked to point out how much better off the industrial worker was than the primitive savage. The underpaid operative, however, showed a strange inability to profit by the advice that if he would just wait long enough everything would work itself out, that in the meantime he was free to make his own contract with his employer, and that above all if he practiced thrift and saw to it that he did not increase a surplus population by marrying too early he would help to vindicate the optimistic prophecies of the Utilitarian school of economic thought. The crack in the armor of the Utilitarian philosopher and his manufacturer enthusiast was being widened by the modifications which John Stuart Mill was making in the accepted creed. Even while reiterating the orthodox position that national education for the working classes would somehow improve their economic position, Mill saw and proclaimed that protective legislation was also necessary. He even went so far as to suggest the eventual abolition of the employing class, and the co-operative association of workers for the manufacturing and marketing of their product.[14] Mill had his supporters, too, within the castle of economic orthodoxy—men who, while in the act of proclaiming that happiness for all, or at least for the greatest number, could best be achieved by *laissez-faire*, spent their days and nights trying to put legislative hedges around the garden of unrestricted competition.

---

* It is interesting to note that this contempt for pauperism was held even more strongly by the lower middle classes—the clerks and small tradesmen and the craftsmen just half a rung on the ladder above the "industrious classes"—than by the aristocracy.

Although people of good will might be baffled, there were things that they could do in addition to distributing temperance tracts. Philanthropy was a big business—even beyond the Aborigines Protective Society and the church missionary societies. In 1844 Sampson Low's report on the charitable (including religious-charitable) organizations of the London metropolitan area alone listed the names of more than 450 such groups. By 1851 eighty-six more had been added to the list. Some of the names are illuminating:

Labourer's Friend Society.
National Truss Society.
British Ladies' Female Emigrant Society.
London Philanthropic Society for providing the Poor with Bread and Coal in Winter.
Metropolitan Association for improving the Dwellings of the Industrious Classes.
Society for the Improvement of the Condition of the Labouring Classes.
The London Female Dormitory and Industrial Institution.
House of Charity for Distressed Persons in London.
Society for the Distribution of Soup during Winter Months.
Society for Establishing Soup Kitchens in the north-west District of the Metropolis.
Association for Promotion of the Relief of Destitution in the Metropolis.
Association for the Aid and Benefit of Dress-makers and Milliners.
The General Domestic Servants Benevolent Institution.

There were some forty Home Missionary societies as of 1851, including the Religious Tract Society (which announced a total distribution of 608,000,000 copies of 112 different tracts in 112 languages and dialects); the Weekly Tract Society; the English Monthly Tract Society, etc.

All of these hundreds of outfits held annual meetings, elected officers, received funds, and distributed moral readings and soup with equal piety and benevolence. There was no ill will in the heart of England, only a great puzzlement and a willingness to trust to palliatives while reality waited in the outer vestibule.

It is clear now that the summer uprisings had been the spontaneous revolt of a desperate people. At the time, however, it was the custom to blame much of the trouble on Chartist agitation—and indeed in its severer aspects the revolt fed and sometimes became indistinguishable from the traditional Chartist line of thought and action. The position of the Chartists in 1842 was crucial.

Since the debacle of 1839 the Chartists had been slowly re-establishing their forces. On May 2d they gathered in force in London to present another monster petition to Parliament. They mustered in Lincoln's Inn Fields and proceeded by way of Holborn and Regent Street to Westminster. The petition of 3,315,702 names (someone must have counted them) was carried on the shoulders of sixteen men. It was too large to get through the door of the House of Commons, and had to be broken up and carried in piecemeal to the House by a series of petitioners. There it was dumped down beside the table until, after a number of speeches—in one of which Macaulay, while approving certain parts of the Charter, said that universal suffrage was incompatible with the very essence of civilization and would lead to a general confiscation of property—the House voted not to receive the petition. The petitioners went home, and that was the end of it. Not quite the end, however.

The Chartist movement, so logical in many ways, carried within itself the germs of its own destruction. What was it really after? In 1836 William Lovett, a Londoner and a skilled cabinetmaker, had been instrumental in founding the London Working Men's Association. Two years later, with the assistance of Thomas Attwood, a rich and economically unorthodox banker, Lovett and this group drafted the six-point People's Charter incorporating the following demands: manhood suffrage, secret ballot, equal electoral districts, payment of representatives in the House of Commons, abolition of the property qualification for membership in Parliament, and annual Parliaments.* The movement gained momentum with the accelerating industrial and agricultural depression of the late 1830's. Stemming in large part from the economic distress of the laborers, it is to be noted that it urged only political reforms, under the assumption that winning votes in Parliament was the best means of redressing social and economic evils. The Reform Bill of 1832, however, had resulted only in disillusion for the masses. It had been hailed at first as a great democratic victory, but it soon became evident that it lodged political power only with those who had already assumed industrial and economic power: the manufacturing middle classes. The rank and file of the people found themselves shut out of their own show, and in bitterness and despair they began to agitate for further political reform.

---

* In 1840 the Duke of Wellington had made his pronouncement on the ballot: "What distinguishes us from other countries is the universal publicity of our conduct, and the open avowal of our sentiments to all mankind; and I should be exceedingly sorry to find men, instead of standing forward openly, and stating their opinions in the face of day, proceeding in a sneaking course, and exercising their elective franchise under a secret mode of voting." One is tempted to quote the old Iron Duke on such points as these, for he was the epitome of a day that was fast dying, and one suspects that he was sometimes aware of it. On this particular issue, however, John Stuart Mill was in agreement with him!

Rapidly the movement divided into several camps, all presumably working for the same thing—the Charter—but separated in method and philosophy. The London group under Lovett's leadership, composed largely of skilled craftsmen and respectable artisans, advocated "moral force" and emphasized a national system of education and self-improvement. The more depressed classes of labor in the metropolis, however, joined in spirit with the other tributaries of the movement which came from the industrial midlands around Birmingham, and still more importantly from the misery-ridden districts of the north—the starving hand-loom weavers, the spinners and knitters in the great textile mills in Lancashire and Yorkshire, and the miners in the coal fields of Durham, Northumberland, and South Wales. With their distress compounded by the aggravations of the New Poor Law and by the government suppression of the emerging trades unions, and with starvation for many almost around the corner, the Chartists in these districts came out openly in favor of "physical force."

Many leaders sprang up. Richard Oastler, the furiously impulsive "Tory Radical," who with the Rev. J. R. Stephens, a tremendously effective orator capable of holding large open-air audiences spellbound, had campaigned violently against the Poor Law. Bronterre O'Brien, "the Chartist Schoolmaster," intellectually the most powerful of the leaders, and another spellbinder (he spoke as a rule for three hours), was a "moral force" man. Joseph Sturge, who chose to lead the Complete Suffrage movement, and who, by thus emphasizing only one aspect of the Charter, was suspect by the all-or-nothing leaders. Thomas Cooper, who, during his stay in prison, composed a long Spenserian poem in ten books, *The Purgatory of Suicides.** There were others, but most important of all was Feargus O'Connor, an Irish squire and former Member of Parliament. Though he never fully identified himself with the "physical force" group, many of his writings and speeches were clear incitements to violence.

---

* Published 1845. In his Preface, Cooper says that the first six stanzas embody a speech he delivered to the colliers on strike in the Staffordshire Potteries, August 15, 1842, just before his arrest and imprisonment. The first stanza runs:

> Slaves, toil no more! Why delve, and moil, and pine,
> To glut the tyrant forgers of your chains?
> Slaves, toil no more! Up, from the midnight mine,
> Summon your swarthy thousands to the plain;—
> Beneath the bright sun marshalled, swell the strain
> Of Liberty:—and, while the lordlings view
> Your banded hosts, with stricken heart and brain,—
> Shout as one man,—"Toil we no more renew,
> Until the Many cease their slavery to the Few!"

All these found technical shelter and presumably common ground under the tent of the National Charter Association. Disputes broke out, however, over questions of policy and action, and before long O'Connor, who sooner or later quarreled with all his fellow leaders, had by-passed the more moderate Lovett and was in popular control of the movement. Under his direction it became flamingly bitter and seditious. He was a flamboyantly able demagogue, with the powerful baritone voice pre-requisite to success in a day of massive torchlight meetings, and a wit which carried home his wealth of vitriolic invective. "You," he would say, "I was just coming to you when I was describing the material of which our spurious aristocracy is composed. You, gentlemen, belong to the big-bellied, little-brained, numbskull aristocracy. How dare you hiss me, you contemptible set of platter-faced, amphibious politicians?" His appeal was to the rancorous mass of operatives and miners rather than to the skilled artisans, and he was even more bitter against the middle classes than against the aristocracy: the factory owners were from the middle classes. Under his leadership great crowds of operatives would gather on the hills to listen to interminable harangues breathing out fire and slaughter against all established authority. However O'Connor might be hated by his fellow leaders, his followers gave him their entire devotion.

The official Chartist organ was O'Connor's *Northern Star*, which at one time had reached a circulation of 50,000. Another of the several journals published on behalf of the cause was J. R. Stephens's *The People's Magazine: a Monthly Journal of Religion, Politics, and Literature*. Representing the milder wing of the movement, this was a pious paper, with articles on religion, religious poetry, tales for children, etc., but these were larded with articles which were an impassioned defense of the suffering poor against privilege. "What are we to do?" it cried. "We, the poor, the heavy-laden, the bewildered and ill-ready, who swarm over the land sorely bestead and scattered, like sheep without a shepherd—what must we do to rid us of our troubles?" The answer was of course to press for the Charter. "The Queen and her babe are doing well," ran one comment in 1841. "Would we could say the same of the wives and little ones of many thousands of her unhappy subjects, whose hard and bitter toil yields her the means of her well-being." One of several "Songs for the People" in this paper ran:

> But alas for the poor! they may plant, they may sow,
> They may gather the grain and the tillage renew;
> But the blessings that God hath seen good to bestow
> Are torn from the millions to fatten the few.

This was the movement, then, which in the summer of 1842 was adding incendiary fuel to the spontaneous series of strikes. Though it was not at the moment apparent to the fearful citizens who watched the turmoil, Chartism was already in decline, defeated in part by the very excess of enthusiasm it fed on.* Jealous of rivalry, it opposed actively, for example, the other contemporary movement working to better the condition of the hungry working classes: the Anti-Corn-Law League. It looked on the League as a tool of the manufacturing interests, used to divert attention from the real causes of distress; and a part of the Chartist program, as we have seen, was to attend League meetings and whenever possible, by making motions from the floor, divert them into Chartist assemblies. This fanaticism led to factional disputes within the group, and above all it alienated the moderate middle-class sentiment which would not have been averse to political modification, but which was badly frightened by the seditious and threatening turn the movement had taken. Divided within, facing a uniform hostility on the part of the middle and upper classes—for once in agreement—and met by swift government action against rioting, Chartism began to fall apart. It was to have one galvanic revival later in the decade, but as working conditions became somewhat better and fuller employment returned with better times, Chartism died as a political force.

Among the arrests following the summer disturbances were those of O'Connor and fifty-eight of his associates and followers. Although prison terms were given to many of the others, O'Connor himself was released because of a technical flaw in one of the early hearings. In general, the Crown Prosecutors showed great leniency in pressing the charges.

There was some light amid the confusion, though it involved a battle over government control of working conditions in the mines and factories, a control which both the predatory practices of the more selfish industrialists and the economic theories which underlay those practices opposed. But nothing is more heartening in the 1840's than the humanitarian passion with which certain leaders drove the House of Commons into appointing commissions of inspection, the fearlessness of those reports, and the way in which Parliament, overwhelmed by the weight of evidence of human slavery at its own doors, implemented those reports by legislative action. Utopia did not arrive overnight, and there

---

* The circulation of the *Northern Star* had by 1841 dropped to 13,580, and by 1842 to 12,500.

Figure 34. Lord Ashley (Shaftesbury), after the painting by Edgar in 1851

was a long series of rear-guard actions on the part of beleaguered privilege, but the issue of the battle was never in doubt. In the front line of the campaign was Lord Ashley, who, with unflagging and Christian zeal, took upon himself in 1842 the cause of the laboring women and children. We must go back to May of this year to see the first of a series of legislative attempts in this decade to pull England out of industrial medievalism.

In May was published, in 296 folio pages, the *First Report of the Commission for Inquiry into the Employment and Condition of Children in Mines and Manufactories*. This report concerned mines, and involved women as well as children. On June 7th Ashley brought the report to the House in a two-hour speech—given calmly, for the evidence needed no oratory to emphasize it—which struck the members with horror.

All over Britain women and children descended into the dank darkness of the coalpits to work as much as thirteen hours a day; in Derbyshire some of the children worked sixteen hours out of the twenty-four, from the time they left home in the morning until they returned at night. In most of the counties children began to work at seven years of age; around Halifax, Bradford, and Leeds, at six; in Derbyshire and South Durham and in Lancashire, at five; and near Oldham as early as four. Scotland and South Wales were no better. Only in "barbarous" Ireland were no children at all employed. In Pembrokeshire, Wales, there were more than 42 per cent as many adult women in the pits as adult men.

Ventilation and drainage were poor; the air was foul and the places of work dusty or damp. The conditions under which women, and more frequently children, drew coal through narrow seams were obscenely revolting. Many worked as "drawers," with a girdle bound round their waists, attached to a chain which passed under their legs and was fastened to the cart. Thus on all fours children went up steep roads through seams usually not more than a yard in height, pulling tubs laden with coal. In some workings "the narrow seams are sometimes 100 to 200 yards from the main roads; so that the females had to crawl backwards and forwards with their small carts in seams in many cases not exceeding 22 to 28 inches in height." One woman testified that "the belt and chain are worse when we are in a family way." Frequently they had to climb eighteen-foot ladders with coal on their backs, varying from three fourths hundredweight to three hundredweight. A sub-commissioner found a six-year-old girl in the pit carrying one half hundredweight of coals and regularly making with this load fourteen times a day a journey equal in distance to the height of St. Paul's Cathedral. Evidence was taken from fathers who had ruptured themselves by straining to lift the coal on their children's backs. Girls from seven to twenty-one worked naked to the waist beside adult colliers who were perfectly naked.

One Robert North testified: "I went into the pit at seven years of age; when I drew by the girdle and chain, the skin was broken and the blood ran down. If we said anything, they would beat us. I have seen many draw at six. They must do it, or be beat. They cannot straighten their backs during the day." Doctors testified to the prevalence of stunted growth and crippled gait, and to the frequency of asthma and "black spit," as well as other spine and lung diseases and inflammation of joints. One clergyman stated ("unwillingly," the *Report* reads!) that he feared that the peculiar bend in the back, and the other physical capabilities necessary to the employment, could not be obtained if the children were set to work at an age later than twelve. Adults were thin and gaunt, with a stooping, shambling walk; their complexions, when their faces were washed, approaching a dirty yellow.

The average wages per week for children of six or seven were 2s. 6d., ranging up to 5s. 4d. for children of twelve to thirteen.

This was the report so devastating in its completeness that there

Figure 35. Child "hurriers" at work in a mine

Figure 36. Girl dragging coal tubs

Figure 37. Hewing coal in 1842
(*These woodcuts are from the official report of the Commission on Mines and Manufactures.*)

seemed no room for explanation or apology. There were tears in the eyes of some of the members when Ashley finished, and Cobden, who had been his inveterate opponent, rushed across the floor to grasp him by the hand. Shortly, by an overwhelming vote, the House passed a bill redressing the worst of the evils. But change came slowly, even at best. Although, according to the House version of the bill, all girls and women were to be excluded from the mines, it was thought sufficient to legislate that boys between the ages of ten and thirteen could be compelled to work only every other day! The employment of boys under ten was prohibited entirely.

The bill then went to the House of Lords, where its slow evisceration began. Ashley had difficulty in finding anyone to sponsor it in the Upper House; the Government would not take sides. Wellington openly opposed it. The point had already been made in the House by Mr. Villiers (the advocate each year of an anti-corn-law bill to prevent suffering) that the proposed bill would throw thousands of women and children out of work. This was the theme taken up in the House of Lords by Lord Londonderry, the coal magnate, who led the attack—abetted by the Earl of Radnor, who objected to all legislative interference with the labor market. Londonderry was particularly indignant that the "disgusting pictorial woodcuts" of the *Report*, showing children drawing coal along the narrow corridors, should have found their way into the boudoirs of refined and delicate ladies who were weakminded enough to sympathize with these "victims of industry."[15] Nevertheless, public sentiment against the whole system of serfdom was so strong that the most they could do was to vitiate the bill as much as possible by amendments. A clause prohibiting apprenticeship (which amounted to open slavery) was deleted, except that a provision was retained under which no apprenticeship could be contracted under ten years of age, and not for a longer period than eight years! The clause limiting the labor of boys under thirteen to alternate days was also deleted.

When the bill was returned to the Commons the amendments of the Lords, despite Ashley's protests, were agreed to. The bill became law on August 10th.

These were the events which were making history in 1842. However, if the space devoted to them in the newspapers is any criterion they aroused little more general discussion than did the long, embarrassed debates in the Commons over the notorious bribery situation in politics, or the advent of a surprised whale in the Thames. Sabbatarians were noting with satisfaction that one John Williams, a murderer who was executed at Shrewsbury, attributed his bad end to Sabbath-breaking and playing at pitch and toss of Sundays—which led him to bad companions, particularly bad women. . . . Lord Hertford died (the original of Thackeray's Lord Steyne)—recognized as one of the most cunning, avaricious, and openly coarse and depraved men of his age, and the rottenness of his seventy-five years was buried at Ragley in a pompous funeral. About the same time the *Spectator* had something to say about the hollow pageantry of noblemen's state funerals (in this case the funeral of the Earl of Munster):[16]

> An imposing procession defiled from Wilton Place, along the high-road towards Putney. The van was led by the parish-beadles in full uniform, and the rear was brought up by the carriages of the Royal Family; the ends of long mourning-scarfs depending like gigantic ear-rings from the corners of the cocked hats of the scarlet-and-gold liveried footmen and coachmen. The centre was occupied by a plumed hearse, gorgeous with the royal arms of England; and to the black cloths which enveloped the horses were pinned satin 'scutcheons, bearing the arrows of the deceased. At the rear of the outriders with their funeral standards . . . was a horseman with an Earl's coronet on a black cushion before him. The sable attendants had all the appearance of being professional and case-hardened to such scenes: the coachmen and footmen looked up uncomfortably at a big cloud over-head that seemed to threaten rain, as if alarmed for their gold lace, scarlet coats, blue velvet inexpressibles, and white silk stockings: if there was any expression of feeling at all, it was that of curiosity, which set people coming up cross-streets or descending the hill from Hyde Park Corner a-running to secure a nearer sight of the pageant. . . .

The summer had been long and fine, and the price of wheat had fortunately fallen to 54s. 7d. per quarter on September 22d. An excellent harvest was expected. . . . A girl committed suicide by throwing herself from the Monument, and an iron screen was erected at the top to prevent a repetition of this sort of thing. . . . A great fire at Liverpool destroyed whole blocks of warehouses at an estimated loss of £700,000. . . . The Fleet and Marshalsea debtors' prisons—the former a debtors' prison for two hundred years—were closed and the prisoners removed to the Queen's prison. A few had been confined in the Fleet for debt for twenty years. . . .

In August there was great public interest in London in the opening of the Thames Tunnel to foot passengers; visitors "of all nations" passed through the tunnel from the Wapping (London) side as far as the

Figure 38. The Monument, Fish Street Hill. Marking the spot where the Great Fire of 1666 started

shaft on the Rotherhithe shore. This vast undertaking, to be completed as soon as circular staircases were put in place on the Surrey side, had been under intermittent construction since the digging of the first shaft in 1825. The 1,200-foot-long borings, 38 feet broad and 22 feet high, had proceeded under the direction of the famous engineer, I. Brunel, who had originally conceived the plan. Lives had been lost and the work delayed when the river broke through the shield several times. The contemplated wagon route was never completed because of the difficulty and expense of constructing adequate approaches, but foot passengers were allowed to pass through for 1d. It was brightly lighted with gas, and the walls of the descending shafts were a little later decorated with paintings of English and colonial scenery and history. The arches were used as bazaars, where goggle-eyed children could buy sweets and colored prints of the tunnel.

Macaulay's *Lays of Ancient Rome* were much admired when they were published in November. "And how can man die better, Than facing fearful odds, For the ashes of his fathers, And the temples of his

Figure 39. Apsley House, Hyde Park Corner. Residence of the Duke of Wellington

gods?" was quoted in every review praising "the spirited performance of the arduous task undertaken." Tennyson's *Collected Poems* in two volumes were noticed at length, and his improvement in poetic power during the decade that he had remained silent was commonly praised. In December was published (3 vols., 27s.) George Borrow's *The Bible in Spain*. Borrow's adventurous story of his experiences during the period in which he had been selling Bibles for the Bible Society was given high praise. Equally high praise was meted out, however, to Samuel Lover's tale of the blundering hero of *Handy Andy*, to William Harrison Ainsworth's *The Miser's Daughter*, and to *The Manœuvering Mother*, by the author of the *History of a Flirt*. The *Athenaeum* referred to the authoress of these volumes (Lady Charlotte Bury) as "many degrees nearer to Miss Austen than any of her contemporaries."

The December theatre included a revival of Congreve's *The Way of the World*, with Mme. Vestris playing Millamant—with the dialogue "purified," and Mrs. Fainall, Mirabel's castoff mistress, turned into a virtuous and injured wife. "The audience," said one dramatic critic, "seemed more puzzled by the plot than dazzled by the dialogue." At Covent Garden Adelaide Kemble (recently Mrs. Sartoris) took final leave of her profession in a revival of the opera *Norma*, in which she made her first appearance a little more than a year earlier. Her success had been triumphant.

On December 10th Macready produced at Drury Lane, with himself, Phelps, and Helen Faucit in the cast, J. W. Marston's *The Patrician's Daughter*. Dickens had written the prologue. This tissue of absurdities received a good deal of attention because it was an attempt to write a tragedy of modern life in five-act, blank-verse structure. The point of the drama turned upon the conflict of the aristocratic and the democratic point of view, developed by a plot most egregiously snobbish and ridiculous. The hero, a plebeian, is rejected by "The Patrician's Daughter," but later manages to get accepted by her; whereupon he in turn rejects the lady on the eve of marriage in the face of her assembled

Figure 40. The Glaciarium. A skating rink of artificial ice, plus artificial scenery

Figure 41. Madame Tussaud's exhibition of waxworks

kindred. This the author calls a "battle for high principles." As described by a contemporary reviewer, the catastrophe caps the climax of improbability and bad taste: the proud earl seeks the base plebian who had taken this despicable revenge, and humbly pleads for his daughter; and the poor dying girl is suffered to follow her father to the house of the lady-killer, at whose feet she dies, exclaiming, as the earl calls the fellow "my son," "I am happy—very happy!" This was one of the more serious efforts of the season. One is not surprised to come across article after article in the papers and magazines lamenting "the decline of the drama."

Good news came from abroad during the latter part of the year. Word was received that Lord Ashburton, on a special mission to the United States, had with admirable diplomatic tact negotiated a treaty which settled the long-disputed boundary question between the north-eastern United States and Canada. It seemed to most people a fair division of territory. Palmerston, in his customary excess of patriotism, carped at the treaty, to be sure, and wrote letters to the *Chronicle* denouncing it as a dire misfortune to Britain and a typical "Yankee Doodle" trick.

Toward the end of November a dispatch arrived which had left Bombay October 15th, giving the peace terms which had been arrived at with the Chinese. The indemnity demanded had risen from $6,000,000 to $21,000,000. Hong Kong was "ceded forever to Her Britannic Majesty." Sir James Graham, the Home Secretary, had come to the conclusion that the Chinese war was one "in which success would not be attended with glory, and in which defeat would be our ruin and our shame." The *Morning Chronicle* put him in his place by asking: "And where is the Englishman who does not carry his head higher from witnessing the stupendous efficacy displayed by his country, which at one and the same time displays her force in the West, in the Levant, and shakes to its center in the extreme East the great empire which inspired Sir James Graham and Sir Robert Peel with such dire apprehension." In the same Bombay dispatch came word that Kabul had been reoccupied in triumph; the disgrace to British arms was in process of being wiped out. The news of peace gave an immediate stimulus to trade in the manufacturing districts. In Manchester the prices of goods suited to the Eastern market were raised.

And so this turbulent year drew to a close.

The Christmas season was very mild. London was crowded with swarms of boys and girls on school holiday, eager for sight-seeing. They visited the Chinese Collection at Hyde Park Corner; they went to the Zoo in Regent's Park; they watched the beautifully painted Panorama of Kabul in Leicester Square, as well as the panoramas of Jerusalem and the Battle of Waterloo in the same building. At the Polytechnic Institution, for the scientifically minded, were a colossal electric machine, a microscope that magnified an incredible number of times, a diving bell, and "dissolving views." They could visit the sculpture gallery, the glyptotheca; and though the weather was too warm for skating in the parks, they could take exercise on a beautiful sheet of artificial ice at the glaciarium in the Baker Street Bazaar. If of a historical turn, they could view the armor and crowns of kings in Westminster Abbey. And everyone saw sooner or later Madame Tussaud's elegant exhibition of waxworks at the Golden Corinthian Saloon, Baker Street—with full-length figures of Mehemet Ali and Lord Palmerston; Her Majesty the Queen; Prince Albert in his military costume; and the group of John Knox reproving Mary Queen of Scots—Mary, Elizabeth, Henry VIII, Luther, and Calvin looking on. For those brave youngsters who would pay the extra sixpence and descend to the Chamber of Horrors in the basement there were the gruesome relics of the French Revolution.

All this—and more—in 1842.

1843 * "To Amuse and Instruct"

NEW YEAR'S NOTES

Court Journal: "Windsor. Her Majesty and his Royal Highness Prince Albert, and suite, walked on the terrace. The Prince of Wales and the Princess Royal were taken for their usual airings."

A Scotsman named McPherson, residing in Pimlico, who had spent several hours drinking with some fellow-countrymen in honor of the old year, was found this morning dead on the stairs of his lodging house.

Mr. Purvis, Whitehall Cottage, Chester-le-Street, gathered in his garden a nosegay composed of carnations, pinks, crimson, pink, yellow and white Chinese roses, double and single stocks, and wallflowers; a great variety of forget-me-nots, pansies, sweet-williams, floxes, and fuchsias—"with a variety of other flowers in great perfection."

IT had been a mild winter so far, so mild that beans were being sown in the open fields in Cumberland in January. Prices were falling, b   so were wages. Unemployment with its accompanying hunger and distress was still a matter of great concern. In London, in the first week

of January, George Wentworth, a silk weaver, was arraigned before
Sir Peter Laurie at Guildhall Police Office for the theft of a handkerchief. He told the court that he had come to London to seek work but
could not find it—and according to what he read of the poorhouses, he
said, they were much worse than the prisons. He was committed to the
treadmill for fourteen days, and he was only one of many committing
small thefts in order to find sanctuary. The general anxiety and disquietude, the restless feeling in the public mind, were reflected in the
discussions in Parliament when it convened. No one had an answer,
although there was a flurry of expected attacks upon the Corn Laws
as the root of all the trouble. Others blamed the income tax and the
financial measures of Peel's government, still others the Poor Laws.
Some advocated emigration as the only hope for an economy pressed
by a rapidly increasing population. A few well-cushioned members were
able to be philosophic about it all in terms of economic cycles, and to
sit back waiting for *laissez-faire* to adjust everything. But in the meantime many were agreeing with Carlyle that unless something was done
the mob, rather than "supply and demand," might take over.

All this, however, was something to read about in the papers for the
great majority of employed Britishers. Paupers and prisoners were
regaled with bread, beef, and porter on Christmas or on New Year's
Day. *Punch* ran two Christmas poems in the same issue. "A Corporation
Carol" began:

> Oh! rest you, merry Aldermen, let nothing you dismay;
> Get up your worships' appetite against next Christmas-day.
> Stout trenchermen of London town, stand to your knives and forks;
> Out-cormorant the cormorants, out-stork the very storks.

The other, attributed to Tom Hood, was called "The Pauper's Christmas
Carol," and ran in part:

> Full of drink and full of meat,
> On our Saviour's natal day,
> Charity's perennial treat;
> Thus I heard a Pauper say:—
> "Ought I not to dance and sing
> Thus supplied with famous cheer?
>   Heighho!
>   I hardly know—
> Christmas comes but once a year.
>
> Fed upon the coarsest fare
> Three hundred days and sixty-four
> But for *one* on viands rare,
> Just as if I wasn't poor!

> Ought I not to bless my stars,
> Warden, clerk, and overseer?
> Heighho!
> I hardly know—
> Christmas comes but once a year.

More fortunate people spent their days behind desks or counters, in office or farmhouse, in the fields, or at the workbench, and when evening came, gathered their families round them to read aloud the latest install-ment of—what? What were people actually reading in these 1840's?

Of new books in 1843 there were a respectable number the titles of which would be familiar—however faintly so—today. Carlyle's *Past and Present* was being reviewed in the magazines. The first installment of Dickens's *Martin Chuzzlewit* was just out, in which he was to carry on (at least it was to seem so to Americans) a guerrilla warfare against the United States. James Silk Buckingham's *The Eastern and Western States of America* fed the kind of fascinated horror with which the English watched their transatlantic cousins.* But there was lighter fare from authors better known than Buckingham. Ainsworth's *Windsor Castle* was running in his magazine; Bulwer's *Last of the Barons* was published in three volumes; Lever's *Jack Hinton* and Surtees's *Handley Cross* were announced. John Stuart Mill appeared with his *System of Logic* and Macaulay with *Critical and Historical Essays*. Thomas Arnold's last (posthumous) volume of *The History of Rome* was pub-lished. Thackeray's *Irish Sketch Book* was enthusiastically reviewed.

Modern Painters, by the twenty-four-year-old John Ruskin, writing as "A Graduate of Oxford," came off the press the first week of May. In 1842 several carping reviews of J. M. W. Turner's paintings in the

---

* At the risk of seeming to overemphasize the attention paid to Americans during these years (an attention riveted, however, by the large number of books written about their folkways), this book is worth a note. Buckingham, who seemed to the *Spectator* (April 8th) to be an "impartial observer, with leanings rather in favour of America than otherwise," drew a dreary picture of the people, socially, morally, and politically. "Foul in feeding, dirty in habits, coarse in manners, devoid of the courtesies of life in themselves and of its conveniences in their houses and very *smart* in their practices, they would appear to have most of the blackguard and the boor. . . . The women are loose in their reading, and scandalous in their discourse. . . ." Buckingham treated "the effects of boarding-houses on morals and manners," "delicacy in a Western steamer," "tip-pling," and "love, marriage, and morals." A part of this mixture of moral evil with social barbarism, mused the reviewer, arose no doubt from the *colonial* origin of the country. "But a good deal of the coarseness and dishonesty of America must be chargeable upon its equality, or the absence of different *classes*." It was during this time, too, that there was a great deal of shocked resentment (which received classic expression in Sydney Smith's sarcastic petition to Congress) over Pennsylvania's repudiation of her debt with England.

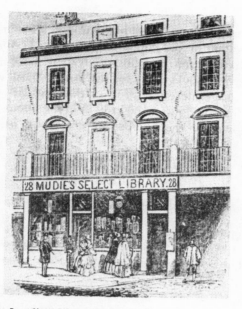

Figure 42. Mudie's Lending Library, started in 1842

Royal Academy Exhibition had filled him with rage. The *Athenaeum* had written: "This gentleman has on former occasions chosen to paint with cream, or chocolate, yolk of egg or currant jelly,—here he uses his whole array of kitchen stuff. . . . We cannot fancy the state of eye, which will permit any one cognizant of Art to treat these rhapsodies as Lord Byron treated 'Christabel'; neither can we believe in any future revolution which shall bring the world round to the opinion of the worshipper, if worshipper such frenzies still possess."[1] Ruskin's anger grew; he girded his loins for battle; and what had first been meant for a pamphlet grew into the first of his volumes in defense of his artistic hero. It must be remembered that Ruskin did not "discover" Turner, who had been rich and well known for many years, tolerated and even praised—if not in the same breath with Wilkie and Maclise—as long as he stuck to painting French rivers and British harbors and landscapes with traditional brown trees in a reasonably conventional way. What had offended the artistic Philistines was his later manner, as shown in the then current "Burial of Wilkie"; his startling chiaroscuro and broad impressionistic use of bright color. The young Ruskin had reason to be pleased with the complimentary way in which his book was reviewed. *Fraser's Magazine* called it "perhaps the most remarkable book which has ever been published in reference to art."

But how many people were reading Ruskin? Obviously not many as yet, for of an edition of 500 copies only 150 had been sold by the end of the year. The question of who was reading what requires further exploration. Leaving books for later discussion, what was the state of newspaper and magazine publication in this decade?

To begin with a few figures: the growth in the number of newspapers published is shown by the number of tax-stamps issued in England alone.*

1840:   49,033,384
1845:   56,433,977
1850:   65,741,271

In 1850 London had twelve registered daily newspapers and eight weekly. There were 222 English provincial newspapers, 102 Irish and 110 Scottish. The average price was 5d. (Some were 6d., others 4d. and 4½ d.)

In terms of prestige as well as of circulation, there was of course just one paper, the *Times*. It grew from an average daily circulation of 21,000 in 1842 to 38,019 in 1850—the latter figure being almost twice as great as that of all its seven daily competitors put together. Under John Walter, III, since his father's death in 1847, and with J. T. Delane as editor since Barnes's death in 1841, it had maintained its position of high influence in all responsible quarters. In sheer amount of reading matter it also exceeded any of its competitors; its eight pages of fine print, rolling, since 1848, from its "Applegarth eight-feeder vertical cylinder press" at the rate of 10,000 copies an hour, contained in each issue some 210,000 words, the equivalent of a sizable octavo volume. Feared by its enemies, cherished by its friends, but read by everyone, it was a staunch supporter of the existing order, hating all forms of radicalism. Yet it was at the same time acutely aware of the current social and industrial evils and was capable of urging humanitarian reforms. It could take the unpopular side of a public cause, as when it waged a campaign against railway speculation in the autumn of 1845, or when it supported the Austrian Government at the time of the Hungarian revolt in 1848. It was suspicious of democratic opinion. Blandly oracular, confidently assured, the *Times* nevertheless shared the violence that afflicted journalism in those days. The *Morning Chronicle* was "a squirt of filthy water." Macaulay it called "Mr. Babbletongue . . . hardly fit

---

* Until 1836 there was a duty of 4d. on every newspaper, at which time it was lowered to 1d. This "tax on knowledge" was not removed until 1855. The duty on advertisements was abolished in 1853.

to fill up one of the vacancies that have occurred by the lamentable death of Her Majesty's two favourite monkeys." And up until 1844 Edward Sterling, "the thunderer," made his rumbling, authoritative leaders a voice from Olympus.

The *Morning Chronicle* (1850 circulation: 3,000) also had great political influence; Palmerston used it against the *Times*. But what the *Times* was to the upper classes, the new *Daily News* (circulation: 4,000) was to the middle classes. This journal was launched with great excitement on January 21, 1846. Like the *Times*, its price was 5d., but in opposition it declared itself a "morning newspaper of liberal politics and thorough independence." Bradbury and Evans, and Joseph Paxton were among the original proprietors. Its great momentary distinction, however, was in securing Dickens as its first editor. A brilliant staff was assembled: W. J. Fox, the great orator and Corn Leaguer, wrote leaders; Leigh Hunt, Charles Mackay, Laman Blanchard, Douglas Jerrold—all were energetically on board. Dickens bustled about briskly, acting very much like an editor—taking care of his own, incidentally, by making his father-in-law, George Hogarth, musical and dramatic critic; and putting his own father, the fat and bumbling John Dickens, in charge of the reporting staff. It should have been clear from the beginning that Dickens, high-strung, tired at the moment but revolving a dozen other schemes in his head, would be no man to endure the thorns in the editorial cushion. Within a month he had withdrawn from the editorship and John Forster had taken over. In April Forster was succeeded by Charles Wentworth Dilke, who had recently withdrawn from the helm of the *Athenaeum*. The *News* reassembled its forces and went on to great success.

Of the other papers, the *Morning Post*—the "Jenkins" of *Punch*—was strong Tory and the mirror of court and fashionable life. *John Bull*, its moral face scrubbed since the old days of Theodore Hook, was still the apoplectic guardian of Toryism and the Established Church. The *Spectator*, under Rintoul's editorship, had a balanced good sense, vitality, and general literate quality that made it one of the best of the weekly journals. The *Athenaeum* carried great weight with its literary criticisms.

The most phenomenally successful paper of the time, however, was the *Illustrated London News*, which, within a year of commencing publication on May 14, 1842, had outdistanced all competitors with a circulation of 66,000. (By 1851 it had a circulation of 100,000.) By its seventh number it had reached 20,000 copies. Its first editor was F. W. N. ("Alphabet") Bailey, but its only true begetter was Herbert

Ingram, once a Northampton news vendor, who conceived the idea of a weekly newspaper carefully avoiding any political commitments, trying as best it could to give the events of the day in a fashion suitable for family reading, yet lively and intelligent. His great idea, of course, was that of illustrating it freely with woodcuts representing the scenes described by the news articles. The first number contained sixteen pages and thirty-two woodcuts, the main one illustrating the destruction of Hamburg by fire. The paper was an immediate success; aimed at the middle classes, it found readers in all classes. Faced by an unparalleled series of technical difficulties in transferring contemporary events to woodblock in time for each Saturday publication, Ingram met those difficulties triumphantly. A new era in picture journalism had begun.* Almost immediately it had its imitator. The *Pictorial Times* started brilliantly in 1843 with Douglas Jerrold as leader writer, Thackeray as critic and reviewer, Mark Lemon as dramatic critic, and Gilbert à Beckett as humorous contributor. Henry Vizetelly was editor. But this paper lasted only four years and then collapsed.

The weekly papers "circulating chiefly among the lower classes," with their mass circulation, are (like their descendants today) a somewhat frightening index of what the popular mind feeds on. The *Weekly Dispatch* was the best of these—the only weekly paper to have correspondents in Paris, Madrid, Dublin, and New York, and the only one to rival the *Illustrated London News* in circulation, claiming also some 60,000 as early as 1843. "Respectable" people frowned on it; the *Illustrated London News* said of it: "It is essentially the organ of the crime districts of England, and its circulation will always be proportioned to the existing amount of depravity in the land. It keeps its venom

---

* The *Illustrated London News* was the occasion of Wordsworth's sonnet which, if it seemed quixotic in 1846, furnishes food for reflection today.

> Discourse was deemed Man's noblest attribute,
> And written words the glory of his hand;
> Then followed Printing with enlarged command
> For thought—dominion vast and absolute
> For spreading truth, and making love expand.
> Now prose and verse sunk into disrepute
> Must lacquey a dumb Art that best can suit
> The taste of this once-intellectual Land.
> A backward movement surely have we here,
> From manhood—back to childhood; for the age—
> Back towards caverned life's first rude career.
> Avaunt this vile abuse of pictured page!
> Must eyes be all in all, the tongue and ear
> Nothing? Heaven keep us from a lower stage!

well set in the teeth of society. . . ." This was mere excess of journalistic zeal, however, spoken at the time of a race for circulation. It did devote much space to police intelligence, and somewhat ostentatiously espoused the cause of the people. It proudly admitted that it had "exposed a great deal of priestcraft—the misdeeds and the rapacity of the Parsons." Its anti-church bias, rather than any indecency, made solid citizens view it with alarm. At this distance—aside from the too-fervid crusading animus which was the journalistic mark of its time—it seems a lively and vigorous newspaper.

The *News of the World*, started in October, 1843 and, selling at 3d., had by 1850 a circulation of 56,000. Like its somewhat less successful competitor, the *Sunday Times*, it was "popular" but not sensational. Although it gave wide general coverage in its eight pages (with much attention to police news), most of it was copied from other newspapers. It fell into the compartments conventional in its day: foreign news, country news, leading articles, metropolitan news, theatrical news, parliamentary news, etc. It is an indication of the fervid interest that all classes, from highest to lowest, had in political affairs and particularly in the debates of Parliament, that in a paper such as the *News of the World*, geared journalistically to a low level, a full page of Parliamentary Report would appear when the Houses were in session.

Bell's Life in London was the sporting paper of the age, concerned with the turf, regattas, prize fights, games of chance, etc. Mr. Dowling, its editor, was said to be "the most graphic and spirited delineator of a prize-fight that the sporting world can boast of." According to one contemporary commentator:[2] "From the regulations of a brutal prize-fight to the etiquette of a genteel game of écarté, this journal is an undoubted authority. Hence it has not a class circulation like many of its weekly contemporaries—it is seen on the table of the peer and the parlour of the public-house—is read alike in the club and the tap-room." The poetry that appeared during these years was "written by a clergyman in the Isle of Wight." This catholicity won the paper its circulation of 24,721 in 1850.

A number of penny unstamped papers were spawned during the 1840's to feed the interest of a public just above the level of literacy. They were four-page folios, usually carrying a rough woodcut at the top of the front page—not infrequently the scene of a murder trial. Thus the *Penny Weekly Dispatch; Clark's Weekly Dispatch;* Edward Lloyd's *Penny Sunday Times and People's Police Gazette; Bell's Penny Dispatch, Sporting and Police Gazette, and Newspaper of Romance and Penny Sunday Chronicle.*

A copy of this last, of February 27, 1842, has on Page One an account entitled "Daring Conspiracy—Attempted Violation," and a story "The Green Man," by M. Jules Janin (continued). Two more stories: "Sister Theresa," from the French of Balzac, and "The Dervise, a Tale of Real Life" (anonymous). Then some police notices, and two more continued stories—all cheap, poor stuff, wretchedly written.

At the bottom of the heap, from the point of view of respectability, were the scurrilous journals the *Age* and the *Satirist*. Each, with feeble circulation, survived only as a scandal and blackmailing sheet. Each was periodically haled into court to defend charges of libel. The first trial under the new libel law* was that of the *Age* in December, 1843, charged with a libel on the Duke of Brunswick, whom the paper had been accusing of homosexuality. The proprietors were found guilty and were sentenced to prison. A little earlier Barnard Gregory of the *Satirist* had been indicted for similar libels against Brunswick.

A strange interlude in the career of the unsavory Gregory had occurred in February, when he had tried to play Hamlet at Covent Garden. He could not be heard in the part because of the tumult of yells and hootings, mingled with applause from a few of his supporters. The management had to suspend the play. By midsummer Gregory was hiding out from the law, and was described in the placards as "about fifty-five years of age . . . has a projecting forehead, giving a lowering expression to the face; eyes darkish colour, nose short and ill-shaped, face round; has an habitual satirical sneer, is high-shouldered, and slightly knock-kneed; voice powerful, with a fawning style of speech . . . manner pompous and vulgar; walk embarrassed and uncertain." A reward was offered for his apprehension, and he was finally seized at Southend in a house where he had been living under an assumed name. He was discovered in a closet in the garret.[3]

Another type of publication in this half-world of London journalism was the *Town*, published by Renton "Baron" Nicholson. It ceased publication in 1842, but was representative of a class of scurrilous salacious publications addressed to the sporting bloods. It pretended to take a high moral tone in its articles dealing with prostitution and "female debasement" in London. It published long, detailed accounts of prize fights (a sport illegal at the time), advertised obscene books, ran

---

* Heretofore the practice was to assume that "the greater the truth, the greater the libel must be." Under Lord Campbell's Act, passed August 18, 1843, the defendant could plead the truth of the charge, and that it was for the public benefit that it was published. Imprisonment was imposed upon those publishing a libel knowing it to be false, or for maliciously publishing a libel.

foul epigrams and poems, and gave notices of the musical and dramatic entertainments at the various saloons—particularly Nicholson's own performances at the Garrick Head, Bow Street, opposite Covent Garden Theatre.

In all this, indecency was making a last stand—as far as public appearance was concerned—against the encroaching morality of a new generation. Readers were now being swamped by the seas of "improving literature for the masses" which were now pouring from the presses. And even in the cheaper catchpenny stuff, which still had an immense sale, most of the horrors, murders, rapes, and suicides were purged of obvious indecencies and were presented in an odor of "poetic justice" and moral teaching.

To turn from the news reporting of the 1840's to the more miscellaneous journalism in papers and magazines is to confront a ground swell of writing so wide in its variations and gradations and so overwhelming in its amount that almost none of it finds its way into the literary histories. Yet for him who would understand the emotional and intellectual temper of more than a modest number of the British public, *Eliza Cook's Journal* is more important than the *Edinburgh Review*.

The number of *weekly* periodical works (not newspapers) issued in London on a Saturday, in 1846, was about seventy-three.* Of these the weekly sale of the more important amounted to almost 400,000 copies, or about 21,000,000 annually.

Two hundred and twenty-seven *monthly* periodical works were sent out on the last day of July, 1845, to every corner of the kingdom from Paternoster Row. Thirty-eight periodical works were published quarterly, making a monthly-and-quarterly total of 265. (This included weekly and monthly "parts" of novels.) A bookseller estimated that the periodical works sold on the last day of the month amounted to 500,000 copies, with 2,000 parcels being dispatched into the country.[4]

Between 1841 and 1851, 845 magazines, reviews, and weekly publications, aside from newspapers, were issued in London and its suburbs —a total which would be still larger with the addition of similar publications in the provinces.[5] Of these, 149 were religious, including a few temperance publications; 85 were cheap journals and magazines for the people, some "elevating," many sensational and romantic, others radi-

---

* Knight's *Penny Magazine*, 1846, p. 233. Knight classifies these as follows: literary papers, 2; economic and social journals, 12; penny and three-halfpenny magazines, 14; tracts, 3; musical, 5; weekly sheets forming separate books, 37.

cal, urging democratic reform or the rights of labor; a number were professional or trade journals such as railway magazines.*

These literary habits of a people need some attempt at classification and description.

At the top stood the well-established quarterlies, well-edited, well-written, if somewhat heavy, ranging across fields of both contemporary and historical significance, with long book reviews or review articles taking off from the "important" books at hand; in most instances, according to the honest custom of the day, giving long extracts from the

---

* Merely to list the names at random of some of these periodical publications is instructive:

The Almanac of the Month: a Review of Everything and Everybody, ed. by G. A. à Beckett; The Annals of Philosophical Discovery and Monthly Reporter of the Progress of Practical Science; The Wesleyan Methodist Magazine (fourth series); The Art Journal; The Artizan: a Monthly Journal of the Operative Arts; Bailey's Universal Railway Guide; The Balloon, or Aerostatic Magazine; The Baptist Examiner; Blackwood's Lady's Magazine and Gazette of the Fashionable World; Bradshaw's General Railway Directory; The British and Foreign Medical Review; The British Critic and Theological Review; The British Protestant; The Builder; The Child's Companion, or Sunday Scholar's Reward; The Children's Missionary Magazine; The Christian Cottager's Magazine; The Church of England Magazine; The Churchman's Monthly Penny Magazine and Guide to Christian Truth; Common Sense; The Cricketer's Companion, containing the scores of . . . the principal matches; The Domestic Economist and Adviser in every Branch of the Family Establishment; The Dramatic and Musical Review; The Earthen Vessel, or Christian Record and Review; The Electrical Magazine; The English Chartist Circular and Temperance Record; Facts and Figures; The Family Economist; The Family Friend; The Family Herald; The Family Journal of Useful Knowledge; The Family Preacher; The Forceps: Journal of Dental Surgery, the Collateral Arts and Sciences, and General Literature; The Friend of the African; The Gas Gazette; Halfpenny London Journal; The Horoscope; Illustrated Juvenile Miscellany; Illustrated Polytechnic Review; Johnston's Penny Fireside Journal; Journal of Gas Lighting; Journal of the Working Classes; Juvenile Christian's Remembrancer; Juvenile Instructor and Companion; Juvenile Missionary Herald; Leisure Moments; Little Magazine of Useful and Entertaining Knowledge; Lloyd's Entertaining Journal; London Entertaining Magazine and Library of Romance; The Lancet; London Teetotaler and General Temperance Intelligencer; Musical Examiner; Patent Journal and Inventor's Magazine; The Penny Pulpit; Peter Parley's Magazine; The Phonetic Friend; The Quarterly Celestial Philosopher, or the Complete Arcana of Astro-Philosophy; The Quarterly Magazine and Literary Journal of the United Ancient Order of Druids; The Ragged School Children's Magazine; The Railway Record: Dialogues of the Gauges; The Reasoner; The Revivalist; Reynold's Miscellany; The Servant's Magazine, or Female Domestic's Instructor; The Teetotal Times; The Thursday Penny Pulpit; Townsend's Monthly Selection of Parisian Costumes; Water Cure Journal and Hygienic Magazine; Who's Who in 1849, etc.; The Working Man's Friend, and Family Instructor; Zadkiel's Magazine: or Record and Review of Astrology, Phrenology, Mesmerism, and Other Sciences; Zion's Trumpet, or, the Penny Spiritual Magazine; The Zoist: a Journal of Cerebral Physiology and Mesmerism.

Not all of these, of course, lived even for the duration of the decade.

works under discussion, from which the reader might form his own opinion. The *Edinburgh Review,* associated with the names of Jeffrey, Brougham, Macaulay, and Sydney Smith; the *Quarterly Review*— Gifford, Kinglake, and Lockhart; the *Westminster Review*—Bowing, John Stuart Mill, George Eliot. But the circulation of the two most important of these magazines in 1841 shows how rarefied must have been the atmosphere in which they were read: the *Edinburgh Review,* 7,000; the *Quarterly Review,* 8,500 (both down from their all-time peak in 1818–19 of 14,000). The others had still fewer purchasers.

Of the monthly magazines, *Fraser's,* with its constellation of Carlyle, Maginn, Mahoney ("Father Prout"), and Thackeray, was the most politically and critically provocative. *Ainsworth's* ran fiction, poetry, and articles of general interest. Laman Blanchard was one of its chief writers, and always there was an installment of a new novel by Ainsworth himself. *Bentley's Miscellaney* published Albert Smith's comic stories and Barham's *Ingoldsby Legends,* theatrical memoirs, and miscellaneous articles and tales featuring illustrations by Cruikshank, Leech, and Crowquill. As the *Law Intelligencer* reviewed the latest issue on January 7, 1843: "Bentley, as usual, has catered well for his readers: he has sentiment for the grave, the lovesick, and the morbid; poetry for those who choose to appreciate it; fun for those who will wallow in it; and wit for those who will understand it." *Blackwood's Magazine* had a great tradition, from John Wilson ("Christopher North") to J. G. Lockhart, and some of the most popular fiction of the day first saw the light there—for example, Bulwer's *The Caxtons.* These were magazines for those who could afford to pay 2s. 6d. for a monthly quota of entertainment and enlightenment. They lay on the library tables of the educated and the well to do.

In the large, however, it was the day of the "family" magazine: the magazine of pious reflections and "daily thoughts"; the magazine of practical household suggestions; or of fiction and sweet poetry meant to be read in the evening after dinner to the assembled wife and children;* or, most typically, a potpourri of sentimental stories, informative articles, fashion hints, and amusing anecdotes.

The *Family Herald* was of this breed. Started in 1842, within seven years it was selling 125,000 copies a week at a penny each.[6] It was meant

---

* Sometimes incongruities crept in here; or perhaps some families could take a more exciting literary diet than others. Witness the illustration at the masthead of the *Illustrated Family Journal* showing the father reading aloud while the mother sews and the children are clustered about in fascinated eagerness—and below is printed the story *The Shot in the Eye: a true story of Texas border life,* with its illustration of a bearded ranger holding at bay with his musket a quaking villain.

THE ILLUSTRATED FAMILY JOURNAL:

No. 13.]　　　　　　　SATURDAY, MAY 31, 1845.　　　　　　　[PRICE TWOPENCE.

THE SHOT IN THE EYE.*

A TRUE STORY OF TEXAS BORDER LIFE.

THESE incidents were all so unaccountable, that I own I felt no little sympathy with the popular association of a supernatural agency in their perpetration. Henry laughed at all this, but insisted that it was a maniac ; and, to account for the peculiar dexterity of his escapes and whole management, related many anecdotes of the proverbial cunning of madmen. The wildest, most absurd, and incredible stories were now afloat among the people concerning this deadly and subtle foe of the Regulators, for it was now universally believed and remarked that it was against them alone that his enmity was directed. The story of Henry was greatly improved upon and added to ; and, as some reports had it, the madman—as others, the bearded ghost—was seen in half-a-dozen places at the same time ; now on foot, stalking with enormous strides across some open glade from thicket to thicket, passing out of sight again before the observer could recover from his surprise : then, mounted, he was seen flying like the shadow of a summer cloud over the prairies, or beneath the gloom of forests, always haggard and lean, dressed in skins with the hair on, and that long, heavy, terrible rifle on his shoulder ! I noticed that there was only one class of men who ventured to assert that they had actually seen with their own eyes these wonderful sights, and that was constructed of those who either had suffered, or from their character and pursuits were most likely to suffer, persecution from the Regulators—the class of hunter emigrants. These men were most industrious in embellishing all the circumstances of character, feats, and relentless hatred to the Regulators, as highly as the excited credulity of the public would bear. They never saw him except in the vicinity of the homes of some one of these hated tyrants. In their versions this being was for ever hovering around them, waiting the moment to strike while they were alone and far from any help.

They carried this thing so far as to attract attention to it, and arouse in the cunning mind of Hinch the same suspicion which had occurred to Henry and myself, namely, that all this was the result of a profoundly acute and thoroughly organized scheme of this class, headed by some man of peculiar personalities and consummate skill, with the object of exterminating or driving off the Regulators. It seemed impossible that, without collusion with many others, the murderer should have been able to so baffle all

* Continued from page 191.

Figure 43. Excitement for all the family

to be "interesting to all, offensive to none," combining instruction and amusement according to formula. Articles on "ill-regulated female labour," on "Parental Affections," and "The Submarine Telescope." Advice to servants as to how to get on with their mistresses. Stories: "The Shepherdess of the Alps"; "Kirkleven, or the Pilgrimage of Grace"; a life of Confucius; "funny" stories; moralizing verses.[7]

Eliza Cook's Journal, established in 1849, was a similar, if slightly more pretentious, publication; it sold for 1½d. Within three or four weeks it had a circulation of 50,000 to 60,000. Eliza Cook had parlayed a very thin talent for homespun verse into a notable popularity. Her poems, appearing each week, were the *raison d'être* of a magazine short on information but long on the kind of inspiration which thousands of her public evidently wanted.

She writes "Ten Years Ago" to memorialize her first published poem:

I gave that song unto the world, with secret hope and fear,—
I longed to try if I could win that world's broad, honest ear;—
'Twas done—applauding words of life came thickly on my way,
And those who caught my holly leaves, flung back a sprig of bay;
"We like your notes," the "people" cried, "Come sing again" and so
My "Christmas Holly" bound me to ye, ten years ago.

She writes a poem "Thank God for Summer," a "Song of June," and thoughts on "Fortune and Love":

Let me live without Fortune, if Providence will it;
For Joy can be found where small treasure is shed;
Those who bear a full cup are most fearful to spill it,
And oftentimes walk with the narrowest tread.

This style infects her prose, as does her opiate philosophy her ideas, in "Make the best of it": "Many an enlightened intellect, many a sensitive spirit, is bound to a wheel of grinding poverty, bitterly restricted in sympathies and hopes, yet wearing the mien and manner of elevated content . . . and a strong lesson it is, when we see a mind and soul of Nature's finest workmanship take the scanty pittance doled out to them by Fortune, and bravely, honourably, and cheerfully 'make the best of it. . . .' Let us . . . emulate the example of a Divine Teacher, and 'make the best of it.'"

Other stories in this first issue are "The Three Hyacinths before Heaven," by "Silverpen," and "Lessons for Little Ones," by Peter Parley, author of "Peter Parley's Annual," "Tales," etc. Parley gets in a boost for his "Annual" in his opening sentence: "Here I am, my little dears, your old friend Peter Parley; you have all read my Annual, I dare say, and will, I doubt not, read it again and again. . . . Every one knows that Peter Parley likes to blend the useful with the instructive; that when he writes a story it is always with a moral aim; that when he writes a book he always has in view to make his little readers *better* as well as wiser."

Dozens of magazines of this kind differed chiefly in the relative proportions of the "instruction and entertainment" they ladled out; they were politically innocent, unless an iteration of the theme "be content with your lot" could be construed as propaganda on behalf of the ruling classes. They all stressed education, piety, and industriousness. Thus the *Family Economist:* a Penny Monthly Magazine, begun in 1848, was "devoted to the Moral, Physical and Domestic Improvement of the Industrious Classes," with a picture of a contented, industrious family on the cover surrounded with such mottoes as "Education Is Second Nature," "Labour Rids Us of Three Great Evils, Irksomeness, Vice, and Poverty." Strangely enough, the useful advice with which this magazine is filled is well written.[8]

The miscellany *Hogg's Weekly Instructor*, published in Edinburgh between 1845 and 1851, says that "the Instructor, though not strictly religious in its character, had its origin . . . in religious feelings and motives," and goes on to reprehend indifference and skepticism. It consists of tales, original and translated, and articles on astronomy, geology, chemistry, botany, electricity, and metaphysics.

The *Working Man's Friend and Family Instructor* (1d., weekly), launched in London in 1850 by John Cassell, declares of itself: "This sort of journal is wanted at the fireside of the Working Man, to improve his evening after his day of toil. Our object has been that of instruction rather than of mere amusement. . . ." But it does include tales (one a continued story by Mary Howitt) as well as short biographies and anecdotes for children. An original feature in this magazine was the publication of "contributions from the working classes" such as "The Educational Apparatus for Working Men" by Henry Janes, cutler, Sheffield; "Eclecticism, and Its Relation to the Present Age" by J. A. Langford, chairmaker, Birmingham; and "The Rationale of Labour," by Edward S. Foster, seventeen, son of a working carter, Sheffield.

In 1842 Hugh Cunningham was publishing the *Mirror* at 2d., which called itself "the father of cheap literature" and the nature of which was adequately described on its title page: "Literature, Amusement, and Instruction: containing original papers; historical narratives; biographical memoirs; manners and customs; topographical descriptions; sketches and tales; anecdotes; select extracts from new and expensive works; poetry, original and selected; the spirit of the Public Journals; discoveries in the arts and sciences," and "etc."

Howitt's Journal began in January, 1847, with a circulation of 25,000, and although it suspended operation at the end of its third half-yearly volume because of the financial instabilities of Howitt's partner, it won a notable reputation in the area of well-written cheap publications. Mrs. Gaskell wrote tales of Manchester life for it under the pseudonym "Cotton Mather Mills, Esq." The Howitts, John and Mary, simple and friendly people, were personally very popular. They had emerged from Quakerism into a wider defense of religious liberty and a dislike of "priestcraft." Howitt's *Aristocracy of England*, by "John Hampden, Jr.," a caustic attack on the British aristocracy, had a large sale; as also had his *Rural Life of England*. Both Howitts were voluminous authors of poetry and descriptive travel books which emphasized their love for the countryside and for old castles and wild legends. Mary Howitt was one of the early English translators of Hans Christian Andersen. Their *Journal*, illustrated with woodcuts, was a typical miscellany which succeeded better than most of its brethren, however, in achieving simultaneous edification and amusement, on a literate level. Far from being Chartist, it was yet alertly aware of and sympathetic with the efforts of workingmen to improve themselves through education; it mingled "Early Spring Pictures" and "Sights in South Germany" with appreciative articles on co-operative movements.

Of the magazines aimed at a feminine audience, the issue of the *Ladies' Own Journal and Miscellany* for June 13, 1846, serves as a type. "A Thing of Shreds and Patches, intended to afford amusement to many—to give offence to none." The Queen's birthday; curious fish, monster of the deep; luxuriant crop of pineapples in the Bahamas; death of the Pope; sea bathing; how to grow grass under trees; London and Paris fashions for June—"plaided silks are now much worn, trimmed with flounces cut on the cross . . . the prevailing colours are green and blue, sky-blue and brown, cerise and white. . . . Chapeaux: mostly decorated with spotted plumes, ribbons, or clouds of gauze, throwing a softened shadow on the countenance"; Mendelssohn and Jenny Lind at a music festival in Aix-la-Chapelle; the nuisance of advertising vans; "Pickings from Punch"; a visit to Messrs. Stephenson's locomotive-engine factory; "Thoughts on Bonnets" (very whimsical); a plea for the hedgehog.

The best known of all these journals was Dickens's weekly magazine *Household Words*, established in 1850, and a "family" miscellany if ever there was one. It was a cozy publication, aimed at both sexes and all ages, which at the same time was to be "the gentle mouthpiece of reform." It ran continued stories by Mrs. Gaskell—and of course stories by Dickens himself; it concerned itself with education and illiteracy, and lacerated its readers' emotions with descriptions of the conditions in workhouses. For the statistically minded it listed, in "Twenty-four hours in a London Hospital," the number of tons and gallons of medicine used annually at St. Bartholomew's.* But above all it was cheery and sentimental.

This cross section of "domestic" publications in the 1840's would be incomplete without mention of the two most prolific and practical of the publishers who carried instruction and edifying entertainment to the cottage door: Charles Knight, and the Chambers brothers, Robert and William.

In 1827 Knight took over the superintendence of the publications of the Society for the Diffusion of Useful Knowledge, which Lord Brougham had been instrumental in organizing. The *Library of Entertaining Knowledge* was begun, and in 1828 the *British Almanac* and its *Companion*. In March, 1832, appeared the first number of the *Penny Magazine*, which by the end of the year reached a sale of 200,000 copies in weekly numbers and monthly parts, representing probably a million readers. After a prosperous career of nine years it began a new series, improved in engraving and printing. The purpose of the *Penny Magazine* was avowedly that of practical instruction and useful information; it contained no stories. Local memories of great men; domestic chemistry; milk; exhibitions of pictures at the National Gallery; memories of great historical events; influence of the oriental character on commerce; what constitutes a steam engine; the camel; a day at a hat factory; how a railway train is propelled; a day at a flint glass factory; a day at a London brewery—these were the subjects which carried information to the people.

By 1845, however, the sale was declining because of the competition of more sensational cheap publications, and in that year the Society-sponsored publication ceased. Knight tried to carry on the *Penny Magazine* under his own name, but had to withdraw it after the sixth monthly part.

According to Knight's own explanation in his "Address to the Reader" in the last number of his *Penny Magazine*, there are those "who

---

* These figures give a clue to the standard remedies of English medicine in the decade: 1,352 gallons of "black draught" (salts and senna); 2,000 pounds of castor oil; 12 tons of linseed meal; 2,700 pounds of salts; 1,000 pounds of senna. This for an average hospital list of 500 patients. Cure constipation and you cure all.

are carrying out the principle of cheap weekly sheets to the disgrace of the system, and who appear to have got considerable hold upon the less informed of the working people, and especially upon the young. . . . There are manufactories in London whence hundreds of reams of vile paper and printing issue weekly. . . . All the garbage that belongs to the history of crime and misery is raked together, to diffuse a moral miasma through the land, in the shape of the most vulgar and brutal fiction . . . the cheap booksellers' shops are filled with such things as 'Newgate, a Romance,' 'The Black Mantle, or the Murder at the Old Jewry,' 'The Spectre of the Hall,' 'The Love-Child,' 'The Feast of Blood,' 'The Convict,' and twenty others, all of the same exciting character to the young and ignorant.*

By 1846, too, the Society for the Diffusion of Useful Knowledge suspended operations because of the fiasco of its *Biographical Dictionary* —by the time the letter "A" was completed the loss was almost £5,000. Its *Penny Encyclopedia*, which was completed in twenty-seven volumes in the spring of 1844, was a great financial loss to Knight but a great publishing triumph. It had originally sold 75,000 weekly parts; at the close of 1843 it had dropped to 20,000.

All this was but a part of Knight's activity. Between 1841 and 1844 he published his illustrated descriptive *London* in weekly numbers totaling 2,500 pages. In 1843 he published his *Life of Shakespeare* and continued working on his edition of the plays. He began his "Book-Club for all Readers" in 1844, issuing a volume every Saturday at a shilling, containing as much as an ordinary octavo volume of 300 pages. By 1849 he had published 186 of these volumes, in which, he said, "no single work, and no portion of a work, can be found that may not safely be put into the hands of the young and uninformed, with the security that it will neither mislead nor corrupt."†

Knight, used to gigantic sales, was disappointed in the reception of the weekly volumes. "There were not twenty volumes that reached a sale of 10,000, and the average sale was scarcely 5,000. Although very generally welcomed by many who were anxious for the enlightenment

---

* Other competitive influences were operating, however, as Knight himself recognizes in another part of his "Address": chiefly the growth of newspaper circulation after the reduction of the stamp duty, and their rapid distribution into every corner of the kingdom by means of the multiplying networks of railways.

† The categories reflect the interests of the readers whom the series attracted; analytical accounts of great writers, English and foreign, 13; biography, 33; general history, 5; English history, 26; geography; travel, and topography, 33; natural history, 17; fine arts and antiquities, 8; arts and sciences, political philosophy, etc., 14; natural theology and philosophy, 15; general literature, 16; original fiction, 6.

of the humbler classes, the humble classes themselves did not find in them the mental aliment for which they hungered. They wanted fiction, and the half-dozen historical novelettes of the series were not of the exciting kind which in a few years became the staple product of the cheap press."[9]

In 1847 he edited, for one year in monthly parts, *Half-Hours with the Best Authors, Selected and Arranged*, introducing his readers to 300 various writers, forty of them living at the time of publication. In the same year he commenced *The Land We Live In*, a monthly illustrated publication, describing "many monuments of the past, but always in connection with the aspects of our latest civilization."

Some months after the *Penny Magazine* appeared, Dr. Thomas Arnold described it as "all ramble-scramble." Said Knight: "It was meant to be so—to touch rapidly and lightly upon many subjects. In the introductory article of the first number I wrote: 'Whatever tends to enlarge the range of observation, to add to the store of facts, to awaken the reason, and lead the imagination into agreeable and innocent trains of thought, may assist in the establishment of a sincere and ardent desire for information.'"

Knight, with his intense eagerness to serve the cause of popular education, must have had an incalculably great effect in raising the standard of reading taste in his generation. The only other influence comparably strong at this level was that of the firm of Robert and William Chambers, in Edinburgh. *Chambers's Edinburgh Journal* appeared almost simultaneously with the *Penny Magazine* in 1832.

The brothers were sons of a prosperous muslin weaver who had been ruined by the introduction of machine-weaving looms. Robert set out as a bookseller at sixteen, later became an author, at twenty wrote *The Traditions of Edinburgh* (1823), and published a *Biographical Dictionary of Eminent Scotsmen* in four volumes in 1832–35. Robert was highly intelligent and broad in his sympathies, William somewhat narrower, platitudinous, and didactic, but together they made an excellent publishing team. Although they were concerned with the intellectual well-being of the working classes, they also thought of themselves as addressing the middle classes. "It was my design," said Robert in the preface to his "Vignettes of Life and Character" published in the journal under the *nom de plume* of Mr. Balderstone, "from the first, to be the essayist of the middle class—that in which I was born and to which I continue to belong."

The conception of the *Edinburgh Journal* was "of a cheap weekly periodical devoted to wholesome popular instruction, blended with original amusing matter." Its success surprised even the most hopeful. At 1½d. it promptly reached a weekly circulation of 50,000, and by 1845, 90,000. The articles were solid and meaty, decidedly on the instructive side, but not written down to the "people." A glance at a table of contents reminds one of other miscellanies: articles on the Chinese; "What is poetry?"; "Two Days in Birmingham"; "Travelling in Spain"; "Recent Decorative Art"; "The Deserts of Africa"; "Electric Communication"; "Siam and the Siamese," etc.—and a whole series of "Familiar Sketches and Moral Essays."

In addition to the histories, biographies, and topographies which Robert poured out over the years, the brothers wrote, with little assistance, in weekly parts, *Information for the People* (1841–42), a solid and respectable series of analytical and descriptive papers; *Papers for the People* (1850–51), "to give a means of self-education to the humble classes"; and a series of miscellaneous tracts. Throughout the first year nearly 70,000 copies of each issue of the *Information* were sold. The plan was completed with Volume II, at the end of the second year.

Papers for the People did admit fiction, less edifying and more sentimentally and romantically popular than the more instructive legends and historical narratives of the *Penny Magazine. Husbands and Wives*, by Mrs. S. C. Hall, was published serially; and a whole succession of "Tales," such as "The Temptation"; "Harriette, or the Rash Reply"; "The Lost Laird—a Tale of '45"; and "Sigismund Temple." They were all very moral and non-sensational but of an entirely different order of prose style from the straightforward, informative articles. One wonders if it was the popularity of such stories as "Sigismund Temple" which enabled the *Journal* to outlive Knight's publications.

A sick father is telling his daughter that he expects to die that night: "Let me, whilst yet I may, feel your sweet breath upon my cheek, the warm pressure of your gentle hand in mine. Darkness is falling upon all things, as upon me; but the earth will reawaken in the smile of the new dawn, and again put on her robe of light and flowers, whilst I can scarcely dare to hope that I shall safely ferry over the dark waters which roll between me and the retreating light of life." He did die, at last.

This is nothing, however, compared with the intricate periods and parentheses in which Sigismund talks to himself. "'Deathbed repentances!' exclaimed the excited young man in a strange, low, beating voice —'deathbed repentances, I have heard bishops preach, are seldom of any value. . . . It would not be seemly,' he added, whilst a bitter sneer curled his white, finely-chiselled lips—'it would not be seemly that Arthur's tardy generosity or justice—exercised at my expense, too,

which makes it all the more pleasant—so suddenly resuscitated by the
near view of a tomb yawning for himself, be made to give the lie to so
salutary and grave a maxim.'" And so on for a full, closely printed page.

In 1844, Robert wrote, with a Dr. Carruthers, *Chambers's Cyclopaedia
of English Literature* in two volumes, treating 832 authors biograph-
ically and critically. This work, later enlarged, was standard for many
years. Before long 130,000 copies had been sold in England alone.

All popular literature was not "edifying," however. Banned from
respectable households yet enormously successful with ladies' maids,
footmen, bakers' apprentices, and factory operatives was a class of
magazines and novels in weekly parts now completely forgotten, and
because of their ephemeral nature difficult to describe historically. They
were of a type different from the conventional fashionable novel of
romance in high society which, however banal, was the stock in trade
of the circulating library and could be found in my lady's chamber as
well as in the scullery maid's locker. These other publications were of
the sensationally horrifying kind, lurid sheets illustrated with exciting
and gruesome woodcuts, telling tales of notorious rogues in "Newgate
Calendar" fashion, stories of passion and betrayal, of hunchbacked
demons and of vampires, of cannibalism and murder and atrocity. One
such magazine, the *London Journal*, was selling 100,000 copies a week
when it was mentioned before the Select Committee on Public Libraries
in 1849. Amid all the horror and violence of these stories there was no
open indecency—indeed, a kind of technical assertion of "moral purpose"—but the witness before the Committee quite properly suspected
that these penny publications had "perhaps a worse tendency than
books positively indecent or immoral."

Volume I of the *London Journal* (1845), for example, amid general
"hints for the table" and "thoughts on temperance," depended for its
staple on articles about "Indian Barbarity," "Mysteries of the Inquisi-
tion," and "A Visit to a Mad-House"; and on stories with such titles
as these: "Was he really hanged until he was dead?"; "The Murderer's
Creek"; "The Haunted House in Yorkshire"; "The Buried Alive," etc.

The *London Journal*, however (like the *New Wonderful Magazine*
of 1848–49, which dealt in rehashes of old murder trials and accounts of
human prodigies and eccentrics), was several cuts above the sensation
sheets sponsored by Edward Lloyd and G. W. M. Reynolds.

Lloyd, who had attempted for a few months in 1842 to compete with
the *Illustrated London News* with a clearly imitative journal, *Lloyd's*

THE
LONDON JOURNAL;
And Weekly Record of Literature, Science, and Art.

No. 4. Vol. I.   FOR THE WEEK ENDING MARCH 22, 1845.   [PRICE ONE PENNY.

TRAVELS IN THE EAST.

Don Sebastian de Villuma, an enlightened Spanish nobleman, has lately published, at Madrid, a narrative of his travels in the East. The work is written in a marvellous style.—simple, elegant, and at times sublime.—a style of a thousand characters, a thousand varying physiognomies, and a thousand sparkling hues. Don Sebastian embarked on board a trading vessel, at Cadiz, and hastened, with a soul full of curiosity and anxiety, to the land of miracles. The wind travelled in the white sails of the gallant vessel, and Sicily soon rose to view. Then appeared the African coast—Tunis, and Carthage, and Saint Louis. How solemn are those scenes—and how sounding are their names! How many varied musings have they awakened in the souls of those different pilgrims who have bowed before them. Beneath the eye, and at the voice of the poet, the dust of Carthage is re-animated, and the palaces are restored; and, with the palaces, and temples, and tribunes, and marbles, rise up the men who peopled them. But we must hasten forward with our author. Malta is now before him—that city chiselled out of a single block of living rock. Athens now appears; bow down to the mountains of Crocus, where the Eurotas has its source;—salute the lofty summits of the hills of Crete. You are now upon the frontiers of Greek antiquity. But we must not linger there;—for, with Byron and Chateaubriand, we have long contem-

plated Greece,—we have looked upon its fine monuments, beneath its light sky—traversed its olive woods—and gazed in admiration upon that ancient land,—that white and perfect statue, "reclining upon a tomb," as Byron says. In Greece, all is mild, all is softened, all full of calm—in nature, as in the writings of the ancients.

But let us change the scene. Don Sebastian doubles Cape Sunium, where Plato taught; and soon catches the moaning of the Cyclades. He now wanders, as it were, amid the islands of the Archipelago. Rhodes smiles upon him, like a tuft of verdure in the bosom of the waves. Already he is in the midst of Oriental dwellings, and Oriental women, with the dark Italian eye, but softer and more loving—calm, simple, and beautiful faces, that have nothing in common with the worn-out and faded beauties of our European saloons. It is by its women that the orient reveals itself to the European traveller for the first time. And now the Spaniard is at Beyrout—one of the most populous towns on the Syrian coast, and so celebrated for the scenes of which it was the theatre in the recent warlike convulsions of the east. The sea—Mount Lebanon—a forest of pines—caravans arriving from Damascus—Jews riding on asses—women on horseback, wrapped in white veils—Arab horsemen flinging the djereed, or javelin—groups of Turks, seated before their

doors, smoking their pipes, or engaged in prayer—and, on the roofs of the houses, stately women and young girls, looking down, with curious eyes, on what is passing below;—these compose the features of Beyrout. The hills take a golden hue from the rays of the sun,—the sea murmurs at their feet,—and a thousand birds sing amid their cedar-nests. The women of Beyrout are beautiful, the horses fine; and the young children are the very pictures of health and happiness.

Leaving Beyrout, Don Sebastian traversed the plains of ancient Tyre, the city fallen beneath the immortal curses of Ezekiel. He visited the lands of Canaan and of Judea—climbed the heights of Zebulon and of Nazareth—skirted the hill of Carmel—beheld the narrow, gloomy, and almost barren valley in which Christ was born—and finally paused on the banks of the river of the Prophets and of the Gospel—on the banks of Jordan! After some discussion, the Arabs whom he encountered in that spot, agreed, as he thought, to conduct him and his attendants to a ford. Upon leaving the Arab encampment, a sort of ceremony was performed for the purpose of ensuring a happy result for the undertaking. There was an uplifting of arms, and a repeating of words, that sounded like formulæ; but there were no prostrations; and it scarcely appeared that the ceremony was of a religious character. The travellers arrived

Figure 44. "Travels in the East" as described for penny readers

Illustrated London Newspaper, was parent to a number of other weekly newspapers which appeared, disappeared, reappeared, and coalesced under other titles. *Lloyd's Penny Sunday Times and People's Police Gazette* (1840–44) was his, as was *Lloyd's Weekly News*. It is difficult sometimes to tell just where his newspapers shade off into miscellanies;

they usually ran stories indistinguishable from those in his more miscellaneous penny publications. *Lloyd's Penny Weekly Miscellany* had a very large circulation in 1842, and in 1844 became *Lloyd's Entertaining Journal*. In 1842 the first issue of *Lloyd's Penny Atlas and Weekly Register of Novel Entertainment* (edited by James Rymer, who wrote many of the stories) ran this exalted Preface:

> . . . true morality—sound reasoning—and exalted sentiments, may be more easily, more effectively, and more pleasantly conveyed to the mind through the medium of works of fiction than by any other means. . . . We have ever found, in our intercourse with our readers, that those fictions in which the innocent—although environed by snares, and nearly brought to destruction by the wicked and designing, ultimately triumphed, and proved the goodness of right over might, were welcomed and read with delight. Can there be a more convincing proof of the ennobling power of Romance, if it be directed in the proper channel? . . . Hence we punish and confound the vicious—hence we defend, applaud, and bring off victorious, the innocent, dealing a poetical, and in our innermost heart believe, a practical justice upon evil doers.

The stories advanced to prove this thesis are "Adventure d'Amour"; "The Assignation"; "The Rival Brothers, or The Secret Marriage"; "The Vampire, or The Midnight Burial"; "Aurelia di Montano, or The Victims of Unhallowed Love"; and "Ada, the Betrayed, or The Murder at the Old Smithy, a Romance of Passion."

The other leading spirit in writing these literary atrocities was G. W. M. Reynolds. He was an active Chartist who had commenced life as a temperance lecturer and was at one time editor of the *Teetotaller* newspaper, but found mass circulation and a larger public more remunerative. He worked all the angles in his *Reynolds' Miscellany*, started in 1846. Amid buttressing articles on science, "How to Read," and "The Moral Elevation of the People" he ran "Wagner the Wehr-Wolf" with its Rosicrucians and Inquisitors; the "Sequel to Don Juan" and "The Parricide, or The Youth's Career of Crime." These serials would later appear in pamphlet form, and finally in bound volumes. He, too, claimed a moral purpose, but Dickens said of him, "His writings are a national reproach." He wrote twenty-six books of fiction which can be dated by the *Cambridge Bibliography of English Literature*, thirty-four others which cannot be dated, and many even the titles of which have disappeared.

The most popular of all his writings, and the book which in periodical parts dragged on interminably through two series to a total of four volumes and 1,650 finely printed, double-column pages, was *The Mys-*

Figure 45. "Gilbert Vernon had precipitated himself from the balcony! . . . His skull was literally beaten in and his hair was covered with his blood and brains!" Illustration from Reynolds: *The Mysteries of London*

teries of London, 1845–47.* This was succeeded by *The Mysteries of the Court of London*, in eight volumes, 1848–56. Here were murders, seductions, rapes, bordello experiences, gambling hells, boozing kens, dens of horrors, executions, body snatchers, suicides galore.

Who read these orgies of journalistic sensationalism and horror? In 1849–50 Henry Mayhew sponsored a series of articles on "Labour and the Poor" for the *Morning Chronicle*. Those investigations reached into the manufacturing districts, and Letter VI reports on the reading habits of the Manchester operatives. The findings concerning cheap literature are important.

---

* Thomas Miller and Laman Blanchard participated in writing the latter half of this series.

Every London publisher knows that Lancashire furnishes no unimportant part of the literary market of England. I was very desirous of ascertaining, therefore, the species of works most in demand amongst the labouring and poorer classes. The libraries in the better parts of the town are of course stocked in much the same way as the libraries in the better parts of London. I wished to ascertain the species of cheap literature most in vogue, and accordingly applied to Mr. Abel Heywood, of Oldham-street, one of the most active and enterprising citizens of Manchester, who supplies not only the smaller booksellers of the town, but those throughout the county, with the cheap works most favoured by the poorer reading classes. The contents of Mr. Heywood's shop are significant. Masses of penny novels and comic song and recitation books are jumbled with sectarian pamphlets and democratic essays. Educational books abound in every variety. Loads of cheap reprints of American authors, seldom or never heard of amid the upper reading classes here, are mingled with editions of the early Puritan divines. Double-columned translations from Sue, Dumas, Sand, Paul Feval, and Frederic Soulie jostle with dream books, scriptural commentaries, Pinnock's Guides, and quantities of cheap music, Sacred Melodists, and Little Warblers. Altogether the literary chaos is very significant of the restless and all-devouring literary appetite which it supplies. Infinitely chequered must be the *morale* of the population who devour with equal gusto dubious Memoirs of Lady Hamilton and authentic narratives of the "Third Appearance of John Wesley's Ghost," duly setting forth the opinions of that eminent shade upon the recent speeches of Dr. Bunting.

So much for the *prima facie* aspect of Mr. Heywood's literary warehouse. I was courteously furnished with details of his business, which throw an unquestionable light upon the taste of the operative reading world of Lancashire.

That species of novel, adorned with woodcuts, and published in penny weekly numbers, claims the foremost place. The contents of these productions are, generally speaking, utterly beneath criticism. They form, so far as I can judge, the English reflection, exaggerated in all its most objectionable features, of the French *Feuilleton Roman*. In these weekly instalments of trash Mr. Heywood is compelled to be a large dealer, as will appear from the following statement:—

Angelina	Average of 6,000 weekly
Almira's Curse	sale. All this mass of lit-
Claude Duval	erary garbage is issued
Eardley Hall	by Lloyd, of London, in
Ella the Outcast	penny numbers.
Gentleman Jack	
Gambler's Wife	
Gallant Tom	
Lady Hamilton	
Mazeppa	
Mildred	

Old Sanctuary
Royal Twins
String of Pearls
The Brigand
The Oath

Of similar works, published also in numbers at 1d. per week, Mr. Heywood sells:—

Adam Bell	
Claude Duval	200
Court of London	400
Gretna Green	1,500
Love Match	460
Mysteries of London	750
Nell Gwynne	1,000
Perkin Warbeck	700
	100

Of the penny weekly journals, some of them, such as *Barker's People*, political and democratic, but the greater number social and instructive, the Lancashire sale is:—

Barker's People	
Reynolds' Miscellany	22,000
Illustrated Family Journal	3,700
London Journal	700
Family Herald	9,000
Home Circle	8,000
Home Journal	1,000
Penny Sunday Times	1,000
Lancashire Beacon	1,000
Plain Speaker	3,000
Potter's Examiner	200
Penny Punch	1,500
The Reasoner	360
Chat	160
	200

Of these publications the *Lancashire Beacon* and the *Reasoner* are avowedly infidel. I have not had an opportunity of seeing the latter, but in the number of the former which I perused, I found nothing more fatal to Christianity than abuse of the Bishop of Manchester. The Lancashire mind is indeed essentially a believing, perhaps an over-believing one. Fanaticism rather than scepticism is the extreme into which it is most likely to hurry. In Ashton-under-Lyne Johanna South-cote's bearded followers still meet under the roof the the New Jerusalem. In remote districts astrologers still watch the influences of the planets; and all quackeries, moral and physical—the remedies of Professor Mes-mer or of Professor Holloway—equally find a clear stage and very great favour.

But to return to the cheap book trade of Lancashire. Of the better

class of weekly publications, generally selling at 1½d., Mr. Heywood
makes the following returns:—

Domestic Journal	600
Eliza Cook's Journal	1,250
Chambers's Journal	900
Chambers's Information for the People	1,200
Hogg's Instructor	60
People's Journal	460

The cheap double-columned edition of Dickens's and Bulwer's books,
sell as follows:—

Dickens	250
Bulwer	200

The sale of *Punch* is 1,200. The *Family Friend* sells 1,500 monthly,
at twopence; the *Family Economist*, 5,000 monthly, at one penny.

In answer to inquiries as to whether he could apportion particular
classes of books to particular classes of readers, Mr. Heywood replied
that the comic or quasi-comic tales, and humorous publications, were
principally bought by shopmen and clerks; that the school of the
monstrous novels, and the more rabid democratic papers, supplied the
literary thirst of the mass of the operatives and that the better weekly
publications were taken by the superior classes of the work-people. The
women were terribly fond of mixed love and raw-head-and-bloody-
bones stories.

This examination of the border lines of literacy leads naturally to
the disturbed problem of education in England, of importance in this
year 1843 because of the defeat of the educational clauses in the Factory
Bill which Lord Ashley tried to bring in.

The startling fact was that in 1841 33 per cent of the men and 49 per
cent of the women marrying in England and Wales signed the marriage
register with a mark.* By 1853 this had fallen to 31 per cent and 45
per cent respectively, but the general average for 1839–48 inclusive
was 40 per cent, both male and female. In the agricultural southeast
division there was slight difference in the male-female proportions of illiteracy; in the northwest manufacturing divisions the number of females
was nearly double that of the males. A rough generalization would be
that those counties were most ignorant in which the population was
least dense. Thus in Middlesex County, incorporating London, the
average for both sexes was only 18 per cent, the lowest anywhere, and
in Surrey only 21 per cent. On the other hand, Monmouth County and

---

* G. R. Porter: *Progress of the Nation*, 1847. Figures taken from the reports
of the Registrar-General.

Bedford County had 59 per cent and 56 per cent respectively.* It was a notorious fact that in the agricultural districts many of the farmers discouraged efforts to educate the laborers. One well-to-do farmer, representative of his class, said: "What have all the schools done for them? . . . What need is there of learning to hold the handles of a plough, or whop a flail upon a thrashing floor? . . . Now, if you lay down a newspaper, and turn your back, the servant takes it up and reads it, and thus neglects his or her work. If you leave an unsealed letter, 'tis ten to one but the servant reads it. All this is the result of the schools, and the bother about reading and moralizing with the working men."†

It is clear that the ability to sign a marriage register did not necessarily indicate a very high threshold of literacy. There must have been many who could spell out their names to whom the simplest newspaper would offer great difficulty. England's much-despised neighbor Ireland had been for many years, according to Robert Chambers, above England with respect to elementary education of the people.‡ Scotland, with a national system of education and a legally endowed school in every parish, had traditionally maintained a high average of literacy.

The situation in England was certainly bad enough. Ashley calculated that in 1842 in England and Wales, 3,180,000 children required education, that 3,120,000 of them required it at public expense, and that of these there were not 845,000 receiving any sort of instruction. In other words, only 23½ per cent of all the children between five and fifteen were being taught at all.§ And with a great mass of those receiving some

---

* Exceptions would be Lancaster, Stafford, and Chester, which were above the average both in density of population and of ignorance.

† Christopher Thomson, *The Autobiography of an Artisan*, 1847. Thomson went on to say that food for the minds of the poor "simultaneously sprang up in the 'Penny Entertaining Library,' 'Penny Magazine,' 'Chambers's Journal,' 'Penny Cyclopaedia,' 'Knight's Store of Knowledge,' the cheap reprints of the poets, 'Chambers's Tracts,' etc. If the villagers were too poor to purchase these books . . . the Book Clubs and Artisans' Libraries reared their heads. . . ."
This is one of several important indications that the audience for any one paper, magazine, or monthly part was much greater than the number of copies sold. It was the custom in many of the public houses for someone who could read to read aloud the paper to the assembled group. This must have happened in many homes too.

‡ *Information for the People*, Vol. II, p. 302. Chambers went on to say: "Education is actively conducted in America, and it is calculated that about a sixth of the people are at school. In most of the states, schools are supported by a tax on property, and the superintendence is intrusted to committees of the rate-payers. In those of the North East, the schools are as one to every 200 of the inhabitants —a proportion, perhaps, exceeded in no part of the world."

§ Ashley, however, counted only the children's schools maintained by the Church of England and by the Nonconformists. If the shabbier and even more

training, the quality of their instruction and the time spent in class were minimal. As late as 1850 Kay estimated that in England and Wales there were 8,000,000 who could neither read nor write—that is, nearly one fourth of the population—and that of all the children between five and fifteen, one half attended no place of instruction.[10] And in Manchester, Ashley pointed out, were 129 pawnbrokers, 769 beer houses, 498 public houses, 309 brothels, and 763 streetwalkers. What was being done about the whole problem of education?

Obviously England had no national system of education. A good deal of attention had been called to the fact that in 1842 Parliament granted £30,000 for the education of the people and £70,000 for the erection of Royal Stables and Royal Dog Kennels at Windsor. The children of the upper and middle classes were tutored privately or trained in private schools of highly varying quality. The poorer classes were dependent largely upon charity schools, most of them poorly organized and badly taught. There were two principal agencies for educating the "industrious classes"—the Church of England's "National Society for Promoting the Education of the Poor in the Principles of the Established Church," and the non-sectarian "British and Foreign School Society," supported by the Nonconformists. Apart from the schools established and maintained by these societies were a small number of free and endowed schools supported by Dissenters. For the most part, education was on a voluntary basis, supported either by the various Nonconformist sects or by small payments made to the masters of common or day schools by the scholars themselves. Even at best, elementary education was a haphazard affair; the teachers were frequently as poor and almost as uneducated as the families from which the children came. In the Church schools, the much-admired "monitor" system was in vogue, under which some of the older children took over the instruction, imparting the benefits of their ignorance to those still more ignorant.* Not until 1841 was a training college for teachers opened by the National Society.

---

desultory day and evening schools supported by payments from the scholars themselves were added to the total number, the percentage would be raised a good deal. In Manchester and Salford, for example, some 33 per cent of the children between five and fifteen were attending some sort of day or evening school; in York, 60 per cent. In Bristol in 1841 some 60 per cent of the children were receiving some kind of instruction. (*Journal of the London Statistical Society*, 1841, pp. 159, 252.) In the country districts, however, the proportion must have been the lowest of all.

* The following remark was made in Bristol in 1841 by a woman commenting on the monitorial system: "I don't like them, because the lads teach, and then they say t'others, 'If you won't gie me summit, I'll have you up afore th' maister';

In addition to the common day schools, many of which charged for instruction, were the Dames' Schools, differing from the former in that the weekly payment for a child ran as low as 5d., instead of 10 or 11d. They were kept by females of the lower classes, one of whom was quoted in the House of Commons as saying, "It's little they pays us and it's little we teaches them." In all these schools there was a strong emphasis on moral and religious instruction; it was the Bible the students learned to read if they learned at all. Reading was emphasized much more than writing, and writing more than arithmetic.* Girls were taught to sew. The various church societies put out cheap one-penny textbooks. In London, however, even the poor schools used Vyse's, Mavor's, and Grey's spelling books, which sold for 1s. 6d. A committee examining popular education in London in 1843 explained this on the basis of "a strong aversion among the middle and lower classes to anything which can in any way be construed into charity."[11]

Most of the children in the poorer districts of England were irregular in attendance, and most of them were taken away from school at an early age to work for wages. In Kingston-upon-Hull in 1841, out of 2,800 children, 595 had left school before the age of ten, 964 at ten and eleven, and 1,108 more between twelve and thirteen. In the same town, of 4,735 minors *who had completed their education*, 823 were unable to read a whole sentence in any printed book, and 2,282 were unable to do any kind of arithmetic.

Still less effective were the Sunday schools, maintained zealously by the different church denominations. Here for a few hours each week children from poverty-stricken homes were taught in religious principles and in reading—and nothing else. Yet in Bristol in 1841 one third of all the schools were Sunday schools.

One other important phenomenon in this maze of educational individualism were the Ragged Schools. The name was descriptive both of the nature of their constituency and of the unconsciously patronizing manner in which it was emphasized. The cause itself was a good one. John Pounds, a crippled cobbler of Portsmouth, began to gather around him and to give elementary instruction to the bedraggled and tattered waifs whom he could bring to his shop. His early amateur efforts grew into a movement; the London City Mission, founded in 1835, took it up; "Ragged Schools" were formed in London and Bristol, and in 1844 the Ragged School Union was founded—the first conference of workers

---

and them as can afford to gie 'em summit does well enough, and them as can't, doesn't do no good." (*Journal of the London Statistical Society*, 1841, p. 161.)

* In Bristol in 1841, out of 598 schools reading was taught in 486; writing in only 292 of them.

convening in a loft over a cowshed in St. Giles's. The first London
school was set up in the Field Lane district of Holborn Hill, one of the
most degraded areas in the City. The children learned little but a
tentative reading of the Bible and certain moral literature. But the
teachers won the confidence of children in districts incredibly depraved
—children whom Lord Ashley described in a speech in the House of
Commons in 1848: "Many of them retire for the night, if they retire
at all, to all manner of places—under dry arches of bridges and viaducts,
under porticoes, sheds, and carts; to outhouses; in sawpits; on staircases;
in the open air, and some in lodging houses." Dickens later made a
touching appeal for the Union in the columns of the *Daily News*. In
1844 Ashley became its president, and devoted to it the energy of his
ethical-religious reforming fervor. In 1848 there were 83 Ragged
Schools, with 8,000 pupils, 124 paid and 929 voluntary teachers. By
1851 the number of schools had increased to 103. Always they were
dependent upon voluntary contributions.

At the adult level, during these years, there was a good deal of
activity among the poorly educated operatives of the industrial districts
in an attempt to create for themselves the educational advantages which
a muddled society had denied them. They organized their own night
schools, their Mutual Improvement Associations. In 1842 the Rev. R. S.
Bayley opened the first "People's College," at Sheffield, and by 1846
more than 1,000 pupils had passed through it. It was conducted by a
committee of working men and taught, among other subjects, Latin,
German, French, elocution, and logic. A second college was established
at Nottingham in 1846. In the village of Edwinstowe was organized the
"Artisan's Library, and Mutual Instruction Society," which held lectures and weekly classes, five nights a week, free to all villagers—teaching reading, writing, arithmetic, music, and drawing.*

In March, 1845, Samuel Smiles, whose book *Self-Help* was to become
in the next decade the bible for all workingmen who aspired to better
their condition, delivered in Leeds, before a mutual Improvement Society, an address on "The Education of the Working Classes." In anticipation of his later book he showed, by citing the lives of famous men,
that "adverse circumstances—even the barrenest poverty—cannot repress
the human intellect and character, if it be determined to rise; that Man

---

* Christopher Thomson: *The Autobiography of an Artisan*, 1847, pp. 21, 344.
In Nottingham, again, the workingmen commenced a number of "Operative
Libraries," housing them in public houses. One in 1849 had: history, 65 vols.;
biography, 80; novels, romances, and tales, 647; voyages, travels, topography, 57;
poetry, plays, and essays, 57; natural philosophy and science, 38. (*The Working
Man's Friend*, 1850, Vol. I, pp. 1f.)

can triumph over circumstances and subject them to his will; that knowledge is no exclusive inheritance of the rich and the leisured classes, but may be attained by all. . . ."[12]

The great mass of the people were not touched by these sporadic efforts of the more ambitious to lift themselves by their own bootstraps, but the persistence of such attempts at self-help in town after town argued a tough core of native intelligence which was determined not to be outflanked by the conditions of an accelerating industrial civilization, or by the suspicions of people such as Melbourne that education of the working classes and the stimulating of subversive republicanism were synonymous. It is not surprising that the first efforts were at a reasonably low intellectual level—these were children learning to walk— nor that Tomlin's *Help to Self-Educators* (1851) missed its market, and failed, when it devoted its columns to "Schelling's Philosophy of Art" and "An Analysis of the Political Economy of Adam Smith and John Mill."

Tied in with this whole movement were the Mechanics' Institutes. In 1850 there were 700 of them, with more than 107,000 members and libraries of nearly 700,000 volumes.[13] But the mechanics who had organized them were progressively crowded out of their own creations, partly because the lectures were frequently over their heads and partly because more and more the lower middle classes took them over for their own entertainment and enlightenment. There was a good deal of resentment about this among the more intelligent operatives, and when, for example, the workingmen of Carlisle started a reading room in 1848, one of their rules was that only a workingman could be a member of the committee.

The difficulties which beset those working for some reasonable system of elementary education in England were brought to a focus in 1843 when the Government, spearheaded by Ashley, brought in its Factory Bill to reduce the working hours of children. The most important feature of the bill was the introduction of compulsory education for factory children. The clauses of the Factory Act of 1833 which had specified a two-hour-per-day education for children had no sufficient provisions for enforcement, and had been openly ignored by the manufacturers. According to the new bill schools were to be established in whose control the Church of England would have the major share. Ashley did not believe in secularized education, and the teaching of moral and religious principles was to be the foundation of the proposed plan.

Then the storm broke. The Roman Catholics, of course, objected.

The more politically powerful Dissenters believed, with some justice, that the proposed system of controls meant that the whole plan would be dominated by the Establishment. Nearly 2,000,000 angry Nonconformists petitioned against the bill. Graham, the Home Secretary, baffled, tried to introduce some clauses modifying the provisions in favor of the Nonconformists, but he did not win their support and succeeded only in angering those who felt that the Church of England should control education. Such a churchman of the old school as Sir R. Inglis told the House that the Church was "the supreme instructress of the people of this country." Hume pointed out that she had, then, performed her office very badly: out of 82,047 prisoners committed in 1838, 77,127 could neither read nor write. Cobden contrasted Westminster from the moral and educational point of view with Manchester, to the great disadvantage of the borough which lay under the immediate influence of a dean and chapter. The superiority in the condition of Manchester he attributed to the Nonconformist ministers and churches.[14] At last, in despair, on June 15th the Home Secretary announced the abandonment of the educational clauses of the bill, and the Factory Bill itself was held over for reintroduction later. "Meanwhile the people perisheth!" wrote Ashley in his diary.

This whole unedifying episode shows how deep the cleavage and suspicion were between Church and Chapel and how ready both sides, but particularly the Dissenters, were to jettison the national welfare in order to salvage sectarian pride—or belief, to give it a gentler name.

Other religious turmoils were disturbing the national scene in this spring of 1843. The Established Church of Scotland was on the point of division. As was usually the case in these church controversies, the issue was not theological but concerned church government. The so-called Non-Intrusion party of the Scottish Church had been protesting for some time over the insistence of Parliament upon the right of lay patronage. This meant, in effect, that individual parishes could not choose their own ministers, but must take one named by a lay patron, usually the local squire.

On May 18th the General Assembly of the Church of Scotland met in Edinburgh, in an atmosphere of tense excitement. As the Non-Intrusion members entered they were greeted with applause from the crowded gallery. A long protest was read, which had been signed by the rebelling ministers and elders, declaring the grounds of their secession. Their leader Dr. Welsh and his party immediately left the hall—169 of them, including lay elders—and marched four abreast, heads high, between lines of cheering spectators waving handkerchiefs, to a hall at Canon Mills. There they were met by some 300 ministers not members of the Assembly; and with great dignity but also with deep emotion they formed the Free Presbyterian Church. The famous Dr. Chalmers was elected its first moderator. On him, as Dr. Welsh said without minimizing the importance of the occasion, "the eyes of the whole Church and country—the eyes of all Christendom—were directed."

Nearly half the Scottish clergy, some 500 out of 1,200, seceded. About £240,000 was raised in less than ten weeks for the erection of new churches and for the support of the seceding clergy.

At Oxford, the battle lines between the Tractarians and the University authorities were becoming more closely drawn. In 1842 Newman had retired to his retreat at Littlemore; in September, 1843, he had resigned the vicarage of St. Mary's, and with it Littlemore chapelry. "Wounded brutes," he said, "creep into some hole to die in, and no one grudges it them. Let me alone, I shall not trouble you long. This was the keen feeling which pierced me." His leadership in the Movement was over. Both friends and enemies became conscious of his flight Romeward.

Pusey became the acknowledged leader of the Movement, and in 1843 he was condemned and censured by the University authorities. On May 14th he preached a sermon at Christ Church in which he made clear his belief in the Real Corporeal Presence of Christ in the elements of the Holy Communion. A commission appointed by the Vice-Chancellor, refusing to hear Pusey's side of the case, declared that the sermon was opposed to the teaching of the Church of England. Pusey refused to retract what he had said, and he was suspended from preaching before the University for two years.

The stress and strain at Oxford during this spring was curiously illustrated at the Commemoration on June 26th. One of the two persons proposed for the honorary degree was Mr. Everett, the American minister. Everett had at one time been a Unitarian preacher. Several members of the Convocation, whose approval was necessary, informed the Vice-Chancellor that they would enter a public *non placet* and demand a scrutiny. Two hours later a strange scene took place in the Sheldonian Theatre. The dissension over Everett's degree coincided with a raucous demonstration put on by the undergraduates against a much-disliked junior proctor. The groans and hisses were so loud and long-continued that the *non placets* were inaudible. Amid the uproar from the gallery the Vice-Chancellor conferred the degrees in dumb show and dissolved the convocation with the prize compositions unread. Mr. Everett's thoughts on his reception at the ancient seat of learning were not recorded.

In the meantime, during this rainy spring, other happenings had held the interest of the English. They were advancing into a decade more significant than most of them realized, but like the life of any person or age it was compounded of jostling events ranging from the trivial to the profoundly important—the trivial often being exciting, and the important, dull.

The whole country had been shocked, however, at the assassination on January 21st of Edward Drummond, Peel's private secretary. As he was walking past the Salopian Coffee-house, a Daniel McNaughton fired a pistol at him, wounding him mortally.* The thing that caused official and public consternation was the assassin's admission that he had thought he was firing at Sir Robert Peel himself. It was a tense moment in a tense year.

But people were concerned, too, about the thick, soupy fog which that very weekend was so opaque that it laid up all shipping in the Thames. And a few days later the wonders of modern science were displayed when a giant blast was set off at Roundown Cliff, next to Shakespeare's Cliff at Dover, to make room for a roadway, instead of a tunnel, for the Southeastern Railway. Four hundred thousand cubic yards of a cliff nearly 400 feet in height were distributed over eighteen acres of beach, to an average depth of fourteen feet. . . . A splendid meteor was noticed in the heavens, and a little later Sir John Herschel described for the papers the tail of a comet which was sweeping across the northern sky. . . . Spain was occupied with the insurrection and civil war which had troubled the nation since Isabella had come to the throne in 1833 under her mother Christina as Regent. Don Carlos, the male claimant, had been defeated. In 1840 Espartero, the victorious general who supported the constitutional party, seized power and Christina fled; but in 1843 he was himself overthrown. Isabella, then thirteen years old, was declared of age.

On March 3d, at seven o'clock in the evening, five wagons, each drawn by four horses, brought through the gateway of the Royal Mint Chinese silver amounting to £1,000,000—the first consignment of the indemnity to be paid by the Celestial Empire. . . . A colliery explosion cost twenty-

---

* McNaughton later escaped execution through a verdict of "insanity"—a verdict which resulted in much headshaking among those who thought that such an appeal was being greatly abused at the time.

NEVER ACTED.
Theatre Royal, Drury Lane.

This Evening SATURDAY, February 11th. 1843,
Her Majesty's Servants will perform
A NEW TRAGIC PLAY,
IN THREE ACTS, called

A BLOT IN THE 'SCUTCHEON.

Thorold, Lord Tresham,	Mr. PHELPS,
Henry, Earl Mertoun,	Mr. ANDERSON,
Austin Tresham,	Mr. HUDSON.
Gerard,	Mr. G. BENNETT,
Andrew,	Mr. MELLON,
Arthur,	Mr. SELBY,
Ralph, (retainers of Lord Tresham)	Mr. YARNOLD,
Joseph,	Mr. C. J. SMITH,
Martin,	Mr. HOWELL,
Walter,	Mr. BENDER,
Mildred Tresham,	Miss HELEN FAUCIT,
Gwendolen Tresham,	Mrs. STIRLING.

AFTER WHICH,
A NEW FARCE,
CALLED THE

Thumping Legacy.

Filippo Geronimo, (an Innkeeper.)	Mr. W. BENNETT,
Jerry Ommous, (his nephew)	Mr. KEELEY,
Bambogetti, Mr. SELBY,	Leoni, Mr. HUDSON,
Brigadier of Carbineers,	Mr. G. BENNETT,
Carbineers,	Messrs. BRADY and PAULO.
Rosetta, (daughter of Filippo,)	Miss P. HORTON.

To conclude with, WEBER'S Romantic Opera of

DER FREISCHUTZ.

Ottocar, (the Prince)	Mr. J. REEVES,
Bernhard, (Head Ranger)	Mr. S. JONES,
Hermit,	Mr. SIMMOND,
Adolph,	Mr. ALLEN,
Caspar,	Mr. STRETTON,
Kilian, (Kinsman to the Head Ranger)	Mr. COMPTON,
Samiel,	Mr. HOWELL.

Witch of the Glen, Mr. STILT. Demon of the Harts, Mr. HARCOURT.
Foresters.—Messrs. Bender, Collet, Gilbeigh, Leigh, Simmonds, Galli, Barclay, Cowbrick,
Williamson, Clifford, Walker, Beale, C. Tett, S. Tett, Warring, Walsh, May, Genge
Ashton, &c. &c.
Peasants.—Messrs. Brady, Sharpe, Paulo, Prierson, Roffey, Burdett, &c.

Linda,	Miss ROMER,
Rose,	Miss P. HORTON,
Bridesmaids,—Mrs. SEBLE,	Miss GOULD, Mrs. WATSON,

Peasants.—Mesdames Byers, C. Byers, Perry, Goward, Boden, Foster, King, Smith,
Emmerson, Ashton, Smithson, Herbert, Reele, Hunt, Greene, Sutton, Carson,
Berringer, Travis, A. Travis, Lee, Smith, Marsano, Maile, &c.

Figure 46. Playbill for Browning's *A Blot in the 'Scutcheon*

seven lives. . . . On the death of Robert Southey, William Wordsworth was pressed to accept the poet laureateship, and did accept. He was seventy-three years of age. . . . The *Illustrated London News* ran a picture of the *Great Northern* steamer, 247 feet long, propelled by Archimedean screw and an engine of 360 horsepower. There were afloat at the time seven other screw vessels, including the *Great Britain*, 3,600 tons and 1,000 horsepower, which Prince Albert was to launch at Bristol later in the summer. She was the largest steamer to cross the Altantic as yet, and was built of iron.

The electric eel died at the Adelaide Galleries; "mortification" was given as the cause, but mortification because of what was not stated. . . . There was great celebration at the official opening of the Thames foot tunnel; two marquees were erected for the accommodation of the directors and proprietors, while some ferrymen hoisted a black flag at the Tunnel Pier to indicate their feelings about unfair competition. Within four days 60,000 persons had passed through the tunnel. A few weeks earlier a curious accident had happened to Mr. Brunel, its chief engineer. While amusing the children of a friend by seeming to pass a half-sovereign piece into his mouth and out at his ear he swallowed the coin and it lodged in his trachea. Surgical assistance proved helpless, and it was not until, on two different occasions, Mr. Brunel was suspended by his heels and shaken that the coin was finally dislodged. . . . *A Blot in the 'Scutcheon* was produced for the first time, at Drury Lane. One critic said that its three acts were better than five, but it would have been better in one, and best left untold. It was "brief, yet tedious, melodramatic without being effective. The unchasteness of the heroine, for whose frailty no palliation is offered, is fatal to dramatic sympathy." . . . On off-nights at Drury Lane, Cobden, Bright, and others were holding weekly meetings of the Anti-Corn-Law League. . . . A great Free Trade banquet was held in Manchester, with 3,400 ladies and gentlemen dining in Free Trade Hall, and 400 in the galleries. . . . Lola Montez performed Spanish dances in the native manner at the Italian opera. There was a protest on the part of some knowing ones who declared that she was not what she seemed, but the newspapers cried "fair play!" and rather liked her. . . . On Easter Monday 18,432 persons visited the British Museum.

On April 25th the new royal steam yacht, 225 feet long, was launched at Pembroke dockyard. The dockyard band struck up "God Save the Queen" and 10,000 voices joined in singing the national anthem. The Queen was not present, having given birth that morning at four o'clock to a princess. The bulletins said that both Queen and infant were doing well.

Figure 47. Going to the Derby

The national excitement of Derby Day arrived—with bishops asking at their clubs, "What horses won?"—and Macready made his final appearance of the season at Drury Lane in *Macbeth*. This also terminated his two-year unsuccessful management of the theater. Serious drama was in a bad way. The "patent monopoly" allowed straight drama to be played only at the two large theaters, Drury Lane and Covent Garden (and at the Haymarket in the summer). If the other theaters wanted to play Shakespeare, for instance, they had to smuggle it in with musical interludes in the form of a "burletta." For the most part they chose to thrive on melodrama and adaptations from the French. The irony was that the two theaters sacred to serious drama were of all places those the least likely to see it successfully performed. The vast spaces of their auditoriums (Drury Lane seated 3,500) immobilized serious acting, or rather demanded that it be so distorted as to lose all dramatic effectiveness. In this year of 1843, however, the patent monopoly came to an end, and hopes were held out for improvement of the drama. How fallacious those hopes were we shall see later.

On June 18th the Duke of Wellington held his annual Waterloo Dinner, gathering around him at Apsley House his surviving officers of the great battle. A vast number of people clustered around the entrance gates to watch the guests assemble. His Royal Highness Prince Albert arrived precisely at ten minutes before eight o'clock. The magnificent silver plateau presented to the Duke by the King of Portugal, twenty-seven feet long, four feet wide, occupied the center of the table. The service of plate used was alternately gold and silver; the unique Dresden porcelain dessert service was a gift from the Emperor of Russia. The military band played "The Old Roast Beef of England." Covers were laid for eighty-five. Many toasts were offered, and the party broke up when Prince Albert left at a quarter past ten.

All through the late winter and spring notices had been appearing in the papers which told of two series of threatening events—one in Wales, the other in Ireland.

A strange popular revolt had broken out in Wales against the injustices of the system of toll roads, and the demonstrations took a dramatically organized form that caught public attention. Crews of night riders dressed like women and called themselves "Rebecca and her daughters" after the scriptural text, "And they blessed Rebekah, and said unto her . . . 'let thy seed possess the gate of those which hate them.'" The attacks on the turnpike tollgates were always made at night and consisted

Figure 48. The Duke of Wellington. From a miniature believed to be by D'Orsay

of the swift demolition of the gate, posts, and tollhouse. As a rule the Rebeccas offered no personal violence to the tollkeepers, and such was their Robin Hood reputation with their friends and neighbors that in spite of offered rewards none of the marauders was apprehended. In the county of Carmarthen between seventy and eighty of the 100 to 150 gates were destroyed, some of them again and again. The trustees of the roads at length had to leave the roads open and free from toll.

The career of this grass-roots rebellion was complicated, before it ran its course, by an accretion of Chartist agitators. Before long the list of grievances had grown to include the New Poor Law, the increase of county taxes, and the alleged extortionate rents taken by landowners for their farms. Lawless elements began to get control; property was fired and an old woman who kept the Hendy gate was murdered in cold blood. The excitement and by this time the fear of the citizenry were reflected in the verdict of the coroner's jury that "the deceased died from suffusion of blood which produced suffocation, but from what cause is to the jurors unknown."

In the end the Government sent a large body of troops down to Wales, London police were imported to ferret out the offenders, and by the latter part of the summer the disturbances declined.

A more potentially serious situation developed this year in Ireland. Daniel O'Connell was making a career, in Parliament and out, of arguing for repeal of the Union. The year 1843 was declared "Repeal Year," and the Repeal Association grew enormously. Cards of membership were issued bearing the names of four places in Ireland where the Irish had won battles against either the Danes or the English. A series of huge meetings took place, the first of them in March, at Trim, with 30,000 people present, whom O'Connell addressed in his florid and inflammatory style. In May he held a demonstration at Nenagh for the North Riding of Tipperary, entering the town after a triumphal march of twenty miles, with an escort of 100,000. It was roses, roses all the way, with women waving handkerchiefs and shouting from the windows. Two miles away, at the Grange, he addressed a meeting not too conservatively estimated at 350,000.* Two weeks later the Repeal papers reported a vast "Kilkenny demonstration" estimating the numbers above 300,000, including 10,000 or 12,000 horsemen.

O'Connell's oratory was much the same on all these occasions. He would begin: "Is there a band within hearing? If there be, let them play up 'God Save the Queen.' " (More than a dozen bands here play the national anthem.) Then references to "That ruffianly Saxon paper, the *Times*." A searing recital of the 300 women, "the loveliness and beauty of Wexford," who had been murdered by Cromwell. "They prayed to the English for humanity, and Cromwell slaughtered them." ("Oh, oh!" and great sensation.) "I am not at all imaginative when I talk of the possibility of such occurrences anew; but yet I assert there is no danger for the women, for the men of Ireland would die to the last in their defense." (Here the entire company rises and cheers for several minutes.) "We were a paltry remnant then; we are millions now." (Renewed cheering.) "Gentlemen, you may soon learn the alternative to live as slaves or die as freemen." ("Hear!" and tremendous cries of "We'll die freemen!") "I say they may trample on me; but it will be my dead body

---

* Irish figures, O'Connell explained: "He often heard it said that it was impossible so many thousand persons could hear him together. He thought there were some forty or fifty thousand persons that heard every word he uttered; or indeed vastly more, for he perceived his voice extended to the very extremes of the crowd."

they will trample on, not the living man." ("Hear!" and most tremendous cheering.)*

Between March and September O'Connell continued his tour of agitation. The climax was to come at a gigantic meeting at Clontarf on October 8th—three miles out of Dublin. The occasion had been announced with great solemnity, and the Irish had been told to come in military formation. On the seventh the Government issued a proclamation forbidding the meeting. Parliament had passed a law in August—the "regulation of firearms bill"—restricting the importation of arms and ammunition, but O'Connell had whipped his followers to white heat with his thinly veiled advocacy of physical force. What would he do in this crisis? His influence hung in the balance.

O'Connell immediately called a special meeting of the Repeal Association, told them there could be no meeting at Clontarf, and at half-past three that afternoon signed a proclamation canceling the demonstration. From that moment his influence was gone, and the movement itself dwindled.

On the fourteenth O'Connell, his son, and others of his leaders were arrested on charges of conspiracy and sedition. His trial did not take place until January, 1844. The jury returned a verdict of "guilty," and he was sentenced to an imprisonment of twelve months. Later his sentence was reversed in the House of Lords, and he was liberated September 4th. But the uncrowned King of Ireland had been dethroned, as far as further Repeal activity was concerned.

Closer home, the year was coming to a close with reasonable quietness. Yet no small furor was being stirred up in medical, religious, and lay circles over mesmerism, or "animal magnetism." At the center of the controversy was Dr. John Elliotson, a brilliant but unorthodox physician (Thackeray gratefully dedicated *Pendennis* to him) who had been dropped in 1839 from the staff of London University for advocating and practicing mesmerism as a technique of operative anesthesia. In 1843

---

* *Punch*, November 4th, ran a burlesque of "The Irish Demosthenes" which might almost have been taken from one of his speeches: "O free born Irishmen! —ah, no!—slaves! . . . This [women's] blood was shed by the Saxons—by those who are now longing to cut your throats—do not dream of cutting theirs. There would be an excuse for you, a strong excuse, a mighty great, an almost total excuse; but you would not be right—not quite right . . . I would not go too far for all the world. Suppose, only suppose, you were to rush to Dublin, storm the Castle, and put the slaves and despots in it to the sword—What should I do? I do not know what I should do . . ." etc.

he published a volume, *Numerous Cases of Surgical Operations without Pain in the Mesmeric State,* giving the case history, among others, of a forty-two-year-old laborer with ulcerated knee who had had his leg amputated by W. Squire Ward in an operation completely successful, without pain. Elliotson claimed other cures under the influence of mesmerism, from "jumping fits" to rheumatism. The *Lancet* called it all "gross humbug," and the medical profession as a whole viewed it with almost frantic suspicion, classifying it with the current vogue for hydrotherapy or "water cures" in Germany, where Dr. Priessnitz made his patients walk barefoot through meadows wet with dew. When the report of Ward and Topham, the mesmerizer, concerning the successful operation was read to the Royal Medical and Chirurgical Society in 1842, the doctors called the claim "irrational, impossible." One declared that he would not believe the facts had he witnessed them himself; other members were anxious to expunge all record of the proceedings from the minute book.[15] There was much talk back and forth about the "physiological fluidum," "adyllic forces," "cerebral sympathy," etc. One writer identified the force with electricity. In the same year mesmerism—also called "somnambulism"—received the support of James Braid, a Scottish doctor who practiced medicine in Manchester in the forties, in his *Neurhypnology, or the Rationale of Nervous Sleep.*

The clergy looked upon mesmerism as a wicked device to suspend and annihilate man's will and conscience. "If there are laws against blasphemy and swearing, and against Sunday trading, there should be laws against necromancy and dealing with familiar spirits." Sermons were preached against it. The Rev. Hugh McNeile in Liverpool published in the *Penny Pulpit* a philippic called "Satanic Agency and Mesmerism." Many people were impressed by the claims of the new "science," however—notably Harriet Martineau, who in seven letters written in 1844 (first published in the *Athenaeum* in 1845) described her prolonged illness, which the best medical attention had been unable to help. She had reached the stage of a desperate dependence upon opiates when, on June 22, 1844, "I found myself, for the first time, under the hands of a mesmerist." At the end of four months she felt quite well, was restored to days and nights of rest. She described her experiences in great detail and cited numerous cases of "recorded cures" of dropsy, paralysis, epilepsy, and other diseases of the brain and nerves. Charlotte Brontë was mesmerized by Miss Martineau, and Elizabeth Barrett admitted that, though "Carlyle calls Harriet Martineau quite mad because of her belief in mesmerism," she herself "was not afraid to say that she quite believed in Harriet Martineau."[16]

Mr. Spencer Hall was Miss Martineau's mesmerist, and in 1843 he became editor of two magazines supporting the cause: the *Phreno-Magnet* and the *Zoist: a Journal of Cerebral Physiology and Mesmerism*. Dr. Elliotson was of course one of his most frequent contributors, and the Martineau case was described at length, Latin being used to describe the symptoms (*"uterus major erat retroversus,"* etc.). One of Elliotson's articles on "Jumping Fits Cured by Mesmerism" gives a curious sidelight on current British medical practice. The patient he was describing had been treated for years by other practitioners in the following manner: "Dr. Watson shaved her head and electrified her. Under the others she was bled in the arm twenty-five times, cupped seventeen times, had two setons, three issues, leeches and blisters without number, and physic without end. . . . One practitioner attended her for a year and gave her carbonate of iron largely, and made her wear bags of steel filings on her back and feet, and silk stockings and gloves; but the filings increased her sufferings when she jumped."[17]

Braid also wrote freely for the *Zoist*. The general drift of the journal was somewhat mystical, but Braid himself believed that the trance was purely a subjective phenomenon. There were reports on the heads of murderers; on cures by mesmerism of heart trouble, insanity, hysteria, epilepsy, etc. Inevitably the embattled defense of mesmerism took on the nature of a cult.

Interest in the hypnotic condition* was generally accompanied by a belief in phrenology, which had a somewhat longer history in England and which was accepted in quarters still suspicious of mesmerism. As Elliotson put it in his book: "Phrenology I have lived to see established, though it had not twenty advocates in this country when I first wrote in its favour." The *Zoist* ran articles also on phrenological investigations, with many charts and such titles as "Doubts on the Organ of Hope," "Morbid Excitement of Veneration, When Small." Benjamin Silliman, M.D., LL.D., "Professor of Chemistry, etc., in Yale College," wrote excitedly from Connecticut, after Mr. Combe had delivered a course of four lectures in New Haven on phrenology, his "Thoughts on the Reasonableness of Phrenology, and Its Claim to the Attention of Scientific Men." Herbert Spencer, in an article published in January, 1844, discussed "A New View of the Functions of Imitation and Benevolence." Later he printed a brief article "On the Situation of the Organ of Amativeness."†

---

* The word "hypnosis" did not come into use until shortly after 1843.

† Spencer was twenty-four years of age at the time. Years later, in his autobiography (Vol. I, p. 227), he explained his more mature conclusion "that, though

There was some controversy over the new Model Prison at Pentonville and its "silent system" which involved the complete isolation of the prisoners from each other. The *Illustrated London News* called this "modern cruelty, designed to impair the health, destroy the constitution and obliterate the mind." . . . John Murray, the well-known publisher, died in his sixty-fifth year. . . . A wet summer raised alarm about the crops; mildew was reported. . . . Father Mathew appeared in England for the first time, and won thousands to the pledge of total abstinence. . . . Colonel Fawcett of the 55th Regiment shot and killed his brother-in-law, Lieutenant Munro, in a duel. He was finally sentenced to twelve months' imprisonment in Newgate. . . . Victoria and Albert visited France and were warmly welcomed and feted.

In London, Balfe's *The Bohemian Girl* was first presented. This tuneful and florid English opera was reprehended as "melodrama on stilts" by one critic, who could not, of course, foresee that it would be translated into French, Italian, and German and would become one of the most enduringly popular of all operas in English.

A great deal of public building was going on in London during the year, none of which made the architectural critics happy—with the exception of the new Houses of Parliament, which were proceeding at a stately rate. The interminably delayed construction of the new British Museum was being carried forward; it was three fourths completed, and everyone wondered what the facade would look like. Would it be as bad as "that architectural abortion, the National Gallery, which disfigures the finest site in London, and is not only paltry and ridiculous to look at but inadequate to the purpose for which it was erected?"[18] Most commentators were equally contemptuous of the new Nelson Column which was rising almost literally inch by inch in the same Trafalgar Square— "that prodigious effort of British taste to give an air of architectural magnificence to the metropolis." During November the public was admitted beyond the hoardings to view the seventeen-foot-high statue of the naval hero before it was elevated to its position on top of its 177-foot column.* A hundred thousand people passed through the enclosure over the week end. *Punch* made fun of the stone colossus, and the *Spectator* wrote of it: "The sculptor, Mr. Bailey . . . has successfully imitated the style of carving peculiar to ship's figureheads. This has enabled him to exhibit that noble superiority to the rules of art, and daring disregard of personal resemblance, for which the dock-yard carvers are celebrated

---

the statements of phrenologists might contain adumbrations of truths, they did not express the truths themselves."

* Landseer's four bronze lions were not completed until 1867.

Figure 49. Trafalgar Square

. . . the feet are made to slope; so that Nelson seems to be in the act of sliding off the rounded top of the pedestal."

The Christmas number of *Punch* included a poem which wrung the hearts of humanitarians across the land. During the summer Elizabeth Barrett had published her touching "Cry of the Children," inspired by the official report on the employment of children in the mines and factories.

> Do ye hear the children weeping, O my brothers,
>   Ere the sorrow comes with years
> . . . .
> They are weeping in the playtime of the others,
>   In the country of the free.

And now Thomas Hood wrote his "Song of the Shirt," calling attention to a class of sweated labor only recently engaging the attention of the reformers: the women in the cheap-clothes trade. It had been reported in the papers that a slop seller, Moses and Son, had prosecuted a poor widow with two children for pawning articles which she had to make up for him. She earned 7s. a week, receiving five farthings for making a shirt and having to procure her own needles. *Punch* had earlier called this to public attention with the verses on "Moses and Co.," and now the "Song of the Shirt," a direct cry of flaming indignation, carried on the campaign in verses beginning:

> With fingers weary and worn,
>   With eyelids heavy and red,
> A woman sat in unwomanly rage,
>   Plying her needle and thread—
> Stitch! stitch! stitch!
>   In poverty, hunger, and dirt,
> And still with a voice of dolorous pitch
>   She sang the "Song of the Shirt!"

All sensitive people were shocked by the disclosures but no one knew quite what to do. The magistrate had given Mr. Moses a bad half-hour, yet official action on the whole problem lagged. Sweated seamstresses continued to sew "a shroud as well as a shirt." As late as 1859 the shirt makers were receiving only 4s. 6d. a dozen.

But Christmas, as *Punch* said elsewhere, comes, like royal births, but once a year. Holly appeared in English windows; Christmas puddings were baked, Dickens published *A Christmas Carol*, and all England, perplexed but hopeful, cried with Tiny Tim: "God bless us, every one."

CHAPTER FOUR

1844 * England's Green and Pleasant Land

I F the "gentle reader" of these pages (to use a Victorianism) had been living in this fourth year of the decade, which would have seemed more important to him: Ashley's attempt to get a Ten Hours' Bill through Parliament or the first visit to England of General Tom Thumb? The first appearance of a book advancing the theory of organic evolution or the new craze of the polka? The revelation of incredibly bad housing and sanitary conditions in the large towns or the visit of the Emperor of Russia? The excellent harvest weather or the depressed condition of the agricultural laborer? The initial meeting of the Society for the Protection and Employment of Distressed Needlewomen or the opening of thirty-seven and a half miles of the Bristol and Gloucester Railway? The publication of Stanley's great *Life* of Thomas Arnold or of Charles Lever's *Tom Burke of Ours?*

The answers would obviously depend upon who the reader was, and where he happened to be living. Was he Friedrich Engels, gathering material for his *exposé* of the British industrial system, or was he (with a slight shift in gender) one Barbara Henrietta White, of Pilton House, Devon, getting married at St. George's, Hanover Square (after a long engagement), to Gartside Tipping, Esq.? Was he Benjamin Disraeli, with Young England gleaming in his eye, or was he Mary V—, aged thirteen, crippled factory worker, giving testimony before the Children's Employment Commission?

All these things were happening simultaneously at the same point in history (narrative is linear, history is solid, as Carlyle knew). But every Englishman, living his little cycle in time in the midst of the vast circumscribed whole, woke each morning to his own hungers and his own hopes, read about or listened to that which seemed to touch him most intimately, ate such dinners as Belgrave Square or Limehouse afforded, and went to bed only more or less dimly aware of the great complex of which he—for himself at least—was the center. The gigantic development of railway transportation which was to bend Britain into a larger economic and cultural whole was still an unrealized though accelerating process in the early forties. Great areas of the population were almost literally unaware of their neighbors. One county could be strangely foreign to the next. If Afghanistan seemed far away from London, so did Dorset from Durham. Yet in these many countries called England there was a deep surge of national life. The 1840's were the matrix of a new culture, and nothing that was human was insignificant.*

If one were searching for the unique catalytic event of 1844, as far as interest shown by both court and cottage was concerned, it would be, oddly enough, the triumphal visit early in the year of General Tom Thumb and his astute manager P. T. Barnum. The enthusiasm in the United States which sent 10,000 people to the docks to see the general off on his voyage to England was equaled by his reception on these distant shores. Thousands of people crowded into Egyptian Hall to watch the little man strut about in his famous imitation of Napoleon and to see him represent "Grecian Statues." Mr. Beaton of Soho built

---

* Some of the more thoughtful commentators were aware how different their age would seem to later generations and prophetically anticipated a very modern complaint. "If posterity judge of the present age by its newspapers," wrote the *Spectator* (May 4, 1844), "they will form a rare opinion of it. . . . Among the news, the rascalities of life occupy a most disproportionate space. The steady unobtrusive exercise of the domestic virtues . . . is the commonplace of life, and affords no salient points to the news-caterer. But the adventures of Lord Huntingtower and the swindling leeches who clung to him . . . the will-forgeries, poisonings, adulteries, stabbing of sheep by clergymen, etc.—these fill up the news-columns as attractively as their dramatized versions do the minor theatres. The rottenness of life is sought out by the newsmonger as the rottenness of cheese is by the epicure."

Figure 50. "General" Tom Thumb, "the American Dwarf"

for his generalship an elegant dress carriage twenty inches high and eleven inches wide, completely furnished in the richest style and drawn by a pair of Shetland ponies. By royal command he appeared before Her Majesty at Buckingham Palace, and the Queen, "*with her own hand,*" presented him with several expensive souvenirs, among which was a gold pencil case with the initials T. T. and his coat of arms engraved on it. *Punch,* always critical of absurdities, could growl ironically about the royal favors shown the "Yankee Dwarf." "We have only to reflect," said he, "upon the countless acts of patronage toward the Arts and Sciences—had only to remember a few of the numerous personal condescensions of the Queen toward men of letters, artists, and philosophers—to be assured that even Tom Thumb would be welcomed with that graceful cordiality which has, heretofore, made Buckingham Palace and Windsor Castle the homes of Poetry and Science." But such carping did nothing to interrupt the midget's spectacularly successful tour, nor did it seem to disturb Buckingham Palace.

When Tom Thumb left for still greater triumphs on the Continent, the Ojibway Indians from the distant spaces of Her Majesty's Canadian kingdom took his place and displayed their prowess in archery at their campground near Regent's Park. After the Ojibways disappeared, fourteen Iowa Indians from the far reaches of the Missouri erected wigwams in Lord's Cricket-ground, and were exhibited, for a consideration, to admiring crowds.

Art also had its curiosity of the year. No less exotic than the Ojibways, to many observers, was Turner's painting "Rain-Steam-Speed" currently on view at the annual exhibition of the Royal Academy. Thackeray, mystified yet captivated, wrote in *Fraser's:* "He has out-prodigied almost all former prodigies. He has made a picture with real rain, behind which is real sunshine, and you expect a rainbow every minute. Meanwhile, there comes a train down upon you, really moving at the rate of fifty miles an hour. . . . All those wonders are performed with means not less wonderful than the effects are. The rain . . . is composed of dots of dirty putty slapped on to the canvas with a trowel; the sunshine scintillates out of very thick, smeary lumps of chrome yellow. The shadows are produced by cool tones of crimson lake, and quiet glazings of vermilion. Although the fire in the steam-engine *looks* as if it were red, I am not prepared to say that it is not painted with cobalt and pea-green. . . . The world has never seen anything like this picture."

Of much wider interest was a new gymnastic exercise accompanied by music. The *Times* had reported a little earlier that in Paris "politics are, for the moment, suspended in public regard, by the new and all-absorbing pursuit—the Polka—a dance recently imported from Bohemia, and which embraces in its qualities the intimacy of the waltz, with the vivacity of the Irish jig." This energetic dance was popularized at Her Majesty's Theatre by Carlotta Grisi and M. Perrot, and soon ecstatic devotees were galloping up and down drawing rooms in 2-4 time. It was danced at Almack's and "at the balls of the nobility and the gentry." Jullien, the melodramatic director of the Promenade Concerts, turned out new polkas one after the other. Ladies wore polka hats, polka

jackets, and polka boots; men wore polka ties. Street ballads were
hawked on the subject:

> Oh! sure the world is all run mad,
> The lean, the fat, the gay, the sad—
> All swear such pleasure they never had,
> Till they did learn the Polka.
>
> *Chorus*
> First cock up your right leg—so,
> Balance on your left great toe,
> Stamp your heels, and off you go
> To the Original Polka. Oh!

Thus was culture served in this year of grace.

The Annual Register found it a matter for congratulation that "the
opening of the year 1844 found the country for the most part in a
thriving and tranquil condition. An increasing revenue and reviving trade
reanimated the spirits of the community after the long period of depression by which the patience of numerous classes had been so severely
tried." Indeed the upswing had begun in the latter half of 1843, and by
New Year's Day the *Illustrated London News* was able to greet its
readers with a song by F. W. N. Bayley and music by Balfe entitled
"A Happy, Happy Year."

> A happy year, O Father dear,
>   (Happy as we are now),
> To shed its sunshine o'er thy head,
>   Its bliss upon thy brow.
> Your honour'd love upon your child
>   Still fondly lavish'd be,
> For that is bliss, oh, Father dear,
>   And sunshine too to me.

When the Queen opened Parliament on February 1st, no stirring
topics of controversy seemed to occupy the official mind, and she was
able to report pleasantly that "the hostilities which took place during
the past year in Scinde [in northwest India] have led to the annexation
of a considerable portion of that country to the British Possessions in the
East." Peel's government seemed to be more firmly seated than ever,
buttressed by an apparent commercial prosperity. Peel reiterated his
opinion that the abolition of the Corn Laws would produce great confusion and distress.

On Easter Monday and the two days following several railway companies introduced reduced-fare excursion tickets, to the great delight of crowds of shopkeepers, clerks, and mechanics, many of whom for the first time could enjoy the delights of railway travel—even as far as the seacoast! Brighton was the favorite destination, but great numbers went also to Dover. At Whitsuntide (May 27th) the London and Brighton Railway repeated the successful experiment. The morning train to Brighton started with forty-five carriages and four engines; at New Cross it was joined by six more carriages and another engine; and at Croyden by another six carriages and a sixth engine. The weather was colder than it had been for years, but all England sought holiday. Immense numbers visited the suburban fairs at Greenwich, Stepney, and Wandsworth. Some 40,000 landed at the Greenwich piers; 30,000 were carried by the Greenwich Railway. The National Gallery was visited by 18,350 persons and the British Museum by 22,000.

Within the month Sir Francis Chantrey's equestrian statue of Wellington before the Royal Exchange was "inaugurated." . . . Albert and Victoria attended the art exhibition of works expected to embellish the walls of the new Houses of Parliament. . . . Albert laid the first stone for the New Hospital for Consumption. . . . Sir James Graham, Home Secretary, brought down a storm of protests when it was revealed that his office had been opening at the Post Office (however legally) certain letters, notably some to Mazzini. *Punch* turned on him savagely, and there were outraged cries of "police state." . . . An institution called "The Dentorium" was established "for the purpose of affording relief at an economical rate to the individuals suffering under affections of the teeth and mouth."

The Emperor of Russia and the King of Saxony visited England at the same time, the former drawing the greater public attention because of the vast extent of his autocratic power over millions of people. He was subjected to the receptions, audiences, reviews, fetes, and state dinners always inflicted upon visiting royalty—including Windsor, the Ascot races, and a huge breakfast-reception at Chiswick given by the Duke of Devonshire, attended by some "seven or eight hundred distinguished noblemen and gentlemen." The huge review in the Great Park at Windsor did not go off so well, owing to mistakes and bad management. One of the blunders concerned the artillery. The Queen disliked firing, and Wellington had ordered the guns to remain silent; but by some mistake they were discharged not far from Her Majesty. The Duke "blew up, and swore lustily," the Queen attempting to pacify him. Greville reported that the Emperor had become bald and bulky, but nevertheless was a fine and grand-looking personage. Greville also noted that he had a keen eye for beauty, "and most of the good-looking women were presented to him." It was considered a democratic touch on the part of the great monarch that he preferred always to sleep on the ground, on a leather tick stuffed with straw, "as being more conducive to health." When, leaving England, he embarked on the steam vessel *Black Eagle*, a sailor carried on board the bundle of straw for His Imperial Majesty's bed.

During the winter and spring, however, events of somewhat greater national importance were shaping up.

Nine nights were consumed in February in the Commons in debate on the Irish question. The report of the closing discussion ran to twenty-six columns in the *Morning Chronicle*, and other papers printed some ten columns of Peel's long speech. One of the problems this time was that of Irish religious disabilities. The Church of England, with all its wealth, served only about one eighth of the Irish population. The Catholic Church, without endowment, lived poorly on the free-will offerings of its constituency. O'Connell argued for the disestablishment of the English Church in Ireland, but that would have left the Catholics as poverty-stricken as before. And opposition was overwhelmingly against a counter-proposal that both churches should be established, for that would have involved a division of endowments between them. Peel's ministry at last decided to propose an act which would legalize bequests for the Catholics, and this was done in December, 1844. However, nine evenings of debate resulted only in the ministerial defeat of Lord John Russell's motion for a committee of the whole House to discuss the state of Ireland! Disraeli expressed the prevalent impatience with the whole Irish question: "It was the Pope one day, potatoes the next."

Of greater national significance was Graham's reintroduction of his bill to regulate the labor of women and children in factories—this time without the educational clauses. The bill as finally passed made certain distinct reforms. Although it lowered from nine to eight years the age at which children might be admitted to factories, it also lowered the working hours of children between the ages of eight and thirteen from nine to six and a half hours. It extended to women the protection hitherto offered to "young people" between thirteen and eighteen; and it set up certain regulations for safeguarding machinery. The hours of work for young people, however, were maintained at the same level as before —twelve. Here arose all the storm and confusion.

The Ten Hours Movement had behind it a history of a dozen years, beginning with Michael Sadler, James Kay, and Richard Oastler in 1831–32.

Oastler, a zealously evangelical Yorkshireman, a Tory, and a Victorian "character" in his own right, was one of the crusading humanitarians who was loathed and loved with equal fervor. A vigorous and romantically flamboyant fighter both against the New Poor Law and the conditions of factory labor, he had been denounced in the House of Lords as a criminal incendiary and was worshiped by those whose condition he sought to alleviate. He had been imprisoned for debt in the Fleet and in the Queen's Prison for more than three years, whence he had issued the *Fleet Papers* in continuation of his campaign. Through friends who felt that he had been imprisoned really for his social views, a subscription was raised to pay his debts, and on February 12, 1844, he was released. He was escorted back to his home in Huddersfield by great crowds of people, with bands playing, and he spoke there to an audience of 15,000. Immediately he began a series of meetings in Yorkshire and Lancaster on behalf of the Ten Hours Bill which Lord Ashley was struggling to get through the Commons.

Ashley had introduced as an amendment to the Government's bill a proposal which would reduce the hours of work for young people from twelve to ten hours. On his side he had no small number of liberal manufacturers who were intelligent enough to see that in the long run their own ends would best be served by such controls. Against this Graham cited 358 masters, "paying wages to the amount of £2,500,000 per annum, who declared that the proposed reduction in working hours would have a ruinous effect upon both capital and wages." But Ashley in his speech moving the amendment laid bare such a series of industrial horrors and painted such a picture of misery, degradation, and despair that sensitive members were panic-stricken and gave a provisional approval to his amendment.

Ashley had at hand the three large folio volumes of the *Second Report of the Children's Employment Commission: Trades and Manufactures*, published the preceding year, which examined the ages at which children were employed in various industries—metal wares, earthenware, glass, hosiery, calico printing, weaving, pin-making, chemicals, etc.—as well as the nature of their employment, their hours of work, wages, number of accidents, and moral condition. The Commissioners pointed out that children frequently began to work at five years of age and regularly between seven and eight, that of the whole number of persons employed in carrying on the "trades and manufactures" a large portion were under thirteen years of age. The apprentice system was in common use, whereby the age of servitude began as early as seven years and ran until twenty-one—a term often passed under circumstances of great hardship and ill-usage and under the condition that the apprentice should receive as payment, during the greater part of his service, only food and clothing.

The hours of work were commonly twelve, frequently extending, however, to fifteen, sixteen, or even eighteen hours consecutively. In the case of young women employed in London millinery and dressmaking establishments, the regular hours during the four months of the busy season were fifteen. The diseases most prevalent in the manufactories were disordered digestion, curvature and distortion of the spine, deformity of the limbs, and diseases of the lungs ending in consumption. A typical case ("No. 61") would be that of Mary Brooks, nine years old, engaged in lace manufacturing in the Nottingham district:

> Can read by spelling, cannot write. . . . When she was little went to a day school; was taught her prayers, to read, and to sew. Goes to St. Peter's Sunday-school; is taught to read and spell, and the catechism by heart. Has learnt two pages of catechism: "Jesus Christ is the Virgin Mary." . . . Has been a threader about two years and a half. Comes sometimes at 6, at 8 or 9 A.M. . . . Never stays later than 9½ P.M.; often leaves earlier than 9; has no regular time for meals; gets tired sometimes at night; they are often sleepy at night; often has the head ache; has a good appetite; sometimes sleeps well and sometimes not. Her legs ache, but not often. Her eyes often pain her very much and sometimes run with water. Sometimes she sees "pretty things" when she shuts her eyes at night.

Mothers who worked in the mills were accustomed to leave their infants in charge of old women or very young children, and the administration of opium "pacifiers" was notoriously general. A Manchester druggist, "of acknowledged respectability,"[1] testified that among the poorer classes there was scarcely a family where the practice did not prevail. Doses of "quietness" would be given to the children to prevent their being troublesome. Young children were often drugged three times a day. In his district he sold retail about five gallons a week of "quietness" and one half gallon of Godfrey's Cordial; the former having 100 drops of laudanum to an ounce, the latter being somewhat stronger. Another brand was Dalby's Carminative. All in all he supplied 700 families a week. The Commissioners found one man in Rochdale who was indignant at the assertion that the practice prevailed to "a great extent" in his district: he knew, as a result of his inquiries, that "out of ten families of operatives, *not more than six* are in the habitual use of opiates."

After the first shock to the House, however, the forces of opposition rallied and voted down Ashley's proposal. It is important to notice both the sources and the nature of that opposition. In the House of Lords, Brougham was the bitter opponent of all factory legislation. "The bill is a travesty of personal liberty," he said. "Women and young persons are capable of making their own bargains, without interference by Government. The sponsors of factory legislation are victims of a misguided and perverted humanity." In the Commons, Nassau Senior opposed the bill on the ground that the work of children in the cotton mills was so light that it was perfectly possible, not to say desirable, for them to work long hours. It kept them off the streets. Edward Baines supported this point of view, saying that although the children were confined for long hours and were deprived of fresh air, and although this made them pale and reduced their vigor, "it rarely brings on disease." Roebuck attacked Ashley as a humanity monger. Hume opposed the bill. John Bright was perhaps the bitterest of Ashley's opponents. Like Cobden, he was opposed vociferously and on principle to all government interference. Cobden complained that the leaders among the operatives of the short-time question had opposed the Anti-Corn-Law League in the manufacturing districts. Bright argued (accurately but with small relevance) that the proposed law would regulate only the factories in the cotton industry* and that abuses in other industries were much worse. It was generally known, too, that parents who had been accustomed to sending their children to work at the earliest possible age for however low a wage were expressing great apprehension of any legislative restrictions. As a matter of fact the most difficult part of enforcing any age rule was the willingness of parents to lie about the ages of their children and even to present forged birth certificates.

Lord John Russell and Macaulay supported the amendment, and great public meetings were held at Bradford, Leeds, and Manchester. But the Government motion to insert "twelve hours" in the bill was rejected in committee, and immediately afterwards the proposal to insert "ten hours" was also rejected. Only when the Ministry reintroduced its bill and threatened to resign if it were not passed did the House come to heel.

It is often forgotten that all the fanaticism in the forties was not displayed by the Chartists, the Irish Repealers, or those who were working for factory reform. The Anti-Corn-Law people were just as virulent as

---

* One is inclined to forget the very limited nature of the proposed reform which resulted in so much acrimony. Whenever the "factory system" is mentioned in contemporary speeches or writing, it meant only the spinning and weaving of cotton. Less than a third of those employed in the textile industries were in cotton manufactories; and the bill ignored the scores of kinds of other manufactories and trades. (See *Companion to the British Almanac*, 1845, p. 88.)

any of the others and just as suspicious of rival schemes to save the country. On the other hand, it has been too generally assumed, both then and more recently, that all opponents of Corn-Law Repeal spent their time lamenting the condition of children in the mines and factories, while its advocates ignored Lancaster to weep with the farm laborers in Dorsetshire and Buckinghamshire. The danger of such oversimplification is illustrated in the scrambling of parties and causes during this vote on the 1844 Ten Hours' proposal. Conservatives, Liberals, and Radicals were inextricably mixed up. As the *Leeds Times* put it: "Lord John Russell and Mr. O'Connell vote with Busfield Ferrand, for Hume and John Bright, with Sir James Graham! The Leaguers support the Tory Ministry and a twelve hours' term of labour, the 'Complete Suffragists' supported Lord Ashley and the ten hours' clause."[2] Party alignments were cut across; Disraeli voted with Ashley, Peel against him. Sixty-one Tories and seventy-eight Whigs and Radicals in British seats voted for Ashley's amendment. In Yorkshire the Tories appeared as upholders of factory reform, but in Lancashire the Members of Parliament who furthered the cause of reform were either Whigs or Radicals.[3]

Greville in his *Memoirs* summarizes the confusion: "I never remember so much excitement as has been caused by Ashley's Ten Hours Bill, nor a more curious political state of things, such intermingling of parties, such a confusion of opposition . . . so much zeal, asperity, and animosity, so many reproaches hurled backwards and forwards. . . . Some voted, not knowing how they ought to vote, and, following those they are accustomed to follow, many who voted against the Government afterwards said they believed they were wrong. Melbourne is all against Ashley; all the political economists, of course. . . . Then Graham gave the greatest offence by taking up a word of the 'Examiner's' last Sunday, and calling it a *Jack Cade legislation*, thus stirring them to fury, and they flew at him like tigers. Ashley made a speech as violent and factious as any of O'Connell's. . . . Ashley will be able to do nothing, but he will go on agitating session after session." In Greville's opinion "a philanthropic agitator is more dangerous than a repealer, either of the Union or the Corn Laws. We are just now overrun with philanthropists, and God knows where it will stop, or whither it will lead us."[4] Against this may be placed Spencer Walpole's observation that it took twenty-five years of legislation to restrict a child of nine to a sixty-nine-hour week, and that only in cotton mills!*

---

* *History of England*, Vol. III, p. 203. Early in 1845 Ashley succeeded in extending the provisions of the 1844 bill to regulate labor in calico printworks and in bleaching grounds.

Closely allied to the conditions of labor in the factories were the living conditions of the operatives in the mushrooming industrial towns, and in London as well. Here again the record is a dismal one, embracing in its bitterness and cruelty no small portion of England's total population. The fetish of private philanthropy on the one hand and a pious encouragement on the other meant to stimulate the poor into a kind of desperate providence and self-help still lingered on, long after the more perceptive leaders saw the potentially lethal nature of the Frankenstein monster which the new machines had created. Legislative control of slum housing and sanitation was delayed year after year, but meanwhile committees and commissions kept piling up the evidence which would one day overwhelm a startled and dilatory Parliament.

What were the conditions in the towns and cities?* It would be well to begin with Manchester, which Friedrich Engels—now living there —called "the classic type of a modern manufacturing town." Lancashire itself contained three fifths of the establishments in England devoted to the spinning and weaving of cotton; there were more than 100 factories in the town of Manchester alone. Manchester was the center of a network of suburbs scarcely distinguishable from the borough proper— Salford, across the river, Pendleton, Upper and Lower Broughton, Cheetham Hill, etc., all of which taken together formed a population of more than 400,000. This ganglion in turn was the center of a still larger accretion of industrial towns, most of them only a short distance away by rail—one-time villages which had boomed into sizable communities: Bolton, Preston, and Chorley, which together had a population (as of 1841) of 114,000, with more than 100 factories; Stalybridge, Ashton, Dunkinfield, and Hyde (total, 80,000); Stockport (50,000). A circle drawn around Manchester, at the distance of an hour's ride, embraced a larger population than a similar circle drawn around London.[5] These purely industrial towns were uniformly and grimly smoke-black-

---

* The following symposium of horrors emerged from the investigations made during the early part of the decade under the direction of such officials as James Kay (later Kay-Shuttleworth), Neil Arnold, Southwood Smith, and above all Edwin Chadwick, secretary to the Poor Law Commission. They were embodied in a series of Parliamentary Papers: *Report on the Sanitary State of the Labouring Classes, as affected chiefly by the situation and construction of their dwellings, in and about the Metropolis. Extracted from the 4th and 5th annual reports of the Poor Law Commissioners,* 1839; *Report . . . from the Poor Law Commissioners on an Inquiry into the Sanitary Condition of the Labouring Population of Great Britain,* 1842; *Report on the Result of a Special Inquiry into the Practice of Interment in Towns,* 1843; *First Report of the Commissioners for Inquiry into the State of Large Towns and Populous Districts,* 1844; *Second Report of the Commissioners,* etc., 1845.

ened, inhabited only by workingmen and petty tradesmen, and were a composite of factories, a few shop-lined streets, and rows of lanes, courts, and alleys. Central Manchester was as much commercial as industrial, composed of offices and warehouses. The factories lined the rivers and canals that cut through the city, and within the shadows of these mills the houses of the operatives stretched like a band around the city. Beyond this circumference of blighted dwellings were the homes of the "masters," the middle-class cotton lords. In and out of this complex went a stream of transients, increasing each year as the railways groped farther into the hinterland. In the early forties it was estimated that the floating population amounted to 100,000 annually.

The factory operatives huddled in a dense mass of houses intersected by narrow lanes from which, in turn, sprang a maze of close courts. Of 647 streets, 248 were unpaved, and 352 contained stagnant pools, heaps of refuse, ordure, etc. The infrequency of scavenging and the neglected state of the courts and alleys gave rise to the practice of using open cesspools and dunghills as places of deposit for all the houses in a given court. There was scarcely a court without a large open cesspool, into which all night soil, ashes, etc., were thrown—a condition which was not confined, incidentally, to the dwellings inhabited by the working classes. Almost no houses, except a few belonging to the wealthy classes, had water closets. In "Little Ireland"* the number of privies averaged two to 250 people. In one part of Manchester the needs of some 7,000 inhabitants were supplied by only thirty-three "necessaries"; in Ashton there was a locality which had only two privies for fifty families. Inhabitants of cellars carried out the filth to the nearest channel, while in many cases the doorways, passages, and pavements were defiled. Some 18,000 people lived in cellars. "I have known," said one investigator, "instances where the wall of a dwelling house has been constantly wet with foetid fluid which has filtered through from a midden, and poisoned the air with its intolerable stench; and the family was never free from sickness." And in the township of Manchester alone there were seventy-seven slaughterhouses—all without regulations. In Bolton there were several courts in which the middens attached to the slaughterhouses were filled with the offal of slaughtered animals, and had not been cleaned in two months.

The overcrowding in these hovels can be imagined. There were 1,500 Manchester cellars where three persons, 738 where four, and 281 where five slept in one bed. Not infrequently as many as nine or ten

---

* Nearly 50,000 Irish were coming every year to England.

people would live in three small rooms. Every twenty-first child was illegitimate.

This was Manchester, a city without a single public park until 1845. Liverpool was worse. There some 40,000 people lived in cellars, and 60,000 in close courts. Out of a population of 223,054 in the 1841 census, 160,000 belonged to the working classes. "I do not know of a single court in Liverpool," wrote W. H. Duncan, M.D., "which communicates with the street or sewer by a covered drain. The fluid contents [of the cesspools] frequently find their way through the mouldering walls. . . . In some instances it even oozes through into the neighboring cellars, filling them with pestilential vapors, and rendering it necessary to dig to receive it. . . . One of these wells, four feet deep, filled with this stinking fluid, was found in one cellar under the bed where the family slept." Houses were built back to back, each having a yard about eighteen feet wide. There were no privies. A "necessary," a sort of tub, had to be emptied every morning. There was no access to the back yards except through the houses; all the dirt and filth which accumulated in the yard had to be carried through the houses. The water supply was miserable. Water was turned on at a low pressure three times a week for one to two and a half hours, and the price to a laboring man was unreasonably high; many of the poorer classes had to buy it from carts at three gallons for a penny.

In Birmingham 2,030 courts contained 12,225 houses—all built back to back. The number of houses in each court varied from four to twenty, and each court had a washhouse, an ashpit, and a single privy at the end. Leeds had one cul-de-sac of thirty-four houses, housing 340 persons. There were three streets in Leeds with a population of 400 to 500 where there was not a usable privy for the whole number. The ordinary size of a sleeping chamber was about five yards square, and it would often be occupied by a man, his wife, and five children. The greatest number of persons living in one house in Leeds was to be found in the lodging-houses for itinerant laborers, where, in some instances, there were as many as five to a bed, with three beds not at all uncommon in one sleeping room. In Bristol 2,800 families were visited, of whom 46 per cent occupied but one room each. In the Old Town in Edinburgh there were neither sewers nor drains, nor even privies belonging to the houses. In consequence all the refuse, garbage, and excrement of at least 50,000 persons were thrown into the gutter every night. Water could be had only from public pumps. Glasgow was no better. Seventy-eight per cent of the population lived in parts of the city as filthy in their squalor as the Wynds of Edinburgh.

Not much wonder the death rate in these towns was high. The average annual mortality for all of Britain was twenty-two per thousand. In Glasgow the death rate was thirty-two per thousand, in Manchester thirty-five, and in Liverpool thirty-five. A newborn child of the working classes had just about one chance in two of reaching the age of five; a child of the higher classes, four chances in five. The average age of death in London was twenty-seven years (with the working classes, twenty-two); in Leeds, twenty-one, in Manchester, eighteen.

London, as might have been expected, was perceptibly better than the new manufacturing towns. Yet it, too, had wide areas of incredible degradation. Some of them lay east of the Tower—Limehouse, Spital-fields, Whitechapel, and Bethnal Green—but others were in the heart of the City, behind the Palace of Westminster, in the fashionable parish of St. George's Hanover Square, and between High Holborn and Oxford Street. This last district of St. Giles (south of Bloomsbury and only a minute's walk from the Strand) incorporated the notorious Seven Dials, where James Catnach had his press—a region of old-clothes shops and secondhand shoeshops. Knight called the inhabitants of this area troglodytes, dwellers in caves, an intermediate species between man and rabbit. The squalor of the Rookery here was notorious—"one dense mass of houses, through which narrow tortuous lanes curve and wind, from which again diverge close courts innumerable. Rooms crowded to suffocation. Stagnant gutters in the middle of the lanes, accumulated piles of garbage and filth choking up the dark passages which open like ratholes upon the highway. . . . Groups of women, with dirty rags hung round them, cower round the doors—the old with wrinkled parchment skin, the young with flushed swollen faces and heavy eyes. The men lounge listlessly about. Shops are almost unknown. Along Broad St., St. Giles, are some provision shops, and opposite the church a gin-shop. . . . They stupefy themselves with gin."[6]

Joseph Toynbee, surgeon, testified before the State of Towns Commission that in the parish of St. George's Hanover Square there were 1,465 families of the laboring classes. Of these, 929 families had only one room for the whole family, and 623 had only one bed for each family. In one family the father, mother, a grown-up son (consumptive), a daughter (scrofulous), and a child slept in one bed. Dr. Smith told of a place called Punderson's Gardens—a long, narrow street in the center of which was an open gutter in which filth of every kind was allowed to accumulate and putrefy. The privies were close upon the footpath of the street; the street was wholly without drainage of any kind. There were nine miles of open sewers in the Tower Hamlets section of London.

Figure 51. A gin palace

In Bethnal Green fifty-seven houses held 580 persons, in some cases as many as thirty persons in a four-room house. Thirty thousand people lived in an area half a mile square. In Shoreditch slops were thrown into the streets because there were no drains to carry them off. In Southwark privies emptied into open sewers. In the neighborhood of Field Lane (described in *Oliver Twist*) some persons had not even cesspools or privies; excrement was thrown into a little back yard, where it was allowed to accumulate for months together. The rate of deaths in the City of London and East London was twenty-seven per thousand; in Whitechapel, thirty per thousand.

Thus also the Saffron Hill district, south of Clerkenwell, in the borough of Finsbury—proverbially the dirtiest in London; the rookeries that abutted on Gray's Inn Road; Ratcliff Highway with its drunken sailors; the night houses of Haymarket and Piccadilly.

The *Times* could exclaim "that within the precincts of wealth, gaiety, and fashion, nigh the regal grandeur of St. James, close on the palatial splendours of Bayswater, on the confines of the old and new aristocratic quarters . . . that there want, and famine, and disease, and vice should

Figure 52. The slums of Smithfield
Victoria and Albert Museum. Crown Copyrig

stalk in all their kindred horrors, consuming body by body, soul by soul! It is indeed a monstrous state of things. . . . God knows, there is much room for action nowadays." Yet whole areas of London were but dimly aware that this sort of thing existed, literally in their own back yards— just as many a Manchester businessman traveled daily from his comfortable home in the suburbs to his office in the city completely unconscious of the depravity and suffering which surrounded him. But as Carlyle pointed out, the disease which came from fetid lanes and cellars was no respecter of persons; the Irish widow in Edinburgh proved her sisterhood with those who refused to help her by infecting seventeen of them with typhus.

And indeed in the more respectable quarters of London worthy citizens had to learn to endure strange and noxious odors. Even where there were sewers, traps did not always work. In the most aristocratic parts of Westminster and in the fashionable squares to the north of Oxford Street, in the Belgrave and Eaton Square districts there were faulty places in the sewers, frequently stopping up the house drains. In and about Cavendish, Bryanstone, Manchester, and Portman Squares "there is so much rottenness and decay that there is no security for the sewers standing from day to day, and to flush them for the removal of their most loathesome deposit might be to bring some of them down altogether." In the hot summer months the Houses of Parliament had to close their windows against the stench which arose from the filthy Thames.

Even royalty moved in an odor of more than sanctity. In 1844 fifty-three overflowing cess pits were discovered under Windsor Castle. And as late as 1848 the drainage of Buckingham Palace was so defective that its precincts "reeked with filth and pestilential odours from the absence of proper sewage." One of the workmen testified: "I was hardly ever in such a set of stinks as I've been in the sewers and underground parts of the Palace."[7]

This cloacal exploration of the forties must continue into one more sordid aspect of a troubled decade. Many people found it difficult to live comfortably; it was difficult for others to die, and get themselves buried, conveniently. London graveyards particularly were more than a metaphorical stench in the nostrils of the body politic.

As early as 1839 one G. A. Walker, a surgeon, had disturbed the placidity of Londoners with his *Gatherings from Graveyards*, in which he described the state of forty-three metropolitan burying places, mincing no words. In 1843 Edwin Chadwick headed a special inquiry of the Commons into the *Practice of Interment in Towns*. And in 1846, little having been accomplished in the meantime, Walker continued the attack in *Burial Ground Incendiarism, or the minute anatomy of grave-digging in London.*

The inherited custom of burying in and around churches had become completely untenable for a large metropolitan center; the saturation point had long since been reached. By 1814 the grounds of St. Margaret's, Westminster, had been declared unfit for use, but they were still used. St. Martin's, with a space 295 feet by 379, had received within ten years 14,000 bodies. In a vault below a Methodist chapel in the New Kent Road from 1,600 to 2,000 bodies were found, not buried, but heaped up in wooden coffins in a space 40 yards long, 25 wide, and 20 high. In the center of a dense population, interments in the two acres belonging to the church of St. George, Hanover Square, had been at the rate of 1,000 corpses a year. Within a distance of 200 yards there were four burying grounds in Clement's Lane in the Strand, where, as Walker reported, "the living breathe on all sides an atmosphere impregnated with the odour of the dead.... The soil of this ground is saturated, absolutely saturated, with human putrescence.... Several bones were lying on the surface of the grave nearest to us ... with long pieces of wood ... nearly as fresh as when interred." Many wagonloads of bones were removed to a receptacle in the northeast corner of the yard. One of the worst places was Enon Chapel in Clement's Lane, built by a Dissenter as a speculation. The upper part of the building, used for public worship, was separated from the lower part by a boarded floor only. This lower part was used as a burying place, and was crowded at one end, even to the top of the ceiling, with dead. Some 12,000 bodies had been buried there in pits, the uppermost of which were covered by only a few inches of earth. A sewer ran angularly across this "burying place." In Buckingham Chapel, Palace Street, about a three minutes' walk from the Palace, one of the burial vaults was underneath a large schoolroom for boys and girls. There were apertures in the boards which admitted light from above. The upper part of the piles of bodies reached within a few inches of the wooden floor.

The removal of decayed bodies, and particularly the burning of coffins, was a generally recognized mode of making room. The scenes of ruthless exhumation with their accompanying indifference not only to public health but to public decency—the shallowness of the graves—the exhalations—the disposal of the bodies—the miasma of putridity which penetrated the surrounding streets—all these are told in a detail which was evidently not too strong for the Victorian stomach, but which, in our more squeamish days, must remain undescribed.* Ultimately, as we shall see, the disclosures led to legislation, and even by 1844 new burial grounds were reaching into what were then the suburbs. Kensal Green Cemetery, a pleasant shady spot of forty-six acres, had been established in 1832. Others followed at Brompton, Highgate, Mile End, Stoke Newington, etc., all the results of private enterprise.

Chadwick's report also furnishes gloomy evidence on the expense and pagan ostentation of contemporary funeral customs. We may pass over the section on "Injuries to the Health of Survivors occasioned by the delay of Interments" to discover that the average price of funerals among the laboring classes was £4. This provided a good elm coffin, bearers to carry it to the grave, and palls and fittings for the mourners. A good "respectable" funeral, however, ran from £60 to £100 and required about twenty men, eight to carry a leaden coffin. Others were "mutes" to carry staves covered with black. There were charges for the velvets attached to the hearse, including feathers, with feathers also for the horses, and charges for the clergyman, the clerk, and the sexton. This kind of funeral was for the tradesmen class and above. When the gentry died, the display was correspondingly more impressive.†

Across the nation, then, the health of towns and particularly the welfare of the laboring population became progressively a matter of official concern. Thoughtful people were reasonably worried lest the race degenerate physically as well as morally. The reformers turned bravely to the task nearest at hand. Some few had the imagination to see that it was not the machine or industrial progress per se which was throwing the social order into confusion, but rather the inability of a nation

---

* He who would read further will find convenient excerpts in Charles Knight's *London*, Vol. IV, pp. 161–76.

† An itemized expense list for the funeral of a person of the middle classes (one Mary Maria ———) is both curious and illuminating. Omitting the cost of each item, the requirements were as follows: elm inner coffin, lined with ruffed super linen; tufted mattress; No. 10 shroud, sheet, cap, and pillow; stout lead coffin, soldering up; lead plate, ditto; six men with lead coffin; two men attending on the surgeons; making up-plumbers; for pair cherubs; ten handles; black screws; brass engraved plate, fine lacquered; six men with case moving down stairs; best pall, lid of feathers; four fine cloaks, nine rich silk bands for gentlemen; nine pairs gentlemen's best kid gloves; two porters and furniture; feathermen, two pages, and wands; hearse and four horses; feathers and velvets for ditto; six hearse pages and truncheons; mourning coach and four horses; feathers and velvets for ditto; two coach pages and wands; two coachmen's cloaks; two velvet hammercloths; fifteen silk bands for two porters, eight pages, three feathermen, and two coachmen; fifteen pairs gloves for ditto; paid dues at St. Margaret's; lead fees ditto; bell and searchers; bearers; sexton; extra digging; grave-marker. The total cost was £60, 19s. 1d.

rooted in land and geared to an agricultural economy to cope with the sudden dislocations caused by a rapidly increasing population and by the transition from country to town which the industrialization of Britain involved.

Such a person was Robert Vaughan, who, in his *Age of Great Cities; or Modern Society viewed in its relation to Intelligence, Morals, and Religion* (1843), made the point that an urban civilization is the one best able to develop man's potential human resources. More than that, an age of great cities becomes in turn an age of improved agriculture. "This has resulted in part from wealth, but still more from mechanical or scientific skill. When the landowners regard cities with jealousy, and are employed in defaming them, they become chargeable with the baseness of ingratitude, or the madness of self-destruction. Lands which bring forth an hundred-fold in the place of thirty-fold, they owe to the science of cities."

Another philosopher of the new order was W. Cooke Taylor, author among other things of *Notes of a Tour in the Manufacturing Districts of Lancashire* (1842) and *Factories and the Factory System* (1844). Reasonably and intelligently he saw, in historical perspective, the factory system as the evolution of a new order of society. "The Factory system is a modern creation," he wrote. "History throws no light on its nature. . . . The steam engine had no precedent, the spinning-jenny is without ancestry, the mule and the power-loom entered on no prepared heritage; they sprang into sudden existence . . . passing so rapidly through their stage of infancy that they had taken their position in the world and firmly established themselves before there was time to prepare a place for their reception." He regards the factory system as "a great fact; established it is, and established it will remain." Never can human force be substituted now for steam power. "Those who declare against machinery must . . . name the machinery with which they would dispense." After describing in gruesome detail the housing conditions in Manchester, he says: "No one denies these fearful evils; but, in the name of common sense, what earthly connection have they with the factory system? They are the obvious results of imperfect policy, incomplete municipal regulations, the want of a building act, the high price of building ground, and the legal difficulties which impede the purchase and leasing of land in small quantities in England."[8] He concludes that the factory system offers "the only means by which England can grow in wealth and greatness, for we have no agricultural produce in surplus for exportation." This is the thesis of an intelligent, moderate man of humane leanings (he viewed with equanimity and even approval the

formation of associations and unions among the operatives in factories),
who saw clearly the inevitability of the change which England was
going through. Yet even he was insufficiently aware of the steps which
society would have to take to accommodate itself to the machine, and
he defended such abuses as the employment of young children for long
hours on the strange grounds that the house accommodations of operatives in large towns were necessarily very limited, and that if the children
were excluded from factories and workshops it was not very clear what
would become of them. His logic is a curious combination of long-range
perception and short-range myopia.

Thus these half-men labored; and England, supported by a tremendous
energy, a certain amount of good luck, and a kind of sinewy national
character which was admired even by those outsiders who had little
affection for it, muddled through into a new world, retaining her self-
respect and gaining the world market simultaneously.

Lest it seem that all England was papered with Parliamentary Blue
Books, it might be well to record briefly the visit of young David Masson
to London in 1844, and something of what he saw there.[9]

He saw Apsley House, and the great carriage drive between Apsley
House and the bridge over the Serpentine at the entry to Kensington
Gardens. He saw the old Duke of Wellington riding along Parliament
Street to the House of Lords, with a groom behind him at a little distance. "He was dressed to the extreme of neatness, in a blue frock-coat
and white trousers, with a hat of peculiarly narrow rim, to which every
now and then he raised his right forefinger in a mechanical way in
acknowledgement of the salutations of reverence. . . . The intense whiteness, the absolute bloodlessness, of his face. It was all bone, marble-
white bone, [with] aquiline nose and strong jaw . . ."

He saw Sir Robert Peel, "a portly, fair-haired gentleman, with a
smiling and somewhat cat-like expression." He toured Cheyne Walk:
"a quaint riverside street of shops and antique houses, looking down
upon the unembanked shore—pleasant enough . . . when the stream was
full, but not so pleasant when the low tide left its margin of mud and
ooze." One could travel from the Strand to Cheyne Row by one of
the river steamboats or by a Chelsea omnibus from the City. Carlyle's
home, he noted, was a neat, oldish house of red brick.

He saw Samuel Rogers, the banker-poet, walking in Hyde Park—"a
slight, aged figure, with a peculiarly wrinkled and rather cankered-

looking visage." (Rogers was then eighty-one, and lived twelve years longer.) He attended an Anti-Corn-Law League meeting at Drury Lane and heard the well-known Unitarian minister and orator W. J. Fox speak. "He played on his voice as if it had been a piano." He saw Daniel O'Connell shortly after he had been liberated by the House of Lords.

At the British Museum he noted the promiscuous assemblage of readers. John Forster was there often enough, and Carlyle more rarely, "when the necessity of consulting some book not to be had elsewhere overcame his nervous sensitiveness to the disturbing sights and sounds of the place." Carlyle's chief horror was "the man with the bassoon nose—who used his handkerchief regardless of all about him." In those days Sir Henry Ellis was the principal librarian, or head of the Museum —a polite little gentleman of the old school. But the gigantic and despotic Italian, Panizzi, was chief of the Department of Printed Books.

Among other spots of interest, Masson visited the celebrated supper halls which were at the same time singing halls—Evans's, and the Cider Cellar in Maiden Lane. He met Douglas Jerrold in 1844: "a little man with a stoop, an eager aquiline look; fair hair." Jerrold, the writer for magazines and one of the chiefs of the *Punch* staff, author of various plays and novels, was at the height of his fame. "Some people," said Masson, "thought of him only as a little, waspish, ill-tempered man, but that is not a fair picture. He was a wit above all others, had a large and generous nature, and could not brook anything petty or mean. A fiery, big-hearted, energetic, generous soul."

No, not all London was occupied with sewers and graveyards. The life of the spirit, as well as the polite life, the fashionable life, and the life of those herded into the courts and alleys, still went on. Mental as well as social anachronisms endured, strange incongruities lived side by side on the streets and in the homes, but who would say that England, or the nineteenth century, was unique in those respects?

The 1840's heard more about the abuses of the factory system than they did about the condition of the agricultural worker. The evils of the big towns were sufficiently delineated; what of the farms and villages? In his Lancashire visits during the depressed days of 1842, W. Cooke Taylor observed that the operative strongly preferred life in the manufacturing centers to that in the countryside from which he came. "He faces starvation rather than return to the farm." Taylor's investigations led him to the conclusion that the state of the agricultural laborer was worse than that of the operative. "There is the same amount of destitution, but not the same amount of respectability." Just what were the conditions in the country districts in 1844?

The third edition of William Howitt's *Rural Life of England* appeared in this year, and it is revealing to follow the progress of his description of "this happy and beautiful island."

He begins with the life of the aristocracy and proceeds through "the pre-eminence of England as a place of country residence"—the delightfulness of the country estates with their parks, lawns, and gardens—the advantages of the climate, "notwithstanding all just cause of complaint." He waxes ecstatic over the enviable position of the English country gentleman, his field pursuits and pleasures: hunting, shooting, coursing. He has much to say about the true wisdom of Izaak Walton, the profound repose of trees, the rich mosaic of fields, the mighty forests, the picturesque halls. This idyllic mood embraces the folkways and amusements of the people: their popular festivals, their social life in the village inn, their wakes and fairs, their sports and pastimes. In Cornwall they still exhibited the old dance of St. George and the Dragon; in Devon they still blessed the orchards on Christmas Eve. Yet many of the simple, hearty old customs were disappearing, and he laments their decay under the conditions of "modern ambition, modern wealth, modern notions of social proprieties, and modern education," which are all "hewing at the root of the poetical and the picturesque."

So far it has been happy going, in Miss Mitford's best manner—an eloquent tribute to the enduring beauties of the English countryside. But soon a different kind of realism begins to break in; Howitt was an accurate as well as a sympathetic observer. The farm laborer, he says, tall, smock-frocked, straw-hatted, ankle-booted, "is as simple, as ignorant, and as laborious a creature as one of the wagon-horses that he drives." He never reads even the weekly papers; he has no books. As likely as not he was unable to read; the Poor Law Commissioners had given a deplorable picture of the educational condition of the agricultural population. In some parts of Essex, Sussex, Kent, Buckinghamshire, Berkshire, etc., schools of any description were unknown. In others not more than one in fifteen of the laborers was able to read. Howitt explains this on the basis of the absence of the gradations in rank and property which existed in the trading and manufacturing districts. "The aristocracy shut themselves up in their houses and parks, and are rarely seen beyond them except in their carriages, driving rapidly to town, or to each other's isolated abodes. . . . The working classes grow up with the sense that they are regarded as necessary implements of agriculture by the aris-

Figure 53. Chatsworth, Derbyshire

tocracy—and they are churlish and uncouth." Most farmers feared the
"over-education of labor," lest the workers should get ideas beyond their
station, and become difficult to manage.

His description of the delights of the hall and the plainness of the
cottage is worth quoting at some length.

> What a mighty space lies between the palace and the cottage in this
> country! ay, what a mighty space between the mansion of the private
> gentleman and the hut of the labourer on his estate! To enter the one:
> to see its stateliness and extent; all its offices, out-buildings, gardens,
> greenhouses, hothouses; its extensive fruit-walls, and the people labour-
> ing to furnish the table simply with fruit, vegetables, and flowers; its
> coach-houses, harness-houses, stables, and all the steeds, draught-
> horses, and saddle-horses, hunters, and ladies' pads, ponies for ladies'
> airing-carriages, and ponies for children; and all the grooms and at-
> tendants thereon; to see the waters for fish, the woods for game, the
> elegant dairy for the supply of milk and cream, curds and butter, and
> the dairy-maids and managers belonging to them;—and then, to enter
> the house itself, and see all its different suites of apartments, drawing-
> rooms, boudoirs, sleeping-rooms, dining and breakfast rooms; its stew-
> ard's, housekeeper's and butler's rooms; its ample kitchens and larders,
> with their stores of provisions, fresh and dried; its stores of costly plate,
> porcelain and crockery apparatus of a hundred kinds; its cellars of wine
> and strong beer; its stores of linen; its library of books, its collections
> of paintings, engravings, and statuary; the jewels, musical instruments,
> and expensive and interminable nick-knackery of the ladies; the guns
> and dogs; and cross-bows, long-bows, nets, and other implements of
> amusement of the gentlemen; all the rich carpeting and fittings-up of
> day-rooms and night-rooms, with every contrivance and luxury which
> a most ingenious and luxurious age can furnish; and all the troops of
> servants, male and female, having their own exclusive offices, to wait
> upon the person of lady or gentleman, upon table, or carriage, or upon

some one ministration of pleasure or necessity: I say, to see all this. and then to enter the cottage of a labourer, we must certainly think that one has too much for the insurance of comfort, or the other must have extremely too little. . . .

When we go into the cottage of the working man, how forcibly are we struck with the difference between his mode of life and our own. There is his tenement of, at most, one or two rooms. His naked walls; bare brick, stone, or mud floor, as it may be; a few wooden, or rush-bottomed chairs; a deal or old oak table; a simple fireplace, with its oven beside it, or, in many parts of the kingdom, no other fireplace than the hearth; a few pots and pans—and you have his whole abode, goods and chattels. He comes home weary from his out-door work, having eaten his dinner under hedge or tree, and seats himself for a few hours with his wife and children, then turns into a rude bed, standing perhaps on the farther side of his only room, and out again before daylight, if it be winter. . . .

Such is the routine of his life, from week to week, and year to year; Sundays, and a few holidays, are white days in his calendar. On them he shaves, and puts on a clean shirt and better coat, drawn from that old chest which contains the whole wardrobe of himself and children; his wife has generally some separate drawer or bandbox, in which to stow her lighter and more fragile gear. Then he walks around his little garden, if he have it; goes with his wife and children to church or meeting; to sit with a neighbour, or have a neighbour look in upon him.

This last, says Howitt, "is cottage life in its best estate; in its unsophisticated and unpauperised condition . . . but how far short of this condition is that of millions in this empire!"

In 1844 the condition of the agricultural laborer was the only exception to the prosperity which had been creeping back to England for the past year; the pressure of insecurity was removed last from the agricultural districts. The large influx of foreign grain in 1842 had depressed the value of the home supply, and the abundant harvest of 1844 again induced a strong and general feeling of depression. Wages were still further reduced; open expressions of discontent appeared among the laborers, and during the summer and autumn the firing of stacks and even barns in the southern counties began again.

Conditions varied somewhat from county to county. In Wiltshire the wages of the agricultural laborer went as low as 8s. a week; in other counties they varied from 7s. to 11s.[10] In Dorsetshire the laborer could get fuel at a reduced price and had his cottage with garden at a low rent; in Somerset his only perquisite was three pints of cider daily. Most laborers succeeded in keeping a pig.

There were few families where the wife and one child or more were not employed in farm labor. Women's wages were about 9d. a day;

girls', 4d. to 6d.; boys', who went to work earlier than girls (as early as the age of seven in some instances), 2d. to 8d. The exploitation of women and children which had stirred up a Parliamentary investigation was at its worst in the "Gang System" or "Castleacre Gangs," under which a general overseer would contract with a farmer to supply a certain number of workers for a stated period. The gangs were composed chiefly of women and children, sleeping where they could and feeding as best they could.* Almost as bad was the "bondage system" of the north of England, on all the large estates in Durham and Northumberland, and in the south of Scotland. Under this rural serfdom no married laborer was permitted to dwell on the estate unless he entered into bond to comply with the system. The miserable hovels of these people were less carefully constructed than the stables of the horses—formed as they usually were of one apartment, open to the roof, with earthen floor, a part of which was occupied by the cow.

The Commissioners found that the lack of sufficient accommodation was universal. Cottages in general had only two bedrooms, and many had only one. Three or four persons not infrequently slept on the same bed. At a village near Blandford there was a cottage of two rooms inhabited by a family of eleven, whose aggregate earnings were 16s. 6d. weekly. They slept in three beds in a bedroom ten feet square. Everywhere the cottages were old, frequently in a state of decay. The floor was always of stone in the southern counties, wet and damp during the winter months. No attention was paid, in the building of cottages, to drainage. And Godfrey's Cordial was used to keep the small children pacified while the mother picked stone or weeded beans in the field. Except for the aristocracy of labor which took care of the horses and was hired on a yearly basis, all other labor was by the day and subject to dismissal at will in slack times of the year.

There were, to be sure, a few "model cottages," to which a good deal of attention was drawn, and some of the great landowners made an honest effort to enable their laborers to live above a mere animal level. Thus the Duke of Bedford on his Bedfordshire estates built fifty-two cottages in 1846–48, and fifty-three more in 1849. He planned a systematic rebuilding until 300 more were erected. Each was built of brick with window lights of cast iron "painted to imitate lead lights," with concrete foundations, iron spouting, and iron conducting pipes which were connected to underground drains made tight with cement. Drains from the sinks conveyed all refuse to a manure tank in a contiguous

---

* In 1867 a Gangs Act prohibited the labor of children under eight!

garden.[11] The rents paid by the tenants were assessed at a rate of 3 per cent return on the outlay, and varied from 1s. to 16d. per week.

Chiefly, however, farm labor eked out a marginal existence on the edge of pauperization, into which it was often thrown when the price of grain fell and the tenant farmers, always complaining of high rents anyway, discharged workmen. Some of the worst conditions, ironically enough, were on the estates of the Earl of Shaftesbury, Ashley's father. This fact was used against Ashley in the Commons, to his great distress; but he was unable to reply, for there was no communication between him and his father, who was contemptuous of his son's piety and humanitarianism.

During all this time the country gentry and aristocracy, on the other side of the gulf fixed between them and their "hinds," lived more than comfortably in a feudal expansiveness which no one of them, however much he might grumble about what seemed to him a growing discrimination against the agricultural interests, ever thought would really disappear. A freshly appreciative and not too naïve account of the folkways of the county families is given in a series of letters[12] written by a young American woman visiting England for the first time in company with her uncle and aunt, who had taken for the year an estate known as Moor Park, in Shropshire, not far from Ludlow Castle. The American visitors were warmly welcomed by the English gentry, and a great deal of the color of the period gets into these letters.

As might have been expected, the visitor was impressed by the quiet charm of the countryside through which she passed on the way to Shrewsbury: "the wonderful solidity of the railways, the absence of dust, the elegance of the large depots and the prettiness of the small ones, the beauty of the country, the lovely hedges, the picturesque [at a distance] cottages scattered on every side, the air of culture, of content, of prosperity . . . the cultivated hills, the beautiful bridges that span the charming little streams, and the odd English and Welsh names that the men call out at every station."

The inn at Shrewsbury, with its sea-coal fire, its little mantelpiece adorned with little old-fashioned jars; the bay window with its white linen shades, the little old-fashioned sideboard with its stuffed owl under a glass case. The oil landscapes under the low ceiling, and an engraving of Leonardo da Vinci with Francis the First.

The household at Moor Park, with its butler, maids, coachman in green coat with gilt buttons; gardener, keeper, porter, cook, scullion. Its daily routine: shooting in the morning for the gentlemen, writing or sewing for the ladies; driving in the afternoon; dinner at six. In the evening a cheerful family party by the drawing-room fire, reading or sewing or playing games with the children. Conversation at a dinner party: "On my right I had Mr. Landon, who is deaf in his left ear; and on my left, Mr. Charleton, who informed me that he was deaf in his right ear." Nevertheless, she had a very pleasant time. "Conundrums were introduced accidentally, and Sir Charles proved himself quite a proficient. Then that never-ending theme of poachers came up. I cannot imagine what English country gentlemen would do were there no poachers. Mention the word, and you set Mr. Betton right off. He fights all his battles o'er again. He enlarges upon the villainy of poachers, upon the ingratitude of poachers, tells anecdotes about poachers, until you grow so nervous that you expect to see a poacher start up and seize the bird upon your plate.

"Naturally the conversation turns upon the day's sport, and you hear how that bird was winged; how another was tailered; how many cock pheasants were shot; how many hen pheasants were deprived of life; how many woodcock were put up; how many partridges flew out of one cover; how many rabbits were killed; who shot well; who shot badly; who missed fire; whose cock pheasant fell with his tail up; whose hen pheasant with her tail down; who shot on this side of the dingle, who on the other, and so forth, and so forth, and so forth, and so on. Then the meet of the previous day takes its turn—who fell in leaping over this hurdle, who in taking that hedge, who fell on his feet, who on his head, where the fox was found, and where killed, and how the sport was spoiled on account of the frost, and how cold it was, and how cold it is, and how cold it is going to be, and how unusual it is, such weather unheard of at this season, and how fine the autumn has been—and then you rise from the table and leave the gentlemen to discuss, more at large, poaching, shooting, hunting, and the cold, unrestrained by female society. After a while they come into the drawing-room and the card-table is taken out, the gentlemen cut to play and the rest look on. They are not a very intellectual set, these country gentlemen, but they are very sociable and pleasant. . . ."

She writes about their neighbors the Landons: "They care only for the narrow sphere in which they live and are utterly without aspirations, provided the hounds meet on the appointed day and Henry's pony is in good order, and Ned gets a mount, Mr. Landon an occasional shooting and his dinner, and Mrs. Landon and Janet their walk after lunch. Europe might be convulsed with revolutions, Asia and Africa submerged, and the Western continent burnt up, for all they would care. . . . George, the eldest son, is expected on Monday from Oxford, where he is studying for a living—for theological students in England have only that in view. He is devoted to cricket and boating, so there will be some new themes for conversation. Never again shall I complain of the want of gallantry of Americans, for you would be shocked to hear these young men talk of young ladies. . . ."

The family arrives home at half-past four in the morning after a dinner and dance at Henley Hall, Sir Charles Cuyler's. "At seven o'clock last evening we were put down before the door of this fine old place. It is by no means kept in the style of Oakley Park or Downton Hall, for Sir Charles had a moderate fortune and an immense family. Still, we were received in the hall by liveried footmen. . . . The butler led us through a long, narrow passageway and throwing open the door announced us. . . .

"A rich white soup first came on; then cod's head and shoulders; after-wards boiled turkey and venison for the large dishes, preceded, however, by various entrées and accompanied by vegetables. Here the dessert is placed on the table with the game, and if you do not take game, creams, jellies, etc., are handed to you immediately and in succession. Before the first cloth is removed, grated cheese and cheese cut into pieces, bis-cuits and bread, and little pats of butter are served. After this come the fruits, fresh and dried, and nuts, etc., more properly, I suppose, called the dessert. It is customary, when you go to dine, to take your own butler or footman, and he offers his services to wait."

She admires the women she meets: "I confess that they have not the beauty of Americans nor the natural grace of French women, nor the taste in dress of both, but the high-born English woman is something quite perfect—elegant, high-bred, affable, warm-hearted, simple, unaf-fected, and accomplished and cultivated to a degree we rarely see." But Miss Myrick "asked me if I could speak Indian."

They go to Ludlow on Fair Day. "You cannot imagine anything so funny. Crowds of quaint-looking people were collected around the market-house to witness the dancing of some young street dancers—two young girls dressed in short dresses and red bodices and two little boys in fantastic costumes. They danced for the amusement of the crowd in the muddy streets, and when they got through went round for ha'pen-nies. To this succeeded ballad-singing on the part of a man and a woman. . . . They sang quaint old ballads, such as you would find in Percy's 'Reliques.' . . ."

Mr. Landon, the parish rector, was not popular. "He gives himself up to hunting, shooting, and fishing, and his kitchen, and it is almost impossible to get him to visit a parishioner even *in extremis*. Though his income is eleven hundred pounds a year, at least, he is very much in debt. At Silvington, another parish in the neighborhood, the rector not only drinks to excess, but is otherwise of the most dissolute habits. The bishop can suspend him, but then the application is attended with great expense and trouble. The parish schools are everywhere neglected—no wonder, then, that the rich go to Rome and the poor to Dissent. . . ." She attends church, where "immediately under the pulpit are four pews lined with red, in which sits the Mayor and Corporation in blue silk gowns trimmed with fur, to which the former adds a red collar. They read the service out of great red books about eighteen inches long, and as they marched out of the church in procession two officials preceded them carrying silver maces. . . . The old clerk keeps a quid of tobacco in his mouth, and after a very long A—men, he spits over toward the Bridges pew. . . ."

Two other foreigners were writing about England in the forties in books published in 1845. Both were dealing with the seamier sides of English life; neither made any impact on the public mind, for Léon Faucher's frank but judicious *Études sur L'Angleterre*[13] was written in French, and Friedrich Engels's *The Condition of the Working-Class in England in 1844* was published in Germany.*

Faucher, who had been for years the leading editor of *Le Courrier Français* in Paris, was recognized as an authority on social economy, finance, and commercial legislation. In the two volumes of his book on England, as one English reviewer pointed out, he did for whole classes what Dickens did for individuals: he depicted the horrors of contrast between the rich and poor on a large scale. His sympathetic English friends were unable to accept his solution of the problem, which lay in a revision of land tenure according to the French pattern, but with his diagnosis they could only agree. The *Spectator* comments in this connection on "the sort of religious colouring which pervades the English mind in regard to the obligation they owe superior position. The traces of our ancient forms and sentiments reveal themselves in spite of the altered habits which now obtain in all ranks, and nowhere more significantly than in the predilection of the lower classes in favour of 'gentle blood.'" It was clear to an English observer, however, that there was a difference of attitude between the English rural inhabitant and the pent-up millworker, and that to generalize on "people at large" was dangerous. The farm laborer might still pull his forelock when the squire passed by; the Birmingham operative, however much he might relish news of the aristocracy and reports of goings on in high life, was less

---

* It was not translated into English until 1885, in an American edition.

servile and much more inclined to heckle his lordship in public meeting. The real snobbery of the day, as Thackeray so well pointed out, lay with the newly arrived middle classes, many of whom yearned for seats near the patrician throne and not infrequently came within sight of it by marrying their daughters of wealth to sons of privilege.

The activity in England of Engels and his friend Karl Marx, the latter of whom spent many days at the British Museum rifling it of materials with which to denounce the capitalistic system it represented, is a good example of one of those historical pockets where the real revolutionary thinking of the century was proceeding unknown to the nation which sheltered it. Engels had settled in Manchester in 1842 as manager of his father's cotton-goods mill. His real interest, however, was in economic and political theory and history, and when he met Marx in London in 1844 he found his spiritual leader, whose concepts of economic materialism and determinism brought to a focus his own revolutionary ideas. Hating business, he kept at it in order to earn the money necessary to support the impecunious Marx and his family. Marx's eyes were turned toward Germany, but Engels, observing the economic slavery of the English proletariat, believed that in England the seeds of world revolution would spring forth. He joined the Chartist movement, only to be disillusioned and angered by the absurd reluctance of the English slave to assert himself by violence. Yet everywhere he found "barbarous indifference, relentless self-seeking on one side and unspeakable misery on the other; social conflict everywhere, a general rush to rob one's fellows under the cloak of law."

He wrote *The Condition of the Working-Class in England in 1844* during this autumn and winter of 1844, in the attempt to describe the crucible in which the inevitable uprising was being shaped—as it seemed to him. Many of the facts he had observed personally, but except for the passages of exhortation there was little that he could not have gained from the fearless investigations the despised middle classes were themselves making into the blank misery of the proletariat. And indeed much of his material was taken from the Parliamentary Reports. In his preface to the English edition of 1892 Engels apologized for the stress he had laid in 1844 on the dictum that "Communism is not a mere party doctrine of the working class, but a theory encompassing the emancipation of society at large, including the capitalist class, from its present narrow conditions." Now he felt that "so long as the wealthy classes not only do not feel the want of emancipation, but strenuously oppose the self-emancipation of the working class, so long the revolution will have to be prepared and fought out by the working class alone."

In 1892 Engels called socialism "that abomination of abominations" (it had become "respectable"), but in 1844 he was willing to credit Owenite socialism, at least, with having contributed to real social progress in England.

Robert Owen, seventy-three years of age in 1844, had been, like Engels, the manager of large cotton mills in Manchester. Later, as part owner of mills in New Lanark, near Glasgow, he had turned much of his profit back into the welfare of his operatives, creating good housing, and establishing schools and even public kitchens for his workmen. Leaving his industry in 1817, he propounded his theory for the salvation of the world and tried to put it into practice. His principle was that of "villages of co-operation," socialist communities where human nature was to flower at its happiest in an atmosphere of mutual labor—without money, private property, or competition. There was something sweet and good about Owen's utopianism, with its eccentric hopefulness and its deep humanity. That it was divinely impractical and unsubstantial did not prevent the hungry workingman from grasping at it eagerly during the thirties and forties. In spite of the suspicion which the movement aroused among those hostile to Owen because of his attack upon religion and his advocacy of freedom of divorce, socialist newspapers were established, socialist lecturers found a wide hearing, and some trusting souls were found to engage in his experiment of socialistic communities. One of these co-operative villages had been established in America, at New Harmony, Indiana, and had failed in 1828, bogged down in confusion, maladministration, and a congenital vagueness. Owen had spent four fifths of his total fortune of £60,000 on this experiment.[14] Other attempts were made in England, notably the one of Harmony Hall or Queenwood at Broughton in Hampshire.

When Alexander Somerville[15] made his series of trips through the countryside in 1842 he visited this community. He found it a thriving place, well-kept, prosperous, with some ninety members holding 1,000 acres on a ninety-nine-year lease. He was impressed by the sober habits and good manners of the co-operators. Here again, however, the £30,000 which had been contributed or lent to the scheme was dissipated; no profits were forthcoming, and the resident members entered upon a most disappointing series of quarrels which resulted in the liquidation of the project in 1845. Only the governor, Mr. Buxton, remained in solitary possession of Harmony Hall against all commands to leave, until he, too, was ejected in 1846 "by a creditor from Liverpool." Owen himself had a way of launching large projects and then ignoring them while he busied himself with some new aspect of his regeneration of the world.

It is ironic that a venture initiated in 1844 by a small group of Owenite enthusiasts who believed that they were following their master's principles should have been reprehended by Owen as being democratic and therefore not in keeping with his communistic or socialistic doctrines, and still more ironic that this experiment, out of all the vast forgotten Owenite schemes, should have been the only one to grow and live into the next century.

The story of Rochdale has often been told. "At the close of the year 1843, on one of those damp, dark, dense, dismal, disagreeable days . . . a few poor weavers out of employ, and nearly out of food, and quite out of heart with the social state, met together to discover what they could do to better their industrial condition."[16] These Lancashire operatives decided to turn merchants and manufacturers. A subscription list was handed round, and a dozen put down a weekly subscription of 2d. each. Thus was born the Rochdale Co-operative, registered in 1844 under act of Parliament as "The Rochdale Society of Equitable Pioneers." Meetings were held and plans made for a co-operative provision store. Everything was to be sold for cash (under the influence of Owen they regarded credit as a social evil, a sign of fraud and corruption), but the profits were to be divided among the members in proportion to their purchases. Their declared objectives involved the future purchasing or building of houses, the manufacture of certain goods, and even the establishing of "a self-supporting home-colony of united interests."

The beginnings were modest, however; the twenty-eight members rented the ground floor of a warehouse in Toad Lane, and there, on December 21, 1844, the "Equitable Pioneers" began business with a scanty arrangement of oatmeal, flour, and sugar. The store also exercised an educational function. Members would meet every evening after working hours to discuss religion and politics—subjects carefully avoided by the Mechanics' Institutes. By 1851 the association had 630 members, with cash sales of £2,785, making a gross profit of £990. And always there was a kind of religious fervor about the idea of co-operation: it was a Way of Life.*

Of quite a different nature, and at the political level, was another movement during these years meant to regenerate England—a movement just as romantic in its way as Owen's but at the opposite end of the

---

* The Rochdale Pioneers were not the first consumers' co-operative organization; their most important innovation was the sharing of profits in proportion to purchases.

philosophic scale. Benjamin Disraeli had gathered around him a group of young Conservatives who called themselves the "Young England" party. It was hardly a party, and it aroused more laughter than fear at the Carleton Club with its advice to the old men to step aside and let the enthusiasm of young take the place of the cold caution of age. Sir James Graham wrote to Croker that he thought "they will return to the crib after prancing, capering, and snorting"—though Graham recognized at the same time the dangerous ability of Disraeli, whose strange blend of oriental mysticism and cynical realism was by way of being a thorn in the side of his fellow Conservatives. In principle Young England was as much a retreat to the glamorous past as was Carlyle's *Past and Present*. Disraeli and his cohorts—Lord John Manners, Bailie Cochrane, George S. Smythe, and others—saw an England under the control of a benevolent aristocracy which would bridge the widening gulf between the classes without in any way disturbing the existing order of things. All was to be expansively paternal and feudal in the most responsible sense. The powerful *Times* wrote leaders on behalf of the movement, and the young gentlemen who were at its center kept talking of knights and keeps, and moved in a self-projected aura of lofty sensibility. The party was to cut across all existing parties, for it considered the Whigs lazy and improvident, Conservatism a sham, and Radicalism a pollution. The *Spectator* wrote approvingly of a dinner at the Manchester Athenaeum at which Disraeli and Manners had sat with the workingmen of Ancoats and Dukinfield, with Disraeli speaking eloquently of the youth of the nation as the "trustees of prosperity," and of education such as that represented by the Athenaeum as being "like the ladder in the patriarch's mystic dream; its base rests on the primeval earth—its crest is lost in the shadowy splendour of the empyrean. . . ."

Manners became the laureate of the movement and wrote of the dream when

> Each knew his place—king, peasant, peer or priest,
> The greatest owned connexion with the least;
> From rank to rank the generous feeling ran,
> And linked society as man to man.
>
> . . . .
>
> Let wealth and commerce, laws and learning die,
> But leave us still our old nobility.[17]

But it was Disraeli who wrote the manifesto of Young England with *Coningsby, or the New Generation*, in 1844. This triple-decker novel, so successful that in three months it went through three editions, was a

Figure 54. Disraeli as a young author

blend of romance and satire in the best Disraeli manner. Contemporaries found satisfaction in making identifications of the characters with living people: the rich and powerful Lord Monmouth was Lord Hertford; Lucian Gay was Theodore Hook; Henry Sidney was Lord John Manners; Smythe was the model for Coningsby, and John Wilson Croker was satirized in the bitter, slashing portrait of the venal and sycophantic Rigby. Sidonia, a blend of Disraeli himself and of Lord Rothschild, was the first of Disraeli's mysterious and philosophical Jews. The story, which deals with the political education of young Coningsby and ends with his entry into Parliament, is unimportant; the virtue—and the popularity —of the novel lay in its brilliant political satire and its presentation of the program of Young England as the hope of the country.

If England was not to be saved in these turbulent years it would not be for lack of sufficient variety of panaceas. Chartism and socialism walking hand in hand, communism around the corner, Young England making a romantic gesture, the Manchester economists preaching the salvation of Free Trade and the Anti-Corn-Law Leaguers threatening economic damnation if repeal did not arrive immediately; humanitarian

THE
ACCOUCHEMENT
OF
HER MAJESTY.

BIRTH OF A PRINCE.

THE TIMES-OFFICE, Tuesday Morning,
Half-past 8 o'Clock.

We have the happiness to announce that the Queen has been safely delivered of a PRINCE.

We are happy to state that Her Majesty is doing well.

We are indebted to the extraordinary power of the Electro-Magnetic Telegraph for the rapid communication of this important announcement.

COURT CIRCULAR.

SECOND EDITION.

THE
ACCOUCHEMENT
OF
HER MAJESTY.

EXPRESS FROM WINDSOR.

THE TIMES-OFFICE, Tuesday Morning,
Half-past 10 o'Clock a.m.

In addition to the intelligence of the auspicious event which we published at half-past 8 o'clock, we have just received the following

OFFICIAL DESPATCH.

" WINDSOR CASTLE, August 6, 1844.
" *Half-past 8 o'Clock a.m.*

"The Queen was safely delivered of a PRINCE this morning at 50 minutes past 7 o'clock.

" Her Majesty and Infant are perfectly well.
" JAMES CLARK, M.D.
" CHARLES LOCOCK, M.D.
" ROBERT FERGUSON, M.D."

Figure 55. Announcement by the *Times* of a royal birth

legislators plugging some of the more obvious gaps in the social structure which the machine was making—and in the midst of it all the ordinary citizen, happily drugged with the Godfrey's Cordial of custom, but wondering wistfully what kind of world lay ahead of him tomorrow. Complacent? Not quite—yet.

While all this was going on the sands of 1844 were running out. Early in July Thomas Campbell was buried in the Poets' Corner of the Abbey. . . . A little later Captain Warner's secret explosive for destroying ships at sea was demonstrated off Brighton before 40,000 intent spectators. Under carefully controlled conditions the mysterious captain blew into the air, from a distance of half a mile, the 300-ton *John of Gaunt*. The Ministry seemed reluctant, however, to pay Warner the £300,000 he demanded before revealing his secret, and finally the public excitement simmered down and disappeared. . . . On August 6th Queen Victoria gave birth to her fourth child—another prince—amid not quite so much general excitement. About this time it was noted that the infant Prince of Wales had an annual income of £73,100. . . . The Marquess of Chandos attained his majority, and the event was celebrated at Stowe and Buckingham with great rejoicing (so the papers said) on the part of the Duke of Buckingham's faithful constituency. Official dinners were given; addresses were presented in the Town Hall; 2,500 inhabitants of nine villages marched past, headed by morris dancers, and were regaled with dinner and strong ale; in the evening a magnificent banquet was served in the state dining room, "refulgent with gold and silver" and with covers for sixty-five guests. Later a grand display of fireworks in the park was witnessed by about 5,000 persons. The celebration lasted two more days, and on the third day the duke gave a dinner to 300 of his tenantry in the tenants' hall. All expressed themselves as grateful and well-pleased.

August 31st was Prince Albert's birthday, and it was marked with the usual amenities. A military band played under his window at Windsor early in the morning; at night the Eastern Terrace, the Gateway, and the adjacent grounds were illuminated with some twelve or fourteen hundred lamps, and there was a brilliant display of fireworks ending in a royal salute. Albert was twenty-five years of age.

In September Daniel O'Connell was released from prison by action of the House of Lords, and was marched in exultant procession through Dublin, riding in a triumphal car composed of platforms on three levels, profusely decorated with purple velvet and gold fringe. O'Connell stood at full height on the topmost stage, some dozen feet above the crowd, and looked a little tired. . . . *The Bohemian Girl* was performed in London for the eighty-first time. . . . Barry, the clown at Astley's, was drawn down the Thames by geese hitched to a tub in which he floated. The road from the new Houses of Parliament to Thames Bank was made almost impassable by the immense crowd gathered to see the feat, and long before the hour fixed upon a number of boats filled with anxious spectators rowed up to Vauxhall Bridge and took up favorable positions there. . . . Louis Philippe visited Victoria, bringing great protestations of friendship and peace (he got the Garter). . . . Word arrived of the election of an unknown Democratic politician named James Knox Polk as President of the United States, he having defeated Henry Clay. . . . And a little earlier, on October 28th, the opening of the Royal Exchange itself. Mr. Tite, the architect, was on hand to greet the party and to conduct Prince Albert through the Exchange. Multiple bands played "See! the Conquering Hero Comes" when Wellington arrived. Politicians and Cabinet members and all sorts of dignitaries were there by the hundreds. The bells in the campanile tower chimed "God Save

Figure 56. The new Royal Exchange

the Queen," in B flat; addresses were presented, and after the heralds had made proclamation the Queen received a slip of parchment from Sir James Graham and said, "in an audible voice," "It is my royal will and pleasure that this building hereafter be called 'the Royal Exchange.'" In the evening the Lord Mayor entertained at the Mansion House four or five hundred visitors, and the lady mayoress gave a ball.

There was some grumbling later about the Corporation of the City of London by those who had had difficulty getting tickets for the ceremony. The Exchange was built for the merchants at large, the press pointed out, complaining that in a bumble spirit of ignorance and insolence the greedy ostentation of the corporate body had swamped the merchants of London. But all this did nothing to dim the gratification that the public took in witnessing the pageantry and its accompanying illuminations that night.

One of the most important events in the history of ideas in the 1840's took place in this year with the publication of an anonymous book, *Vestiges of the Natural History of Creation*. Not until 1884, thirteen years after its author's death, was it publicly admitted to be the work of Robert Chambers, the protean Edinburgh publisher and author. Its effect on the public mind was that of a minor earthquake; by 1853 it had gone through ten large editions. Never had a scientifically dubious

Figure 57. Robert Chambers

book contained so much truth, and never was the truth accepted by so many on the basis of mistaken evidence. Religious orthodoxy fought it as it would have fought a literal devil. Many thoughtful people, from Matthew Arnold to Tennyson, began their long journey of reconciliation between two religious wastelands, "one dead, the other powerless to be born," of which the *Vestiges*, though not the only inciting cause, was in the forties the chief focal force. The book was, very simply, a popular presentation of the theory of organic evolution.

The idea of evolution was of course not new. Charles Lyell in his *Principles of Geology* (1830–33), though he had very modest views of the earth's antiquity, had refuted the "catastrophic" theory of geological science and had identified the changes in the earth's surface with laws of subsidence, elevation, and erosion rather than with the spasms of earthquakes and volcanic eruptions. Lyell had been revolted, however, by the Lamarckian intimations of organic evolution. But more than he knew he paved the way for Chambers, and, more importantly, for Charles Darwin. By 1844 Darwin, still publishing in successive volumes his *Zoology of the Voyage of the "Beagle"* and, in this year, his *Geological Observations on the Volcanic Islands visited during the voyage of* the "*Beagle*," had expanded to a length of 231 handwritten folio pages the brief sketch of his theory of natural selection which he had first written out in 1842. Only a few friends knew about it, and fifteen years were to pass before the *Origin of Species* would burst upon a startled yet receptive world.

Thus the concept of evolution was already in the air. On the very eve of the publication of the *Vestiges* a meeting at York of the British Association for the Advancement of Science had been thrown into a dither by a violent battle between theologians and geologists over Buckland's *Treatise on Promoting Religion by the Study of Natural Philosophy*. The controversy between the Dean of York and Adam Sedgwick, professor of geology at Cambridge, became so bitter that it was doubtful whether they should be asked to sit down at the same table at dinner. At length George Hudson, the "Railway King," and host for the dinner, resolved the situation for the moment by saying to the professors: "Why, gentlemen, I'm really very sorry, gentlemen, the affair can't be managed, gentlemen; but"—smiling and bowing—"the fact is, gentlemen, I've talked the thing over with the Corporation, and —*we've decided for Moses and the Dean!*"[18]

And now the *Vestiges* set up mutterings in religious and scientific circles. It was a very clear and well-written account, according to Chambers's understanding, of the creation of the world, the continuous development of the species from the lowest to the highest order of plants and animals, and the gradual ascent of man. It was generally recognized that his theory was founded on Lamarck's, but his friendly critics found the author of *Vestiges* more plausible. It is worth noting today that he suggested that electricity had something to do with producing organization as regards structure: the first step in the creation of life, he said, was a "chemico-electric operation, in which simple germinal vesicles were produced."

At this distance the reader is impressed by the length to which Chambers went in conciliating his religious opposition. The iterated theme of the book (which was nevertheless ignored by hostile critics, as Chambers ruefully kept pointing out later) was that although the Creator, whom the author treats very reverently, had not created each individual species, He had established the natural laws under which the development of species took place. "How can we suppose," he asked, "that the august Being, who brought all these countless worlds into form by the simple establishment of a natural principle flowing from His mind, was to interfere personally and specially on every occasion when a new shell-fish or reptile was to be ushered into existence on one of those worlds?" Yet this was the gage of battle to the orthodox who believed that the age of the world could be dated as of a few thousand years ago and that God had given in six calendar days special creation to each living thing. What was to happen to the Garden of Eden and the Fall of Man? The vials of clerical wrath were poured out and Chambers, caught in the cross fire between the religiously orthodox and the scientists who found his structure of evidence unbelievable, could turn only to the general public, an amazing number of whom liked what he had to say.

The reception of the book, both favorable and unfavorable, is an important index to the intellectual temper of the time. Lockhart wrote to Croker that "it is a work of extraordinary knowledge and ability, dashed with apparently mad extravagance—the effect, however, bringing into form all the elements of infidelity scattered through the modern tomes of Geology, Botany, Zoology, etc., and written so clearly and powerfully that the *savans* anticipate an outburst of orthodox wrath upon their whole clique." Croker replied: "You must get the *Vestiges* reviewed. I, in my happy ignorance, think it very shallow humbug . . . an odious, disgusting, revolting, and irrational theory." The *Quarterly* did not review the book.

Huxley was irritated by "the prodigious ignorance and thoroughly unscientific habit of mind manifested by the writer." Darwin admired its powerful and brilliant style, but thought the geology bad and the zoology worse. Yet in the preface to the sixth edition (1872) of the *Origin of Species* he said: "In my opinion, it has done excellent service in this country in calling attention to the subject, in removing prejudice, and in thus preparing the ground for the reception of analogous views." Sedgwick attacked the book viciously in the *Edinburgh Review*. The *Athenaeum* classed it with the popular errors of "Alchemy, Astrology, Witchcraft, Mesmerism, Southcotianism, Phrenology, and other kindred humbugs." The *Eclectic* and the *British Quarterly* tore their hair over its heresies. It was preached against from pulpits, and attacked in pamphlets. But the *Spectator* reviewed it favorably, as did the *Prospective* and the *Westminster Review*.

S. R. Bosanquet published a fifty-six-page attack called *Vestiges of the Natural History of Creation; its Argument examined and exposed*, in which he spoke of the *Vestiges* as having "all the graces of the accomplished harlot. Her song is like the syren for its melody and attractive sweetness. . . . But she is a foul and filthy thing, whose touch is taint, whose breath is contamination." Chambers answered this and other hostile criticisms in a 198-page reply: *Explanations: a Sequel to*

"*Vestiges.*" Here he complained with the most equable good temper not so much about disagreement as misrepresentation, and reasserted his belief in a Deity who, under his explanation, "becomes a defined instead of a capricious being."

Far from being a tempest in a teapot, the controversy, anticipating Darwin, underlined what was to become one of the central spiritual uncertainties of the Victorian age.

The November fogs this year were even more intense than usual, and on Thursday, the twenty-first, the worst fog within the memory of man descended on London. In the afternoon the mingled vapor and smoke grew thicker and thicker until it was literally pitch-dark. Torches appeared on all the streets. In the Strand and along other busy thoroughfares carriages were led by the drivers on foot. Omnibuses ceased to run, and river traffic was entirely suspended. Every good guidebook to London during these years described the fogs as if they were as much a part of the local scene as the Abbey or Hyde Park—as indeed they were. Sometimes they were just white mist, sometimes bottle-green, and sometimes pea-soup yellow—the fog itself, arising in part from imperfect drainage, being impregnated with the smoke from hundreds of thousands of blazing coal fires in homes, factories, breweries, chemical works, and steamboats.*

With December the worst fogs passed, bright cold weather came, and on a Sunday 5,000 persons ventured on the ice of the Serpentine in Hyde Park, notwithstanding the fact that the ice was only an inch and a half

---

* There was a lively, humorous description of a London fog in *Cruikshank's Comic Almanack* for November, 1841: "Now, the sun, after a vain attempt to catch a glimpse of St. Paul's, or the Monument, gives it up in despair. . . . Now, invisible cabmen drive unseen horses along viewless thoroughfares, and omnibuses go, flitting like so many Flying Dutchmen, through the mist and fog. . . . Now, wood-pavements are in nice condition; particularly that in the pleasing bend by St. Giles's church; where

> They slip now who never slipped before;
> And they who always slipped now slip the more.

Now, the man 'wot lights the lamps' in St. James's Park is in a regular state of bewilderment, and not infrequently is found running up one of the saplings instead of the lamp-post. . . . Now, Charing Cross is as difficult to navigate as the Northwest passage, and the parks are impossible; hackney coaches drive up against church windows; old men tumble down cellar holes; old women and children stand crying up against lamp-posts, lost within a street of their own homes . . . in short, the town is in such a state of commotion and panic, that it only requires a well-organized banditti to carry off all London into the next county."

Figure 58. A November fog

thick and that the icemen of the Royal Humane Society issued repeated cautions. Numbers broke through the ice, but no fatal accident occurred. A few nights later an entirely different kind of accident occurred—a tragic one—when, during a ballet at Drury Lane, the dress of the dancer Clara Webster caught fire from an exposed gaslight at stage level, and, enveloped in flames, she burned to death in view of the terrified audience.

As 1844 drew to a close it was becoming more and more evident that a new kind of boom was in the making. The miles of iron rails which the railway entrepreneurs had thrown across the countryside had grown in more than arithmetical progression. This year had been unparalleled for the production of new railway schemes; as England came out of its financial depression it was caught and held by the romantic practicality of steam locomotion. In 1842 only three new lines had been sanctioned; in 1843, three more lines; but in 1844 twenty-six projected lines totaling

800 miles were approved by Parliamentary committees. During the year 173 miles of new railway had been opened by thirteen lines. And Parliament had invited still further investment by requiring only one twentieth, instead of one tenth, of the total amount of capital to be deposited before a railway bill could be introduced.* Before long the country was to be caught in a frenzy of speculation which would be one of the wonders and horrors of the age. The bait of egregious profit was already being dangled before the noses of the susceptible.

No one paid much attention to Wordsworth's sonnet against the spoliation which he thought the Kendal and Windermere Railway was threatening to the Lake Country (it was not one of the laureate's happiest effusions),† nor to his subsequent letter to the *Morning Post* on the same subject, in which he succeeded in implying that the only people capable of enjoying the mountain scenery were poets, or at the very least those who had been born and bred in the district. No good was to be had "by transferring at once uneducated persons in large bodies" to such spots. Better not tempt "artisans and labourers, and the humbler class of shopkeepers, to ramble to a distance." Said one commentator: "It seems that Mr. Wordsworth thinks that there ought to be preserves of poets, as there are of partridges. . . . There is poetry in the very railway, as some among the contemned 'operatives' could perhaps teach."

Railway travel up to now had been pretty much of an adventure, and not always comfortable. Third-class carriages in particular had been shamefully inadequate, open to the air and unprotected against wet or cold—with shallow backless seats or no seats at all. In 1844 Gladstone, then president of the Board of Trade, got through the Commons a "cheap trains act" which proved very popular. From now on each railway was required to run at least one train each day in each direction with provisions for third-class passengers at a rate of 1d. per mile—such carriages to be protected from the weather. Gladstone resisted, however, the running of third-class carriages on Sunday (though first- and second-class travelers could ride on Sunday) on the grounds that "the working respectable mechanic would not choose the Lord's day for travelling, and were it otherwise it would be bad policy in government to encourage such a system. The observance of the Sabbath is the main support of

---

* By 1845, however, the original requirement of a one-tenth deposit had been restored.

　† Is then no nook of English ground secure
　　From rash assault? Schemes of retirement sown
　In youth, and 'mid the busy world kept pure
　　As when their earliest flowers of hope were blown,
　Must perish;—how can they this blight endure? etc.

religion." Mr. Sheild quite properly pointed out that the question therefore seemed to be "whether Dives Should travel on a Sunday and Lazarus should not." Another provision of the bill of 1844 was that the electric telegraph should be established on all lines of railway; it had already been installed on the Great Western Lines.

And so 1844 slid imperceptibly into 1845. Those interested in studying balance sheets at the end of the year found that the total exports of the United Kingdom of £131,833,391 had exceeded those of the year before by some £18,000,000. There was peace at home and, except for border incidents halfway round the world, peace abroad. The latest arrival in the royal family had been christened, and at Windsor Victoria and Albert watched the old year out with quiet hearts.

PART TWO

1845 - 1848

* * *

CRISIS

CHAPTER FIVE

1845 * Steam; Smoke; Speed

"FORTY-FIVE," said the *Spectator* in the first week of the new year, "is a critical age for men, maidens, and centuries. . . . Our expectations . . . are not excessive. Perhaps it is well that they are not. 'Blessed,' says a supplementary beatitude, 'are they who expect little, for they shall not be disappointed.'"

Yet the year began with a kind of statistical optimism. Trade was good and the cost of living was down. Wheat, which had reached 64s. in 1841, was now 46s. The unprecedented growth in railway construction was absorbing surplus labor, and for the first time in years there was a greater demand for workmen than there was supply. Crime had diminished. There had been 3,000 fewer convictions in 1844 than in the year previous, and 5,000 fewer than in 1842. And 1845 was to show a still further decline, over 1844, of 2,000 such cases. Pauperism had decreased 20 per cent as compared with 1843. The surplus population had been reduced by 70,000 people who had emigrated to the colonies or to the United States during the year. The old Merry England seemed to be just around the corner as the life of the decade reached midstream.

Even crime was being overtaken by invention, this time in the shocking case of the Salt Hill murder. A woman by the name of Sarah Hart had been discovered on New Year's night in the last agonies of prussic-acid poisoning. A Quaker named John Tawell, suspected of being her paramour and murderer, left suddenly for London from the Slough Station of the Great Western Railway. His description was sent by "galvanic telegraph" along the lines to London, where he was met by waiting policemen upon his arrival. The case, with its protracted trial and ultimate execution of Tawell, created great excitement, but the method of the murderer's apprehension held the public attention almost as much as the crime itself. Still further interest was aroused a little later when a game of chess was played over the telegraph lines of the South Western Railway between London and Portsmouth, a distance of eighty-eight miles. The game was abandoned as drawn after nine hours.

For the most part, less spectacular events crowded the newspapers read at the English breakfast tables during these early weeks. On New Year's Day Victoria and Albert had graciously distributed bounty to the poor at Windsor; tables fifty feet long, loaded with joints of beef, plum puddings, potatoes, bread, and ale, held largesse for some 330 families. . . . A whole week's festivities were needed at Badminton to celebrate the coming of age of the Marquis of Worcester, son of the Duke of Beaufort. Royalty honored the mansion with its presence; thirty-five guests sat down to banquet in the brilliantly illuminated Great Hall, and 200 of the tenantry feasted in the servants' hall of the old baronial mansion. Later a great ox was roasted, and the revelry continued. . . . A monster eight-foot, thirteen-ton bell, cast for York Minster, was placed on exhibit. . . . It was considered worthy of record in the public prints that 5,143 teeth were extracted in the London Hospital during 1844 (without anesthesia, of course). . . . Three new magazines were announced for January: *Douglas Jerrold's Shilling Magazine*, *Parker's London Magazine*, and *George Cruikshank's Table-Book*. . . . *Antigone* was presented with great acclaim at Covent Garden, with Mendelssohn's music. . . . The play *Honesty* was produced at Drury Lane, and was withdrawn; it seemed, said one reviewer, not to be the best policy.

In January, too, the Queen and her Consort paid a visit to the Duke of Buckingham at Stowe, where they were entertained with a magnificence truly regal. There, and later in the year on a trip to his native country of Coburg, Albert was drawn by his hosts into the sport of deer killing *à la battue*, with the Queen present. Under this system carnage became a festival. At Coburg, after the queens and duchesses had entered a sort of pavilion and the gentlemen had taken up their positions beside a table stacked with ammunition, men acting as beaters drove the frightened deer into the enclosure, after which the sportsmen strewed the field with dead and dying animals. In the intervals necessary to allow lesser huntsmen to cut the throats of the stricken deer and to drive others into the stockade, a military band played lively polkas and national airs. This continued for two hours, and then the ladies departed through a carefully arranged avenue of dead beasts. Stout English hearts devoted to true sportsmanship, reading this, were somewhat comforted to learn that Victoria wept, and with difficulty kept her chair. The press commented bitterly on the occasion, *Punch* being particularly savage. A butcher wrote a letter to the *Morning Chronicle* after the earlier *battue* at Stowe, offering, in order to save trouble and expense, to let the nobility visit his slaughterhouse and there "have the felicity of terminating the existence of any of those herbiferi most commonly devoted to a man's consumption they might choose."

About this same time one of the great prize fights of the generation took place—"a decaying sport," as the papers called it. Caunt, a man of gigantic height and the champion of England, was defeated by Bendigo of Nottingham in an eighty-eight-round contest lasting two hours and thirty-eight minutes—"when Caunt he could not rise," as the ballad put it. Pugilism, one notes in this connection, had been outlawed as a brutalizing sport, and it was necessary for the "bloods" who were in attendance at this bout to change the location of the fight three times in order to evade the sheriffs who were determined to break it up.

Religious tensions were increasing during the early part of the year, reaching their climax at last on the floor of the House of Commons.

The Tractarian dispute still kept the Church of England in turmoil. In January, when the Rev. Mr. Courtenay of St. Sidwell's, Exeter, had persisted in wearing a surplice in the pulpit, many of his congregation angrily left the church service. At the end of the service, when Mr. Courtenay emerged, he was hooted and yelled at by a crowd of 2,000 people who had been waiting through a torrential downpour to revile him. Police had to make a lane for him through the crowd.

In Oxford, at the center of the Movement, W. G. Ward was publicly condemned at a convocation on February 13th for writing his book *The Ideal of a Christian Church Considered*—the charge being that it was inconsistent with subscription to the Thirty-nine Articles. At the same time his degrees were taken from him amid a chorus of *non-placets*. Ward spoke bootlessly for an hour in his own defense, pointing out that the penalty of "degradation" had not been meted out even to those who had left Oxford to enter the Church of Rome. He was overwhelmed by a two-to-one vote, and emerged from the storm of cheering, counter-cheering, and hissing to take what small comfort he could from the applause of the undergraduates assembled outside the Sheldonian Theatre. Gladstone had voted for Ward, Ashley against him.

"Mr. Newman," it was noted, "did not vote, nor was he present." For Newman, at Littlemore, was waiting for the sign which would lead him from the Church he had tried to revive into the arms of the Church toward which, he now felt, his whole career had been taking him. On the night of October 9th, in his little red-hung oratory, Newman made his confession to Father Dominic and was received into what seemed to him the only Church of Christ. The Church of England had received a great blow; there were many to revile Newman but there were also many to lament the loss. Ward followed Newman, as did Manning later. Keble and Pusey had been silenced. Orthodox Anglicanism was triumphant in its own kind of authoritarianism; and it was aided both by public prejudice and by an emerging secularism which, however romantic many of its manifestations were, saw that the medieval road was not the one which led to solution of the nineteenth-century quandry. Yet the Oxford Movement left its mark. Its fragments flew far and pierced deep.

In a still wider context the great universities were the object of increasing criticism. On April 10th Mr. Christie, M.P. for Weymouth, moved for a royal commission of inquiry into the state of education in the English universities.* The *Athenaeum* in reviewing Charles Lyell's two-volume *Travels in North America* took occasion to point out "the inefficiency, absurdity, and injustice of the present educational system at Oxford and Cambridge—a system rather of hollow pretensions than real advantages, in which enormous revenues are directed to the sealing the mouths of professors, the keeping down the number of students to a minimum, and offering a bonus to the indolence and immorality of its members." These hard words were not entirely unjustified, for the universities were in a bad period of intellectual obstructionism. Even many of those who cherished the classical concept of studies felt that some slight gesture might be made to modern science, particularly. The classics and mathematics comprehended the whole range of secular knowledge as far as the ancient seats of learning were concerned. The Vice-Chancellor had urged that a century should pass before new discoveries in science should be admitted to the curriculum.

---

* The commission was not appointed until 1850, and did not report until 1852.

Lyell was led to comment on the English system of higher education through questions he had been asked by friends in the United States.* His complaint was that Oxford was really twenty-four small colleges rather than a university, and that, if the colleges were small, two or three individuals, and occasionally a single instructor, might be called upon to give lectures in all the departments of human knowledge embraced in an academic course of four years. Thus one instructor would give lectures or examinations on the writings of the Greek and Roman historians, philosophers, and poets, together with logic, mathematics, and theology. Even worse, it seemed to him, had been the progressive transfer of instruction from the permanent to the collegiate and temporary teacher, the latter chiefly clerical, abiding his time only until he could reach some ecclesiastical preferment. And now the tutors were in process of being superseded to no small degree by private tutors or "crammers," chosen by the young men themselves to prepare them for examination. In 1841 one fifth of the resident students had this kind of assistance, paying for it more than £10,000 a year.

Since 1839, at which time examinations had been pointed even more sharply toward mathematics, theology, and the classics, the sciences, never notably strong, had been in danger of extinction. Some of the authorities were opposed to the cultivation of the physical sciences on principle, on account of their alleged irreligious tendency. Chemistry and botany attracted, between 1840 and 1844, from three to seven students; mineralogy and geology, "still taught by the same professor who, fifteen years before, had attracted crowded audiences," from ten to twelve; political economy still fewer. At Cambridge the professors of chemistry and anatomy had been able to muster only six or seven pupils; the chairs of Modern History, and of the Application of Machinery to the Arts, once numbering audiences of several hundreds, had been in like manner deserted.

Five years later, in 1850, out of 1,600 students at Oxford the average attendance at the modern history course was eight; at the chemistry courses, five; at botany, six. And the interlocking of Church and education was so strong that Dissenters were still as a matter of course excluded —from attendance at Oxford and from degrees at Cambridge. As the Dissenting public grew in numbers and in importance many thoughtful university graduates, aware that Anglicanism had no exclusive yield of brains, became worried about the disabilities suffered by those from

---

* He visited Harvard, and wrote with great approval of its 400 students and thirty-two professors.

whose number, like it or not, many future leaders of the nation were to come.

But as far as religious disabilities were concerned, it was an Irish problem which was keeping the House of Commons up nights during the early part of the 1845 session. Peel introduced a bill for Government support of poverty-stricken Maynooth College to the extent of £30,000 a year. The assumption was that since Catholic Ireland was going to have clergy anyway, it might be better for all concerned if it were a reasonably well-educated clergy. Moreover, the grant represented no real change in policy, only an increase beyond the £9,000 which Parliament had earlier voted Maynooth. But immediately the battle lines were drawn with a vitriolic intensity understandable only in the light of a traditional mistrust of the Irish, and, still more, of a deep-rooted reluctance to give state assistance to Catholic education. Dissenters and Anglicans alike held protest meetings the length and breadth of the land.* Thousands of petitions poured in against the bill, deploring the audacity of those who would establish Popery in England. "I believe," thundered Dr. Candlish in Edinburgh, "so sure as I believe in God's word to be true, a judgment must overtake this nation if we homologate this great sin."

The debate on the second reading of the bill occupied six nights in the Commons and three nights in the Upper House. Disraeli launched another sardonic philippic at Peel's policy and personal conduct. Ashley opposed the measure. Colonel Sibthorp made a speech punctuated by the uproarious laughter of the House in which he declared he could not know whether Peel was a Protestant, a Romanist, or a Mahomedan; in any event, he had lost all confidence in "that man" at the head of the Government. But Lord John Russell supported the measure, as did Gladstone on grounds of "justice," although the latter's conscience made him resign office because the proposal was incompatible both with his earlier opinions and with the pledges under which he had been returned to Parliament. Macaulay advocated it warmly, pointing out the inconsistency of those who had supported the small grant but objected to the present addition; who were quite willing to subsidize what they considered error, provided only it was subsidized in a mean and shabby manner. "The Orangeman raises his war-whoop," he said. "Exeter Hall sets up its bray; Mr. McNeile shudders to see more costly cheer than ever provided for the priests of Baal at the table of the Queen;

---

* In the course of the controversy, figures were published concerning the number of congregations of Dissenters in the country: Wesleyan Methodists, 4,700; Independents, 2,550; Baptists, 1,713; Free Church and Secession Communities of Scotland, 1,200. Total, 10,163.

Figure 59. Sir Robert Peel

and the Protestant operatives of Dublin call for impeachment in exceedingly bad English."

The last night of the debate did not terminate in the House of Lords until 4 A.M., when, wrote a reporter, "the light of a summer's dawn blending with the beams of almost expiring tapers, fell on a crowded, exhausted, and yet anxious assembly." The Commons had passed the second reading by a safe majority of 147, and the Lords approved the bill by a majority of 157. The victory made it much easier for Sir James Graham, shortly after, to get approval of his less-controversial bill to provide education for the Irish middle classes through the establishment of three colleges in the north, west, and south of Ireland, each to offer good and cheap education to "Catholic, Protestant, and Dissenter alike."

Speaking for three hours and a half, Sir Robert Peel made his annual financial statement and introduced his budget for 1845, which was generally compared with his brilliant budget of 1842. Backed by good times (exports rose a million-and-a-half pounds in 1845) and a surplus from the previous year of £3,357,000, he was able to undertake another large free-trade operation on duties. To be sure, he had to recommend the retention of the income tax for another three years. But he removed all duties on British exports, and slashed the import duties heavily. The duty was removed entirely on 430 out of 813 items. Some of these were products as remote as whale fins and zebrawood, but they included also the critical raw materials of silk, flax, and cotton wool, and the reduction of the sugar duty. The duty on glass, which ran from 200 to 300 per cent of the value of the article, was also abolished. The window tax, however—that discriminatory survival of a more primitive civilization—was retained. Peel estimated that out of 3,400,000 houses in Great Britain, not more than 450,000 were charged with window duty; but it was notorious that the tax set a premium on bad construction, and that the poor, to evade the tax, closed up many windows necessary for light and ventilation.* Its remission was not to come until 1851.

Since there were few people who in one way or another did not stand to profit by the budget, it passed without difficulty. Free trade was on its way. Disraeli made the salty comment that Peel had caught the Whigs in bathing and had run away with their clothes, but there was general approval, including that of the *Times*. Peel was understandably self-assured about it all, and the *Times* called attention to this when it said: "It would be hard on him, and human nature itself, to expect that he should not do the thing rather grandly. It is not his fault that he acts the Goddess of Plenty, and wields his cornucopia with an air."

All this time, however, there were rumblings of distant thunder. Where would all this free-trade business end? Was Peel a Tory or was he leading his so-called Conservative party up the garden path? When Mr. C. P. Villiers brought on his annual motion for a committee on the Corn Laws, Peel opposed it and the motion was rejected, as it had been year by year in the past. But shrewd commentators had observed the direction in which Peel was moving. The landed interests put up fingers to test the wind and went home to quiver with indignation and to grumble in their beards about political traitors. *Punch* ran one cartoon showing Peel dressed in costume for the Queen's fancy-dress ball and asking:

---

* The sliding scale reached, at 8 windows, 2s. 3½d. per window; at 39 windows, 7s. 6¾d.; at 500, 2s. 7¼d. In many cases the houses exempt were those used as warehouses by wealthy proprietors, and those old buildings, occupied by the poor, the windows of which were boarded up. In one instance there were twenty windows shut up in a house occupied by twenty-seven families. The Duke of Wellington paid on Apsley House (annual rental, £2,000) a tax of £37; or 2⅜ per cent; Francis Beazley, plasterer (rent, £32), paid £6, or 20 per cent.

"How do you like the new W(h)ig?"—and another showing Papa Cobden leading little-boy Peel in a free-trade walk. Cobden: "Come along, Master Robert, do step out." Master Robert: "That's all very well, but you know I cannot go as fast as you do." By this time both Victoria and Albert, who had become very fond of Peel, were devout free-traders. It had been noticed, too, that once when Cobden had finished one of his masterly speeches in the House against the Corn Laws, and everyone had expected Peel to answer him, Peel sat silent, muttering something about "let him answer who can."

As a matter of fact Peel was an enigma to many of his contemporaries. He had never been a popular party leader, but had dominated his party simply by virtue of being the greatest statesman of his generation—plus a cool ability to crack Conservative heads on occasion. Cold, awkward, and shy in personal relationships, his inner warmth seldom broke through, and even his followers frequently found him unsympathetic. It was he who had reconstituted the Tories as Conservatives, and many of them were somewhat restive under the new designation. As Tories they knew where they stood on any given issue; as Peelites they were constantly being surprised by realignments of supposedly entrenched positions. Ultra-Tory, Ultra-Radical, High Churchman, and Dissenter attacked him because he was impervious to the particular bigotry of each. The landed aristocracy could never quite forgive him his background of Lancashire manufacture. He was commonly attacked as inconsistent, was labeled a man who acted expediently and not on principle except as it was suggested to him by passing circumstance. By "principle" his enemies meant party consistency, but the result was that at the moment when, in the early months of 1845, the Conservative position seemed impregnable, there was a secret quivering fear that Peel was ruining the party from within. One sympathetic observer called him "the embodied reflex of the public mind of England,"[1] and history would be able to make an impartial survey of his great reforms. Nevertheless, it was difficult for his embattled colleagues to understand a man who would put the welfare of the nation above political ambition and who would revise his earlier opinions in the light of new conditions. It was the fate of the Conservatives that they could not do without him and that with him they were about to commit suicide.

Being at all levels a political animal, the Englishman followed with intense interest the Corn Law agitation and the ministerial crisis to which the sequence of national events led in 1845.

Never had the Anti-Corn-Law League been so active. Long before the formal organization of the League in 1838—indeed ever since the first passage of the new Corn Laws in 1815—complaints had been mounting against the "bread tax." In the twenties Ebenezer Elliott, the master founder of Sheffield, wrote his Corn Law Rhymes in bald, primitive, powerful verse reminiscent of Blake's angrier moments:

> Bread-taxed weaver, all may see
> What that tax hath done for thee,
> And thy children vilely led,
> Singing hymns for shameful bread,
> Till the stones of every street
> Know their little naked feet.

The movement for repeal gained impetus when Cobden was elected to Parliament, and it was still further strengthened on the floor of the House when John Bright, the Quaker son of a Rochdale miller, was returned as member for Durham in 1843. Bright's ability lay in the powerful oratory by which he could move large audiences. Cobden, less histrionic if no less fervid, was a master of persuasion. With transparent honesty and simplicity, and with a singular graphic power to marshall facts and illustrations into a logical and irrefutable structure of evidence, he won friends to his cause. Gradually their concerted efforts, exercised with an incredible devotion and a concentration not unlike narrowness, bore fruit. The easiest task had been to convince the industrial midlands that the Corn Laws interfered with the growth of trade and had raised the price of food. At the same time the Leaguers attacked the landlords as the root of all evil, and wept over the debased condition of the agricultural laborer. Wide use was made of the speech of such a laborer at a League meeting: "I be protected, and I be starving." Later the campaign was extended to London, and the long series of public meetings was held in Drury Lane and Covent Garden theaters. Unremittingly assemblies were held up and down the land, in town or village, wherever dissatisfied farmers or operatives could be brought together to hear a League orator denounce the Corn Laws as the ruination of Britain.

All this activity was supported by a swelling tide of gifts. In 1843 the League collected £50,000 for propaganda purposes; in 1844, £100,000, and in 1845 it was well on the way toward an additional £250,000. During one week in 1843, 400,000 tracts were sent out for distribution, a total of 9,000,000 to date. One of the events of May, 1845, was the great Free-Trade Bazaar held in Covent Garden Theatre. The whole area of the pit and stage was boarded over and the auditorium transformed into a vast Gothic hall, crowded with objects of manufacture. One hundred thousand people visited the bazaar in seventeen days, and the sales from the stalls added some £25,000 to the funds of the League.

Despite all this activity the outlook for the League from 1843 to the middle of 1845 was not encouraging. Abundant harvests, steady corn prices, and general prosperity made it difficult to maintain enthusiasm for the cause in either town or country; and the prospect of winning a majority in Parliament seemed increasingly remote. But in midsummer of 1845 it was becoming clear that heavy and too-frequent rains were going to create a lower-than-average harvest. Even more disturbing news began to filter in from the provinces. A strange disease was rotting the potatoes in the ground. By October it was clear that the blight was spreading rapidly and that most of the Irish crop was suffering catastrophe. In Tipperary and Cork it had made fearful ravages and was extending into other counties. The chief food of some 6,000,000 people in the British Isles was being wiped out.

Two things were clear: public or private charity would have to operate to save lives, and additional food would have to be imported from abroad. On October 13th Peel wrote to Graham: "I have no confidence in such remedies as the prohibition of exports or the stoppage of distilleries. The removal of impediments to import is the only effectual remedy." At a Cabinet meeting on November 1st Peel recorded as his opinion that the existing restrictions on the free importation of grain could not be maintained "in full operation." Later in the month Lord John Russell put the Whigs on record with his famous Edinburgh letter to his constituents in London, in which he urged putting an end to the Corn Laws, which had "proved to be the blight of commerce, the bane of agriculture, the source of bitter division among classes, the cause of penury, fever, mortality, and crime among the people." Cobden gloated, and reproached the Government with waiting to repeal the Corn Laws until a period of famine, "when Palace Yard should be crowded with famishing thousands."

The cause of the noble upholders of protection was not helped at this time by a pronouncement of the Duke of Norfolk. This gentleman came in for a good deal of attention by recommending the use of curry powder by those who had nothing to eat. His Grace told an audience in all seriousness that curry powder is to the Hindu what potatoes are to the Irishman (he forgot to mention the rice). A pinch of this powder—and he had tried it himself—if put into water to make a kind of soup, warms the stomach indescribably, he said, and a man without food "can go to bed comfortably on it." His auditors at the Protectionist dinner had the decency to laugh and cheer ironically. The *Examiner*, commenting on the suggestion, said that it preferred to recommend simple pepper instead of curry, "because there is an idea of luxury in the name of curry, which might startle many frugal minds."

Peel was in a quandary. He could not, in this crisis, suggest the removal of the sliding scale of duty and the substitution of a low fixed duty. Nothing but total and outright repeal would satisfy a population facing famine. Only three of Peel's cabinet, however, would support such a drastic proposal. Steadily the Prime Minister exercised strong efforts to win the others over, and it was just at this juncture, on December 4th, that the *Times* published its cataclysmic disclosure. "The decision of the Cabinet is no longer a secret," it said. "Parliament, it is confidently reported, is to be summoned for the first week in January; and the Royal Speech will recommend an immediate consideration of the Corn Laws, preparatory to their total repeal." Lord Aberdeen, Secretary for Foreign Affairs, had at a moment when the Cabinet seemed near agreement given the information to Delane, the editor of the *Times*. The irony was that even as the story appeared, Peel had become convinced that sufficient agreement was impossible, and the decision had been made to resign. Yet what was a mistaken announcement at the moment was eventually to prove true.

So on December 6th Peel resigned, and the Queen asked Russell to form a ministry. This was not quite what the noble leader of the Opposition had hoped for. He would much rather have placed upon the Conservatives the responsibility for introducing the repeal which he himself wanted, but which his party was by no means unanimous in favoring; for the great Whig landlords would oppose repeal to the bitter end. Moreover, the Whigs suffered under a House minority of 100, and therefore repeal under their leadership could have been attained only with Peel's support, a support which the retiring minister was shrewd enough not to promise. After a rather feeble attempt to form a ministry, Russell announced his inability to do so because Lord Grey would not hear of Palmerston's taking the Foreign Office, and Palmerston would accept no other portfolio. Thus, as Disraeli put it, Lord John "handed back with courtesy the poisoned chalice to Sir Robert." Peel went immediately to Windsor and told the Queen he would accept office. Before the year was out he had reconstituted his cabinet, Lord Stanley being the only one of the former ministers who refused to serve. Gladstone replaced him at the Colonial Office. Peel was happy. "I feel like a man coming back to life," he wrote. He did not suspect the political catastrophe which lay ahead.

While all this was happening in political circles at home, English affairs abroad were not very exciting. True, Sir Charles Napier had led an expedition against the mountain desert tribes to the north of Scinde, and had been pleased to report in his dispatch: "The moral effect of this expedition has been to spread a wholesome respect for our armies among the neighbouring nations. . . . The chiefs and their tribes who held out have been deservedly plundered by the troops which I had despatched in all directions to intercept their retreat with their baggage, cattle, and household furniture; almost everything has been taken, except what was in possession of their women and children, who have been in no way molested."

In the United States Mr. James K. Polk had been inaugurated as eleventh President. In his address he took notice of the adoption by Congress of joint resolutions for the annexation of Texas and, more important to the English, he described the current status of the discussions about the Oregon Territory. This boundary dispute had been the subject of prolonged negotiations between the two countries. England wanted to settle for the 49th parallel, but Polk, who had been elected on the slogan "fifty-four forty or fight," declared truculently that "our title to the country of the Oregon is clear and unquestionable, and already are our people preparing to perfect that title by occupying it with their wives and children." The *Times* declared that "Oregon will never be wrested from the British Crown, to which it belongs, but by war." Buchanan, whom Polk appointed as Secretary of State, took a milder tone, and the negotiations were reopened. But a suggested compromise failed, and by December diplomatic sparks were again flying back and forth across the Atlantic. Not until 1846 did the wisdom and good judgment of Aberdeen prevail, and threatened war was averted by an agreement which made the 49th parallel the boundary line on the mainland, but which reserved Vancouver Island for Britain and made the Columbia free for navigation to both countries.

The current nationalistic temper of at least a part of the United States could be judged by a set of resolutions adopted this summer in Philadelphia by the National Convention of Native Americans: "Believing that the greatest source of evil in this respect is to be found in the rapid influx of ignorant foreigners, and the facility with which they are converted into citizens, be it resolved that no foreigner hereafter coming to these United States shall be allowed to exercise the elective franchise, until he shall have been a resident here at least twenty-one years."

Also from abroad came the news of several devastating fires—one at Pittsburgh, Pennsylvania, which burned 1,200 houses and destroyed (so the report ran) "both the Monongahela Bridge and the University."

Another in New York leveled the Bowery Theatre (for the fourth time). And within a week of each other, two gigantic conflagrations swept over Quebec. The first of these wiped out one third of the city; the second, half of the city that remained.

At home, as winter disappeared into spring and spring into summer, the average Englishman (a faceless creature who keeps disappearing as one approaches him) was getting born, teething, being whipped at school, finding a profession or a job, getting married, rearing a family, and, if he was lucky, becoming eventually a slippered pantaloon. Sometimes, too, he was dying; and the spring of 1845 saw the death of two famous wits—one in poverty and in middle life, the other in the ripeness of years and position. Thomas Hood died at forty-six, after a long illness from tuberculosis, loved by all who knew him. "Of all humourists," said the obituaries, "he was the most poetical." He had poured himself out, in the punning fashion of the day, into "Whims and Oddities," "Comic Annuals," and at the last "Hood's Own" magazine. His jokes and poems had an edge, however: witness the immortal "Miss Kilmansegg." His humanity was deep and there was nothing of the charlatan about him. In 1845 he was still best remembered for the "Song of the Shirt," perhaps of all poems in the decade the one to make the deepest impact on the largest number of people. The pension of £100 which Peel granted him toward the end came too late to do him any good but was given to his widow, who herself died a year later.

The other death was that of Sydney Smith, in his seventy-seventh year, canon of St. Paul's and rector of Combe Florey, Somersetshire. Smith's long and distinguished career had included participation in the founding of the *Edinburgh Review* and the writing of many articles for that quarterly, on everything from prison discipline to Methodism to Irish bulls. He had been an extremely popular preacher and had been taken up by the fashionable world, where his wit and learning made him feared as well as admired. He was devastating in controversy and brilliant in conversation; his *bon mots* would have made a stock in trade for a dozen lesser humorists. Men were complimented to be made the butt of his remarks. Amiable, enjoying the good things of life, he was an inveterate diner-out in London society. Fanny Kemble knew him well, and tells in her *Records of Later Life* how, when being visited by some illustrious guests at his place in Somersetshire, he had a pair of horns fastened on his jackass in order, he said, to give the place a more noble and parklike appearance. It was Smith who, endeavoring to find an appropriate subject of conversation for the Archbishop of York, next to whom he was seated at dinner, asked: "Pray, my lord, how long do you think it took Nebuchadnezzar to get into condition again after his turn out at grass?"

The usual stream of books ran from the presses in 1845. Dickens had no major work in hand, and Thackeray, who had just finished in *Fraser's*, December last, his brilliant tour de force *Barry Lyndon*, was scribbling the memoirs of Jeames de la Pluche for *Punch*. Carlyle gave birth to his sizable *Cromwell's Letters and Speeches, with Elucidations*, which won respectful attention from the reviewers. Browning had published No. 7 of his *Bells and Pomegranates, Dramatic Romances and Lyrics*. One of the poetical events of the year was the revised and amplified edition of Philip James Bailey's *Festus*—first published six years earlier when the author was only twenty-three. The original 10,000 lines had grown and were to grow still more until they reached a super-epic length of some 40,000. Bailey called it "a summary of the world's combined moral and physical conditions, estimated on a theory of spiritual things." Structurally it consisted of twelve books of "twelve or more groups, celestial, astral, interstellar, and terrestrial, solar, planetary and one other, the sphere of the Infernals." All this was presented in fifty-two "scenes." It began:

> Parent of spheres, who filling once all space,
> God bidding, threwest off all cloaking clouds,
> To thee intolerable, of nebulous heat,
> The planetary fires; which, gathered there
> In narrowing circlets, imminent o'er the void, etc.

The surprising thing is the great vogue which this clumsy, inflated philosophical dissertation enjoyed. It was, of course, highly moral, and its sheer bulk must have awed contemporary readers, surprised that from one small brain such things could flow. In his *Spirit of the Age* (1844), a series of chapters by several hands on contemporary authors, R. H. Horne praised *Festus* as having "the passion of true poetry," and abounding in fine passages.*

Disraeli's *Sybil, or The Two Nations* was, however, the great publishing success of 1845; the novel went through three editions within the year. In general it met with a more tepid critical reception than

---

* Horne had published his own epic *Orion* in 1843. He insisted that it be sold at one farthing and stipulated that no copy should be sold to any person who pronounced it "Orion." Edgar Allan Poe wrote that "in all that regards the loftiest and holiest attributes of the true Poetry, *Orion* has never been excelled."

Coningsby. It lacked the personal hits which had helped the earlier book. Moreover its social analysis of the poor versus the rich in the turbulent days following Victoria's accession was used to fill the interstices of a conventionally romantic story dealing with an estate kept wrongfully from its true owners, with missing papers, and other such Minerva Press paraphernalia—"a transcript," as one reviewer said, "of blue-book incident and adventure." "Philosophical Young England," said another, "can imagine only two modes of amalgamating the Two Nations—killing off the poor, or making them rich." Yet Disraeli's scenes of fashionable life were good, with less of the yeasty rhetoric which marred his earlier volumes. His social conscience remained keen if somewhat paradoxical.

On February 7th, just as the British Museum was being closed, a man calling himself William Lloyd seized a piece of granite from one of the cases and smashed into a thousand fragments the famous Portland Vase, a distinguished specimen of Greek art found near Rome and deposited in the Museum in 1810 by the Duke of Portland. There seemed to be no motive for the vandalism beyond an alleged delirium "arising from intemperance." Under a strange provision of the law at the time Lloyd could not be prosecuted for destroying the vase; the Wilful Damage Act covered only property under the value of £5! The result was that he was fined £3, the value of the case within which the vase stood. Someone paid his fine, and he was released after a few hours' imprisonment.

The London season came on, and with it a great deal of activity. Barry's new fountains began to play in much-maligned Trafalgar Square, the waterspouts reaching a height of forty feet. The fountains were only useful, declared Colonel Sibthorp, as a receptacle for dead dogs and cats. . . . The enlightened management of Phelps and Mrs. Warner continued to present Shakespeare in excellent taste at Sadler's Wells. Macready, back from America after three years, opened with *Hamlet* to great crowds at the Princess Theatre—replacing Charlotte Cushman and Edwin Forrest, from the United States, who had been playing *Macbeth*. Forrest was hissed as well as applauded, but Miss Cushman was a complete success. She was praised particularly for her "terrible energy" in the part of Lady Macbeth. The Adelphi combined melodrama and the farce of *Mrs. Caudle at Home and Abroad*. The Lyceum devoted itself to a burlesque of *The Forty Thieves*, and the Haymarket presented farces interlarded with John Barry's comic songs.

Vauxhall, perennially on the verge of being closed out, came back with a new lease on life. Once again its myriads of lamps and its blaze of fireworks delighted the public. The Hermit still sat, a little seedy, in his cell, and Neptune rode triumphant in his car. The refreshments, it was reported, were no longer diaphanous. . . . The Colosseum, closed for many months, was reopened with new model scenery of Mont Blanc and an entirely new glyptotheca, or museum of sculpture. The Ascending Room still raised spectators to the upper level to view the Grand Picture of London and the new Panorama of London by Night—the latter of which held young and old enthralled with its fleecy clouds sailing steadily along, the reflection of the bridge lights on the Thames, the brilliancy of the shops in Cheapside and Ludgate Hill, the colored lights of the chemists' shops, and the flaring naked gaslights in the open stalls and markets.

The new Hungerford Suspension Bridge was opened with flags flying and guns firing, and before dusk, on that May 1st, 25,000 persons had crossed it. . . . The next day, at Yarmouth, more than 100 lives were lost when the suspension bridge there collapsed, overcrowded chiefly with children gathered to watch a clown from Cooke's Equestrian Circus imitate Barry's feat of crossing the river in a tub drawn by four geese. . . . The Queen and Albert opened to public view the series of frescoes painted by British artists in adornment of the Garden Pavilion at Buckingham Palace—a sort of test run for the proposed frescoes for the Houses of Parliament. The subject, treated by Stanfield, Eastlake, Maclise, Landseer, and others, was Milton's *Comus*. There was agreement that English artists, unused to fresco, had much to learn about the medium. . . . Sir John Franklin left for the Arctic in H.M.S. *Erebus* and *Terror* to "penetrate the icy fastnesses of the North, and to circumnavigate America." Disaster and death lay ahead of him.

At the new port of Birkenhead, rapidly growing into a great town, a revolutionary experiment in town planning was developing under the benevolent leadership of the Birkenhead Dock Company. The area was being laid out with well-arranged streets, public grounds, and even with a complete system of drainage. The dwellings for the workpeople were a series of "flats" rather than cottages, each with a living room, two bedrooms, and its own yard. Ventilation was carefully planned, as was also a plentiful supply of water. Gas was led in for light. Everything was fireproof. Yet with all this it was expected that the landlord would receive a return of 8 or 10 per cent on his investment.

Thomas Carlyle wrote to the *Times* in angry opposition to the post-office opening of Mazzini's letters. "He is a man," said Carlyle, "of genius and virtue, a man of sterling veracity, humanity, and nobleness of mind. . . . Whether the extraneous Austrian Emperor and miserable old chimera of a Pope shall maintain themselves in Italy, or be obliged to decamp from Italy, is not a question in the least vital to Englishmen. But it is a question vital to us that sealed letters in an English post office be, as we all fancied they were, respected as things sacred. . . ." The Carlyles had known Mazzini for some nine years—ever since he had first come as a political exile to England, to direct from there the network of intrigues through which he hoped to free his beloved Italy from the Austrian tyrant. He was in London in 1845, and came frequently to Cheyne Row for tea or dinner. Once this autumn, during a tempestuous September storm, Jane found him standing meekly on the doorstep with water oozing out of his doeskin boots "in a manner frightful to behold." Certainly no man to be afraid of! But Mazzini burned with a pure revolutionary flame, idealistic, high-minded, sensitive—living only for the unification of Italy under a republican government. Everyone who knew him felt his charm; even his vaguest flights of philosophizing were always tempered with a kind of playfulness. And the English in 1845 were more indignant about the possible existence of a police-spy system than they were fearful of foreign revolutionaries.

One Edward Riley, a worker in a dust yard in Maiden Lane, London, came unexpectedly into a fortune of £50,000. His first act was to have a tailor and a bootmaker measure his fellow dustmen for suits and shoes. He next supplied each of them with a joint of meat for his Sunday dinner, and said that he planned to give a dinner to all the dustmen in London, illuminating the front of his house for the occasion.

These were the curiosa of England in the summer of 1845, the subjects of conversation in home and shop. But your shopkeeper, if he had any kind of reserve capital (and even if he hadn't), was likely to be much more interested during these months, and to be sharing, in the growing hysteria which was seizing everyone from clerk to clergy: the great railway boom!

No part of the industrial revolution was more dramatically real than the engines and coaches which were rushing at a terrifying yet exhilarating speed up and down the miles of iron rails which laced the country. Almost overnight, it seemed, the old English road had disappeared. Sir Archibald Alison described with a good deal of nostalgia the last posting journey he made from London to his home in Glasgow before the railroads took over. He traveled in his own carriage with post horses, going only eighty miles a day, and taking five days for the journey. "On the

Figure 60. Viaduct on the Sheffield and Manchester Railway, with arches 136 feet high

road you never went less than nine miles an hour. When the horses drove up to the inn-door, the next pair walked out of the stable-yard with the post-boy already seated. . . . The inns were on a level with these luxuries of locomotion. Nothing could exceed their cleanness, elegance, and comfort. . . . A cheerful fire, reflected from nicely papered walls, luxurious sofas, easy-chairs, and shining mahogany furniture, awaited you at the moment of your arrival."[2] The cost of posting down in this style for a gentleman and lady, with their servant and a maid, from London to Edinburgh, was about £45. Now all this elegance and comfort were vanishing before the snorting iron horse, belching cinders and black clouds of smoke as he rushed over viaducts, through tunnels, and between angry gashes in the hills. Soon the old days of the road would belong only to Dickens and the Christmas post card. In 1844 Dover and London were at last connected by rail, and in July, 1845, a railway was opened all the way from London to Cambridge and Ely. Plans were being made for a railway tunnel under London from Paddington to the City. Because of the railroads, only five of what had once been twenty-eight Royal Mail coaches now left the Central Post Office every evening. The old glory was departed.

Yet surprisingly few people were rueful about the change. There were of course die-hards other than William Wordsworth. In spite of the stupendous prices paid for rights of way, some landowners stubbornly refused to let iron monsters desecrate their fields. Skirmishes occurred between surveyors and the shock troops of the regimented tenantry. The Tory *John Bull* had written earlier:

> Does anybody mean to say that decent people, passengers who would use their own carriages . . . would consent to be hurried along through the air upon a railroad . . . ; or is it to be imagined that women . . . would endure the fatigue, and misery, and danger, not only to themselves, but their children and families, of being dragged through the air at the rate of twenty miles an hour, all their lives being at the mercy of a tin pipe, or a copper boiler, or the accidental dropping of a pebble on the line of way? We denounce the mania as destructive of the country in a thousand particulars—the whole face of the kingdom is to be tattooed with these odious deformities—huge mounds are to intersect our beautiful valleys; the noise and stench of locomotive steam-engines are to disturb the quietude of the peasant, the farmer and the gentleman; and the roaring of bullocks, the bleating of sheep and the grunting of pigs to keep up one continual uproar through the night along the lines of these most dangerous and disfiguring abominations. . . .

John Bull's double in Parliament, Colonel Sibthorp, set his face against all railways, calling them "public frauds and private robberies," and stating his belief that "the displacement of traffic, disturbance of business, and destruction of employment, which they had produced, had materially increased the distress of the country." He hated, he said, "the very name of a railway—he hated it as he hated the devil."

The country was warned that the smoke would kill the birds and that the noise would make the terrified cows go dry; that foxes and pheasants would be exterminated; that vegetation would be destroyed; that elderly gentlemen would be run over and horses slaughtered; that noxious fumes would smother passengers to death in the tunnels. Eton masters, fearful that the railway would destroy the discipline of the school, proposed to screen the Great Western for four miles with walls ten feet high. Dr. Routh, president of Magdalen College, Oxford, was so opposed to railways that he declined to take any official cognizance of their existence. And Ruskin wrote: "The whole system of railroad travelling is addressed to people who, being in a hurry, are therefore, for the time being, miserable. No one would travel in that manner who could help it—who had time to go leisurely over hills and between hedges, instead of through tunnels and between banks. . . . It transmutes a man from a traveller into a living parcel. . . . Keep them [the railways] out of the way, take them through the ugliest country you can find, and spend nothing upon them but for safety and speed."[3]

But in 1840 the Great Western Railway had fitted up for Victoria and Albert a splendid carriage twenty-one feet long, divided into three compartments, the saloon "handsomely arranged with hanging sofas of carved wood in the rich style of Louis XIV . . . the walls fitted up with rich crimson and white silk and exquisitely executed paintings." Not until 1842 did the Queen venture her first trip, with Mr. Brunel himself driving the engine from Slough to London. Then she said: "I am quite charmed with it," and the royal accolade was given.

The question of safety was by no means an academic one in the decade. He who entrained lived dangerously, with fifteen times as many chances of cracking up somewhere along the way as did a traveler on the German railways, for example. In 1841 there were twenty-nine accidents for which the railroads themselves could be held responsible through collision or running off the track, resulting in twenty-four deaths and seventy-one cases of injury. During the last *half year* of 1851, with roughly four times as many miles of track, the ratio had been reduced; in thirty-six accidents, thirty-eight were killed from causes beyond their own control, and 230 injured. But in this year 1845 there were seventeen accidents, of all kinds, on nine railways within a single week in August, resulting in a few fatalities and many injuries. The week before there had been nine, and the week following there were eight. *Punch* suggested a new invention to be called "The Railway Pocket Companion, containing a small bottle of water, a tumbler, a complete set of surgical instruments, a packet of lint, and directions for making a will." The sense of danger was increased by the fact that once the carriage was closed and the train under way there was no possibility of communication either between carriage and carriage or carriage and locomotive. One Mr. J. C. Roberts was somewhat ahead of his time when he invented an electromagnetic emergency signal by means of which a wire, passing through all the carriages to the engine, with a switch in each carriage, acted on the steam whistle.[4]

Speeds had been stepped up in the meantime. In 1840 it took five and a half hours to travel from London to Birmingham by the fastest train, a distance of 112 miles, with five intermediate stops—an average of twenty miles an hour. By 1843 the average express speed was 26.1 miles per hour, and by 1848, 37.2 miles per hour, with the London and South-Western Express making 44.5 miles per hour. In this same year, as a stunt, the "Courier" locomotive on the Great Western traveled a distance of fifty-three miles at a rate of sixty-seven miles per hour.

The early traveler gained speed, however, at the expense of comfort. First-class carriages had antimacassars, comfortable cushions, and foot warmers in cold weather, but no lamps for night journeys. The seats

Figure 61. London and Northwestern Railway Station, Euston Square

of the second-class carriages were severely hard boards, while third-class passengers (until 1844) rode, often without seats, in open box cars, entirely exposed to wind and rain. Yet it must be remembered that travel by horse coach was not all idyllic. The advantages of the new mode of travel were pointed out by F. S. Williams:

> There is now no hazard, as there was then, of being informed that there is "no room"—there are no importunities from extortionate guards to satisfy—no clambering over dirty wheels—no hurting one's shins on sharp irons—no wedging of one's-self amidst piles of luggage on a lofty unsheltered platform, around which numerous legs hung dangling like a dozen brace of black and white grouse; while, if it rains, it is not necessary for one's own comfort that the drip of our umbrella should be turned into a neighbour's neck. And it is at the same time a pleasant thought to many that while the train bowls along over the iron road, there is no plying of the whip, no foaming mouths, nor turgid veins of generous steeds; but that the giant power which thus swiftly bears us onwards has bones of brass and iron, and nerves and muscles that cannot tire.[5]

In design and equipment the first-class carriages resembled for some time a gentleman's horse carriage transposed to rails. It was the custom, too, for the gentry and nobility to bring their own coaches on board flatcars, and thus to ride in the comfort and solitary grandeur to which they had been accustomed on the road.

The gloomy prognostications of the railway haters became little more than an obbligato to the great symphony of steam and speed. Though many people lived and died within sound of the passing trains without ever being carried by them into the next county, thousands who had never known real travel began to discover their own country. The great railway engineers such as George Stephenson (connected with thirty-four lines) and Sir I. Brunel (connected with fourteen) were romantic heroes in a new aristocracy. The opening of a new line was an occasion of public holiday, with celebrations, dinners, and speeches. When the Grand Junction Railway was opened to public travel, people assembled in vast multitudes along the whole line (ninety-seven miles), and "the different stations, for some days, had all the appearance of so many country fairs." Railway stations began to dot the countryside, replacing the old coaching inns, which went into a decline. London in 1844 had ten railway termini and seven stations.* The Blackwall Railway between the Minories and Brunswick Wharf at Blackwall, three and a half miles long, was carried over London most of the way on an arched viaduct of brickwork. The carriages were drawn on an endless rope, with two engines at each end of the line. The Euston Station for the Birmingham Railway (or London and North Western, as it became after 1844) was perhaps the most splendid, with its massive Doric entrance, its columns eight feet six inches in diameter and seventy feet high, its elaborate booking offices, its lofty and highly decorated great hall with a circular refreshment table in the center. Others, such as the Paddington Station of 1845, had the dignified beauty of a series of simple arches. In the provinces an excess of bad taste too often led the early Victorians to ignore the clean, functional beauty of the railways themselves, with their cuttings, their bridges and viaducts so simply and beautifully proportioned, and to perpetrate stations in the Sir Walter Scott manner, or in Anglicized Italianate. "Gothic" enginehouses sprang up, and castellated signal towers.

To sense something of the multiple thrills enjoyed by the Englishman traveling by train in the forties, one need only accompany him vicariously in one of the contemporary guidebooks.† Thus, for example, *The Great Western, Bristol and Exeter Railway Guides, containing a topographical, antiquarian, and geological account of the country, and of the towns and villages in the neighborhood of the railways; with a*

---

* The railways: Birmingham, Eastern Counties, Blackwall, Greenwich, Dover, Croydon, Brighton, South Western, Great Western, and West London.
† Bradshaw published his first timetable in 1839 and his first *Monthly Railway Guide* in 1841. Thomas Cook ran his first advertised excursion train in 1841.

Figure 62. Croydon's "Gothic" engine house

preliminary description of the construction of the Great Western and other railways, illustrated with numerous and accurate engravings on wood. It was assumed, properly enough, that the neophyte in railway travel did not know his England, and that he would be interested, mile by mile, in the breweries he passed, in the country halls and estates (with thumbnail descriptions of their owners), and in the villages (with complete history of the village churches).

The 1844 edition of *Osborne's Guide to Grand Junction, or Birmingham, Liverpool and Manchester Railway*, is a typical product of the day. It begins with a long history of "the rise and progress of railways," with many diagrams showing the construction of the malleable-iron rails, the laying of track, the signal apparatus, couplings, brakes (spelled "breaks" at the time), engines, boilers, etc. Then a history of the Grand Junction Railway itself. Then "Regulations": both first- and second-class coaches have seats on the roof for the accommodation of those who prefer riding outside. No smoking in any of the coaches. And then the trip begins.

Having taken your place, and made all ready, you are now at ease to observe what is going on, provided there be time. The scene is one which cannot fail to be interesting. I shall suppose you mounted on the box seat. You look round, and see several engines with red-hot fires in their bodies, and volumes of steam issuing from their tall chimneys. One of them moves slowly toward you. The huge creature bellows, at first, like an elephant. Deep, slow, and terrific are the hoarse heavings that it makes. It passes by your train of carriages, and going to the head of them, slips from one line to the other, and backing to the train, is fastened to it. There it is, roaring, groaning, and grunting, like a sea-horse, and spouting up steam like a whale. You feel a deep, strong, tremulous motion throughout the train, and a loud jingling rattle is heard, analogous to what is experienced in a cotton mill. . . . The guard is in his box at the back of the first carriage; a bell is rung as a signal for starting, and you are off.

As we get under way our guide gives us innocently a horrific glimpse into the future, when "Orators, Lecturers, and Missionaries will be multiplied, and will travel the length and breadth of the land in the same time that they used to go from one town to another." Less terrifyingly, "Villages and small towns will gradually exchange their dialect for the national tongue, by the increased frequency of communion with other places and persons."

Farther along, the *Guide* identifies residences and statues and describes all the viaducts, cuttings, and grades. It points out "Aston Hall, the property of Keeling Greenway, Esq., of Warwick," and immortalizes its owner by declaring that he "expended about £2,000 in opposing, and preventing, the line passing through his park." It gives the net incomes of the various curacies. It describes the factories and coalpits of Staffordshire, with elucidation of the lives, wages, and intemperate habits of the miners.

We pass Bilston (pop. *ca.* 15,000):

The whole district round about here is a mass of apparent disorganization, confusion and ruin. By day we see nothing but the remains of the disembowelling of the earth; heaps of stones, clay, coal, cinders, and ashes, as if a volcano had burst out and covered the country with its lava; furnaces, chimneys, forges, and iron works, beds of burning coal, coal pits with their engines and apparatus, and waggons conveying loads of stone and coal in every direction, attended by men, women, and boys, dressed as if they were accustomed to live in the earth. The whole is constantly enveloped in the gloom of one perpetual cloud of smoke, which bedims and darkens the country for miles around.

By night the country is lit up by fires. On all sides, the blazes of the furnaces, forges, coal pits, coke beds, and lime kilns, are seen terrifically glaring through the awful darkness. The rushing and roaring of the

Figure 63. "The Excursion Train Galop"

blasts of the furnaces, the clankings and crashings of the steam engines
. . . the rattling and rumbling of the rolling mills . . . give the stranger
the most fearful and awful notions of the place. From a hill near the
town, toward Sedgley, at night, nearly *200 blast furnaces* . . . may be
seen. . . .

We pass Wolverhampton. At its Free Grammar School was educated
"the celebrated Dr. Abernathy, the great founder of the indigestion system in medicine." And so alternating between descriptions of fine parks
and shabby mining towns we reach Birmingham.

Thus the railway traveler in the middle of the decade explored his England, conscious that all around him still other lines were feeling their way across the countryside—some shooting out to end nowhere, others completing articulations with existent roads. All at an enormous outlay of capital. In England and Wales the railways were capitalized at an average of £64,453 per mile.* The preliminary expenses in each case —getting the bills through Parliament, paying surveyors, paying barristers in the struggle with canal owners and others interested in preventing the railways from being authorized or extended—were £4,000 per mile. The cost of the right of way usually ran from £3,000 to £6,500 per mile; in the case of the London and Brighton Railway (opened in 1841) it ran to £8,000, and with three other lines to £14,000.

Nevertheless, authorized and extended they were, amid the greatest national furor since the South Sea Bubble. In 1841 the country had some 1,600 miles of railway. By 1845 the figure was 2,400; and by the end of 1851, 6,890. To the sixty-six steam railways and branches in operation in Great Britain in 1840 had been added, according to Bradshaw, eighty-two more by 1848. In the meantime, however, there were many amalgamations which reduced the total number. In 1843 seventy railroads had conveyed 25,000,000 passengers; in the *last half* of 1851 the railroads carried 47,500,000 passengers.

This phenomenal growth, however, hints only dimly at the frenzy of speculation in mid-decade. The railroads sanctioned by Parliament were as follows:

Year	No. sanctioned	Miles	Capitalization
1844	26	797	£11,121,000
1845	120	2,883	43,800,000
1846	270	4,538	132,000,000
1847	184	1,354	38,000,000

Of this total of 9,572 miles, 1,560 were abandoned by consent of Parliament in 1850.

The story of those lines proposed in addition to the above, but not sanctioned, takes us to the heart of the "railway mania" of 1845, when gambling in shares became the pursuit of everyone from lord to lackey.

In January sixteen new lines were registered with the Board of Trade for submission to Parliamentary committees. By April, fifty-two more companies had been added to the total, and the craze was reaching

---

* In the United States at the same time the cost per mile was the equivalent of £13,000. It is true that the English road was better laid.

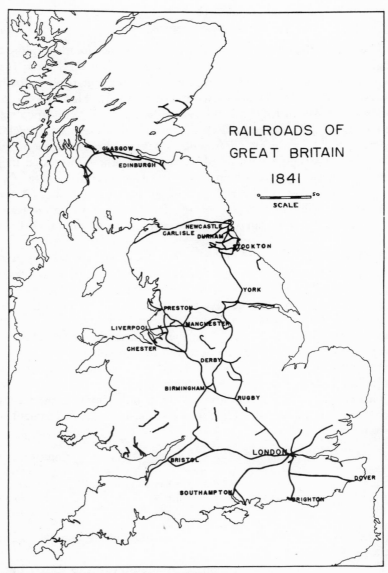

Figure 64. Map: Railroads of Great Britain, 1841

fever height. Everyone wanted to get in on the huge profits which were dangled before the noses of prospective subscribers. The writers of prospectuses composed prose epics of the glories which Christendom would know under the reign of rail—particularly if the shares to the West Diddlesex Junction of five and a half miles were subscribed promptly. Forgotten hamlets saw their commercial future ruined if they

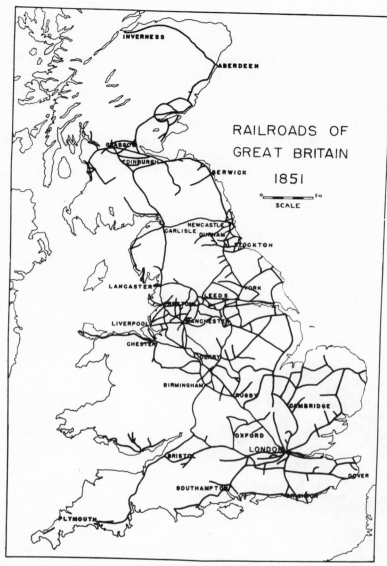

Figure 65. Map: Railroads of Great Britain, 1851

did not share in the new lines of communication. All sorts of parallel and competing lines were registered, as well as lines beginning nowhere and ending in a cattle track. Money was abundant, interest rates were low, and the most exalted and exemplary citizens were being listed as directors of the proposed welter of lines. Investment soon pyramided into speculation; shares were bought and sold for the rapidly increasing premium they commanded. When Parliament called for a return to show the number of persons who had subscribed more than £2,000 to railway ventures, the published list included bishops and barkeeps, butchers and bankers, vicars and coachmen, footmen and peers. Servants wrote for shares in their masters' names; Jeames became independently wealthy on his paper profits.

Sensible men knew that it could not last, but they forgot their good sense and scrambled for scrip. Before 1845 there had been three papers devoted solely to railway news. By the end of the year some thirty such papers, daily and weekly, were on sale, swollen with railway advertisements: Railway Expresses, Railway Globes, Railway Examiners, Railway Mails, Railway Reviews. The other journals shared in the increment; on November 29, 1845, the *Gazette* put out 225 pages, on December 15th, 583 pages. The *Times*, while editorially warning its readers against the mania, received for advertisements, in the one week ending October 18, £6,687. The *Iron Times* collected as much as two shillings a line for its insertions. "Lines which passed by barren districts and by waste heaths, the termini of which were uninhabitable places, reached a high

Figure 66. John Leech: "The Railway Juggernaut of 1845"

premium."[7] The Welsh Midland announced in its prospectus 160 provisional committeemen.

In September 457 new schemes for railways were registered. The climax came on November 30th, the last day for new proposals to be submitted for presentation to Parliament the following year. It fell on a Sunday, and up until the last minute draftsmen and printers worked day and night preparing the plans. One drafting committee imported 400 lithographers from Belgium and still failed to complete all its plans. The Eastern Counties Railway ran eighteen or twenty special trains; engines were kept with steam up to bring in the last-minute proposals of the projectors. By eleven o'clock at night at the Board of Trade offices the clerks were unable to keep up with the arrivals. The entrance hall became packed. Just after the doors were closed at twelve a post chaise drove up with reeking horses to the entrance, three men alighted and rushed down the passage with armfuls of huge plans. When the attendant opened the door to tell them it was too late, they took advantage of the moment to throw in all their papers, breaking the passage light in the process. The plans were thrown back at them into the street.

When the shouting of that November night had died away and the captains and railway kings had departed, it was discovered that 800 projected railways were in the hands of Parliament, seeking a capital of £258,009,000*—which was just about the amount of the annual national income! The promoters of 514 schemes which could not make the deadline declared that they would submit their proposals to Parliament in 1846.

This was the mania of 1845, satirized by *Punch* in story and cartoon, and lamented by responsible observers.

At the center of the whole railway boom and idolized by its devotees was a former linen draper from York: George Hudson, "the Railway King." Having inherited some property as a young man, he turned to politics, and in 1833 became treasurer of a York Railway Committee to promote a line between Leeds and Selby. When, three years later, the line between York, Leeds, and London was established, Hudson was made chairman of the board. A year later he was elected Lord Mayor of York, and he was on his way. "Mak all t'railways cum t'York" was the locally impregnable thesis with which he started operations.

Success seemed to attend everything he touched, and rapidly his

---

* So reported authoritatively by the Railway Commissioners in 1847. The *Times*, carried away in spite of itself, had reported 1,428 companies, and a capital of £701,243,208.

empire grew. Francis at the time summarized his career in the days of the expanding railway universe:

> In little more than ten years . . . it may be seen that Mr. Hudson had originated the York and North Midland; that he had proved his opinion by the shares he subscribed . . . that he was the author of an Eastern route to Edinburgh; that he carried out a reform in one railway at a saving of 20 per cent; that he joined the capital of three undertakings, and effected an enormous saving; that he bought half one railway and subscribed 2,000 shares to forward another to Scotland; that he largely increased the dividends of the Midland proprietary; that he aided in purchasing the York and Darlington; that he leased the Hull and Selby; that he bought a grand estate which was then esteemed necessary to the welfare of the shareholders; that he never raised his voice against competition; and that his name, moreover, was never connected with a company not meant to be carried out. His influence extended seventy-six miles over the York and North Midland; fifty-one miles over the Hull and Selby and Leeds and Selby; over the North Midland, Midland Counties, and another, one hundred and seventy-eight miles; over the Newcastle and Darlington, and the Great North of England, one hundred and eleven miles; while over . . . [others] it affected nearly six hundred more, making a total of 1,016 miles, all of which were successful in developing traffic, and equally successful in paying good dividends.[8]

To success like this every shareholder's knee must bow, and when Hudson gained a seat in Parliament at an exciting by-election in 1845 and subsequently moved to London, he became socially the lion which he had been professionally. Amid a storm of adulation made concrete by a public testimonial which reached the sum of £30,000 in three months, he bought Albert House (where the Albert Gate gave into Hyde Park) for £15,000 and furnished and decorated it for £14,000.[9]

By 1845 this rough, burly, short-necked, arrogant, thick-spoken Yorkshireman was not only a millionaire, but was also, in the manipulation of his vast holdings, the symbol of the success which could come to those willing to gamble in railways. Dukes and Members of Parliament hung on his every word. The Marquis of Northampton gave a reception open to Fellows of the Royal Society, and Prince Albert came to be introduced to the Napoleon of the Railways. Wrote a contemporary: "England's greatest authors, greatest sculptors, greatest painters, greatest inventors, greatest philanthropists, greatest statesmen, greatest physicians, greatest engineers, greatest captains, jostled each other in the crowded rooms." Wellington sought his advice. "When he rose in wrath, boards of directors were scattered before him; when he spoke in anger, shareholders denied their own proposals." Hudson was King.

Figure 67. George Hudson, "the man wot knows how to get up the steam," by HB

In all this morass of worship it went unnoticed that Hudson had achieved no small part of his success by a very simple device: that of paying dividends out of capital. According to extant laws, no professional auditing was required. If shareholders wanted to conduct their own audits they were at liberty to do so—but none of Hudson's awed colleagues made a move in that direction as yet, being more than happy with the fat dividends which kept rolling in. The day of reckoning would come, but for the moment it was roses, roses all the way.

One of the titillating experiments of 1845 was the Atmospheric Railway, which came in for a great deal of both favorable and antagonistic comment. One such railway had been opened between Dalkey and Killiney, in the vicinity of Dublin, in 1844, and another was built on a line between Croydon and London in the current year. The principle was that of exhausting the air in a continuous tube between the tracks, to which the carriage was connected and by means of which vacuum it was carried along. It seemed to work for a time, and had great advantages of smoothness and safety. But it proved expensive, and it was difficult to maintain the vacuum. All sorts of valves were tried—leather, water, copper, none of them practically successful, and the attempt was abandoned after a short time. Another similar device—atmospheric pressure this time—was tried on the South Devon line in 1848. This also failed.

Amid all the speculating, railways were getting built and were changing the face of England. President Tyler earlier in the year had said of the telegraph: "Space and time are annihilated," and to a somewhat lesser extent people felt that way about railways. It was not merely that tourists were now able to visit easily and quickly the more scenic portions of their own country or that tired shopkeepers could flee easily to Brighton for the week end. Distant suburbia was brought closer to the cities and large towns. The regrouping of population made necessary by the growth of new industrial centers was accelerated. Letters which had earlier taken days on the road now arrived overnight. London got cheaper coal and fresher food. Above all in importance was the fluidity of transportation needed to support the economy of a nation rapidly becoming in fact the workshop of the world. And best of all, this new hope of abundance and prosperity brought its own romance with it, an exalted conception of a world in which British industriousness combined with "Steam's triumphal car" would supply the markets while "Peace and Improvement" shed a civilizing light over all. Thus sang the popular poet Dr. Charles Mackay:

No poetry in Railways! foolish thought
Of a dull brain, to no fine music wrought,
By Mammon dazzled, though the people prize
The gold untold, yet shall not we despise
The triumphs of our time, or fail to see
Of pregnant mind, the fruitful progeny
Ushering the daylight of the world's new morn.

. . . .

Blessings on Science, and her handmaid Steam!
They make Utopia only half a dream;
And show the fervent, of capacious souls,
Who watch the ball of Progress as it rolls,

That all as yet completed, or begun,
Is but the dawning that precedes the sun.

But England was a small island. The seas were wide. More than locomotives were needed, and in these years the steamship also was becoming
more and more important to the national economy. The problems here
were more difficult, and sails were to be the staple of the merchant fleet
for many years. Not until the latter part of the century was steam to
come into general use at sea. In 1858 the ratio of sail to steam was still
about forty-five to one.

The first transatlantic crossings by steam had been achieved in 1819
by the *Savannah*, an American packet of 320 tons, using an auxiliary
ninety-horsepower engine. (All through the decade of the forties steamships carried sail, both for added speed and for not-infrequent emergency.) By 1838 England had the *Great Western* and a year later her
rival the *British Queen*. These were wooden ships, the *Great Western*
of 1,320 gross tons and a length of 235 feet. With her 400-horsepower
engine she could travel at a rate of nine knots; her voyages averaged
fifteen days from Liverpool to New York and thirteen days homeward.
In 1838, too, came the first Atlantic crossings of the *Sirius*, the *Royal
William*, and the *Liverpool*, the latter a ship of 1,050 tons, capable of
carrying fifty saloon passengers and 150 tons of cargo. In this year the
Cunard Line was formed by Samuel Cunard, a Halifax Quaker who got
the Government steam mail contract and began immediately to build
four Cunarders.

The ill-fated *President*, a big ship for her day (2,366 tons), made her
first voyage to New York in 1840, the same year as the *Britannia*, in
which Charles Dickens was to travel two years later—a ship of 1,156
gross tons, a speed of eight and one half knots, and accommodation for
115 cabin passengers. Competing transatlantic fares on all these paddle-
wheel ships averaged £30 by mid-decade. Even first-class accommodations were rugged, by present-day standards. Second-class passengers
lived in a single compartment with two tiers of wooden berths all the
way around it—with no provision for division of the sexes. On the emigrant ships the passenger in the early forties had to supply his own food
and cooking utensils. Cooking was done on deck. Chickens were kept
on deck in coops, and "a special deckhouse with padded sides was provided for accommodation of the ship's cow, whose milk was reserved for
ladies, children, and invalids."[10]

Much attention was drawn during this year 1845 to the *Great Britain*
of Bristol, designed by Sir I. Brunel, the builder of the Great Western
Railway. Its plan incorporated several distinct innovations. It was an

Figure 68. The *Great Western* steamship
British Crown Copyright. Science Museum, London.

Figure 69. The *Great Britain* steamship
British Crown Copyright. Science Museum, London.

iron ship of 2,984 tons' displacement and was driven by the new screw propeller at a speed of twelve knots. The screw had six arms, each about seven feet long, and was connected to a propeller shaft geared by chains to low-pressure engines. She was 322 feet long, had six masts, and was equipped with five watertight bulkheads, then a novelty. Completed in 1843, her gigantic bulk prevented her being brought to London until her Bristol locks had been widened. On Saturday, January 25th, she anchored off Blackwell, having made her journey steadily and successfully through heavy seas. The screw, it was proved, did not suffer, as did paddle wheels in stormy weather, by being lifted out of the water. Thousands of people, including Her Majesty, visited this "interesting monster." Particular attention was drawn to the vast saloon, where 300 people could dine at long tables running the length of the apartment. The *Great Britain* left for Liverpool on June 12th, whence, on July 26th, she started her first trip across the Atlantic with sixty passengers and more than 800 tons of cargo. She steamed well, and reached New York in fourteen days, twenty-one hours.

Every mile of rail and every horsepower of steam was underlining for the awed Englishman in these years an optimistic belief in Progress. The revolution in production and distribution, the ability to supply across the world new markets made necessary by increased production at home—all this was interpreted as a moral and esthetic as well as a commercial accomplishment. The phrase "live steam" was the symbol of the new age in more ways than one.

Other conquests of nature were being made in the forties. Some of them were laughed at, but incredulity was tempered with a fascinated expectation. Who could tell what wonders the next year might bring?

The idea of human flight was as ancient as Icarus, and balloons had been a scientifically amusing stunt ever since the eighteenth century, as well as a perennial attraction at Vauxhall and Cremorne Gardens. Others had more recently investigated the problems of mechanical flight. Sir George Cayley, in 1810, had asserted that air flight "with a velocity of from 20 to 100 miles per hour" was within the realms of possibility, basing his statement on his own careful calculations concerning "aerial navigation." In 1843 Mr. Monck Mason proposed to propel balloons by the Archimedean screw. He constructed a large egg-shaped balloon under which he suspended an oblong car. At the end of an iron axle he placed a screw propeller. With a model which he constructed (and that was as far as he got) the screw was set in motion by clockwork, and actually propelled the balloon around the room.* In the same year Mr. William Henson burst upon a startled world with his proposal for an "aerial steam carriage," a contraption in which a car was attached to a huge rectangular wing with an area of 4,500 square feet covered with oiled silk or canvas, and with a rudder like the tail of a bird to make the machine ascend or descend. In point of fact it was in many respects not unlike the early monoplanes of more than sixty years later. He proposed to start his machine by running it down the side of a hill, after which it was to be maintained in flight by a steam engine of twenty-five to thirty horsepower driving two propellers.

This again did not get beyond the model stage, although in 1848, after Henson had retired and turned the work over to a collaborator, John Stringfellow, a revised version succeeded in accomplishing, with a small steam engine, the first power-driven model flight in history. In 1843 he tried to form the "Aerial Transit Company," which was provisionally approved amid raucous laughter by the House of Commons, but which through lack of funds never really got organized. The announcement of Henson's "Ariel" was a ten days' wonder. A writer in the *Times* praised it as "a very scientific conception." *Punch* burlesqued it, and many fanciful and comic prints of the machine in flight were produced. Ridicule reached its height in a pamphlet called "The Full particulars of the Aerial Steam Carriage which is intended to convey Passengers, Troops, and Government Despatches to China and India in a Few Days"[11]—than which proposal, absurdity could go no further.

Still other marvels poured into the Patent Office and even reached production in the forties. In 1842 a Mr. Bain invented an electric clock. "Since last Christmas Eve," said *Bradshaw's Manchester Journal* on January 29th, "a large illuminated electric clock (in front of the London Polytechnic Institution in Regent Street) has been going day and night, with perfect success, by the agency of a galvanic current. Of all the discoveries of the present age there are few, if any, so extraordinary as this." Electromagnets were used to make and break the circuit which moved the second hand of the clock.

Gutta-percha had first been brought to England in 1843. Within a few years it was competing with the better-known India rubber for insulation, waterproof raincoats, cricket balls, buffers for railway car-

---

* Contemporary interest in this sort of thing is illustrated by the launching of the magazine *The Balloon; or Aerostatic Magazine*, in 1845, edited by H. Coxwell and H. Wells.

Figure 70. Henson's "Ariel" in supposed flight
British Crown Copyright. Science Museum, London.

riages, molds for electrotyping (another development of the forties), and even for filling hollow teeth. Mr. F. Whishaw exhibited to the British Association his Telakouphanon, or speaking trumpet, of gutta-percha, by means of which "the voice can be conveyed quite audibly for at least three-quarters of a mile." *Hereapath's Journal and Railway Magazine* advertised in 1843 the "Patent Elastic (Caoutchouc) Pavement Co." ready to execute orders for paving blocks one eighth to three inches thick, which "make a firm, substantial, and elastic pavement for court-yards, basements, foot-paths, and for preventing the escape of unwhole-some effluvia from the vaults of churches; for sea and wharf walls, stable floors," etc.

The use of gas for lighting was being extended rapidly; London had in 1842 eighteen public gasworks and twelve public gas companies.* But electricity also was on its way. In 1845 the first arc light was patented in England, and although its expense of operation by batteries made it impractical, it gave such brilliant illumination when tried experimentally

---

* These burned 180,000 tons of coal annually, supplying gas to about 134,300 private burners and 30,000 public or street customers. Three hundred and eighty lamplighters were employed. (C. Knight: *London*, Vol. IV, p. 233.)

in Trafalgar Square that it amazed the spectators. In 1849 Mr. Herder, of Plymouth, gave demonstrations of his carbon arc light from the top of the Devenport Column. At a distance of three and a half miles, so said the "several scientific gentlemen" who took observations, the light "cast a strong shadow, and writing could be distinctly read by it."

And in 1845, to return to the current year, the *Illustrated London News* ran a picture and a description of Mr. Beningfield's Electric Gun, "Siva," which, according to experiments conducted during June "to the satisfaction of many distinguished persons," could discharge five-eighth-inch bullets at the rate of 1,000 per minute, with a force sufficient to penetrate three-inch boards at twenty yards. The invention involved "the application of gases exploded by galvanic electricity." It is strange that more should not have been heard about this marvelously destructive weapon; but with this one appearance it seems to have dropped out of history.

Another event of the year was the first use of Lord Rosse's new telescope with its six-foot lens and its heavy and elaborate mountings weighing four tons. It had a focal length of fifty-four feet and with its supports was seven times as heavy as the four-foot telescope of Sir William Herschel—the largest that had been constructed up to that time. The Dean of Ely walked through the tube—it is a pleasant picture—with his umbrella up. Jupiter, it was said, looked like a coach light through the instrument.

The real frontiers of science were being pushed forward during these years by Sir John Herschel (son of Sir William) who, like his father, was a famous astronomer, but was also a well-known chemist. He identified the lavender rays of the spectrum and paved the way for the discovery of fluorescence by announcing in 1845 "epipolic dispersion" as exhibited by sulphate of quinine. He was the first person to apply the terms "positive" and "negative" to photographic images. He spent his declining years in translating the *Iliad* into English verse.

Even more important was Michael Faraday, who in 1841 first described to the Royal Society his great discovery of the induction of electric currents, and who in 1845 began his significant researches into the effect of magnetism on polarized light. By the end of the year he had described fully the properties of dimagnetic bodies.

Politically, economically, industrially, and financially, 1845 was a year full of turmoil and yeastiness. Two events late in December highlighted as many aspects of this ferment. One was the announcement of a stupendous railway bridge to be built across the Mersey at Runcorn; five wet arches of 280 feet span, and 168 dry arches of thirty feet span (a total of 2,480 yards of arching), a project of construction "so gigantic as to be without parallel in engineering." The other was the huge meeting of the Anti-Corn-Law League at the Town Hall in Manchester to begin the raising of £250,000 for the League. Before the meeting broke up £62,000 had been subscribed.

Dickens's *Cricket on the Hearth* appeared on the bookstalls for the Christmas trade, and the chirrupy story of the cricket and the kettle with its assorted pathos, mystery, and melodrama warmed the hearts of some critics and chilled others. It could hardly fail to be popular, however, and before you could say "Hollywood" it was appearing simultaneously in dramatic form on six London stages—only one version, however, having been authorized by Dickens, that of the Keeleys at the Lyceum. A few weeks earlier Dickens had produced with a company of fellow authors and amateurs *Every Man in His Humour* for a fashionable benefit audience. Macready had reluctantly directed the play, and the result was reviewed as highly meritorious. All agreed that Dickens himself was brilliant as Bobadil, and Mark Lemon excellent as Brainworm. The cast was a roll call of literary London; John Forster, Douglas Jerrold, John Leech, and Frank Stone also participated. In the boxes, the Dukes of Devonshire and Cambridge, Prince Albert and Lord Morpeth looked on complacently. Lord Melbourne, however, present in a box with Mrs. Norton and Lady Duff Gordon, was heard to exclaim in a stentorian voice across the pit between the acts: "I knew this play would be dull, but that it would be so damnably dull as this I did not suppose!"

1846 * Political Crisis

ENGLAND AND THE ARTS. ADVERTISEMENTS

O LD Jeremy Bentham, dead in 1832, had been residing ever since
with Dr. Southwood Smith, to whom he had willed his body for anatomical study. As R. H. Horne put it in 1844: "The head and face were
preserved by a peculiar process, but the latter, being found painful in
expression, is covered with a wax mask admirably executed and a correct
likeness. The skeleton also was preserved; and the whole clothed in the
ordinary dress worn by the philosopher (according to his own express
desire), presenting him as nearly as he was while living. Seated smiling
in a large mahogany case with a glass front, the homely figure, with its
long snow-white hair, broadbrimmed hat, and thick ash-plant walking
stick . . . may be seen by anyone who takes an interest. . . ."[1]

In the winter and spring of 1846 the old gentleman's pleasant if mask-
like smile could have been interpreted as beneficent approval of the final
abolition of the Corn Laws and a triumph of the school of thought to
which he had given his name. But the path toward repeal was strewn with
the debris of bitter argument and the wreckage of a political party.

At the beginning of the Parliamentary session Peel introduced his budget and with it a proposal to reduce the duties on grain to a nominal one-shilling tax by 1849. In the meantime the duties were to operate under a greatly decreased sliding scale. So intense was the focus of interest on the Corn Laws that it almost escaped notice that at the same time he was suggesting the complete removal of tariff from forty-six other items, and a heavy reduction in the case of some 140 more. Everyone knew that the Corn Laws would somehow be repealed; the current Irish famine was only accelerating the process. Yet the embattled country gentlemen were not giving up without a long-delaying action.

All through the Christmas holidays the Protectionists had been busy organizing meetings of protest, with assorted dukes and earls in the various chairs. The meetings were symposia of anger, horror, and disgust. Abuse of Peel and the cry of "traitor" were uniform parts of the proceedings. At the same time the rich Anti-Corn-Law League was holding assemblies marked by an air of preliminary triumph. More impressive than any of these to the ordinary observer, however, was a spontaneous gathering on January 5th of some thousand agricultural laborers at Goatacre, in Wiltshire. These men and their families met under the jurisdiction of no propaganda agency and listened to none but their own speakers. Hence the impressiveness both of their descriptions of distress and of their moderation of tone.

The *Times*, a strong advocate of repeal, reported the meeting fully. The people assembled at a crossroads in the inclemency of a winter night unmistakably anxious, hungry, and in want. The speakers described in plain language the nature of their miseries. David Kell, the chairman, said that he had only 6s. a week to keep himself, a wife, and two small children—not half enough to support life. Past forty years of age, he had never been able to purchase a pound of good slaughtered beef. He knew what veal was, but he had never had any of that. "Dissatisfied minds have brought all these people here tonight," he said. "I am sure I should not have walked all the way up here from Christian-Malford, through lanes and paths full of mud and dirt, if it hadn't been for that." Charles Vines made a speech in which he said that his average income for the past two years was 7s. 1¼d. per week, upon which he had to support a wife and six children. He concluded by singing several verses of Thomas Hood's "Song of the Labourer":

> No parish money, nor parish loaf,
>   No pauper badge for me;
> I'm a son of the soil, by rightful toil,
>   Entitled to my fee.

> No alms I ask—give me my task:
>> For will, or arm, or leg.
> I'm strong and bold, and to this I'll hold—
>> To work, and not to beg.
>>> *[Loud cheering]*

William Parry declared that he maintained himself, his wife, and six children on 8s. a week. Advised to send one of his children to the workhouse, he could not decide which one to send; they all cried, "Don't send me, Father! Don't send me!" and "was not that enough to try a man, without the pressure of starvation?"

In a fashion as dignified as that of any Protectionist gathering the crowd passed a motion petitioning the Queen to abolish the Corn Laws. It was a simple and touching scene, but the echoes of this meeting and of others like it reached as far as Westminster. The Corn Laws were doomed.

Peel's opponents, among whom were many of his own party, delayed action on the bill as long as possible, but the coalition of his Conservative supporters, the Radicals, and the more liberal Whigs turned the tide. Aware that he would be under bitter personal attack because of his change of views (Disraeli led the pack of the Opposition), Peel told the House: "I will not undertake to direct the course of the vessel by observations taken in the year 1842. I will reserve to myself the unfettered power of judging what will be for the public interest. I do not desire to be the minister of England; but while I am minister of England I will hold office by no servile tenure; I will hold office unshackled by any other obligation than that of consulting the public interests and providing for the public safety." The cheers for this came chiefly from Opposition benches.

Not until May 15th did the bill reach its third reading, on which day it was passed by a majority of ninety-eight and turned over to the House of Lords. The Lords showed some disposition toward endless debate, the Duke of Richmond voicing the typical complaint that the Anti-Corn-Law League was in process of destroying the Church and every other institution in the country. It was Wellington who made the speech which bluntly put them in their place.

Wellington's position here was anomalous, as was indeed his position in English society during his declining years. On the one hand he was worshiped as the great warrior and hero of Waterloo; no one man in the kingdom had a greater prestige during this period. At the same time it was generally recognized that he was becoming increasingly irritable and testy, and that his social and political instincts belonged to a day which was past. The interesting point is that the duke was aware of this last. Secure in the adulation which was his on every side, and which he had come to take for granted, he won respect for his unshakable honesty, and even for his bluntness. No orator, he said laconically what he had to say, and sat down; but no one ever doubted his meaning. All his instincts were against the abolition of the Corn Laws. He made no secret of this. In a memorandum written in November he had said: "I am one of those who think the continuance of the Corn Laws essential to the agriculture of the country in its existing state, and particularly to that of Ireland, and a benefit to the whole community." Privately he could grumble: "Rotten potatoes have done it all; they put Peel in his damned fright." But when the chips were down, Wellington made it clear that to support Peel's government and the Throne was his "only object in public life." To save the Queen from inconvenience in any way he considered of more importance than the Corn Laws.

When his fellow Lords showed signs of restiveness, the duke told them more plainly than they had ever been told before just what they ought not to attempt. Public opinion, he said, had pronounced itself so clearly for the Bill that even to debate it would be a waste of time. If they attempted to stand alone, to place themselves in opposition to a large majority in the Commons and to the Crown, they would assume "a position in which they ought not and could not stand, as they would be powerless." With that he stopped, and the chastened Peers hurried to give the Bill their approval.

On the same night, however, as the House of Lords was passing the Corn Law Bill, Peel was coming to the end of his ministerial career by defeat in the Commons. As early as January he had agreed to bring in a bill which would reduce the mounting lawlessness in Ireland. Hunger and starvation were accompanied there by a series of outbreaks against person and property. Arms were being sold to the peasantry; homes were being attacked and fired into; personal assaults were reaching dangerous proportions; homicides were growing in number. Famine riots were breaking out in many towns. In Clonmel, wrote a correspondent, "we have cannon at either end of the town, and the streets are full of soldiers and police. This morning the mob broke into every baker's shop in the place, and took out all the food they could lay their hands on. The banks and shops are shut, and the town in a state of siege." At the same time in Carrick-on-Suir the populace broke into the provision shops, ironically enough at the very moment when carts were passing through the streets carrying grain for export—a kind of paradox not uncommon in modern society!

Hence the Ministry's Irish Coercion Bill with its restrictive proposals, one of its more inflammatory clauses being a curfew law which provided the punishment of transportation for anyone caught out between sunset and sunrise. Even in February this seemed severe. By June it was still more obvious that soup kitchens were needed more than coercive legislation. But Peel was committed to the Bill, and with it he went down to defeat on the night of June 25th by a majority of seventy-three.

Peel resigned, and in his closing address startled the House by paying tribute to his one-time bitter enemy. "Sir," he said, "the name which ought to be, and which will be associated with the success of these measures, is the name of a man who, acting, I believe, from pure and disinterested motives, has advocated their cause with untiring energy, and by appeals to reason, enforced by an eloquence the more to be admired because it was unaffected and unadorned . . . the name of Richard Cobden.

"I shall surrender power," he went on, "severely censured, I fear, by many honourable men . . . I shall leave a name execrated, I know, by every monopolist who, professing honourable opinions, would maintain protection for his own individual benefit. But it may be that I shall be sometimes remembered with expressions of good-will, in those places which are the abodes of men whose lot it is to labour and earn their daily bread by the sweat of their brow; in such places, perhaps my name may be remembered with expressions of good-will, when they who inhabit them recruit their exhausted strength with abundant and untaxed food, the sweeter because no longer leavened with a sense of injustice."

Thus Peel drove a wedge down the middle of his party. The "Peelites" stayed by him, a party within a party. Gladstone, Graham, Cardwell, and Sidney Herbert were among the faithful. The old Toryism of Church and State found its leaders in the wily and able Disraeli and Lord George Bentinck. Disraeli was not yet fully trusted; so Bentinck became the avowed leader of the opposition, astonishing all who had known him only as an ardent and inveterate turfman during the nearly twenty years he had sat in the House, by moving with an appalling, if naïve, energy into the political arena. He had a capacity for slashing revengeful attack which appealed at the moment to the angry Tories.* His aggressiveness was more remarkable than his wisdom.

---

* By this time the shades of distinction in the Tory-Conservative and Whig-Liberal labels began to have meaning. The old Tories had much more in common with the ancient Whigs of the landed aristocracy (both concerned over the preservation of the landed interests and the worship of British institutions—which meant no changes inimical to the welfare of the ruling classes) than they did

All that Peel had left was the respect and affection of those who admired the statesmanship of a man to whom the welfare of his country meant more than his own career. *Punch's* change of attitude is significant here. *Punch*, which reflected accurately the prejudices of the middle classes against Puseyism, O'Connell and Repeal, Chartism, Prince Albert, the servility of the *Morning Post;* which was anti-Graham, anti-American, anti-Brougham, and which in 1844 had identified Peel with Pecksniff, had nothing but praise for the minister's repeal of the Corn Laws. *Punch*, incidentally, had improved vastly during the last few years in the quality of its wit and satire. Its political cartoons were something to be reckoned with, and it was deserting its earlier plethora of egregious puns for a kind of punditry (or pun-ditry, as it would have parenthesized in 1841).

When Lord John Russell's cabinet was announced it was discovered that the lion and the lamb had lain down together: Lord Grey accepted the colonial secretaryship while Palmerston moved unopposed into the Foreign Office.

In the meantime Fielden was unable to carry in the Commons the second reading of the Ten Hours Bill previously introduced by Lord Ashley. Ashley himself had resigned because, although he had become an Anti-Corn-Law man, he had been elected on a platform of protection, and his conscience would not allow him to vote against his Dorset constituency. Fielden's bill was defeated at this crucial point by a majority of only ten—118 fewer, it is to be noticed, than had defeated the same bill in 1844. It was supported this year by "a queer combination of Whigs and Tories against the Peelites and their allies, the Manchester Radicals."[2] The Protectionists thus failed only by a narrow margin to inflict reprisal upon their enemies the manufacturers.

While the political revolution of 1846 was getting itself accomplished a busy Parliament was nearly swamped by the flood of applications for railway bills which had to be screened through multiple committees. Of the 561 petitions submitted, it actually sanctioned the construction of 270 new railways or additions. Yet a curious reaction had already begun to set in. The first tremor had been noticed when, in the latter months of 1845, the Bank of England raised its interest rate. With the

---

with Peel's new Conservative wing, which was indistinguishable in many respects from the more liberal and radical element among the Whigs. Those to whom party was a religion were incensed over the emphasis upon measures and men at the expense of traditional political alignments.

approval, too, of each set of plans it became necessary for the stock-
holders of each projected railway to make a down payment of 10 per
cent on its capitalization. This necessity, which should not have been
too obscure to speculators, caused the collapse of many purely gambling
ventures and the bankruptcy of many individuals, from merchants to
retired clergymen, who had gambled in shares. Those who had been
talking learnedly and glibly of gradients, cuttings, and gauges suddenly
ran for cover. Railway scrip became almost impossible to dispose of. Railway bills already proposed could not be withdrawn without the approval
of Parliament, and so began the strange spectacle of bills being opposed
by the very shareholders who had applied for them. Preferring to lose
what they had already invested rather than to throw good money after
bad, they asked Parliament to reject their applications promptly. The
Government announced a measure under which a majority vote of the
shareholders in any company would compel the directors to dissolve it.
Legitimate schemes sometimes suffered the fate of purely fly-by-night
ventures.*

George Hudson still maintained his vast prestige, however, and an
ability both to inspire confidence and to ride down ruthlessly any of his
timid directors. The *Times* had said in March: "Probably there is not a
single new company at this moment in which the majority of shareholders would not vote for abandonment." Yet under Hudson's whip the
shareholders in the Midland Company gave their approval to twenty-six
bills they had before Parliament. A few days later his York and North
Midland sanctioned six bills and at the same time he induced the Newcastle and Darlington Company to approve of seven bills and accompanying agreements. Half an hour later he took his seat as the controlling
power on the board of the Newcastle and Berwick. Within two days
he had obtained the consent of shareholders to forty bills, involving an
expenditure of about £10,000,000.

Later in the year, at a triumphal dinner given by Hudson, his Tory

---

* A parody of *Childe Harold* appeared at this time, one verse of which ran:

> And then and there were hurryings to and fro,
>   And anxious thoughts, and signs of sad distress.
> Faces all pale, that but an hour ago
>   Smiled at the thoughts of their own craftiness.
>   And there were sudden partings, such as press
> The coin from hungry pockets—mutual sighs
>   Of brokers and their clients. Who can guess
> How many a stag already panting flies,
> When upon times so bright such awful panics rise?

Quoted in F. S. Williams: *Our Iron Roads*, 1852, p. 62. A "stag" was one who
purchased shares solely in the hope of speculative profit.

friend Bentinck estimated that the railways were daily giving employment to 200,000 laborers at wages averaging 22s. 6d. a week. Railway construction had indeed absorbed much of the surplus labor, and the appearance of the railway laborer or "navvy" (navigator) was one of the social as well as economic phenomena of the time.

The men who dug earth, blasted tunnels, and laid rails formed a class new to the country. Coming chiefly from the hills of Lancashire and Yorkshire (with an infiltration of Irish) and the fens of Lincolnshire, they were physically hardy but were ignorant and brutalized. They formed a clan of their own, living in filthy hovels along the right of way. They were depraved and reckless. In a report made to Parliament in 1846 by Edwin Chadwick they were described as drunken and dissolute, afflicted universally by "loathsome forms of disease." They drank whisky by the tumbler, calling it "white beer." They earned a high wage, and spent it—much of it being drained off, however, by the extortionate "truck" or company-shop system. What was left was spent in a debauch following payday. As a class they spread terror throughout the countryside, defying gamekeepers and driving country gentlemen to despair with their depredations. Policemen were killed, and the rural police officers were helpless. Chadwick recommended legislative interference, but Parliament did nothing.

Yet amid all the confusion and financial panic, the railways were being built. Stock in the railways for which Acts of Parliament were obtained in 1846 amounted to £90,298,430. Short lines were reaching out to touch longer ones, consolidations were being made, networks being established. And it was during 1846 that the "battle of the gauges" reached its climax.

Books were written, dozens of pamphlets published, and the railway journals packed with articles concerning the struggle between the proponents of wide gauge versus narrow gauge: seven feet as against four feet eight and a half inches. At times the campaign reached a pitch of rancor hardly equaled by debates at Westminster. Sir I. Brunel had engineered the wide gauge for the Great Western and battled valiantly to make it the uniform standard, even though the other railways had, for the most part, adopted the narrower gauge. The variety of gauges then obtaining made travel and the shipment of goods very complicated; at junction points both travelers and freight had to be transhipped at great expense of effort and time. Finally a royal commission of investigation was appointed and reported to Parliament in May. It found the broad gauge preferable in respect to speed and the narrow gauge better for the transport of goods, the general advantage being on the side of the narrow gauge. Above all, uniformity was essential for the comfort and even the safety of passengers. And so, with customary British compromise, the Gauge Act of 1846 made the narrow gauge the standard for the future, but allowed the whole system of the Great Western not only to keep its present gauge but to use it for further branches or extensions. Mixed gauge was tried in some instances, a third rail being laid.*

The development of the electric telegraph had paralleled that of the railway, and, like the railway, thrilled all England. It had been invented by Wheatstone (his first patent was taken out in 1837) and it was developed, with some dispute as to the relative part each had in the invention, by Wheatstone and Cooke. In 1840 Wheatstone had made improvements which reduced the number of wires to two; by 1844 Bain's "Electro-Magnetic Printing Telegraph" was in practical operation in the South Western Railway. It printed by means of numbers on an electrically motivated type wheel. Dramatic announcements were made and thieves as well as murderers captured through the agency of the new invention. In 1846 the Electric Telegraph Company was incorporated, with its central establishment immediately behind the Bank of England. It held a patent for fourteen years, and charged £20 per mile for the use of the lines. "There have now been established," ran its first official circular, "in Edinburgh, Manchester, Liverpool, Glasgow, Hull, and Newcastle, Subscription News Rooms, for the accommodation of the mercantile and professional interests, to which is transmitted by electric telegraph the latest intelligence." Rates: for 20 words, 1d. per mile for the first 50 miles; ½d. for the second 50; ¼d. for any distance beyond 100 miles. London to Edinburgh: 13s. for 20 words.† By 1848 the company had laid down 2,500 miles of wire and had 1,000 men in its employ, with fifty-seven clerks sending and receiving messages, "independent of those occupied in printing communications to the newspapers."

"Progress," wrote William Johnstone, "can hardly beat this, let what will happen. In this matter we may rest satisfied that science has done her utmost. The force of nature and of art can no further go."[3]

Still other inventions were brought forward in 1846. Captain Warner's long-range shell failed miserably in an official experiment (declared capable of hitting objects at eight miles, it failed to carry three miles); but guncotton, invented the year before by a Swiss chemist, Professor Christian Schönbein, was tested in England and reported on favorably. It had four times the explosive force of gunpowder. In this same year,

---

* Not until 1892 was the broad gauge abolished on the Great Western.

† Contemporary rates in the United States were much lower. Ten words from New York to Boston (220 miles) cost twenty cents.

too, a London corset manufacturer named Thomas bought the English patent on the sewing machine invented by the American, Elias Howe, two years before. He engaged Howe to adapt the machine for his manufacturing purposes.* In the area of pure science, M. Leverrier, solely on the basis of calculation, announced the discovery of a new planet which proved to be the outermost one found up to that time in the solar system. The Berlin Observatory, using Leverrier's figures, located the planet in its telescope. It was named Neptune.

Amid the welter of politics and starvation at home, foreign news attracted little interest in 1846. The first Sikh war was brought to a successful conclusion and was followed by the annexation of the Punjab to the British Empire. It had involved some fierce and bloody battles, however, and the rejoicing in England was mixed with a good deal of complaining about the heavy losses. The Sikhs had in the field an able army of 30,000, which inflicted upon the British 2,383 casualties in one engagement.

Indignation had been aroused in England over the occupation of Cracow by Austria, and Palmerston had merely voiced public sentiment with his expression of sympathy for the Poles and his declaration that the occupation was a violation of the Treaty of Vienna. Satisfaction was felt, on the other hand, over the long-delayed settlement of the Oregon dispute with the United States; on June 12th the Senate had accepted the English compromise solution. The English were watching carefully, too, the war declared by the United States against Mexico on May 13th. Beginning as a "defense" of Texas, it speedily involved the taking of New Mexico (an area including also the present states of Utah and Nevada). Moreover, the energetic and independent activity of John C. Fremont had added California, with its 1,200 foreign residents, to the total area captured. On June 15th a proclamation was issued at Sonoma inviting all peaceable and good citizens of California to assist in establishing a republican government. Shortly Fremont's California Battalion brought this area under its control, although not until July 9th did a courier bring word to Fremont that war had broken out between Mexico and the United States! The English watched these seizures of ancient

---

* Howe pawned his American patent rights in England and returned penniless to the United States in 1849. As early as 1841 a poor French tailor, Thimmonier, had some eighty sewing machines of his own operating in Paris. Strangely enough the sewing machine, though exhibited at the Crystal Palace in 1851, did not come into general use until some time later.

Figure 71. Richard Doyle: "The Land of Liberty." From *Punch*

Spanish territory with some reprehension; the new phrase "manifest destiny" did not sound so pious on American as on English lips.

Things were not dull at home. For those who could purchase or rent, new books were announced daily. Melville's *Narrative of a Four Months' Residence among the Natives of the Marquesas Islands* (later called *Typee*) received a good deal of attention. The public was not sure how much was fact and how much fancy but it had, as always, an avid appetite for picturesque descriptions of the strange and far away. George Grote, banker and M.P., published the first two of what were to be twelve volumes of his *History of Greece*, "the first attempt at a philosophical history of Greece." G. P. R. James and Mrs. Gore came out with their annual or semi-annual three-volume (31s. 6d.) novels; the former with *The Step-Mother* and the latter with *Peers and Parvenus*, a repetition, in her lazy, smart style, of the themes of previous stories dealing with the improbabilities of highly artificial fashionables. It did not stretch the mind, and it found a ready public.

Mary Ann Evans (George Eliot) completed and published a translation of Strauss's *Life of Jesus*. Ruskin issued the second volume of *Modern Painters*. Thackeray's *Notes of a Journey from Cornhill to Grand Cairo* (still as by M. A. Titmarsh) was welcomed as an unsentimental and humorous comment on the Near East. A little volume of poems by Currer, Ellis, and Acton Bell (the Brontë sisters) was published, as was Browning's *Luria*. Walter Savage Landor's collected and amplified *Imaginary Conversations* met with approval. And one Edward Lear, who was currently giving drawing lessons to Queen Victoria, published almost unnoticed *A Book of Nonsense*.

Sir Edward Bulwer Lytton published under an elaborate but transparent anonymity his *New Timon*, a satirical poem dealing with contemporary figures, which went into its third edition in three months in spite of the pounding it took from critics. The reviewer in the *Athenaeum* pretended to believe that its glowing verbiage was a bad and shameless imitation of Bulwer Lytton. *Hood's Magazine*, to be sure, praised its extravagantly as "one of the most remarkable poems of the present generation . . . a great poet is at length before the world." But blurbs like this were pulverized by the *Spectator*. The story and persons, it said, were drawn from the circulating library and its incidental matter was that of the flashy "article"; of true poetry there was none. The poem won a footnote in literary history, however, because of its tasteless attack upon Albert Tennyson and because of Tennyson's reply. Bulwer Lytton wrote:

> Let school-miss Alfred vent her chaste delight
> On darling rooms, so warm and bright.
>
> A quaint farrago of absurd conceits
> Out-babying Wordsworth and out-glittering Keats.
>
> No tawdry grace shall womanize my pen,
> Even in love-song men should write for men.

How could a government, asked the poet, "pension Tennyson while it starves a Knowles"? Tennyson, who had recently with some embarrassment accepted a civil list pension of £200 a year, and who had earlier suppressed as puerile his "Lines to a Darling Room," furiously if uncharacteristically replied in *Punch* of February 28th with a poem "The New Timon, and the Poets," signed "Alcibiades."

> I *thought* we knew him: What, it's you,
>   The padded man—that wears the stays—
>
> Who kiss'd the girls and thrill'd the boys,
>   With dandy pathos when you wrote,
> A Lion, you, that made a noise,
>   And shook a mane en papillotes.
>
> .   .   .   .
>
> And what with spite and what with fears,
>   You cannot let a body be:
> It's always ringing in your ears,
>   "They call this man as good as me."
>
> What profits now to understand
>   The merits of a spotless shirt—
> A dapper boot—a little hand—
>   If half the little soul is dirt?

A week later, however, Tennyson repented his wrath and sent some supplementary lines to *Punch*:

> And *I* too talk, and lose the touch
>   I talk of. Surely, after all
> The noblest answer unto such
>   Is kindly silence when they brawl.

The first issue of the liberal *Daily News*, with Dickens as editor, appeared with great eclat on January 21st. . . . Two wrecks were reported in February: one of the emigrant ship *Cataraqui*, sunk at the entrance to Bass's Straights with 414 lives lost; and the complete destruction, without loss of life, of the steamship *Great Liverpool*, off Cape Finisterre. The *Great Liverpool* was one of the squadron of the Peninsular and Oriental Steam Navigation Company (P and O) which had been organized in 1841. . . . Cambridge won the annual Oxford-Cambridge boat race on the Thames in April. . . . A testimonial of more than £13,000 was given to Rowland Hill in recognition of his services in reforming the postage. . . . At the Exeter Hall meetings the British and Foreign Bible Society announced receipts for the year of £101,305 and the issuance of 1,441,651 Bibles—500,000 more than the previous year. . . . Complaints were multiplying about the snail-like progress of the printed catalogue of books in the British Museum under the autocratic direction of Panizzi. The last catalogue, printed in 1823 in seven volumes, had been interleaved to forty-eight folio volumes. There was only one copy of it for the 230 persons who daily attended the reading room. . . .

Louis Napoleon, the nephew of Napoleon I, imprisoned at the fortress of Ham since his abortive revolt of 1840, made a dramatic escape by dressing himself as a laborer and walking past the guards with a plank over his shoulder. He came immediately to England—the home of all famous Continental exiles. It was reported that his government, embarrassed by having to continue to imprison him, was not too unhappy at his escape. . . . Public anger was stirred by the death of a soldier who had received a punishment of 150 lashes. So strong was the sentiment of the people in favor of the complete abolition of flogging in the armed services that Wellington, as commander in chief, was able to stop Parliamentary action only by announcing that in the future fifty lashes would be the maximum. Russell, supported by the duke, argued on the floor of the Commons that if flogging were abolished the high state of discipline, of which the British Army was justly proud, might be lost. . . . The first all-England cricket eleven, made up of the best professionals of the day, was organized. It visited in its first three years some forty districts, playing matches against local teams. . . . A young medical graduate named Thomas Henry Huxley, age twenty-one, was made assistant surgeon of H.M.S. *Rattlesnake*, about to set out for surveying work in Torres Strait. The year before, the young man had published his first scientific paper, announcing the discovery of the layer of cells in the inner sheath of hair which was henceforth to be known as "Huxley's layer."

On May 25th another daughter—the fifth child, Helena Augusta Victoria—was born to the Queen. People were not unduly excited by the royal event.

An American troup of burnt-cork musicians and entertainers called

Figure 72. The Ethiopian serenaders

the Ethiopian Serenaders appeared at the Hanover Square Rooms. Dressed in white waistcoats and cravats, they sat in a row playing two banjos, the accordion, tambourine, and bones—singing glees and telling jokes interspersed with imitations, comical noises, and ventriloquism. Their close harmony seemed to curious observers more sophisticated than primitive, but their songs ("Come, Darkies, Sing," "The Sugar-cane Queen," "Lucy Neal," and "Ole Bull and Ole Dan Tucker") were much enjoyed. Their Railroad Overture, a ludicrous imitation of a steam engine getting under way, had the audiences in the aisles—or whatever the Victorian equivalent of that was. . . . In more dignified fashion Rachel, once more in England, was packing St. James's Theatre with her performance of Camille in Corneille's *Les Horaces*. She still exercised her almost hypnotic control over audiences, who found in her restrained passion and vehemence "one of the most superb pieces of acting we ever witnessed." She was equally successful later in Racine's *Phèdre*.

General Tom Thumb also reappeared in London in April, triumphantly as ever. This time he was on display in the Egyptian Hall during the day and at the Lyceum Theatre at night, where he appeared in *Hop-o'-My-Thumb*, to the great delight, apparently, of all who saw him.

Across the passageway from the general, in Egyptian Hall, the painter Robert Benjamin Haydon was displaying his two latest gigantic canvases: "The Banishment of Aristides" and "The Burning of Rome by Nero," two pictures which Haydon had hoped would be selected for the New Houses of Parliament. He had been ignored in the competition, and was now appealing to the public. The *Times* was gentle, and praised ("the drawing is grand and the characters most felicitous"). The other papers carried severely critical notices. The picture of Nero fiddling was called "a colossal caricature: coarse alike in idea and execution." The "Aristides" was damned as having the wish for sublimity without the attainment. The artist's advertisement in the *Times* had urged visitors to "go up into the gallery of the room, in order to see the full effect of the flame of the burning city . . . Haydon has devoted forty-two years to improve the taste of the people; and let every Briton who has pluck in his bosom and a shilling in his pocket crowd to his works during the Easter week."

But the public refused to crowd, and the distracted Haydon watched them pass his room in streams to have a look at the mighty midget performing across the way. He rushed to the *Times* again to insert another notice: "*Exquisite Feeling of the English People for High Art*—General Tom Thumb last week received 12,000 people, who paid him £600: B. R. Haydon . . . was honoured by the visits of 133½, producing £5 13s. 6d., being a reward for painting two of his finest works. . . ."

In his journal he wrote:

April 4. Receipts 1st day, "Christ entering Jerusalem," 1820 [his finest picture], £19 16s.

Figure 73. Haydon's "The Banishment of Aristides"

> Receipts, 1st day, "Banishment of Aristides," £1 1s. 6d.
> "In God I trust: Amen."

and on April 13th:

> Receipts of £1 3s. 6d. . . . They rush by thousands to see Tom
> Thumb. They push—they fight—they scream—they faint—
> they cry "Help!" and "Murder!" They see my bills and
> caravans, but they do not heed them; their eyes are on them,
> but their sense is gone. It is an insanity—a *rabies furor*—a
> dream—of which I would not have believed Englishmen could
> be guilty.

It was the end of a long and tragic career. Racked by poverty, disowned by the public he sought to elevate, scorned by critics, Haydon was a pathetic and melancholy fighter for a heroic art in which his own imaginative limitations denied him success. Tender and pious, he suffered because he could not support his family adequately. He would spend any cash in hand for more huge canvases on which to paint pictures no home or even hall could ever hang. He had had an early success of a kind; when he would paint pictures of a moderate size he could find purchasers. Thus his "Napoleon on St. Helena," which he repeated, according to his own testimony, thirteen times.

His self-appointed mission was to restore to England the concept of sublime art in the grand manner. On behalf of this ideal, with a tremendous vigor and with the truculent arrogance of a prophet, he wrote and lectured incessantly, always controversial, estranging even those who wanted to help him. For years he engaged in a running battle with the Royal Academy, which had refused to accept him, in defense of what he called "high art." He wanted art to be noble and inspiring, but the pictures which he painted to illustrate those ideals seemed to others merely empty and pretentious. Courageous, energetic, he struggled bravely with adverse circumstances, never losing faith in himself or in his artistic ideals.

At the very last, hounded by creditors, he received £50 forwarded from a special fund by Sir Robert Peel, who had taken time in the midst of his ministerial crisis to honor a worthy artist. But despair was settling on this noble egoist, and on June 22d he reached the end of the road. About noon Haydon's sixteen-year-old daughter found him lying in his studio in a pool of his own blood, a bullet in his brain and his throat slashed through with a razor. He lay immediately in front of one of his colossal historical pictures, "Alfred the Great and the First British Jury." Facing his large picture he had placed on a small easel a portrait of his wife.

Figure 74. Exhibition of the Royal Academy (the Royal private view)

The last entries in the diary which he had kept for many years and which now lay open at an adjoining table ran: "June 21.—Slept horribly, prayed in sorrow, and got up in agitation. June 22.—God forgive me: Amen.—Finis. B. R. Haydon. 'Stretch me no longer on this rough world!'—*Lear*. The end of the twenty-sixth volume."

What was the position of the arts in England in the mid-forties? If there is any relationship between art and the national character of a period one can learn much by studying what was created and still more by what was approved.

Portraiture, of course, furnished the staple of the Victorian artist's livelihood, but the exhibition pictures were another story—and the word "story" is used advisedly. Witness, for example, the leading paintings in the Royal Academy Exhibition of 1846, the mere listing of which dusts off some then popular but now forgotten names, and the titles of which are the clue to the art interests of a public which at least knew what it liked. The Exhibition was held each May in the National Gallery, an admittedly crowded, inadequate, and ugly building in Trafalgar Square. In 1841 the total permanent collection consisted of 166 pictures, of which forty were by native artists. By 1849 it had grown to include 216 paintings. A guidebook of 1841, with more frankness than is usually found in such compendiums, said, "Let us assume a little modesty, and until we have a collection fit to be seen, pray sink the name of National, and adopt one more suited to the humbleness of our pretensions. When we say that the building is worthy of the collection, and each of the other, our readers will not expect much praise from us. Mr. Wilkins's [building] . . . offends against good taste and architectural beauty. . . . If the observer can look upon Mr. Wilkins's abortion without nausea—why, he has a stronger stomach and less taste than we give him credit for."

In 1846 Maclise's large picture "The Ordeal by Touch" was praised as the greatest work of the Exhibition. It was a theatrically expressed subject painted in the artist's metallic manner; the accused, with his face averted, had just touched the corpse, from which the blood was starting. . . . Mulready presented a little episode from the Vicar of Wakefield: "Choosing the Wedding Gown." "For richness and splendour of colour, exquisite finish, and luminous depth of tone," wrote an ecstatic critic, "it is inimitable. The Dutch painters must 'pale their ineffectual fires' before its glowing brightness." . . . Etty, the English Rubens, offered the "Choice of Paris" and "Circe and the Syrens." . . . Turner had six pictures which included a couple of "Whalers" and a pyrotechnical "Angel in the Sun." . . . Leslie had a "Scene from Roderick Random"—reading the will—as well as a portrait of Dickens as "Captain Bobadil." . . . Edwin Landseer showed four animal pictures, including the "Stag at Bay." . . . Eastlake a delicate "Visit to the Nun." . . . Webster showed "Good Night," a country family at supper. . . . W. P. Frith, "Madame Jourdain discovering her Husband at the Dinner which he gave to the Belle Marquise and the Count Dorante"—a comic scene. . . . Redgrave, "Sunday Morning—the Walk from Church." . . . E. M. Ward, the "Disgrace of Clarendon," and A. Egg, "Buckingham Rebuffed."

This is enough to give the clue. English art of the time, even at its best, was highly domesticated. It fell into two large categories: the *genre* and the historical. The historical was not the "high" art of the rejected Haydon but pleased by its "human interest" and was essentially literary. Indeed literature itself was a staple source for subjects: *Don Quixote*, *Gil Blas*, the plays of Molière and Shakespeare, and above all just at this moment the *Vicar of Wakefield*, were rifled for themes. Scenes from Sterne, Smollett, and Fielding appeared on many canvases.

Genre art, whether of subjects drawn from novels or invented by the painter, was the most popular of all. It had to tell a story, and the

Figure 75. C. R. Leslie: "Sancho and the Duchess"

Figure 76. Daniel Maclise: "Malvolio"

Figure 77. William Etty: "Bathers Surprised"

Figure 78. William Etty: "The Penitent

ed with sentiment and warm associations; the
.... Above all, art must be the handmaiden of
..... it did not teach a lesson, it must at least appeal to serious
minds and must avoid the taint of profligacy which an Englishman somehow associated with the artistic nature. The chief exception to this rule
was William Etty, a remarkably pure-minded man, we are told, who
was fascinated by the beauty of the undraped female form and turned
out painting after painting of remarkably realistic nudes, whose warm,
voluptuous flesh tints startled and yet allured the public even while
offending it. As Thackeray said, Etty was quite unabashed by the
squeamishness "exhibited in the highest quarter," and he recommended
looking at the artist's pictures closely, though, "considering all things,
it requires some courage to do so."

Thackeray, who reviewed each annual exhibition through the first
half of the decade, was a perceptive critic. "The English now paint
from the *heart* more than of old," he said. "They do not aim at such
great subjects as heretofore, or at subjects which the world is pleased
to call great, viz., tales from Hume or Gibbon of royal personages
under various circumstances of battle, murder, and sudden death. . . .
The heroic has been deposed; and our artists, in place, cultivate the
pathetic and the familiar. . . . The younger painters are content to
exercise their art on subjects far less exalted: a gentle sentiment, an
agreeable, quiet incident, a tea-table tragedy, or a bread-and-butter
idyl. . . . Bread and butter can be digested by very many . . . [unlike]
Prometheus on his rock, or Orestes in his strait-waistcoat, or Hector
dragged behind Achilles' car, or Britannia, guarded by Religion and
Neptune, welcoming General Tomkins in the Temple of Glory. . . ."[4]
A little later, however, Thackeray attacks the insipidity, the vulgariza-
tion, the domestication, the namby-pamby quality of much contemporary
painting—"the milk-and-water of human kindness," he called it. To this
he made an interesting exception in Edwin Landseer, whose stags, dogs,
horses, cats, and lions treated pictorially an analogy between the characters of men and animals—and whose paintings and drawings, incidentally, were great favorites of Victoria and Albert.

Although subject was more important than treatment, contemporary
academicians had great technical competence of the hard, niggling, realistic sort which public taste approved. Broad handling was considered
bad painting; the more stilted, "worked-up," and finished paintings of
Constable, for example, were admired more greatly than the free force
of his superb studies for those paintings.

The brown dimness of the landscape painting of the earlier period had

Figure 79. J. M. W. Turner: "Peace: Burial at Sea" (of Sir David Wilkie)

disappeared. The earlier Turner had taught his lesson, and great warmth of color flooded the paintings of the period. Yet the general acceptance of the rule of infinite detail created chiefly a baffled aversion when artists were confronted with the later Turner. By mid-decade Turner, who had from the beginning tried to catch the whole range of the chromatic scale in his purples, his hot reds, and his luminous golds, was pushing his intense lights and his impressionistic forms to a length which excited wonder but, in most quarters, little admiration. His bold laying on of masses of color, his studied avoidance of any detailed realization, the rapid breadth which he achieved with his palette knife—all this was attributed by the more charitable to his failing eyesight and declining health. It is true that in his last few years (he died in 1851) both his mind and his health were disappearing; but long before that he had become what friendly critics called "caviare to the multitude."[5] The strange thing was, however, that the mulitude seemed to approve of him more than did his fellow painters.

In 1846 a young man named Millais, aged seventeen, exhibited for the first time at the Royal Academy, his picture being "Pizarro Seizing the Inca of Peru." Pre-Raphaelitism, however, was as yet unbegotten.

If painting was trivial in these years, sculpture was moribund. The two most popular pieces of statuary in the forties—as became clear when they were exhibited at the Crystal Palace—were Power's "Greek Slave" and Kiss's "Amazon," the former a chained girl whose embarrassed modesty only called attention to her nudity; the latter a huge representation of a female on horseback repelling with her spear the attack of a panther. The "Amazon" had a kind of lustrous vitality, but it was the size of the creation that impressed the public. In general that statuary which was most gargantuan in conception was considered best.

The year 1846 showed one celebrated exception to this rule, however, as far as the united criticism of the press and of competent observers was concerned. It concerned Wyatt's mammoth statue of the Duke of Wellington.

Largely through the insistence of Sir Frederic Trench, Wyatt had been commissioned to make an equestrian statue of Wellington to be placed on top of the "triumphal" archway (what triumph is not recorded) opposite Apsley House and the main entrance to Hyde Park. Using metal from captured cannon, Wyatt had modeled and cast a statue twenty-seven feet high, weighing almost forty tons, and costing £25,000. A fierce controversy raged for weeks concerning both the merits of the statue and the appropriateness of placing it in its aerial position on Constitution Hill.

The engineering feat merely of lifting the colossus to its pedestal made people throng the streets on the day it was drawn to Hyde Park Corner by twenty-nine brewery horses driven by ten sturdy draymen in full professional costume, one "wearing upon his breast a Waterloo medal." The horses were crowned with laurel; a large group of distinguished personages were assembled in a stand; others gathered at Apsley House to witness the installation; giant cranes heaved the huge mass into place; the duke himself appeared upon his balcony and smiled approval.

The awkward horse with its sodden-looking rider looked even worse than was expected. *Punch* declared that the horse would be a nightmare to all Londoners; others wondered if the duke would enjoy looking out his windows to see himself mocked in bronze. But Wellington showed great irritation when it was suggested that the statue be removed, and it was allowed to stand astride its arch.*

---

* It was not removed until taken to Aldershot in 1884.

THE ILLUSTRATED LONDON NEWS

No. 241.—Vol. IX.] FOR THE WEEK ENDING SATURDAY, OCTOBER 3, 1846. [SIXPENCE.

Figure 80. Wyatt's colossal statue of Wellington

If there was some confusion of styles during the forties, architecture, at least, had not arrived at the stage of grotesqueness which it was to reach later in the century. Though devoted always to the picturesque, the Victorians had not yet allowed picturesqueness to verge on the bizarre. As a matter of fact some nobly successful buildings were planted solidly on English soil during the decade. If academic rather than idiomatic, imitative rather than in the vernacular, they are still respectable.

Of the two styles current in the period—Graeco-Roman and Gothic —the classical was dominant in public buildings during the early years. When Victoria came to the throne, London, like any other large city, was a complex of the ugly and the beautiful. There were the old eighteenth-century squares with their clean, quiet architecture. The City was studded with Christopher Wren churches and grandly overlaid with the Regency contributions of John Nash; Nash had been responsible for Buckingham Palace but he had also created the impressively colonnaded Quadrant of Regent Street. By the forties, scholarship and architectural taste had made the classical revival the dominant tendency. Sir Robert Smirke's British Museum, with its impressive façade of Ionic columns (to be opened in 1847), was of this school, as was Sir William Tite's Royal Exchange, a combination of a Roman portico and an Italian building. This was decorated with a sculptured frieze by R. A. Westmacott which consisted of an allegorical tableau with Commerce, ten feet high, as the central figure. Admittedly the most triumphant success of the Victorian classical school was St. George's Hall in Liverpool, designed by H. L. Elmes with great forcefulness and simplicity, immensely beautiful in its handling of mass and proportion.

Side by side with the classical appeared the Italianate, which had a great vogue as being more pictorial. Even Decimus Burton's Athenaeum Club, allegedly Greek, was touched with Italianate overtones. Philip Hardwick placed behind the great classical porticoes of Euston Station its magnificent Great Hall in an elaborate Italian manner. And Sir Charles Barry, who was essentially a classicist, produced the new Barry Italian in the Travellers' Club, the Reform Club, and in the Manchester Athenaeum. Shop fronts were turned into highly ornamented Italian

Figure 81. The Quadrant, and part of Regent Street

windows and entrances. Even the rows of houses which were springing up in the suburbs were adaptations of Italian villas. Paddington became the locus of a florid Italian grandeur; the new Kensington Gardens Road sprouted mansions with campanile towers and loggias. All this Italian palazzo mode was traced back to Barry and his clubhouses. Even this, however, was better than the deadly monotony which marked street after street of London houses. J. McCulloch noted in 1851[6] that "until a comparatively late period the external appearance of the houses of London was little in harmony with the wealth of their occupiers and the richness of their interiors. Internal comfort was long the only, as it still is . . . the grand object of the Londoners. . . . Hence it was that the interminable rows of dull-looking brick houses . . . led strangers to remark that the best streets resembled long walls pierced with holes for doors and windows." The houses for the most part were built of brick. "But within the last few years those in the principal streets have been mostly plastered or stuccoed over, and their fronts made so exactly to imitate the finest freestone, that it is sometimes no easy matter to distinguish between them."

Steadily encroaching upon the classical-Italianate, however, was the Gothic revival, which had moved out of the period when it leaned upon mere external effect and was in process of becoming as academic as the classical had been. The great missionary for Gothic in the early forties was A. W. Pugin, a Catholic convert who, with the kind of superhuman energy and gusto which were so much a part of the Victorian character,

Figure 82. St. George's Hall, Liverpool. Elmes, architect

Figure 83. The Athenaeum Club, Pall Mall

turned Gothic into a religious crusade: Gothic was the only Christian
architecture.* Not only did he sprinkle England with Gothic churches
but he wrote constantly on behalf of his cause. His *Contrasts, or a parallel between the architecture of the 15th and 19th Centuries,* published
in 1836 (second edition, 1841), was a biting satirical attack upon
so-called pagan architecture. In more than one instance he made a successful point about the extraordinary architectural conglomeration peculiar to the day. His chapter on "The Present Degraded State of
Ecclesiastical Buildings" is a savage exposure of the state of neglect into
which England's great churches had fallen. "Westminster Abbey itself,"
he wrote, ". . . is in a lamentable state of neglect, and is continually
being disfigured by the erection of more vile masses of marble. Having
occasion lately to examine the interior of this wonderful church, I was
disgusted beyond measure at perceiving that the chapel of St. Paul had
been half filled up with a huge figure of James Watt, sitting in an arm-
chair on an enormous square pedestal, with some tasteless ornaments,
which, being totally unlike any Greek or Roman foliage, I suppose to
have been intended by the sculptor to be Gothic. This is the production
of no less a personage than S. F. Chantrey." In an appendix he pointed

---

* It is worth noting that this zeal for Gothic had little connection with the
medieval revival in religion of the Oxford Movement. Newman liked Gothic, but
was chiefly concerned with the uses of a church building. In *Discourses on the
Scope and Nature of University Education* he said: ". . . a revival of an almost-
forgotten architecture, which is at present taking place in our own country, in
France, and in Germany, may in some way or other run away with us into this
or that error. . . ."

out that on the first of May, 1841, the contents of the font in the parish church of St. Helen's, York, were: "three dusters, a sponge, a hammer, several pieces of old rope, some portions of old books, a hand broom, several tin candle sockets and candle ends, besides a large deposit of dirt."

A zeal like this left its mark. In a few years Ruskin came along to support the thesis that great art could be created only by a noble and devout people, and that great art was Gothic by definition. In the *Seven Lamps of Architecture*, 1849, Ruskin argued eloquently for Gothic, never quite succeeding in making clear in just what way it was to represent organically or symbolically a nation devoted to trade. He confused his admirers almost as much as he inspired them. The inspiration took hold, however, and as the Gothic revival spread, Ruskin's sanction was used for much which revolted him. Many years later he wrote in his *Stones of Venice:*

> I would rather for my own part that no architects had ever con-descended to adopt one of the views suggested in this book. I have had indirect influence on nearly every cheap villa builder between this and Bromley, and there is scarcely a public-house near the Crystal Palace but sells its gin and bitters under pseudo-Victorian capitals copied from the Church of the Madonna of Health of the Miracles. And one of my principal motives for leaving my present house is that it is surrounded everywhere by the accursed Frankenstein monsters of, indirectly, my own making.[7]

For Pugin led to Gilbert Scott, and Scott created the Albert Memorial, and beyond the Albert Memorial lay the wastelands of Victorian and Builder's Gothic, where all the sentimental bad taste of a nation converged on public and domestic creations the horrors of which only time and war have laid waste.

In the meantime the real architectural creations went unrecognized as such: the beautiful clean-arched viaducts which the engineers were making as a path for the iron horse; the simple and functional bridges, both suspension and tubular. And, more formally, such a building as the London Coal Exchange, opened in 1849. In this building erected for the most obvious of dingily commercial uses J. D. Bunning, behind a commonplace stone exterior, threw up a domed inner court of articulated cast iron and glass which not only anticipated in time the Crystal Palace, but had a unique architectural integrity of its own.

The 1840's, however, saw the creation of one great set of buildings in Tudor Gothic: the new Houses of Parliament, begun in 1840 and formally opened in 1852. The competition among architects was won by Barry, who turned from his classical and Italianate manner to con-

Figure 84. Villa in the "cottage" style

ceive and execute what was the most important architectural work of
the nineteenth century. Ruskin could frown on it and call it in this
year "the absurdest and emptiest piece of filigree, and as it were eternal
foolscap in freestone," but other competent judges found it a masterly
piece of designing—its one weakness perhaps being a too-monotonous
repetition of exterior detail and the lack of relief or contrast in broad
surfaces. Barry secured the services of Pugin and turned over to him
the ornamentation and detail. The building contains the best work of
the two men: Barry's massive grasp of fundamental plan and function
and Pugin's rich knowledge of Gothic decoration.

And what of music in these years? There was plenty of it, and a
kind for every taste.

As far as the writing of music was concerned, the early Victorian
years were the nadir of British composition. The home-grown composers
were energetic and prolific, but Sterndale Bennett's decorously refined
and undistinguished concertos and oratorios were as high as England
seemed to be able to reach. Balfe's thin and popular *Bohemian Girl*, out
of the thirty operas he wrote, was the peak of his own and of English
operatic achievement. The cantata was perhaps the most distinctive Victorian achievement in music. It was completely and piously respectable
and gave a public which looked with suspicion upon the theater an
opportunity to indulge in mildly theatrical emotions.

It was left to foreigners to supply the real musical talent of the age.
Here it could not be said that the English were unappreciative. To
be sure, Bach was unknown, though Bennett tried to introduce him

and even organized a Bach Society in 1849. It was Handel who came close to dominating English musical performance during these years, in spite of the encroaching popularity of Mendelssohn. Yet the great musical event of 1846 was the presentation at the Birmingham Festival of Mendelssohn's *Elijah*, conducted by the composer himself with an orchestra of 126 instruments and a provincial chorus of 272 singers. At the conclusion of the Festival, two mornings after the presentation of *Elijah*, 3,000 persons crowded into the Town Hall to hear the *Messiah*. It was Mendelssohn's last visit to England; he died the next year.

Liszt had been given an enthusiastic reception on his second visit in 1841, appearing before the Queen. Chopin gave recitals in Manchester, Glasgow, and Edinburgh, as well as in London, in 1848. Berlioz in 1847 conducted Balfe's new opera, *The Maid of Honor*, at Drury Lane. And in the early years of the reign the elder Johann Strauss had dazzled the public with his Viennese waltzes, visiting many of the provincial towns.*

English opera made small headway against the overwhelming popularity of Italian opera. Wallace's *Maritana* (1845) was the only close rival to *The Bohemian Girl*, and when Drury Lane opened as an English opera house in 1847, in competition with the Italian opera at Covent Garden, it survived only a year. Rossini, Bellini, Donizetti, and more recently Verdi were the staple of operatic performance, and the favorite performers, year after year, were the great tenor Mario, the basso Lablache, and the sopranos Grisi and Garcia. In the ballet Cerito, Taglioni, and Fanny Elssler were perennially welcomed. As we shall see, Jenny Lind took England by storm on her first appearance in 1847. During the forties those who liked good music had to bring both their composers and performers across the channel.

Nevertheless a taste for music, good and bad, and particularly for singing, extended deep into every corner of Britain. London had its Philharmonic Society, and a flourishing Handel Society. Choral singing flourished in Birmingham and its neighborhood, and the Birmingham Choral Society conducted subscription concerts throughout the forties. Liverpool had a number of concert halls, one of which held nearly 3,000 people. Hereford sponsored musical festivals. London had a Beethoven Quartet Society as well as innumerable *Soirées Musicales*. In 1843 Manchester had seen the first meeting of the Lancashire and

---

* When Strauss died in 1848 the *Critic* ran the following notice: "The death of this great hero of the ball-room was an irreparable loss. He died in Vienna, leaving a family of six children and scarcely enough property in ready money to defray the funeral expenses. His wife is still living, but they have been separated for years—no uncommon thing in Vienna."

Figure 85. The Birmingham Musical Festival: the Great Hall

Cheshire Workmen's Singing Classes at Free Trade Hall, with 1,500 performers, and in 1845 the first of a series of concerts for the working classes conducted by the Lancashire and Cheshire Philharmonic Institution.

Singing societies multiplied in every part of the kingdom, aided by the invention of the tonic-sol-fa system. Since 1842 John Hullah had been conducting his gigantic singing classes at Exeter Hall; 25,000 pupils passed under his baton between 1842 and 1860. The hall held 4,000, and frequently he had as many as 2,000 singers combining their voices before crowded audiences. So successful was this venture that in 1850 a special hall—St. Martin's, in Charles Street—holding 3,000 was built for the purpose.

The most popular conductor of the period was a melodramatic Frenchman by the name of Louis Antoine Jullien, who began giving summer concerts at Drury Lane in 1840 and whose "Concerts d'Hiver" became an annual institution after 1842. He was above all a popularizer who made waltzes, polkas, and army quadrilles the staple of his programs, and who enlivened the proceedings by re-enforcing the percussion instruments with explosives and fireworks. He used a jeweled baton and ostentatiously donned kid gloves handed to him on a silver tray. At the conclusion of a performance he would sink back exhausted into a gilt-and-red-velvet chair. *Punch* called him "the Napoleon of Quadrille," crediting him with the intention of bringing out *Stabat Mater* waltzes and a *Dead March* gallopade.

> Demon of discord, with mustaches cloven—
> Arch-impudent *improver* of Beethoven—
> Tricksy professor of *charlatanerie*—
> Inventor of musical artillery—

But Jullien was as much genius as charlatan. Along with his melodramatic effects he smuggled in a good deal of Beethoven and Mozart, and probably did more than any other person of his time to popularize good symphonic music.

It was an age, too, when musical entertainers had a great vogue; the songs which they popularized were sold in thousands of cheap booklets and sung everywhere. The concerts of John Orlando Parry, harpist, pianist, and singer, became almost a craze. The *Illustrated London News,* reviewing a performance in May, 1846, said: "He is a pianist of forty-hand power, to whom every school of music is familiar. He has three distinct qualities of voice, which enable him to imitate the high notes of the soprano, and the deep tones of the basso, with the intervening tone register, in a most extraordinary manner. The 'Somnambula' (a Mesmeric opera compressed) and the 'Family Argument' (Foreign Affairs) are acceptable additions to his repertoire. An imitation of the 'Maniac' song, 'I saw her walking on the wall,' elicited peals of laughter. We may add," continued this estimable family newspaper, "that John Parry is as much esteemed for his excellent private qualities as he has been distinguished in his public career." The extent of his public recognition is pointed up in an announcement that he was to appear in Birmingham, on the Saturday following the Festival, in concert with Grisi, Mario, and Lablache.

Another and even more popular singer and song writer was Henry Russell, who wrote more than 800 songs and in company with another prolific poet and song writer, Charles Mackay, began to give entertainments in England about 1841, after his return from the United States. In that country while playing the organ at the Presbyterian Church in Rochester, New York (as he testifies in his memoirs), he discovered that sacred music played quickly "makes the best kind of secular music." By playing "Old Hundredth" very fast he produced the air of "Get out o' de way, Ole Dan Tucker." "My Good Ship! Come Home! Come Home!" (a Christmas carol in the days of Henry VIII) became "Buffalo Girls! Come out Tonight!" and "Hark! the Vesper Hymn Is Stealing" was turned into "Lubly Rosa! Sambo Come!"

When Russell opened at the Hanover Square Rooms in London, crowded houses heard his "Gambler's Wife," "The Ship on Fire," and "The Maniac." As for "Cheer! Boys, Cheer!," "The Ivy Green," and "A Life on the Ocean Wave," he modestly testifies that they "were to be heard on every barrel organ and hurdy-gurdy in the city, and were whistled and sung by young and old alike."[8] His best-known pieces were "The Gambler's Wife" (an obvious didacticism); "The Maniac" (a protest against the iniquities of private lunatic asylums); "Man the Lifeboat"; "The Old Arm-Chair" (words by Eliza Cook); "The Ship on Fire"; "The Slave Ship"; "There's a Good Time Coming"; "Cheer! Boys, Cheer!"; and "To the West." The words of the last three were written by Charles Mackay and were his most popular pieces. Of "To the West" Russell boasted, perhaps a little too enthusiastically, that it created such a furor at the time of the emigrations that it "induced many thousands of people to turn attention to the promises held out by the New World." But "There's a Good Time Coming" was, as we know by independent testimony, sung on the emigrant ships by the perplexed travelers who were seeking a new life.

There's a good time coming, boys, a good time coming:
We may not live to see the day, But earth shall glisten in the ray
Of the good time coming:
Cannonballs may aid the truth, But thought's a weapon stronger:
We'll win our battle by its aid;—Wait a little longer.

. . . .

The pen shall supersede the sword,
And right, not might, shall be the lord
In the good time coming
Worth, not truth, shall rule mankind,
And be acknowledged stronger . . .

The other ran

Cheer! boys, cheer! no more of idle sorrow—
Courage! true hearts shall bear us on our way,
Hope points before, and shows the bright tomorrow,
Let us forget the darkness of today.

And

To the West! to the West! to the land of the free,
Where the mighty Missouri rolls down to the sea,
Where a man is a man, if he's willing to toil,
And the humblest may gather the fruits of the soil.

The popular songs of the day leaned heavily on two themes. The first was that of melodramatic horror, as in "The Maniac":

No! by heav'n, no! by heav'n, I am not mad!
Oh! release me, Oh! release me . . .

Ay, laugh ye fiends, laugh, laugh ye fiends!
Yes, by heav'n,—yes, by heav'n, they've driven me mad!

And in "The Slave Ship":

Gloomily stood the captain, with his arms upon his breast,
And his eyebrow firmly knotted and his iron lips compressed:—
"Are all well whipp'd below there?" "Ay, ay," the seaman said.
"Heave up the worthless lubbers, the dying and the dead" . . .

The other vein was that of heavily-charged sentiment, as in Eliza Cook's "Old Arm-Chair":

I love it, I love it, and who shall dare
To chide me for loving that old arm-chair.
I've treasur'd it long as a holy prize,
I've bedew'd it with tears, I've embalmed it with sighs . . .

Yet at this distance one has the surprising experience of recognizing many of the lyrics, which became for several generations a part of the national folkways both in England and America. Thus

A life on the ocean wave! A home on the rolling deep!
Where the scatter'd waters rave, And the winds their revels keep!

Also the American George Morris's

Woodman spare that tree—
Touch not a single bough—
In youth it sheltered me,
And I'll protect it now.

And Mary Howitt's

"Will you walk into my parlour?" said a spider to a fly,
"'Tis the prettiest little parlour that ever you did spy."

When the Victorian family gathered around the piano in the evening, songs even more sentimental were available and popular. "Take back those gems you gave me, I prized them but for thee"; "One kindly word before we part, One word besides farewell"; "The heart bow'd down by weight of woe, To weakest hopes will cling"; and "I heard her angel voice grow faint, and knew that Death was near." *Punch* satirized the prevailing lugubriousness by suggesting as the typical title "Brush back that briny tear."

Perhaps the most popular song of the decade was a catchy nonsense ditty called "Trab, Trab, Trab"—sung by Fräulein Jetty Treffz at Jullien's Promenade Concerts in 1849–50 and repeated *ad nauseam* until by December, 1850, the critics were referring to it as a "horror and detestation."

> One day while gently riding,
> > To reach my fair one's home
> I found her fondly waiting,
> > And when she saw me come
> She cried aloud with glee,
> > "My lov'd one haste to me!"—
> Trab, trab, trab, trab my gallant steed,
> > And bring my love to me.
> > > Trab, trab, etc.

Comic songs and singers were no less popular. Sam Cowell, who was going strong in the forties, made a great hit with "The Ratcatcher's Daughter" and with "Vilikins and His Dinah," which the great comic entertainer Robson had introduced at the Olympic Theatre:

> It is of a rich merchant I am going for to tell,
> > Who had for a daughter an unkimmon nice gal.
> Her name it was Dinah, just sixteen years old,
> With a wery large fortune in silver and gold.
> > Ri-toorali, toorali toorali, da.

Another of Cowell's successes was his burlesque of *Hamlet:*

> Hamlet lov'd a maid—Calumny had pass'd her—
> She never had play'd tricks, 'Cause nobody had ask'd her;
> Madness seiz'd her wits, Poor Lord Chamb'rlain's daughter—
> She jumped into a pond, And went to heav'n by water.
> > Tooral looral lay, etc.[9]

This brings us into the region of the "Caves of Harmony" and the supper clubs—the antecedents of the music halls—of which more later. For the moment it is enough to say that not all these songs were of a kind to be placed in the hands of a Victorian daughter and sung in the family circle. But somewhere, somehow, all found music that they liked, from Beethoven to Dr. Mackay, LL.D. And who will say that the "popular" song has made great progress in a hundred years?

The summer was hot beyond all belief; on July 4th the temperature in London was 95° in the shade. All who could, fled to the seashore, where again midsummer madness set in. There were angry letters to the *Times* concerning the indelicate way in which bathing was conducted at Ramsgate. Ladies frolicked about in the sea, and even danced polkas in their bathing dresses as if entirely removed from the gaze of the male sex—who, on the contrary (complained the correspondents), crowded the beach. Better police supervision was suggested.

After several weeks of drought the heat wave broke with a terrific thunderstorm on August 1st, accompanied by great hailstones which did severe damage. At Buckingham Palace the roof of the picture gallery was totally destroyed. Seven thousand panes of glass were broken in the Houses of Parliament and Westminster Hall; at Burford's Panorama, 10,000 panes. The skylights in the Quadrant and the Burlington Arcade were shattered. At Ditton Park, the residence of the Duke of Buccleuch, 2,000 windows were broken.

The promise of the harvest, however, seemed reasonably hopeful, with the important exception of the potato crop. The disease had appeared earlier than last year and its ravages were more extensive; potatoes failed in England and Scotland as well as in Ireland. In Ireland the prospect of a second year's famine was terrifying. All winter and spring the Irish had been suffering from the effects of the 1845 famine. Since the previous November nearly £1,000,000 had been spent for relief, and by November of 1846 the number of people engaged in public works was 150,000. It soon became evident that pounding rocks on roads was not the way for a famishing people to conserve its strength, and public works were rapidly withdrawn in favor of direct relief. Disease followed in the wake of starvation; fever and dysentery decimated whole local populations. The newspapers were filled with reports of violence and depredation. The Government poured large supplies of Indian corn into the country (and taught the natives how to use the unfamiliar grain), but few dared to imagine what another year of privation would result in. The peasantry were arming, it was reported, almost to a man—for what acts of desperation no one knew.

At the same time those professionally committed to making propaganda for repeal of the Union redoubled their efforts. Yet there was division in the ranks, and, more importantly, in the leadership. Daniel O'Connell was old and sick and it now seemed that in spite of his inflammatory speeches he had never been in favor of "physical force." This moderation was not liked by the Young Ireland wing of the movement, which broke from O'Connell under the more fiery leadership of Smith O'Brien. Its members walked away from Old Ireland at Conciliation Hall in Dublin and set up for themselves in a building in Abbey Street. John Mitchel, afterward editor of the *United Irishman*, was another extremist. He published plans of the forthcoming insurrection, described "how street-fighting should be conducted, how and where the barricades were to be erected, how the women were to be taught to throw vitriol from the windows on the Queen's troops, and to fling broken bottles before the cavalry, how the walls of houses were to be perforated for sharpshooters."[10] While the Government was trying to keep life in his fellow Irishmen by means of public rations, O'Brien made his triumphal entry into Limerick on an elaborate car drawn by six horses, with 300,000 cheering in the streets (an Irish estimate by the *Limerick Reporter*).

In August a futile attack—the seventh—was made on the life of Louis Philippe. . . . The Scott Monument in Edinburgh was inaugurated in the midst of a driving rain. . . . Westminster Bridge, in bad condition, was closed to carriage traffic, and plans for a new bridge were announced. . . . Thirty-nine persons drowned in a coal mine when it was flooded after a violent storm. . . . Three public parks were opened simultaneously in Manchester—the first parks in the city. . . . The *Great Britain* steamship, carrying 181 passengers and a crew of ninety (the largest number yet to start across the Atlantic), got off her course and went aground in Dundrum Bay off the coast of Ireland. No passengers were injured, but there the great vessel stuck until the next year, when she was finally floated off. . . . In London the wooden paving in Cheapside was being taken up as too slippery and dangerous to horses. At the same time Fleet Street was closed to traffic, and there was much complaining about the excavations which always seemed to be appearing in the busiest thoroughfares.

Street repairs were not the only hazard to London traffic. Even more objectionable were the advertising vans—a subject which involves the whole vexed problem of advertising in the forties. If songs are a clue toward understanding a people, their advertisements bring one even closer to the tangibilities and immediacies of life as it went on from day to day. What people tried to sell to each other and how they tried to sell it is more than an episode in the life of any decade. A new flush toilet has social significance. A nostrum can indicate the digestive life of a nation. An advertisement for a governess can open whole vistas of comparative economics as well as a view of polite education in the forties. The renowned and scholarly Porson had said that a single Athenian newspaper would be worth all the commentaries on Aristophanes put together.

In 1846 Sir Peter Lawrie, the popular magistrate, was making an attempt to grapple with the "enormous nuisance" of the advertising van. Any Englishman wandering through the streets of London, or any other large town, was likely to have hand bills by the dozen thrust at him; and he was used to seeing all available blank walls, hoardings, and fences plastered with great placards shouting, in gigantic type and flaming colors, everything from the virtue of Guinness's Dublin Stout to gentlemen's walking clothes to the latest attraction at the Lyceum or the Queen's Theatre. Thus the *Domestic Tale*, with one man shooting another on the quarter-deck of a vessel in flames, or the grand fight between grenadiers and Jacobite conspirators in the *Miser's Daughter;* or a view of the "tremendous Khyber Pass" as it might be seen nightly, "with Lady Sale at the top of it brandishing a pistol in either hand, beneath the cocked and levelled terrors of which a row of turbaned Orientals kneel on either side of the heroine."[11] The so-called external paper hangers or bill-stickers were almost a corporate body of their own, with strict rules of tenure and priority.

More recently the "peripatetic placard" had been introduced: at first just one man walking the streets holding aloft a banner calling attention to the latest issue of the *Weekly Dispatch* or to some patent medicine. Next came the man with the advertisements on boards hanging before and behind; Dickens seems to have been the first to give him the title of sandwich man. Soon it was discovered that the public impact was greater if a dozen men in a row carried identical such advertisements. And shortly the vehicular advertisement—bigger and better—succeeded the pedestrian. A colossal seven-foot hat was set on wheels and pulled through the streets by a broken-down horse.* A huge perambulating obelisk was inscribed in honor of cheap "washable wigs." A complicated structure of Gothic arches and niches contained dummies wearing the stuffed-out dresses of the day—the whole revolving slowly on its pedestal by means of some internal clockwork construction. The *Times* described a great military tableau on wheels which exhorted the public to emulate the conduct of a gentleman in a field marshal's uniform giving a dinner to five or six other military men—all field marshals like himself —"who were in raptures like himself over a few blue-and-white plates which the host was emphatically declaring he had purchased recently, in 'cash down,' for a mere trifle." Thus to the hazard of traveling on foot among the sandwich men was added the vehicular congestion of the advertising vans, some of them reaching "nearly as high as a second-floor window."

Aside from the more spectacular street displays the newspapers and

---

* This was the hat which annoyed Carlyle in *Past and Present*. The hatter, he said, "has not attempted to *make* better hats, as he was appointed by the Universe to do . . . but his whole industry is turned to *persuade* us that he has made such."

Figure 86. The perambulating hat

magazines were of course the chief outlet for the man who had something to sell. To read the advertisements of the forties is to come almost tangibly in contact with the everyday Englishman, his aspirations and his comforts, his snobberies and his fears, his vanities and his digestive complaints.

The first page of any English newspaper was a human record—even beyond the cryptic cries of the "personal" columns. Cooks wanted at £30 a year and governesses at £20; bankruptcies of upholsterers, linen drapers, chemists, and druggists, booksellers, tobacconists, and grocers; noblemen wanting valets, footmen, housemaids—and ditto wanting positions. Lea and Perrins's Worcestershire Sauce, "prepared from the recipe of a nobleman in the county"; Schweppe's soda waters and ginger beer; Pears's pale amber soap; magic and phantasmagoria lanterns; Ne Plus Ultra Pins, with perfect solid head and smooth, adamantine points; Spencer's Pulmonic Elixir; ivory table knives, 11s. a dozen; Ricket's Patent Calorifere Gas Stoves; the Vesta Patent Stove—"a Madeira climate in England." For railway and coach travelers, Wray's Aromatic Spice Plasters for the Chest; for the bald, Professor Browne's Ventilating Invisible Peruke; for the toothless, the new artificial teeth offered by Mr. Howard, dentist-surgeon: "teeth which will never decay, installed by a method which does not require the extraction of old roots and is free from wires, springs, and ligatures." And always, in newspaper or magazine, the rhymed advertisements of the aggressive Moses and Son, "Tailors,

ROWLAND'S MACASSAR OIL.

This ELEGANT, FRAGRANT, and PELLUCID OIL, in its *preservative, restorative,* and *beautifying* qualities, is unequalled over the whole world. It *preserves* and *reproduces* the *hair,* even at a late period of life; prevents it from *turning grey.* or if so changed, *restores it to its original colour;* frees it from *scurf* and *impurity,* and renders it *soft, silky, curly,* and *glossy.* It preserves its virtues unimpaired by the change of climate, and is alike in use from the frigid to the torrid zone—from the assemblies of St. Petersburg to those of Calcutta and the remote East.

Its value is of course enhanced by being used at an early period of life; and to CHILDREN it is especially recommended as forming the basis of A BEAUTIFUL HEAD OF HAIR.

CAUTION.—Numerous *pernicious* compounds are universally sold as "MACASSAR OIL." To ensure the *genuine* article, see that the bottle is enclosed in a wrapper, (a steel engraving of exquisite workmanship,) on which are engraved these words, in *two* lines—

ROWLAND'S
MACASSAR OIL.

*** As a further protection, the words "*Rowland's Macassar Oil*" are engraved on the back of the envelope nearly 1,500 times, containing 29,028 letters—WITHOUT THIS NONE ARE GENUINE.

Price 3s. 6d.; 7s.; Family Bottles, (equal to four sm ll,) 10s. 6d. and double that size, 21s. per bottle.

ROWLANDS' KALYDOR,

An ORIENTAL BOTANICAL PREPARATION of singular efficacy for rendering the SKIN peculiarly SOFT and FAIR, and for bestowing a delicate roseate hue on the COMPLEXION.

Utterly pure and free from all mineral or metallic admixture, it exerts the most *soothing, gentle, cooling,* and *purifying* action on the skin; and by its agency on the pores and minute secretory vessels, dispels all impurities from the surface, allays every tendency to inflammation, and thus most effectually dissipates all REDNESS, TAN, PIMPLES, BLOTCHES, SPOTS, FRECKLES, and other Cutaneous Visitations. Its constant use will transform the *bilious* and *clouded* aspect to one of *clear* and *spotless white;* while it invests the NECK, HANDS, and ARMS with *delicacy* and *fairness,* and perpetuates the charms which it bestows to the most advanced period of life. In travelling; during the heat and dust of summer; and as a preservative against the frosts of winter, its virtues have long and extensively been acknowledged.

It is alike prized by GENTLEMEN who suffer from tenderness after shaving, as affording the most grateful alleviation of the part affected.

Sold in half-pint bottles, at 4s. 6d. each; and in pints, at 8s. 6d. each, duty included.

ROWLANDS' ODONTO,

A FRAGRANT WHITE POWDER, *prepared solely from Oriental Herbs* of inestimable virtue, for *strengthening, preserving* and *cleansing the teeth.*

It eradicates the factitious formation of tartar, and by the removal of that extraneous substance lends a *salutary growth and freshness to the gums.* It removes from the surface of the teeth the spots of incipient decay, *polishes and preserves the enamel,* substituting for discolour and the aspect of impurity, the *most pure and pearl-like whiteness;* while, from its salubrious and disinfecting qualities, it gives *sweetness and perfume to the breath* bestowing at once *cleanliness,* and the *appearance and reality of health.*

Price 2s. 9d. per Box, duty included.

NOTICE.—It is necessary on purchasing either Article to see that the word "**ROWLANDS'**" is on the Envelope. For the Protection of the Public from Fraud and Imposition, the *Hon. Commissioners of Her Majesty's Stamps* have authorized the Proprietors to have their Names engraven on the Government Stamp, which is affixed to the *KALYDOR* and *ODONTO,* thus—**A. ROWLAND & SON, 20, Hatton Garden.**

*** *All without are spurious Imitations.*

Be sure to ask for "ROWLANDS'" Articles.

Sold by the Proprietors, and by all Chemists and Perfumers.

Figure 87. Beauty by the bottle

Woolen Drapers, Hosiers, Furriers, Hatters, Boot and Shoe Makers, etc.," at 154–5–6–7 the Minories. Take at random one of the New Year's messages of this house, addressed to "John Bull":

> Mr. Bull,—We return you our thanks, as we ought
> For your vast and your lasting amount of support.
> . . . .
> And, in truth, you've not tarnish'd the fame you have won
> In your liberal favours to Moses and Son.
> . . . .
> The warehouse of Moses and Son you have made
> The Glory of Commerce, the Wonder of Trade.
> . . . .
> Our waistcoats shall rival all others by far,
> And our Trowsers shall prove that our House is the star.
> . . . .
> We certainly think we had better conclude,
> In hopes you'll support (as you ever have done)
> The vast trading House of
> ### E. MOSES & SON

The appeal to vanity was no discovery of the 1840's. For years the advertising pages had published the seducements of Mr. Rowland with his Macassar Oil for the Hair, and his Kalydor: "An Oriental Botanical Preparation of singular efficiency for rendering the Skin peculiarly Soft and Fair, and for bestowing a delicate roseate hue on the Complexion." His oil—the elegant, the fragrant, the pellucid—not only "preserves and reproduces the hair," but also prevents its turning gray, or, if so changed, restores it to its original color. Mr. Rowland was much concerned with cautioning his clientele against pernicious compounds "universally sold as 'Macassar Oil'" and with urging them to make sure that the bottle had his own engraved label. He never thought it worth while to tell them that his oil had never seen a Macassar nut, but was made of one pound of olive oil to one dram of oil of origanum.* He was doubtless pleased, as any advertiser would be, when the comedian Joseph Grimaldi tried successfully on the stage the experiment of turning a wooden box into a hair trunk, with the aid of one double bottle.

If vanity was a powerful motive, the appeal to fear and pain, compounded with the suggestion that in using X's nostrum you were hobnobbing with your fellow sufferers among the nobility, was even stronger. The patent-medicine advertisements of the day, completely unregulated, are a study in the grotesque. The sales were astronomical.

---

* These and other disillusioning analyses from the *Druggist's General Receipt Book,* 1850 edition.

For Locock's Pulmonic Wafers, during the month of January, 1847, one house in London paid the vendor £700—and the wafers were a compound of morphia and ipecacuanha.[12] *Hannay's Royal Almanack for 1846* contained a catalogue of patent medicines sold in Oxford Street, London: 783 different medicinal nostrums for human use. Pills, 190;

 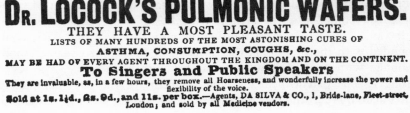
Figures 88 and 89. Cures for everything

Holloway's Pills.

CURE OF A DISORDERED LIVER AND STOMACH, WHEN IN A MOST HOPELESS STATE.

Extract of a Letter from Mr Matthew Harvey, of Chapel Hall, Airdie, Scotland, dated the 15th of January, 1850.

To Professor Holloway.

SIR,—Your valuable Pills have been the means, with God's blessing, of restoring me to a state of perfect health, and at a time when I thought I was on the brink of the grave. I had consulted several eminent Doctors, who, after doing what they could for me, stated that they considered my case as hopeless. I ought to say that I had been suffering from a liver and stomach complaint of long standing, which during the last two years got so much worse, that every one considered my condition as hopeless. I, as a last resource, got a box of your pills, which soon gave relief, and by persevering in their use for some weeks, together with rubbing night and morning your Ointment ver my chest and stomach, and right side, I have by their means alone got completely cured, and to the astonishment of myself and everybody who knows me.

(Signed)   MATTHEW HARVEY.

CURE OF A CASE OF WEAKNESS AND DEBILITY OF FOUR YEARS' STANDING.

Extract of a Letter from Mr William Smith, of No. 5, Little Thomas Street, Gibson Street, Lambeth, dated Dec 12th, 1849.

To Professor Holloway

SIR,— I beg to inform you that for nearly five years I hardly knew what it was to have a day's health, suffering from extreme weakness and debility, with constant nervous headaches, giddiness, and sickness of the stomach, together with a great depression of spirits. I used to think that nothing could benefit me, as I had been to many medical men, some of whom, after doing all that was in their power, informed me that they considered that I had some spinal complaint beyond the reach of cure, together with a very disordered state of the stomach, and liver, making my case so complicated that nothing could be done for me. One day, being unusually ill and in a dejected state, I saw your pills advertised, and resolved to give them a trial, more perhaps from curiosity than with a hope of being cured, however I soon found myself better by taking them, and so I went on persevering in their use for six months, when I am happy to say they effected a perfect cure.

(Signed)   WILLIAM SMITH,
(frequently called EDWARD)

A CURE OF ASTHMA, OF TWENTY YEARS' STANDING.

Extract of a Letter from Mr J. K. Heydon, 78, King Street, Sydney, dated 10th of November, 1842.

To Professor Holloway.

SIR,—I have the pleasure to inform you that many extraordinary cures of Asthma have been effected here by means of your pills. One is that of a Lady residing near the "Razorback," who after having for twenty years been unable to make the slightest exertion, suffering very fearfully from shortness of breath, coughing, and spitting, but is now, to use her own expression, able to run up the top of that mountain. Another case is that of r Caton, Tailor, Hutchinson's Buildings, Clarence street, who was so dreadfully bad that he was confined entirely to his bedroom for six months, prior to his commencing with your pills, and attended regularly by his medical man, who pronounced him to be in a dying state, yet he, likewise, to my knowledge, has been restored to perfect health by the use of your pills, and rubbing your ointment night and morning into his chest.

(Signed)   J. H. KEYDON.

THE EARL OF ALDBOROUGH CURED OF A LIVER AND STOMACH COMPLAINT.

Extract of a Letter from his Lordship, dated Villa Messina, Leghorn, 21st February, 1845.

To Professor Holloway.

SIR,—Various circumstances prevented the possibility of my handing you before this time for your politeness in sending me your pills as you did. I now take this opportunity of sending you an order for the amount, and, at the same time, to add that your pills have effected a cure of a disorder in my Liver and Stomach, which all the most eminent of the Faculty at home, and all over the Continent, had not been able to effect; nay, not even the waters of Carlsbad and Marienbad. I wish to have another box and a pot of ointment, in case any of my family should ever require either.

Your most obliged and obedient Servant,
(Signed)   ALDBOROUGH.

These celebrated Pills are wonderfully efficacious in the following Complaints.

Ague	Female Irregularities	Scrofula, or King's Evil
Asthma	Fevers of all kinds	Sore Throats
Bilious complaints	Fits	Stone and Gravel
Blotches on the skin	Gout	Secondary symptoms
Bowel complaints	Headache	Tic-Douloureux
Colics	Indigestion	Tumours
Constipation of the	Inflammation	Ulcers
Bowels	Jaundice	Venereal Affections
Consumption	Liver Complaints	Worms of all kinds
Debility	Lumbago	Weakness, from what-
Dropsy	Piles	ever cause, &c. &c.
Dysentery	Rheumatism	
Erysipelas	Retention of urine	

N.B.—Directions for the guidance of patient in every disorder are affixed to each box.

lozenges, 80; tinctures, elixirs, and drops, 74; plasters, liniments, and ointments, 100; besides various powders, balsams, and liquids.

The leading proprietary medicines were Parr's Life Pills, Morison's Pills, Holloway's Pills and Ointments, and Cockle's Antibilious Pills.

The family of Parr dated, according to the house biography, from the old days: an engraving showed the original Parr, "at the age of 152," being introduced to King Charles II. Another woodcut showed him gathering herbs and looking very much like Christ with his long gown and staff. In his current advertisements Parr leaned heavily on testimonials; a fifty-page book containing these was available to interested persons, who could learn there, according to attested cases, that six boxes would cure cancer as well as nervous complaints and giddiness and that one R. W. Richardson, a schoolmaster and a walking wreck until he came across Parr, had been cured of (1) a cough of three years' duration; (2) a nervous affection; (3) costiveness; (4) a forty-year-old rheumatism; and (5) a scorbutic humor of forty-four years' duration.

The medications of James Morison had behind them the authority of the British College of Health, in Hamilton Place, a foundation created, strangely enough, by Morison himself. The researches of this institution led it to announce that all diseases lay in the blood stream, and that all could be eradicated by the use of the Vegetable Universal Medicine. Such was the secret power of equal parts of aloes and cream of tartar. In his last illness, it was recorded, Morison followed his own advice; he rejected all other medicine, took more pills as he grew worse, and was in the very act of calling for a fresh box when he died.

"Professor" Holloway was a tradesman who jumped from behind a counter to the highest scientific eminence both in pills and ointment. His grateful clients testified to cures of diseases that included (in part only) ague, asthma, bilious complaints, bowel complaints, cholera, constipation, debility, dropsy, erysipelas, fevers of all kinds, gout, jaundice, liver complaints, piles—to go only halfway through the alphabetical list! An analysis of the ointment showed a compound chiefly of olive oil, lard, and resin, mixed with small quantities of wax and turpentine; and of the pills, aloes with some rhubarb, saffron, and Glauber's salt. The story ran that during the Great Exhibition, Holloway had gained admission to Gore House and made use of the reluctant George Augustus Sala to obtain an introduction to Thackeray. Thackeray appeared to understand the name imperfectly, and complimented the professor in the same strain he would have used in the case of a distinguished military officer. Holloway, confused, had to explain that he was not a general, but merely Professor Holloway. "Oh well," said Thackeray, "I made a very natural mistake, for you, too, must have killed your thousands."

Cockle had the distinction of listing among the patients he had saved some whom all the world thought dead. As a whole, the list of his patrons gave a discouraging insight into the bilious tendencies of the upper classes. His grateful patients included ten dukes, five marquises, fifteen earls, seven viscounts, sixteen barons, one archbishop, thirteen bishops, six dignified clergymen, thirty-two Members of Parliament. Lord Melbourne was one, as was almost each member of his former Cabinet. Colonel Sibthorp was another "martyr to bile."

The list of nostrums could be extended indefinitely. To select a few: Collis Browne's Chlorodyne (a mixture of chloroform, Indian hemp, and morphia—in one ounce there was the equivalent of twelve full medical doses of morphia and thirty-six full doses of chloroform); Barry's Revalenta Arabica, good for everything from asthma to vertigo (and consisting solely of lentils ground to a fine powder); Dr. Kitchener's Peristaltic Persuaders (rhubarb and oil of caraway).

Worsdell's Vegetable Restorative Pills—testimonial: "Sarah, wife of James Broadbent, of Quick-hedge, near Mossley, was for two years in a very weak and languid condition. She had advice and medicine from several doctors, without obtaining the least relief. . . . After taking eight pills, she voided a tapeworm of great length. She has been so remarkably benefitted, that her husband says he is better pleased than if he had received a present of twenty pounds."

Congreve's Balsamic Elixir—testimonial: "Notwithstanding I had been lately married, I found it impossible to sleep on the same pillow with my husband, but was obliged to be supported with bolsters in nearly an upright position. *This, to a person in the situation I then was, was extremely unpleasant.*" But after a quart bottle of elixir, she was enabled to lie down in bed (as attested by her husband).[13]

Baker's Patent Antidote for the Prevention of Sea-Sickness—certification by the steward of the good ship *Ocean:* "This is to certify, that Baker's Patent Antidote was taken by a young lady going to Rotterdam in the *Ocean,* who found great relief from a single dose, having a heavy sea on at the time and likewise several gentlemen. I think myself that the Antidote is a very excellent medicine to take.—F. Willis, Steward."

It was claimed that 40,000 bottles of Atkinson's Infant Preservative were sold annually, its active ingredient being laudanum. It was forced on the public attention by "the portrait of a female, far gone in the family way, in the act of pouring the anti-Malthusian fluid down the throat of a struggling baby with a spoon."

We have noticed earlier how even the sedate *Times* opened its advertising columns to such quack books as *The Confessional, a Medical Pamphlet*—"on Melancholy . . . Mental and Physical Debility, arising

from anxiety, grief, ennui, dissipation, gourmandism, love, and religion";
and *Manhood: the Cause of its Premature Decline, with Plain Directions
for its Perfect Restoration*. It is with a sense of incongruity, however,
that one meets in *The Kentish Independent*, the subtitle of which was
"A Family Newspaper," a notice of the much-advertised "Cordial Balm
of Syriacum" in the column next to the notice of a "Select Establishment
for the Education of a limited number of Young Ladies, conducted by
the Misses Gollop." For the Cordial Balm was a specific for the "renova-
tion of the impaired functions of life, and is exclusively directed to the
cure of such complaints as arise from a disorganization of the Generative
System, whether constitutional or acquired, loss of sexual power, and
syphilitic disease. . . . How many at eighteen receive the impression of
the seeds of syphilitic disease itself?" And immediately beneath: "Perry's
Purifying Specific Pills . . . the most certain ever discovered for every
stage and symptom of the Venereal Disease, in both sexes"—so on to the
description of more specific symptoms. Evangelicalism seemed less concerned with this sort of thing, in the forties, than with trying to keep
the trains from running on Sunday.

Doubtless the advertising efforts of the early Victorians, could they
have reviewed them a century later when millions would be spent to
establish the superiority of a cigarette indistinguishable from any other,
would have seemed as naïve as present-day practices. But they had the
correct instincts, and what they did sold everything from pens to
purgatives.

The hot, brilliant summer came to a close, the season ended, the boat
trains were crowded with families leaving for their annual trip to the
Continent, and on the moors and uplands the grouse were being flushed
out of their coverts. And on Saturday, September 12th, Elizabeth Barrett
and Robert Browning were married quietly in Marylebone Church, without benefit of Mr. Barrett's presence. A week later they were on their
way to Italy. What was eventually to be known as the most romantic
marriage of the century did not even make the *Annual Register*. Nor
was much attention attracted by Newman's departure for Rome, where
he went to undergo a course of discipline preparatory to being ordained
in the Church of Rome.

In October Dickens put out the first of twenty green-covered monthly
installments of his new novel, *Dombey and Son*. From the first it sold
famously; readers and critics alike were delighted to see Dickens "at
home again" with a major work in the vein best suited to him. Slowly

the massive outlines of the Firm of Dombey, "Wholesale, Retail, and for Exportation," took shape; all the Dickensian bustle and humor came alive. Eccentric and lovable and pathetic and haughty and arrogant characters sprang forth—characters instinct with so much vividness and gusto that readers could safely ignore the typically complicated and melodramatic plot which Dickens concocted to imbed his people in.

Six weeks later Thackeray, slowly gathering his forces for the major literary attempt of his career, met the Christmas trade with his little story of *Mrs. Perkins's Ball*, a Titmarshian mélange of kindly satire and humor, with the young Perkinses stealing macaroons on the sly; with Miss Bunion, the ugly, fashionable authoress; Mr. Menchin, the serious young barrister of the Western Circuit; and Mulligan, the improvident Irishman who tags along with Titmarsh to the ball and ends by staying to insult his host. The text of the story served chiefly to support Thackeray's own gay illustrations. It was pleasantly received.

The foggy November disappeared into a cold December; by the tenth, the mercury was fourteen degrees below the freezing point. The Thames had ice in mid-channel. A heavy snow fell; Newcastle was cut off from its communications; the Carlisle trains were brought to a standstill, with the passengers making their escape on foot in the middle of a dark, cold night.

The Covent Garden Theatre was being reconstructed and redecorated for a new and rival Italian opera company which was to make its appearance. . . . Paris fashions for the new year were announced the day after Christmas: skirts were a little fuller; cloaks and mantles were still made in velvet; bonnets were frequently ornamented with feathers or worn with a short veil; the morning and visiting dresses were made quite tight around the waist; the large, spreading patterns currently in vogue used moiré Gothique, rich damask, satine velvet, silk shot in a thousand different colors.

There was a mild tempest of dispute about the cleaning of the pictures in the National Gallery: would the process ruin the pictures or would it merely bring them back to their original brightness of color?* . . . Considerable anxiety was being felt about the Arctic expedition of Sir John Franklin. It had sailed in June, 1845, and no word had been heard from it since December of that year. . . . The last oil lights disappeared from Grosvenor Square and were replaced by gas.

On the last day of the old year wheat was selling at 88s. per quarter in the Uxbridge Market. Many English as well as Irish tightened their belts against a hard winter.

---

* Exactly the same dispute was current in the summer of 1948.

CHAPTER SEVEN

1847 * Food and Famine

ITEMS OF THE NEW YEAR:

It is ushered in by a heavy fog of the pea-soup variety.

Twenty-two policemen are dismissed for having been drunk on Christmas day.

A Dr. J. Wolff is committed for fraudulently pretending to draw corns. He calls himself a "chiropodist."

A new "patent mile-index" for cabs is inaugurated—the first meter for fares.

Announcement is made of the first major operation performed in London with the use of ether anesthesia.

FOR centuries medical science had been searching for some means of alleviating the pain which was the nightmare horror accompanying all surgical operations—a shrieking, screaming, cursing, strapped-down-to-the-table horror which flooded every operating room, threw patients into shock, and unnerved the surgeon, whose skill in those days was equated with speed. He was the best who could extract a stone in fifty-four seconds or amputate a leg in two minutes. Yet all the skill of medical research had brought the profession little further than Shakespeare's poppy and mandragora. Opium and above all whisky were recognized narcotics but well known to be dangerous as well. Mesmerism was feared or scorned by reputable doctors. The patient who endured surgery as late as 1846 faced torture which human means could do little to help— this in spite of the fact that ether (though not its pain-destroying properties) had been discovered in the sixteenth century and that in 1818 Michael Faraday had published in the *Journal of Science and Art* an account of the pain-removing effects of ether, which he compared with those of laughing gas.

It is impossible to exaggerate, then, the cataclysmic impact of the discovery of a Yankee dentist in 1846, the report of which sped across the Atlantic, and the English confirmation of which was carried in the columns of the *Lancet* for January 2d.

Extract from a private letter from Dr. Bigelow of Boston to Dr. Francis Boott of London, November 28, 1846:

My Dear Boott: I send you an account of a new anodyne process lately introduced here, which promises to be one of the important discoveries of the present age. It has rendered many patients insensible to pain during surgical operations, and other causes of suffering. Limbs and breasts have been amputated, arteries tied, tumours extirpated, and many hundreds of teeth extracted, without any consciousness of the least pain on the part of the patient.

The inventor is Dr. Morton, a dentist of this city, and the process consists of the inhalation of the vapour of ether to the point of intoxication. I send you the *Boston Daily Advertiser*, which contains an article . . . relating to the discovery.

An extract from the *Advertiser:*

On the 16th of October, 1846, an operation [the first] was performed at the [Massachusetts General] hospital, upon a patient who had inhaled a preparation administered by Dr. Morton, a dentist of this city, with the alleged intention of producing insensibility to pain. Dr. Morton was understood to have extracted teeth under similar circumstances, without the knowledge of the patient. The present operation was performed by Dr. Warren, and though comparatively slight, involved an incision near the lower jaw, of some inches in extent. . . . On the following day the vapour was administered to another patient with complete success. A fatty tumour, of considerable size, was removed by Dr. Hayward from the arm of a woman, near the deltoid muscle. The operation lasted four or five minutes, during which time the patient displayed occasional marks of uneasiness; but upon subsequently regaining her consciousness, professed not only to have felt no pain, but to have been insensible to surrounding objects. . . . On Saturday, November the 7th, at the Massachusetts General Hospital, the right leg of a young girl was amputated above the knee. . . .

Just below this the *Lancet* printed a letter written to Dr. Boott by Robert Liston, one of the most brilliant and famous of contemporary London surgeons, concerning the first operation to be performed in London with ether. "I tried the ether inhalation today," he wrote, "in a case of amputation of the thigh, and in another requiring evulsion of both sides of the great toenail, one of the most painful operations in surgery, and with the most perfect and satisfactory results." It is worth noting that the amputation so skillfully performed by Dr. Liston was made necessary by the infection of an abscess which developed after the doctor had earlier probed it, according to common practice, with his unsterile fingers—and also that in the audience watching the operation was a young student by the name of Joseph Lister.

Early in January Dr. Lansdowne, of the Bristol General Hospital, used ether anesthesia in amputating a young man's leg. The leg was separated from the body in one minute, but the operation was reported as a "long" one, taking fifteen minutes altogether. By the middle of the month major and minor operations had been performed at University College Hospital, King's College Hospital, Guy's Hospital, St. George's Hospital, the Westminster Hospital, and hospitals in Cambridge, Dublin, Birmingham, and Edinburgh—as well as by many individuals in private practice. The discovery was acclaimed universally as the greatest blessing of the ages for humanity. In the first six months of 1847 the *Lancet* had 107 references to ether anesthesia.

The human tragedy accompanying this great discovery was the bitter quarrel which developed among the Americans seeking to establish their fame and fortune by proving each his own right to the title of benefactor of mankind. It began on a sour note when Morton and his apparent collaborator Charles Thomas Jackson, a well-known Boston chemist and scientist, tried to patent jointly the use of ether as an anesthetic. This early proved impossible, but the waters of discovery were further muddied by the claims of another dentist, Horace Wells, to be the first person to use ether operatively. Morton and Jackson quarreled, and together with Wells engaged in a three-cornered, protracted series of recriminations, charges, and countercharges involving litigation and ending in a most unedifying blackening of character for all concerned.

England also had her claimants: In January, 1847, Dr. R. H. Collyer wrote to the *Lancet* asserting that "years since, I gave the process of inhalation to produce unconsciousness to the world [*sic*]." He had publicly advocated it, he said, since 1842, and had published information

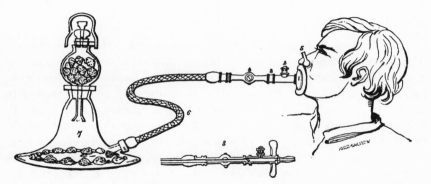

Figure 90. One of the first ether inhalers. From *The Lancet*, January 16, 1847

concerning it in 1843 (he did not say where). At the same time Thomas Dudley wrote to assert that twenty years ago a Dr. Hickman, residing at Shiffnal, had successfully performed experiments with sulphureted ether on animals. The next week, Thomas Lee asserted that as early as 1802 or 1803, Dr. Graham (of "celestial-bed" and "earth-sweating" panacea fame) used to inhale an ounce or two of ether several times a day for its sedative effects. And back in the United States it became clear after a time that an American country practitioner, Dr. Crawford W. Long of Jefferson, Georgia, in 1842 had really performed the first painless operation under ether, but had published nothing about it and was not interested in making claims of priority.

Toward the end of the year the famous Edinburgh obstetrician James Young Simpson introduced the use of chloroform to relieve the pangs of childbirth. Before long chloroform, praised for its "delicious taste," had largely supplanted the use of ether in England as a general anesthetic. By 1850 it was stated in Edinburgh that chloroform had been used in many thousands of cases without a single accident traceable to its use.

Thus, with its minor cacophony of human pettiness, the great medical revolution of the age took place. "In six months," Liston cried after an amputation at University College Hospital, "no operation will be performed without this previous preparation." Within the year Liston himself—a robust and energetic man—was dead at fifty-two of an aortic aneurism brought on, it was said, by "having unduly exerted himself in some violent calisthenic exercises, in which he was accustomed to indulge."

It was noticed briefly in the newspapers in January that cholera had broken out on the shores of the Red Sea, and it was feared that it would soon visit Egypt.

The year began gloomily enough for many of Her Majesty's subjects. The tide of commercial prosperity seemed to have ebbed in the cotton-manufacturing industry. A partial failure of the American cotton crop had raised the price of raw material until it was half again as high as in 1846. Mills closed down and operatives were thrown out of work. In Manchester alone 5,500 workers were dismissed and 13,500 were working short time. Seventeen mills had stopped entirely and sixty-eight were operating only partially. In the whole industry nearly half the workers were employed on short time and some 23,000 were unemployed. By March the average number of working hours was seven. The price of grain, too, had been fluctuating wildly. In the first week of January it was 64s. 3d.; by March it had reached 78s.; by May, 100s.

With many of the mills working only part time, it seemed to the advocates of the Ten Hours Bill an opportune moment to press their cause. Ashley was out of Parliament; so John Fielden introduced the bill. Few men could have made their support more impressive. As one of the largest cotton spinners in England, whose entire income depended upon his industrial profits, Fielden declared that he would rather throw manufactures to the wind than hesitate between private interests and the lives of little children. Russell, now Prime Minister, supported the bill. A converted Macaulay declared that it was the duty of legislators to protect health and morals by restrictive laws. On February 17th it passed its second reading by 195 to 87; on May 3d its final reading by 151 to 88. A willing House of Lords approved, and the bill became law. During the discussion in the Commons, Ashley had lingered in the lobby, reluctant to enter the House. As he wrote in his diary: "I . . . should have been nervously excited to reply, and grieved by inability to do so." On the evening of the third reading he wrote: "What reward shall we give unto the Lord for all the benefits He has conferred upon us?"

Events were to prove that Ashley's exultation was somewhat premature. The bill stipulated after May, 1848, when the law was to go into effect, a fifty-eight-hour week for young persons thirteen to eighteen, and for all females. But the act did not say ten continuous hours per day, and thus a loophole was left for the manufacturers to continue the relay system, under which the operatives could be called to work on shifts so irregular that inspectors were unable to police the factories adequately. Even where the law was obeyed technically, the fact that "protected" women and young people worked early in the morning and late at night defeated the purpose of the legislation. Not until 1850, after a bitter battle, in which he was attacked savagely by the very people he was trying to help, was Ashley able to reach even the compromise of a literal ten-and-a-half-hour day.

Meanwhile the Irish famine was reaching its grim climax.

Pestilence and disease walked hand in hand with starvation. Typhus was spreading rapidly in Dublin. Want, nakedness, and cold were mowing down the people. In many instances the dead were left unburied and the living and the dead lay side by side. The coroners of Cork resolved to hold no more inquests on persons dying in the streets of famine or fever. Within one week there were ninety-five deaths in the union workhouse of Lurgan—one-eighth of its entire number of inhabitants. Women and children were to be seen on the decks of steamers trying to appease their hunger with the turnips half-eaten by the cattle on board. In Coachford parish 4,000 out of 6,000 had not received one substantial meal a day in six months; out of 300 families not less than an average of three in each family had fever, dysentery, or dropsy. As horses died of starvation, the people ate them greedily. Reports indicated that people were dying at the rate of 1,000 a week. In March it was estimated that 240,000 had already perished. And closer home similar if less severe distress was felt in western Scotland, whose inhabitants. like the Irish, depended largely upon the potato for food. Even at such places as Exeter and Taunton there were food riots because of the high price of bread, and incendiarism began again in Cambridgeshire.

In the face of this emergency Parliament moved swiftly to relieve the distress. As soon as the session opened on January 21st it unanimously suspended the operation of the Corn Laws and the Navigation Laws, the latter of which had meant that except under certain reciprocal agreements imports could be made only in British ships manned by British sailors. It was clear, too, that the maintenance of public work on the roads did little except make the roads impassable to traffic and aggravate the already-starving condition of the workers. Hence the laborers on relief works, 734,000 of whom were employed in March, were reduced by June to 28,000. In place of this, temporary relief committees were organized throughout Ireland, supported in part by each locality, in part by voluntary gifts, and in part by Government subsidy. The Society of Friends contributed largely, and great quantities of meal and flour were donated by Americans. Three million daily rations were being distributed at one period. At the same time the Irish Poor Laws were revised to permit relief outside the workhouse.*

---

* Those Members of Parliament who protested that this measure would ruin the landowners, who would have to pay increased taxes to support such relief,

Parliament was forced to pass one restrictive measure for Ireland. Crimes of violence had increased with the growing famine. Homicides, attempts on life, and the firing of dwellings had tripled in the first six months of 1847, until no landed proprietor, bailiff, agent, or steward in the counties of Clare, Limerick, or Tipperary was safe against outrage on the part of the armed bodies of men who prowled nocturnally about the countryside. Thus was passed the Coercion Bill, which invested the lord-lieutenant with extraordinary powers to suppress crime and outrage. This bill, introduced by the new ministry, was in effect the same bill upon which Peel's government had gone down to defeat the year before!

Emigration, a perennial remedy for an underfed Ireland, expanded enormously during these disastrous years. Many Irishmen came to England; Liverpool was choked with them and they roamed the streets of London in increasing numbers. The greater proportion of emigrants, however, went abroad to Canada, Australia, and particularly to the United States, which even then seemed the land of opportunity.

It was estimated that during the three years 1847–49, 182,000 persons emigrated to Canada and 550,000 to the United States—most of them Irish.* The totals, year by year, as estimated in addition to the official records of the Emigration Commissioners, ran:[1]

1842:	151,600 (a depression year)
1843:	112,738
1844:	111,910
1845:	153,622
1846:	220,576
1847:	300,000

were met by those who openly rejoiced that the Irish landlord, traditionally poor and encumbered and traditionally zealous in squeezing the last shilling out of his poverty-stricken tenant farmers, would at last be forced either to assume some of the burden of relief or else, under the Encumbered Estates Act, be forced to sell his properties. The hope for Ireland, many believed, lay in abolition of small tenant holdings, where the farms were frequently too small to support life, and the consolidation of land into large estates upon which the former tenant farmers would be employed, at a living wage, as laborers. The problem was not to be solved this simply; the Irish land question was to heckle England far beyond the forties.

* Spencer Walpole: *History of England*, Vol. V, p. 457. Exact emigration figures are almost impossible to obtain, for in addition to those who went out through government channels were many thousands who made their own arrangements and therefore did not appear in official figures.

Australia, with its high land prices (£1 per acre, as against $1.25 in the United States), and the inclination of Australian employers, used to convict labor, to treat immigrants as serfs, did not beckon attractively. Of those who emigrated in 1848–49, three fourths went to the United States, and only one fourth to the British Colonies. Only a small part of the total number went to Australia. The advantages of the United States for the artisan were pointed out in the "preliminary dissertation" (by John Hill Burton) in the *Emigrant's Manual*:

The uniformity with which, in the United States, mechanical and engineering enterprise keeps up to the program of population and territorial expansion, must ever render it such a field for the better kind of artisan emigrants as our colonies can never compete with. No plan for the sale or occupation of wastelands, no arrangements for balancing capital with labour, will accomplish for Australia or Canada what the shipping, the railways, the roads, the bridges, the canals, the rapidly-growing cities, with their waterpipes, gasworks, and harbours, do to make the States a field of never-failing industrial enterprise. . . . Nowhere is intelligence or good conduct more highly prized. Idleness, pride of birth, and depravity, meet no countenance. In a word, no one need cross the Atlantic unless possessing hands and a will to work, along with an earnest determination to achieve respectability of character.

The rigors of the transatlantic voyage would have been discouraging to anyone not driven by desperation. In the interest of the Australian colonies the Colonial Land and Emigration Commission paid the fare of emigrants to Australia—a matter of some £17. Those going to the Americas had no subsidy, and paid steerage fares of £5 6s. (first-class fares ran from £12 to £20). Bread, water, and fuel—one gallon of water and one pound of bread per day—were furnished by the ship. Beyond that the steerage passenger had to provide everything for himself: food, cooking utensils, mattress, and bedding.* The passage to North America took an average of six to eight weeks, and could take twelve weeks, in ships carrying from 50 to 500 passengers. The Commission selected every emigrant for Australia and provided a medical officer for each ship. No such controls were exercised over an emigrant ship to the Americas, which was entirely a private affair. The results as far as sanitation and overcrowding were concerned could be imagined.

---

* One handbook for emigrants (*Emigration*, by Thomas Rawlings, Liverpool, second edition, 1846) advised coarse ticking, filled with fresh straw. It further warned against frauds: "Any man that offers to board and lodge you for less than three dollars (12s. English money) by the week, or two dollars 50 cents (ten shillings) permanent, be assured he cannot be an *honest* man."

This year of 1847 was the period of great mortality among emigrants; some 50,000 were supposed to have died in the process of trying to find a new life. Weakened by malnutrition, herded together on shipboard, the steerage passengers offered little resistance to typhus. One official wrote:

> Out of the 4,000 or 5,000 emigrants that have left since Sunday, at least 2,000 will fall sick somewhere before three weeks are over. They ought to have accommodation for 2,000 sick at least in Montreal and Quebec, as all the Cork and Liverpool passengers are half-dead from starvation and want before embarking; and the least bowel complaint, which is sure to come with change of food, finishes them without a struggle. I never saw people so indifferent to life; they would continue in the same berth with a dead person until the seamen or captain dragged out the corpse with boathooks. Good God! what evils will befall the cities wherever they alight! Hot weather will increase the evil. . . .

The Quebec correspondent of the *Morning Chronicle* wrote on July 24th to say that up to that time, of the 57,000 emigrants who had arrived since May 8th, 7,000 were dead of typhus. Of those, 2,200 had died at sea and 1,000 after arrival but before landing. The sufferers were almost, without exception, Irish, and more arrivals were coming daily and hourly. Fever was also raging in Montreal, carrying off great numbers of inhabitants.

Thus were the "anxious classes" of 1847 decimated in the great exodus.

Meanwhile, in spite of scattered food riots at home, most Englishmen, particularly if they belonged to the privileged classes, were unaware of the famine at their door except as they were asked for contributions to benevolent funds. By way of contrast, the normal ebb and flow of life in the comfortable houses is reflected, during this critical year, in the letters written home to the United States by Mrs. George Bancroft, wife of the American minister to the Court of St. James's.[2] She and her husband had made their debut in London "on November last in the midst of an orange-colored fog, in which you could not see your hand before you." They dined at Lord Palmerston's with the Marquis of Lansdowne, Lord and Lady Russell, Earl and Countess Grey. "Their manners are perfectly simple," she reports, "and I entirely forget, except when their historic names fall upon my ear, that I am with the proud aristocracy of England . . . a decided impression of ability and agreeable manners, but of excellence and the domestic virtues."

She discovers that "a 'lady's' maid is a *very great* character indeed, and would be much more unwilling to take her tea with, or speak familiarly to, a footman or housemaid than I should. My greatest mistakes in England have been committed toward these high dignitaries, my own maid and the butler, whose grandeur I entirely misappreciated and ignored. . . . She has her fire made for her, and loaf sugar in her tea, which she and Cates [the butler] sip in solitary majesty."

She finds it a great mystery as to how people get to know each other in London. "Persons talk to you whom you do not know, for no one is introduced, as a general rule. . . . It is a great puzzle to a stranger, but has its conveniences for the English themselves." She visits Westminster School, where in the schoolroom "were two bundles of rods . . . daily used, as indeed the broken twigs scattered upon the floor plainly showed. . . . These young men looked to me as old as our collegians. . . ." She dines at the Palace. "The Queen and the Prince sit in the middle of a long table, and I was just opposite to the Prince . . . I talked to my neighbors as at any other dinner, but the Queen spoke to no one but Prince Albert." But after dinner Victoria conversed with each of the guests, as did Albert.

In May the Bancrofts went to "a concert at Mr. Hudson's, the great 'king,' who has just made an immense fortune from railway stocks, and is now desirous to get into society. These things are managed in a curious way here. A *nouveau-riche* gets several ladies of fashion to patronize their entertainment and invite all the guests. Our invitation was from Lady Parke, who wrote me two notes about it, saying that she would be happy to see me at Mrs. Hudson's splendid mansion, where would be the best music and society of London; and, true enough, there was the Duke of Wellington and all the world. Lady Parke stood at the entrance of the splendid suite of rooms to receive the guests and introduce them to their host and hostess."

They saw Rachel in *Phèdre;* Grisi and Alboni and Tamburini in the *Semiramide.* "Grisi, so statuesque and so graceful, delights the eye, the ear, and the soul. She is sculpture, poetry, and music at the same time." They met Mr. Brooke, the Rajah of Sarawak, who was at the moment "the lion of London." Brooke was a curious adventurer and army man who had gone out in the service of the East India Company and had landed in Borneo, where he had helped the Rajah suppress a rebellion of several Dyak tribes in the province of Sarawak—and had been rewarded not merely with the title of Rajah of Sarawak but with the actual rule of the province. He had attempted, with British naval help, to stamp out piracy in the surrounding waters, and had just returned to England at the height of his glamorous reputation. Later this fabulous person was to run foul of a Parliamentary investigation concerning his operations in Borneo, on charges later to be declared "not proven." His hereditary rajahship, however, was to fall upon his descendants into the twentieth century, and Sarawak was to continue as a British crown colony.

In a letter of February 21st, Mrs. Bancroft writes: "The next day, Thursday, there was a grand opera for the benefit of the Irish"—the only mention made in her whole correspondence for 1847 of the tragedy which was being enacted across the Irish Sea.

The Englishman of even modestly comfortable means was eating well these days. If he were a real success in trade or belonged to the gentility, he was eating better than well—he was indulging in the gargantuan succession of dinners and suppers which must have laid many a Briton prematurely in his grave, or at the very least have made him ripe for Cockle and his antibilious pills. One can understand the prevalence of "peristaltic persuaders" after studying a typical dinner menu of the non-anxious classes.

The most colorful figure in the realm of cookery during the forties was a temperamental but brilliant French chef, Alexis Soyer. In 1841 Soyer had taken possession of the elaborate kitchens (designed by himself) in the new Reform Club, and for ten years he turned out for the worshipful members a stream of delicacies such as London had never known. Gastronomy did not know his peer; he was continually inventing new and ever more elaborate and artistic dishes. His special dinners were spoken of with awe. When he prepared the famous dinner at the Reform Club in 1846 for the Egyptian Ibrahim Pasha the papers paid as much attention to the menu as to the speeches. And well they might; the dessert alone was a chef's triumph. Called the *Crème d'Egypte à l'Ibrahim Pasha*, it was described by the *Morning Post* as "a pyramid about two and a half feet high, made of light meringue cake, in imitation of solid stones, surrounded with grapes and other fruits, but representing only the four angles of the pyramid through sheets of waved sugar, to show, to the greatest advantage, an elegant cream *à l'ananas*, on the top of which was resting a highly-finished portrait of the illustrious stranger's father, Mehemet Ali, carefully drawn on a round-shaped satin carton, the exact size of the top of the cream."[3] Beneath this portrait, in the cream and apparently under glass, was a portrait of Ibrahim Pasha, carefully transferred from wafer paper to the jelly, its seemingly gilt frame made of *eau de vie de Dantzic* and gold water mixed with the jelly. No one of the guests dared to begin to eat the masterpiece.

On another occasion Soyer invented his "hundred-guinea dish" for

Figure 91. Alexis Soyer, from a painting by his wife

a banquet at York, with the Queen and Consort in attendance. It was composed as follows:

   5 Turtle heads, part of fins and green fat
 24 Capons, the two small *noix* from each side of the middle of the back only used, being the most delicate part of every bird
 18 Turkeys, the same
 18 Fatted Pullets, the same
 16 Fowls, the same
 10 Grouse
 20 Pheasants, *noix* only
 45 Partridges, the same
  6 Plovers, whole
100 Snipes, *noix* only
 36 Quail, whole
 40 Woodcocks, *noix* only
 36 Pigeons, the same
 72 Larks stuffed
    Ortolans from Belgium

The *garniture*, consisting of cockscombs, truffles, mushrooms, crawfish, olives, American asparagus, *croustades* (paste crust), sweetbreads, *quenelles de volaille* (strip of slices of fowl), green mangoes, and a new sauce.

This elegant and gastronomically dramatic chef was better known to the public than most of the clubmen for whom he prepared his famous dishes. He made and allowed Crosse and Blackwell to market a bottled sauce, of which he sent review bottles to the press—and did not receive a single bad notice! Next came Soyer's relish, which sold for seventy years; then his meat extract "Ozmazone"; then his bottled "Nectar." Each concoction was greeted with delight. He invented a "magic stove"— pocket model—on which a noble marquis cooked a meal on top of one of the pyramids.

Strangely enough, Soyer had a social conscience in a decade when hunger was at many people's door. In 1847 he headed a public subscription for soup kitchens for the poor, and himself established such a kitchen in Leicester Square, where he dispensed forty to fifty gallons of soup to 2,000 to 3,000 people daily. In the midst of the Irish famine he went to Dublin and supervised the building of a model soup kitchen. Between April and mid-August, 1,147,279 rations were distributed there, consisting of 2,868,197 pounds of food—an average of 8,750 rations daily from the one kitchen—at a cost of £7,768. Under the plan of preparing food in different depots the cost would have been double. On Soyer's return from Ireland his admirers gave him a splendid dinner at the London Tavern, complete with bumpers and oratory.

Best of all, for the housewife who wanted to emulate the Reform Club kitchens, he wrote cookbooks. The first of these, published in 1846, was the *Gastronomic Regenerator*. Most of the 2,000 elaborate recipes were aimed at the "Kitchens of the Wealthy," and the book cost a guinea. Nevertheless, 2,000 copies were sold in a few months, and by 1849 it had reached a sixth edition. The *Times* in reviewing it said:

> For ten months he laboured at the pyramid which the remotest posterity shall applaud; and during the whole of that period he was intent upon providing the countless meals which a living generation have already approved and fully digested. Talk of the labours of a Prime Minister or Lord Chancellor! Sir R. Peel was not an idle man. Lord Brougham was a tolerably busy one. Could either, we ask, in the short space of ten months . . . have written the *Gastronomic Regenerator*, and furnished 25,000 dinners, 38 banquets of importance, comprising above 70,000 dishes, besides providing daily for sixty servants, and receiving the visits of 15,000 strangers, all too eager to inspect the renowned altar of a great apician temple? All this did M. Soyer.

When Soyer was in Ireland he compiled a 6d. booklet of fifty pages: *Charitable Cookery, or the Poor Man's Regenerator*, which urged people to use the outside of vegetables. The profits from the sale of the book he gave to charity.

Soyer's most useful book for the middle-class housewife was *The Modern Housewife, or Ménagère* (1849), a collection of nearly a thousand simplified recipes "for the economic and judicious preparation of every need of the day." Within two weeks it went into a second edition of 6,000; by 1851 it had reached its twenty-first thousand.

The recipes were interlarded with imaginary conversations and letters which cast a good deal of light on the eating customs of the day. The culinary progress of a family the head of which begins as simple shopkeeper and advances to prosperous merchanthood is traced in a series of bills of fare illustrating the various stages of the progress.

Mrs. B. tells the story. "When I was first married and commencing business, and our means were limited, the following was our system of living:

Sunday's Dinner—Roast-Beef, Potatoes, Greens, and Yorkshire Pudding.
Monday—Hashed Beef and Potatoes.
Tuesday—Broiled Beef and Bones, Vegetables, and spotted Dick Pudding.
Wednesday—Fish if cheap, Chops and Vegetables.
Thursday—Boiled Pork, Peas, Pudding, and Greens.
Friday—Pea Soup, Remains of Pork.
Saturday—Stewed Steak with Suet Dumpling."

After the first two years business increased, "and having the three young men [clerks] to dine with us, we were of course obliged to increase our expenditure." Moreover, Mrs. B. had in the interim accompanied her husband to France, "where my culinary ideas received a great improvement."

The new plan:

Sunday—Pot-au-Feu, Fish—Haunch of Mutton, or a quarter of Lamb, or other good joint—Two Vegetables—Pastry and a Fruit Pudding —a little Dessert.
Monday—Vermicelli Soup made from the Pot-au-Feu of the day previous—The Bouilli of the Pot-au-Feu—Remains of the Mutton— Two Vegetables—Fruit Tart.
Tuesday—Fish—Shoulder of Veal Stuffed—Roast Pigeons, or Leveret or Curry—Two Vegetables—Apples with Rice, and light Pastry.
Wednesday—Spring Soup—Roast Fowls, Remains of Veal minced, and poached Eggs—Two Vegetables—Rowley Powley Pudding.
Thursday—Roast Beef—Remains of Fowl—Two Vegetables—Sweet Omelet.

Friday—Fish—Shoulder of Lamb—Mirotan of Beef—Two Vegetables—
    Baked Pudding.
Saturday—Mutton Broth—Broiled Neck Mutton—Liver and Bacon—
    Two Vegetables—Currant Pudding.

The B's parties at that time never consisted of more than ten, and they had

Julienne Soup—Fish—A quarter of Lamb—Vegetables, Cutlets—Vegetables, Bacon and Beans—Boiled Turkey, Pheasant, Jelly or Cream—
Pastry—Lobster Salad—Omelet or Soufflé—Dessert, etc.

"Now," says Mrs. B., "we dine alone, except when Mr. B. invites somebody to dine with him, which is most generally the case. Our daily bill of fare consists of something like the following:

"One Soup or Fish, generally alternate—One Remove, either Joint or Poultry—One Entrée—Two Vegetables—Pudding or Tart—A little Dessert.

"This may seem a great deal for two persons; but when you remember that we almost invariably have one or two to dine with us, and the remains are required for the breakfast, lunch, nursery, and servants' dinners, you will perceive that the dinner is the principal expense of the establishment. . . ."

A party for one or two persons in these lusher days went like this:

First Course
One soup, say Purée of Artichokes—One Fish, Cod Slices in Oyster
    Sauce—Remove with Smelts or White Bait.
Removes—Saddle of Mutton—Turkey in Celery Sauce.
Two Entrées—Cutlets à la Provençale—Sweetbreads larded in any White
    Sauce.
Two Vegetables—Greens—Kale—Potatoes on the Sideboard.

Second Course
Two Roasts—Partridges—Wild Ducks.
    Jelly of Fruit—Cheesecakes—Meringue à la Crème—Vegetable—
    French Salad on the Sideboard.
Removes—Ice Pudding—Beignet Soufflé.
    Dessert of eleven dishes.

This is doing pretty well for the merchant class. For an account of an average dinner party at one of the "best-mounted" private homes, however, one must turn to a book published in 1851 by Chapman and Hall: *London at Table; or how, when, and where to dine and order a dinner; and where to avoid dining. With practical hints to cooks. To which is appended the butler's and yacht steward's manual, and truisms for the million.* Says this lively author:

You order your carriage, which lands you within five minutes of the appointed time at your host's door, and after passing through the hall lined with servants in and out of livery, you are ushered into the presence-room. About ten minutes after, dinner is announced, and your hat is taken from you as you descend the stairs to enter the drawing-room. To enter the drawing-room without your hat is a solecism, except perhaps in what Theodore Hook used to term the wild uninhabited parts of London. A delicate soup and turtle are handed round, nothing on the tables except flowers and preserved fruits in old Dresden baskets, a bill of fare placed next to every person, a turbot with lobster and Dutch sauces, and a portion of red mullet with Cardinal sauce are offered to each guest; cucumber and the essential cruet-stands bringing up the rear. The "flying dishes," as the modern cooks call the oyster or marrow patés, follow the fish. The entrées are carried around, a *suprême de volaille aux truffes*, a sweetbread au jus, lamb cutlets, with asparagus, peas, a *fricandeau a l'oseille;* carefully avoid what are called flank dishes, which if placed on the table, are usually cold, and are quite unnecessary; either venison, roast saddle of mutton, or stewed beef à la jardinière, are then produced, the accessories being salad, beetroot, vegetables, French and English mustard. A Turkey poult, duckling, or green goose, commences the second course, peas and asparagus following in their course; plover's eggs in aspic jelly, a mayonaise of fowl succeed; a *macédoine* of fruit, *meranges à la crème*, a marasquino jelly, and a chocolate cream, form the sweets. Sardines, salad, beetroot, celery anchovy, and plain butter and cheese, for those who are gothic enough to eat it. Two ices, cherry-water, and pine-apple cream, with the fruit of the season, furnish the dessert. Two servants or more according to the number of the party, must attend exclusively to the wine; sherry Madeira, and champagne, must ever be flowing during dinner. Coffee, hot and strong, ought always to be served in the dining-room with liqueurs. . . .*

All the eating in early Victorian days was not done in the pages of Dickens.

But he who read the revelations about adulteration of food as they were published by Arthur Hill Hassall, M.D., in the pages of the *Lancet*

---

* Although coffee imports into England quadrupled between 1824 and 1850, there was still five times as much tea (liquid measure) drunk as there was coffee. The difficulty of getting a cup of good coffee in England was the despair of gourmets; Soyer gives very specific directions for making it. Most coffee was heavily adulterated with chicory. William Kitchiner, the author of another contemporary cookbook, complains in his 1845 edition: "Coffee as used on the Continent, serves the double purpose of an agreeable tonic, and an exhilarating beverage. . . . Coffee, as drunk in England, debilitates the Stomach, and produces a slight nausea. In France and Italy it is made strong from the best coffee, and is poured out hot and transparent. In England it is usually made from bad coffee, served out tepid and muddy, and drowned in a deluge of water, and sometimes deserves the title . . . 'a base, black, thick, nasty, bitter, stinking Puddle Water.' "

beginning in 1851, might pardonably have had his misgivings about the most aristocratic dinner. The findings of the Sanitary Commission as they were finally collected in Hassall's volume *Food and Its Adulterations* (1855) gave damning evidence concerning the cynical cupidity of food manufacturers and merchants.

Some of the reports were:

Disgusting insects, acari, were present in 35 out of 36 samples of brown sugar tested; sporules of fungi in ten cases. Mustard, in every case, was adulterated with immense quantities of wheaten flour, highly colored with tumeric. Starch and wheat flour (amounting to nearly 50 per cent) were detected in 46 out of 56 samples of cocoa; ten contained earthy coloring matter. Of 26 samples of milk, 12 were genuine, the rest were adulterated with water up to 50 per cent. Red lead was present in 13 out of 28 samples of cayenne pepper; red ochre was present in seven more samples. Only six out of 33 samples of preserved fruits and vegetables were free from contamination with copper. Colored sugar confectionery uniformly contained chromate of lead. All coffee contained chicory or roasted grain. Bread uniformly contained alum to make it hold more water and thus weigh more.

The wonder is that so many people lived on! In a sketch for *Punch* written in 1848, Thackeray purported to be a man driven almost to suicide by the terror inspired by the reports that almost everything he eats, and even the air he breathes, is full of poison. He can buy, in a certain place, coffee that is guaranteed non-poisonous, but "if my milk is poisoned, my bread ditto, the air which I breathe poisoned . . . if my Thames is a regular Lethe, in which every eel is a mortal writhing serpent, and every white bait a small dose of death, what is the odds of taking a little more pyroligneous acid in my coffee?"

Newspaper commentators noted the general public apathy during the year toward foreign affairs. The United States was winning progressive victories over her Mexican foe; Switzerland was engaged in a quick civil war; and there had earlier been a good deal of international intrigue at high levels over the age-old question of the Spanish marriages—whom should the crowned heads of Europe pick as a husband for Isabella?—with Palmerston unable to convince the other European governments that Guizot and Louis Philippe had acted perfidiously. Anglo-French relationships were considerably strained. In another direction one commentator in the press pointed out the encroaching threat of Russia. "It is frightful," he said, "to take up the map of Europe, and mark the slow, insidious, but certain progress of Russia, as the incarnation of brute power, here crushing a republic, there absorbing a state, in another direction annexing a province, by force or fraud, advancing always, encroaching on Germany on the west, stopped nowhere but by the ocean. . . ."[4] But all this seemed far away to the English public of 1847.

There was more interest in a curious revelation which arose incidentally out of a lawsuit in which Alexander Dumas was involved: the great French writer had agreed with certain publishers not to write, during the ensuing five years, more than eighteen volumes of romances per annum. They were chagrined to discover that he was currently publishing, outside his agreement, six other works in various journals, to say nothing of the independent novel *Les Trois Mousquetaires*.

For those who liked to read of lurid happenings (and who didn't?) there was the Murder of the Year: the killing in France of the Duchess of Praslin by her husband the duke. Literally pages of fine print in the most respectable English journals were devoted to this *cause célèbre*. Diagrams of the lady's bedroom were published, showing the furniture overturned in the struggle and the trail of blood leading to the duke's bedroom. Detailed descriptions were given of the multiple dagger wounds under which the lady had expired. Letters and diaries of both parties were published showing the domestic tensions of the household: the jealousy over a governess, disputes over the training of the nine children who were the issue of the marriage. Every word of the police examination was printed, as was the duke's tacit confession of his guilt and the account of his suicide by poisoning. Because of its titled participants the affair had shaken France deeply, and English journalists were aided in their researches by the massive quarto volume of 226 pages printed by order of the French Court of Peers, detailing all the facts. The *affaire Praslin* furnished delightfully gruesome summer reading; it had all the elements of the classic crime: titled rank, savagery, sex, domestic infelicity, and yet obscurity of sufficient motive.

The London theatrical or rather musical season had been particularly brilliant. The old war horses of acting were doing their best at the smaller theaters to stem the tide of complaints about the "decline of the drama"; but their best consisted of intelligent revivals: Macready and Charlotte Cushman in Shakespeare at the Princess'; Mrs. Warner in *The School for Scandal* at the Marylebone; Phelps in Shakespeare at Sadler's Wells. Fanny Kemble, now Mrs. Butler, reappeared briefly from retirement as Julia in Knowles's *Hunchback*, and was welcomed enthusiastically by a devoted public—at £500 for six nights. The Keeleys played popular comedy at the Haymarket, as did Mme. Vestris, Charles Matthews, Buckstone, and company at the redecorated Lyceum. The real comic success of the year was a new farce *Box and Cox*, made by J. M. Morton out of two French originals. This play about the landlady who lets a room twice over, once to a hatter who is out all day and again to a printer who is out all night, was very popular, but few suspected that it would have the phenomenal career which lay ahead of it.

Italian opera was the real rage, and the theater-going public was edified by the spectacle of two competing companies. A revolution had occurred under Lumley's management at Her Majesty's in the Haymarket, and there had been a general desertion of singers, including Grisi, Mario, and Tamburini (and the entire orchestra) to the newly established Royal Italian Opera at Covent Garden. The new company, augmented from abroad and with the advantage of a completely remodeled and redecorated theater,* was of unprecedented strength and completeness. Lumley, on the other hand, retained in ballet the great Taglioni, Carlotta Grisi, and Cerito, and he recruited from abroad an amazingly competent group of singers—notably the contralto Alboni. Balfe conducted the orchestra.

A few people wondered how long the available public could support two such huge houses in the repetition of hackneyed pieces by Donizetti, Bellini, Rossini, and Verdi. The situation was further complicated later in the year when Jullien began a season of grand opera in English at Drury Lane, with an orchestra directed by Berlioz. He rode along comfortably for a time on the great sensation caused by an English tenor whom he had imported from Italy: Sims Reeves.†

The dramatic and musical event of the century, however, was the much-heralded appearance at Her Majesty's Theatre of Jenny Lind.

The Swedish Nightingale's first appearance on an English stage was on the night of May 4th as Alice in an Italian version of Meyerbeer's *Robert le Diable*. Expectations had been high, so high as to create apprehensions on the part of judicious critics, who wondered if Miss Lind's great continental reputation could be justified. Tickets had been sold at enormous prices. As curtain time approached, crowds jammed the piazza

---

* The house held more than 3,000. Ecstatic descriptions were given of its grand staircase, painted in imitation of Sienna marble, its colossal chandelier, its elaborately painted ceiling. It had 188 private boxes and seated 440 persons in the pit—"all the seats, as indeed in the gallery, having backs." This was an innovation.

† Drury Lane had earlier in the year closed a dreary season under the management of Alfred Bunn—a medley of English opera, ballet, and melodrama plus elephants.

Figure 92. Jenny Lind

in the Haymarket to watch the string of carriages discharge their passengers. Her Majesty arrived and was cheered heartily. Inside the theater the music began, the curtain was drawn, and Jenny Lind appeared in pilgrim's garb. "The uproar which followed her entrance," said the *Times*, "is something to be remembered, not described. The whole crowded mass displayed a power of lungs truly astounding, and hats and handkerchiefs waved from all parts." So far, however, it was still expectation. Then the not-too-beautiful but sweetly charming girl began her first aria.

Reading at this distance the reports of Jenny Lind's singing one wonders if such vocal mastery and acting skill were really humanly possible. The anticipation was nothing to the event itself. Hardened critics melted like schoolboys and went home to hunt their dictionaries for superlatives. Rapture verged on madness; ecstasy made the reviewers almost incoherent as they lamented that there were no words to describe the wonder adequately. Certainly the singer's success had never been equaled in musical history. "We have arrived at a new state of our theatrical experience," wrote one of the more restrained critics. "A new perception of musical art has burst upon us; it is as though we now learned for the first time what singing really is, and have been, with all our fancied knowledge and taste, groping, till now, in darkness and error."[5]

Adulation dwelt upon the singer's faultlessness, purity, and delicacy of execution; it reveled in her pianissimos, her ethereal diminuendos, her sustained notes; it lingered over her perfection of tone and articulation—a tone full and sweet and yet vibrating and penetrating. Her softest whisper was audible in all parts of the house. Every passage was as highly finished "as if it proceeded from the violin of a Paganini or a Sivori." And as an actress she was not merely graceful and expressive; her air of ingenuousness and engaging modesty and goodness were equaled by an ability to express the most delicate shades of feeling. She seemed equally good in moods of softness and gentleness and in scenes demanding energy and passion. "She possesses every vocal gift of nature and art," wrote another critic, who admitted that he had joined with the audience in "such bursts of irrepressible delight as would scarcely look like sanity in cool description." Even *Punch* fell under the enchantment, forgot to be funny, and breathlessly dropped to its knees: "To endeavour to give any description of her charms as a singer and actress would be as vain as to endeavour to represent the brilliance of the sun with a ha-porth of gamboge. . . . We might as well send for a pot of paint in order to paint the lily, or cover a sovereign with a layer of Dutch metal, as endeavour to paint Jenny Lind's splendid achievements in their appropriate colours."

In short, England was in a mild delirium. The crush at the doors of the theater on every night of her performance was terrific. The singer's portraits and statuettes were in every shopwindow. There were "Jenny Lind" cigars and "Lindiana" silks. Devotees in distant parts of the kingdom hired special railway trains in which to make the pilgrimage to London. Nor was the bliss of her public reduced at all by the knowledge that Mademoiselle Lind's private character was just as admirable as her vocal powers. Morality hand in hand with genius—what good Victorian could fail to be enthusiastic?

Meanwhile life—and death—went on. An uncommonly large number of wives fed their husbands arsenic in 1847. . . . George Robins, the eccentric and good-humored auctioneer who had presided at important sales for more than fifty years, died, as did Macvey Napier, editor of the current seventh edition of the *Encyclopaedia Britannica* and for twenty years editor of the *Edinburgh Review*. John Walter, publisher of the *Times*, died at the age of seventy and was succeeded by his son bearing the same name. Daniel O'Connell, weary and old, died at Genoa, en route to Rome, the city to which he had piously willed his heart. His body was brought back to Dublin, with 50,000 people following in the funeral train; the Rev. Mr. Miley preached the funeral sermon with tears flowing down his cheeks. The writers of obituaries remembered O'Connell's great physical strength and industriousness, his large and cordial fellowship, his humor and cunning, his dramatic use of the mythical Irish past in his appeals to his fellow countrymen, his embodiment of intolerable Irish grievances. But even before his death O'Connell's occupation was gone. His own movement had swept past him and was in the hands of younger leaders.

On Easter Monday the great new Birkenhead Docks on the Mersey were opened "with public rejoicings," followed by a dinner and grand ball. Attention was called again to the symmetrical and comfortable model town which had been created to house the workmen—complete with parks and well-lighted houses equipped with a steady water supply and indoor toilets. . . . The emigrant ship *Exmouth*, bound for Quebec, was lost off the coast of Scotland with 240 on board. . . . Ashley chaired the annual meeting of the Ragged School Union, the report of which announced that the Union had educated 4,476 children in 1846—more than twice as many as the year previous. . . . Both Houses of Parliament adjourned for Derby Day. It was noted that the opening of a new line of railway from London Bridge to Epsom added some thousands to the crowd at the races, "but greatly deteriorated from the aristocratic air of the assemblage."

It was reported that "Mr. Alfred Tennyson, the poet, is undergoing cold-water treatment at Umberslade Hall, near Birmingham." His poem *The Princess* was published just at the end of December, too late for the Christmas trade or to be reviewed in 1847. His poems of 1842 reached their fourth edition this year. . . . New Oxford Street was opened to the public on the evening of March 6th. Its construction had necessitated doing away with a part of the more squalid section of St. Giles. . . . A family of bushmen from South Africa was put on display at Egyptian Hall for the enlightenment of the curious. . . . One reason advanced for the frequency of railway accidents was that the lines were now running eighteen-ton engines over tracks laid down for eight-to-twelve-ton engines. . . . The peak of the railway speculation was over. The 184 Railway Acts of 1847 sanctioned 1,354 miles of new road, at an expense of

Figure 93. George Cruikshank

£38,000,000, less than a third as much as the previous year. Of those approved in 1846, however, many were being built. Between October, 1846, and October, 1847, 783½ miles were brought into operation.

The year 1847 was notable for its literary activity. *Dombey and Son* was still being bought by its monthly enthusiasts, and on January 1st had appeared the initial yellow-colored installment of the first full-blown novel by Michael Angelo Titmarsh, writing for the first time under his real name of W. M. Thackeray. Its subtitle, "Pen and Pencil Sketches of English Society," was still reminiscent of Titmarsh and did not indicate adequately the broad plan in terms of which the new novel was conceived. But from the moment Becky Sharp threw the copy of Johnson's *Dictionary* through the carriage window in the direction of Miss Pinkerton, the little green-eyed heroine of the "novel without a hero" brought the story alive. Soon Jane Carlyle was writing to her husband that *Vanity Fair* was "very good indeed, beats Dickens out of the world." The reviewers of the early numbers were kind if not extended in their notices. The *Morning Chronicle* said: "Everything is simple, natural, and unaffected. The very spirit of society is distilled by the alembic of genius into drops which sparkle before the reader's eye." The *Daily News*, of which Dickens had been editor, was gently patronizing: "The public offerings of M.A.T. are ever pleasantly welcome to us. . . . He is the prince of etchers and sketchers." The novel caught on slowly, but before long an increasing number of perceptive readers were admiring the cool astringency with which Thackeray viewed the grotesqueries and hypocrisies and inanities of life's battles, and at the same time the way in which he combined with the acidulous an infiltration of love and pity. Thackeray, who needed badly a popular success, had one on his hands. He was also concluding the *Snobs of England* for *Punch* and was beginning for the same magazine *Punch's Prize Novelists*—including a burlesque of Bulwer Lytton under the title: "George de Barnwell, by Sir E. L. B. L. BB. LL. BBB. LLL.," and one of Disraeli called "Codlingsby, by B. de Shrewsbury, Esq."

Melville's *Omoo* was published in England—its first appearance anywhere—and was declared equal to its predecessors. . . . William H. Prescott's *Conquest of Peru* received good notices, as did George Cruikshank's *The Bottle*. This was a Hogarthian story in eight engraved plates of St. Giles and Gin Lane, revealing the several stages of drunkenness, from the taking of the first drop to the final drunken murder—by which time the drunkard's son and daughter were living a life of vice and the murderous, maniacal father was ready for Bedlam. Cruikshank followed this series of engraved tracts with the no less pitiless *The Drunkard's Children*. . . . Young Anthony Trollope published his first three-volume novel, *The Macdermots of Ballycloran*. The reviewers appreciated his naturalness and reality and his aptitude for dialogue, but compared him unfavorably with his famous mother. "He seems, however, to possess a view of humour," said one critic.

Disraeli's new novel, *Tancred; or, The New Crusade*, was obviously not up to his better performances. It was a philosophical, poetico-political extravaganza—picturesque, sonorous, chivalric (said the *Athenaeum*); an Eastern tale blending adventure and a kind of lyrical extravagance which, in terms of story, came to nothing. Sidonia, the all-wise Jew, reappeared, and gave Tancred instructions for his trip to Jerusalem, where he aspired to "penetrate the great Asian mystery." As always, Disraeli was better in the scenes of sardonic humor and sarcasm which occurred in the early part of the book. In one notable scene he burlesqued Chambers's *Vestiges of Creation* as *The Revelations of Chaos*. Lady Constance was trying to describe the book to Tancred: "First, there was nothing," she said, "then there was something; then—I forget the next—

Figure 94. Cruikshank's *The Bottle* (Plate VI)
"*Fearful quarrels, and brutal violence, are the natural consequences of the use of the bottle.*"

Figure 95. From *The Drunkard's Children* (Plate I)
"*Neglected by their parents, educated only in the streets, and falling into the hands of wretches who live upon the vices of others, they are led to the gin shop, to drink at that fountain which nourishes every species of crime.*"

I think there were shells, then fishes; then we came—let me see—did we come next? . . . And the next change there will be something very superior to us—something with wings. Oh! that's it: we were fishes, and I believe we shall be crows."

Most puzzling to the reviewers was the sudden appearance in print of the three Bells: *Agnes Grey*, by Acton Bell; *Wuthering Heights*, by Ellis Bell; and *Jane Eyre*, by Currer Bell. The identity of the sisters Brontë—Ann, Emily, and Charlotte—was not recognized. In general, it was said, "the Bells seem to affect painful and exceptional subjects," and "in spite of its truth to life in the remote nooks and corners of England, 'Wuthering Heights' is a disagreeable story." *Agnes Grey* seemed more acceptable to one reviewer, as not being such a gloomy fiction elaborated with dismal minuteness. Other reviewers found the incidents and persons of *Wuthering Heights* too coarse and disagreeable to be attractive. *Jane Eyre* received more respectful attention: even those who did not like the melodramatics of the story recognized its power and its ability to excite strong interest—in spite of its "sordidness," its "low tone of behaviour," and its "inability to attract sympathy for either heroine or hero." The *Quarterly Review*, however, thundered against the book in a fashion more Victorian than Victoria herself: "Jane Eyre is throughout the personification of an unregenerate and undisciplined spirit. . . . Altogether the autobiography of Jane Eyre is pre-eminently an anti-Christian composition. There is throughout it a murmuring against the comforts of the rich and against the privations of the poor, which is a murmuring of God's appointment—there is a proud and perpetual assertion of the rights of man, for which we find no authority in God's word or in God's providence. We do not hesitate to say that the tone of mind and thought which has overthrown and violated every code human and divine abroad, and fostered Chartism and rebellion at home, is the same which has also written *Jane Eyre*."

The appearance of so much memorable writing in this year of 1847 should not obscure the fact that the longer notices were given to lesser books, or that in a monthly list, selected at random, of sixty-six new books, one out of every four was religious: collections of sermons, meditations, ecclesiastical history, etc. Great sections of the reading public were still serious and pious folk who could take their morality straight, if need be.

This was clearly reflected in religious circles this year in what was known as the Hampden Controversy. Dr. Hampden was Regius Professor of Divinity at Oxford, where his liberal, latitudinarian views had brought on his condemnation by the University as early as 1836. The tumult had died down but had not been forgotten by the High Church party; and when Lord John Russell appointed Hampden as Bishop of Hereford the old, smothered flames burst out again. Thirteen bishops sent a protest to Russell, declaring that the nomination had created great alarm in the Church, and that its consummation might provoke a feeling hostile to the supremacy of the Crown. Almost immediately 485 laymen supported the protest, and the Bishop of Exeter sent Russell an arrogant and threatening note. Since the appointment of bishops lay wholly within the control of the Crown, Russell refused to bow to clerical and University blackmail. Hampden's appointment was confirmed and the back-yard revolution suppressed.

Another survival of ancient religious prejudice came into view with the election to Parliament of Baron Lionel Rothschild for the City of London. Although there was no law to prevent the election of a Jew to the House of Commons, there was no provision for swearing in one who could not take his oath "on the true faith of a Christian." Since 1830 measures to enable Jews to sit in Parliament had several times been passed by the Commons but rejected by the Lords. The anomalies of the present situation were such, however, that Lord John Russell brought in a resolution affirming the eligibility of Jews to all offices to which Roman Catholics were eligible by law. Ashley opposed the bill on the ground of "religious truth," but Gladstone favored it. Disraeli argued for it on the basis of the closeness of Judaism to Christianity. But the bill was not brought in until the next year, and even then nothing happened. Rothschild was elected again in 1849 and attempted to take his seat in 1850, but withdrew when the Speaker refused to swear him upon the Old Testament only. Another election in 1852 proved equally bootless; it was not until 1858 that an act of Parliament permitted the distinguished Jewish financier to take his seat in the Commons.

A late spring slid into a beautiful summer. In June the fine weather and the prospects of a bumper harvest both in England and Ireland began to lower corn prices. Bakers announced a reduction in the price of bread. On the first Monday in June wheat dropped six or seven shillings; on Friday five or six shillings more; by May 17th, fifteen to sixteen shillings lower still. At the end of August, wheat had fallen from its high of 102s. to 50s. a quarter.

By this time Parliament had been prorogued to allow for the first general election in six years. The public seemed apathetic, and although the Whigs gained some seats, and the Peelites held their own, there was no important change. The only surprising events were the return of

Feargus O'Connor, and the defeat of Macaulay in his Edinburgh election. Macaulay's open scorn for narrow sectarian views, and particularly his advocacy of the grant to the Catholic College of Maynooth, had told against him.

Much more important than the desultory election were the signs of an approaching economic crisis. It arose through a combination of causes: the immense inflation of railway speculation, the pressure of a distressed cotton industry, and, more recently, the failure of corn speculators when grain prices declined so precipitously. Gold was being withdrawn steadily from the Bank of England, and by August the reserve was alarmingly low. The Bank found it necessary to raise its rate of discount to 6, 7, and 8 per cent—and the panic was on. Many merchants and manufacturers were unable to fulfill their contracts; September was marked by a series of failures among the principal mercantile houses. Large firms in Manchester, Liverpool, and Glasgow were obliged to suspend, and with each new failure the pressure in the money market tightened. Railway shares were unsalable. By October 1st the City was in great distress and disorder, with the worst yet to come. More firms failed, and on October 18th the Royal Bank of Liverpool stopped payment. This was followed by other bank failures across the country. People began to wonder about the Bank of England itself.

Finally the Bank, hampered until now by legislation of 1844 which had divorced the banking and the issue-of-currency departments, was allowed by Government to extend the amount of its loans on approved security. This action, which might well have been taken earlier, eased the crisis immediately. Nevertheless, the pressure on the merchants remained severe, and November saw a large if dwindling number of failures. By the last of the month, however, Russell was able to report the gradual revival of confidence. Foreign bullion began to come in along with orders; the number of men employed increased. Though money was still dear—8 per cent was charged—food remained cheap, and the prospects for the winter were hopeful.

The Queen and Albert made their trip to Scotland in August, this time by sea in the royal yacht. . . . The Duke of Buckingham found it necessary to go to the Continent for some years; through his reckless expenditures he had incurred liabilities of £1,800,000. All his personal effects, down to and including his poultry, were attached. . . . Albert, who had been elected Chancellor of Cambridge University, was installed with great dignity and ceremony, Victoria looking on. Wordsworth composed an Installation Ode, set to music by Professor Walmisley, which was sung at the occasion. It was not one of the laureate's major efforts. . . . The boilers of the *Cricket*, a halfpenny steamboat taking passengers from the Strand to London Bridge, exploded, killing six and seriously injuring twelve. At the inquest it developed that the engineer was accustomed to tie down the safety valve in order to get a higher pressure of steam. . . . The *Great Britain*, by a massive engineering effort, was floated off her sands in Dundrum Bay. . . . The explosion of a gun-cotton mill at Faversham killed twenty-four people. . . . A man committed suicide by leaping from the Whispering Gallery of St. Paul's. . . . The theatrical manager Alfred Bunn, who had been satirized mercilessly by *Punch*, produced a burlesque magazine in imitation of *Punch*, largely devoted to anathematizing Wronghead (Douglas Jerrold), Sleekhead (Gilbert à Beckett), and Thickhead (Mark Lemon).

Shakespeare's birthplace was sold at public auction for £2,000 to a committee which immediately turned it over to the Government, which in turn accepted it as a national trust. . . . Announcement was made in November that three expeditions would sail for the Arctic in search of Sir John Franklin—one in a few days to Bering Strait; a second the next spring to Baffin Bay, under command of Sir James Ross; the third an overland expedition under the direction of Sir John Richardson. . . . In November Harvey's "Fraternal Democrats" gave a reception in London to the delegate of a Belgian group "which styled itself the Democratic Association to promote Brotherhood Among the Nations." The delegate was "our esteemed friend and brother, Dr. Marx." The occasion was not noticed by the British press.

Albert Smith, humorist and editor of the *Man in the Moon*, made an almost fatal balloon ascent with Mr. Gypson from Vauxhall Gardens—a night ascent with fireworks, attached below the basket, sending out cascades of colored flame when the balloon had reached a proper height. When they were at an altitude of nearly 7,000 feet the valve parted from the bag and the balloon began to drop with an appalling velocity. The upper netting kept firm, and so the occupants descended rapidly as in a parachute, landing eventually in a street not more than a mile from the Gardens, scratched and bruised but otherwise unhurt.

Ralph Waldo Emerson arrived at Liverpool for a winter's lecture tour in Manchester and other provincial cities. Manchester listened to two series, one at the Athenaeum on "Men Representative of Great Ideas," the other at the Mechanics' Institution on a variety of subjects. The December 11th issue of *Howitt's Journal* contained a report of his lectures on "Swedenborg, the Mystic" and "Montaigne, the Sceptic." The

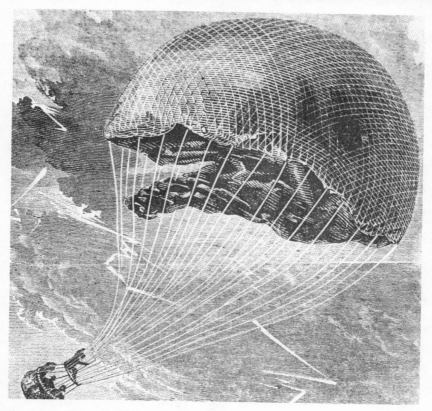

Figure 96. Albert Smith's perilous balloon ascent

correspondent reported Emerson as being thin and spare, with a prominent profile. "The tones of his voice are nasal and American; but now
and then they come out with musical richness and depth . . . his delivery
is indifferent and careless. . . . What I distasted most was the woodenness
of the face . . . his voice hardly varied, his countenance still less." The
listener expressed honest disappointment in the lecture—a misty subject
treated in a misty manner. He was all enthusiasm for the lecture on
Montaigne, however: "It was a noble lecture. Though every sentence
was (as before) loaded with meaning, I understood him throughout. . . .
It is curious to trace back, and perceive how one's admiration and appre-
ciation of him grow. His voice, his delivery, his very carelessness of his
audience . . . seem to become endeared to one, as forming part of the
individual Emerson. . . . The lecture which seems to have given the most
universal satisfaction (I may even use the word delight) was one delivered at the Mechanics' Institution, 'On Domestic Life'. . . ."

Carlyle wrote of his friend, however: "I rather think his popularity
is not very great hitherto. His doctrines are too airy and thin for
the solid, practical heads of the Lancashire region. We had immense

talking together here, but found he did not give us much to chew the cud upon. . . ."

The question of public health was worrying Britain in the closing weeks of 1847. Little reports trickled into the papers indicating the steady approach of cholera. Whole families, it was said, were leaving Moscow for Germany and France, and the greatest apprehension was felt in Warsaw. One fatal case of Asiatic cholera was reported from Malta. In England every great center was in an unusually bad state of health. Manchester and Birmingham were suffering epidemic fever. Liverpool, flooded with Irish, had a total of 5,669 deaths in the last quarter of the year among a population of 225,000. Edinburgh was reported in a vile condition. The sanitation of London, a perennial problem, was arousing increasing concern—particularly the condition of the slaughterhouses within the City. The *Illustrated London News* (November 20th) quoted a letter describing the slaughterhouses in Whitechapel:

> The butchers' shops are chiefly pent-houses, projecting from their dwellings into the causeway. They are separated from each other by alternate passages leading into extensive chambers, where the animals are killed. Down these passages you will generally see an open gutter, running with hot water and blood in about equal quantities. . . . The smell baffles description. . . . I have seen blood, black and clotted, in large heaps in the gutter, in a summer sun. . . . I have seen entrails and manure lying just on the causeway, with infection and putridity on every side . . . and this within ten minutes' walk of the very heart of the City of London, in the very centre of its population. . . !

In December an epidemic of influenza seized England and Scotland. The mortality in London during the first week of the month exceeded the normal average by 134 per cent, and the disease was spreading as the year ended. In Scotland schools and colleges were suspended; in Glasgow 70 policemen out of 480 were laid up with fever and influenza. The *Times* warned: "The epidemic now raging is said, on good grounds, to be sometimes the precursor of cholera. . . . Everybody must remember how belated and baffled we were in 1832. Fifteen years, half a generation, has passed, and are we now better prepared?" Deaths all over England had been 166,000 in 1845; they were 215,000 in the year just ending.[6]

The holly, according to people well enough to notice it, was unusually beautiful this year, its berries very red, its leaves a deep rich green. But much of England ruefully sat out the old year with its feet in warm water, suffering influenza and awaiting cholera. By and large it had been a grim year, this 1847. What lay ahead in 1848?

1848 * Revolution and Escape

CARLYLE, in 1848: "The human race has now reached its final stage of jackassification."

At the close of the year Charles Greville wrote in his journal: "This *Annus Mirabilis*, as it may well be called, is at last over, and one cannot but feel glad at getting rid of a year which has been so pregnant with every sort of mischief. Revolutions, ruin, sickness, and death have ravaged the world publicly and privately; every species of folly and wickedness seems to have been let loose to riot on the earth." As clerk of the Privy Council and a specialist (to be sure a very lively and engaging specialist) in the intricate "who's in—who's out" of politics, Greville was likely to view with jaundiced eye any threat to the established order, whether in England or on the Continent.

Eighteen forty-eight was indeed a year of decision at home and abroad, and there were times when honest British citizens locked their doors and went dubiously to bed, fearful of what the morning might bring. But for the most part the times seemed exciting rather than dangerous to the ordinary man. Most of that which was likely to inspire terror was going on across the Channel in countries which, thank God, were not like England, and were sufficiently far away. Besides, the contradictory day-by-day reports were so intricate, so fragmentary and confused that it may be doubted whether many tried to grasp the full implication of what was happening. It would be difficult enough for later historians to disentangle; to the English newspaper reader it was a great deal of sound and fury signifying no one knew quite what, except that there was blood in the streets, crowns were toppling all over Europe, and not a little kingly and princely flotsam was being washed up on English shores.

The year began in England on a note of uneasiness. Within a period of five or six weeks some 500,000 out of 2,100,000 Londoners had been smitten by the influenza. And in spite of the reassurances of her "citizen king," France had given periodic reason for some large talk about possible war, until every severe thunderstorm over the British Isles began to sound to an already-fevered populace like the guns of invasion. This tension was not eased by the public release of a letter written by the Duke of Wellington a year earlier on the subject of Britain's defenses. The duke, who took his duties as commander in chief seriously, was alarmed at the paucity of coast defense and at the ease, therefore, with which an invading force (guess who?) might land flotillas of steam war vessels overnight and march on London. The naval dockyards and arsenals were not half garrisoned, said he, and "excepting immediately under the forts of Dover Castle, there is not a spot on the coast on which infantry might not be thrown on shore, at any time, with any wind, and in any weather. . . . I hope," he concluded, "that the Almighty may protect me from being the witness of the tragedy which I cannot persuade my contemporaries to take measures to avert."

The *Times* scoffed at this, yet Parliament began to move toward a heavily increased subsidy for both army and navy. Then, before much could be done, the political explosion across the Channel removed any immediate danger. For some little time the French were too busy at home and too eager to have friends abroad to shake a fist at perfidious Albion.

Of the revolutions which were this year to run across Europe like a train of Greek fire the one in France was of the most immediate and consuming interest to the English. It came with an incredible suddenness. Guizot's stiffly conservative ministry had been in power since 1840 and seemed unshakable. Louis Philippe, essentially commercial and middle class in his interests, was not a popular king. He was despised by men of intellect and hated by a proletariat which viewed with disgust the electoral corruption by which privilege was maintained. Yet with a kind of amiable selfishness and a shrewd opportunistic craftiness he had been able to maintain a political equilibrium. What Louis and his ministers underestimated was the ground swell of republicanism led by such men as Louis Blanc, the socialist leader who had agitated steadily on behalf of the workingmen against a government of the bourgeoisie. Few indeed suspected that the decay of the government or the force of the opposition was such as to make possible the February revolution.

It began with the prohibition by the ministry of a reform banquet scheduled to be held on the night of February 22d. Crowds of students and workingmen assembled in the streets in protest and a few barricades were thrown up, but troops appeared and nothing serious happened.

The next day the crowds multiplied and tempers wore thin. By ten o'clock some 6,000 men, chiefly students in blouses, thronged the riverside before the Chamber of Deputies. The soldiers inflicted a few saber wounds, but appeared reluctant to charge. More street barricades appeared, hastily constructed of paving blocks, store fronts, trees, and whatever else was at hand. The National Guard was called out, but to the consternation of the authorities they joined the crowds in throwing up their hats, singing the *Marseillaise*, and shouting in favor of reform. They marched to the Tuileries to declare their sentiments, and the Government quaked in its boots. The King, under strenuous advice, dismissed Guizot and promised reform—but too late. Nervous troops fired on a crowd, fifty-two persons fell dead or wounded, and at night the maddened mob marched the streets with torches crying for vengeance: "To arms! to arms!" Now it was "to the barricades!" in earnest. Every tree on the boulevards was felled to build defenses; determined men and women bivouacked in the streets and mounted guard at the barriers.

On the morning of Thursday the twenty-fourth M. de Rémusat burst in on the royal family at breakfast to announce that troops and people were fighting not more than 300 yards away. The King donned his uniform and showed himself on horseback to his unenthusiastic army and to a sullen National Guard, then hustled back to his apartments. By one o'clock proclamations were posted in the streets declaring his abdication in favor of his child grandson the Comte de Paris, with the Duchesse d'Orléans as Regent. The duchesse bravely appeared with her children before a demoralized Chamber of Deputies just in time to watch the hurried exit of most of the members before the unruly mob which burst into the Chamber. The claims of the young count never had a chance of being accepted. Amid the confusion a provisional government was declared, including the names of Ledru-Rollin, a left-wing radical, and the more moderate M. de Lamartine, poet, historian, and orator.

In the meantime Louis Philippe had fled with his family, just a little in advance of the mob of rioters who broke into and pillaged the Tuileries, scattering draperies and dresses in the garden, and burning the furniture in the Rue Rivoli. When the throne upon which Louis Philippe had first sat as King of the French was thrust into the fire, the shouts were thunderous. Within a few hours the republic was proclaimed.

The ex-King and Queen were landed damply by the steamer *Express* at Newhaven, Sussex, on the morning of March 3d. Louis Philippe had passed as an Englishman, dressed in a rough pea jacket with a common red-and-white "comforter" around his neck, and sporting a week's growth of beard. Thus "Mr. Smith" found sanctuary. "The people," wrote the *Spectator*, "would have . . . escorted him politely to the frontier. He preferred dodging the great nation in a chase without pursuers. The poet and minister Lamartine would have read him an exalted farewell lecture: but the poet was defeated in his high-tragedy vein by the ludicrous and gratuitous panic of the dispersion. . . . He comes for shelter, with his cajoling tongue in his cheek: he returns to us, even on deposition, 'with pleasure'; he continues to know all sorts of obscure gentlemen by name: he shakes hands all round; and addresses a knot of anonymous sight-seers as 'the British nation.' There is not a puffing advertiser, nor even a playhouse manager, that better understands the art of humbug. No one better knows that an Englishman's most esteemed delights are—to be known correctly by name, to shake hands with a king, and to be considered as 'the British nation.' . . . He has fallen on his true social designation—he is properly one of the Smiths."

Guizot followed "Mr. Smith" into English exile. When, at the Théâtre de la République (formerly the Théâtre Français) Rachel whipped her audience into a frenzy of emotion with her solemn and inspired chant of the *Marseillaise*, it was the whole of the Provisional Government that sat in the box immediately opposite the loge of the ex-royal family, now tenanted by solid bourgeoisie.

After the first few days of the revolution Lamartine's influence worked for a time successfully on the side of moderation. There had been a moment when it seemed that the mob would insist on the red flag rather than the French tricolor. But a constitution was formed, incorporating universal suffrage and secret ballot, and for a time Lamartine was able to combine adverse elements into a unified government.

Figure 97. Louis Philippe
Figure 98. John Leech's comment on the abdication. From *Punch*

Thus far the revolution had proceeded without the blood baths of 1789. Before long, however, the National Workshops, organized as a provisional measure of relief for unemployed workmen, sank under the weight of their own impracticality.* The laboring classes began to feel that the glorious revolution had been a farce, and by mid-April the left wing, led by Louis Blanc and Ledru-Rollin, was threatening further trouble. The situation reached a minor climax in May, when the National Guard came to the rescue and the incipient revolt seemed to be stamped out. Elections were held for the National Assembly, Louis Napoleon being returned for Paris and for three other departments.

But the unrest grew with the abolition of the National Workshops and June saw a left-wing revolution, with barricades once more in the streets and blood in the gutters. General Cavaignac was given dictatorial powers by the assembly. Between June 23d and 26th Paris saw the most terrible street fighting it had ever known. Ten thousand were killed or wounded and 11,000 prisoners taken. The revolt of the socialistic republicans was squelched, but only at the cost of their enduring hatred. A temporary military dictatorship was formed under General Cavaignac, with Lamartine rapidly losing his influence.

---

* In Lyon the *Ateliers Nationaux* cost the city 1,650,000f.; the work done was estimated at a value of 30,000f.

The elections for president were not held until December, at which time foreign observers were amazed to see that Louis Napoleon, mouthing pious democratic sentiments, was chosen over Cavaignac by 5,000,000 votes to 1,500,000. A rabid electorate which had shed its blood for liberty, equality, fraternity, fell under the spell of a name which, however glorious, could be associated only with empire. The "hero of the tame eagle" was much less a man than his uncle except, as the event would prove, in his ambition. In this same month Greville wrote: "And now there is a pretty general opinion that he will be Emperor before long."

How did England feel about all this? Lord John Russell hastened to give assurances that England would not interfere with the internal problems of France. Palmerston, used to dealing with French ministers whose tricks he understood, and somewhat fearful of the effect that universal suffrage in France might have upon the English non-voting population, still could write "*Vive* Lamartine!" His contempt for Louis Philippe was vindicated. By the end of 1848 there was much to support the view that the revolution was something of an accident, and that "France is retracing her steps as fast as she can, scrambling, crestfallen, perplexed, and half-ruined, out of the abyss into which she suffered herself to be plunged."[1]

France was only the beginning. The storm which had lashed the Paris streets was breaking all over Europe. Its lightnings played about crowned heads. Princes and potentates scuttled for safety and found suddenly that they had always believed in constitutional governments for their peoples. The tidal wave of freedom, as well as of nationalism, was rising, and for a time it seemed that tyranny was washed away, that constitutional representation and freedom of the press would bring to subject peoples from the Baltic to the Mediterranean a political liberty which absolutism had denied them.

In March the people rose in Berlin and the King of Prussia, Frederick William IV, attempted to stem the tide by adopting the revolutionary flag of national unity and making liberal addresses to students and soldiers. He announced, moreover, that he was taking upon himself the task of reuniting Germany as one empire: "Henceforth," he declared, "'Prussia' will be merged in 'Germany'." At the same time he allowed the Constituent Assembly to draft a liberal constitution. He was greeted everywhere with the acclamations of those who did not suspect that he would soon repudiate his liberal concessions. It became clear, however, that even his desire for a united Germany was not so strong as his fear of placing power in the hands of the people.

The immediate result of the Berlin revolt was that William, Prince of Prussia (brother of the King), became the scapegoat for the clashes between army and people. He fled to England, and the princes of several states granted constitutions to their peoples.

In Bavaria the old king, Louis I, had been living for two years in senile infatuation with Lola Montez. To please the fascinating adventuress he had made her Countess Landsberg, much against popular sentiment, and particularly against the will of the Jesuits, who were a strong political power in Bavaria. Lola, a fighter for her own power, became involved in acrimonious disputes. The students paraded in front of her home shouting "Perish the whore!" Eventually she was forced to flee to Switzerland, predicting, accurately, that the King would follow her. This he did in March, abdicating in favor of his son Maximilian II. For once the crash of thrones had a hectic romantic accompaniment.

In this same fatal month of March the great Austrian Empire appeared on the verge of dissolution. The Hapsburg Ferdinand I, the weak and vacillating "Dumpling King," was on the throne; but Metternich was his minister—Metternich the wily, the unscrupulous, the pitiless, the reactionary. Here again the spring fever of revolution brought impatient people into the streets of Vienna, surging into the Diet and making demands for constitutional government. Their proposals were turned down, and massacre and bitter fighting were the issue of the refusal. Metternich resigned and took the already-beaten path to England. The "cretin" king was compliant. He promised civil liberties, drove out in his landau, and was surrounded by a now-joyous mob. He was so agitated that he begged with tears to be taken back to the palace; the people dismissed the horses and drew him home themselves. But within two months another revolt had forced the Emperor to flee to Innsbruck, and thence to Bohemia. By December he had been forced to abdicate and was succeeded by his nephew Francis Joseph I.

In the meantime other parts of the polyglot Hapsburg Empire had wrung concessions from the Emperor. Hungary demanded virtual independence from Austria and received a modern democratic constitution. The Czechs of Bohemia insisted upon a constituent assembly, and the Emperor conceded all. The flame of national revolt against Hapsburg domination was burning, too, in Italy—Lombardy and Venice revolted. And the independent states of Italy—Tuscany, Naples, and the Papal States—had already launched their own revolts against their ruling princes. So violent was the crisis in Rome that later in the year the notilliberal Pope Pius IX had to scurry away in disguise, leaving his temporal power behind.

By early spring, therefore, revolution seemed everywhere successful. Constitutions had been promised right and left. But Ferdinand was not Austria, unhappily for the revolting states. The generals took over in the field, national jealousies and enmities were played against each other, and the bright hopes dissolved into an aftermath of bitterness and despair.

The Hungarian revolt had been led by the brilliant patriot Kossuth, backed by the more moderate and less dramatic but no less able Francis Deák, whose wise leadership eventually helped Hungary win a constitution. Kossuth was the fiery, the persuasive one, whose impassioned appeals demanding sweeping democratic reforms inflamed the imagination of the people. For a time he was the spirit of revolution incarnate. Kossuth was really leading a Magyar revolt which, if successful, would have allowed the Magyars to dominate the Slovaks, Croatians, and Roumanians within the borders of Hungary. The Hapsburgs cannily exploited existing racial tensions. Civil war burst out when Jellachich, governor of the Hungarian province of Croatia, led an army against the Magyars. But only when Russia eventually threw in her weight with Austria did the war, which extended into 1849, close with Hungarian defeat and the flight of Kossuth.

The initial successes of the Italian provinces of Austria against the Hapsburgs also proved illusory. The Austrian general, Radetzky, was able to deal with the rebels singly. And when the Sardinian army, drawn into war against Austria in its attempt to take leadership in the unification of Italy, was defeated early in 1849, King Charles Albert abdicated in favor of his son, Victor Emmanuel II. Rapidly the republics of Florence, Rome, and Venice capitulated. Mazzini, who had rushed back to Milan from London when the revolution broke in 1848, had moved on to Rome to help establish the republic there. That was crushed by the French in 1849, and Mazzini once more found his way to England. Reaction was in the saddle. The kings or their successors crept back to their rehabilitated thrones.

The confusion of these kaleidoscopic events was reflected in the disconnected day-by-day reports as they reached the Englishman in the pages of his newspapers. Although Louis Philippe and family were given a warm reception by the royal family,* those entrusted with the affairs of state were watching the turmoil with wary eye. The progress of events was marked most clearly for the ordinary non-political citizen by

---

* But the estate at Claremont assigned to them proved to have poisonous water-pipes, and they retreated precipitantly with upset digestions to London.

Figure 99. Lord Palmerston, from a drawing by George Richmond

the stream of refugees who hurried to what *Punch* called "The Asylum of Europe."* The list was impressively long, and by no means of uniform political complexion. It included Louis Philippe and Louis Blanc, the Prince of Prussia and Ledru-Rollin, Guizot and Kossuth, Metternich and Mazzini. Below official levels the sympathy of much of the British public lay with the revolutionaries rather than with the royal exiles. And at the official level there was always Palmerston, embarrassing both his Queen and his fellow cabinet members by what seemed ill-considered expressions of sympathy for the downtrodden peoples of Europe.

Palmerston delighted the man on the street as much as he irritated his

---

* Come, all ye kings kick'd out of doors
    By foreign insurrection.
Oh! come to Britain's peaceful shores
    For safety and protection.
Ye Ministers, obliged to run
    From climes too hot to hold you,
Come to John Bull, each mother's son—
    Let her stout arms enfold you.

colleagues. Highhanded, determined above all to maintain the prestige of England abroad, gay and debonair and reckless, an energetic and successful bluffer reveling in the delicate poker game of European politics, he nevertheless stood firmly on the side of constitutional liberties on the Continent. Early in the year he had blundered badly, as his fellow ministers and even the larger portion of the press saw it,* in hurrying off a note to Spain urging with more than paternal favor the granting of increased liberties to the Spanish people—a note which resulted in the prompt dismissal by the Spanish Court of the English minister Sir Henry Bulwer and created a ministerial scandal at home. A little later Palmerston urged that both Lombardy and Venetia should be severed from the Austrian Empire. It emerged also that he had been sending war matériel to the Italian rebels. All this was without official sanction of any kind. Russell writhed but was unable to do anything about it; Palmerston never seemed to have time to submit his communications for royal approval. When the Queen, distracted, came as close as a constitutional monarch could to exclaiming "Will no one rid me of this pestilent minister?" Russell had to point out to her that Palmerston's prestige with the people and his competence in a government not noted for its over-all strength made it impossible to dismiss him. There was nothing to do but to live in hot water and try to like it. When Disraeli and others took several nights in the House of Commons to impeach Palmerston's foreign policy as being anti-French and pro-Russian, the foreign minister met a five-hour speech of Mr. Anstey's with a five-hour speech of his own in which he reviewed his whole parliamentary career—it reminded him, he said jocularly, of a drowning man's vision of his past life. "I hold," he said, "that the real policy of England . . . is to be the champion of justice and right, pursuing that course with moderation and prudence, not becoming the Quixote of the world, but giving the weight of her moral sanction and support wherever she thinks that justice is, and whenever she thinks that wrong has been done."

Parliament was sufficiently perturbed by the Continental conflagration to pass a Removal of Aliens Bill aimed at "aliens of disreputable character, whose presence and conduct may be deemed dangerous to the peace and social order of these realms." It seemed a matter of no importance at the time—indeed almost no one knew of it—that England was comfortably harboring two intellectual German exiles who were drafting in the early weeks of the year the most inflammatory document not merely of the decade but of the century. Karl Marx and Friedrich Engels

---

* The *Spectator* referred to his "ostentatious patriotism" and said, "He piques himself so in getting out of scrapes that he is eager to get into them."

sent to a London printer, just a few weeks before the outbreak of the French revolution, the German text of the *Communist Manifesto*, beginning: "The history of all hitherto existing society is the history of class struggles," and ending: "Workingmen of all countries, unite!" Not all of the significant events in the biography of a nation appear in its formal record.

Amid the cataclysmic European happenings of 1848 it seemed of relatively small importance that the United States completed her conquest of the Mexican armies and annexed to her territories the areas which form the present states of California, Utah, Arizona, and New Mexico; or that General Zachary Taylor, the hero of the Mexican War, won the election for the presidency over his democratic rival, General Lewis Cass of Michigan.

There was a good deal of self-congratulation among the English in 1848, much thanksgiving that England was not as other nations. The terror on the Continent seemed far from English shores. Nevertheless, there was enough to worry about at home, and in at least two instances during the spring and summer there were threats of violence which seemed to echo briefly the sinister events across the Channel. The Chartists were again on the move, and Ireland was at the point of active rebellion.

The threatened Chartist revolution, which someone called "a bad translation of a French piece," has its background and its prologue. The background was that of continuing industrial depression. Prices were down but work was scarce. The closing of cotton manufactories threw many out of work; in Manchester there were half as many entirely unemployed or working only short time as there were working full time. March saw riots in Manchester and Glasgow; large mobs assembled on the Glasgow green and attacked the shops of gunsmiths and provision dealers. Not until the soldiery had fired on the crowd did it disperse amid a few cries of "Down with the Queen" and *"Vive la République."* Obviously events across the Channel were having a repercussion.

In London on March 6th there was a curious unorganized and abortive riot in Trafalgar Square. One Charles Cochrane had called a meeting to protest against the income tax, of all things! When the meeting was declared illegal, Mr. Cochrane wisely did not put in appearance. By one o'clock a heterogeneous crowd of some 15,000, followers and spectators, had gathered in the square, many of them younger ragamuffins and thieves who took advantage of the occasion to tear up the wooden fence around the still-unfinished Nelson Column and to engage in sporadic fights with the police. The disturbance quieted down by midnight without reaching any serious crisis.

All this time the Chartist rumblings were growing louder under the leadership of the Irishman Feargus O'Connor. He was an egotistical and frantic enthusiast—another descendant of Irish kings—whose fanatical speeches, fanned by the success of the French Revolution, were consolidating the forces of Chartism, which had been moribund for several years and were now about to be resurrected in one last frenetic gesture. O'Connor was a Member of Parliament, where his speeches were taken less than seriously; but with the assistance of a still more violent agitator, Ernest Jones, he had succeeded in calling a grand Chartist National Convention in London. The plan was to march on the House of Commons with a giant petition bearing more than 5,000,000 signatures. On March 13th a sort of test flight was made with a gathering on Kennington Common. But a heavy rain came on and cleared the common in an hour, the inflammatory speeches washed out.

April came and with it the huge meeting scheduled for the tenth. Some 150,000 were to assemble, again on Kennington Common (on the Surrey side of the Thames, just across the river at Blackfriar's Bridge). They were to listen to the conventional tirades and were then to accompany the petition back across the river to the doors of the House of Commons. The report was that the marchers had been advised to procure arms and weapons.

All this seemed serious enough to warrant official protective preparation. The Commissioners of Police, some days previous, posted placards throughout London forbidding the procession. The defense of the City was turned over to the Duke of Wellington, who proceeded energetically to lay out his plan of campaign. Troops were stationed at strategic points—government offices were manned; the Bank of England was packed with troops and artillery and strengthened with sandbags. Twelve hundred infantry were kept at Deptford Dockyards, and thirty pieces of field artillery were held in readiness at the Tower, to be sent by special river steamers to any point of acute disturbance. Very wisely, however, the troops were to be kept out of sight, and the seeming control of the situation to be entrusted to the regular police and to a provisional army of 170,000 special constables, many of whom were to be deployed at the various bridges.

The morning of April 10th dawned fair and bright over a watchful and somewhat fearful city. Shops were closed and the streets were deserted except for curious sight-seers and the thousands of white-badged

and bestaved constables who rather self-consciously patrolled the ave-
nues. It was democracy come alive, for all London had turned out in
defense of home and fireside. Peers of Parliament paraded with middle-
class burghers; butlers and merchants and shopkeepers marched together
—some with umbrellas, to the merriment of onlookers. Louis Napoleon,
who would in nine months be President of all France, wore a white
armband and policed Piccadilly.

The Chartists assembled at various points—Russell Square, Whitechapel, and elsewhere—and were allowed to pass unmolested across
Blackfriar's Bridge to the common. Meanwhile the Convention met at

Figure 100. A special constable. From *Punch*

its hall in Fitzroy Square, where O'Connor addressed the assembly in a rambling and curiously equivocal speech. He had come to the determination, he said, to attend the meeting in spite of the Government injunction, and take the responsibility on himself, in the event of any physical force on the part of the Government, to persuade the people not to bring themselves into collision with the authorities. Other more violent speakers expressed some surprise at this declaration of the chairman, but delegates were elected to present the petition (declared by O'Connor to contain 5,600,000 signatures), and those elected representatives piled into a twenty-foot van, commodious enough to "afford comfortable accommodation to the delegates, as well as to several representatives of the press." The car, inscribed with such Chartist mottoes as "Liberty is worth living for and worth dying for," was hauled to the meeting by "six farm horses of superior breed, and in the highest possible condition." It was followed by a four-wheel cab bearing the monster petition, and thus the cavalcade moved across the bridge to the place of meeting.

There the prophesied scores of thousands of participants had dwindled unaccountably to some 23,000, including spectators. O'Connor presented himself, to the prolonged cheers of the multitude, and spoke with much self-praise and in vague generalities about "Liberty" and "Rights of the People." He then urged his followers to disperse peaceably, since the Government had taken possession of the metropolitan bridges. The "executive" of the Chartist Association would convey the petition to the House of Commons. The mob began to show signs of dissatisfaction, as did some of the delegates in the van. Speakers sprang up to insist that the petition should be accompanied by the people until opposed by the military. Squabbles broke out, and the uproar was such that only those nearest the platform could hear what was going on. The situation was not eased by the noise of a competing crowd of 5,000 "Irish Confederates," headed by a handsome green flag and drawn up at one side of the common to listen to its own speeches. But those Chartists within hearing distance voted approval to a collateral petition to the Commons—one of the most strangely worded revolutionary documents on record. It began: "The humble petition of the inhabitants of the metropolis of England . . . showeth," and begged "your honourable House" to reject a proposed measure relating to sedition. Then at a quarter past one the meeting was declared adjourned; the four large bundles forming the petition were piled into two cabs and taken by the Executive Committee to the House of Commons. By two o'clock the only occupants of the common were some boys playing at trapball.

As the crowd started back across the river it discovered that the police would allow it to pass only in small groups. There was crowding on the approaches; the police went into action and some heads were broken; a few special constables were roughly handled by the Chartists, several of them being deprived of their staves. A good many arrests were made on the City side of the bridge, but in a very short time London was quiet again, the crowds dispersed.

The Chartists who expected their petition to be taken at face value reckoned without their Parliamentary hosts. The House delegated the petition to a committee of tellers who returned with the announcement that the document contained only 1,975,496 signatures instead of an alleged 5,706,000. They further reported that many of the signatures were written in the same hand, and that they included the names of Her Majesty, the Duke of Wellington, Sir Robert Peel, and Colonel Sibthorp, among others. (Colonel Sibthorp, the eternal Tory, grew apoplectic with rage at this indignity.) Moreover, some names were inserted which seemed, so the tellers said, fictitious, such as "No cheese," "Pug-nose," "Flatnose"—to say nothing of some obscenities "which your committee will not hazard offending the House by repeating."

And so Chartism broke up amid ridicule and roars of caustic laughter. Although there were a few troublesome isolated outbursts later in the year, it was seen no more as an organized movement. The comfortable feeling of middle-class solidarity was enhanced; men congratulated one another on the dispersal of a non-English phenomenon. But what of the discontent which lay behind Chartism? Many of the nearly 2,000,000 signatures *were* real, and the hopelessness which they reflected was no less real. Thoughtful people other than Carlyle saw that discontent could not be muffled by laughter, that the basic question, "What will you do to save me from the shadow of this death?" somehow had to have an answer, and that it would trouble the dreams of sensitive Englishmen until it was answered.

What saved England from the whirlpool of revolution that engulfed the Continent in 1848? Here was a country in which six sevenths of the adult male population could not vote and where the representation in the Commons was so unfairly distributed that the great congested center of Manchester, with twice the population of Buckinghamshire, returned only two members as against the latter's eleven. Hunger and possible starvation looked just as ghastly to the Liverpool Irishman or the Glasgow operative as it did to the French workman. "It is quite new," wrote Greville, "to hear any Englishman coolly recommend assassination." How did England escape catastrophe?

In the first place, the Chartist leadership was divided within its own house. Such "moral force" men as Lovett would have nothing to do with the seditious threats of those who urged violent opposition to the Government. The leadership of the "physical force" group was itself vacillating: witness Feargus O'Connor's performance on Kennington Common. There was, too, a new and growing class of superior artisans—notably those essential to the great engineering developments in factories and railways—who wooed respectability, trusted in the developing organization of trade unionism to secure their rights, and threw their social weight with the middle classes. And, unlike the French, the English middle classes were one with the aristocracy in defense of the established order; the householders who patrolled the streets on April 10th as special constables were more important as symbols of a national *esprit* than they knew. Moreover, England had an aristocracy of which even the more stiff-necked members had the sense to bow constitutionally before the inevitable, and many of whom exerted themselves actively to temper the winds of distress. The energetic philanthropic and liberal efforts of such men as Lord Ashley, Sir William Molesworth, Lord Morpeth, and Lord Dudley Stuart (friend of Poland and champion of Kossuth) told heavily. The repeal of the Corn Laws, too, had come just in time; and there had never been any question about the freedom of the British press. The result of all this was that even the underprivileged Englishman felt that he was living under a constitutional government, that he could appeal to a sympathetic Queen and her "most honourable ministers" for relief. Hence an almost pathetic faith in monster petitions. Street barricades were simply not an Englishman's way of life. He might march endlessly with angry banners, but under such a friendly monarchy he would never tear up his own trees in Hyde Park to block Constitution Hill.

Ireland was another matter, not merely in her more aggravated sufferings but also in her spirit of rebellion. In 1848 the Irish lid came close to blowing off.

The revolutions in Europe quickened the pulse of every Irish republican and made him feel that his hour was at hand. Small matter that a congratulatory mission sent to Paris, seeking sympathy and possible aid, was turned away coolly by Lamartine, who made it very clear that France wished to be at peace with *all parts* of the British Empire. There were plenty of firebrands at home to whip up a conflagration: Duffy, Davis, Meagher, John Mitchel, and Smith O'Brien. Irish patriotism reached its shrillest pitch in Mitchel's *United Irishmen,* currently a much more vociferous and popular newspaper than the *Nation.* Every

Saturday Mitchel addressed a letter "To the Earl of Clarendon, Her Majesty's Executioner-General and Butcher-General of Ireland" and published plans for the approaching insurrection; street fighting and barricades *were* in the Irish pattern. "I have a mission," he wrote in an April epistle to Clarendon, "to bear a hand in the final destruction of the bloody old 'British empire.' . . . Against that Engine of Hell a thousand thousand ghosts of my slaughtered countrymen shriek nightly for vengeance. . . . And Heaven has heard it. . . . Thank God, they are arming. Young men everywhere in Ireland begin to love the clear glancing of the steel, and to cherish their dainty rifles as the very apple of their eyes."

At this point the Government supplemented its Coercion Bill by a Treason-Felony Act which resulted in the arrest of O'Brien, Meagher, and Mitchel on charges of seditious libel. At O'Brien's trial, as at Meagher's, the jury failed to agree, but Mitchel was found guilty and sentenced to fourteen years' transportation. His followers, however, increased the fury of their agitation; revolutionary clubs were organized, pikes were on sale at every other shop, scythes were sharpened into lethal weapons, and a general insurrection was indicated by early autumn.

But on July 22d the House of Commons suspended the Habeas Corpus Act for Ireland, moving the bill through all its stages in an afternoon. This made possible the immediate arrest of Smith O'Brien and his confederates, who promptly left Dublin and scattered through the provinces to organize resistance. The constabulary—a military more than a police force—caught up with O'Brien about two miles north of Ballingary, on the mountainous edge of Tipperary. There occurred the famous battle of Widow McCormack's Cabbage Patch. The constabulary, numbering about fifty men, met on a hill road a straggling Irish army of some 500 peasantry, accompanied by half as many women urging them to violence against the constables. The latter barricaded themselves in the house of Mrs. McCormack while the insurgents ranged themselves behind the garden wall. The widow had been away from home and arrived to find her house, in which were five of her children, under siege. She was refused admittance by the police. Briskly she sought out O'Brien, crouching behind the wall, and induced him to advance and hold parley with the police—according to some accounts, by seizing him by the collar and propelling him across the yard. The discussion through the barricaded windows proved inconclusive. O'Brien returned to his cover behind the wall, the waiting army of camp followers fled in all directions, and the firing began—the blunderbusses and fowling pieces of the ragged Irish against the muskets of the constabulary. The issue was not long in doubt: seven of the courageous but foolhardy rebels were

Figure 101. The battle of Widow McCormack's Cabbage Patch

killed and others wounded. Shortly the miscellaneous rabble of pikemen and scythemen retreated and the battle was over. It was the high point of the Irish Revolution of 1848.

O'Brien, deserted by his comrades, was hunted for a week through the Irish countryside, where he was concealed by the peasantry. At last he was recognized by a guard at the Thurles Railway Station—a Mr. Hulme—and was quietly arrested. He was sentenced to death at his trial for high treason with a recommendation for mercy; the sentence was commuted to transportation for life, and the rebellion was over. Great Britain had rounded the revolutionary corner of the decade.

At the Colosseum in London the new panorama of London by moonlight showed quiet streets and a peaceful sky; the red glow from the windows of the houses was that of domestic felicity rather than the communistic flame of blood and terror.

During these turbulent spring and summer months the basic flow of English life was little disturbed. The new Glasgow Athenaeum, with a membership of 1,900, held its first meeting—an establishment "for the mental and social improvement of the young men of Glasgow, in literary and scientific knowledge." A grand soirée was held, with 3,000 to 4,000 present, and Mr. Charles Dickens in the chair. "The sovereignty of man lies hid in knowledge" read a gold inscription. . . . The Art-Union called for an Exposition of British Manufactures and Industrial Arts. . . . George Hudson laid the foundation stone at his new Sunderland Docks. . . . The hit of the theatrical season was a new five-act play by Mr. Lovell (author of *Love's Sacrifice* and *Look Before You Leap*), called *The Wife's Secret.* . . . Robert Houdin, the great magician, appeared at the St. James's Theatre. . . . The Jenny Lind fever hit the metropolis again. . . . Chopin gave a recital in London. . . . A new steam engine for thrashing grain was introduced. . . . A Chinese junk anchored at the East India Docks was visited by Victoria and Albert, Wellington, Metternich, Jenny Lind, and the Prince of Prussia (not all at the same time). . . . The first ball of a series of six at Almack's (with ten lady patronesses) was held in May. . . . Emerson gave a series of lectures at Exeter Hall on "Napoleon," "Domestic Life," and "Shakespeare." . . . Berlioz gave a concert at Drury Lane of his own pieces, conducting his "Inauguration Symphony," "Harold in Italy," and a "Chorus of Souls in Purgatory." His romantically descriptive music was a subject of contemporary controversy. . . . So hot was the dispute about the domination of the English stage by foreign performers that when a French company presented Dumas's *Count of Monte Cristo* at Drury Lane the audience hooted, whistled, and shrieked during the three hours the play was being performed in dumb show. . . . An enterprising showman at Leeds got hold of the clothes of a recently hanged murderer, stuffed them out with a wax figure, and put it on display. When doubt was expressed as to the authenticity of the relics, he imported the actual hangman, who gave detailed accounts of the hanging with explanations as to why the criminal's death agonies had been unduly protracted.

It was decided to kill an elephant who had murdered his keeper at the Liverpool Zoological Gardens. Two ounces of prussic acid and twenty-five grains of aconite administered in a bun gave him only a slight uneasiness for five minutes. A detachment of the Third Rifles was sent for; fifteen men fired; the elephant staggered and leaned against his den; fifteen more fired, whereupon he died instantly.

Amid the jeers of the more sophisticated press, Coventry staged a revival of the Lady Godiva Procession at its fair. The pageantry was elaborate, with one Mrs. Warton impersonating the Countess Godiva in a tight pink dress, her husband playing the part of the Black Prince. All the citizenry were "peeping Toms" on this occasion.

Queen Victoria gave birth to Princess Louise on March 18th.

The concern about public health grew more tense during 1848. The cholera was creeping closer during the summer. It was reported raging in

Moscow, where it had caused 728 deaths in one week in June. By September it had reached Hamburg and Paris. Lord Morpeth had tried unsuccessfully to get approval of a Public Health Act in 1847. He revived the bill this year, and it passed Parliament in an emasculated form which made it little more than a permissive act. Local committees or borough authorities could, if they chose, regulate water supply, control cemeteries, and construct sewers. The activities of these boards were under the jurisdiction of a central Board of Health of which Edwin Chadwick was a member, but that board had no power to compel action. Nevertheless, in a fumbling and inadequate way some good was done, despite the almost immediate creation of a Private Enterprise Society whose function was to resist wherever possible the operation of the Act.

Reports of Commissioners for the last ten years had made almost ocularly vivid the need for sanitary reforms in towns both large and small. The investigators entered into the problems of sewerage, drainage, paving, cleansing, removal of nuisances, supply of water, arrangement of buildings and streets, and interments in towns. They showed that in the more populous towns the poorer districts were almost entirely lacking in underground drainage. They underlined the need of surveys: in such towns as Rochdale and Bolton no one knew what direction the sewers followed. In some of the towns sanitary regulations were under the control of as many as three distinct boards of commissioners and four distinct boards of surveyors. The incredible foulness of the close courts and the back-to-back houses in the poorer sections of the towns had been laid bare by chapter and verse. In Liverpool there were 2,398 courts, containing a population of 68,345 persons. In these courts 1,272 cellars were occupied by 6,290 persons. Of the occupied cellars in streets, as distinct from courts, 2,848 were described as damp, 140 as wet. The water supply to flush even the open drains and sewers was universally ineffectual. At Bath there were four local acts in force to control sewers and paving, with the result that in one street the carriageway was half paved, the other half macadamized, and the two halves on different levels!

Towns could be smelled out by their public nuisances. In Sunderland there were 182 public receptacles for dung and filth of all kinds, usually situated in the narrow streets and lanes occupied by the poorer classes; in some cases they were actually in the basement stories of dwelling houses. Birmingham had 1,600 pigsties within its borough limits. Of 40,000 houses in Birmingham, only 8,000 had water laid on; in Newcastle the proportion was one in twelve. In Bristol, out of 130,000 inhabitants, only 5,000 of the most wealthy had running water in their houses.

One of the poorer streets of Liverpool had 1,585 inhabitants in a space which gave but six square yards to each.

Data like these had filled huge folio volumes of the Parliamentary Blue Books. Only now was officialdom making feeble gestures to correct the more flagrant evils. And worst of all, London itself was not included in the Public Health Act! London presented a problem of infinite complexity in statutes, privileges, interests, and governing bodies. Up to 1847 it had seven sewerage districts, each under a separate body of commissioners.* Most of the 270,000 houses in London had cesspools under them, sometimes three or four. Mr. J. Phillips, testifying before the Metropolitan Sewers Commission, said in 1847:

> There are hundreds, I may say thousands, of houses in this metropolis which have *no drainage whatever*, and the greater part of them have stinking, overflowing cesspools. And there are also hundreds of streets, courts, and alleys, that have no sewers; and how the drainage and filth is cleaned away, and how the poor miserable inhabitants live in such places is hard to tell.
>
> In pursuance of my duties, from time to time, I have visited very many places where filth was lying scattered about the rooms, vaults, cellars, areas, and yards, so thick, and so deep, that it was hardly possible to move for it. I have also seen in such places human beings living and sleeping in such rooms with filth from overflowing cesspools exuding and running down the walls and over the floors. . . .[2]

To add to the accumulated putridity there were 138 registered slaughterhouses within the city limits, in fifty-eight of which slaughtering took place in vaults and cellars. "How overwhelming an amount of organic decomposition must be furnished by these out of the blood and offal merely of those 450,000 sheep and 60,000 cattle which annually pass over Blackfriars Bridge alone, can neither be estimated nor conceived." It was little wonder that in an atmosphere like this other diseases, in addition to cholera, made deep ravages. In spite of the knowledge of vaccination, 6,903 people died in Britain in 1848 from smallpox alone.

John Simon, the London medical health officer, in making his report to the Commissioners of Sewers in 1849, spoke of the typhus which was endemic in many quarters of the city. In a few houses of Seven Step Alley there occurred, in 1847, 163 cases of fever. It was just as bad in many other quarters, some of them verging on the wealthiest thoroughfares: thus in Plumtree Court and Blackhorse Alley, in Holborn; in Hangingsword Alley and Peahen Court, in Bear Lane and Friar's Alley. One of the worst was the Devil's Acre in Westminster, almost literally under

---

* Late in 1847, under a Metropolitan Sewers Act, the seven boards were merged into one consolidated commission of twenty-three members.

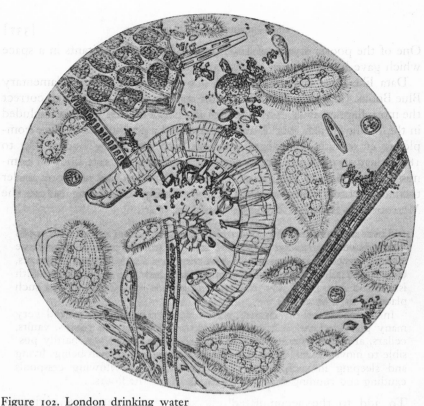

Figure 102. London drinking water

"This engraving exhibits the organic matter, living and dead, especially the Thames Paramecium, contained in the water as supplied by the Lambeth Company. Drawn with the Camera Lucida, and magnified 220 diameters."

the shadows of the Abbey towers. "It is too true," said Simon, "that among these classes there are swarms of men and women who have yet to learn that human beings should dwell differently from cattle. . . . Men and women, boys and girls, in scores using jointly one single, common privy; grown persons of both sexes sleeping in common with their married parents; a woman suffering travail in the midst of the males and females of three several families of fellow lodgers in a single room. . . ."

As far as drainage was concerned, all the London sewers emptied into the Thames, whence six of the nine independent water companies drew their supplies of water for the metropolis. Two thirds of the companies had no system of filtration. There was no pressure system; the water was pumped into domestic cisterns. It would seem, said Simon mildly enough, "that the sanitary purposes of drainage are but imperfectly achieved where the outfall of sewerage is into a tidal river passing through the heart of a densely-peopled metropolis." Sixty sewers had outlets into the Thames; with one exception none of the City sewer outlets was covered, and the deposits ran in open channels upon the shore. Some sewers were higher than the cesspools they were supposed to drain. And as for the Thames, most of the sewers emptied themselves only at time of low water; as the tide rose, the outlets were closed and the sewage was dammed back. The sewage was carried *up* the Thames by the rising tide, washing the banks of the river. As a result, to call the Thames an "open sewer" was less metaphorical than literal.

All this became a matter of vital importance as the year progressed and the cholera came nearer. Yet very little was done about it. The near-panic induced by the thought of an epidemic of cholera was aggravated by a complete lack of knowledge about the causes of the disease. The germ theory of disease was still in the womb of time, and all sorts of ingenious explanations were advanced as to the source of the trouble. Water or food supplies were seldom mentioned; the consensus of opinion among the best authorities was in favor of the "zymotic" theory: that cholera was carried by an atmosphere impregnated with "pestilential miasmata." Few believed that it was contagious. Wrote Dr. E. V. Mainwaring in the *Lancet* (and other authorities agreed with him): "I consider that the disease is probably caused by persons inhaling a noxious gas. . . . A residence in a swampy situation, on the banks of stagnant and dirty water, canals, or near foul drains," etc., are the causes.* In November the *Lancet* declared: "We have abundantly shown that the Serpentine, the St. James's Canal, and the pool of pestilence in the Queen's private gardens are the great 'plague-works' of the West End of London." The Serpentine was an "Augean ditch" with its "accumulated abominations"—fifty acres of putrescent mud. About the same time the magazine printed a theory of M. Fourcault, presented to the Academy of Medicine: that Asiatic cholera is a disease "caused by the non-equilibration of the atmospheric electricity and terrestrial magnetism, which produces a rapid subtraction of the material principle of life."

Momentary publicity was given to the announcement in the *Medical Gazette*[3] that "Mr. Brittan, lecturer on anatomy at the Bristol Medical School, in a series of investigations, undertaken with Mr. J. G. Swayne, has observed the constant occurrence [under the microscope] of certain peculiar bodies, hitherto undescribed, as "characteristic constituents of cholera evacuations," also "the discovery of similar bodies in the atmosphere of districts infested with cholera." Microscopic pathologists

---

* In 1849 Henry Mayhew noted, however, that where the "zymotic" influences were the worst—Belgravia and Tyburnia—the cholera was least destructive.

seemed to consider the research important, but, as we shall see, official-dom declared against it. The truth was almost in hand, and it escaped.

The remedies used for cholera were as many as the theories of its communication. They varied from the use of calomel and tartar emetic to packing in a wet sheet, drinking three small cups of pure olive oil, and taking carbonate of soda—"a speedy and effectual antidote to the poison of the disease." The best advice was that there was no objection to the use of disinfectants for removing disagreeable odors, but that there was no evidence to show that they would destroy the "poison" of contagious diseases. But however diverse the theories, all people held in common the fear of the approaching epidemic.

Meanwhile, however, interesting things kept happening. There was a great deal of curiosity about the public auctions held at Stowe in August to liquidate the estate of the bankrupt Duke of Buckingham. People wandered about the extensive and elaborately decorated grounds, studded with temples, obelisks, grottoes, and bridges. Memories arose of the elaborate and expensive entertainment which the duke had offered Victoria and Albert on their notable visit to Stowe two years earlier—an extravagance which compounded, though it did not precipitate, the duke's financial collapse. The visitors noticed the two trees which Albert had planted near the Temple of Victory on that visit. Bidders bought one of the most elaborate collections of works of art, furniture, and curios outside a museum—portraits, chalices, vases, chimney pieces, Sèvres and Dresden china, inlaid tables, gilt beds, forests of chandeliers, oceans of plate, a Huygens clock (for fifty-one guineas) said to have cost the duke no less than a thousand guineas. The Chandos portrait of Shakespeare was sold to Lord Ellesmere for 355 guineas. A picture of Henry VIII by Holbein sold for £94 10s. and one of Nell Gwyn by Lely for £105.

Marryat the novelist and George Stephenson the famous engineer died within a week of each other in August. . . . George Bentinck, recently resigned as leader of the Protectionist group of the Conservative party, was found dead in one of the fields of his estate. . . . A shocking accident occurred in the Irish Channel when the emigrant ship *Ocean Monarch* burned to the waterline and 178 people lost their lives. . . . Announcement was made of a new park to be built at Battersea, across the Thames —two and a quarter miles long by one mile wide. . . . The fishermen of Cromarty Firth were thrown into excitement by the discovery of a school of bottle-nosed whales gamboling in the shallow water off their shores. Armed with guns and pitchforks, men, women, and children rushed into the waves and killed about seventy of the whales. . . . Mr. Green made his 201st balloon ascent, this time at the Hippodrome in Paris, accompanied by four persons and a monkey. The latter descended in a parachute.

In London the Vernon Gallery of English pictures—100 of them—was given to the nation and placed on display in the basement of the National Gallery. . . . There was a good deal of architectural regret over the removal of the arcade of the Regent Street Quadrant, John Nash's noble contribution to the London scene. But it darkened the shop windows and furnished, underneath, a loitering place for undesirable characters, and so design was sacrificed to morality and commercial practicality. The 270 painted cast-iron pillars were sold for railway purposes. . . . The thrill of the concert season at Drury Lane was Jullien's presentation of "God Save the Queen" with four bands. Five thousand persons packed themselves into a theater meant to hold 3,000 and demanded four encores.

Vanity Fair had run its course in monthly numbers, and was being reviewed as a completed whole in the press. Some of the critics took exception to what seemed to them Thackeray's mean view of human nature, but most of them praised his style, his quietness "in a literary age which has a tendency to mistake spasm for force," and by and large found it "one of the most remarkable works of modern fiction." *Pendennis*, which was just beginning to appear, seemed to them to open with even greater promise than did *Vanity Fair*.

Mill's *Political Economy* was recognized as one of the great books of the generation. Mill had invited comparison with Adam Smith's *Wealth of Nations*, and the comparisons made were favorable. . . . It was believed that Lytton's archaeology spoiled the fiction of his newly published *Harold*. . . . The terrible unmelodramatic truth of Mrs. Gaskell's *Mary Barton*, her picture of life among the working classes, was praised. Said *Fraser's Magazine:* "Had we wit and wisdom enough, we should placard its sheets on every wall, and have them read aloud from every pulpit, till a nation, calling itself Christian, began to act upon the awful facts contained in it." . . . Tennyson's *Princess* was both praised and damned. The judicious found rare and genuine beauty in the lyric passages but condemned its general design and plan. . . . Cruikshank published the eight plates of his *Drunkard's Children*, accompanied by an illustrative narrative in Spenserian verse by Dr. Charles Mackay.

The first two volumes of Macaulay's *History of England from the Accession of James II* had been awaited eagerly, and when the book appeared in November the first impression was sold out in three days. It was evident that even the brilliant Macaulay would have difficulty completing his plan within the reaches of a single lifetime; it took two large volumes to cover the three years' reign of King James. Macaulay, a man of mudsucker memory, was afflicted with almost total recall. "He is like nothing in the world," wrote Fanny Kemble of his conversation, "but Bayle's Dictionary, continued down to the present time, and purified from all objectionable matter. Such a Niagara of information did surely never pour from the lips of mortal man!"[4] All this wealth of knowledge he poured into his history in discursive form—picturesque details, argumentative discussion, fluent illustrations. Beyond that was a superb delineation of character and a masterly skill in analyzing as well as assembling evidence—even though a good portion of that evidence was carefully drawn to prove a preconceived thesis. But to a generation anxious to be shown the course of its advance into material well-being and to have its complacency fed by a recognition that Progress was not only the Englishman's heritage but that its future prospects were illimitable, Macaulay brought great comfort. Above all he made vivid and clear what a historian like Carlyle could make only vivid; under his hands "the dry bones lived." All the reviewers mentioned his lively account of the social condition of England at the accession of James II— a tapestry of real life which was quite outside the realm of dignified dullness which had traditionally been considered appropriate to history.

In November, too, died the man who was Home Secretary when Macaulay began his Parliamentary career: William Lamb, second Viscount Melbourne. Although Lord Melbourne was only sixty-nine and had been Prime Minister when Victoria was crowned, he seemed to belong to another day; his health and political activity had both declined rapidly since he left office in 1841. He had always been in spirit more a part of the eighteenth century or the Regency than of the Victorian age. People remembered his early domestic difficulties with Lady Caroline Lamb, who had been infatuated with Byron; his defense of the suit brought against him by the husband of Mrs. Norton; his easy, indolent manner which took the world much as it found it; his paradoxical taste for greatness and goodness, a taste founded on rich and wide reading but combined with a sensuality and a cynical observation of man's follies and vices; the decay of Whig strength under his too-expedient leadership. They remembered, too, his lack of vanity or desire for honors, and the patriotic and tactful devotion with which, as Prime Minister, he entered upon the education of a young queen; how his deference and his entertaining conversation captivated Victoria, who liked the frankness and honesty with which he would tell her his opinions, and whose affection for him allowed him to talk to her with

Figure 103. Thomas Babington Macaulay

Figure 104. William Ewart Gladstone

Figure 105. Lord Brougham

Figure 106. Michael Faraday

a license she would have permitted no one else. "He was never really well fitted for political life," wrote Greville, "for he had a great deal too much candour, and was too fastidious to be a good party man. . . . And still less was he fit to be the leader of a party and the head of a Government, for he had neither the strong convictions, nor the eager ambition, nor the firmness and resolution which such a post requires." Yet Greville disliked the "coarse, vulgar, and to a great degree unjust" obituary which the *Times* printed—a notice which damned with faint praise: "He was indolent; he might have been corrupt. He was a man of easy virtue; he might have been a reckless profligate. He co-operated with Mr. O'Connell; but he had grace enough left to be ashamed of the alliance. He was lavish of title; but he did not quite swamp the House of Lords." But the Queen wrote: "One cannot forget how good and kind and amiable he was."

Public curiosity at the moment was about equally divided between the exhibition of Staite's new patent electric light in Trafalgar Square, which flooded the Square with a dazzling beam equal to that of 900 wax candles, as white as a sunbeam,* and the reported discovery of a sea serpent off the Cape of Good Hope.

---

* It used the principle of the carbon arc, powered by galvanic batteries. Its maintenance was too expensive to be practical.

Figure 107. Exhibition of the electric light in Trafalgar Square

Figure 108. The sea serpent

The latter episode was reported in an official letter from Captain McQuhae, of H.M.S. *Daedalus*. At 5 P.M. on August 6th, in latitude 24° 44′ S. and longitude 9° 22′ E., the weather dark and cloudy, four officers on the quarter-deck saw clearly something very unusual approaching the ship from before the beam. In the captain's own words:

> It was discovered to be an enormous serpent, with head and shoulders kept about four feet constantly above the surface of the sea, and as nearly as we could approximate . . . there was at the very least 60 feet of the animal *à fleur d'eau*, no portion of which was, to our perception, used in propelling it through the water, either by vertical or horizontal undulation. It passed rapidly, but so close under our lee quarter, that had it been a man of my acquaintance I should have easily recognized his features with the naked eye; and it did not, either in approaching the ship or after it had passed our wake, deviate in the slightest degree from its course to the S.W., which it held on at the pace of from 12 to 15 miles per hour, apparently on some determined purpose.
>
> The diameter of the serpent was about 15 or 16 inches behind the head, which was, without any doubt, that of a snake, and it was never, during the 20 minutes that it continued in sight of our glasses, once below the surface of the water; its colour a dark brown, with yellowish white about the throat. It had no fins, but something like the mane of a horse, or rather a bunch of sea-weed, washed about its back.

The captain's drawing was reproduced in the pages of the *Illustrated London News*, and the controversy was on. Mr. Owen, a professor of comparative anatomy, argued that the creature must have been a very large and disconcerted seal which had floated down on an iceberg and was then swimming in search of a resting place. The professor then went on to show by learned reasoning that a sea serpent was an impossibility in nature. Captain McQuhae replied indignantly, and gave further data which tended to refute Professor Owen's cavalier dismissal of the episode. There the case rested, the public having to make up its own mind, as it has always had to do, about the existence of such a monster of the deep.

A ripple of excitement larger than the event itself was caused by a sordid trial at the Worship Street Police Office. Messrs. Moses and Son, the advertising clothiers, had haled into court a poor woman named Sarah Ladd on the charge of stealing six calico shirts entrusted to her for sewing. The incident called public attention to the fact that seamstresses received fifteen pence a dozen for making shirts, or about three and three fourths pence a day. The press was indignant; *Punch* recalled Hood's "Song of the Shirt" and cited another case of an Emma Mounser who, in order to support an unemployed husband and two children, had pawned seventeen shirts for the making of which she was supposed to receive from Moses and Son two and a half pence apiece, or fourpence a day. Moses and Son declared that competition forced them to sell as cheaply as their neighbors, hence their starvation wages.

This sort of thing, symptomatic of still deeper abysses in the sweatshop trades, was the stimulus which caused a small group of devoted if impetuous men, enthusiastic for social reform, to launch a crusade which was to carry beyond mid-century and then to dissolve because of forces beyond their control.

J. M. Ludlow was a lawyer who had agitated for the repeal of the Corn Laws and was the one who taught the others what they learned about socialism. John Frederick Denison Maurice, whom Ludlow called "the central figure of the movement, towering spiritually by head and shoulders over all the rest," had taken orders in the Church of England and was currently professor of English literature and history at King's College, London. Just this year he had been instrumental in founding Queen's College. Later on he was to face charges of heterodoxy initiated against him by the *Quarterly Review* in 1851; his simplicity and gentleness would not allow him to believe that God would damn anyone to eternal punishment. For him religion was nothing if it had no social implications, and he burned with a pure and holy flame against injustice and social wrong. The third of the trio, who, like the others, was strongly under the influence of Carlyle's social thundering, was Charles Kingsley, the energetic and full-blooded Broad Church clergyman and exponent of "Muscular Christianity" who was currently publishing his social novel *Yeast* in *Fraser's Magazine*. Kingsley was another of those passionate Victorians extending himself in a multitude of directions, not the least important of which was the campaign for social betterment. None of these men liked the violence of Chartism, but they saw that some reasonable facsimile of relief must be extended to a suffering proletariat. Their remedy was Christian Socialism—and for them these words were synonymous rather than mutually exclusive.

On the morning of the Chartist fiasco of April 10th Kingsley had come up to London from his parish in Eversley, Hampshire, curious about what was happening. That evening he discussed with his friend Maurice and with Ludlow, whom he had just met, what might be done about the whole confused situation. Discussion led to immediate action. Kingsley sat up until four in the morning writing posting placards "to speak a word for God with." Already plans had been laid to issue a series of *Tracts for the Times*. Thus Christian Socialism was born, and on the streets of London appeared an address to the "Workmen of England," signed by "A Working Parson."

By May 6th they began the publication of the first of their periodical papers under the title *Politics for the People*. The series lasted only three months, but in that interval they had drawn into their columns such influential names as those of Richard Whately, the Archbishop of Dublin; Richard Trench, then a colleague of Maurice at King's College; and Arthur P. Stanley, afterward Dean of Westminster. Kingsley wrote under the pseudonym of "Parson Lot," the name he was to use later in his exposé of the sweatshop system, "Cheap Clothes and Nasty."

There was a kind of generous mistiness about the enthusiasm of these men. (Ruskin called Maurice "puzzle-headed, and, though in a beautiful manner, wrong-headed.") Their "socialism" connoted only mildly what the word came to mean to most people. It recognized the right of private property, did not depend upon the state for its reforms, and was by no means an attempt to lift the workman out of his class. Its hope was to stimulate him to self-endeavor, and frequently it took the form of workers' co-operatives. It did have a lyrical-ethical fervor, however, which dignified both religion and the social cause for which it worked. In 1848 all was in its first fine careless rapture; it remained to be seen how far and how long the English wage earner would follow the leadership, however inspirational, of a group of churchmen.

Another movement, artistic this time, and also to develop into some importance, had its roots in 1848. Reform—political, religious, social, artistic—was more deeply a part of the early Victorian temperament than was the complacency of which it has been consistently and smugly accused. Art, too, could become a Cause.

In 1848 [wrote William Michael Rossetti years later] there were four young students in the Royal Academy Schools—John Everett Millais and William Holman Hunt in the Life-school, Thomas Woolner in the Sculpture-school, and Dante Gabriel Rossetti in the Antique-school. . . . These young men [Woolner, the eldest, was twenty-three; Millais, the youngest, was nineteen] were all capable and ambitious: they had all, except Rossetti, exhibited something, to which (more especially in the case of Millais) the Art-authorities and the public had not proved wholly indifferent. They entertained a hearty contempt for much of the art—flimsy, frivolous, and conventional—which they saw in practice around them; and wanted to show forth what was in them in the way of solid and fresh thought and invention, and the intimate study of and strict adherence to Nature. The young men came together, interchanged ideas, and were joined by two other youthful Painter-Students, James Collinson and Frederic George Stephens, and also myself, who was not an Artist. So there were seven men forming the Praeraphaelite Brotherhood. I will not debate at any length why the term Praeraphaelite was adopted. There was much defiance in it, some banter, some sense, a great deal of resolute purpose, a large opening for misinterpretations, and a *carte-blanche* invitation for abuse. After thus constituting themselves, what they had to do was to design, paint, and model, and one of them in especial, Dante Rossetti, to write poetry; and they did it with a will.[5]

The Brotherhood was not to come into notice until the exhibitions of 1849, but it was already busy on the paintings which would cause more than a little furor in artistic circles.

Although there were no Praslins to murder or be murdered in England in 1848, nor any noble scandals to be uncovered, the atrocious killings at Stanford Hall near Norwich, late in November, were close enough to the gentry, and savage enough in themselves, to be a ten days' wonder. The mansion was the home of Mr. Isaac Jermy, the recorder of Norwich—a large building in the Norman style, with a moat around it. At half-past eight in the evening Mr. Jermy walked through the hall to the front of the building. Just as he was re-entering the porch a man wrapped up in a cloak and wearing a mask fired a pistol at him, killing him instantly. The masked intruder then went into the house through the servants' entry. There he met the butler, whom he warned back by waving his pistols. At the turn of the passage he was met by Mr. Jermy's son. The man fired at him, hitting him squarely in the breast. Young Mr. Jermy died on the spot. As young Mrs. Jermy came and leaned over the body of her husband, another shot shivered one of her arms and entered her breast. A maid, Eliza Chestney, was courageous enough to run to the passage to see what was happening. She received a shot in the thigh. Then, having killed two men and having severely wounded two women, the murderer made his escape. Mrs. Jermy, the more seriously injured of the two, lost her arm, but lived.

Suspicion pointed to a man named Rush, a neighboring farmer with whom Mr. Jermy had had disputes. The butler testified that the glass door by which the murderer passed into the house was one by which Rush was in the habit of entering, without knocking or ringing. A superintendent of police found in Rush's bedroom a long black wig which would have served to conceal his face. The most important evidence at the inquest, however, was that of a young woman calling herself Emily James, who had lived in Rush's house originally as a governess, later as his mistress. She first told a story of Rush's having been in his house all evening. Later she confessed that he had been out between eight and nine. When he returned he was deadly pale and much agitated. "If anyone asks for me," he told her, "say that I was out not more than ten minutes."

At the examination Rush violently denied all. He was bound over for trial in the early months of the next year, and on the basis of the preliminary evidence, any assiduous reader of murder accounts would have been able to predict what the outcome would be.

The last months of a tumultuous year were enlivened by the news, long-delayed in transit, of the discovery of gold in California early in 1848. So far there had not been many details, and the first reports had been received skeptically in England. But letters began to arrive telling how the gold fever was rising. As early as July there had been 4,000 people digging and sifting, and the number had increased greatly since. All pursuits were being abandoned except that of gold hunting. Monterey was nearly deserted; with few exceptions all the male inhabitants had gone to dig for gold. Ships arriving on the coast were immediately deserted by their crews. San Francisco had merely a skeleton population. Sonora, San Jose, and Santa Cruz were deserted. "Every bowl, tray, warming pan, and piggin have gone to the mines—everything, in short, that has a scoop in it that will hold sand and water." "Thus far," said one dispatch communicated to Congress by President Polk, "all who have returned have brought back two, three, and four, and some as much as ten thousand dollars' cash in gold dust. It is now so abundant, and coin so scarce, that it can be bought at nine dollars an ounce. One man found 800 dollars in one day. I have seen many persons from there, and all agree that from 50 to 100 dollars per day can be made by any person who is willing to work." Another report said: "Men often give an ounce of gold, which is worth at our Mint 18 dollars or more, for a bottle of brandy, a box of soda powders, or a plug of tobacco. . . . I know seven men who worked seven weeks and two days, Sundays excepted, on Feather River, they employed on an average 50 Indians, and got out in these seven weeks and two days 275 pounds of pure gold."

The *Morning Herald* received a letter from a "gold finder" in person, sent from the new El Dorado. "In the spring of the year," he wrote, "some settlers were excavating a mill-race in the neighborhood of the Sacramento, a river about thirty miles to the north of San Francisco. . . . In the course of their work they met with several pieces of heavy yellow-coloured metal, which . . . were speedily discovered to be gold of great purity. . . . All hands hastened to the 'diggings'—the expressive but in-elegant name given to the gold country." Prices of goods were sky-rocketing. "A blanket that cost 16s. sold for more than £20. . . . Bowie knives, worth from 8s. to 12s. each, sold for £12 sterling. A searcher in four weeks made £1,200. One man left, after a few day's collecting, with 25 lb. weight of gold, and another is said to have sent down 125 lb."

So the first ecstatic reports flowed in, though the real fever was not to come until the next year. It is not recorded that California had yet organized a Chamber of Commerce, but a London journal reported: "Independently of its gold, which, plentiful as it now appears, may soon be exhausted, the country and the climate are admirable; and in a few years California promises to be one of the most flourishing states of the Union, and the emporium of a magnificent trade with all parts of the world. . . . California seems destined to rival even Europe in the romance of its history." In England ships were being fitted out for emigrants, and scores of spectators formed joint-stock companies. Many tradesmen were selling their goods and embarking as adventurers for the new Gold Coast.

At the very end of the year fearful predictions were being made about the cholera. It had reached England in October; a score of cases had been reported in London between the seventh and the fourteenth. A week later Edinburgh had forty cases, thirty of them fatal. By the

Figure 109. The grocer's shop at Christmas

twenty-eighth Scotland had 222 cases, 128 fatal. Fifty-four new cases appeared in London during the first week of November; in the same week there were thirty-four deaths. So it mounted. By the middle of November the official returns showed 1,109 cases, with 563 deaths.

By December 31st 1,105 had died from cholera in England alone, and the worst was yet to come. But the *Illustrated London News* brought out a Christmas supplement, filled with jolly engravings of the making of the Christmas pudding, with pictures of the Christmas holly cart and Father Christmas, and a full-page plate of the Christmas tree at Windsor Castle surrounded by Victoria, Albert, and five admiring children. "The Oldest Inhabitant" described the streets at Christmastime: the butcher's windows where every carcass was adorned with ribbons, wreaths, or sprigs of holly; the poulterer's, with its tempting chickens, geese, and turkeys; the grocer's, beplastered with placards announcing the arrival of millions of pounds of currants and raisins for pudding-loving people: "There's a good time coming, boys—Raisins will be cheap at Robinson's!"

Famine and hunger in many homes? Yes. Revolutions abroad and threats of revolt at home. Distress in towns and depression in the countryside. Epidemic disease stalking every street. All this—but side by side with gloom and despair, happiness and contentment and the churning life of an industrious nation working its way somehow—never quite sure how, but working—toward the haven of rest and prosperity and security which must await those who keep their feet dry, spend no more than they earn, and are convinced beyond all argument that the heart of Old England is sound!

Before the bells had rung the old year out everyone knew that trade and business were improving perceptibly. Five thousand miles of railway were open for traffic, and 175,000 navvies were building 2,000 miles more. The four-pound loaf of bread was selling at the low price of 7½ d. Look hopefully toward 1849, Charles Greville!

PART THREE

1849-1851

* * *

THIS BRAVE

NEW WORLD

1849 * Authorship and the Reading Public

MONDAY, January 1st. Sky overcast, with cold east wind and showers. Average temperature, 31½°.

The year started gloomily enough. No one complained about the weather, for non-rheumatic Englishmen had learned from childhood to endure patiently raw, dark January days. But the undercurrent of concern about the cholera was growing stronger. The disease, striking with seeming blindness, had killed 575 in England and 2,523 in Scotland during the last months of 1848, and there were indications that it had by no means reached its climax. By the second week in January the weekly table of mortality showed 101 deaths in London and 356 in Scotland. The authorities were being attacked on every side for their sluggishness in taking precautionary measures to meet the disease.

On New Year's Day a report was made which emphasized the imminence of tragedy but also revealed a dark corner of administrative malfeasance. At Tooting, on the southern outskirts of London, there was an asylum which received pauper children from many of the largest metropolitan parishes. Here, over stagnant ditches and beside filthy surface drains, were dormitories for some 1,500 boys and girls who lived—as the subsequent investigation showed—poorly clothed and poorly fed, under abysmal conditions of overcrowding and of poor ventilation. Within a fortnight 229 children had contracted cholera, and before the disease had run its course 150 of them were dead. Mr. Peter Drouet, manager of the establishment and the one to whom the children had been farmed out, was tried on charges of manslaughter. He was freed by a jury whom the judge had instructed to the effect that the children might have died of cholera had they never been at Tooting at all!

New theories sprang up to account for the disease. The "zymotic" explanation (that of a noxious gas similar to hydrogen produced by the decomposition of water, especially foul water) found general acceptance. A correspondent of the *Morning Chronicle* suggested an "anti-zymotic" theory: that cholera was caused by the absence of ozone in the atmosphere. More particularly, attention of the medical profession was drawn to the announcement, mentioned earlier, of Dr. Brittan and Mr. J. G. Swayne of Bristol, who described the "fungoid cellules" which they had discovered under the microscope in the effusions of cholera patients and in tainted water. Other pathologists corroborated this discovery of "annular bodies" in the shape of a disc, with a cupped form, in the discharges of patients as well as in drinking water obtained in cholera districts. In no "healthy" water did they discover such bodies. A Dr. Budd, also of Bristol, urged that the disease might be restrained if all discharges from the sick were received "into some chemical fluid known to be fatal to beings of the fungus tribe." And since "water is the principal way through which this poison finds its way into the human body . . . so is the procuring pure water for drink the first and most effectual means of preventing its action." Thus close did the micropathologists of 1849 come to identifying the germ theory of disease and anticipating Koch and his discovery of the microorganism of cholera thirty-five years later. But the "Cholera Committee" appointed by the Royal College of Physicians effectively squelched Messrs. Brittan and Swayne in a report which concluded that the bodies found and described by them "are not the cause of cholera, and have no exclusive connection with that disease; or, in other words, that the whole theory of the disease which has recently been propounded is erroneous."

Even lay observers, however, saw that the disease had some relation to filth, poor drainage, and poor sanitation in general, and that its worst ravages in London occurred in the lower districts swept by the Thames— the "open sewer" which was still the chief source of water supply for the City. "We are paying the Companies collectively," wrote the *Spectator*, "£340,000 per annum for . . . a more or less concentrated solution of native guano:" But the provisions of the Health Act of 1848 did not apply to London, and its citizens could only wait fearfully for the plague to spread, and inform themselves meanwhile of the symptoms which marked its onslaught: the diarrhea, the colicky pains and cramps, the trembling and dizziness, the vomiting, the husky whisper—and finally the clammy sweating, the sunken eyes, the black lips, and the bluish skin.

The continuing news from California, during the early part of the year, furnished one distraction from the growing fear of cholera. Englishmen read eagerly the reports which were printed on every hand concerning the wealth which lay open to all comers. Hundreds of them took ship to join the great Gold Rush of 1849. All the newspapers printed lengthy reports from the gold fields, or "diggins," as they were learning to call them. "The people are running over the country and picking gold out of the earth here and there," wrote one correspondent, "just as a thousand hogs, let loose in a forest, would root up ground-nuts. Some get eight or ten ounces a day, and the least active one or two. . . . I know a man who got out of a basin in a rock, not larger than a wash-bowl, 2½ lb. of gold in 15 minutes." Within three weeks twenty-four vessels had sailed from New York for the gold country. At the same time fifty more ships were entered in the shipping list of New York with a San Francisco destination. In a short time 451 ships, barques, brigs, schooners, and steamers were counted in a single day as they lay anchored in the cove of San Francisco—a village which had changed almost overnight to a rude city, and within a year would have schools, churches, and even two large theaters.

Word came back that the *Crescent City* had sailed from New Orleans for New York with $500,000 worth of gold dust on board. By June and July prospectors were reaching San Francisco at the rate of a thousand a week. Prices were staggeringly high, it was reported. Spades and shovels were selling for nine and ten dollars; flour, sixty dollars a barrel; coffee, two dollars a pound; eggs, three dollars a dozen. One hotel in San Francisco, it was reported, was renting for $95,000 a year, and

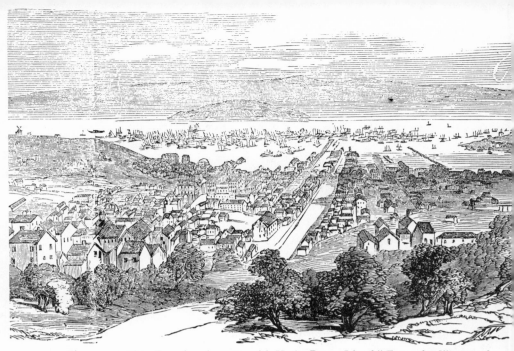

Figure 110. "San Francisco in 1851, with Yerba Buena Island." From the *Illustrated London News*

large single rooms in the same hotel were renting for $18,000 a year each.* There were sinister items, too, on the periphery: many of the inhabitants were sick with fever, and several parties of overland immigrants had been murdered, it was reported, by Apache Indians. The trip to California was long and arduous. The voyage around Cape Horn was one of four months and 17,000 miles. Those eager to save time disembarked at Chagres and crossed the Isthmus of Panama to tranship for San Francisco—a dangerous and difficult land journey, but one which enabled the emigrant to go from New York to San Francisco in thirty-seven days.

"It is impossible," wrote the Philadelphia correspondent of the

---

* In the still-primitive reaches of Ohio, however, food was very cheap, from the point of view of a wistful Englishman. During 1849 Joseph Barker sent back to his journal *The People*, published at Leeds, a series of letters written during the investigative tour which he was making in the United States. Once, near Akron, he and his brother put up overnight at the farmhouse of a comfortably prosperous farmer. They enjoyed "good, dry, comfortable beds. Breakfasted at 6:00 on fish, mutton, apple pie, bread and butter, milk and honey, preserved apples, apple sauce, preserved peaches, peach sauce, pickled cucumbers, boiled beet, sweet-potatoes, coffee, etc. The charge for bed and breakfast for three persons, and for two pecks of oats and a sack-full of hay for the horse was one dollar!" This was sixpence less than he had paid for the accommodation of his horse one night in England, and sixpence less than he once paid in London for bed and supper "for my solitary self."

Morning Chronicle, "to convey any idea of the excitement." In England, "From London to California Direct" began to be a standing heading in the London ship advertisements. Liverpool and Glasgow also announced many vessels leaving on the long voyage around the Cape. English mills created prefabricated, demountable houses of corrugated iron, each with three dwelling rooms and one storeroom, and these were shipped to the rapidly growing towns of the gold country. Gold Rush songs, such as the comic "Race to California," were published and sung in England. "The California or Golden Polka" was announced. A farce, *Cockneys in*

CALIFORNIA;

THE FEAST OF GOLD.

A New Comic Song,

Written by Henry Valentine,

SUNG BY MESSRS. CARROL, WARDE, MARTIN, MILLS,

And all the Principal Comic Singers,

Figure 111. An English gold-rush song

California, became very popular at the Adelphi. Books were hurriedly published to inform the curious: *Four Months Among the Gold Finders*, *The Gold Seeker's Manual*, and *The Emigrant's Guide to California*. *Punch* wrote poems about California and rattled off a steady stream of jokes about the gold seekers. The excitement and romance of the new El Dorado was one of the wonders of 1849.

The early part of the year saw the opening of the Islington cattle market to the north of town. It was hoped that the use of these new and spacious facilities would result ultimately in the abandoning of Smithfield Market in the center of the city, the noise and confusion and stench of which were reprehended by all as a public nuisance. . . . On February 3d a great banquet was held in Manchester to celebrate the demise, at midnight, of the Corn Laws. Three thousand guests crowded Free Trade Hall, and were regaled with speeches by Messrs. Villiers, Cobden, Bright, and others. . . . Seventy-five people perished in a colliery explosion near Barnsley. . . . A false rumor of fire in a Glasgow theater sent gallery patrons stampeding down a narrow stairway. Sixty-five were trampled and smothered to death. . . . The American barque *Floridian* was wrecked in a terrific storm in the English Channel, and of the crew and some 200 immigrant passengers, only four were saved. . . . The United States Congress was reported as discussing a project to establish telegraphic communication across the Atlantic to Europe, and to form a similar line across the American continent—as well as a line of railway from the Great Lakes to the Pacific. . . . "Professor Mulder," said the *Illustrated London News*, "so well known by his discovery of proteine (a much controverted substance) has just fulminated a solemn condemnation of the potato. 'As an article of food,' says the learned chemist, 'this tuber is not nourishing, and is the cause of the moral and physical degradation of the nations who make use of it.'" . . . The first numbers of two new magazines were announced: *Eliza Cook's Journal* and the *Journal of Design* (the latter distinguished by inserted specimens of textiles and wallpapers). . . . A "new patent calisthenic chest-expander" was advertised.

Mudie's Circulating Library, which had been operating since 1842 in a little shop in Upper King Street, off Bloomsbury Square, announced new additions to its stock. Mudie's had been the first of the lending libraries to go beyond the meager array of fiction which was the staple of such institutions* and provide for its readers a complete range of new books in history, biography, travels, poetry, and theology. The charge was a guinea a year for one volume, which could be exchanged as frequently as desired. This winter Mudie's advertised "from twenty to one hundred copies of every good new work . . . Macaulay's *England*, Layard's *Nineveh*, Warburton's *Prince Rupert*, Prince Adelbert's *Travels*, Curzon's *Monasteries of the Levant; Mary Barton, Mordaunt Hall, My Uncle the Curate*, etc."

What books did Englishmen read in the 1840's? What kind of libraries did people have access to? What represented a good sale for a successful work? What was the size of an average edition? Who were the popular authors? How well received in this decade were the writers who were to become known as the Great Victorians, and what were the now-forgotten names which were then household words? With books, as with magazines, the answers to these too-little-explored questions take one to the heart of early Victorian culture.

To begin with, there were several factors controlling the distribution of books. The size of the reading public beyond the newspapers and cheap magazines was limited. Out of a total population of over 18,000,000, 40 per cent of the adults could not write their own names. Moreover, the cost of a standard three-decker novel was 31s. 6d.—astronomical enough to keep it off the shelves of any but the well to do and to throw the burden of circulation upon the lending libraries. As we shall see, there were notable efforts during these years on the part of many publishers to make cheap editions of good works available to the modest purse, but for the most part sales, according to modern standards, were small, and the profits of authorship in most cases not large.

English book-reading habits were essentially serious. As noted earlier, of the 45,000 books listed by the *London Catalogue* as published between 1816 and 1851, 10,300 were works on divinity. Sermons were bought, and presumably read. Newman's *Tract 90* (of controversial interest to be sure) sold 12,000 copies before it finally went out of print in 1846. And in 1847 the publisher Virtue made a profit of £4,000 from the publication of a series of lectures delivered by one Dr. John Cumming at Exeter Hall on the subject of the Apocalypse. In a list of 117 new books noted in the Athenaeum on October 23, 1841, thirty-nine were on religious subjects, eleven were poetry, ten medical, thirteen travel, and only sixteen were novels. Religion aside, the *London Catalogue* listed more

---

* A count of ten circulating libraries in 1837 showed a total of 2,192 books, of which 1,008 were "imitations of 'fashionable novels.' " There were 166 of Walter Scott "and such." (*Journal of the London Statistical Society*, Vol. I, p. 485.)

books of history and geography than of fiction: 4,900 as against 3,500. Indeed there were almost as many books of drama and poetry (3,400) as of fiction. Some 2,500 medical books found print in this period; 1,850 of biography; and 2,450 of science. There were 1,400 in the category of "moral sciences"—which included such diverse subjects as philology and domestic economy. The arts had 2,460 titles. Books at this level were bought, by and large, for their edifying and informing effect rather than their entertainment value.

Editions were not large. The chief sale of popular works was confined to the circulating libraries and book clubs, and averaged from 500 to 2,000 copies—the first being a good sale for a work of reasonable merit, the second an extraordinary sale for a work of a very popular author.* Only 2,500 copies of Thackeray's *Henry Esmond*, for example, were printed in 1852.

On the other hand, large numbers of certain expensive books were sold if they happened to catch on. The first two volumes of Macaulay's *History* (at 32s.) ran through five editions and 18,000 copies within six months of its first publication. Longman's wrote Macaulay a check for £20,000 in royalties (some of them an advance) on Volumes III and IV within eleven weeks after publication. And in December, 1849, Murray held his annual trade sale at the Albion Tavern. In one evening the trade agreed in advance to take, among others, the following books:

Lord Campbell's *Chief Justices of England* (2 vols.):	2,000 copies
Layard's *Nineveh and Its Remains* (2 vols., 36s.):	1,400 copies
Byron's *Works* (1 vol.):	1,400 copies
Borrow's *Lavengro* (3 vols., 31s. 6d.):	1,300 copies
Grote's *History of Greece* (Vols. V and VI, 32s.):	750 copies
Curzon's *Monasteries of the Levant* (2d ed., 15s.).	750 copies

Simultaneously Murray announced Ranke's *History of Prussia* (3 vols., 36s.); Washington Irving's *Columbus and His Companions* (3 vols., 31s. 6d.); and the ninth edition of Hallam's *Europe in the Middle Ages* (3 vols., 36s.). None of these books was either light or cheap reading for the masses, and all sold well.

Borrow's sales represented a greater-than-average popularity. Four editions of the *Zincali*, of 750 each, had been published between 1841 and 1846. One thousand copies were printed of the first edition of *The Bible in Spain* (3 vols.) in 1843. This made such a sensation that editions

---

* The *Journal of the London Statistical Society*, Vol. VI, p. 57, declared that the sale of books in England was injured by the constant influx of foreign reprints. Libraries on the coast and as far as forty miles inland "are supplied entirely by pirated editions."

two to six were published during the same year. Seven thousand copies were sold altogether. Murray printed 3,000 copies of *Lavengro*, and when it finally reached the booksellers in 1851, 2,145 copies had been sold to the trade. This time, however, it took twenty-five years to clear away the rest of the first edition.

At the other end of the intellectual scale were the "gothic" novels, many of them published first in parts and later in volume form, scribbled by the score for belowstairs readers, full of stereotyped horrors, seductions, and fearsome midnight adventures. Even the names of their authors have been lost in the cloacae of literary history, and the books have gone down the drain of time just as completely as have their opposites, the streams of "edifying" bilge. But like the "improving" literature, these counterparts in the 1840's of the Minerva Press are evidence of a taste which must be reckoned with if one is not to oversimplify the history of national reading habits. Many of the titles never reached the dignity of being listed in the otherwise complete *London Catalogue:* Mrs. Elizabeth Bennett's *Gipsey Bride; or, The Miser's Daughter,* (1844), and *The Broken Heart; or, The Village Bridal* (1844). Thomas Frost's *The Black Mask; or, The Mysterious Robber* (1850), and *Paul the Poacher* (1853). Malcolm J. Rymer's *Woman's Life; or, The Trials of the Heart* (1844–45). Thomas Peckett Prest's *Fatherless Fanny; or, The Mysterious Orphan* (1841); *The Maniac Father; or, The Victim of Seduction* (1842); and *The Skeleton Clutch; or, The Goblet of Gore* (1842).

Of the sixty-one novels that Thomas Prest wrote between 1841 and 1851, his version of the Sweeney Todd legend under the mild title of *The String of Pearls* (*A Romance*) was the most spectacular. In one form or another this horrific tale of the demon barber and his victims continued to titillate Victorian readers for generations. Complete with all the possible gruesome details, the story dealt with a barber who jettisoned his better-fed customers through a trapdoor into the basement, where they were dismembered and baked into meat pies—pies the flavor of which was beyond praise, and which were devoured eagerly by lawyers and their clerks and apprentices in Bell's Yard. The public revelation of Todd's industrious cannibalism came at a moment when the eager crowd of clients were digging into a fresh batch of pies, laughing "as they smacked their lips and sucked in all the golopshious gravy of the pies, which by-the-way appeared to be all delicious veal that time. . . ." The immediate reaction of the customers when they were informed of the nature of their feast was described in anatomical detail. Prest was no man to flinch from the realistic necessities of his theme.

Rymer, who also wrote under the name of Errym, reached his apothe-

osis in *Varney the Vampire; or, The Feast of Blood* (reprinted in 1847)
—a story which makes Stoker's later *Dracula* seem like a nursery tale.
Something of a major climax was reached in the very first of the 220
chapters:

> The figure turns half round, and the light falls upon its face. It is
> perfectly white—perfectly bloodless. The eyes look like polished tin;
> the lips are drawn back, and the principal feature next to those dreadful
> eyes is the teeth—projecting like those of some wild animal, hideously,
> glaringly white and fang-like. It approaches the bed with a strange
> gliding movement. It clashes together its long nails that literally appear
> to hang from the finger ends. No sound comes from its lips. . . .
> The storm has ceased—all is still. The winds are hushed; the church
> clock proclaims the hour of one; a hissing sound comes from the throat
> of the hideous being and he raises his long gaunt arms—the lips move.
> He advances. The girl places one small foot from the bed on the floor.
> She is unconsciously dragging the clothing with her. The door of the
> room is in that direction—can she reach it?
> With a sudden rush that could not be foreseen—with a strange
> howling cry that was enough to awaken terror in every breast, the
> figure seized the long tresses of her hair and twining them round his
> bony hands he held her to the bed. Then she screamed—Heaven granted
> her then the power to scream. Shriek followed shriek in rapid succes-
> sion. The bed clothes fell in a heap by the side of the bed—she was
> dragged by her long silken hair completely on to it again. Her beautiful
> rounded limbs quivered with the agony of her soul. The glassy horrible
> eyes of the figure ran over the angelic form with a hideous satisfaction
> —horrible profanation. He drags her head to the bed's edge. He forces it
> back by the long hair still entwined in his grasp. With a plunge he
> seizes her neck in his fang-like teeth—a gush of blood and a hideous
> sucking noise follows. *The girl has swooned and the vampire is at his
> hideous repast!*[1]

At this distance it is difficult to determine the extent to which all this
stuff was read. The list of titles is overwhelmingly long, however, and
if one can judge by the sales of Lloyd's penny dreadfuls, in which form
many books of this kind first appeared, the market was huge. Human
nature being what it is, it may be suspected that not a few of these
thrillers were smuggled into sedate households by younger readers.

At a more respectable level there were novels and romances for all
tastes. The influence of Scott was strong, and the historical romance had
a great vogue, from Bulwer Lytton to Disraeli to William Harrison
Ainsworth and G. P. R. James. Ainsworth wrote in 1849 that a one-
shilling reissue of his earlier *Rookwood* "promises wonders—nearly 6,000
were subscribed in the City alone yesterday. This exclusive of agents,
etc., which will treble that amount." The indefatigable James wrote, over

a long career, a total of 199 volumes (seventy-five novels), of which the first editions usually ran 1,000 to 1,500 copies. When he got three to four novels ahead of his publishers, Smith and Elder, they asked him to restrict his annual output, whereupon he indignantly parted company with them. Disraeli's *Coningsby* went through three editions in three months. Charlotte Brontë's *Jane Eyre*, published in three volumes in October, 1847, reached a fourth edition by 1850. The average run of Bulwer Lytton's novels was 2,250 to 2,700 (the last for *Harold*). For those who liked novels of the sea there was the prolific Marryat (who died in 1848); and for those who preferred farce plus military adventure, Charles Lever. And the superficial "fashionable" novel, of the silver-fork school, lived on into the forties in the glittering, facile stories of Mrs. Gore. Mrs. Frances Trollope continued to support her family by turning out an average of two novels a year. Her son Anthony had just begun to publish his first stories in modestly sized editions which as yet made no great splash in the world of letters. Of *The Macdermots of Ballycloran* (1847), 400 copies were published; of *The Kellys and the O'Kellys* (1848) 375 copies, of which, six months later, 150 had been sold. Barchester and success were still around the corner. Nor would anyone have been able to recognize the future Wilkie Collins in his first novel, published in 1850 when he was twenty-six: *Antonina: or, The Fall of Rome. A Romance of the Fifth Century*.

Another young man who started a notable literary career in 1850 was "Captain" Mayne Reid, an Irish adventurer who had fought in America during the Mexican War, and had gone to England in 1849. The press compared his first novel, *The Rifle Rangers; or Adventures of an Officer in Southern Mexico*, with those of Fenimore Cooper. The year 1851 saw the publication of his second novel, *Scalp Hunters,** and in the same year appeared the first of his boys' books of adventure: *The Desert Home, or English Family Robinson*.

Most of Herman Melville's books appeared in England in advance of their publication in the United States. Murray recorded that he printed 5,000 copies of *Typee* and sold 4,104; of *Omoo*, 4,000 copies and sold 2,512. Only 100 copies were printed of *Mardi*, and of *The Whale* (later *Moby Dick*) in 1851, only 500 copies. But reissued in a 2s., 6d. series, *Typee* sold 4,000 copies in 1847 and *Omoo* 2,500 the same year. *Mardi*, in 1849, was praised by the English reviewers, though Sir Walter Farquhar wrote to Lord Ashley that the tone of Melville's books "is reprehensible throughout . . . they are not works that any mother would like

---

* In 1900 his widow wrote: "Over a million copies of this work have been sold in Great Britain alone."

Figure 112. Charles Dickens in the early forties
Figure 113. W. M. Thackeray in 1848, from a drawing by D'Orsay

to see in the hands of her daughters, and as such are not suited to lie on the drawing-room table."

Dickens, of course, was the Great Novelist of the time, with Thackeray, in point of general popularity, panting behind a poor second. While *Dombey and Son* was selling its 30,000 copies per monthly issue in 1846–48, *Vanity Fair* did no better than 7,000. Dickens had become the national literary hero while Thackeray had been struggling anonymously in the magazines as Michael Angelo Titmarsh. Not until *Vanity Fair* did Thackeray begin to hear himself mentioned in the same breath with Dickens, and then only by the relatively few and perceptive. Their later rivalry was a personal and artistic one only. Thackeray sold his thousands, and made more than a comfortable living, but Dickens sold his tens of thousands.

It was the custom of popular authors in those days to bring out each year, for the Christmas trade, a separately published story. *The Chimes*, Dickens's Christmas book of 1844, sold 20,000 copies at once; his *Christmas Carol*, a year earlier, had been in its sixth thousand by December 24. Before the year 1844 was over it sold some 15,000 copies. His *Battle of Life*, in December, 1845, sold 23,000 copies within twenty-four hours. Thackeray, on the other hand, sold 3,000 copies of the first edition of *The Kickleburys on the Rhine*, his Christmas book for 1850, and 2,000 of *Mrs. Perkins's Ball*, his offering for 1847.

David Copperfield and *Pendennis* were both appearing in monthly parts in 1849—each of them autobiographical. There again Dickens's lusty vividness, his carefully brewed recipe of humor, pathos, and melodrama, triumphed in popular favor over Thackeray's quieter, mellower, retrospective method.* Thackeray's admirers among the judicious were many, but numbers of the critics carped at the preponderance of his "unpleasant" characters (he had no conventional heroes); and the public preferred the juicy vitality of Dickens's eccentrics to Thackeray's more critically humorous commentary on life. The Victorians knew satire and liked it; humorous exaggeration they delighted in; tears were a benediction to them. But irony, which was the heart of Thackeray's method, left them uneasy. Blacks and whites were more comfortable than grays.

A curious legend has grown up that the Victorians were a restrained and sedate people, living in an atmosphere of gloomy if bustling activity. Nothing could be further from the truth. The energy which was their dominant characteristic included a high and romantic relish and gusto.† Nothing proves this more clearly than the abandon with which the middle classes (who were buying the books) gave themselves to the woes and delights of fictional heroes and heroines. Such a public figure

---

* Dickens was disappointed by the early sale of 25,000 copies per month, a circulation which grew much larger as the book caught on.

† Where, for example, does one get such a sense of hearty eating and drinking as in the Victorian novel? With Dickens particularly the digestive juices flow freely. It fairly snows meat and drink and plum pudding and jolly, steaming, self-sacrificial turkeys.

Figure 114. Dickens reading to his friends from his own writings

as Dickens wrote always under a sense of high responsibility to the accepted conventions of middle-class morality; books that were read aloud at the family fireside must be free from any possible offense. But once protected by an assurance that no book of a respected author could bring a blush to a young lady's cheek, readers were quite willing to let themselves wallow in a sentimental carousal. Nor was this unbuttoning of the emotions limited to the obscure or the ignorant. Forster, Landor, and Tom Hood all wept over the death of Little Nell in the *Old Curiosity Shop*. Macready begged Dickens to save her life, and when the fatal stroke fell he said that it "gave a dead chill to my blood." Daniel O'Connell broke into tears, said "He should not have killed her," and threw the book out the window. Mrs. Henry Siddons found Francis Jeffrey with his head on the table, his eyes suffused with tears. "You'll be sorry to hear," he told her, "that little Nelly, Boz's little Nelly, is dead." Even Carlyle was deeply moved. Dickens wrote Forster: "Nobody shall miss her like I shall. It is such a very painful thing to me, that I really cannot express my sorrow." When Paul Dombey passed to his reward in one of the most egregiously sentimental deathbed scenes prior to that of Little Eva, Jeffrey wrote Dickens: "I have sobbed and cried over it last night and again this morning." Macready, when he saw Dickens for the first time after Paul's death, could not speak for sobs. Nor was Dickens himself less generous in blubbering manfully for the distresses of rival fictional characters. "I cried most bitterly," he wrote to Thackeray, "over your affecting picture of that cock-boat manned by babies,[2] and shall never forget it." The Victorian heart was easily lacerated. Both laughter and tears lay near the surface.

With a few notable exceptions, poetry had hard sledding in the 1840's. Byron, to be sure, was perennially popular, and Wordsworth had many enthusiastic readers. By 1850 the 1836–37 six-volume edition of the latter's poems had been reprinted at least six times. Yet in 1842 (the year before he became poet laureate) Wordsworth could get his publisher Moxon to assume the risk of only 2,000 copies of his new volume. Browning had to swim upstream against a depressing lack of recognition. With the exception of *Strafford*, all his poems up to *Christmas-Eve and Easter-Day*, in 1850, were published at his father's expense, and of the latter volume the sale flagged after the first 200 copies had been disposed of. Moxon, known as the "publisher of poets," declined publication of Elizabeth Barrett's poems in 1843, saying that Tennyson was the only poet he did not lose by.

Tennyson was rapidly becoming the most respectably distinguished poet of the time. He had retired into a decade of hurt silence upon the unfavorable reception of his poems of 1833. In the early forties, after he had lost heavily in a "Patent Decorated Carving and Sculpture Co.," he became hypochrondriac and took to hydropathy, a medical craze of the time in Germany which had spread to England. The theory of the cure was that medicine of every kind was a false interference with nature, and that water, externally and internally, would cure every disease. In 1844 Tennyson wrote: "I am in an Hydropathy Establishment near Cheltenham. . . . Much poison has come out of me, which no physic ever would have brought to light. . . ." As late as 1848 Fitzgerald could say: "Tennyson is emerged half-cured, or half-destroyed, from a water establishment; has gone to a new Doctor who gives him iron pills; and altogether this really great man thinks more about his bowels and nerves than about the laureate wreath he was born to inherit."

In the meantime, however, his poems of 1842 had been kindly received and had sold 500 copies in the first two month—considered a highly promising sale. A reprint of 1,000 copies was issued in 1843, and a seventh edition appeared in 1851. *The Princess*, in 1847, sold out its first edition of 2,000 copies, went into another printing the next year, and reached a fourth by 1851. *In Memoriam* was published in 1850 in an edition of 5,000. Moxon saw to it that the authorship of the anonymous volume was generally known, and two more editions were issued the same year; a fourth and a fifth, the latter of 5,000 copies, appeared in 1851. When in 1850 Tennyson succeeded Wordsworth to the laureateship he was well on his way to becoming not only the official but also the definitive poetic spokesman for his age. When, much later, 50,000 copies of *Enoch Arden* were sold during the first year of its publication, it seemed only a reasonable tribute to the man who epitomized in his verse the prejudices, doubts, affirmations, and sentiments of a generation.

Yet Tennyson was not the most popular poet of the forties. More households possessed copies of Eliza Cook, Charles Swain, Robert Montgomery, Martin Tupper, and even Philip James Bailey than of Tennyson.

Swain, like Miss Cook, was a "people's" poet whose volumes of verse ran through multiple editions, of whom Southey declared: "If ever man were born to be a poet, he was." His *Dramatic Chapters, Poems, and Songs* of 1848 was reviewed in the *Literary Gazette* as follows: "Every critical opinion in England . . . has proclaimed in perfect unison the true poetic genius of Charles Swain. . . . The spirit and the force, and the tenderness, and the pathos, and the originality of Swain's compositions are acknowledged and re-echoed on every hand." The reviewer quoted

Figure 115. Alfred Tennyson from a portrait by Samuel Laurence in 1839

Figure 116. Robert Browning in the late thirties

Figure 117. Thomas Carlyle in 1841

Figure 118. John Ruskin in 1843

from such poems as "The Cottage Window," "A Sigh," "Near Thee," "There's a Duty," and "The Snow." One verse of "The Snow" ran:

A new creation without a stain—
Lovely as Heaven's pure domain!
But ah! like the many fair hopes of our years,
It glitters awhile—and then melts into tears.

Robert Montgomery published numerous sermons and theological works but was best known for his poem *Satan*, which, published in 1830, reached its tenth edition in 1842. Macaulay in a notice in the *Edinburgh Review* pulverized Montgomery as merely a pious versifier. His unmixed contempt did not disturb the public which bought Montgomery's volumes by the thousands. *Woman, the Angel of Life,* saw its fifth edition in 1841. This was the poem which Thackeray had reviewed as a young man in 1833, annihilating its florid sentimentality and perpetrating, with complete success, the astounding trick of printing its last fourteen lines in reverse to show that the poem made as much sense read backward as forward.

Even more grandiloquent was Philip James Bailey, whose *Festus, a Poem,* published in 1839, was reprinted in 1845 (as we have seen earlier) with additions and a selection of press notices. (It ultimately reached a twelfth edition.) This inglorious though not mute Milton had a great popularity. Somehow his spongy rhetoric gave people the illusion that they were plumbing philosophical depths.

The people's real laureate, however—the voice of middle-class England, whose books were to be found on the drawing-room tables of all the semi-intelligentsia—was Martin F. Tupper, whose appalling facility at banal moralizing carried him into an unprecedented popularity. His best-known book, *Proverbial Philosophy*, went through fifty editions, selling nearly half a million copies in England and a million in the United States. Mediocrity has never had greater reward. Tupper was admired by the Queen and her Consort; the King of Prussia sent him a gold medal for his services to humanity and science; he was admitted as Fellow of the Royal Society, and received the D.C.L. at Oxford. Upon the death of Wordsworth it was known that Tupper would be willing to become poet laureate, and indeed such an impressive person as James Garbett, professor of poetry at Oxford, urged his claims. The *Spectator* bracketed him with Wordsworth, Tennyson, and Browning, and said that Tupper had won for himself the vacant throne waiting for him amidst the immortals.

Tupper himself was a friendly, sanguine man, not unimpressed by his own success, and driven by a majestic urge to do good.[3] He oozed

Figure 119. Martin Tupper

verse as easily as most men draw breath. Few public occasions were not followed by a poem of Tupper's in the pages of the morning newspapers. When a lunatic attacked the Queen, Tupper rushed home to write:

> O dastard! Thus to strike that brow
> Anointed and so fair.

When he once fell out of a carriage he wrote a poem on the moral lessons to be learned in carriage accidents. At the time of the Great Exhibition he turned out an "Exhibition Hymn" beginning "Hurrah! for honest Industry, hurrah! for handy Skill," which was set to music and printed in twenty-five languages.

Much of his energy was poured into the construction of his most successful work, *Proverbial Philosophy*. This was little more than a potpourri of truisms embedded in a kind of rhythmic prose which he called poetry. Reviewers compared him with Solomon, finding great moral beauty in his platitudinous commonplaces:

> Yea, there is no cosmetic like a holy conscience.
>
> . . . .
>
> With his mother's milk the young child drinketh Education.
> Patience is the first great lesson; he may learn it at the breast.
>
> . . . .
>
> There is a limit to enjoyment, though the sources of wealth be bound-
>   less:

And the choicest pleasures of life lie within the ring of moderation.

. . . .

For a good book is the best of friends, the same today and forever.

Somewhere in the maze of these moralizings, and their enthusiastic acceptance by scores of thousands of readers, lies one of the keys to the understanding of the age. Like any universally popular work, *Proverbial Philosophy* created as well as fed a taste. To those suspicious of poetry as such it seemed to make an esoteric art simple and edifying at the same time. Its morality, aimed at home and fireside, buttressed and gave a kind of ratification to the pious codes by which middle-class England lived. Its banalities were simple and unostentatious, its soporific qualities eminently respectable. Years later Tupper came to be as much derided as he had been praised earlier, but during these middle years of the century he gave an intellectually unsophisticated public reassurance and comfort.

It is impossible to estimate the relationship between the sale of a book and its number of readers in the 1840's, except to say that the latter would be proportionately greater than today. This was especially true of the three-volume, guinea-and-a-half novels, which depended almost entirely upon the circulating libraries for their support. From Mudie's and similar enterprises at one end of the scale, through the libraries of the 720 Mechanics' Institutes with their 120,000 members and 815,000 volumes of books,[4] down to the modest bookshelves of the coffeehouses, which were finding it increasingly advantageous to supply books as well as newspapers for their customers—all were in the business of making reading matter available to those for whom the purchase of a single novel would have meant an extortionate expenditure.

But if the middle-class reader would accept cheap reprints, he who read a book in the forties could also buy. In 1851 the *London Catalogue* listed 1,400 volumes issued by publishers in cheap "libraries" at a cost of one to six shillings. Thus Bohn's *Library* ("antiquarian, classical, ecclesiastical, illustrated, scientific, and standard"); Murray's *Home and Colonial Library* and his *Family Library;* Lardner's *Cabinet Cyclopaedia,* published by Longman's; Pickering's *Aldine Poets;* Knight's *Library of Interesting Knowledge;* and Chambers's *Papers for the People.* Although a reasonable balance of novels was maintained in these series, the great bulk of them was informational and serious in character: history, biography, travel, antiquarianism. Of forty-nine titles advertised by Murray in his *Home and Colonial Library* in 1851, twenty-one were travels and accounts of strange countries, thirteen were biography or history, and only seven were fiction. The list included Borrow's *Bible in Spain,* Southey's *Lives* of Cromwell and Bunyan, Darwin's *Voyage of a Naturalist Round the World,* Irving's *Tales of a Traveller,* and Thomas Campbell's *Short Lives of the British Poets.* The most important fictional series was Bentley's *Standard Novels,* in which was published between 1841 and 1851 some forty novels by Theodore Hook, Fenimore Cooper, Mrs. Gore, Captain Marryat, and a host of lesser writers.

The development of the railways encouraged the sale of books of all kinds. Until 1848 no systematic attempt had been made to supply passengers with either books or papers at the railway stations. In that year W. H. Smith got the exclusive right to sell books and papers on the Birmingham Railway. His first bookstall was at Euston Station. Shortly he had the franchise for the entire London and Northwestern System. By 1849 the station library at the Paddington terminus contained 1,000 volumes, chiefly works of fiction. Here, for the charge of 1d., a passenger had free access to the use of the library while waiting for trains, and for slightly more could take a volume with him on his journey, turning it in at his destination. To meet this new demand Routledge launched his *Railway Library*—novels by Cooper, James, Hawthorne, James Grant, Dumas, and others. Murray advertised his "Literature for the Rail"— "works of sound information and innocent amusement."

An article in the *Times* of August 9, 1851, by one Samuel Phillips, a staff writer, gives an illuminating answer to the question "what do people read on railways?" Phillips's "Literature of the Rail" was the result of a week's exploration into railway termini. He first found that, with few exceptions, unmitigated rubbish encumbered the bookshelves of almost every bookstall he visited in London. As he proceeded north, however, he saw "a wholesome change. At the North-Western terminus [Euston] . . . we poked in vain for trash. We asked for something 'highly coloured.' The bookseller politely presented us with Kügler's *Handbook of Painting.*" He was offered Prescott's *Mexico,* Murray's *Handbook of France,* and Coleridge's *Table Talk.* No Eugene Sues for love or money. Macaulay sold rapidly, he was told, as did Layard's *Nineveh. Stokers and Pokers,* a sketch of the London and Northwestern Railway, published in Murray's *Colonial Library,* sold 2,000 copies. The Bishop of Exeter's pamphlet on "Baptismal Regeneration" and Baptist Noel's book on the Church "had an unlimited sale at Euston-square."

Ladies, he discovered, were not great purchasers of good books at railway stations. "This season they have been greedy in their demand for *The Female Jesuit.* . . . If they do by chance purchase a really serious book it is invariably a religious one. There is a regular sale on the line for what are termed Low Church books."

Phillips found as he went farther north that "Yorkshire is not partial to poetry." And "it is difficult to sell a valuable book at any of the stands between Derby, Leeds, and Manchester. Religious books hardly find a purchaser at Liverpool, while at Manchester, at the other end of the line, they are in great demand. *Sophisms of Free Trade*, by Serjeant Byles, sold at all the stations to the extent of some hundreds.

"Descending to the cheaper volumes. . . . Weale's series of practical scientific works, published at 1s. and 2s. each, have sold thousands of copies. . . . Longman's *Traveller's Library*, price 1s., found a market at once. A thousand copies of *Warren Hastings* were disposed of as quickly as they could be supplied; of *Lord Clive* 750 copies have been sold . . . [and] three thousand of Washington Irving's works. . . ."

What kinds of libraries were available to the Englishman in the 1840's? Almost none for the use of which he did not have to pay a fee or from which he could borrow books. The elaborate and lengthy *Report from the Select Committee on Public Libraries*, ordered printed by the House of Commons in 1849, revealed some discouraging comparative facts. France, it was discovered, had 107 public libraries with an aggregate of nearly 4,000,000 volumes; the Prussian States, 44; Austria, 48; and even the United States 81 public libraries of 5,000 volumes and up. To all these admission was granted unrestrictedly, while in Great Britain there was only one library equally accessible: the Chetham Library in Manchester. There were no free lending libraries in Great Britain of any kind. At Oxford no books were ever removed from the Bodleian Library, and only M.A.'s and those of higher degrees were allowed to use the books when in the library. An undergraduate could not even read the books in the Bodleian unless he got special permission. In 1849 Cambridge gave to undergraduates the privilege of taking books out of the University library on the recommendation of the college tutors.*[5]

The Mechanics' libraries were all subscription libraries, and the institutes were so predominantly supported and used by the middle and "respectable" classes that workingmen began to feel uncomfortable in such surroundings. At Nottingham, for example, the workingmen commenced in 1849 a number of "Operative Libraries," keeping them in public houses. The stock of one of them, supported by small contributions from the members, included: history, 65 volumes; biography, 80; novels and romances, 647; voyages, travels, and topography, 57; poetry, plays, and essays, 57; natural philosophy, science, etc., 38.[6]

---

* The separate college libraries were of course available to undergraduates.

Figure 120. The British Museum on a holiday. About 1845, while the new building was under construction

Figure 121. The British Museum reading room

The British Museum, with its 435,000 books (in 1849) was of course the most important library in London. It also was the subject of a Parliamentary investigation in 1849, at which Thomas Carlyle testified and was sharply critical of the reading arrangements. He thought that novel readers and the insane ought to be put off by themselves, so as not to distract serious readers.[7] The reading room of the British Museum (like the present one) did attract some curious visitors. Charles Knight, describing the room and what he called its "inmates,"[8] observed that "some queer enough customers are among them, God knows. . . . The briefless barrister, the clergyman who cannot get a living, the doctor whom no patient will trust, the half-pay midshipman, all betake themselves to some branch of bookmaking; and many yet more eccentric adventurers . . . may be seen seeking in this workshop of letters a haven of repose." He notes "the monomaniacs who occasionally stray hitherward. . . . They are a strange set, these discoverers and editors of old MSS.; testy and wayward with all—continually squabbling among themselves. . . ." No lights were allowed in the reading room, for fear of accidents. On many a day dark, rolling fogs sent people home long before closing time.

Culturally then, in spite of the fact that there were published in the United Kingdom in the ten-year period some 32,000 books, England was highly stratified, and had succeeded in making good books very difficult for the ordinary man to borrow. In 1850 William Ewart, who had talked Parliament into appointing the 1849 Committee on Public Libraries, saw through the Commons the first Public Libraries Act. It was little more than a bill to enable town councils to establish libraries and museums and it applied only to municipal boroughs in England. But it was an attempt to improve a bad situation, and it became law—over the protests of the ubiquitously cantankerous Colonel Sibthorp, who said that this was merely an attempt to impose a general increase of taxation. He did not like reading at all, he declared publicly, and had hated it when at Oxford.

"I'm five years old today, Papa," said a child in the 1840's. "Five years nearer your grave, my boy," replied the father.

The aggressive Moral Tale still cast a stern shadow, often a fearful, gloomy shadow, over the prescribed reading for young early Victorians. Life was a jungle of moral hazards in which threatening vices lurked to snatch the wayward childish foot. It was possible to escape disaster, these books pointed out, only by treading a line of rectitude so narrow and so ascetic that many young readers must have wondered whether it would not be better to give up at once, and accept the dubious delights of the primrose path. But the gallows always stood at the end of that path, whereas the highroad of morality led in ascending order to a satisfied conscience, public esteem, and an indubitable financial success. One must assume that these sugarcoated tracts for children played some part in strengthening a somewhat puzzled evangelical solemnity. Yet one must assume, too, that many children escaped them or that the resilience of childhood triumphed over them, else the Victorian solemnity would have been impenetrable.

In the hands of such able writers as Miss Edgeworth, Mrs. Barbauld, and Mrs. Sherwood, the edifying tale had a kind of literary quality noticeably absent from the work of most of their contemporaries and successors. The dead level of this sort of thing is seen, rather, in such a series of rhymes as *The City Apprentices; or, Industry and Idleness Exemplified*, by the Rev. T. B. Murray, M.A., published in 1846. Following Hogarth (afar off), the clerical instructor delineates the careers of Thomas Idle and Francis Goodchild. It would be no shock to a properly conditioned child to learn that the latter became Lord Mayor of London or that the former was brought to execution at Tyburn. And the reader who wanted documentation was referred, in the course of the stanza which ran

> The hurrying crowd, the tolling bell,
>   The frame of death erected nigh,
> All, with a fatal meaning, tell,
>   Yon wretched culprit comes to die . . .

to "Note G" in the back of the book, which gave verbatim for the inquiring child the address always delivered to prisoners the night before their execution.

An example of a less terrifying and more widely perpetrated type of ethical instruction for children was Robert Huish's *Our Grandmamma's Clock . . . being a series of moral tales for the edification and improvement of youth.* This little volume, which reached its second edition in 1842, told in barefaced detail such stories as those of "Frederic and Theodore Thompson; or, The Evil Consequences of Extravagance"; "Emma Darlington; or, The Folly of Vanity"; "Richard Careless; or, The Certainty of Punishment by God for Crime"; and "Anthony Curtis; or, The Injurious Consequences of Pride." The estimable author began his address to his young readers: "For you, ye joyous ones, who are standing at the entrance of life, basking in the sunshine of an apparently unclouded future, the following pages have been written, with the hope that the perusal of them may be attended with advantage, not only to the formation of your intellectual character, but also to the promotion of your terrestrial welfare." And the first story opened with the following literary ingenuity: " 'Huzza! Huzza! Huzza!' So shouted the younger branches of Mr. Hamilton's family. . . ."

With the forties, however, a new type of literature began to appear on the child's bookshelf: the Matter-of-Fact Tale. It was the age of information—information about strange and far-off foreign lands and peoples, about nature and its wonders—technology and its accomplishments. Such popular school histories as *Mrs. Markham's* and Lady Callcott's *Little Arthur* were compendiums of hard facts, although "Mama" Markham did temper her facts by "conversations" with her three children, whose task it was to ask questions about the undigested statements which had just been presented to them.*

The most phenomenally successful writer of such information books for children was Peter Parley, an American named Samuel Griswold Goodrich. During the early thirties he turned out five or six volumes a year. These were pirated in England and his pseudonym borrowed by English authors. At least six English Peter Parleys have been identified— not a surprising imitation in view of the fact that in thirty years more than 7,000,000 copies of about 120 *genuine* Parleys were sold.[9] Goodrich, since he did not have to moralize, could be simply and interestingly direct in his stories and his accounts of foreign lands and customs. His descriptions of the alligator, of the reindeer, of Niagara Falls, of tigers and tiger-hunting; his stories about the Chinese or the Poles; his brief histories of the Knights Templars or Thomas à Becket—all these avoided condescension and could be swallowed by young readers without loss of self-respect.

Goodrich, who loved a good fact, set his face sternly against fairy tales and old legends. During the forties in England he and his imitators had to face a growing tide of criticism that his books, as he put the hostile argument, "seek only to instruct the understanding of [my] readers, without making an effort to please their imagination, or to call out their affections. . . . My object in writing," he went on, "is to make children wiser and better; but I know that I can do nothing towards this end without pleasing them." Later he wrote: "In England . . . the feeling against my juvenile works was so strong among the conservatives, that a formal attempt was made to put them down by reviving the old nursery books.

---

* Murray shared with Mrs. Markham's widower during 1847 a profit of about £1,400 a year. (George Paston: *At John Murray's: Records of a Literary Circle, 1843–92*, 1932, p. 71.)

. . . A quaint, quiet, scholarly old gentleman, called Mr. Felix Summerly—a dear lover of children—was invented to preside over the enterprise. . . ."

This Felix Summerly was in fact Henry Cole, afterward Sir Henry, one of the founders of the Royal College of Music, the Albert Hall, and the South Kensington Museum. During the forties he published, in series, "Felix Summerly's *Home Treasury* of Books, Pictures, Toys, etc., purposed to cultivate the Affections, Fancy, Imagination, and Taste of Children. . . ." "The many tales," continued the announcement, "sung or said from time immemorial, which appealed to the other and certainly not less important elements of a little child's mind, its fancy, imagination, sympathetic affection, are almost all gone out of memory, and are scarcely to be obtained." Under the impetus of this new crusade the Percy Society published in 1846 an enlarged edition of *Nursery Rhymes of England*, and in 1849 J. O. Halliwell published his *Popular Rhymes and Nursery Tales*.

Thus Jack the Giant-Killer, Red Riding Hood, Cinderella, and Beauty and the Beast crept back into respectability. Writers such as Mary and William Howitt lived on both sides of the fence with equanimity. In 1846 Mary translated Hans Christian Andersen under the title *Wonderful Stories for Children*, and in 1849 she presented the same children with *Our Cousins in Ohio*, an informative account of a visit with some American relatives. In this Battle of the Children's Books all young readers profited.

In reviewing the literature of the last half of 1848 and the first half of 1849 the *Illustrated London News* said: "These are not days for literary excitement. . . . In the palmy days of the *Edinburgh* and *Quarterly*, the conversation in every man's mouth was the tone, temper, and ability of the last review. Literary criticism was a subject alike for the drawing-room and the club. Now, who asks, except on rare occasions, which is the grand article in the last *Quarterly?* Railroads and revolutions have put the finishing stroke to his sort of excitement, which had been gradually declining for many years past." Yet the same year had seen the publication of two volumes of Macaulay's *History* and of part of Harriet Martineau's *History of England During the Thirty Years' Peace;* volumes five and six of Grote's *History of Greece; Shirley*, "by the author of *Jane Eyre*," and sizable installments of *David Copperfield* and *Pendennis*. Two other major books were widely reviewed in 1849: Ruskin's *Seven Lamps of Architecture* and Layard's *Nineveh*.

One of the most thrilling literary events of the year was Austen Henry Layard's account of the discovery and initial excavation of Nineveh, as published in his *Nineveh and Its Remains: with an Account of a Visit to the Chaldean Christians and Kurdistan, and the Yezidis or Devil-Worshippers; and an Inquiry into the Manners and Arts of the Ancient Assyrians* (2 vols.). Layard was an enthusiastic thirty-two-year-old explorer and diplomat, rather than an archaeologist, who possessed the right combination of tenacity and ingenuity needed to surmount the many difficulties which beset an excavator of ancient ruins in those days. His account of the discovery of the site of Nineveh and of the excitement of excavating the inscriptions and sculptures caused intense interest in England, for Layard was a good travel writer as well as a persevering explorer. The *Times* called the book "the most extraordinary work of the present age." A third "edition" was announced in April. Within twelve months nearly 8,000 copies were sold, and for some time the author's half-share of the profit amounted to about £1,500 a year. The clergy took comfort in Layard's assurances that the circumference of Nineveh was exactly that mentioned by the prophet Isaiah: it was pleasant to have the truth of biblical history scientifically reaffirmed.

Later in 1849 another volume by Layard, *Illustrations of the Monuments of Nineveh*, came from the press, and in August he started on a second expedition, which took him to the ruins of Babylon and the mounds of southern Mesopotamia. Already he had started to send back the statues of winged bulls and of kings which were to form the greater part of the collection of Assyrian antiquities in the British Museum.

By the time Ruskin's *Seven Lamps of Architecture* appeared in May, the fourth edition of Vol. I and the second edition of Vol. II of *Modern Painters* had been announced. Ruskin's stature as an art and architectural critic was beginning to be recognized, even by those who disagreed with him violently. *Blackwood's* called the *Seven Lamps* "verbose, tedious, obscure, and extravagant." The critics for *Athenaeum* and the *Spectator* took exception to the author's eccentricities and to his "infirmities of temper," as well as to his excessive stress on the didactically-historical interpretation of architecture. But both professed having received some pleasant if violent intellectual exercise, and the latter praised him for "awakening the moral feelings which it is the province of art to keep alive." The architects and architectural writers were for the most part angry or contemptuous. "What funny fal-lal is all this!" wrote George Wightwick in the *Architect*. Yet the Gothic revival then in progress was strengthened immeasurably by Ruskin's eloquent defense of the spiritual qualities of Gothic.

Early in the year appeared a little volume of poetry: *The Strayed Reveller, and Other Poems,* by "A." Some of the reviewers complained about the anonymous poet's "unintelligibility"; others praised his evident poetic power and quoted "The Forsaken Merman" and "To Fausta" to prove it. Young Matthew Arnold himself received pleasant letters of congratulation from his friends.

In May the Overland Mail brought news of the annexation of the Punjab. The announcement created no surprise, for it was generally felt that the treachery and daring of the Sikhs had threatened the loss of British authority in every part of India. Thus quietly a territory of 100,000 square miles and three and a half million inhabitants was added to Her Majesty's territories. It was noted that the net annual revenue of the acquired lands would be about a million pounds.

The Exhibition of the Royal Academy, which opened this same month, was the first at which pictures by members of the new Pre-Raphaelite Brotherhood were shown. The Brotherhood had not been publicly announced, but it was holding regular and enthusiastic meetings and was even contemplating a communal household. William Michael Rossetti suggested that " 'P.R.B.' might be written on the bell and stand for 'please ring the bell' to the profane." Millais's painting, "Lorenzo and Isabella" (after Keats's "Eve of St. Agnes") and Holman Hunt's "Rienzi Vowing Revenge over His Brother's Corpse," received a good deal of attention from the critics, who, although critical of what they called "an affectation of medieval uncouthness," were in general gratifyingly commendatory. Hunt sold the "Rienzi" for 160 guineas. Dante Gabriel Rossetti exhibited his "Girlhood of Mary Virgin" at the same time at the Free Exhibition near Hyde Park Corner. It, too, drew a good deal of favorable notice because of its "sacred mysticism." The storm of systematic abuse which would break against the Brotherhood in 1850 was still beyond the horizon.

Troubled news came from across the Atlantic this spring in connection with the Astor House riots in New York. On May 7th Macready, on tour of the United States, had appeared in *Macbeth* at the Astor House Theatre. On the same evening his rival American actor, Edwin Forrest, played the same role at another theater. Forrest, stupidly jealous of Macready and angered by hostile criticism which he had received in London—criticism which he attributed to Macready's instigation—was supported by a crew of ruffians who broke up the Englishman's per-

Figure 122. Dante Gabriel Rossetti: "The Girlhood of Mary Virgin"

formance by hissing and throwing rotten eggs, potatoes, and pennies at the stage.

Macready, in excusably high dudgeon, planned to leave New York, but was persuaded by some embarrassed citizens (among whom, according to the *New York Tribune*, were Washington Irving and Herman Melville) to continue his engagement. On the evening of the tenth he was to appear again in *Macbeth*. All possible precautions were taken to prevent trouble. Some 300 policemen were stationed in the theater, and the patrons entered the house through a hollow square of police. When Macready appeared, the hoots and hisses of the enemy were drowned

Figure 123. The Astor House riot in New York. From the *Illustrated London News*

by the cheers of the respectable majority of the audience. A few arrests were made, and the play went on amid a great deal of confusion.

Outside the theater, Astor Place and the adjoining Bowery were filled with angry crowds. Hundreds of persons packed Broadway. Before long the mob began to throw paving stones through the theater windows. The police dragged off some dozen of the ringleaders, and repeated this procedure several times. The shower of stones continued, however, beating down the barricades which had been placed at some of the windows. The National Guard made an appearance but was driven up Broadway by the mob throwing stones. The soldiers re-formed their ranks and, as the crowd continued to press upon them, attempted an abortive bayonet charge. At last, after issuing repeated warnings to the crowd, General Sandford gave orders to fire. Some twenty persons were killed, and more than thirty wounded. Not until cannon loaded with grapeshot were brought up was there any assurance that order would be restored.

Macready himself escaped to Boston on the morning of the eleventh, riding as far as New Rochelle on horseback, disguised as a soldier. Respectable American citizens were covered with shame, but a Mr. Mike Walsh addressed an audience described as 30,000 strong and denounced "the murderous attack on unoffending citizens." Obviously more was involved here than strife between rival aestheticians of the drama. The shades of '76 were invoked; one of the placards which had been posted ran: "Americans! arouse! The great Crisis has come! Decide now whether English Aristocrats and Foreign rule shall triumph in this,

America's, metropolis, or whether her own sons, whose Fathers once compelled the base-born miscreants to succumb, shall meanly lick the hand that strikes, and allow themselves to be deprived of liberty of opinion—so dear to every true American heart." It is perhaps significant that Mike Walsh was a Tammany Hall celebrity, and that the list of the dead included such names as Cahan, Kearnin, McGuire, and Kelley.

The episode did much to confirm the concept of American barbarity in the minds of the English, but the *Spectator* (no enthusiast for the United States) reminded its readers of similar if less bloody anti-Gallican riots at Drury Lane Theatre when Mr. Jullien tried to establish a French company at that house.

Spring turned into a pleasant summer which indicated a better-than-average harvest. . . . A new musical instrument was announced by its inventor, a Mr. Saxe—to be known as the saxophone. . . . Prince Albert laid the cornerstone for the Licensed Victuallers' Asylum. . . . The name of Lola Montez popped up again in the news. She was charged at the Marlborough Street Police Office with bigamy in marrying lately Mr. Heald, a young officer in the guards. Crowds filled the office at the hearing. The proceedings were adjourned, and by the time they were resumed Montez was in Barcelona, being implored by the young Mr. Heald for forgiveness. The *Formento* of Barcelona reported later: "Lola has been able to catch her faithless husband, and has brought him back to the conjugal roof." . . . Liverpool and Birmingham staged musical festivals, and Birmingham an exposition of arts and manufactures. . . . The Queen visited Ireland for the first time, and was received with satisfying enthusiasm.

The summer saw the exposure and financial collapse of George Hudson, the Railway King. His manipulation of shares, his paying dividends out of capital, his juggling of accounts had at last caught up with him, and now, belatedly, Parliament was considering a bill to enforce the auditing of railway accounts. Amid a great odor of righteous indignation the companies which Hudson had ruled instituted investigations. Attempting to explain himself before the Commons, he assured the House that if he had been guilty of error it had not been intentionally. In his published defense he described "the circumstances in which I find myself placed—circumstances to me of a most painful nature, but in which I have become involved without the slightest idea on my part that I was doing anything deserving of reprehension." The directors of his companies pressed him for restitution. One by one his vast estates, assessed at a value of £700,000, were sold. Only his membership in the House prevented his imprisonment for debt.

Thus was the glory departed. Acrimonious and piously angry voices were raised on every side. Charles Greville wrote: "The exposure that has just been made of Hudson's railway delinquency has excited a great sensation, and no small satisfaction. In the City all seem glad of his fall, and most people rejoice at the degradation of a purse-proud, vulgar upstart, who had nothing to recommend him but his ill-gotten wealth." In his home town of York, where everyone had bowed before him, Hudson's name was taken from the aldermanic roll, and Hudson Street was renamed Railway Street. However culpable Hudson may have been, he was clearly made a scapegoat by those in influential quarters who had encouraged and abetted and had been enriched by his gigantic gambles. Many responsible journals pointed out that Hudson was as much the victim of his former sycophants as of his own naïve disregard for financial proprieties. They lamented the sordid way in which those who had been eager to ride to fame and fortune on the Hudsonian coattails now joined to revile him in his disgrace. Carlyle in "Hudson's Statue," one of the most sardonic of his *Latter-Day Pamphlets*, impaled the hollow morality of those who had subscribed £25,000 to a Hudson memorial, only to repudiate now the king they had in fact created. At this distance there is no little pathos in the career of the Yorkshire linen draper who was little worse if no better than the railway gamblers for whose greed he had become the symbol.

Two notable murders, and the subsequent execution of the criminals, captured an extraordinary amount of attention in 1849. On March 31st the *Illustrated London News* ran the following story, headed "Tragedy in Liverpool."

> About twelve o'clock on Wednesday, a boy named William Bradshaw was passing the house of Captain Hinrichson, who is in the employ of Messrs. James Aikin and Son, and master of the ship *Duncan*, at present in Calcutta, when he heard a deep moaning, often repeated, and in consequence gave notice to the police; before whose arrival, however, some persons who had forced an entrance found three persons, lying on the floor, weltering in blood—their moans, at the time, being of the most pitiable description. Life not being extinct, they were conveyed to the Southern Hospital. The house was then searched, and in the back cellar was found the body of a child, lying on the floor, in a pool of blood, with its throat cut, and being quite dead. The three bodies found in the front parlour were those of Mrs. Hinrichson, her eldest daughter, of about seven or eight years of age, and her servant

woman. They were all dreadfully beaten about the head and body. On the forehead of Mrs. Hinrichson there had been a dreadful blow inflicted, the forehead being laid open a depth of two or three inches. . . . The servant also had received similar wounds on the head and face. The body of the child also presented a most dreadful appearance. The poor little creature's head seemed to have been beaten to a jelly by the inhuman ruffian. She has since died.

The sufferers were all insensible, and therefore unable to make any communication which would throw light upon this shocking occurrence. The wounds were inflicted with the fire-irons. As yet the affair is a complete mystery.

The servant girl who survived for a few days what proved to be a quadruple murder identified the attacker as one John Gleeson, a new lodger in the house. No motive for the murders could be established at the trial, but the judge angrily disallowed a plea of insanity, and Gleeson was executed at Kirkdale on September 15th. A crowd estimated at 100,000 watched the proceedings. The railway company ran cheap trains, all of which were densely packed. Madame Tussaud had a repre·sentative there to acquire Gleeson's clothes for exhibition. Mr. Bally, "the eminent phrenologist," was present to take a cast of the prisoner's head. "All the vacant ground in front of the prison and spreading down to the canal," ran one account, "presented much the same appearance with respect to numbers as Aintree, or Epsom on the Cup or Derby Day. . . . Never in the history of capital punishment in Lancashire has the execution of a criminal excited the same interest in the public mind."

Yet the Gleeson affair, as one journalist put it brilliantly, "paled into insignificance" before the Manning murder case in London this same year. Readers followed hungrily the accounts of the murder, the trial, and the executions through hundreds of inches of news columns. Diagrams were published showing the spot of the murder and the position on the floor under which the body was buried. Artists were present at the trial to sketch for the illustrated papers the features of the culprits, and tens of thousands of curious onlookers made holiday at Horsemonger Lane when the death trap was finally sprung. Public interest was focused throughout on the personalities of the two murderers themselves. One was a woman, a steel-willed Lady Macbeth. And here were all the elements of an illicit relationship, premeditation, flight and capture, the reported (and exaggerated) beauty of the murderess, the mutual recriminations of the culprits as the hour of execution drew near.

On August 9th one Patrick O'Connor, a selfish petty usurer and an officer of the Customs, reasonably well to do, left his lodgings in Mile End Road. When he did not return after some days, handbills were cir-

Figure 124. The Mannings, drawn in court by Robert Cruikshank

A. Wall at the bottom of the kitchen-stairs, on which spots of blood were discovered, and near which it is supposed the air-gun was discharged.
C. Iron-barred window, through which the shadow of the Mannings was reflected on the garden-wall, late on the night of the murder.
D. Entrance to the kitchen where the body was found.

Figure 125. View of the kitchen where O'Connor's body was found

culated offering a reward for his discovery. It was known that O'Connor had an improper connection with a Maria Manning, wife of George Frederick Manning, formerly a guard on the Great Western Railway. It was soon ascertained that this "Swiss lady" had, since the disappearance, visited O'Connor's lodgings and gone through his boxes and drawers. Suspicion was therefore turned toward the Mannings, and when officers went to their house at 3 Miniver Place, Bermondsey, they found it empty, the furniture and effects having been hastily sold.

An initial search of the premises and a good deal of digging in the garden revealed nothing. One of the officers observed, however, fresh cement around some of the flagstones of the kitchen floor. The stones were raised, and underneath lay the body of the murdered man, his legs doubled up and tied to his haunches. He had been buried in quicklime; final identification could be made only through a set of false teeth. A bullet was discovered near the temple, and some eighteen severe wounds had been inflicted upon the head.

Mrs. Manning was traced to Edinburgh and arrested there. From the beginning she displayed not the slightest emotion or alarm, and declared not only her innocence but even her ignorance of the crime—although money and railway shares belonging to O'Connor were found in her possession. She was brought to London and lodged in Horsemonger Lane Gaol—a large woman, with dark hair and eyes and somewhat masculine features.

Big rewards were offered for the detection of Manning, and he was at last discovered and arrested on the island of Jersey some two weeks later. He immediately related the particulars of the murder, which, he said, had been wholly planned and perpetrated by his wife. The hole in the kitchen floor had been dug days in advance and covered with boards. The victim had several times walked over it in the interim and had inquired for what purpose it had been dug—never receiving, however, quite the correct answer! Manning himself was a bullheaded, thick-necked man, with a large fat underjaw. Unlike his impassive wife, he appeared nervous and dejected.

The case proceeded rapidly to trial amid a furor of public attention. The shovel used to dig the grave was identified, the purchase of quick-lime proved. A bloody crowbar was brought into evidence. The Central Criminal Court at Newgate was crowded when the jury, after a delib-eration of forty-five minutes, brought in a verdict of "Guilty!" Justice Cresswell put on the black cap and began to pronounce the sentence. At this point Mrs. Manning broke in excitedly to declare again her inno-cence and her love for O'Connor. "If I had wished to commit murder," she exclaimed, "how much more likely is it that I should have murdered that man [pointing to her husband], who had made my life a hell upon earth ever since I have known him." Manning said nothing. The judge completed the sentence.

The detail in which the London press reported this whole affair reflected a universal fascinated interest. Notes were printed which had passed between the Mannings in prison, he declaring again her guilt and giving her religious advice, she reminding him vaguely that the murder had been committed by "that young man from Jersey," and denying him his request for a last interview.

The Mannings were executed at nine o'clock on November 13th in front of Horsemonger Lane Gaol. The *Times* devoted four long, closely-printed columns to the event, including the last moments of the criminals before they were led forth. Manning was calm, resigned to his fate. His wife maintained her "diabolical self-possession" and "walked to her doom with firm, unfaltering step," dressed in a handsome black satin gown.

A crowd of 30,000 thronged Horsemonger Lane and its vicinity. For days past the immediate neighborhood of the prison had presented the aspects of a great fair, so large were the hordes of people collected there. Now, said the *Times*, "the surrounding beer shops were crowded. Windows commanding a view of the scaffold rose to a Californian price. Platforms were run up in every direction," many of them dangerously flimsy. Five hundred police were on the ground on the evening before the execution, "in ample time for the immense streams of people, men, women, and children, that began pouring down towards the scene of the execution as midnight approached. . . . From that great seething mass there rises a ceaseless din of sounds and war of tongues—voices in every note, shrill whistles, and slang calls. . . . On the outskirts of this great mass of human beings were . . . a very different class of people—men and women too—who had paid their two or three guineas to gratify a morbid curiosity, and who, from the fashionable clubs at the west end, and from their luxurious homes, came to fill the windows, the gardens, and the housetops," watching the proceedings with opera glasses leveled.

At last the fatal procession ascended the scaffold, and a gleam of sunshine fell upon the platform as Calcraft the executioner placed the nightcaps over the prisoners' heads and drew the bolt.

More than 2,500,000 copies of broadsheets describing the "last moments," the execution, the "confessions," and carrying a rhymed set of verses, were sold at the time. Society laid away its black satin dresses for the season.

Figure 126. An execution at Newgate

The same issue of the *Times* that carried the extended account of the execution printed also an angry letter from Charles Dickens, who had viewed the proceedings with unmitigated horror.

I was a witness of the execution at Horsemonger Lane this morning. I went there with the intention of observing the crowd gathered to behold it, and I had excellent opportunities of doing so, at intervals all through the night, and continuously from daybreak until the spectacle was over. . . . I believe that a sight so inconceivably awful as the wickedness and levity of the immense crowd collected at that execution this morning could be imagined by no man, and could be presented in no heathen land under the sun. . . . When I came upon the scene at midnight, the *shrillness* of the cries and howls that were raised from time to time, denoting that they came from a concourse of boys and girls already assembled in the best places, made my blood run cold. As the night went on, screeching, and laughing, and yelling in strong chorus of parodies on Negro melodies, with substitutions of "Mrs. Manning" for "Susannah," and the like, were added to these. When the day dawned, thieves, low prostitutes, ruffians, and vagabonds of every kind, flocked on to the ground, with every variety of offensive and foul behaviour. Fightings, faintings, whistlings, imitations of Punch, brutal jokes, tumultuous demonstrations of indecent delight when swooning women were dragged out of the crowd by the police with their dresses disordered, gave a new zest to the general entertainment. When the sun rose brightly—as it did—it gilded thousands upon thousands of upturned faces, so inexpressibly odious in their brutal mirth or callousness, that a man had cause to feel ashamed of the shape he wore, and to shrink from himself, as fashioned in the image of the Devil. . . .*

While all this was going on every Englishman who woke in the morning with unfevered brow had good reason to be thankful. During the summer the mysterious and terrifying scourge of the cholera reached its height. The mortality lists grew steadily through July and August in London, from 152 in the first week of July to 1,272 in the last week in August. On September 8th the London weekly list reached its climax of 2,026, and began thereafter to decline. In England and Wales 55,201 deaths were attributed to cholera during the latter part of 1848 and the whole of 1849. It was much more fatal in the large towns than it had been during the 1831–32 epidemic. The deaths in London alone during the third quarter of 1849 were 12,847. Although officials were still devoted to the "zymotic theory," it was observed that the disease struck most severely those districts with defective drainage and polluted water.

By November 10th the Queen was able to issue a proclamation appointing the fifteenth of the month as a day of thanksgiving for the cessation of the epidemic. On the same day Sir John Simon read his first annual report on the sanitary condition of the City of London—a devastating analysis which the *Times* printed in full in multiple columns.

Amid the turmoil of the expiring year there were those who noticed and admired the first blooming of the gigantic water lily (*Victoria Regia*) at Chatsworth. . . . Prince Albert, as president of the Royal Society of Arts, suggested a grand Exhibition in London of the Arts and Manufactures of All Nations—to take place during the spring or summer of 1851. It was thought that it would be necessary to construct buildings for the purpose, perhaps in Hyde Park. . . . The opening of the new Coal Exchange in Lower Thames Street was marked by a royal visit to the city by barge, the first such splendid civic ceremony since the "inaugural" of the New Royal Exchange in 1844. Albert did the honors, walking hand in hand with the young Prince of Wales and the Princess Royal. . . . Sir James Ross returned from his fruitless search for the Franklin expedition. . . . A hundred British vessels were reported in harbor on November 1st at San Francisco, a city which had grown from a population of 500 to an estimated 15,000 within a year. . . . The first bronze plaque was placed on the seemingly never-to-be-finished Nelson

---

* As noted earlier, public executions were not abolished in England until 1868.

Figures 127 and 128. Richard Doyle, in *Punch*

Column in Trafalgar Square. . . . Chopin died in Paris at the age of thirty-nine.

Earlier in the year, in June, Lady Blessington had died suddenly in Paris of apoplexy, just at the time when the sale of her furniture and effects in Gore House had been completed. Those public auctions had been melancholy affairs for the friends who remembered the brilliance of the Blessington salon in Kensington, whither had flocked all the famous men of the day. Thackeray visited the sale and wrote gloomily: "I have just come away from a dismal sight; Gore House full of snobs looking at the furniture . . . , brutes keeping their hats on in the kind old drawing room—I longed to knock some of them off, and say, 'Sir, be civil in a lady's room! . . . There was one of the servants there, not a powdered one, but a butler, a *whatdoyoucallit*. My heart melted towards him and I gave him a pound. Ah! it was a strange, sad picture of *Vanity Fair*. My mind is all boiling up with it. . . ." Writing his impressions of the sale to his mistress, Lady Blessington's French valet said: "M. Thackeray came also, and had tears in his eyes on leaving. He is perhaps the only person whom I have seen really affected by your departure."

The December weather was dark, cold, and frosty across all England. But the *Illustrated London News* was able to mingle a pleasant warning with its New Year's greetings to its readers. "The dangers of the approaching year seem to be," it said, "not the dangers of adversity, but of prosperity." It was a risk most Englishmen were ready to assume.

1850 * Metropolis

RICHARD Roe woke early in his Kensington home on New Year's morning, 1850. The weather was unusually raw and cold, even for a London winter. Since Mr. Roe was subject to head colds—and already he felt sniffles coming on—he was oppressed by a mild sense of outrage. He sneezed, loudly. This was no way for a person of importance to begin the New Year.

Mr. Roe knew that he was important. It was he whose vote the Parliamentary orators argued long nights in the House to gain. It was he whose soul the immense machinery of the Establishment wrestled to make safe. It was for Mr. Roe that publishers announced their new books, that theatrical managers concocted newer and more amazing entertainments, that old Parr advertised his Life Pills. The manufacturers of Patent Stoves, Patent Exercisers, and Patent Boots, the makers of greatcoats and pianofortes, watches and umbrellas, wallpapers and ginger brandy—all had their eye on Mr. Roe.

And Mr. Roe had his eye (a little bloodshot) on them. Later, sitting before a hot breakfast, he opened his newspaper to see whether or not the country was doing right by him. What did he read, on this first day of the new half-century? Or *was* it the new half-century? The *Times* had said yes; the *Spectator* had pooh-poohed the *Times* for being so dim-witted as not to see that 1850 was the closing year of the former half of the century, not the opening of the latter half. This morning the *Times* retracted.

What was the condition of England as the papers reflected it to Mr. Roe's somewhat febrile and rhinitic gaze? Not bad. In perspective it could be seen that the steady revival of trade during 1849 had marked it as the first year of returning prosperity after a long and dismal period of adversity. There had been a conspicuous revival in export trade. The new gold was beginning to come in from the United States, and great markets were opening up there, as in India, for cotton thread, calicoes, linen goods. Industrial England was humming. And on January 1st 5,996 miles of railway were in operation—an increase of 1,013 miles over the previous year. On the other hand, the cost of living had been going down. Wheat, which in 1847 had sold for 69s. 9d. the quarter, had dropped year by year to 50s., to 44s., and was now selling for 39s. 5d.

The farmers, to be sure, were grumbling about the decline in the price of grain. Protectionists held angry meetings all over the country. Some 12,000 people attended a great county Protectionist rally in the castle yard at Lincoln—nobility, gentry, farmers, laborers. Fights broke out at a similar meeting in Reading, and at Stafford a sizable riot arose between the farmers who were holding the meeting and the townsmen who approved of cheap bread. The battle was carried into the town square. Numbers were severely hurt. Lord Talbot stayed in the chair amid yells, hisses, and hootings from the free traders. Someone threw a large stone at him, and the policemen were totally unable to quell the disturbance. The mob tore up benches with which they armed themselves. The police were overpowered and the rioters outside began battering in the door with paving stones. At this juncture Lord Talbot achieved a masterpiece of decorum and understatement: he declared the meeting dissolved!

At other gatherings, noble lords capped their arguments by personal attacks on Sir Robert Peel. "I entertain," said Earl Stanhope at a Seven Oaks meeting, "the utmost contempt for his character and conduct." Disraeli was in the midst of all this, eloquently and shrewdly consolidating his gains, capitalizing always on the mistakes of his opposition. Since the death of Lord George Bentinck, it was noted, Disraeli had constructed a new Tory party, already numbering some two hundred

Figure 129. Great Protectionist meeting in Drury Lane Theatre

and fifty. Someone called it "a party without statesmen," and Peel "a statesman without a party."

For most people, however, the year opened auspiciously—even for the deserving poor at Windsor, where the Queen and Prince Albert, with their children, "personally witnessed" the distribution of Her Majesty's New Year's gifts of food and clothing and received, so the reports ran, "respectful gratitude." In London, on the same day, great crowds went skating on the thin ice in the parks. Soyer, the famous chef of the Reform Club, had a very narrow escape. He fell through the ice in St. James's Park into sixteen feet of water. Iceman Martin of the Humane Society's rescue crew got him out. Mr. M'Cann, surgeon to the Society, immediately placed him in a hot bath and "administered a glass of whisky." In a few hours he was able to be removed to his own residence in a cab. Next day he donated ten pounds to the Humane Society.

And so England turned the corner into 1850, with prosperity beckoning in the near distance. It was to be a year of unpredictable yet important public events, but politically a quiet year—except for Palmerston's histrionic, tub-thumping engagement with Greece in the strange affair of Don Pacifico. Even here Palmerston's highhanded actions had an inner consistency—his belligerent concern for the genus Englishman under whatever flag—but as usual he overextended himself, to the embarrassment and irritation of his colleagues. And, as usual, he salvaged his position and reputation at the lost moment, jauntily and triumphantly.

David "Don" Pacifico was a Portuguese Jew who was a native of Gibraltar and therefore a British citizen. He had been living in Athens, where in 1847 his house had been sacked on Easter Sunday in an anti-Semitic riot. Pacifico's somewhat extravagant claim for damages of £31,500 had been looked at skeptically by the Greek Government, and in spite of Palmerston's efforts no settlement had been reached by January, 1850. At that time Palmerston as foreign minister, with an ostentatious disregard of potential international repercussion, ordered the British fleet in the Mediterranean to proceed to Athens. When the Greeks did not respond to a twenty-four-hour ultimatum, the British began to seize Greek merchant ships, and by the middle of February had some forty vessels in custody.

Palmerston suspected French influence in the whole matter, and during the subsequent arbitrations in which France was intermediary, resumed his coercion against the Greek Government, which could only capitulate to superior British force and pay the bill. The whole affair produced a tremendous sensation at home. The Cabinet was annoyed at Palmerston's bullying operations and was fearful, at one stage, of a major war. Lord John Russell was of no mind to break up the Government, however, and seems to have hoped that the Queen would take the initiative and dismiss Palmerston. The House of Lords, led by Stanley in an all-night debate, passed a vote of censure. Everyone wondered what Palmerston would do. When the question was brought to the Commons he defended himself in a brilliant four-and-three-quarter-hour speech—the famous *civis Romanus sum* speech—in which he forced the lion to roar heartily: any British subject had a right to British protection in any part of the world. The House of Commons, by a majority of forty-six, approved Palmerston's policy. In the end, therefore, with a sublime irony, Palmerston strengthened the position of the Government which in desperation had been eager to throw him overboard.

Sir Robert Peel spoke during that last debate in the Commons, spoke moderately and generously, condemning Palmerston in sorrow rather than in anger. It was his last speech. That same afternoon, riding for exercise up Constitution Hill, he was thrown from his horse. He lingered three days in agony, and died on the night of Tuesday, July 2d. The shock to the nation was profound. His bitterest enemies kept silence in the face of the nearly unanimous tribute to the character of a great statesman. "When we remember," wrote Greville in his journal, "that Peel was an object of bitter hatred to one great party, that he was never liked by the other party, and that he had no popular and ingratiating qualities, and very few intimate friends, it is surprising to see the warm and universal feeling which his death has elicited. It is a prodigious testimony to the greatness of his capacity, to the profound conviction of his public usefulness and importance, and of the purity of the motives by which his public conduct has been guided."[1]

During Peel's last hours there stood before his outer gate, waiting for bulletins, a silent crowd of poor people—mechanics and laborers, women in shabby shawls, with tears in their eyes. *Punch*, which had attacked Peel viciously and consistently, suffered twinges of conscience and proposed a memorial of loaves of cheap bread piled high. Street ballads were hawked which ran

> The poor have long praised and blessed him
> Now tears wet each eye, while in sorrow they sigh,
> He is gone, is Sir Robert, God rest him.

Four other deaths this year marked the passing of another generation. Louis Philippe died in August in exile at Claremont, more quietly than most kings or ex-kings, closing a career, said the *Spectator*, "singularly combining the felicitous and the unworthy." Informed that he was about to die, he spent some of his last moments dictating, with great clearness, the closing pages of his memoirs.

Earlier, in January, Francis Jeffrey had died in the ripeness of years, remembered chiefly for his aggressive journalism in the early decades of the century. In April, Madame Tussaud and William Wordsworth died within three days of each other, each belonging to another age, she in her ninety-sixth and he in his eighty-first year. The poet's long, autobiographical work, *The Prelude*, was published posthumously this year. Reviewers recognized it as a remarkable work. The question of Wordsworth's successor to the laureateship was discussed widely. The *Athenaeum* suggested that, since a queen was on the throne, a proper appointment would be that of Elizabeth Barrett Browning, than whom "no living poet of either sex . . . can prefer a higher claim."

The Queen delayed the appointment, but later in the year Alfred Tennyson was named to the post, amid general approval. In the meantime *In Memoriam* had been published and the Victorian public had found in that poem the perfect expression of its hopes and fears, its yearning doubts, its grim optimisms. When Tennyson met frankly the confusions of intellectual life in an age tormented by suspicions of its own self-satisfaction, when he embraced "the larger hope," he replaced the multiple spiritual frustrations of thoughtful readers with a cry which "faced the spectres of the mind and laid them." The laureate wreath seemed the only proper accolade for the poet who could find for a generation hungry to reconcile heart and head "a sentinel" who

> . . . whispers to the worlds of space,
> In the deep night, that all is well.

Yet the battle between the evolutionists and the advocates of special creation went on. This year Hugh Miller published his *Footprints of the Creator*, an attempt to vindicate geologically the theory of creation by miracle as against the hypothesis of "creation by law" proposed by Chambers in his *Vestiges of the Natural History of Creation*. Darwin in 1850 was still refining his theories for the *Origin of Species*.

Down in Chelsea Carlyle set himself furiously against any rising tide of optimism. He began in January the monthly publication of his *Latter-Day Pamphlets*. Reviewing the strident excesses of the first two of these, "The Present Time" and "Model Prisons," both of which advocated the jettisoning of democracy in favor of a vague, benevolent dictatorship, the *Athenaeum* declared that it was almost ashamed to deal with them at all. The general impression, as Froude put it, was that Carlyle had taken to whisky.

Other happenings were discussed at the breakfast tables of thousands of Mr. Roes during the early part of the year. The "Lion Queen" was chewed to death by a tiger which she had introduced into the cage in her lion-taming performance. . . . The price of illuminating gas in the City was reduced to four shillings per 1,000 cubic feet. Although it took twelve companies to supply greater London, gas was used chiefly in shops and warehouses. It had found its way as yet into very few homes. . . . A plebeian stag hunt was staged in Camden Town, east of Regent's Park. One afternoon the inhabitants were astonished to see a fine red deer running down the streets at full speed, pursued by two riders on horses that had evidently done a hard day's work. With five hounds at his haunches the stag dashed into the house containing Mr. Prior's stove-grate manufactory, and was there secured. The strange scene attracted thousands of persons and it took a dozen policemen to save Mr. Prior's fence railings from destruction. . . . A demonstration was made of a "Patent Impulsoria," a sort of substitute for railway engines, on which four horses, working a treadmill-engine, pulled a

Figure 130. Hyde Park

Figures 130, 131. London Amusing Itself. By Gavarni, from *Gavarni in London*

Figure 131. The soirée

train at a speed of fifteen miles an hour. . . . A curious tale arrived from New York (appearing there in "a respectable newspaper entitled *The Friend*") that the Dauphin of France, son of Louis XVI, who had for many years been reported dead, was now a chieftain and missionary among the Menominee Indians of Wisconsin! . . . The opening of the tubular Britannia Bridge (a railway bridge 1,500 feet long) across the Menai Straits was hailed as a great engineering achievement. The press was full of statistics—tonnages, lengths, number of rivets (2,000,000 of them). . . . "Charles" Marx and Friedrich Engels wrote a long letter to the *Spectator* complaining about the Prussian spies and English informers who were plaguing their lives in London. . . . A process of photography on glass was announced; by means of a coating of egg albumen, sensitized with silver, glass negatives could now be made.

England suffered through the coldest March within the memory of man. The Easter weather was bitter—"a *North*-Easter," the wags called it. But Easter Monday turned suddenly beautiful, and enormous crowds flocked to the parks and traveled down to Greenwich to see the traditional fair with its acrobats, clowns, and puppets. The proceedings were enlivened this year by a pitched battle between some soldiers of the Royal Artillery, who attacked one of the traveling theaters, and the crowd which took the part of the performers. The police were called in and, as so often seemed to happen, were driven back. Only when soldiers from Woolwich charged the rebels in grand military style, using cutlasses with some freedom, was the mob dispersed.

The London season was inaugurated by Victoria's giving birth to a seventh child. The boy was named Arthur, which pleased everyone as being sufficiently English. In Parliament Sir Robert Inglis expressed his approbation, a little optimistically, at the additions which were "each year" being made to the list of princes.

What kind of place was London in this season of 1850? In a sense, a great, clamorous, congested city of more than two and a quarter million inhabitants. In another sense, an accretion of villages looking for a metropolis, for London had grown with a rugged individualism which defied planning. When in 1848 the Health of Towns Act established a general Board of Health for the purpose of improving the sanitary condition of towns and populous places, London, as we have seen, was exempted from the provisions of that act. So great was the opposition from the parish vestries, so great the popular outcry against "centralization," that London was "left to the enjoyment of the ancient nuisances"

Figure 132. General view of London from the Southwark side

(as Charles Knight put it) until 1855. Except for the City, there was really no uniform local government; each parish, without visible boundary, dominated its local affairs. Even the degree of centralization represented by the seven bodies called "Commissioners of Sewers" had seemed excessive to many. No two parishes were governed alike. In the middle of the century there were eighty-four paving boards in London, nineteen of them in one parish. Eight water companies and twelve gas companies supplied the utilities for the metropolitan area. The lighting of the parish of Lambeth was under the charge of nine local trusts. The affairs of St. Mary, Newington, were under the control of thirteen boards or trusts.[2] To understand the anachronisms and paradoxes of London in mid-century one must remember how much of an eighteenth-century city it was. There was not, as yet, even municipal fire protection; the fire brigades were maintained by the insurance companies, and technically had no obligation to put out fires except those attacking insured buildings. There were 838 fires in London in 1849, in which twenty-six lives were lost.

To Europeans it seemed merely an ugly city of dirty red brick, grimed with the smoke of a million fires which hung over it like a pall. Even in the newer areas, where it was becoming fashionable to cover the brick with stucco, the houses stayed fresh only a short time. The public buildings, built chiefly of granite, monotonously similar, were a uniform dirty gray; the new Houses of Parliament were smoke-blackened before they were finished. By way of compensation there were, of course, the squares and the parks, which every Londoner knew and loved—the parks, open

Figure 133. Hyde Park Corner and Apsley House

Figure 134. Belgrave Square

to all, the squares, with their enclosed trees and greensward, barricaded against the footprints of the vulgar. Hyde Park and Rotten Row in high season was one of the spectacles of London. It reached its full glory on a Sunday afternoon in spring. About five o'clock the throng of carriages became thickest, when the elite, elegantly arrayed, promenaded—dukes, merchants, barristers, and bankers bowing to their friends. Tall footmen, shining in scarlet and lace; beautiful females strolling under (sometimes) blue skies on the Elysian turf, listening to the band of the Royal Horseguards play Meyerbeer and Rossini. It was very stylish, but styles changed slowly in Britain. An irreverent American, Nathaniel Parker Willis, observed in the mid-forties that "the men have the same tight cravats, coats too small, overbrushed whiskers, and look of being excessively washed. . . . The blind beggars tell the same stories, and are led by the same dogs; but what is stranger than all this sameness is that the ladies look the same! The fashions have perhaps changed—in the milliners' shops! But the *Englishing* that is done to French bonnets after they are bought, or the English way in which they are worn . . . gives the fair occupants of the splendid carriages of London the very same look they had ten years ago."[3]

There were, incidentally, strenuous efforts during the forties to extend that well-scrubbed look to the lower classes, whose opportunities for bathing were notoriously few. The first public bath and washhouse was opened in George Street, Easton Square, in 1846, by voluntary contributions. Speedily it became self-supporting, and three similar institutions were launched within the next few years. In 1850 an elaborate bath and washhouse was opened in St. Marylebone. It contained 107 separate baths, with vapor and shower baths in addition—to say nothing of two large swimming baths. The washhouses contained eighty-nine pairs of washtubs and boilers. The price of hot baths varied from 2d. to 6d. (the latter for a "first-class" bath). The inveterate statistician Mayhew reported 96,726 baths taken in the George Street establishment in 1849.

London was many cities. As defined by the Registrar-General, it was an area of 115 square miles—including all places within five miles of the Post Office. As defined by the London District Post: (1) The Central Metropolis (hourly delivery of letters after midday); (2) the six-delivery Metropolis (three miles from the General Post Office); (3) the six-mile Metropolis; and (4) the twelve-mile Metropolis—the extreme range of the London District Post. The Metropolis of the Metropolitan Commissioners of Police: 96 square miles. The metropolis of the Hackney-Carriage Act (which controlled fares): within five miles of the General Post Office. "There were other districts for the registration and exercise of votes, parliamentary or municipal; ecclesiastical and educational districts; a complication of parochial, extra-parochial, and chartered districts. A world of sub-divisions and sub-sub-divisions often with preposterous and arbitrary distinctions."[4]

In spite of its congested districts it was an open London by present-day standards. Notting Hill and Shepherd's Bush were next door to the country, beautiful and picturesque. It was a country walk to Hammersmith, Acton, and Kensal Green. Chelsea (without embankment) was a suburban village. In central London the contrasts were even more striking. As a contemporary put it: "If you walk along Regent-street, it is a city of gorgeous shops—if you turn into the West, of parks and palaces—if you traverse St. Giles, of gin and dirt,—again, in Belgravia it is rich and grand—in Pimlico it is poor and pretentious—in Russell-square it is well-to-do—in Islington it is plain and pious."[5] The fashionable districts began at Charing Cross and Leicester Square and ran westward to Hyde Park and northward to Regent's Park. The districts eastward of Charing Cross and Leicester Square were all considered unfashionable, and were inhabited chiefly by merchants. In the West End, the line of Waterloo Place and Regent Street formed the handsomest street in London. West of this were Hanover, Berkeley, Grosvenor, Cavendish, and Portman squares, containing the solid homes of the aristocracy. In Pall Mall were the famous clubs, and clubdom was as native to the British culture as any other aspect of London life. Here were the Oxford and Cambridge, the Army and Navy, the Carlton, the Reform, the Travellers', the Athenaeum—with their lordly halls, splendid carpets, roomy armchairs, doors covered with cloth to prevent the noise of their opening and shutting, mahogany furniture, elaborate kitchens out of which appeared superb five-shilling dinners, crowds of servants. All was elegant, substantial, comfortable.

Cheek by jowl with all this were some of the most degraded slums in London, of which we have already seen a good deal. The worst of these were St. Giles's (partially demolished when the extension to Oxford Street was put through in the forties), Clerkenwell (Limehouse was there), Whitechapel, and Westminster. Here were rookeries, like honeycombs, perforated by blind courts and alleys. Rows of crumbling houses, squalid children, haggard men, gutters overflowing with filth. The Statistical Society reported that in Church Lane were twenty-seven buildings, of which twelve were dwellings. The population of those twelve was, in 1847, 463. One of the worst districts was Saffron Hill, north of Holborn Hill, through the east part of which ran Fleet Ditch, an unsavory black stream of fetid water—really a wide, deep, open sewer, causing an intolerable stench in summer. Equally bad, however, was the area near Westminster Abbey, containing the famous Pye Street—as depraved as St. Giles's. Here in 190 houses 700 families of 3,000 persons lived.

The smells of London, with its open sewers, the products of which the Thames regurgitated upon her banks, were not confined to the slums. In 1848 the *Daily News* ran a story with the heading "Stink Traps." It said: "A person with the slightest sense of smell might walk through the streets of London blindfold, and point out the exact locality of these danger-valves of our streets. If not able to detect the nuisance in Regent-street, we would direct their course over Trafalgar-square, and just in front of Northumberland House they will find two most magnificent gullyholes, which have lately never failed to warn our nostrils of the dangers lurking near. . . . Pestilential gases . . . are exhaled from this unclean mouth of the Strand and St. Martin's-lane sewers."

Yet somehow Londoners learned to live with this and to ignore it. Even the depressing dinginess of the wharf-side approach to the City up the crowded Thames impressed them less than the beauty of the seven bridges connecting the north with the Surrey side. Much admired, too, were the elegant station buildings at the railway termini. The Great Western terminus with its regal splendor—its immense mirrors, velvet sofas, bronzes, waiting women in full dress; its windows as large as doors, of one piece of pier glass.

The traffic on the busy London streets awed or terrified all beholders. The main streets were either paved with granite blocks or were macadamized (some few had wooden blocks, on which horses slipped). Up and down these too-narrow thoroughfares clattered the innumerably miscellaneous vehicles which composed London traffic: clumsy but capacious omnibuses, seating twelve persons inside, and as many more on the "knife-board" roof (1,500 of them in London in 1850); hackney coaches (more than 600), each carrying four passengers; cabriolets, licensed to carry two persons; broad-tired wagons of all descriptions, from the good old Saxon wain with as many as six horses, to the brewers' drays, to the hundreds of coal wagons; carts of all imaginable sizes—manure carts, butchers' carts, tradesmen's carts, advertising vans. All these drove, said James Grant, "at as furious a rate as if on an unfrequented turnpike, [so] that you have sometimes to wait a considerable period before you can venture to cross from one side to the other, and then only by making the greatest possible haste."[6] The sounds of all this traffic merged into one continuous pounding roar, which David Masson, when he first came to London in 1843, called "the roar of

Piccadilly, heard from Green Park. Ceaselessly on your ear . . . there comes a roar or boom, as if all the noises of all the wheels of all the carriages in creation were mingled and ground together into one subdued, hoarse, moaning hum. . . . All day, and, I believe, all night, it goes on. . . ."[7] As far as one could look down Fleet Street there was nothing but a dark, confused, quickly moving mass of men, horses, and vehicles. At Pall Mall, opposite Her Majesty's Theatre, 800 carriages passed every hour. On London Bridge the number of vehicles passing every twelve hours was 13,000. On Westminster Bridge the annual traffic was estimated at 8,000,000 horses. Not infrequently the omnibuses, cabs, gigs, carts, drays, and wagons would run into a traffic jam; a fallen horse would stall vehicles for half a mile.

Horses being what they are, and the mud in wet weather and the dust in dry weather (even on paved roads) being notoriously bad, London streets were consistently dirty. The crossing sweeper who swept a path for you from curb to curb was a necessary part of the London scene.

The windows of the shops which lined these streets were crowded with displays, and all the stores went in uniformly for elaborate illumination by means of gas jets. "London shops," said Charles Knight, had "a character of magnificence which has drawn forth expressions of wonder from many a pen."[8] He must have been thinking of the more elegant emporiums in Bond Street and Regent Street, and in New

Figure 135. A new shop in Regent Street

Oxford Street, with their large plate-glass windows and ornate Italianate exteriors. Bakers' shops, butchers' shops, grocers' shops, the latter "redolent of plate-glass and gas-lights. . . . The grocer is no longer content to place a solitary box of raisins, a chest which may or may not contain tea, and a few other articles, in his window. He has his extensive prairie of moist sugar, crossed with rivulets of preserved lemon-peel; his samples of tea are contained in elegant little polished vases, guarded by mandarins in splendid attire; his coffee is exhibited in various states and qualities; he has a highly polished steam-engine in his window, to imply that he sells so much coffee that he must have steam power to grind it."

Chemists' shops, or, as they ought more properly to be called, said Knight, druggists' shops. "Most London walkers will remember the time when the large red, and green, and yellow bottles, shedding a ghastly light on the passers-by, were the chief indications of a Druggist's shop; but now the plate-glass window exhibits a most profuse array of knick-knacks, not only such as pertain to 'doctors' stuff,' but lozenges, perfumery, soda-water, powders, etc." Drapers' shops, and shops where objects made of gutta-percha were sold. The first sample of gutta-percha was sent into England in 1843, discovered by an Englishman in the forests of Singapore. By 1850 the following articles were being made from it: shoe soles, tubes, pumps, covering for wire, picture frames, imitation carved wood, flower vases, lifeboats, sou'wester hats, liquid in bottles for cuts and wounds, stethoscopes, battery cells, speaking trumpets, tiller ropes, etc.

Public houses, taverns, and gin palaces—highly decorated and splendid, with a dazzling array of gas lamps on the outside and even more inside. There were 4,000 licensed public houses in London in 1843.

Most shopmen were taking down their shutters by six o'clock in the morning. As evening came, the gas jets were lighted in one shop after another; none closed until seven or eight o'clock, and some stayed open until ten or eleven.

Beyond these were the busy, noisy, odoriferous markets: Covent Garden for flowers, fruits, and vegetables; Smithfield for cattle, sheep, and pigs; Billingsgate for fish. The latter occupied a nook near the Custom House and was a wholesale market for fish dealers. It opened each morning at five o'clock amid a scene of indescribable noise, confusion, and filth, reeking with water-front smells, brilliantly lighted with streaming flames of gas.

No small share of the London shops was given over to the delights of eating. There were the large and respectable taverns such as the London in Bishopgate Street; the Crown and Anchor in the Strand; the Thatched

House in St. James's Street. The chop or dining houses did an enormous trade, each usually developing a reputation for the excellence of certain dishes—boiled beef, chops, or beefsteaks. Thus Dolly's Chop-house in Paternoster Row; Dr. Johnson's Tavern in Bolt Court; and the Mitre in Fleet Street. The general charge for a bowl (an English pint) of mock-turtle soup was from tenpence to a shilling, including a slice of bread. A plate of roast or boiled beef was sixpence, mutton and pork the same. Porter or ale for a penny, and a pie or pudding for threepence. Cheese, twopence. A substantial dinner, therefore, cost about two shillings in one of the better eating houses.

The growth in the number of coffeehouses in London during the last quarter of a century had been phenomenal. In the early forties there were some 1,800 of them, of all classes, catering to all kinds of people. Many served coffee from one to threepence a cup, and some were open from 4 A.M. to 11 P.M. Few of them sold intoxicating liquors, and all of them took in for their customers the daily and weekly papers—metropolitan and provincial—as well as magazines. More recently, by popular demand, the coffee shops had been compelled to sell cooked meat, or to cook gratis a chop for the man who brought it with him.

If the carriage thoroughfares of London were crowded, the sidewalks must have been more so. In addition to the ordinary pedestrians the throngs were swollen by an incredible number of street hawkers and peddlers. Advertising men paced the streets, frequently in lines, carrying banners or sandwich boards fore and aft, proclaiming the merits of every conceivable article of merchandise. Professional beggars estimated at 35,000 in number wandered about the streets. Thirty thousand men, women, and children were employed in the costermonger trade, selling fruits, vegetables, and fish from little carts. A thousand old-clothes men roamed London; 500 sellers of water-cress; 300 cats'-meat men; 1,000 bone-grabbers and mudlarks; 300 sellers of hot baked potatoes. There were some 300 portable coffee stalls in the streets; 1,000 street museums; and thousands of street performers and showmen—Punch-and-Judy shows, jugglers, acrobats, tumblers, fat boys, and dwarfs; German bands, barrel organists (complete with monkeys), ballad singers, playbill salesmen, tinkers, chair-umbrella-and-clock menders; sellers of stationery, songs, last dying speeches, tubs, pails, crockery, blacking, lucifers, corn salves, brooms, razors, dog collars, dogs, birds, coals. Even the sale of ice cream in the streets was instituted in the summer of 1850. All these street sellers made up, Henry Mayhew estimated, some 30,000 adults. Altogether, about one-fortieth part of the population of London was getting its living in the streets.* Most of them existed in ignorance and want, and many of them in vice. "Of all these street-people," wrote Mayhew, "the coster-mongers form by far the largest and certainly the most broadly marked class. They appear to be a distinct race . . . seldom associating with any other of the street-folks, and being all known to each other." They were nearly all Chartists. Only one tenth of the couples living together and carrying on the costermonger trade were married. Though not many could read, they liked to be read to, and they liked best to listen to Reynolds's periodicals, particularly the "Mysteries of the Court of London."

The self-styled "aristocracy of the street sellers" were the "patterers," or the men who cried the ballads, the "last dying speeches," etc., in the streets. There were two categories of these: "running patterers" and "standing patterers" who required a "pitch" or fixed locality. These last were mainly dealers in nostrums and street "wonders." They stopped at corners with a large pictorial placard raised on a pole, glowing with a highly colored exaggeration of the interesting pamphlets they had for sale: "The Life of Calcraft, the Hangman," "The Diabolical Practices of Dr. ——— on his Patients when in a state of Mesmerism," "The Secret Doings of the White House, Soho," etc.

Sellers of ballads and songs had been a part of the London scene for a long time, but during the forties what were known as "long songs" rose and flourished. "Popular songs! Three yards for a penny!" was the cry. The running patterers usually dealt in murders, seductions, "criminal conversations," explosions, deaths of public characters. Notorious murders were the "great goes." Good fires were next best to murders. Street "ballads on a subject" always concerned a political, criminal, or exciting public event. The gallows literature consisted of "Sorrowful Lamentations," "Last Dying Speech," and "Confession, and Execution" of criminals.

Most of this erudition emanated from Seven Dials, where the leader in the field for many years had been James Catnach. He died in 1841, but the Catnach Press was carried on by his sister in partnership with a James

---

* These figures come from Mayhew's classic work *London Labour and the London Poor*, 2 vols., 1851. This book was an expansion of an investigation which Mayhew had undertaken, with collaborators, for the *London Chronicle* in 1849—an amazingly careful and detailed research into every aspect of the life of the poor in London. It gives infinitely elaborate statistics, case histories, etc., and was recognized at the time to be a sociological document of prime importance. A third volume was added in 1861. The original *Chronicle* articles included the provinces and foreign countries, as well as London. Mayhew did the London part of it; Charles Mackay the country section; and Shirley Brooks the foreign part.

Figures 136–143. London street sellers, from the daguerreotypes by

Figure 136. The street stationer   Figure 137. The street seller of crockery ware

Figure 138. The London coffee stall   Figure 139. The baked-potato man

Figure 140. The London dustman

Figure 141. The London costermonger

Figure 142. Long-song seller

Figure 143. Song illustrations

Paul. John Pitts was Catnach's great rival in the printing of street literature. The sheets of songs were illustrated with crude woodcuts selected without any regard for their fitness to the subject. "The Heart that can feel for another" was illustrated by a savage-looking lion; "The London Oyster Girl" by a portrait of Sir Walter Raleigh; "Bright Hours are in store for us yet" by a tailpiece of an urn on which was inscribed "Finis." The illustration of "The Sun that lights the roses" was an engraving of a worried-looking man ramming a sword down the throat of a wild boar.

"Few of the residents in London, but chiefly those in the quieter streets," wrote Mayhew, "have not been aroused, and most frequently

MURDER OF CAPTAIN LAWSON.

CRUEL AND INHUMAN MURDER,
LAST NIGHT.

Figures 144 and 145. Street "cocks" and ballads

in the evening, by a hurly-burly on each side of the street. An attentive listening will not lead anyone to an accurate knowledge of what the clamour is about. It is from a 'mob' or 'school' of running patterers. . . . It is not possible to ascertain with any certitude what the patterers are so anxious to sell, for only a few leading words are audible, as 'Horrible,' 'Dreadful,' 'Murder,' 'One penny,' 'Love,' 'Mysterious,' 'Seduction,' 'Nine children,' 'Coal-cellar,' 'Pool of blood.' . . ." When there were no "popular murders" the patterers sold "cocks," or fictitious accounts of fearful happenings, such as "Horrible murder and mutilation of Lucy Game, aged fifteen, by her cruel brother, William Game, aged ten, of Westmill, Hertfordshire. His committal and confession, with a copy

COPY OF VERSES ON THE LATE
DREADFUL FIRE
In James Street, Lisson Grove.

PRAY give ear you feeling Christians,
    For a moment pray attend,
List, oh, listen with attention,
    To those lines which here are penned,
Concerning of a dreadful fire,
    As I will unfold to you ;
The which occurred on Saturday Morn.,
    In Great James St., Lisson Grove.

————CHORUS————

The dreadful sight it was bewildering,
    Awful and sad you may suppose,
A Father and his lovely children,
    Burned to death in Lisson Grove.

At 1 o'clock on Saturday morning,
    Oh ! how dreadful to relate,
They also did without warning,
    Meet with their unhappy fate,
They soundly in their beds was sleeping,
    And no power could them save,
Now their friends for them are weeping
    While they sleep in Lisson Grove.

In health and youth they did retire,
    To their beds on Saturday night, .
E're occurred the dreadful fire,
    Which did the neighbourhood affright·
The nurse who did attend the children,
    That night her precious life lost there
And also the tender Father,
    And his three little children dear.

Oh, what may occur to-morrow,
    None of us on earth can tell,
There may be much pain and sorrow,
    In the home wherein we dwell ;
God above is all sufficient,
    For to keep us from alarms,
He is willing to protect us,
    Guide & guard us from all harm.

That fatal night when they retired,
    And their tender eyelids closed,
The house e're morning would be fired,
    While they did sleep in sweet repose ;
They for a moment had no morning,
    They did not dream of sad alarms,
They did not think before the warning,
    They would sleep in deaths' cold arms

Oh ! God receive their souls in glory,
    There to dwell for ever more ;
This distressing dreadful story,
    Causes many to deplore.
Six poor souls from hence was hurried,
    Their earthly days was at an end,
Their bodies in the earth lie buried,
    And their spirits up to Heaven ascend

London :—Printed and Published by H. SUCH,
    123, Union Street, Borough.
    Where all the new Songs may be
    had as soon as Published

Figure 145.

Figure 146. A "life, trial, and execution" broadside

of a letter sent to his affectionate parents." Or "Full particulars of the poisonings in Essex—the whole family poisoned by the female servant. Confession of her guilt—Was seduced by her master—Revenged herself on the family."

The London streets may have been ugly and crowded, but they could never have been boring.

And so the sun rose and set each day, this spring of 1850, on a conglomerate London, overgrown, underorganized, dirty, crowded, monotonously ugly, and massively dull in suburbia—but also busy, alive, and beneath its soot, and in spite of some of its misbegotten contemporary architecture, full of the charm of past centuries, with quiet squares and green parks and, within a few minutes' ride, country vistas. Royalty lived at its center; from Westminster, Government laid down the policies which ruled the little island and its growing network of empire; the threads of world commerce and banking were knit in the City; literature, art, and entertainment found their publics within easy reach. It was metropolis in the biggest nineteenth-century sense.

And so Mr. Richard Roe, being a London businessman of the upper-middle classes, breakfasted at nine, read his morning newspaper and his mail, and then started for his office in the City. He lunched at midday. By four or five o'clock he was home in Kensington again, dining with his family around him. At seven the maid served tea. Supper at ten—after the children were in bed—a meal not unlike dinner, with cold cuts instead of a hot joint. This was the routine, broken in August by the yearly mark of gentility: a trip to the seaside. In the evenings in London supper was delayed until a later hour if the Roes were out at some entertainment. There were multiple kinds of entertainment which the Roes could find at hand in this year of grace.

There were theaters for every taste, seventeen of them. Well, almost every taste. Many respectable citizens stayed away from them altogether, and many dissenting sects looked upon the theater in any guise as a den of iniquity. Others, who had no moral scruples against the theater as an institution, found the contemporary stage so banal that they avoided it merely for that reason. Certainly English drama in the forties had reached a nadir. Nothing is more common in the periodical literature of the time than articles on the "decline of the stage." Each critic had his own answer, and probably all of them were right: there were no new English dramas of the highest class; there were few good actors or actresses; the star system had ruined the stage; Italian opera, patronized

Figure 147. Haymarket Theatre

Figure 148. Covent Garden Theatre

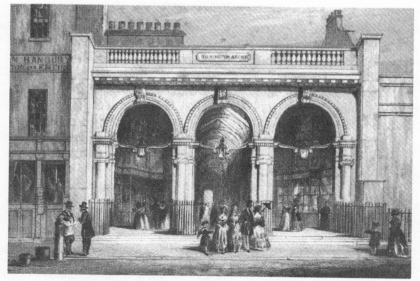

Figure 149. Burlington Arcade

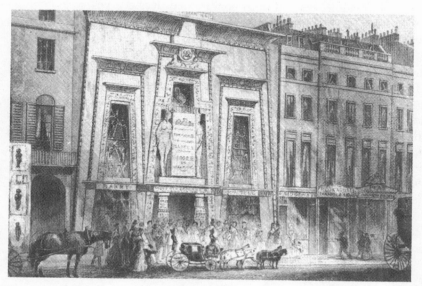

Figure 150. Egyptian Hall, with Tom Thumb's carriage

by the Queen, had smothered legitimate drama; people preferred spectacle to drama; prices were too high; the theaters were dirty and uncomfortable and were frequented by prostitutes; evening concerts, private
music parties at home, and the influx of cheap books and periodicals had
drained off the audiences; even the cigar shops and the prodigious increase of smokers were to blame! No one argued that the theater was
in anything but a bad way.

What was the actual situation in 1850? Except for sporadic productions of Shakespeare by Macready at the Haymarket, Samuel Phelps at
Sadler's Wells, and Charles Kean at the Princess' (where he had taken
over the management just this year and had launched his "archaeological"
revivals) the only legitimate drama of stature consisted also of revivals
of earlier plays: Moore's *Gamester*, Webster's *Duchess of Malfi*, Home's
Douglas, and some of Bulwer Lytton's better pieces such as *The Lady
of Lyons* and *Richelieu*. Otherwise the stage was absorbed by weak
dramatizations of Scott's and Dickens's novels, by some sterile "original"
romantic comedies, by scores of comedies rifled from the French, and
above all by melodrama and farce and extravaganza. Mme. Vestris and
Charles Mathews at the Lyceum were making an honest effort to restore
dignity and taste to the English stage, but were fighting a losing financial
battle.

Certainly audiences had been conditioned over the years to the presentation of farce and spectacle. As we have seen, up to 1843 only the
two patent theaters, Drury Lane and Covent Garden, could legally
present legitimate drama. If the minor theaters wanted to play serious
drama, Shakespeare, for example, they had to smuggle it under the guise
of a "burletta," which meant a doggerel rewriting of the lines and the
addition of a musical accompaniment larded with trombone solos and
acrobatic feats. By the 1840's the situation had become so absurd and
the evasions so open that the abrogation of the patent monopoly was
little more than a recognition of an existing situation. Still the native
drama languished; a depraved taste for "burlettas" had been formed.
Drury Lane and Covent Garden were so huge (each had seats for more
than 3,000) that the importance of the play itself, however much the
actor might rant, was minimized. More attention was given to spectacular
scenic effects than to the plays. Moreover, the rents were so high that
no manager could make the houses pay.

The result was that during the forties the larger houses were given
over to Italian opera, which was the current craze—"the morbid love of
the aristocracy," wrote one critic, "for everything foreign." During the
season of 1850 rival opera companies were competing at Covent Garden

Figure 151. Drury Lane Theatre: wrestling scene in *As You Like It*

Figure 152. Astley's Amphitheatre

and Her Majesty's Theatre—to say nothing of a company presenting French opera at the St. James's. The theatrical triumphs of these years for the audiences which jammed Covent Garden and filled the four tiers of boxes at Her Majesty's were Sontag, Grisi, Alboni, Mario, and Tamburini; in operas by Weber, Meyerbeer, Rossini, and Verdi; with Carlotta Grisi, Cerito, and Taglioni dancing the ballets. New operas by Auber, Halévy, and Gluck were also produced in 1850, and Sontag received an ovation as Miranda in *La Tempesta* (based on Shakespeare's *Tempest*) with a libretto by Scribe done into Italian from the French, and a score by Halévy!

The smaller theaters were left to their farces, melodramas, and extravaganzas, with an occasional interpolation of a more pretentious piece such as George Henry Lewes's *Noble Heart*, a Byronic play filled with much talk and little action, which was nevertheless produced "with triumphant success" at the Olympic. Buckstone, the leading comic actor of the time, was writing farces in 1850 (*Leap-Year*); young Tom Taylor was dramatizing the *Vicar of Wakefield*, and young Dion Boucicault producing his comedy *The Irish Diamond*. Douglas Jerrold kept turning out hack pieces full of wit but with little characterization or action; and Mark Lemon presented at the Adelphi his farce *The School for Tigers*.

Always there were the melodramas, such as *Jessie Gray* at the Adelphi, *Frankenstein* and *The Mendicant Son* at the Marylebone, and *Alvarez; or, The Heart-Wreck* at the Strand. The latter was by Francis Talfourd and involved a wronged husband and a heartless seducer who pursued his career, as one reviewer put it, "with an indomitable energy seldom witnessed even on the stage." It would be difficult to find a theatrical literature more dismally bad than the buffoonery which passed for farce in these Victorian years, the dreary tragedies imitating outworn Elizabethan models, or the grotesqueries of melodrama. The theater had lost touch with life, and was panting out a debased dramatic existence for the sake of audiences which knew no better. The real literary talent of the time was being poured into other channels. Not only were the rewards greater for fiction writing, but the novelist could claim a social respectability denied the playwright. When a Browning or a Tennyson did turn to the theater, it was as an avocation, and his accomplishment was derivative and lifeless. It is worth noting, however, that the young man who was to lead the way toward a regeneration in the theater produced his first play in 1851. Tom Robertson's *A Night's Adventure* was withdrawn after four performances.

If anything, the provinces were in a worse way than London, starving as they were on third-rate plays performed by inferior actors. Nevertheless, every sizable town had its theater or theaters—Birmingham, Liverpool, Manchester, Bristol, Newcastle, Portsmouth, Plymouth—and occasionally a Macready or a Phelps or the Keans would tour the provinces and bring them a spark of theatrical life.

There were good reasons why many a respectable Victorian stayed away from the theatre. Prostitutes used the lounges and saloons of the theatres as places for making assignations openly. "What avails it," wrote one angry correspondent to the *Theatrical Times*, "that a father takes his son to listen to the moral sentiments of a Shakespeare if the youth's eyes are to be diverted from the stage by the meretricious deportment of shameless impudence? Besides [he continues somewhat anticlimactically] the trampling to and fro distract the attention, and oftentime render what is spoken on the stage inaudible."

In 1841 the writer of "Theatrical Intelligence" for the *Daily Dispatch* condemned, at Drury Lane, "as against public morality . . . the *Tableaux Vivans*, or living statues, as they are somewhat absurdly called, which have night after night been allowed to pollute those boards once trodden by a Garrick and a Kemble. Where, we ask, in the name of common decency are these things to end? Are we to calmly suffer our mothers or our sisters to sit and witness human figures—but one remove from a state of nudity—standing in positions which, if represented by the artist's skill, would justly call down a prosecution from the Society for the Suppression of Vice? Are French *filles de joies*—our English phrase, though more expressive, is less decorous—to exhibit themselves in a manner equally repulsive and disgusting to the gaze of a British public? . . ." One of Macready's crusades during his managership of Drury Lane in 1842 was a strenuous moral attempt to clean up the grosser aspects of theatre life by banishing the parade of prostitutes and making the saloon "a fit resort for any gentleman or lady."

Another ground for complaint was the length of the performance; triple or quadruple features were the norm. Performances began about seven o'clock and often ran for five or six hours. Tragedy, comedy, farce, melodrama, and spectacle were all huddled together, not merely on subsequent nights, but on the same evening. Thus a typical program at the Adelphi would be first a dramatization of Dickens's *Christmas Carol*, followed by the burletta *Antony and Cleopatra Married and Settled*, followed by a "new romantic drama in two acts (founded on the French)," *Ulrica; or, The Prisoner of State*, and concluding with *Richard the Third:* "in which all the sanguinary acts of that Tyrant's

Life are compressed into One cruelly startling *Act*." The price for all this: boxes, 4s; pit, 2s; gallery, 1s. When Phelps presented Browning's *Blot in the 'Scutcheon* at Drury Lane in 1843 the play was followed first by a farce called *The Thumping Legacy*, and finally by Weber's opera *Der Freischutz* complete!

It may be that the enjoyment of the theater as a social institution in these days reached its height in the so-called "people's theatres," such as the Surrey and the Victoria (the "Vic"). The latter had the largest gallery in London, and into it would crowd (at threepence a head) costermongers and laborers—men, women, children, and babes in arms— to watch the goriest melodramas and the most outrageous farces. The atmosphere was stifling and sweaty, the noise uproarious. The audience would hurl advice at the actors on the stage and would punctuate the play by shouted comments on the action. All waited for the grand climax of the evening, when they would join loudly in songs led by a very resourceful actor.

One of the most notable acting careers of the century drew toward a close in 1850. Macready had begun his extended series of farewell per- formances the previous year and was continuing them now at the Hay- market, filling the theater with his performances as Macbeth, Hamlet, Shylock, Lear, Richelieu, and Virginius. He was a strenuous, thoughtful, high-minded man, irritable and inordinately vain and self-torturing but possessing great integrity both as man and actor. As actor and manager he had worked to restore the drama as an art, lamenting always the current decay of cultivated patronage and the progress of foreign inno- vation. Estimates of his acting differed. He was primarily an "intel- lectual" actor, with a cultivated intelligence. Apparently his creative powers were not great, but his portrayals were bold and animated. Searching for realism in his reading of lines, he seemed abrupt and jerky to a generation of theatergoers brought up on the rotund oratory of an older school. Fanny Kemble had a cordial esteem for Macready as a man, but did not have a very high opinion of his merits as an actor. "He growls and prowls," she wrote, "and roams and foams, about the stage, in every direction, like a tiger in his cage, so that I never know on what side of me he means to be." She played opposite him in *Macbeth* and *Othello*, and *Hamlet* in 1848, and lived in constant dread of his stage violence. In *Macbeth*, she said, he pinched her black and blue, and crushed a finger which she had injured earlier. "And as for that smothering in bed, 'Heaven have mercy upon me!' as poor Desdemona says."

Macready's last regular performance was in *Lear* early in 1851, with Victoria and Albert in the royal box. When he came forward to give his

Figure 153. Macready delivering his farewell address

farewell speech at the end, he was greeted with such tumult and enthusiasm that he could scarcely continue. On February 26th he played *Macbeth* for his own benefit, realizing £906. Thus he retired in a great odor of dramatic sanctity and acclaim. Six hundred one-guinea tickets were sold for his farewell dinner on March 1st. Sir Edward Bulwer Lytton presided, and Forster read a sonnet written by Tennyson for the occasion. Macready inserted all the speeches (including the punctuations of "loud cheers") in his diary.

For those who wanted to combine cigars and drinks with an entertainment sufficiently low to shock the "respectable" there were a number of "supper clubs" in London. The music halls or variety shows, as they were to be enjoyed in later years, were just coming into being at the turn of the half-century.* Their unexpurgated equivalents in the 1840's were The Coal Hole, in a court off the Strand; The Cider Cellars, next to the stage door of the Adelphi in Maiden Lane; and Evans's, at the western corner of the Covent Garden Piazza. The Coal Hole was probably Thackeray's Cave of Harmony, where Colonel Newcome took Clive and was outraged by the songs. Here, it was said, a young fellow called Cave was the first to introduce to England the American banjo as an accompaniment for the voice. The Cider Cellars was the prototype of

---

* The first music hall proper was the Canterbury Arms Saloon, opposite the Houses of Parliament, on the Surrey side. It opened in 1848.

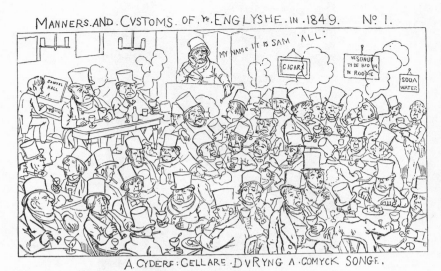

A·CYDERE·CELLARE·DVRYNG·A·COMYCK·SONGE.

Figure 154. The Cider Cellars, by Doyle

the Back Kitchen of *Pendennis*. Here, to a crowd of men enjoying oysters, welsh rabbits, cigars, brandy, and stout, a man named Ross sang ribald songs—notably the ballad "Sam Hall," which was for a whole season the talk of the town. David Masson remembered seeing him, sitting in a kind of raised box or pulpit in one corner of the room—"a strange, gruesome figure, in ragged clothes, with a battered old hat on his head, his face stained and grimed to represent a chimney-sweep's and a piece of short black pipe in his mouth. Removing his pipe, and looking round with a dull, brutal scowl or glare, he begins his slow chaunt of the condemned felon, whose last night in prison has come, and who is to be hanged the next morning":

> My name it is Sam Hall, I'm a thief!
> My name it is Sam Hall, I'm a thief!
> My name it is Sam Hall,
> And I've robbed both great and small
> And my greeting is to all,
> Damn your eyes!
>
> They've shut me up in quod, up in quod,
> They've shut me up in quod, up in quod,
> They've shut me up in quod
> For killing of a sod
> They have, so help me God,
> Damn their eyes!
>
> The parson he will come, he will come,
> The parson he will come, he will come,

The parson he will come,
And he'll look so bloody glum,
And he'll talk of Kingdom Come—
Damn his eyes!

The sheriff he'll come too, he'll come too,
The sheriff he'll come too, he'll come too,
    The sheriff he'll come too,
    With all his ghastly crew,
    Their bloody work to do,
Damn their eyes!

Then as up the drop I go, up I go,
Then as up the drop I go, up I go,
    Then as up the drop I go,
    The swine down there below
    Will say, "we told you so!"
Damn their eyes!

And now I'm going to hell, going to hell!
And now I'm going to hell, going to hell!
    And now I'm going to hell,
    But what a bloody sell
    If you all go there as well!
Damn your eyes!

Punch reported the performance in its "Mr. Pips his Diary": "Ross . . . did sit upon the platform leaning over the back of a chair, so making believe that he was on his way to Tyburn. . . . Strange to think what a hit this song of Sam Hall hath made, and how it has taken the town, and how popular it is, not only among tavern haunters and frequenters of the night houses, but also with the gentry and aristocracy, who do vote it a thing to be heard, although a blackguard!"

The best known of all these places was Evans's, presided over by a "Paddy" Green. It was here that the old German, Herr von Joel, used to imitate pigs and barnyard fowl; and here the famous comic singer Sam Cowell sang his inimitable burlesque of *Hamlet*.

All this was vulgar, sometimes bawdy, eminently reprehensible by later Victorian standards. But all the gustiness had not yet gone out of life, and these supper saloons were attended by prominent men who, a generation later, would have shunned them. Thackeray used to be there, and Horace Mayhew, Leech and Jerrold, Albert Smith and Augustus Sala. They were the night clubs of the forties.

More notorious in the half-world of London sporting society of boxing, gambling, drinking, and wenching was a strange figure called "Baron" Renton Nicholson. For some time he edited a scandalous sheet

called *The Town,* and in 1841 he launched his "Judge and Jury Society" at the Garrick's Head Tavern in Bow Street. Imprisoned for debt
after a few years, he emerged later on to reactivate his Society in 1851
at The Coal Hole. In his autobiography Nicholson boasted that "members of both Houses of Parliament, statesmen, poets, actors of high
repute . . . have visited the Judge and Jury Society. It has been no uncommon occurrence to see the jury composed of noble lords and
M.P.'s."[9] The entertainment was a parody of the law courts and was
presided over ·by Nicholson himself as the Lord Chief Justice, in full
wig and gown—assisted by actors as leading barristers and witnesses. The
cases had all to do with rape or divorce ("crim. con.") and Edmund
Yates described the entertainment as "clever, but so full of grossness and
indecency, expressed and implied, as to render it wholly disgusting."[10]

This was for the man about town of 1850—pretty clearly not for
Mr. Roe and certainly not for his family. Was there nothing instructive
as well as amusing in London, to which a man *might* take his wife and
daughters? A great deal.

The perennial Vauxhall Gardens were still a fairyland for the respectable, who patronized it on fine summer evenings to walk its groves,
look at the fake-bearded hermit in his "property" cave, admire the fireworks and illuminations, listen to the two bands, observe the jugglers,
acrobats, and balloon ascensions, and partake of the expensive transparent ham and the oleaginous salad; and perhaps to watch an acrobat calling
himself Joel il Diavolo make an astounding descent from the top of the
Campanile, riding down a wire surrounded by blazing fireworks. Cremorne Gardens were even more popular with the youth of the period
as being cheaper and livelier; they also had fireworks and balloon ascensions, secluded grottoes and bowers, statues and fountains—and in addition a large circular dancing platform.

Those who liked natural history could visit the Zoological Gardens
in Regent's Park and see, among other exotic beasts, the pair of hippo-
potami presented by His Highness the late Pasha of Egypt. And at the
Surrey Zoological Gardens in Newington one could see in summer (in
addition to the animals) such exciting exhibitions as the "Storming of
Bajodos," the "Capture of Chinese War Junks," and the "Eruption of
Etna and Vesuvius."

For those interested in the wonders of science there was the Polytechnic Institution in Regent Street, with its famous diving bell and
diver, its working models of steam engines, its oxyhydrogen microscope,
dissolving views, galvanic batteries and electrical apparatus, photogenic
drawing, and optical illusions. Lectures on the arts and sciences were

Figure 155. Cross section of Wyld's model of the globe

given at regular intervals during the day. The Egyptian Saloon in the British Museum drew many visitors; new gigantic sculptures from Nineveh were arriving steadily. In 1851 Mr. Wyld erected in the spaces of Leicester Square his huge model of the globe, "one of the most pleasingly instructive sights in the metropolis" according to the guidebooks. Its dome was sixty-five feet in diameter, and the interior was covered with a relief map of the world on the scale of ten miles to the inch, showing the hills and valleys, mountains and volcanoes, land and water, all "appropriately coloured." Visitors (appropriately lectured at) gazed upon this wonder from four galleries reached by a winding staircase. Always, of course, there was Madame Tussaud's (with the figures of Mr. and Mrs. Manning added this year). And Astley's Royal Amphitheatre, "patronized by Her Most Gracious Majesty the Queen, Prince Albert, and Royal Family," with brilliant feats of horsemanship, bottle equilibrists, pantomimes, ropedancers, and weight lifters. Currently exhibited there was "the unabated career of Lord Byron's Poem of *Mazeppa* and the *Wild Horse*."

Most popular of all the entertainments, if one can judge by their number, were the cycloramas, panoramas, cosmoramas, and dioramas. These were vast areas of canvas covered either opaquely or translucently with such scenes as the Lisbon earthquake, at the Colosseum (the building mentioned earlier, with its conservatories, waterfalls, aviaries, Swiss cottages, and grottoes), where the visitor was elevated in the "rising room" to a level with the summit of the panorama. The earthquake was accompanied by a crescendo performance on the Apollonicon (a great organ with 1,900 pipes). "The manner in which the earth heaved and was rent," wrote Yates, "the buildings toppled over, and the sea rose,

Figure 156. The Gothic Aviary at the Colosseum

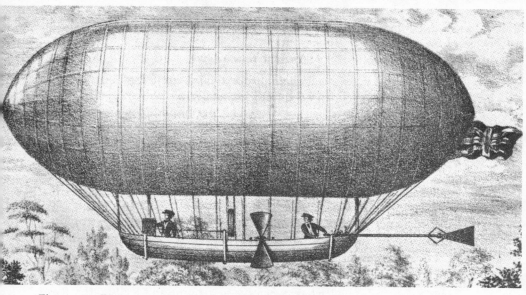

Figure 157. Bell's patent "locomotive" balloon
British Crown Copyright. Science Museum, London.

was most cleverly contrived, and had a most terrifying effect upon the spectators; frightful rumblings, proceeding apparently from under your feet, increased the horror." In 1848 the Colosseum had exhibited more quietly a panorama of "Paris by Moonlight." As reported by the *Literary Gazette*, "the effects of direct and reflected light are so extraordinary that no description can convey an idea of them. The public buildings, the palaces, the streets stretching into the country, the gardens, bridges, and *Places*, the quais, and the houses, all lit with lamps or other flames; and the moonlight shed on the river, fountains, and atmosphere are wonderfully managed. Every pane is as clearly illuminated as in the reality . . . absolutely marvellous." At the diorama in Regent's Park spectators sat in a revolving theater which brought into view two scenes in perspective, each 80 feet by 40 feet, painted both in transparency and in solid color. The lighting effects were particularly admired.

There were many other panoramic exhibitions. Some were painted on vast rolls of canvas which unfolded before the spectator's eyes while a lecturer expatiated on the beauties of the scenes represented. The Easter Exhibitions in 1850 included the "Overland Route to India" at the Gallery of Illustration ("sublime and picturesque scenery, beautiful aerial effects, richness of colour"); a "Panorama of the Nile" at Egyptian Hall, as well as Banvard's "Panorama of the Ohio" (on canvas 1,200 yards in length); and Burford's "Panorama of the Arctic Expedition." A little later Albert Smith was to thrill and amuse large audiences with his "Ascent of Mont Blanc."

Modern science as well as art had extended itself for the edification and delight of the Englishman and his family in the forties. One wondered how much further such incredible accomplishments could go. A hint of the future was given, perhaps, in the ascent this summer, from Vauxhall, of Mr. H. Bell in his patent aerial machine—a fifty-foot-long cylindrical balloon with conical ends, with a car beneath it in the shape of a boat, the whole driven through the air, and its flight controlled, by hand-operated screw propellers. No one looked on it as much more than a stunt.*

All through the year plans for the Great Exhibition of 1851 were progressing steadily. In January a "Royal Commission for the Promotion of the Exhibition of the Works of Industry of All Nations" had been appointed, under the leadership of Prince Albert. Very soon the selection of a site in Hyde Park between the Serpentine and Kensington Road stirred up a bitter if short controversy. Aristocratic gentlemen whose windows looked upon the park shivered at the prospect, said the *Athenaeum*, "that the people should come into the people's park for the people's own great occasion." Colonel Sibthorp set himself sternly against the whole proposal. In the course of a debate in the Commons he prayed that some hailstorm or visitation of lightning might descend to defeat the ill-advised project. He warned the people to beware of thieves, pickpockets, and whoremongers when the foreigners came. "Take care," he said, "of your wives and daughters; take care of your lives and property." But the Commission went bravely on with its plans.

In July the *Daily News* announced that after long deliberation the plans of Joseph Paxton, well-known gardener to the Duke of Devonshire, had been selected for the building. Mr. Paxton had already built successfully a great glass conservatory at Chatsworth. The framework was to be of iron, with glass panels. Modern improvements in glassmaking had made it possible to roll four-foot sheets of plate glass at a reasonable cost. The building was to contain, on the main floor alone, seven miles of tables and was to be 1,848 feet long. It was suggested that this be extended to 1,851 feet, and everyone saw the symbolic fitness of the proposal.

---

* Someone published this year a burlesque issue of the *Times* "as it may be in 1950," and had great sport advertising "rapid aerial flights," regularly scheduled from Trafalgar Square to India and China. Another mock advertisement ran: "*Singular Curiosity*. To be seen alive, at 229, New Regent Street, a remarkably fine specimen of that noble animal, the Horse . . . supposed to be the last of that species which formerly drew the cabs, broughams, etc., of the metropolis." Again: "*The Tunnel through the Alps*. The largest train ever remembered . . . passed through this tunnel yesterday morning, conveying pleasure parties from France to Italy." What fun to imagine the incredible as happening a century hence!

Figure 158. The Crystal Palace in its early stages of construction

In March Lord Mayor Farncombe gave a banquet in London to Prince Albert and the mayors of most of the boroughs of the United Kingdom, in order to further the project. Later in the year the Lord Mayor of York, together with the municipalities of the United Kingdom, reciprocated, and Albert attended a magnificent festival which was declared a landmark in civic history. Soyer planned and prepared the dinner and decorated the Guildhall with huge ornamental designs. A large emblematic vase twenty feet high showed Britannia receiving specimens of industry from Europe, Asia, Africa, and America. The bill of fare for the dinner read like a banquet for the gods rather than for mortal mayors. For the royal table Soyer created his "hundred-guinea dish," replete with turtles' heads, woodcocks, the choice portions of 100 snipe, and six dozen larks.

By November the structural iron for what was beginning to be called the Crystal Palace was taking shape. There was general praise for Prince Albert's leadership and imagination in conceiving and fostering the project. Almost imperceptibly, over the years, the public attitude toward Albert was mellowing. There was still opposition to him, but his early stiffness and eccentricity (to English eyes) were beginning to be forgotten. His quiet, hard work, his sponsoring of science and the arts, his faithful performance of the monotonous public duties that hedged a consort were beginning to be recognized. He was being made over, it seemed, in the Victorian image. This year the *Spectator* praised him as "not only a gentleman who adorns his station with singular propriety and good taste, but also one who lends to royalty the most tangible functions of utility. In Prince Albert the public recognizes not only a decorous but a useful servant." "God bless my dearest Albert, God bless my dearest country," wrote Victoria in her diary.

On January 1st appeared the initial number of a new magazine called *The Germ: Thoughts toward Nature in Poetry, Literature and Art* containing among other things poems by Christina Rossetti and poems and articles by Dante Gabriel Rossetti and William Michael Rossetti. It was the first public indication that the principles of the Pre-Raphaelite Brotherhood embraced literature as well as art. In the second issue, a month later, Rossetti's poem "The Blessed Damozel" was printed. But the magazine withered for lack of support, and disappeared after the fourth number. Gradually, however, people were coming to recognize the significance of the initials PRB, and when the critics realized that they were confronted not merely with a group of eccentric artists,

Figure 159. John Everett Millais: "Christ in the House of His Parents"

but with artists who were eccentric according to defined and heterodox principles, their fury descended. When the spring exhibition of the Royal Academy arrived, and Rossetti, Hunt, and Millais all showed pictures, the *Times*, the *Examiner*, and the *Daily News* were definitely hostile. Their bitterness seemed to be most virulent against Millais, whose "Christ in the House of His Parents" was abusively condemned. The critic for the *Athenaeum* was perhaps the most savage of all. He wrote:

> This school of English youths has, it may be granted, ambition—but not of that well-regulated order which, measuring the object to be attained by the resources possessed, qualifies itself for achievement. Their ambition is an unhealthy thirst, which seeks *notoriety* by means of mere conceit. Abruptness, singularity, uncouthness are the counters with which they play for fame. Their trick is to defy the principles of beauty and the recognized axioms of taste. . . . What a wilful misapplication of powers is that which affects to treat the human form in the primitive and artless manner of the Middle Ages, while minor accessories are elaborated to a refinement of imitation which belongs to the latest days of executive art! . . . Mr. Millais, in his picture without a name which represents a Holy Family in the interior of the carpenter's shop, has been most successful in the least dignified features of his presentment,—and in giving to the higher forms, characters and meanings a circumstantial Art-language from which we recoil with loathing and disgust. There are many to whom his work will seem a pictorial blasphemy.

Household Words called the female figure "so horrible in her ugliness that she would stand out from the rest of the company as a monster in the vilest cabaret in France."

This would have seemed enough to trim the wings of youthful exuberance and idealism. At this juncture the critics, enraged by the Brotherhood's contemptuous rejection of academism and by what seemed a mystical devotion to medievalism, did not observe how, in many ways, the Pre-Raphaelites really were of their time. Like the stuffiest of the R.A.'s, they dredged history, legend, and literature for their themes—"The Scapegoat," "Paolo and Francesca," "King Arthur and the Weeping Queens," "The Wedding of St. George and the Princess Sabra," "Dante's Vision of Rachel and Leah," "Lorenzo and Isabella," "Ophelia." Their pictures told stories, taught morals (in a somewhat agitated fashion). Even their passion for precise and elaborate details was the sort of thing which the Victorians admired. Yet their hard, brilliant, primary colors were at variance with the contemporary fashion; and above all, the critics were offended by what seemed their affected simplicity and their cramped style. The Pre-Raphaelites needed a champion to give an aesthetic sanction to their artistic belief and to declare its *rationale*. In the next year, 1851, he appeared—in the shape of John Ruskin.

During the May Exhibition of that year the *Times* had returned to the attack in a long, ranting critique. "That morbid infatuation," it said, "which sacrifices truth, beauty, and genuine feeling to mere eccentricity, deserves no quarter at the hands of the public."* On May 13th and 30th the *Times* published two letters from Ruskin in explanation and defense of the new art. Ruskin disclaimed acquaintance with any of the artists, and his comments were not unqualified praise. He did acquit them, however, of the charge of "false perspective," and praised their "marvellous truth in detail and splendour in colour." And as far as their antiquarianism went: "They intend to return to early days in this one point only—that, as far as in them lies, they will draw either what they see, or what they suppose might have been the actual facts of the scene they desire to represent, irrespective of any conventional rules of picture-making; and they have chosen their unfortunate though not inaccurate name because all artists did this before Raphael's time, and after Raphael's time did *not* this, but sought to paint fair pictures, rather than represent stern facts. . . ."

---

* The Pre-Raphaelite pictures exhibited in the Academy of 1851 were: Millais's "Mariana, The Return of the Dove to the Ark," and "The Woodman's Daughter"; Holman Hunt's "Valentine Rescuing Sylvia from Proteus"; and Collins's "Convent Thoughts."

Later in the year Ruskin published his pamphlet *Pre-Raphaelitism*, in which he returned to the defense. Help like this from the best-known art critic of his time, at such a moment, was a tremendous encouragement to the struggling young painters.

The House of Commons in the new Palace of Parliament was completed this year. There was some difficulty about acoustics, which necessitated changes. The Victoria Tower was growing steadily. . . . The Sabbatarians rather unexpectedly carried in the House of Commons an order abolishing the Sunday delivery of mail, but so great was the protest over the resultant inconveniences that the order was unostentatiously withdrawn. . . . The great Koh-i-noor diamond, now Her Majesty's by gift of the East India Co., through right of conquest, arrived from Delhi under heavy guard. . . . Jenny Lind, who had retired from the stage, left from Liverpool for a concert tour in the United States under the management of P. T. Barnum. She was to receive £200 for each of the 150 performances. Her visit in Liverpool preliminary to sailing became a sort of royal progress. Upon her arrival in America 50,000 idolatrous enthusiasts lined the piers. The first ticket for her first concert in Boston sold at auction for $625. Miss Lind was pleased but somewhat unnerved by her reception. Her first rehearsal was interrupted by the slow booming of a hundred-gun salute at the Battery in celebration of California's entry into the Union. . . . Mr. Green made a balloon ascension riding a horse suspended from the cordage, this is spite of the protests from the S.P.C.A. . . . A John Peters was convicted for stealing a duck from Kensington Gardens and was sentenced to three months' imprisonment. . . . August came, and Parliament was prorogued in time for the hunting season. The grouse, it was reported, were numerous, and in exceedingly good condition. . . . The annual complaints (reassuring to British manhood) came from Brighton about the indecent curiosity of men concerning women sea bathers.

The first issue of Charles Dickens's new journal *Household Words* had appeared in March. It proved to be essentially another miscellany of serial novels, poetry, and essays on such subjects as knight-errantry, piracy, and heathen customs of burial. Some important books were published: Browning's *Christmas-Eve and Easter-Day* was received with the usual tempered praise which approved the poet's originality and condemned his obscurity. Bayard Taylor's *Eldorado; or, Adventures in the Path of Empire* was appreciated as the best and liveliest of the scores of books concerning California. Mudie's advertised an increase of 12,000 volumes per year to their library: 25 to 250 copies each of the best current books. Being added at the moment were 50 copies of *In Memoriam*, 50 of Albert Smith's *Constantinople*, 50 of the *Life of Southey* by his son, and additional copies of Ruskin's *Modern Painters* and Macaulay's *England*.

In August the anonymous novel *Alton Locke* created a great impression. Some reviews devoted pages to praising its powerful and exciting qualities, its vivid scenes and characters. Others, such as the *Edinburgh Review*, condemned it severely. *Blackwood's* denounced it as "a bare-faced and impudent assumption of a specific profession by a person who knows no more about tailoring or 'slop-selling' than he has learnt from certain letters in the *Morning Chronicle*," but devoted thirty-six columns to its discussion. The conservatives in general looked upon the doctrines of Christian Socialism as inflammatory and subversive. Kingsley used the career of his hero—a tailor, Chartist (reformed at last), and people's poet—to give a realistic picture of the mistakes and errors of workingmen, but chiefly to call attention to their sufferings. He wanted to arouse the attention of a class of readers wider than that which saw the Parliamentary Blue Books and official reports. *Alton Locke* was Christian Socialism fictionized.

The crusade for social betterment on the part of the group which now included Maurice, Laidlow, Kingsley, and Thomas Hughes had not been spectacularly successful. Somehow the workingman himself had reservations about clerical efforts to improve his moral and social status. The journal *Politics for the People*, begun in 1848, had died an early death. The *Tracts for Christian Socialists* and the magazine *The Christian Socialist*, both of 1850, did not do much better. Kingsley's most famous diatribe against the abuses of the tailoring trade, *Cheap Clothes and Nasty* ("by Parson Lot"), was published as a separate pamphlet in January. It was written at white heat. Kingsley's indignation had been aroused by the contrast between the luxurious plate-glass shops in Regent Street and the verminous attics in which sweated labor made clothes (sometimes plague-infected clothes) for those shops.

Out of this activity grew the Working Tailors' Association in 1850, an attempt at co-operative production more strictly Owenite in its principles than was the Rochdale system. An Association advertisement ran:

> A few Journeyman Tailors, anxious to rescue themselves and their class from the miseries and degradation consequent on unlimited competition, and from the abuse of the powers of capital . . . have resolved

Figure 160. Cardinal Wiseman

to seek a remedy in their own exertions, rather than in any Parliamentary enactment. . . . They have, therefore, united together on the Co-operative principle. . . . They are mutually bound to devote one-third of their net profits to the extension of their numbers.[11]

This was the first of some dozen similar associations: builder's, printers', bakers', pianoforte makers', needlewoman's, etc. None of them survived long. The Christian Socialist movement as a whole was treated contemptuously by large sections of both Church and laity, and at best seemed a quixotic attempt to lift the workman by his own bootstraps. But it helped to secure the enactment of a bill in 1852 which removed the disabilities of co-operatives and made possible their future growth. Even more importantly it was the symptom of an aroused social conscience more widely spread, without which the starving worker would have continued to suffer in anguished poverty.

The great religious excitement of 1850, however, was on a less idealistic level, and involved ancient prejudices.

Late in October the Pope announced that he was establishing a Roman Catholic hierarchy in England, with Dr. Wiseman as Archbishop of Westminister. The whole of England and Wales was to be made into an archiepiscopal province of the Church, divided into thirteen bishoprics. The tempest which ensued engulfed all England and was incredibly fierce. Reactions ranged from that of the *Times*, which was contemptuous if resentful, to a shrillness of alarm and execration which issued from all classes, from statesman to street ragamuffin. At the very least the papal action was considered impudent and absurd; at worst, subversive and traitorous. All the long history of Catholic-Protestant strife in England revived in one massive popular outburst.

By early November the cry of "No-Popery" was in full swing

throughout the land.* Wiseman issued an imprudent "pastoral" in which he referred to "this noble act of Apostolic authority." The Bishop of London called for public "protesting and petitioning." Lord John Russell in an open letter to the Bishop of Durham denounced the aggression of the Pope as "insolent and insidious . . . inconsistent with the Queen's supremacy, with the rights of our bishops and clergy, and with the spiritual independence of the nation. . . . The feeling has become national in its extent, headlong in the fervor of its alarm and of its anger at the encroachment of Popery and the intrusion of an alien authority."

The hubbub grew. Bishops sent letters to their clergy; the clergy made representations to the bishops. There were scores of official "addresses" of protest to the Queen. The City of London, Oxford University, and Cambridge University sent a joint deputation to address Her Majesty in person at Windsor. There was a huge meeting of the citizens of London at the Guildhall; there were parish meetings, town meetings, county meetings. A contemporary statistician listed the total number of meetings up to December 31st as 6,700. Great Protestant demonstrations sprang up in the provinces. Some 8,000 met in the Castle Yard at York, the high sheriff presiding. The Reverend Hugh McNeile of Liverpool, a man of fanatical energy, rose in his pulpit to call for the punishment of death upon those priests who administered the confessional. Even the Tractarians were pulled into the fray and anti-Tractarian philippics were delivered against the snake within the bosom. *Punch* thundered steadily and tempestuously in its columns and suggested in a letter to Russell that any person accepting from the Pope any ecclesiastical title should suffer the penalty of high treason. The Catholics maintained an attitude of injured dignity. Henry Edward Manning, a High Church leader, resigned his benefice and his archdeaconry, and the following April was received into the Roman Catholic Church. On Wiseman's death in 1865 he was to become cardinal and archbishop.

Guy Fawkes Day came while the fever was at its height and gave a new character to the bonfires and fireworks of the traditional proceedings. The great pageant of the day issued into Fleet Street about noon. A colossal figure of Guy Fawkes, sixteen feet in height, was drawn in a van by two horses and had to bow down to pass through Temple Bar. An effigy of Wiseman, dressed in the canonical robes, was paraded all through the town and was burned at night on Bethnal Green in a huge bonfire. The flames lit up banners displaying the slogan "The Queen, God bless her, and no Popery." Similar demonstrations took place in

---

* The *Publisher's Circular* listed seventy-eight works on the Papal Controversy published between the fourteenth and the thirtieth of November.

dozens of towns and villages, indulged in by many to whom the religious issues must have been dim indeed. National and anti-foreign sentiments had been stirred up, rather than pious ones.

The chief question was: What should be done about it? And to that no one seemed to have an adequate answer. None of the existent laws applied to the situation, and when even the more rabid statesmen sat down to think it over they saw the difficulties of passing new legislation to prevent the Pope from having spiritual influence over his communion, or to unfrock his bishops. About this time Wiseman published a moderate and conciliatory announcement, and gradually the storm aroused by the "Papal Aggression" blew itself out. The next year Parliament passed a watered-down Ecclesiastical Titles Bill which forbade Catholic priests under penalty of a fine of £100 to take territorial titles. This seemed to salve the public anger, even though everyone knew that the application of the law would never be invoked. The whole thing was one of the stranger and at the same time more revealing episodes of the decade, showing how near the surface national emotions lay.

Another happening during the latter part of the year underlined the popular hatred of foreign oppression. The Austrian general Marshal Haynau came to London. His operations against the Hungarians had gained him the title of "Butcher Haynau," and it was generally believed that the flogging of women had been one of his pastimes. On a visit to the great brewery of Barclay and Perkins he was recognized by the workmen, who ran out with brooms and sticks crying, "Down with the Austrian butcher!" He received very rough treatment; missiles were thrown at him and his clothes nearly torn off his back; he was even dragged along by his luxuriant mustaches. In terrified flight, he ran into a public house and barricaded himself in one of the bedrooms. The crowd by this time had grown to several hundred, and it was only with the help of the police that the old man was rescued.

The episode was reported in great detail, and with a good deal of secret satisfaction, in many quarters. Barclay and Perkins refused to discipline their men for the attack. The most that they would do "in order that the excitement may be allayed in every possible manner," was to obliterate Haynau's signature from the guestbook!

While all this national steam was blowing off, the great basic pulse-beat of English life went on undisturbed. The customary festivities were indulged in at the opening of the Chippenham cheese market, with 400 tons of cheese brought to the first day's market. . . . The Marble Arch at Buckingham Palace was torn down, to be re-erected at Cumberland Gate, Hyde Park. . . . Richard Manks of Warwickshire walked 1,000 miles in 1,000 hours—a mile every hour on the hour. . . . People read with interest of the trial of Professor Webster of Harvard College, U.S.A., who had murdered a Dr. Parkman and had burned his dismembered body in a laboratory furnace.

Christmas came at the appointed time, and the Christmas book trade included a fanciful, graceful little story attributed to Ruskin: *The King of the Golden River*, with illustrations by Richard Doyle. It was more than humorous; it had "the moral purpose of showing the superiority of kindness to riches." The *Illustrated London News* issued a holiday supplement with a descriptive article by John Oxenford: "The Grocer's Shop on Christmas Eve," which entered fully into the mysteries and delights of pudding making. In its review of the past year the same paper found cause for tempered satisfaction: "Calm in the midst of turmoil—at peace when her neighbors are either in actual warfare with one another, or engaged in preparations for it—Great Britain has offered to the perplexed nations of the world an example worthy of their imitation. Her old civilization—by many deemed so old as to be effete—has bequeathed her many evils to endure or remove—an immense debt, a fearful pauperism, an uneducated multitude, a divided Church, and an impatient public spirit. . . . But the past year . . . has shown that the energy and resources of the British people are unsurpassed by those of any people in the world. . . . While taxes have been diminished and expenses increased, the national revenue, under the operation of the wise principles of Free Trade, has presented a surplus scarcely expected. . . . Pauperism and crime have alike diminished; and every able and willing hand has found remunerative employment. . . . Those who predicted their own ruin have not been ruined."

On New Year's Eve Londoners opened their windows at midnight to hear the bells of St. Paul's, the bells of Bow, the bells of all the churches across the parish distances of the great city. This time they had Tennyson at hand to remind them that the year was dying in the frosty night, and, in terms of the noblest Victorian aspiration, to order the wild and happy bells to "ring out the feud of rich and poor" and "the thousand wars of old," and to ring in "redress to all mankind" and "the thousand years of peace." Who could ask for more a century later?

CHAPTER ELEVEN

1851 * The Crystal Palace: Utopia Around the Corner

Gather, ye Nations, gather! From forge, and mine, and mill!
 Come, Science and Invention; Come, Industry and Skill!
Come with your woven wonders, the blossoms of the loom,
That rival Nature's fairest flowers in all but their perfume;
Come with your brass and iron, Your silver and your gold,
And arts that change the face of earth, unknown to men of old.
Gather, ye Nations, gather! From ev'ry clime and soil,
The New Confederation, the Jubilee of toil.
        —WORDS BY CHARLES MACKAY. MUSIC BY HENRY RUSSELL

I T was the year of the Great Exhibition of the Works of Industry of All Nations. Crystal Palace year, and optimism was twopence a ton. Britannia, placing an uncertain foot upon the detritus of the Hungry Forties, kept her eyes up, looked upon all that she had made, and found it good. Her statesmen and orators declared the event in dithyrambic prose, her poets sang it, her most cynical journalists opened the flood-

[443]

gates of ecstatic praise, and her people, from Queen to commoner,
thrilled to the great national festival of all time. Its filaments ran into
every corner of the British Isles and around the world; hopes and aspirations beyond compare found excited focus beneath the glass roof in
Hyde Park. The grandchildren of these Victorians, looking back upon
it a hundred years later, would find here a good deal that was silly, more
that was fatuous, and, in the light of later events, not a little that was
naïve and even pathetic. But at the moment every Englishman who had
a shilling to spend was able to see the best show of his life. If he drew
from it a moral, that was no more than he had been trained to do. If he
made sweeping predictions about an illusory future, that was no more,
in all humanity, than one should allow a decade which had been reeling
along the rim of threatened disaster.

The idea and the final realization of the Great Exhibition were the
work of some of those titanic Victorians whose energy, imagination, and
determination knew no bounds. Prince Albert was its titular father, and
he got the praise. The real work, and most of the ideas, belonged to
others—Henry Cole, for example. Cole, whom we met earlier as "Felix
Summerly," was much more than a writer of children's books. He was
an assistant keeper at the Record Office, the reorganizer of the Post
Office, editor of numerous periodicals (among them the current *Journal
of Design and Manufactures*), designer of prize tea services, an etcher
and a water-color painter. He was profoundly interested in the improvement of British industrial design, and the foreordained promoter of
exhibitions celebrating such design. Under his leadership the Society of
Arts had held an exhibition of art manufactures in 1847, another in 1848,
and a third (the most successful of all) in 1849. Both Manchester and
Birmingham had held separate similar exhibitions. All was set for the
gigantic effort of 1851, which Cole conceived and the Royal Consort
took under his wing. The Royal Commission was appointed and began
to operate; Cole was a member, prodding, pushing, facilitating. At last
a building committee was appointed and it invited the submission of
designs.

That the building came into being as the Crystal Palace was almost
an accident. Of the 245 plans submitted, the committee approved of
none and proceeded to draw up its own plans and indeed to invite bids
from building contractors for what, if it had materialized, would have
been a misbegotten monstrosity in brick—a hideous thing which it would
have been impossible to erect within the allotted time. The plans were
published and met with scorn and derision. The committee was uneasy,
but didn't know what to do. At just this moment, only a few days

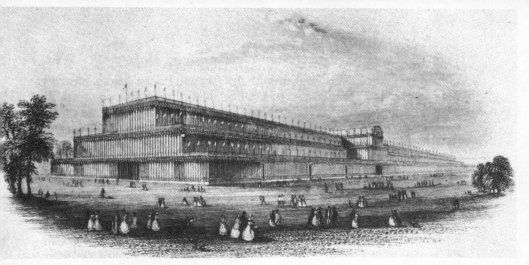

Figure 161. The Crystal Palace

before the bids were to be received, the indefatigable Cole enlisted the interest of Joseph Paxton, whose reputation as an architect in glass and whose accomplishments in general were poorly described by his title of head gardener to the Duke of Devonshire. Paxton and his men worked seven days and nights, and just before the deadline the committee had before it the plans for a huge palace of glass. While deliberations proceeded, Paxton was shrewd enough to publish an engraving of his plan in the *Illustrated London News*. It was greeted with such unanimous and enthusiastic approval that the committee could only sweep aside its own design and accept Paxton's proposal.

That conception had everything. Using iron and glass, in standardized and interchangeable sizes, it could be built within the time limit. It could be taken down afterward (a stipulation of the Commission) with relatively small effort and with a high salvage value. The interior space, with its galleries, was perfect for exhibition purposes. And above all it was a daring, imaginative creation—soaring, ethereal, brilliant. The diehards who resisted the idea of *any* building in Hyde Park had complained about the necessity of cutting down trees. So Paxton incorporated in his plan a great transept which would enclose the large elms, alive.* This was the only major change since he had jotted down his original design on blotting paper while attending a committee meeting of the Midland Railway!

---

* *Punch* lamented the threatened loss:

> Albert! spare those trees,
> Mind where you fix your show;
> For mercy's sake, don't, please,
> Go spoiling Rotten Row.

And so ground was broken and the Crystal Palace began to grow. Messrs. Fox and Henderson, the builders, had promised to complete the structure by January 1, 1851. They had twenty-two weeks to erect a gigantic building covering eighteen acres, with a mile and three quarters of exhibition galleries. The statistics were staggering: length, 1,851 feet; width, 456 feet, with a huge vaulted transept 408 feet long. The height of the nave, 64 feet; of the transept, 108 feet. Total area of the ground floor, 772,824 square feet; of the galleries, 217,100 square feet. Total cubic contents, 33,000,000 feet. Materials used: 900,000 square feet of glass weighing 400 tons, in standardized panes four feet long and one foot wide; 3,300 iron columns; 2,224 girders; 205 miles of sash bars. The contract price (with right of salvage) was £79,800. (Because of modifications this was somewhat exceeded.)

The assembling of the building was ingenious and its erection rapid. New machinery was designed to groove the "Paxton gutters," which served both as frames for the glass and led the rainwater to the hollow iron supporting columns. These in turn carried it to the iron pipes which were both the structural base of the building and the main drainage system. No mortar and no bricks were used. Adjustable louvers provided ventilation.

Thousands of people flocked to the Park to watch the rising girders throw their tracery against the sky. There were still carpers who complained that the building would not be safe: a hailstorm or even a stiff wind would break the glass; gunfire across the Park would collapse it; the structure would buckle under the weight of people in the galleries; the vibration either of moving machinery or of the large pipe organs would shake the glass out like cards. Even those who liked the building had moments of doubt; nothing like this had ever been tried in architectural history. But Paxton knew what he was doing. Even before the building was completed a hail-and-windstorm did not move a single pane of glass. Huge carts filled with cannon balls, weighing eight tons, were rolled in tests up and down the galleries with impunity. The whole corps of Royal Sappers and Miners marched over and around the bays in close order, and even marked time "in the most trying manner." Still the construction suffered no injury.

While this mountain of iron and glass was being thrown up, one little incident occurred which showed that British individualism was by no means dead. The episode of Mrs. Hicks and her cottage in Hyde Park started an inordinate amount of official machinery moving. Since 1843 Mrs. Ann Hicks had been selling apples and ginger beer from a stall in Hyde Park. Gradually she had extended her stall until it became a

sort of hidden cottage. She had had several disputes with the Park authorities, and now that the Exhibition rules permitted no peddling of refreshments she was given notice to get out. She refused to move, saying it was
her ground. Sibthorp, still thundering in Parliament against the Exhibition (it was "morally, religiously, and socially a great curse to the
country, sucking up all its wealth, causing gross desecration of the
Sabbath, demoralizing the people, and disuniting parties")—Sibthorp
cited the case of Mrs. Hicks as evidence of criminal mismanagement and
trespass upon ancient English rights. The Duke of Wellington, who
was ranger of the Park, was consulted, and he engaged in some little
correspondence on the matter. He recommended that Lord Seymour
take legal advice. At last the entire affair was put in the hands of the
solicitors of the Board, and despite Mrs. Hicks's claim that she held her
stall by gift to her family from George the Second she was evicted. The
danger to the Great Exhibition was avoided.

Rapidly the Palace drew toward completion, and the crates and boxes
of exhibitors began to arrive from all over the world. Everything had
been thought of. There were large refreshment rooms, from which
Messrs. Schweppe (who paid £5,500 for the privilege) were to dispense, as it proved, some £75,557 worth of refreshments—bread, cake,
buns (1,804,698 of them), pickles, hams, jellies, and coffee (14,299
pounds); and 1,092,337 bottles of non-intoxicating beverages: soda
water, lemonade, ginger beer, to say nothing of thirty-seven tons of
salt. "Waiting rooms" had been thought of. During the time of the
Exhibition, said the *Official Catalogue* with a nice scientific precision,
827,820 or 14 per cent of the visitors paid for the use of these conveniences, "in addition to an equal if not larger proportion of gentlemen
who made use of the urinals, of which no account was kept. No apology
is needed," continued the official voice, "for publishing these facts,
which . . . strongly impressed all concerned in the management . . . with
the sufferings which must be endured by all, but more especially by
females . . . on account of the want of them."

The first day of May had been set for the opening of the Great
Exhibition. Long before that time arrived, London, and more than
London, was electric with anticipation. Yet no matter what happened
from here on, the metropolitan scene had been graced by a most astonishing architectural accomplishment. The Crystal Palace, perfect in
proportion, balance, symmetry, was incredibly modern and incredibly
beautiful. It rose tier upon tier of slender columns and arches. The long
perspective of girders and trusses—all functional and all exposed—created
a repetitive lacelike pattern. All was light and cheerful and airy, the lines

Figure 162. Joseph Paxton

Figure 163. Going to the Exhibition

were clean and sharp, and the flags of all nations, fluttering from various levels of roof top, broke any possible severity of the exterior. The glass sparkled in the sunlight against the dull background of London stone and brick. Here in the middle of the nineteenth century, when English architecture was becoming less and less creative if more and more ingenious, was an anachronistic miracle of design, a complete integration of material and form and function. England was not to see its architectural equal for generations, for although Paxton was to urge similar construction for more ordinary uses, it was thought of even by its enthusiasts as a kind of gallant trick. It was big, and therefore good, but it was as impermanent (the public at first believed) as the new ugly façades of Kensington were enduring.*

May Day. Since early morning people had been pouring into town by every conceivable road and railway. Already strange-bearded foreigners were appearing in numbers on the streets. The South Eastern Railway, with the co-operation of the Northern Railway Company of France, had started one tidal service per day, each way, between England and France, bringing Paris within an eleven hours' continuous journey of London. The *Morning Chronicle* ran articles in parallel columns in English, French, and German. But the English were there, too, and in force. The day dawned brightly, crisp and cool. By six o'clock, the hour fixed for the opening of the Park gates, streams of carriages were pouring in from the outlying districts. They reached westward through Kensington to Hammersmith, eastward to Long Acre. Only season ticket holders were to be allowed inside the Palace for the opening ceremonies, but by eleven o'clock the Park with all its approaches was a sea of heads. By noon half a million people were massed in the Park—all waiting hopefully, in that best of British outdoor traditions, to catch a glimpse of the royal procession.

Inside the Crystal Palace the ticket holders,† who had thronged in when the doors were opened at nine o'clock, gazed in wonderment at the vaulted glass heights, the elms in leaf under their arching canopy, the long rows of columns, the sweep of the galleries, the tantalizing vistas of the crowded exhibits, and waited for the trumpets which would an-

---

* It lasted, after its removal the next year to Sydenham, until its destruction by fire in 1936.

† Season tickets had been sold for £3 (gentlemen) and £2 (ladies). After the first three weeks general admission was lowered to a shilling, except for week ends: on Fridays it was 2s. 6d.; on Saturdays, 5s.

Figure 164. Opening of the Great Exhibition, May 1st

Figure 165. South transept

Figure 166. Interior of transept

Figure 167. Main avenue, looking east

Figure 168. Main avenue, looking west

Figure 169. Kiss's "Amazon" (German)

Figure 170. Power's "Greek Slave" (American)

Figure 171. E. Davis's "Venus and Cupid" (English)

Figure 172. Statuary in the main avenue (Belgian)

Figure 173. Ornamental chimney piece (English)

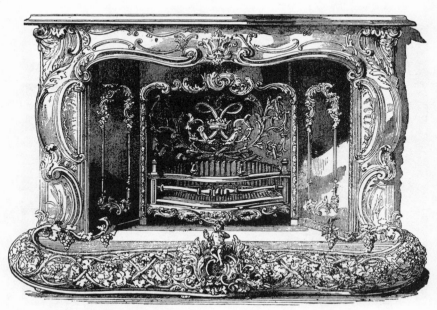

Figure 174. Fireplace (English)

Figure 175. Cabinet (English)

Figure 176. Four-foot vase in silver electroplate. Prince Albert awarding palm of honor to successful industry (English)

Figure 177. Group of plate (English)

Figure 178. Mahogany sideboard (English)

Figure 179. Walnut chairs (Canadian)

Figure 180. The "dreamer's" chair, in papier-mâché (English)
Figure 181. Ridgway and Co's cabinet water-closet (English)

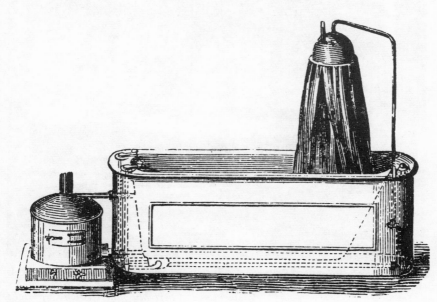

Figure 182. Copper bath (English)

Figure 183. Portable steam engine, threshing machine, and grain drill (English)
Victoria and Albert Museum. Crown Copyright

Figure 184. Crompton's "Folkstone" locomotive, with six-foot driving wheels (English)

Victoria and Albert Museum. Crown Copyright

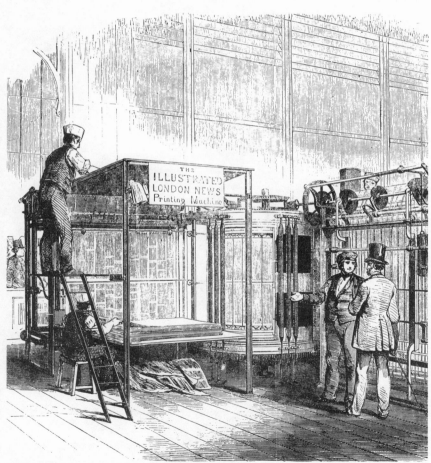

Figure 185. Applegarth's vertical printing press

Figure 186. McCormick's reaper

Figure 187. Model of floating Seamen's Church at Philadelphia (American)

nounce the Queen's arrival. Other notabilities kept arriving. The Duke of Wellington—this was his eighty-second birthday—was seen in the northeastern part of the transept, surrounded, as usual, by a bevy of beautiful ladies. Someone introduced Mr. Cobden to him; it was evidently the first time the two had met!

A sudden shower broke, but soon passed, and as the battery across the Serpentine fired a salute and the royal carriages drew up, the sun broke through brilliantly. It caught the fluttering pennons on the roof top. The Palace gleamed with a fairy-tale brilliance. The Queen appeared with Prince Albert, the Prince of Wales, and the Princess Royal. She took her seat under the central arch on a throne covered with a magnificent crimson brocaded elephant cloth, and the ceremony began.

Albert read a dullish report of the Commission proceedings: there were 15,000 exhibitors, half of them British; forty foreign countries were participating; the Exhibition was divided into four great classes, (1) Raw Materials; (2) Machinery; (3) Manufactures; (4) Sculpture and Fine Arts; there were ten miles of frontage for the display of goods. The Queen read a brief reply, indicating a concern for "the welfare of my people and the common interests of the human race." The Archbishop of Canterbury prayed at proper and eloquent length. The five organs and a vast choir delivered the Hallelujah Chorus, and the Great Exhibition was declared open. Away went the boundary ropes, and for some two hours the distinguished ticket holders acted like any Derby Day crowd. "All was push, squeeze, cram, and chaos," wrote one reporter. "All order was forgotten now; everybody struggled to see the Great Diamond, and the Throne, and the Crystal Fountain. . . . People jostled, shoved, elbowed, apologized, accepted the apology. . . . A great number rushed into the refreshment rooms, clamouring, not in vain, for ices and jellies. . . ."

A strange incident occurred as the official procession began its tour of the exhibits. Across the line of the foreign ambassadors and ministers and through the distinguished circle with which court etiquette had surrounded the throne burst a little Chinese dressed in superb mandarin costume. Advancing close to the Queen, he salaamed deeply. Her Majesty, a little puzzled, but curious and pleased, acknowledged the obeisance and placed the foreign potentate between the Archbishop of Canterbury and the Comptroller of the Household. In that position he paraded the building; later, Prince Albert was heard to ask for an introduction. Only subsequently was it learned that the "mandarin" was a sailor off the Chinese junk which had been anchored at the East India docks for some time. There, advertising himself as "the Acting Imperial

Representative of China," he and his crew were exhibiting a "Museum of Curiosities" and giving nightly performances (admission one shilling) of Chinese swordplay. Thus, not inappropriately, did the magnificent and the grotesque rub shoulders on this exalted occasion.

The Exhibition was open; what did it contain? A microcosm of the period we have been surveying: its eager amazement at its own accomplishments; its fantastic advance, within the century, into mechanical control of its environment. And at the same time its debauchery of taste; its equal admiration of the noble and the meretricious; its romantic love of the colossal and the infinitesimal, from the twenty-one-foot statue of Victoria in zinc to the delicate "real artificial" flowers placed in the hands of a marble "Veiled Vestal." From one point of view the Great Exhibition was a marvelous tribute to human ingenuity; from another, a compendium of ugliness and bad taste almost terrifying in its effrontery. At one end the sleek efficiency of the modern locomotive and of intricate textile machinery, the marvels of Shepherd's electric clock, Rosse's telescope, and Applegarth's vertical printing machine, capable of turning out 10,000 sheets of the *Illustrated London News* each hour before the eyes of astonished spectators. At the other end, hideous monstrosities of furniture, atrocious statuary, and a group of stuffed cats seated on chairs and drinking tea at a table. The Great Exhibition was the Victorian paradox sheathed in glass.

The surprises began even before one entered the building. On the greensward toward Kensington loomed Marochetti's huge figure of Richard Cœur de Lion. One wove his way past enormous anchors, monoliths of granite, masses of coal as large as cottages. Once inside, the eye was caught by the vast length of the central vista. Standing by the central Crystal Fountain, a towering, four-ton mass of crystal glass twenty-seven feet high, one saw in diminishing perspective a huge pile of Canadian timber, a giant stone cross, a great, intricate, arching cast-iron dome constructed by the Coalbrookdale Co., the huge lenses of a lighthouse, a mass of zinc weighing 16,400 pounds, a great bell, a massive wine jar, a rubber boat with pontoons, the Koh-i-noor diamond in its gilded iron cage—all flanked by numerous fountains and by group after group of statuary dominated by a colossal equestrian figure of Godefroy de Bouillon.

Certainly it was the heyday of science, and British machinery was by far the most important feature of the Exhibition. Nasmyth's steam hammer, which was revolutionizing the forging and stamping of iron— capable, with slight adjustments, of delivering a terrific blow of 500 tons or of cracking lightly an eggshell. Improved Jacquard looms, hydraulic presses, Bessemer's centrifugal pump, steam mills for crushing sugar cane, soda-water machines, diving suits, models of the iron bridges, Krupp's steel cannon, Willis's grand organ of 4,500 pipes, portable steam engines, patent iron thrashing machines, seed drills, improved electric telegraphs (including Bakewell's copying telegraph, which delivered facsimile copies at the other end of the line). Adorno's cigarette machine, which could turn out automatically eighty cigarettes a minute with greater neatness than could be done by hand—but "on the English market there is scarcely any demand for cigarettes." And the "silent alarum bedstead," guaranteed to dump the sleeper out of bed at a given hour and deposit him, if he so chose, in a bath of cold water.

Silks, ribbons, Sèvres porcelain, Aubusson carpets, Beauvais tapestries, artificial flowers, and pianofortes from France. Porcelain bowls and landscapes in ivory from China. Cutlery from Belgium; engraved goblets from Bohemia; massive intricately carved Gothic furniture from Austria; elaborate ornamental plate and great malachite wares from Russia; jewels and boat models from India; watches from Switzerland. And from everywhere a plethora of ornately designed objects meant to look artistic. Inkstands that looked like thistles; flower stands so encrusted with ornament as to disguise their usefulness; chairs with arms and backs made of antlers, to embrace dangerously anyone so foolhardy as to sit in them; fireplaces repulsively elaborate; clocks with their faces lost amid sculptured figures; papier-mâché "dreamer's" chairs that were nightmares; sideboards, tables, bedsteads the function of which was hidden under grotesque embellishments and carvings. And everywhere cupids holding up candelabra, centerpieces, cornices. No chair leg dared be a chair leg: it must be an outsize bear's or lion's paw. No piano but looked naked unless every inch was covered with carved scrollwork. It was sterile design ostentatiously gone to artistic hell.

In the midst of all these morbidities the American part of the exhibit came in for a great deal of criticism. Evidently the Yankees had talked too loudly of their expectations, and were slow in making good their claims. When the Exhibition opened, the extensive display spaces they had demanded were filled with a mere scattering of objects—chiefly ungraceful if sturdy carriages; ship models and rocking chairs; and raw materials and produce such as huge blocks of copper ore, Indian corn, and flour. A long line of barrels of fine flour did not add much to the enlightenment of nations. The London press uniformly poked acid fun at the inadequacies of the American exhibit, just as they were amused by the model of the floating Seamen's Church the original of which navigated the Delaware off Philadelphia. As time went on, however,

and objects of greater merit began to arrive, their tone changed somewhat. Some beautiful and simply designed gold ornaments came from
New York—made from fresh California gold. The Colt revolver excited
military men, although it did not get even honorable mention among
the awards. The Goodyear Company displayed a remarkable array of
articles manufactured from the new India rubber "vulcanized" by a new
sulphurizing process,* and there was universal recognition that the
McCormick reaper, capable of reaping an acre or more of grain per
hour, might help to change the face of English agriculture. Everyone
admitted, too, that the American photographs and daguerreotypes had
a beauty, clarity, and brilliance beyond those of any other country.

Important photographic innovations had been introduced recently and
were being experimented with in Britain as well as in the United States.†
The process of sensitizing an emulsion of egg white on glass and thus
making possible the production of glass rather than paper negatives
was being superseded by the use of collodion as an emulsion. The new
glass pictures were called Hyalotypes. And Mr. Talbot had recently
produced, with great clarity, the photographic image of printed words
on a piece of paper attached to the rim of a rapidly revolving wheel:
the lens of the camera was opened just as a powerful electric flash
illuminated the whirling disk. It was the first really instantaneous
photography.

Two things happened during that summer which sent the Americans
home happier than they might otherwise have been. A Yankee named
Mr. Newell had placed on exhibit an "unpickable" lock. He offered
£500 to the person who could succeed in picking it, but no one collected the reward. By way of demonstrating his own ability he accepted
two long-standing challenges of English lockmakers. He first opened,
with great ease, the patent lock of the famous Messrs. Chubb. He then
opened the "unpickable" lock of the Messrs. Bramah, and claimed their
£200 reward. The chagrined lockmakers were inclined not to pay him,
but an impartial jury of arbitration declared for Mr. Newell, and the
money was turned over to him.

The other event was the unexpected and demoralizing defeat inflicted
upon the crack yachts of the aristocratic British yacht clubs by the
schooner yacht *America* in the great Cowes Regatta for the purse of All
Nations. "No Englishman ever dreamed," said the *Times*, "that any
nation could produce a yacht with the least pretensions to match the

---

* Mr. Macintosh also exhibited a variety of garments waterproofed with the
same material.
† Daguerre died in Paris that summer.

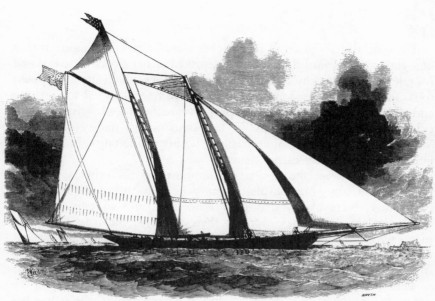

Figure 188. The yacht *America*

efforts of White, Camper, Ratsey, and other eminent builders." But it
simply was no race. The 100-ton *America*, of unusual design, ran away
from the field and crossed the finish line eight minutes and one mile
ahead of its nearest competitor. The good sportsmanship of the British
was impeccable, and they expressed real admiration for the American
craft. It was particularly noted that after the race, when the *America*
passed the royal steamer, its blue-and-white ensign was hauled down.
Commodore Stephens took off his hat, and all his crew stood at attention until they had passed the royal party—"a mark of respect to the
Queen," said the *Times* nobly, "not the less becoming because it was
bestowed by Republicans."

The only defense that can be entered for the Fine Arts section of the
British part of the Exhibition is to say that its vulgarity and tastelessness
were equaled by the other nations. The statuary as a whole was deplorable. The two most popular statues in the Crystal Palace (both drew huge
crowds) were the "Amazon" by Professor A. Kiss, of Berlin, and the
"Greek Slave" by Hiram Powers, an American who had lingered too
long (or not long enough) in Italy. The former was a gargantuan piece,
in zinc, of a heroic female figure on a frightened horse, leveling a lance
at a tigress which was climbing up and over the horse's shoulder. It was
a tremendously energetic conception, startlingly real and dramatic. Both
its size and its subject fascinated the spectators who swarmed about
its base.

The official description of the "Greek Slave" ran: "The figure is that of a young and beautiful Greek girl, deprived of her clothes and exposed for sale to some wealthy Eastern barbarian, before whom she is supposed to stand with an expression of sorrowful dejection, mingled with shame and disgust." The figure was ill-proportioned and awkwardly posed; evidently what caught the public taste was not its nudity (the early Victorians took acres of nude statuary without flinching), but its titillating and respectably carnal theme.

Beyond this were the vast artistic morasses of the other sculptured figures in tin, zinc, marble, plaster—most of them, when not intimidatingly huge, were bland, artistically innocuous, and stiltedly imitative of classical models. They were at their worst in the mawkish *genre* pieces which told a story, usually pathetic: "The Unhappy Child," weeping over his broken drum; "The Boy Attacked by a Serpent"; "The Mourners": a dead knight being wept over by his horse and his widow.

This essential cheapness of sculptural taste was paralleled by the ornate commonness of commercial and industrial design—the worse because with the beginnings of mass production such atrocities were entering every Victorian household. Wood carving by machinery, the fact that papier-mâché could be molded into any extravagant form and that cast-iron scrollwork could be applied cheaply to any second-rate stove, meant merely the multiplication of horrors. The Victorian liked to think of this excess of ornament, of scrollwork, of tracery and interlacings as being "cinquecento." It was, in fact, Renaissance gone to seed (mingled with a large infusion of rococo) and reproduced in a bizarre and fantastic mingling of styles so overloaded with a profusion of detail as to sink under the weight of its artistic iniquities. The worst excesses of "Victorian Gothic" were still ahead, but they were to represent only a mutation in an inferiority of taste already soundly established.

Even in 1851, however, there were voices to cry out in this wilderness of bad taste. Samuel Warren, in his rapturously chaotic *Lily and the Bee, An Apologue of the Crystal Palace* might exclaim in wonder over the "Greek Slave"

> Brethren ye bring us a form of Beauty, and in chains!
> Look ye yourselves upon her loveliness!
> Ponder her thrilling tale of grief!—
> She is not mute, O marble eloquent!
> She pleads! She pleads!

But others were more critical of contemporary artistic manners. One journal[1] took a dim view of English imitative design in general. "For want of this application of inventive and original taste to handicraft," it said, "the latter, left unaided and in the dark, has had, through a series of generations, to resort to mere copying of favourite models of former periods. . . . Thus we have constant boastings of pure *cinque cento*, pure *Renaissance*, pure Elizabethan, pure Louis Quatorze, and most abundantly of pure *rococo*, as though these were passports to honour and favour, instead of simple confessions of bankruptcy in idea, and almost hopeless extinction of inventive faculty." The same publication took exception to the "Greek Slave," although it knew it was running "counter to the opinion of the majority of the critics of the day." Another paper spoke regretfully of "the prodigious amount of ugliness it [the Exhibition, and particularly the English part of it] contained, especially in decorative manufactures."[2] William Morris, a young man of seventeen, "stood aghast at the appalling ugliness of the objects exhibited, the heaviness, tastelessness, and rococo banality of the entire display."[3]

In an article entitled "Recent Decorative Art"[4] Chambers's *Papers for the People* inveighed against the sordid pretense of ornament which was "stuck on. In the more expensive . . . [grates, stoves, etc.] there is free recourse to nondescript, to Louis Quatorze and Quinze, not to speak of *pseudo*-Gothic puerilities. . . . In papier-mâché applied architecturally the perils of facility become graver . . . we have sham-classic, Gothic, Elizabethan work, sham-stone moldings and tracery; sham-stone pillars; all is papier-mâché, *carton-pierre*. For the present is the age of shams; at all events in architecture. The one idea suggesting itself to our minds after making a mechanical discovery is, how to turn it to profit as a *sham?* . . . Works of art are *tacked on* to works of utility. One idea is lost amid a host of conflicting ones. . . . To the endeavour at imparting a decorative aspect to our works in the baser metals—iron, brass, etc.— fidelity of character and directness of expression have been strangers. . . . Instead of an article *itself* ornamental, it must be, if 'decorative,' *something else*. . . . Everywhere, if not frightful, our forms are tame, overloaded, or broken up; inharmonised into unity. . . . In the more elaborate candlestick or centre-piece, instead of clear enunciation of the structural features, and subservience of decoration thereto, there prevails indiscriminate addition of ornament everywhere, and combinations without plan or meaning for a whole."

This is sound criticism in design for any age. In 1851, however, it seemed merely a sour note in the symphony of adulation for British decorative art.

It was a great summer for London, for England, for all the world: the thoughts of Englishmen were nothing if not global these days. Foreigners kept coming to admire; Flaubert wrote to Ernest Chevalier about the

Great Exhibition, admitting that "despite the universal admiration it was really fine." Special excursion trains from the provinces brought to London hordes of laborers and farmers in smocks who had never been outside their own counties before. One eighty-four-year-old woman, Mary Callinack, walked 300 miles from Penzance in Cornwall to see the Exhibition, carrying a basket on her head. When she arrived, she insisted on paying her respects personally to the Lord Mayor. The Lord Mayor: "What induced you to come to London?" Mrs. Callinack: "I had a little matter to attend to as well as to see the Exhibition." The Lord Mayor gave her a sovereign so that she could return to Land's End by rail.

Not the least attractive of the side shows that clustered around the Great Exhibition was Alexis Soyer's *Gastronomic Symposium of all Nations* in Gore House, across the road from the Crystal Palace. It was really a restaurant to feed the visitors, but Soyer's romantic genius made it a restaurant transfigured. With a lavish hand he spent great sums in alteration, improvement, and reconstruction. He made a small Vauxhall of the grounds, with statues, fortunetellers, grottoes, and a monster American bar for sherry cobblers, mint juleps, brandy smash, and other exotic transatlantic drinks to forty in number. The dining saloon, which seated 1,500, was called the "Encampment of All Nations." George Augustus Sala painted on the walls of the grand staircase a mural, which included people of importance from Wellington to Napoleon to Dickens, Thackeray, George Cruikshank, Jerrold, Dumas, Victor Hugo, John Bright, Cobden, and General Tom Thumb. This Soyer called, to Sala's disgust, a "Demisemitragicomigrotesquepanofanofanifunnisympo-siorama." The food, for those who dared the decorations, was up to Soyer's best culinary standards. And even the Ethiopian Serenaders were there to entertain the guests.

Soyer persuaded Jullien to join him in continuing the place as a winter garden after the Exhibition closed. But the man who inspected the place preliminary to granting a license was horrified by the noise and gaiety. "A more dissipated place," he said, "or a more dangerous place for the morals of young persons" he had never entered. Soyer, deeply offended, closed the Symposium on October 14th, and began bombarding the press with angry letters. The venture ended with a heavy deficit.

Never had there been such crowds in London streets. In July the Queen, accompanied by Prince Albert, honored the Corporation of London with her presence at an entertainment at the Guildhall. During the customary State Procession through Pall Mall, up the Strand, and through the City streets to the Guildhall, the crush of patriotic subjects obeying the almost pathological English impulse to look at royalty was so great that one man was trampled to death.

The famous writers of the day lifted their voices in paens of praise for the Crystal Palace. Martin Tupper wrote his *Hymn for All Nations* and saw that it was translated into twenty-five languages, including the Ojibway. Thackeray wrote a vivacious *May-Day Ode,* the first and last stanzas of which ran:

> But yesterday a naked sod
> The dandies sneered from Rotten Row,
> And cantered o'er it to and fro:
> And see 'tis done!
> As though 'twere by a wizard's rod
> A blazing arch of lucid glass
> Leaps like a fountain from the grass
> To meet the sun!
>
> . . . .
>
> Swell, organ, swell your trumpet blast,
> March, Queen and Royal pageant, march
> By splendid aisle and springing arch
> Of this fair Hall:
> And see! above the fabric vast,
> God's boundless Heaven is bending blue,
> God's peaceful sunlight's beaming through,
> And shines o'er all!

The laureate contributed his official *Ode:*

> Till each man find his own in all men's good,
> And all men work in noble brotherhood,
> Breaking their mailed fleets and armed towers,
> And ruling by obeying Nature's powers,
> And gathering all the fruits of earth and crown'd
> with all her flowers.

The one common note in all the rhapsodies was a determined insistence that such a fraternization of nations was bound to usher in a new era, not merely of prosperity but also of mutual understanding and brotherhood and peace. Occasionally the theme of self-congratulation and national pride came to the surface, and a writer would apostrophize "the country of Wedgwood, of Arkwright, and of Watt—the seat of the most advanced manufacturing processes, the focus of unlimited capital, the spot whence laden vessels radiate in every direction, the country whose flag floats above more wealth than any rival state can boast, whose scientific men have led the way in the pursuit of wealth, whose legislators have stood in the van of political progress. . . ."[5] This may not have been seemly, but it was rapidly becoming true. More deeply bitten, however, was the pious hope that what was really just an exhibition by the various nations of products frequently competitive would by a kind of celestial osmosis become the basis of enduring peace and good will. "It has made us," ran the leader in one paper, "understand one another better than we did before; broken down the ancient barriers of jealousy and exclusiveness; obliterated the rancourous remembrances of bygone wars; softened the lingering asperities of traditional hatred. . . ."[6]

The *Athenaeum* was even more rhetorical: "The tale of Hyde Park in 1851 will fall on the page of history. Fallen thrones will lie around it: here the Saturnalia of power,—there the wild excess of popular freedom . . . everywhere anarchy, repression, conspiracy, darkness, dismay, and death. In the midst of all these struggling spirits rises up the great figure of the Crystal Palace, to redeem the age."[7]

Victoria, on the evening of May 1st, wrote in her private diary: "One felt,—as so many did whom I have since spoken to—filled with devotion, —more so than by any service I have ever heard. The tremendous cheers, the joy expressed in every face, the immensity of the building, the mixture of palms, flowers, trees, statues, fountains,—the organ (with 200 instruments and 600 voices, which sounded like nothing), and my beloved husband the author of this 'Peace-Festival,' which united the industry of all the nations of the earth,—all this was moving indeed, and it was and is a day to live for ever."

Against subsequent history all these intimations of Utopia seem very remote, unreal, and wistfully pathetic. But in the Crystal Palace the age sat for its daguerreotype, and its dreams of world power walking hand in hand with world peace were just as true to itself as were its grubbier, more provincial tendencies. No one paid much attention, this year, to the difficulties which Her Majesty's armies were having with the Kaffirs in faraway Africa, or to Mr. Roebuck's declaration in the Commons: "We have no business in Kaffraria, except on the understanding that we are going to plant there a people of high intelligence, and this can only be done by the gradual annihilation of the native population. It is an utter pretense to talk of humanity, and the principles of the Christian religion, and the Decalogue; the black man must vanish in the face of the white." Gladstone's protest against this point of view received just as little attention. Everyone was busy watching his imagination expand under the impact of this first Festival of Britain.

Thrilling as the Crystal Palace was, people did have time to think of other things in 1851. Papal aggression was still on the minds of many, though not a few were beginning to be weary of the fuss. Wiseman kept on appointing his bishops.* Parliamentary politics were dull during most of the year. The old debates dragged on: deceased wife's sister reared her head again in the House of Lords, and was met, successfully, with the same old arguments out of Leviticus. The Commons devoted hours to what the press called ironically "the great chicory debate," during which a great deal of emphatic nonsense was delivered from the floor. The adulteration of coffee with chicory had become almost universal: it appeared in thirty-one out of thirty-four samples tested. The chickory growers insisted, with startling accuracy, that coffee drinkers had learned to prefer the adulterated product; the coffee merchants were clamoring for a heavy duty on chicory. And this tempest in a coffeepot was further complicated by the concern of the chicory interests that inferior adulterations were being substituted for chicory: roasted grain, beans, potatoes, and even unmentionable filth!

Lord John Russell did succeed in abolishing the window tax. It was recognized as damagingly discriminatory, but it had brought in annually a sum of £1,856,000, and it was necessary to replace it with a tax on inhabited houses. The shakiness of Russell's government during this session, and the confusion of parties produced by the Free Trade issue and the continued independence of the Peelites, resulted in a strange ministerial crisis. Defeated on several issues, Russell tried to resign. Lord Stanley, however, coyly refused to form a government, and Russell returned to office, as Greville pointed out, "damaged, weak, and unpopular; his party nervous, frightened, uneasy." *Punch* ran a cartoon showing the shipwrecked ministers, stranded on a raft, being saved by the "Exhibition Steamer." There was a good deal of truth in it.

Miscellanea: Mary Godwin Shelley died, aged fifty-three; as did also Lady Augusta Leigh, Byron's sister, aged sixty-nine. James Fenimore Cooper died in Cooperstown, New York. . . . Mr. Hullah's imperishable choral concerts included, in January, several sacred compositions by M. Gounod, "a young Frenchman whose name is just beginning to be heard in the musical world." At the same time Gounod's new opera *Sapho* was warmly received in Paris. . . . St. Paul's was opened for the

---

* Tom Moore's lament twenty-five years earlier was applied to 1851:

> What! still those two infernal questions,
>   That with our meals, our slumbers mix;
> That spoil our tempers and digestions—
>   Eternal Corn and Catholics?
>
> Gods! were there ever two such bores
>   Nothing else talk'd of, night or morn;
> Nothing *in* doors or *out* of doors,
>   But endless Catholics and Corn!

first time to visitors without pay. . . . Boucicault's comedy *Love in a Maze* was greeted as a happy omen for the English stage by those tired of adaptations from the French. . . . The Society for the Propagation of the Gospel in Foreign Parts celebrated its 150th anniversary. . . . An American, Asa Whitney, described to English audiences in glowing terms the prospect of building a transcontinental railway in the United States. . . . San Francisco was swept by a fire which was the most severe of three within the year. It leveled the buildings in thirteen blocks. . . . Sixty-one lives were lost in a coalpit explosion at Paisley (there were ten bad colliery accidents in 1851, and eight severe railway accidents). . . . The Lady Godiva procession at Coventry was celebrated with great splendor before a crowd of 60,000. . . . Thackeray lectured to distinguished audiences on *English Humourists of the Eighteenth Century*. . . . The *Athenaeum* ran a very cordial appraisal of the Pre-Raphaelites—perhaps because William Michael Rossetti was now art critic for that paper! . . . Sir Edward Bulwer Lytton's *Not So Bad as We Seem* was performed at Devonshire House, with Victoria and Albert in attendance, by a brilliant amateur cast: Charles Dickens, Douglas Jerrold, John Forster, Mark Lemon, Charles Knight, Wilkie Collins, John Tenniel, and Augustus Egg, A.R.A.

Book publishing enjoyed a good year, buttressed by scores of illustrated and descriptive Guides for visitors. Hawthorne's *House of Seven Gables* appeared and the author was ranked "amongst the most original and complete novelists that have appeared in modern times."[8] Melville's *The Whale* (later *Moby Dick*) puzzled the reviewers, who saw in it only an ill-compounded mixture of romance and matter of fact, full of harassing and absurd manifestations of bad taste. Young George Meredith published his first volume of poems; it was greeted as having much promise, though "it betrays the young writer." Carlyle published his *Life of John Sterling*. It was condemned by the pious as an unfruitful excursion into religious dubieties.

A volume of sermons appeared by Dr. Vaughn, head master of Harrow School and Chaplain in Ordinary to the Queen. Doubtless many people read them, just as they had listened to them approvingly earlier. The capacity of the serious Victorian to absorb punishment from lecturers and preachers must have been extraordinary. Dr. Vaughn's pulpit style ran as follows: "If that [eternal] damnation consisted only or chiefly in the infliction of external suffering; if the awful images by which the Scriptures have sought to bring home to human understanding the realities of that retribution . . . were to be literally interpreted, and regarded as constituting the whole of that misery which they faintly typify; then, certainly, the sentence might vary in its duration with each individual case, and admit in every instance of an ultimate however remote termination." The sermons also terminated remotely.

The greater profit in bookselling, however, lay with such works as Walter Scott's novels. In March the copyright to those novels was sold for £15,000, even though the copyright had not more than twenty years to run—in the case of *Waverley*, only five years. Between 1848 and March, 1851, 4,760 sets of the novels had been sold, 4,360 sets of the poetry, and 2,610 sets of Lockhart's *Life*. Since 1829 the *Waverley Novels* had sold 78,270 sets; the poetry, 41,340; and the *Life*, 26,860. In the People's Edition, 7,115,197 weekly sheets of the novels had been sold.

Whitsuntide early in June produced dismal weather for those who had planned to celebrate the holiday out of doors. A constant soaking drizzle from morning to night kept the sight-seers at home, reducing attendance even at the Crystal Palace. The previous Saturday, however, had been fine, and great crowds saw the flower shows of the Horticultural Society at Chiswick and of the Royal Botanic Society in Regent's Park. The rhododendrons and azaleas surpassed those of former years in beauty, and the Regent's Park display had the added attraction of a new floral wonder: the Chinese peony tree, brilliant with 500 colossal flowers. The holiday crowds were much interested, too, in Prince Albert's model cottage at the margin of Hyde Park. This building, with its galleried porch, outside staircase, well-pitched roof, and picturesquely grouped chimneys, was erected by Albert as a "group of dwellings for the poor." It used several innovations in construction, notably hollow brick, which made possible the use of lighter foundations. The floors and interior walls were made of glazed brick, insuring both insulation and easy cleaning. There were four living units under the one roof, the rent of each being only 5s. a week. Since the whole building cost only £500, this promised a good return on a philanthropic investment.

The wet spring ran into a hot summer. Farmers were predicting a better than average harvest. In early July the thermometer in Hyde Park read 90° in the shade. But a little later, on July 28th, a sudden access of wet weather, with the sky shrouded in clouds, spoiled completely the view of a total eclipse of the sun which observers had been anticipating.

As October drew near, the papers began to discuss the problem of "what to do with the Crystal Palace." The public had come to love it and there was a good deal of sentiment in favor of keeping it where it was. Paxton suggested that it might be made into a winter garden. But

Figure 189. Prince Albert's model lodginghouse

the Commissioners held to their original promise to dismantle the building, and rapidly the time grew near when the Great Exhibition would have to close.*

On October 7th 109,915 people saw the Exhibition, the largest crowd to date. The eleventh was the last day on which the public was admitted. The crowds gathered in the central court at five o'clock as the evening shadows were advancing. The waters of the Crystal Fountain ceased to play, and as the great clock struck the hour all the organs burst forth (not quite in unison) with "God Save the Queen." Ringing bells then warned the visitors to depart. They did so slowly and regretfully; not until six-thirty were the guards able to clear the building.

The official closing ceremonies came on the fifteenth, with a group of invited guests present to see the Commission give the medal awards. The Queen did not attend, and the ceremony was short and simple. The day was dark; pelting showers had set in early in the morning and had continued steadily. But before eleven o'clock 20,000 people had assembled, crowding the galleries and staircases and climbing onto the statuary to gain vantage points. Prince Albert and the various committees and commissions arrived. Albert, attired in plain morning dress, was greeted with cheers and shouts.

The report of the juries was read. They had considered more than

---

* The Palace was purchased by a newly organized group of investors and was re-erected in Sydenham, a good deal extended in size.

1,000,000 articles of 17,000 exhibitors, and had awarded more than 3,000 medals. Albert made a short statement, reiterating his expectation that the Great Exhibition, "by showing our mutual dependence upon each other, [will] be a happy means of promoting unity among nations, and peace and good-will among the various races of mankind." He was heard by only a few of the vast assemblage, but he was cheered repeatedly. The Bishop of London prayed solemnly ("peace and brotherly love" again). At the conclusion the organ, orchestra, and a great choir burst into the Hallelujah Chorus. The Great Exhibition of 1851 was over.

More than 6,000,000 people had seen the exhibits, paying total entrance fees of £356,000. The Exhibition had made a profit of £86,000, of which £831 came from taking charge of umbrellas!

The newspapers were lamenting in October that with the closing of the Crystal Palace there was nothing left for people to get excited about. Relief for this vacuum came rapidly on October 25th, when the exiled Hungarian national hero, Louis Kossuth, landed at Southampton. The story of Kossuth's progress through England and his reception in the various towns shows how strong British sympathy still was for the revolutionaries of central Europe—the sympathy, that is, of the middle and lower classes. The upper classes viewed with alarm such public demonstrations on behalf of radical foreigners. Thus the *Daily News* championed Kossuth; the *Times* was coolly satirical, sometimes acidulous.

There was much in the career and personality of Kossuth to explain the storm of popular demonstrations which greeted him in England. During the fierce days of 1848–49 he had been the energetic leader of the Hungarian revolt against Austria. The new emperor, Francis Joseph, had proclaimed him a traitor. When the Hungarian revolt was defeated by the Austrian forces in 1849, Kossuth fled to Italy. There he was honorably interned and at last allowed to embark for England.

Kossuth cast England under the spell of his oratory. During an earlier political imprisonment he had learned English with the aid of a volume of Shakespeare, and so he brought to his audiences now the full, rich flavor of their own Elizabethan heritage. He was a man of medium height, slight, with oval face, high forehead, and bluish-gray eyes. He wore whiskers and a heavy mustache. He delivered his speeches clearly and distinctly in his beautiful, logical, if somewhat florid, English, and a three-hour talk was not unusual for him. The fact that emotion occasionally overcame him as he spoke of the disgrace of his country did not at all reduce his effectiveness. From the beginning his audiences were huge and their enthusiasm unbounded.

The dignitaries of the various towns he visited delighted to honor

Figure 190. Louis Kossuth

him, until his tour, to the consternation of those who disapproved of him, took on the aspect of a semi-official series of municipal receptions. At Southampton the route of his entry into towns was lined by delighted crowds. He addressed them briefly from a balcony. When the band somewhat inappropriately played "Auld Lang Syne," the people joined in the chorus and Kossuth asked the mayor what the air was that so awakened popular sympathy. The mayor extricated himself by explaining that it was a song "customarily sung on occasions of cordial welcome." In the afternoon Kossuth addressed the Corporation in the Town Hall, and was presented with a large flag of the Hungarian Republic.

The triumphal tour began. The Corporation of London held a meeting in his honor, and his progress through the streets to the Guildhall was lined with cheering thousands of people. His audience greeted him with excited shouts. He next returned to Southampton, there to deliver a more elaborate three-hour speech, with Mr. Cobden and Lord Dudley Stuart on the platform as "assistant guests." Then next to Winchester, for a great banquet and attendant speechmaking on the part of many local and invited notables. Then to Manchester and Liverpool, and to Birmingham, where even the less sympathizing accounts placed the numbers of those who watched his procession under the triumphal arches at 75,000. Back again in London he addressed the Trades Unions at Copenhagen Fields, Islington. There "respectable artisans"—some 12,000 of them—formed a huge parade in Russell Square and marched through the streets out to the Fields. The *Times* conservatively described the crowd as one of 25,000; the *Morning Chronicle* estimated it at 50,000; the demonstrators themselves at 100,000.

It was in connection with the great excitement of Kossuth's reception in England that Palmerston, always sensitive to the public pulse and usually aware just how far he could go safely in displaying his contempt and hatred for foreign oppressors, overplayed his hand. The Government was already somewhat worried, for Austria was naturally annoyed at the enthusiasm which had greeted the exile. Palmerston had intended to receive Kossuth at his estate, but the Cabinet forbade him to do so. Palmerston then did receive a deputation of English from Finsbury and Islington and listened sympathetically while they read an address which declared the emperors of Russia and Austria despots, tyrants, and odious assassins. This created great alarm at Court, and the Queen would have liked to dismiss Palmerston. He was saved by Russell, who knew how generally unpopular such a dismissal, over such an issue and at that moment, would have been. But more critical events were brewing, which would at last blow Palmerston out of office.

The time was approaching when Louis Napoleon's four-year term as President of the French Republic would come to an end. The Constitution made it impossible for him to be re-elected; but he determined to remain in power, and in a sudden order of December 2d, dissolved the Assembly, abrogated the Constitution, and threw into prison the political leaders who were opposed to him. England was astonished to receive by midday the telegraphic communication: "Paris in a state of siege. The President re-establishes universal suffrage, and appeals to the people." While appealing to the electorate, however, Napoleon saw to it that the army was under tight control and issued thinly veiled instructions as to how *it* should vote. Nor was the chance given to the voters to cast ballots for anyone else; it was the familiar dictator's tactic: "Do you want me or don't you want me?" All this behind a lusty smoke screen of declarations on behalf of the people's welfare. The whole move was freely interpreted in England as one of unmitigated despotism; nor was anyone surprised when Napoleon was swept into new office by an overwhelming vote.

In the meantime official England, under Victoria's strong insistence, was playing a policy of careful neutrality. Just at this point Palmerston created an intolerable situation for the Government. He expressed in conversation to Walewski, the French ambassador in London, his belief that the President was fully justified in his *coup d'état,* in view of the plots that were hatching against him. Walewski wrote home what Palmerston had said. The British ambassador in Paris learned of it, wrote to Russell, and the cycle was complete. This indiscretion could not be ignored. The Queen was in a high temper, and the day before Christmas the *Times* announced that on the twenty-second Palmerston had been dismissed, with full Cabinet approval, from the foreign secretaryship. Lord Granville was appointed in his place. *Punch,* the consistent friend of Hungary and Kossuth and hater of Louis Napoleon, expressed its regret over the loss of the "strong man of the Cabinet." Many of those who did not have to live with Palmerston officially agreed with *Punch.*

The prompt receipt of all this exciting news from abroad was made possible by the completion, within the last few months, of the telegraphic cable between Dover and Calais. It had been laid the year before, but almost as soon as communication was established the cable broke. New and better cable had been woven of wires covered with gutta-percha and sheathed in twisted iron wire, and now the line was in operation. It was considered one of the wonders of the world.

In the waning months of the year not a little amusement was aroused by the appearance in London of several females from the United States, disciples of a Mrs. Bloomer and devoted to the task of spreading the gospel of Bloomerism among the benighted women of the British Isles. They held lectures and demonstrations, and some of the converted appeared in Piccadilly and elsewhere in a dress described as consisting of "something between a gipsy hat and a 'wideawake' of straw; a white collar turned down upon a velvet coatee of Lincoln green, buttoning tight around the waist, but open, and showing a frilled shirt front at the bosom, the sleeves fitting the arms closely and the skirts descending to the knee; the 'bloomers' are exceedingly full to the knee, but tight from there to the ankle, where they are drawn close." *Punch,* which had applied its wit with damnable iteration on behalf of the No-Popery campaign until public interest began to die, took over Bloomerism as its new *bête noir* and lambasted it from every conceivable comic point

Figure 191. Louis Napoleon

of view—and from some which tried to be comic but weren't. The whole thing was one of the few amusing public events in the latter part of 1851.

Lately official confirmation had come from New South Wales of the discovery of vast, rich gold fields. Already the rush from the Australian towns to the diggings had begun. Observers were concerned lest Australia go the wicked way of California: news had come from San Francisco of the establishment of Vigilance Committees and of lynch law. . . . The first *practical* adoption of an improved electric light was made by the Lancashire and Yorkshire Railway Company, which planned thus to illuminate the several tunnels along its line. . . . The annual Cattle Show of the Smithfield Club was held in December at the Bazaar in Baker Street. It was a democratic display by lord and farmer, here in the heart of London—and a symptom that even metropolitan England was still not far from the soil. It was noted that this year the animals were not so obscenely overgrown with fat as in previous exhibits. . . . The latest party (the tenth) in search of Sir John Franklin's expedition in the Arctic wilds returned unsuccessful. That expedition

BLOOMERISM—AN AMERICAN CUSTOM.

Figure 192. *Punch* on "Bloomerism"

had now been out five years, with provisions for only three or four years. Hope for their survival was dwindling fast. . . .* J. M. W. Turner died in his seventy-sixth year, and his artistic career was reviewed at length as being one of England's greatest. Particular emphasis was laid, however, on the earlier paintings rather than the later ones. . . . The declining days of the year were lightened by a report from Edinburgh concerning the "mesmeric mania" which had gripped that city in recent months.[9] Fashionable society had been greatly agitated; its parties had been converted into "scenes of experiments on the mental functions. Noblemen, members of the learned professions, and respectable citizens, have been amusing themselves in private. . . . The result has been an increased degree of nervousness in many individuals." . . .

So 1851 drew to a close. England took a long look backward, and a longer look ahead. This was a census year, and the statistics were encouraging. The population of Great Britain was now 20,793,000—an increase within the last decade of more than 2,100,000. Most of this growth had been in England alone, which now numbered 16,734,000. In Ireland the

---

* Other searching expeditions went out in subsequent years. Not until 1859 was definite confirmation made of the death of Franklin and his party.

number of people had dropped more than a million and a half from its 1841 census of 8,175,000. Fever, famine, and emigration had taken their toll. One of the more significant indications of the continuing shift of population from country to town was the accelerated growth of the midland cities. Manchester went from 300,000 to 400,000; Liverpool from 290,000 to 390,000; Birmingham from 180,000 to 230,000. London itself had increased by 415,000 or 21 per cent. It now had a population of 2,363,000.

National prosperity was pounding at the door if indeed it was not already inside. The official value of imports had jumped 60 per cent between 1841 and 1850; the value of exports had almost doubled in the same length of time (from £101,750,000 to £197,309,000). Even the Government had been able to show a surplus for the year ending in April, 1851, of two and a half million pounds. A surplus of nearly two million was estimated for the next year.

Perhaps the prophets celebrating the symbol of the Crystal Palace were right! Perhaps Great Britain was over the hump of economic depression, of famine and plague, of social injustices and unemployment, of political aberration. Perhaps her steamships sailing the seven seas, her gleaming railways, the millions of tons of cotton which her smoking mills were engulfing and sending back across the sea lanes of the world as finished fabric, her inventiveness and energy and solidity, her comfortable growing assurance that this was the best of all possible worlds and that the Englishman was God's anointed creation—perhaps all this *was* Utopia, and not just a wild surmise! It was at least a pleasant thought to carry into 1852.

True, food was given on Christmas Day from the Leicester Square soup kitchen to 10,000 poor families—roast beef, plum pudding, tea, coffee, and sugar. But the deserving poor were appointed to their place so that one could be generous at holiday time. And on Tuesday night the chapels in London and across the provinces were overflowing with people watching the old year out in thanksgiving, and waiting for the new year with quiet hope.

Dawn came rolling once more out of the North Sea as it had a decade earlier, over Regent's Park and Piccadilly and (this time) the great glass palace in Hyde Park; through the silent suburban villages, over the moors and farms and great towns, across the headlands into the Irish Sea. Death was under that dawn, and birth, and life. England had begun a new decade.

CHAPTER TWELVE

1841-1851 * Panorama

ONE hundred years rolled by, and the observer who has been seeing the sights, hearing the noises, and smelling the smells of a vanished generation may reasonably ask what it all meant: this crucial, crowded, kaleidoscopic decade of the 1840's. What was this Englishman of a century ago?—illusioned, disillusioned; worried, complacent; sagacious, silly; mature, adolescent; confident, bewildered; sensitive, cruel. Living in the midst of that historical cliché, a "transitional" age, what was peculiar to him and his time? Of what larger continuum was he a part?

It should be clear to one who has lived this many pages in the interstices of history that the Englishman he has been meeting was primarily *homo sapiens* (a major thesis for any historical interpretation): for that is exactly what Peel and Palmerston, mesmerism and anesthesia, "Sam Hall" and Morison's Pills, cholera and railroads, Tupper and Tennyson add up to. As we have said, he spent his time going to bed and getting up, eating and drinking, begetting children, nursing toothaches, reading small print by dim lights—and worrying a little (when he had time) about his soul. If he seems strange to us it is because we are so close to him that we are more aware of his differences. But if he went in 1850 to see the Arab snake charmers and the hippopotamus in the zoo at Regent's Park, so did his great-grandchildren a century later. If his curiosity was aroused by an advertisement in the *Times* ("*The greatest Wonder of the Age. Cantelo's Royal Incubator. . . . Chickens always hatching. Exhibited by command of Her Majesty, His Royal Highness Prince Albert, and Royal Family at Windsor Castle, and to thousands of ladies and gentlemen equally astonished and delighted*")—his same descendants were impressed by the same kind of royal approval. If he trampled his neighbor in the milling crowds watching royalty proceed through the streets to the opening of a new public bath, he had his parallel a century later.

He lived in the midst of paradoxes, some of them inherited and some self-created, and was undismayed. Many of those paradoxes were the price he paid for belonging to the human race; others were peculiarly British. *Punch* identified some of them in 1841 in his description of "What an Englishman Likes":

> An Englishman likes a variety of things. For instance, nothing is more to his liking than:
>
> To talk largely about Art, and to have the worst statues and monuments that ever disgraced a metropolis!
>
> To inveigh against the grinding tyrannies practised upon poor needlewomen and shop tailors, and yet to patronize the shop where cheap shirts and clothes are sold!
>
> To purchase a bargain, whether he is in want of it or not!
>
> To reward native talent, with which view he supports Italian operas, French plays, German singers, and in fact gives gold to the foreigners in exchange for the brass they bring him!
>
> To talk sneeringly against tuft-hunting and all tuft-hunters, and yet next to running after a lord, nothing delights him more than to be seen in company with one!
>
> To boast of his cleanliness, and to leave uncovered (as in the Thames) the biggest sewer in the world!
>
> To admit the utility of education, and yet to exclude from its benefits every one who is not of the same creed as himself!
>
> To grumble, no matter whether he is right or wrong, crying or laughing, working or playing, gaining a victory or smarting under a national humiliation, paying or being paid—still he must grumble!

Many years later, in 1948, the then Princess Elizabeth opened the Exhibition at Marble Arch which marked the centenary of the first Public Health Act. She pointed out, with commendable pride, how a century of steady progress "due to wise Acts of Parliament and to the increase of knowledge and to public enlightenment, have worked an almost miraculous change in the health of the people." Today five times as many children survive their infancy as in 1848. The expectation of life at birth has risen by twenty years. "The death rate from tuberculosis is one fifth of what it was in 1860," she said, "and there has been an equally remarkable decrease in deaths from most of the other dangerous diseases." But even while she spoke, the habitués of the British Museum were drinking water from the public drinking cup chained to the tap under the portico; and in the washroom were using the institutional roller towel, renewed each Monday morning. That they felt very comfortable in their anachronism was even more characteristically English than was their immunity to germs.

In a decade when everything was changing, nothing was more notable than the Englishman's traditional resistance to profound change—unless it was his ability to come to terms with it once it became inevitable. Intensely individual and loving liberty, he based that liberty on an endless series of social inequalities. Cherishing political freedom, he could afford to adore the feudal trappings with which he draped the crown whose power he had progressively been limiting. Proud that revolution had stayed away from his shores, he preached *laissez-faire* and then spent his time concocting political and social reforms that controverted the dominant economic theories but increased the range of social justice. Few of these reforms were based, however, on any theory that was "democratic" as the mid-nineteenth century understood that term. The state recognized a minimum responsibility to the indigent (no one should starve), and a plethora of private charitable agencies showed a concern for the underprivileged. Yet men so different as Dickens and Lord Ashley were representative of a large group which trusted private benevolence more than it did organized agencies, and wanted nothing done which would disturb the *status quo* of social classes. That the Englishman could still believe that everything could happen according to the good old way of doing things, that "precedent to precedent" could proceed with immutable regularity, was perhaps one of the reasons why, amid all kinds of threatening cataclysms, he continued to believe in the unbelievable and at last made an approximation of it come true.

Certainly it was a reforming age. The *Athenaeum* in 1851, while admitting the evils which had come in the wake of industrialism, pointed out that those evils were being attacked with more or less success: "We have already satisfied ourselves that even calico-spinners have souls as well as bodies. . . . The refinements in the art of government, and the extension of the means of observation, have laid bare the rotten parts of our system with greater minuteness than has ever been attained in any other country or time; and like a deformed child which sees its own distorted figure for the first time in a faithful mirror, we have been filled with terror by the contemplation not of a new, but of a newly-reflected image." So the age threw itself upon political reforms, social reforms, religious reforms. A reforming decade produced its prophets and its panaceas. Carlyle, Ruskin, and Newman with their retreat, each in his own way, to the Middle Ages: hero worship, art, and the medieval church. Chartism, Disraeli's "Young England" movement, the Anti-Corn Law League, the Co-operative movement, evangelicalism, Christian Socialism, even Manchester economics—each was looked upon by its enthusiasts as the road to happiness, prosperity, and peace.

Behind this enthusiasm for social and political amelioration was a moral earnestness which was as secular as it was pious. It invaded literature, art, and politics as well as religion. Even trade expansion and colonization were coming to be thought of as existing for the greater glory of England and therefore as a divine dispensation. A decrease in drunkenness and a growth in exports were equated as moral benefits. At this point a certain intellectual confusion was bound to enter, involving some self-delusions but as yet a relatively small amount of hypocrisy. When the Englishman in the 1840's was mistaken, his mistake was usually based on what seemed to him the highest of moral principles.

This earnestness was a part of the pervasive temper of energy and enthusiasm which was perhaps the most striking single feature of the early Victorian personality. No matter whether you were distributing religious tracts by the million, writing multiple-volume histories, poetry, or novels, arguing for the secret ballot or for the repeal of something or other, preaching sermons, designing cathedrals or Crystal Palaces, building railroads, making cloth in Manchester or iron in Birmingham, or merely eating a gargantuan dinner, you did it with a complete absorption of interest and with a boundless energy. Macaulay, Mill, Ruskin, Dickens, Disraeli, Paxton, Ashley, Knight, Hudson, O'Connell, Kingsley, Peel, Browning, Cole (to rehearse quite at random some of the names of the forties)—each did more in a lifetime than a dozen men in a lesser age. The decade threw up "characters" on every hand. Nor is it sufficient to explain all this activity by reference to the solemn obligation to "work, for the night cometh" which popular religion laid upon the Victorian conscience. Evangelicalism and Dissent undoubtedly helped to create the code of hard work, and the entrepreneurs of industry found it profitable to encourage it. But agnostics worked just as hard as the puritans. The answer lies rather in the whole complex of the times, with the exhilarating awareness that the contemporary Englishman was living in an expanding (English) universe, that the world's great oyster was his, and that all one had to do was to hang on to the coattails of Progress to be ushered into an Elysium where every prospect pleases.

"Victorianism," in its drabber, more conventionalized sense, had not yet demoralized the Englishman of the forties. To be sure, the decade was essentially serious: it had to grapple with severe problems, and there were many in the mines and shops and factories who felt no euphoria as they contemplated their future prospects. Still others, wistful intellectuals, found the reconciliation of doubt and belief difficult and drifted between the two worlds of faith and spiritual disillusion. Some of them took flight to Rome, some to a different kind of medievalism. Still others grappled with their doubts in daylight and laid them. But it is by no means primarily an age of doubt; it is rather an age emerging from a period of political and social turmoil into one where Hope, a maiden decorously dressed, beckons from the near horizon. It had been the Hungry Forties for many, the Anxious Forties for others; but by mid-century all were looking expectantly toward what they believed would be the Fabulous Fifties.

It is not surprising that a decade stirred by so many crosscurrents, so full of life and aggressiveness, so hungry for certitude and yet not quite sure of its own standards, should be a romantic one. Romanticism invaded art and religion. It was built into the Italianate-Classical architecture and still more into the emerging neo-Gothic. Music was romantic, and literature. We have seen how gustily the Englishman of the forties laughed and wept. The two great figures in poetry and the novel, Tennyson and Dickens, wrote on the one hand of medieval knights and ladies and on the other of melodramatic villains, tender heroines, and comic eccentrics. At the lesser literary levels reams of sentimental poetry and horrific as well as sentimental fiction were engorged by avid readers. Melodrama and farce were the staples of the theaters.

As the Great Exhibition abundantly showed, contemporary household design was romanticism gone to seed. The intricate, the ornate, the elaborate in decoration were laid upon objects so essentially solid and British that the result was the grotesque. Good taste was disappearing into an orgy of bastard rococo. And even in men's dress the transition from the gay dandyism of the Regency to the dull monotony of black was not yet complete. Impressive "chimney-pot" silk hats were worn, and in the mid-decade blue frock coats, with white drill trousers and straps, were still fashionable. Loud-checked trousers were common; ornately patterned waistcoats were in style.

People in the forties could give themselves heartily to the emotion at hand. Their aggressiveness may have hidden at times an inner bewilderment, their romanticism a secret instability. But however sedate the great middle classes were to become they were as yet far from complacent. There was work to be done and they were doing it.

The Great Exhibition of 1851 was not merely the climax of a decade: it was also the symbol of British aspiration at mid-century. Here were all its halting defects of taste, its meretricious as well as its genuine accomplishments; its aesthetic obliquities and its groping, wistful hopes. Here were Production, Invention, Achievement. Here was the sign to the nations that Britain was ready to accept what every good Englishman knew she deserved: world recognition of her mighty industrial power. Had she not flung across her countryside, within the decade, 5,000 miles of shining rails? Had not the new industry of machinery and machine tools doubled and trebled? Were not her steamships in multiplying numbers furrowing the sea lanes to bring back raw materials to be woven and stamped into products once again to be shipped to the world markets hungrily awaiting her production? And were not those markets merely a due reward for the supremacy of British culture and institutions and initiative?

A great deal had happened in the last fifty years. "At home," said the liberal *Spectator* at the beginning of 1851, "the half-century has changed the aspect of society: where all was Tory suppression at the beginning, all is thrown open now. We have gained freedom, political, religious, and commercial; food, clothes, and lodging are cheaper; the appliances of life, intellectual and material, pleasurable and useful, have multiplied in every class. We have clubs for the wealthy, athenaeums and mechanics' institutes for the humble; the factory system, which dresses the women of the working class like the ladies of the last century, is the creation of the epoch which has given us railways, steamships, electric telegraphs, the Rosse telescope, photography; 'mesmerism' says the *Post*, and 'chloroform'; also, cries the American, California. . . . Standing on the threshold of another half-century, we ask in an admiring but not an exacting spirit what in that period will be the unforeseen equivalents of chloroform and photography; of the oxyhydrogen microscope, and Crosse's electrical magic; of the electric telegraph, of the steam-ship, and the railway." What more, in other words, could a Festival of Britain in 1951 possibly celebrate?

In this accession of confidence it is best to leave the early Victorians—

in their hopes, bedded with some lingering apprehensions, in their cupidities and philanthropies, their intellectual and emotional confusions, and their very real wisdom. If they have a comfortable sense that they are not as other people they mean it as a tribute to English character and not as a reflection upon God's handiwork elsewhere. Peace was here, and prosperity, and a queen still young was on the throne, of whom the laureate could write in 1851:

> Her court was pure; her life serene;
>   God gave her peace; her land reposed;
> A thousand claims to reverence closed
>   In her as Mother, Wife, and Queen.

Peace, repose, serenity. The throne reaching down a friendly hand to the Victorian family. The Victorian family confident against the future. The future—silent within the circle of its own enigmas.

CHAPTER ONE

1. G. D. H. Cole and R. Postgate: *The Common People*, 1946, p. 305.
2. "English Fragments," *Pictures of Travel*, Vol. II, 1828.
3. Quoted by William Howitt: *The Rural Life of England*, 2d ed., 1840, pp. 110–11.
4. Quoted by D. C. Somervell: *English Thought in the Nineteenth Century*, 1929, p. 28.
5. R. F. Wearmouth: *Methodism and the Working-Class Movements of England*, 1937.
6. See *First Impressions of England and Its People*, an observing book by an intelligent Scotsman, Hugh Miller, 1847.
7. E. E. Kellett: *Religion and Life in the Early Victorian Age*, 1938, p. 29.
8. Vol. I, Chap. VII, sec. 152.
9. Richard L. Evans: *A Century of "Mormonism" in Great Britain*. Deseret News Press, Salt Lake City, 1932, p. 244.
10. *The Mormons: a Contemporary History*, 1851, p. 249.
11. J. L. and B. Hammond, *Lord Shaftesbury*, 1923, p. 66.
12. *Ibid.*, p. 241.
13. Wilfred Ward: *W. G. Ward and the Oxford Movement*, 1889, p. 136.
14. Experiences of a practicing photographer in 1840. Quoted in Lucia Moholy: *A Hundred Years of Photography*, 1939.
15. Alex Straaser: *Victorian Photography*, 1942.
16. Spencer Walpole: *History of England*, 5 vols., 1878–86, Vol. IV, p. 66.
17. *Records of Later Life*, 2d ed., 3 vols., 1882, Vol. II, pp. 99–100, 102.
18. Charles Greville, *Memoirs of the Reign of Queen Victoria, Second Part*, 3 vols., 1885, Vol. II, pp. 51–52.

CHAPTER TWO

1. Greville: *Ibid.*, Vol. II, p. 86.
2. *Spectator*, May 28, 1842.
3. *London Labour and the London Poor*, Vols. I and II, 1851. Vol. III, 1861. Vol. I, p. 284.
4. British Museum, Collection of Ballads.
5. *Journal of Mary Frampton*, ed. Harriot G. Mundy, second edition, 1885, p. 415.
6. *Spectator*, June 4, 1842.
7. See Jane Grey Perkins: *Life of Mrs. Norton*, 1909.
8. By Arthur Freeling [1840].
9. Léon Faucher: *Études sur L'Angleterre*, Paris, 1845.
10. For these quotations from the Home Office Papers, 45, see R. F. Wearmouth: *Methodism and the Working-Class of England*, 1937, pp. 133–34.
11. *Memoirs, Second Part*, Vol. II, p. 119.
12. *Past and Present*, Bk. I. Chap. 3; "Manchester Insurrection."
13. *Journal of the London Statistical Society*, May, 1848, p. 119.
14. *Edinburgh Review*, April, 1845.
15. See his pamphlet: *A Letter to Lord Ashley*, 1842.
16. April 2, 1842.

CHAPTER THREE

1. May 14, 1842.
2. *London Journal*, 1845, Vol. I, p. 158.
3. *Pictorial Times*, August 19, 1843.
4. *London Journal*, 1845, Vol. I, p. 407.
5. *Tercentenary Handlist of English and Welsh Newspapers, Magazines, and Reviews*, published by the *Times*, 1920.
6. *Report from the Select Committee on Public Libraries*, 1849, p. 178.
7. The summary of this first issue is given in *Early Victorian England*, 2 vols., 1934, Vol. II, p. 70.
8. Q. D. Leavis: *Fiction and the Reading Public*, 1932, p. 174.
9. *Passages from the Life of Charles Knight*, condensed from *Passages from a Working Life*, 1864-65. N. Y., 1874, p. 328.
10. *Household Words*, 1850, Vol. I, p. 82.
11. *Journal of the London Statistical Society*, 1843, p. 213.
12. *Autobiography of Samuel Smiles*, ed. Thomas Mackay, 1905, p. 131.
13. *Early Victorian England*, Vol. II, p. 72.
14. C. S. Home: *Nonconformity in the 19th Century*, 1907, p. 74.
15. *Account of a Case of a Successful Amputation of the Thigh . . .* , 1843.
16. Margaret Goldsmith: *Franz Anton Mesmer*, N. Y., 1934, p. 223.
17. *Zoist*, Vol. I (March, 1843–January, 1844), p. 455.
18. *Spectator*, September 30, p. 932.

CHAPTER FOUR

1. *Second Report of the Commissioners for Inquiring into the State of Large Towns and Populous Districts*, 1845, pp. 61–62.
2. March 30, 1844. Quoted by B. L. Hutchins and A. Harrison: *A History of Factory Legislation*, 1903, p. 69.
3. See G. D. H. Cole: *Chartist Portraits*, 1941, p. 104.
4. *Memoirs of the Reign of Queen Victoria, Second Part*, 1885, Vol. II, pp. 236-37.
5. Léon Faucher: *Manchester in 1844*, 1844, p. 15.
6. Charles Knight: *London*, 6 vols., 1841-44, Vol. III, pp. 263f.
7. Henry Mayhew: *London Labour and the London Poor*, 2 vols., 1851, Vol. II, p. 402.
8. *Factories and the Factory System*, p. 40.
9. *Memories of London in the 'Forties*, 1908.
10. This and subsequent material are taken from *Reports of the Special Assistant Poor Law Commissioners on the Employment of Women and Children in Agriculture*, 1843. These reports covered Wiltshire, Dorsetshire, Devonshire, and Somersetshire.
11. C. K. Hartshorne: *The System of Cottage Building pursued by his Grace the Duke of Bedford* [1849].
12. *Victorian Days in England: Letters of an American Girl, 1851-52*, by Anna Maria Fay. Boston and New York, 1923.
13. Paris, 1845. 2 tom. A translation of part of this, however, taken from earlier articles in the *Revue des Deux Mondes*, was published in England in 1844 as *Manchester in 1844*. (See above.)
14. Arthur E. Bestor, Jr.: *Backwoods Utopias*, N. Y., 1950.

15. See his *Whistler at the Plough,* Manchester, 1852, pp. 107f.
16. G. J. Holyoake: *Thirty-three Years of Co-operation in Rochdale,* 9th ed., 1882, p. 2.
17. "England's Trust," published in his *Poems of 1850.*
18. R. S. Lambert: *The Railway King,* 1934.

CHAPTER FIVE

1. *Spectator,* 1845, pp. 373–74.
2. *Some Account of My Life and Writings,* 2 vols., 1873, Vol. I, p. 415.
3. *Seven Lamps of Architecture,* 1849.
4. Leigh Hunt: *Readings for Railways* [1850].
5. F. S. Williams: *Our Iron Roads,* 1852, p. 280.
6. *Companion to the Almanac,* 1841.
7. John Francis: *A History of the English Railway,* 2 vols., 1851, Vol. II, p. 151.
8. *Ibid.,* Vol. II, p. 216.
9. See the excellent biography of Hudson by Lambert: *The Railway King,* pp. 171f.
10. F. C. Bowen: *A Century of Atlantic Travel,* 1931.
11. See M. J. B. Davy: *Henson and Stringfellow,* 1931, p. 42.

CHAPTER SIX

1. *A New Spirit of the Age,* 1907 ed., pp. 62–63.
2. Elie Halévy: *The Age of Peel and Cobden,* 1947, p. 119.
3. *England as It Is,* 1851, p. 253.
4. *The Pictorial Times,* May 13, 1843.
5. Richard and Samuel Redgrave: *A Century of British Painters,* 1947 ed., p. 263. A very useful and intelligent book, first published in 1866.
6. *Geographical Dictionary,* pp. 11–13.
7. Letter to the *Pall Mall Gazette,* March 16, 1872.
8. *Cheer! Boys, Cheer! Memories of Men and Music* [1895], p. 188.
9. "120 Popular Comic Songs sung by Sam Cowell," in an edition of *Dalcorn's Musical Miracles* [1851].
10. Obituary of William Smith O'Brien, the *Times,* June 20, 1864.
11. These particular posters are described by Charles Knight in his *London,* 6 vols., 1841–44, Vol. V, p. 34.
12. *The Lancet,* May 29, 1847.
13. This, like the following case, from the *Edinburgh Review,* LXXVII (1843), pp. 6–7.

CHAPTER SEVEN

1. *The Emigrants' Manual,* Edinburgh, 1851.
2. *Letters from England, 1846–49,* by Elizabeth Davis Bancroft, N. Y., 1904.
3. Quoted by Helen Morris: *Portrait of a Chef: The Life of Alexis Soyer,* 1938. This book is a mine of lively information about Soyer.
4. *Illustrated London News,* November 6, 1847.
5. *Ibid.,* May 8th.
6. *Journal of the London Statistical Society,* 1848, p. 166.

CHAPTER EIGHT

1. Greville: *Memoirs of the Reign of Queen Victoria, Second Part*, Vol. III, p. 257.
2. Quoted by Henry Jephson: *The Sanitary Evolution of London*, 1907, pp. 18–19.
3. Quoted by the *Critic*, October 1, 1849.
4. *Records of Later Life*, Vol. II, p. 153.
5. W. M. Rossetti: *Praeraphaelite Diaries and Letters*, 1900, pp. 206–7.

CHAPTER NINE

1. Quoted in E. S. Turner: *Boys Will Be Boys* [1950], p. 24.
2. In "The Curate's Walk," *Punch*, November 27, 1847.
3. For a vivacious biography of Tupper, see Derek Hudson: *Martin Tupper, His Rise and Fall*, 1949.
4. According to returns prepared by Dr. Hudson, Secretary of the Manchester Athenaeum, in 1851, and quoted by Charles Knight: *The Old Printer and the Modern Press*, 1854, p. 306.
5. *Report from the Select Committee on Public Libraries*, 1849.
6. *The Working Man's Friend and Family Instructor*, Vol. I (January to March, 1850).
7. *Report of the Commissioners appointed to inquire into the condition and government of the British Museum*, 1850.
8. *London*, 6 vols., 1841–44, Vol. IV, pp. 391f.
9. F. J. Harvey Darton: *Children's Books in England*, Cambridge, 1932, p. 233.

CHAPTER TEN

1. *Memoirs of the Reign of Queen Victoria, Second Part*, Vol. III, p. 349.
2. See Henry Jephson: *The Sanitary Evolution of London*, 1907, pp. 12f.
3. N. P. Willis: *Famous Persons and Famous Places*, 1854, p. 187.
4. Mayhew: *London Labour and the London Poor*, Vol. II, p. 416.
5. J. Ewing Ritchie: *The Night Side of London*, 1857, p. 66.
6. [James Grant]: *The Great Metropolis*, N. Y. and London, 2 vols., 1837, Vol. I, p. 8.
7. Masson: *Memories of London in the 'Forties*, p. 21.
8. Charles Knight: *London*, 6 vols., 1841–44, Vol. V, pp. 389f.
9. *The Lord Chief Baron Nicholson: An Autobiography*, 1860, p. 285.
10. *Edmund Yates: His Recollections and Experiences*, 2 vols., 1884, Vol. I, p. 172.
11. *The Weekly Tribune: A Journal of Education, Colonization, Politics, and Social Progress*, June 15, 1850.

CHAPTER ELEVEN

1. *The Crystal Palace and Its Contents; an Illustrated Cyclopaedia of the Great Exhibition*, October 11, 1851, pp. 22–23.
2. *Spectator*, November 8, 1851, p. 1074.
3. Peter Quennell: *Victorian Panorama*, 1937, pp. 103–4.
4. No. 65, 1850, pp. 4f.

5. *The Crystal Palace and Its Contents*, p. 282.
6. *Illustrated London News*, May 3, 1851, p. 343.
7. No. 1251, October 18, 1851, p. 1094.
8. *Athenaeum*, May 24th, p. 548.
9. John Hughes Bennett:. *The Mesmeric Mania of 1851*, Edinburgh, 1851.

INDEX

à Beckett, Gilbert, 50, 108, 112, *note;* 314
Aberdeen, Lord, 208, 209
Aborigine's Protective Society, 19
Adamson, Robert, 37
advertisements, 275–84
  coarseness, 6
  newspaper, 15–16
aeronautics. *See* aviation.
Afghanistan, war in, 8, 17, 100
Africa, 470
Age, The, 110
Age of Great Cities, by Vaughan, 169
Agnes Grey, by Brontë, 311
agriculture. *See* farming
Ainsworth, William Harrison, 54, 59, 97,
  104, 113, 365
Akbar Khan, 17
Albert, Prince, 7, 9, 29, 186, 295, 468
  at the Crystal Palace, 461
  birthday, 186
  father of the Crystal Palace, 444
  free trader, 205
  growth in public favor, 434
  influence, 69
  visit to France, 146
Albert Edward, Prince. *See* Prince of
  Wales
Albert Memorial, 266
alcoholism. *See* drunkenness
aliens, bill for removal, 326
Almack's, 152, 335
Alton Locke, by Kingsley, 438
America and the Americans. *See* United
  States
*America—Historical, Statistical and
  Descriptive,* by Buckingham, 20
American Notes, by Dickens, 81
America's Cup, 464–65
Amoy, 18
amusements, 21
Andromaque, 47
anesthesia, 286–89
Anglican Church. *See* Church, Established
"animal magnetism." *See* mesmerism
Anti-Corn Law Bill, 94
Anti-Corn Law League, 46, 61, 90, 138, 158,
  171, 205–06, 239, 240
Antonina, by Collins, 365
archaeology, 381
architecture, 262, 381
  Gothic, 266
aristocracy, 8, 69, 172, 176, 179, 183, 198,
  294, 338, 406
  homes of, 173
Aristocracy of England, by Howitt, 117

army, flogging in, 5, 251
Arnold, Matthew, 7, 31, 188, 382
Arnold, Thomas, 23, 24, 33, *note;* 81, 104,
  120
  biography of, 149
arson in country districts, 149, 174
art, 255
  Pre-Raphaelite. *See* Pre-Raphaelitism;
    also names of arts
Arthur, Prince, birth of, 402
Ashburton, Lord, 100
Ashley, Lord (later Earl of Shaftesbury),
  7, 19, 26, 30, 61, 91, 129, 132–34, 149,
  156, 157, 158, 159, *note;* 176, 200, 243,
  290, 312, 332, 484
Asiatic cholera. *See* cholera
Association for the Relief of the Poor in
  London, 10
Astley's Royal Amphitheatre, 8, 429
Astor House Riots in New York, 382–85
astrologers, 127
"Asylum of Europe," 325
Athenaeum, 107
Atmospheric Railway, 230
Attwood, Thomas, 87
Australia, gold rush to, 479
Austrian Empire, 323, 326, 441, 477. *See
  also* Hungary
authors. *See* books
Autobiography of an Artisan, by Thomson,
  129, *note;* 132, *note*
aviation, attempts, 234
  balloons, 432; fatal ascent, 314

Bailey, F. W. N. ("Alphabet"), 108
Bailey, Philip James, 211, 369, 371
Balfe, 267, 268, 304
ball in Buckingham Palace, 67
ballads, hawking of, 6
  "Sam Hall," 426–27
ballet, 268, 304
balloons. *See* aviation
ballot. *See* suffrage
Bancroft, Mrs. George, 294–96
Bank of England, 243, 313
  discount rate, 313
Barbauld, Mrs., 378
Barham, 113
Barnes, Thomas, 35, 106
Barnum, P. T., 150, 437
Barrett, Elizabeth. *See* Browning, Elizabeth
Barry, Sir Charles, 263, 267
Barry Lyndon, by Thackeray, 211
bathing, sea, 273–74, 437
Battle of Life, by Dickens, 366

Bavaria, King of, 323
Bayley, F. W. N., 153
beards, 80
Bedford, Duke of, 175
Belle Assemblée, 78
Bell's Life in London, 109
Bells, Acton, Ellis, and Currer. *See* Brontës
Bells and Pomegranates, by Browning, 211
Bennett, Sterndale, 267
Bentham, Jeremy, 238
Bentinck, Lord George, 242, 340
Berlioz, Hector, 268, 304, 335
betterment, social. *See* reforms
Bible in Spain, The, by Borrow, 97, 362
Bibles, distribution of, 25
  production of, 251
Billingsgate, 3
Biographical Dictionary, 118
Birkenhead, 213, 307
birth control, 85
Blanc, Louis, 319, 321, 325
Blanchard, Laman, 107, 113, 125, *note*
Blessington, Countess of, 74–75, 393
Bloomer, Mrs. Amelia, and Bloomerism, 478
Blot in the 'Scutcheon, by Browning, 138, 424
Bohemian Girl, The, by Balfe, 146, 186, 267, 268
Bonaparte, Louis. *See* Louis Napoleon
Book of Nonsense, A, by Lear, 249
books, 15, 53, 104, 211, 249, 308–12, 361, 380–82, 437–38, 472
  by women, 73, 78
  cheap editions, 373
  children's, 377–80
  Christmas, 76, 237, 285, 367, 442
  copyright, international, 81
  etiquette, 72, 76
  "horror," 363
  novels in weekly parts, 122
  on the United States. *See* United States
  read by laboring men, 125–26
  religious, 23, 361
  sale, 373; at railway stations, 374–75
  school. *See* education
  sensational, 119, 122, 124, 363
  sentimentalism in, 121
  sermons, 23
  weekly parts, 122
Borrow, George, 7, 97, 362
Bosanquet, S. R., 190
Bottle, The, by Cruikshank, 309
Boucicault, Dion (Lee Moreton), 47, 422, 472
boundary dispute, northeast, with the United States, 21
boundary dispute, Oregon, settlement, 104
boxing. *See* prizefighting

Bradshaw's Railway Guide, 57, 112, *note;* 220
Braid, Dr. James, 144
bread, prices, 312
bribery in politics, 94–95
bridges, Menai Straits, 402
  Mersey, 236
  See also London
Bright, John, 7, 26, 138, 158, 206
Britannia Bridge, Menai Straits, 402
British Almanac and Its Companion, 118
British Museum, 146, 212, 263, 377, 429
broadsheets, 65, 414
Brontë (Bell), Charlotte, 7, 144, 311, 365
Brontë (Bell) sisters, 73, 249, 311
Brooke, Rajah of Sarawak, 295
Brooks, Shirley, 411, *note*
Brotherhood, Pre-Raphaelite. *See* Pre-Raphaelitism
Brougham, Lord, 118, 158
Browning, Elizabeth Barrett, 73, 144, 147, 285, 368
  and Robert, 26, 284
  mentioned for laureateship, 399
Browning, Robert, *xiii*, 7, 27, 37, 53, 211, 239, 285, 424
Brummell, Beau, 7
Brunel, Sir I., 138, 217, 219, 232, 245
Brunswick, Duke of, 110
Buckingham, Duke of, 196, 313
  sale of effects, 340
Buckingham, James Silk, 20, 104
Buckingham Palace, 166, 213, 263
  ball, 67
Buckstone, 304
budgets, 203, 239
Bulwer Lytton, Edward, 47, 71, 74, 104, 249, 341, 365, 420, 472
Bunning, J. D., 266
Burnes, Captain Alexander, 17
burnings. *See* arson
Burton, Decimus, 263
Bury, Lady Charlotte, 73, 97
business, depression, 82, 97, 290, 313, 327; of 1837, 10
  improvement, 352, 396
Byron, Lord, 75, 368, 429

cabinet. *See* ministry
cable, Dover-Calais, 478
  transatlantic, proposed, 360
California, gold discovery and rush, 349–50, 357–60
"Calotypes," 36–37
Cambridge University, decline of, 200
Campbell, Thomas, 5, 6, 185
Canton, 18
Cardigan, Lord, 5, 6,
Carlyle, Jane, 308

Carlyle, Thomas, 7, 31, 47, 103, 104, 113, 144, 150, 170, 183, 211, 213, 308, 315, 331, 342, 347, 400
gospel of work, 22
Catholic Church. *See* Roman Catholic Church
Catholicity, 33
Catnach, James, 163, 413
Cavaignac, General, 322
Cayley, Sir George, 233
census, 56, 480
Chadwick, Edwin, 7, 166, 245, 336
Chalmers, Dr., 135
Chambers, Robert, 118, 120, 187, 189, 309, 400
Chambers, William, 118, 120
Chambers's Cyclopedia of English Literature, 122
Chambers's Edinburgh Journal, 120
Chantrey, Sir Francis, 265–66
chapels. *See* Dissenters
Charitable Cookery, or the Poor Man's Regenerator, 299
charity. *See* philanthropy
Charles Albert, King of Sardinia, 324
Chartism, 10, 11, 23, 86, 141, 180, 327, 328
National Charter Association, 88
petition, monster, and end of Chartism, 87, 328–32
cheese for the Queen, 9
child labor. *See* labor
children, books for, 377–80
Infant Custody Bill, 74
"pacifiers," 157, 175
Chimes, The, by Dickens, 366
China, missionaries in, 19
Opium War, 8, 17, 18, 100
chloroform, use of, 289
cholera, 289, 316, 335–36, 339, 350–51, 355–56, 392
Chopin, Frédéric, 268, 335, 393
Christian Socialism, 23, 346–47, 438
Christmas books. *See* books
Christmas Carol, A, by Dickens, 148, 366
Christmas Eve and Easter Day, by Browning, 437
Christmas pantomimes, 8
Christmas poems in *Punch*, 103
church, the. *See* religion; also names of denominations
Church, Established (Anglican Church; Church of England), 23
Anglicanism (Orthodoxy; High Church), 24, 200
Apostolic Succession, 30, 32
Broad, 24
complacency, 30
Evangelical wing, 24
interlocking with education, 201
Latitudinarianism, 32

Church (*Cont.*)
school societies, 130
Thirty-Nine Articles, 33
Toryism, 24
turmoil in, 199
Church, Roman Catholic. *See* Roman Catholic Church
Church, Scottish. *See* Established Church of Scotland
cities, growth of, 169, 481
Civis Romanus Sum speech of Palmerston, 398
clergymen, 178–79
clothing. *See* fashions
Clough, Arthur Hugh, 31
Cobden, Richard, 7, 45, 61, 94, 134, 138, 158, 205, 206, 207, 242
Cockle's Antibilious Pills, 202
coffee, 471
coffee and tea, 302, *note*
Cole, Henry (Felix Summerly), 380, 444
Collier, John Payne, 59
Collins (painter), 436, *note*
Collins, Wilkie, 365
Collinson, James, 348
colonies and colonialism, 17, 19, 470, 485
Combe, George, *Notes on the United States of America*, 20
commerce, 17, 22, 57, 197, 204, 396, 481
revival, 153
See also business
Communism, 180
Communist Manifesto, 327
Complete Suffrage movement, 88
Condition-of-England Question, 12, 83, 180
Condition of the Working Class in England in 1844, by Engels, 179
conduct. *See* morality
Congreve, 97
Coningsby, or the New Generation, by Disraeli, 183, 212, 365
Conquest of Peru, The, by Prescott, 309
Conservatives (Tories), 183, 205, 242, 396
conservatism, *xiii*, 5, 484
contemporary record, *xv*
Cook, Eliza, 73, 111, 115, 271, 360, 369
Cook, Thomas, 220
cook books, 298–99
cookery. *See* food
Cooper, James Fenimore, 20, 471
Cooper, Thomas, 88
co-operatives, 23, 85, 181, 182, 439
copyright, international, 81
corn. *See* wheat
Corn Law Rhymes, by Elliott, 206
Corn Laws, 45, 61, 90, 103, 153, 158, 207, 238
end of, 360
suspension, 291
See also Anti-Corn Law League

cosmetics, 79
cost of living, 197
"cottages, model," 175
cotton industry, 158, *note*
    depression, 290
cotton supply, 19
Count of Monte Cristo, The, by Dumas,
    335
Court Magazine, 78
courts, police, 14
Covent Garden, 268, 285, 420
Cowell, Sam, 273, 427
cricket, 251
Cricket on the Hearth, The, by Dickens,
    237
crime, increase in, 84
    lessened, 197
crisis, economic. *See* business; finance
Critical and Historical Essays, by Macaulay,
    104
Crockford's, 3
Croker, John Wilson, 183, 184, 190
Cromwell's Letters and Speeches, by
    Carlyle, 211
crop failures, 52
    See also famine; Ireland
Crown and people, 68
Cruikshank, George, 25, 50, 309, 341
Cruikshank's Comic Almanac, 191, *note*
Crystal Palace, 266, 432, 443–82
    arts and handicrafts sections, 465–67
    awards, 474–75
    exhibits, 462; American, 463
culture of the time, *xiv*
curry powder for hunger, 2–7
Cushman, Charlotte, 212, 303
customs, country families', 176
    old, disappearance of, 172

Daguerre, 37, 464
Daily News, London, 107, 250
dancing, 77, 152
dandies, 7
Darwin, Charles, 7, 31, 56, 188, 190, 191, 400
    books by, 188, 189
David Copperfield, by Dickens, 367
Deák, Francis, 324
death rate, 163, 484
deceased wife's sister bill, 471
debtors' prisons, 95
deer killing à la battue, 199
defenses, 318
Delane, John T., 35, 106
depression, business. *See* business
Derby, Epsom, 140, 307
Dickens, Charles, 6, 7, 23, 54, 57, 74, 98,
    104, 107, 117, 132, 148, 179, 211, 237,
    250, 276, 285, 308, 334, 366, 368, 437,
    484, 486
    account of a public execution, 391

visit to America, 81
dinner-party menu, 300–01
diplomacy, triumphs of, 100
disaster, predictions of, 62
diseases, germ theory, 356
diseases of labor. *See* labor
Disraeli, Benjamin, 7, 17, 45, 74, 150, 155,
    183, 202, 204, 208, 211, 240, 242, 309,
    312, 365, 396
Dissenters, chapel; description by Ruskin,
    27
    churches and membership, 26
    disabilities of, 26
    number of, 202
Dombey and Son, by Dickens, 285, 308, 366
domesticity, 69
domestics, 57
    discrimination against Irish, 16
Don Pacifico affair, 397–98
d'Orsay, Count, 7, 75
Dost Mohammed, 17
Doyle, Richard, 442
dress. *See* fashions
Drummond, Edward, murder of, 133
Drunkard's Children, The, by Cruikshank,
    309
drunkenness, 12, 103
Drury Lane, 8, 198, 268, 420
dueling, 5
Dumas, Alexandre, 303, 335

earthquake, prediction of, 62
eating. *See* food
Ecclesiastical Titles Act, 441
economic and social philosophies, 23
economic depression. *See* business
economic theory, Manchester, 85
Edgeworth, Maria, 73, 378
Edinburgh Review, 111
education, 128
    adult, 121, 132
    books, school, 131
    compulsory, bill for, 133
    Dames' Schools, 131
    higher, criticism of, 201
    interlocking with the Established Church,
        201
    monitorial system, 130
    neglect of, 129
    "People's Colleges," 132
    popular, 120
    public-school, 23
    Ragged Schools, 131
    self, 121, 132
Edward VII. *See* Prince of Wales
Egypt, foray in, 9
election, general. *See* politics
electricity, coming of, 235, 344, 479
Elijah, by Mendelssohn, 268
Eliot, George, 7, 249

Eliza Cook's Journal, 111, 115, 360
Elizabeth II, Queen, 483–84
Elliott, Ebenezer, 206
Elliottson, Dr. John, 143, 145
Ellis, Sarah, 71
Ellsler, Fanny, 74, 268
Elmes, H. L., 263
Emerson, Ralph Waldo, 314–15, 335
emigration, 103, 197
  increase in, 84
  movement for, 13
Empire, the, 17
Encyclopaedia Britannica, 307
end of the world, prediction of, 14
Engels, Friedrich, 149, 160, 179–81, 326–27, 402
Enoch Arden, by Tennyson, 369
enterprise, individual, 5
entertainments, 21
equalitarianism, 5, 27
"Equitable Pioneers," 182
Established Church. *See* Church, Established
Established Church of Scotland, division of, 134
ether anesthesia, 286–89
etiquette, books of, 72, 76, 77
Etty, William, 256
Études sur l'Angleterre, by Faucher, 179
Evangelicals, 26
evangelism, societies for, 25
Everett, Edward, 135
Every Man in His Humour, 237
evolution, organic, 149, 188, 400
executions, public, 65, 387
  account by Dickens, 391
Exeter Hall, 25, *note;* 269
exports. *See* commerce

factories. *See* manufactures
Factories and the Factory System, by Taylor, 169
Factory Bill and Act, 128, 133
factory labor. *See* labor
Family Economist, 116
Family Herald, 113
"family" magazines, 113
famine, 286–316
  See also Ireland
Faraday, Michael, 26, 236, 287
farming labor, 171, 174; "bondage" system, 175; distress, 174, 239; illiteracy, 129; wages, 174
farming life, strenuous, 22
fashion magazines, 78
fashions, men's, 7, 80, 486
  women's, 285
Faucher, Leon, 179
Ferdinand I, Emperor of Austria-Hungary, 323

Festus, by Bailey, 211, 371
fiction. *See* books
Fielden, John, 290
finance, crisis of 1837, 58
  See also budgets
First Report of the Commission for Inquiry Into the Employment and Condition of Children in Manufactories, 91
Fitzgerald, Edward, 369
Flaubert, Gustave, 467–68
Fleet Prison, 95
flogging in the armed services, 5, 251
folkways. *See* customs
food, 286–316
  adulteration, 302
  menus, 296, 299, 300
  prices, 8
Food and Its Adulteration, 302
Footprints of the Creator, by Miller, 400
foreign affairs, 302
foreigners, attitude toward, 5
Forrest, Edwin, 212
  Astor Place riots in New York, 382–85
Forster, John, 74, 107, 171, 237
Fox, W. J., 107, 171
France, *coup d'état* of Louis Napoleon, 477
  defiance of England, 9
  King of. *See* Louis Philippe
  relations with, 302
Francis Joseph I, Emperor of Austria-Hungary, 323, 475
Franklin, Sir John, 213, 285, 314, 392, 479
Frederick William IV, King of Prussia, 53, 59, 322
Free Presbyterian Church, 135
free trade. *See* tariff
Free Trade Bazaar, 206–07
Frost, John, 10
Froude, Richard Hurrell, 31
funerals, 95, 168

gas lighting, 235, 285, 400
Gaskell, Mary, 26, 117, 118, 341
Gastronomic Regenerator, The, 298
Gatherings from Cemeteries, by Walker, 166
gentlemen, country. *See* aristocracy
Germ, The, 434
germ theory of disease, 356
Germany, Revolution of 1848, 322–23
Gladstone, William Ewart, 7, 19, 24, 31, 46, 61, 193, 200, 202, 312, 470
Gleeson murder case, 387
globe, model of, 429
gold discoveries. *See* Australia; California
gold withdrawal from the Bank of England, 313
Good, Daniel, murder case, 64–66
Goodrich, Samuel G. 379
Gore, Mrs., 54, 73, 249, 365

Gore House, 75, 393
Gothic architecture, 266
"Gothic" novels, 363
Gounod, Charles Francois, 471
government. *See* ministries
Graham, Sir James, 46, 100, 134, 154, 155, 183, 203
grain. *See* wheat
Granville, Lord, 478
Great Britain (steamship), 138, 231
Great Exhibition of 1851. *See* Crystal Palace
Great Liverpool (steamship), 251
Greece, Don Pacifico affair, 397–98
"Greek Slave" of Power, 261, 466–67
Gregory, Barnard, 6, 110
Greville, Charles, *Memoirs*, 53, 60, 76, 83–84, 154, 159, 317, 322, 331, 344, 386, 399, 471
Grey, Earl, 208, 243
Grisi, Carlotta, 152, 268, 270, 304, 422
Grote, George, 249
Grote, Mrs. George, 73
Guizot, M., 9, 302, 318, 320, 325
guncotton, invention of, 246
gutta-percha, 234, 409
Guy Fawkes Day, 440

Half-Hours With the Best Authors, 120
Hall, Mrs. S. C. 73, 121
Hall, Spencer, 145
Hamlet, 212
Hampden, Dr., and the Hampden Controversy, 311–12
Handel, 268
Handley Cross, by Surtees, 104
Handy Andy, by Lover, 97
Hardwick, Philip, 263
Harmony Hall, 181
Harold, by Bulwer Lytton, 341, 365
Hassall, Dr. Arthur Hill, 301–02
Hawthorne, Nathaniel, 472
Haydon, Benjamin Robert, career and suicide, 252–55
Haynau, Marshal, 441
health, public, 168, 316, 336
improvement in, 483–84
Heine, Heinrich, 21
Helena, Princess, birth of, 251
help, domestic. *See* domestics
Henry Esmond, by Thackeray, 362
Henson, William, 234
Heroes and Hero Worship, by Carlyle, 53
Herschel, Sir John, 36, *note;* 136, 236
Herschel, Sir William, 236
Hertford, Lord, 95
Hicks, Mrs. Ann, of Hyde Park, 446–47
Hill, David Octavius, 37
Hill, Rowland, 251
history, content of, *xiv*

making of, *xiv*
History of a Flirt, by Bury, 97
History of England from the Accession of James II, by Macaulay, 341–43, 362
History of Greece, by Grote, 249
History of Rome, by Arnold, 104
History of the Thirty Years' Peace, by Martineau, 73
Hogarth, 49
Hogg's Weekly Instructor, 116
Holloway's Pills and Ointments, 282
Home Missionary Society, 25, *note*
Honesty, 198
Hong Kong, 18, 100
Hood, Thomas, 50, 103, 147, 210, 239
Hook, Theodore, 6, 184
Horner, R. H., 211
Houdin, Robert, 335
hours of labor. *See* labor
Household Words, 117, 437
Houses of Parliament, 4, 146, 154, 213, 266, 437
housing, 161, 163, 213, 337, 473
"model cottages," 175
Howe, Elias, 247
Howitt, John, 117
Howitt, Mary, 73, 116, 117, 380
Howitt, William, 172, 174, 380
Howitt's Journal, 117, 380
Hudson, George, 189, 227, 244, 295
exposure and failure, 385–86
Hullah, John, 81, 269, 471
humanitarianism, 50, 90, 106
narrow, 25
See also philanthropy
humor, 22
Hunchback, The, 303
Hungary, 323, 324, 475
revolution, 106
hunger, curry powder for, 207
Hunt, Leigh, 107
Hunt, William Holman, 348, 382, 435, 436, *note*
Husbands and Wives, 121
Huxley, Thomas, 190, 251
hypocrisy, national, 5
Hyde Park, 446–47
hydropathy, 369
hypnotism. *See* mesmerism

Ideal of a Christian Church Considered, by Ward, 199
illiteracy, 128, 172, 361
Illustrated London News, 107, 108
illustrated newspapers. *See* newspapers
Imaginary Conversations, by Landor, 249
immigration of Irish, 161, *note*
immorality. *See* morality
imports. *See* commerce
In Memoriam, by Tennyson, 369, 399

income tax, 103, 204
indecency. *See* morality
India, 153, 247, 382
Indians, American, visit of, 152
individualism, 5
industrial depression. *See* business
Industrial Revolution, 214
industrialization, 169, 484
industry, 22
    See also manufactures
Infant Custody Bill, 74
infants. *See* children
influenza, 316, 318
information, search for, 119
Information for the People, 121
Ingoldsby Legends, by Barham, 113
Ingram, Herbert, 108
inns, 215, 219
instruction, popular, in magazines, 121
interest rate, 243
intoxication. *See* drunkenness
inventions, 16, 234, 246
Ireland, Battle of Widow McCormack's
    Cabbage Patch, 333
    Coercion Bill, 242, 292, 333
    debate on, in the Commons, 155
    education bill, 203
    emigration from, 292; to England, 161
        note
    famine, *xiv*, 52, 207, 239, 274, 291; and
        lawlessness, 241, 292
    liquor consumption, 13, *note*
    literacy, 129
    population, loss of, 13, *note*
    religion, problem of, 202
    religious disabilities, 155
    repeal of the Union, agitation for, 13,
        142, 274
    unrest, 327, 332
    violence in time of famine, 292
    visit by the Queen, 385
    voters, registration of, 34
    Young Ireland, 274
Irish, discrimination against, 16
Irish Sketch Book, by Thackeray, 104
Irvingites, 29
Italy, 323, 324
    unification, 214

Jack Hinton, by Lever, 104
Jackson, Charles Thomas, 288
James, G. P. R., 54, 249, 364–65
Jameson, Mrs., 73
Jane Eyre, by Brontë (Bell), 311, 365
Jeffrey, Francis, 399
Jermy murder case, 348–49
Jerròld, Douglas, 50, 107, 108, 171, 237, 314
Jews, barred from Parliament, 312
John Bull, 107
Journal of Design and Manufacture, 80,

note; 360
journalism. *See* newspapers
Jullien, Louis Antoine, 152, 270, 304, 341,
    385, 468

Kabul. *See* Afghanistan
Kalydor, 16
Kay-Shuttleworth, James, 155, 160
Kean, Charles, 420
Keble, 30, 200
Kemble, Adelaide, 47, 73, 97
Kemble, Mr. and Mrs. Charles, 47
Kemble, Fanny, 73, 210, 303, 342
Kent, Duchess of, 67
King of the Golden River, The, by Ruskin,
    442
Kingsley, Charles, 7, 24, 347, 438
Knight, Charles, 59, 118, 119, 163, 168, *note*
Knowles, 303
Koh-i-noor diamond, 437
Kossuth, Louis, 325, 475–77

labor, agricultural. *See* farming labor
    and religion, 25, 27
    artisan class, growth of, 332
    child, 155, 158; bill to reduce hours,
        133; inquiry into, 91; poem by E.
        Barrett, 147
    degradation of, 11
    demand for, 197
    disorders, 10, 82–84
    diseases, 157
    factory, 158
    gospel of work, Carlyle's, 22
    hours, 290
    laws, 91; proposed, 155
    living conditions, 160
    "navvies," 245
    railway, 245
    strikes, 82–84, 89
    sweatshop, 438–39
    Ten Hours Bill, 149, 155, 243, 290
    unemployment, 57, 58, 82, 102
    unions, 170, 332
    women's, 346; inquiry into, 91; sweated,
        147
Ladies' Cabinet, 78
Ladies' Own Journal and Miscellany, 117
Lady of Lyons, The, 47
laissez faire, 23, 85, 103
Lamartine, 320, 322, 332
Lamb, Lady Caroline, 342
Land We Live In, The, 120
Landor, Walter Savage, 74, 249
Landseer, Edwin, 146, *note;* 259
Last of the Barons, by Bulwer Lytton, 104
Latter-Day Pamphlets, by Carlyle, 386, 400
Latter-Day Saints. *See* Mormons
Lavengro, by Borrow, 363
Layard, Austen Henry, 381

Lays of Ancient Rome, by Macaulay, 96
Lear, Edward, 249
Ledru-Rollin, 320, 321, 325
Leigh, Lady Augusta, 471
Lemon, Mark, 50, 108, 237, 314
Lever, Charles, 54, 104, 149, 365
libel law, new, 110
Liberal-Conservatives, 45, *note*
Liberalism, 30
libraries, lending (public), 360, 375–77, 438
Library of Entertaining Knowledge, 118
life, daily, 8
Life of Jesus, by Strauss, 249
Life of John Sterling, by Carlyle, 472
Life of Shakespeare, by Knight, 119
lighting by gas, 235, 285, 400
lighting, stage, 60, *note*
likings of an Englishman, 482–83
Lind, Jenny, 268, 335, 437
    furor, 304–07
Lister, Joseph, 288
Liston, Dr. Robert, 288, 289
Liszt, Franz, 35, 268
literacy. *See* illiteracy
literature. *See* books; magazines
living conditions, 161
Livingstone, David, 7
Lloyd, Edward, 123–24
Lockhart, 190, 473
London, 395–442
    ballads and songs, 411
    bathing in, 405
    beggars, 410
    bridges, 407
    buildings, 146, 264, 403
    cemeteries, 166
    clubs, 406
    districts, 403; fashionable, 406
    entertainments, 417
    fire protection, 403
    fog, 191
    government, 402–03
    habits, 417
    hawkers, 410
    health, 402
    Lord Mayor's Day, 53
    markets, 409
    music halls, 425
    noise, 407
    parks, 403–05
    "patterers," 411
    pavements, 408
    peddlers, 410
    Polytechnic Institute, 428
    population, 56
    public houses, 409
    restaurants and taverns, 410
    sanitation, 166, 316, 337, 407
    scientific exhibitions, 432

London (*Cont.*)
    sewers, 338–39, 407
    shops, 408–09
    shows, street, 411
    sights, 170
    slaughterhouses, 316, 337
    slums, 163, 406
    Smithfield, 3
    spaces, open, 403–05
    "supper clubs," 45
    taverns and restaurants, 410
    theaters, 417–32
    Trafalgar Square, 4
    traffic, 407
    water supply, 338, 357
    Zoological Gardens, 428
London, by Knight, 119, 168, *note*
London Assurance, 47
London at Table, 300–02
London Journal, 122
London Labour and the London Poor, by
    Mayhew, 411, *note*
London Library, 47
Londonderry, Lord, 94
Long, Dr. Crawford W., 289
Louis I, King of Bavaria, 323
Louis Napoleon, 14, 251, 322
    coup d'état, 477–78
    election as President of France, 322
Louis Philippe, King, 186, 275, 302, 318–
    19, 324, 325
    abdication and flight to England, 320
    death, 399
Louise, Princess, birth of, 335
Lover, Samuel, 97
Lovett, William, 87, 88, 89
Luddites, 83
Ludlow, J. M., 346
Luria, by Browning, 249
Lyell, Charles, 188, 200

Macassar Oil, Rowland's, 16, 279
Macaulay, Thomas B., 7, 87, 96, 104, 158,
    202, 290, 313, 341–43, 362
Macbeth, 140, 212
Macdermots of Ballycloran, The, by Trol-
    lope, 309
machinery, use of, 160, 170
Mackay, Charles, 56, 101, 230, 270, 273, 341,
    411, *note;* 443
Maclise, 256
MacNaghton, Sir W., 17
Macready, 6, 47, 60, 74, 81, 98, 140, 212,
    237, 303, 368, 420
    Astor Place riots in New York, 382–85
    retirement, 424–46
magazines, 6, 106, 123–24, 198
    "family," 113
    fashion, 78
    influential, 112

magazines (*Cont.*)
  monthly, 111, 113
  weekly, 111; penny weeklies, 127
  women's, 117
Maginn, 113
"magnetism, animal." *See* mesmerism
Mahoney ("Father Prout"), 113
Maid of Honor, The, by Balfe, 268
Man in the Moon, 314
Manchester economic theory, 85
Manners, Lord John, 183
manners. *See* etiquette
Manning, Henry Edward, Cardinal, 200, 440
Manning murder case, 387–91
Manoeuvering Mother, The, by Bury, 97
manufactures, 16, 56, 59, 160
  bills, factory, 85
  labor, 90
Maritana, by Wallace, 68
marriage, view of, 72
marriage to deceased wife's sister, law on, 61
Marryat, Frederick, 54, 340
Marshalsea Prison, 95
Marston, J. W., 98
Martin Chuzzlewit, by Dickens, 104
Martineau, Harriet, 73, 144
Marx, Karl, 180, 314, 326–27, 402
Mary Barton, by Gaskell, 341
Mason, Monck, 233
Masson, David, 120, 407, 426
Mathew, Father Theobald, 12, 146
Matthews, Charles, 304
Maurice, John Frederick Denison, 346–47
Mayhew, Henry, 50, 125, 405
Maximilian II, King of Bavaria, 324
Maynooth College, bill for support, 202, 313
Mazzini, 154, 214–15, 324
M'Leod, Alexander, case of, 21
McNeile, Rev. Hugh, 440
Mechanics' Institutes, 133, 182, 373
medicines, 118
  patent. *See* nostrums
Mehemet Ali, 9
Melbourne, Lord, 34, 46, 47, 133, 237
  death, 342
  in divorce action, 74
Melville, Herman, 249, 365, 472
Memoirs by Greville. *See* Greville, Charles
Menai Straits Bridge, 402
Mendelssohn, 268
Meredith, George, 472
Mersey Bridge, 236
mesmerism, 143, 480
Messiah, by Mendelssohn, 268
Metternich, 323, 325
Mexican War, 247
middle class, 71, 72, 87, 89, 90, 120, 180, 332

  reading, 367–68, 371
Mill, John Stuart, 7, 31, 85, 87, *note;* 104, 341
Millais, John Everett, 261, 348, 382, 435, 436, *note*
Miller, Hugh, 400
Miller, Thomas, 125
mines, labor conditions in, 90, 92
ministry
  crisis of 1851, 471
  fall of Melbourne's, 46
  Peel's, 46, 208, 242
  Russell's, 243
  See also names of Ministers
minstrels, American, 252
Mirror, The, 116
Miser's Daughter, The, by Ainsworth, 97
missionaries and missionary societies, 25
  in China, 19
Mitchel, John, 274, 332, 333
Mitford, Miss, 172
Moby Dick, by Melville, 365, 472
"model cottages," 175
Modern Housewife, or Ménagère, 249
Modern Painters, by Ruskin, 249, 381
Molesworth, Sir William, 332
money, purchasing power, 8
Money, 47
Montez, Lola, 138, 323
Montgomery, Robert, 369
Moor Park, 126
"Moral Tales," 377
morality, 70, 111
  colonial and commercial, 19
  private and public, 5
Moreton, Lee. *See* Boucicault, Dion
Morison, James, and his pills, 282
Mormons, 29
Morning Chronicle, London, 107
Morning Post, London, 101
Morpeth, Lord, 332, 336
Morris, George P., 272
Morris, William, 32, 467
mortality rate, 163, 484
Morton, Dr., 287
Morton, J. M., 304
Moses & Son, 147, 277–79, 346
Mothers of England, by Ellis, 71
Mrs. Perkins's Ball, by Thackeray, 285
Mudie's Circulating Library, 360, 438
murders, Gleeson case, 387
  Good case, 64–66
  Jermy case, 348–40
  Manning case, 387–91
  Parkman case, 442
  Praslin case, 303
  Salt Hill case, 198
Murray, John, 146
"muscular Christianity," 347
music, 268, 304

music halls, 273
Mysteries of London, The, by Reynolds, 124–25

Nanking, treaty of, 18
Napier, Commodore, 34
Napier, Sir Charles, 209
Napoleon III. *See* Louis Napoleon
National Charter Association. *See* Chartism
National Gallery, 146, 255
natural selection, 189
Navigation Laws, suspension of, 291
"navvies," 245
navy, flogging in, 251
Nelson Column, 4, 146
Neptune, discovery of, 247
New Harmony, Indiana, 181
New Poor Law, 11, 87, 141
New Royal Exchange. *See* Royal Exchange
New Timon, by Bulwer Lytton, 249
New York, Astor Place riots, 382–85
"Newgate Calendar," 122
Newman, Cardinal, 7, 23, 30–33, *note;* 135, 265, *note;* 285, 361
    joins the Roman Catholic Church, 200
News of the World, 109
newspapers, 6, 7, 106
    advertising, 15–16, 277
    and periodicals, in the United States and in the United Kingdom, 20, *note*
    illustrated, 108
    minor, 109
Nicholson, "Baron" Renton, 6, 111, 427–28
night clubs, 171
Nineveh and Its Remains, 381
No-Popery agitation, 30
nobility. *See* aristocracy
Noncomformists. *See* Dissenters
Norfolk, Duke of, 207
Norma, 47, 98
Norton, Mrs. Caroline, 74, 342
nostrums, 16, 280–84
Notes of a Journey from Cornhill to Grand Cairo, by Thackeray, 249
Notes of a Tour in the Manufacturing Districts of Lancashire, by Taylor, 169
Notes on the United States of America, by Combe, 20
novels. *See* books

Oastler, Richard, 88, 155, 156
O'Brien, Bronterre, 88
O'Brien, Smith, 274, 332, 333
O'Connell, Daniel, 5, 12, 142, 143, 155, 171, 274, 344
    death, 307
O'Connor, Feargus, 10, 88, 90, 313, 328
Old Curiosity Shop, The, by Dickens, 368
Omoo, by Melville, 309

opera, in English, 268, 304
    Italian, 304, 410–20
Opium War. *See* China
Oregon boundary dispute, 209
    settlement, 249
Origin of Species, by Darwin, 189, 190, 400
Orion, by Horner, 211, *note*
Ottoman Empire; support of, 9
Owen, Robert, 23, 181
Owenite Socialism, 151
Oxford Movement, 30, 32, 33, 135, 199, 265, *note*
Oxford University, 135
    decline of, 200
    opposition to Oxford Movement, 33

"pacifiers." *See* children
Paganini, 8
painters and painting, 255–56
    See also Pre-Raphaelitism
Palmerston, Lord, *xiii,* 19, 30, 47, 100, 107, 243, 322, 325, 326, 397–98, 477
    Civis Romanus sum speech, 398
    dismissal, 478
panaceas, political, 184
panoramas, 430
pantomimes, Christmas, 8
Papal States, 323
Papers for the People, 121
Paris, riots in, 319–22
Parker, Nathaniel Willis, 405
Parkman murder case, 442
Parley, Peter, 115, 379
Parliament, meeting of, 13, 34, 46, 60, 103, 153
    proroguing of, 35, 312, 437
    reforms, proposed, 87
    "rotten boroughs," 331
    summoning of, 208
Parliament, Houses of. *See* Houses of Parliament
Parry, John Orlando, 270
Parris Life Pills, 282
parties, political. *See* politics; names of parties
Past and Present, by Carlyle, 84, 104, 183
patent medicines. *See* nostrums
Patrician's Daughter, The, by Marson, 98
pauperism. *See* poverty
Paxton, Joseph, 107, 432, 445, 449, 473
Peel, Sir Robert, 19, 35, 46, 50, 60, 61, 100, 103, 153, 155, 170, 204, 208, 209, 240, 243, 255, 292, 396
    death, 398
    downfall of ministry, 241
Peers and Parvenus, by Mrs. Gore, 249
Pendennis, by Thackeray, 143, 341, 367, 425
Penny Encyclopedia, 119
Penny Magazine, 118, 120, 121

penny postage, 46
People's Charter. *See* Chartism
Phèdre, 295
Phelps, Samuel, 420
philanthropy, 84, 86
philosophies, social and economic, 23, 25
photography, 35–36, 402, 464
phrenology, 145
Pictorial Times; The, 108
pills. *See* nostrums
Pippa Passes, by Browning, 53
Pius IX, 439
planning, town, 213
Playfair Papers, 21
plays. *See* theatre, the; *also* names of actors,
    actresses, authors, and theatres
pleasures, 21
"Plug Plot," 83
poet laureateship, 138, 369, 399
poetry, 368–73
Poland, 247
police courts, 14
political economy, 85
Political Economy, by Mill, 341
politics, 13, 34
    bribery in, 94–95
    crisis in, 238–85
    election, general, 45, 312
    panaceas, 184
    party distinctions, 242, *note*
    revolution of 1846, 244
    scrambling of parties, 159
    See also names of parties
Politics for the People, 347, 438
Polk, President James K., 186, 209
polka, the, 152
poor, the. *See* poverty
Poor Law of 1834, 84, *note*
Poor Law, New. *See* New Poor Law
Poor-Law Commission, 82
poor-law prisons, 84
poorhouses, 103
Pope, the. *See* Pius IX
population, 56, 480–81
Portland Vase, smashing of, 212
postage, penny, 46
postage reform, 251
potato famine in Ireland. *See* Ireland—
    famine
potatoes, crop failure, 207, 274
    disease, 207
poverty, 9, 12, 25, 58, 82–84
    attitude toward, 25
    decline in, 197
    Punch as advocate of reform, 50
    Wellington statement on, 50
Power, Hiram, 261, 465–67
Praslin, Duchess of, murder, 303
Pre-Raphaelitism, 261, 348, 382, 434, 472
Pre-Raphaelitism, by Ruskin, 437

Prelude, The, by Wordsworth, 399
Presbyterian Church, Free, 135
Prescott, William H., 309
President (steamship), loss of, 34, 231
Prest, Thomas Peckett, 363
prices, 8
    California, 357
    falling, 102
Prince of Wales, 102, 185–86
    birth of, 53
Princess, The, by Tennyson, 307, 341, 369
Princess Royal, 102
Principles of Geology, by Lyell, 188
prisons, 146
    debtors', 95
    poor-law, 84
privies, 161, 162, 163, 164
prizefighting, 199
    illegal, 111–12
progress, 233
proletariat, the, 180
prophecies of disaster, 62
prosperity, 174, 203–04, 481
prostitutes, 6, 60, 111
    at the theatre, 423
protection. *See* tariff
"Prout, Father," 113
Proverbial Philosophy, by Tupper, 371–73
Prussia, King of. *See* Frederick William IV
Public Health Act, 483
public houses, number of, 12
public-school education, 23
pugilism. *See* prizefighting
Pugin, A. W., 264, 266, 267
Punch, 143, *note*; 171, 243
    advocate of the poor, 50
    first issue, 49
Purgatory of Suicides, The, by Cooper, 88
Pusey and Puseyism, 7, 30, 31, 33, 135, 200

Queen, the. *See* Victoria
Queen's prisons, 95
Queenwood, 181

Rachel, 47, 252, 295, 320
Radetzky, General, 324
Radicalism, 183
Ragged School Union, 307
"Railway King." *See* Hudson, George
railways, 16, 47, 57, 154
    accidents, 217
    advantages of, 218
    advertising, 226
    Atmospheric, 23
    book sales at stations, 374–75
    cost of, 223
    denunciation of, 216
    extension, 150, 161, 192, 214, 222, 230, 244,
        245, 308, 352, 396, 487
    gauges, "battle" of, 245

railways (Cont.)
  guides, 220. See also Bradshaw
  journey on, 221
  labor, 245
  speculation in shares, 223, 244, 307
  speeds, 217
  Sunday trains, 285
  travel conditions, 193
reading. See books; magazines; newspapers
record, contemporary, xv
Reeves, Sims, 304
reform, 485
Reform Bill of 1832, 87
Reform Club, 296
reformers, 23, 158, 159
reforms, political, 87
Regency, the, 5
Reid, Mayne, 365
religion, 23
  and labor, 25, 27
  Dissenters, 24
  Hampden controversy, 311-12
  literature, 23
  romanticism in, 7
  tensions, 199
    See also names of churches, contro-
    versies, etc.
religiosity, 23
remedies for diseases, 118
Removal of Aliens Bill, 325
revenue, national, 442, 481
Revolution, Industrial, 214
Revolutions of 1848 in Europe, 25, 317-52
Reynolds, G. W. M., 124
Reynolds's Miscellany, 124
riots, labor, 82-84
Robertson, Tom, 422
Robins, George, 306
Rochdale, 182
Rogers, Samuel, 120-21
Roman Catholic Church, controversy over
    appointment of Wiseman, 439-40
  Ecclesiastical Titles Bill, 441
  movement toward, 30, 31
  No-Popery agitation, 30
romances, weekly parts, 122
Romanticism, 7, 486
Rookwood, by James, 364
Roose's telescope, 236
Rossetti, Christina, 434
Rossetti, Dante G., 348, 382, 434
Rossetti, William M., 348, 382, 434, 472
Rothschild, Baron Lionel, 312
Rowland & Son, 16
Rowland's Macassar Oil, 270
Royal Academy, 254, 382, 435, 436, note
Royal Exchange, 4, 59, 154, 186, 263
royalty. See Crown, the; personal names
    and titles
rubber, 234-35, 409, 464

Rural Life of England, by Howitt, 117, 172
Ruskin, John, 7, 23, 26, 27, 32, 105, 216, 249,
    266, 267, 347, 380, 381, 436, 437, 442
Russell, Henry, 270-71, 443
Russell, Lord John, 25, note; 50, 61, 155,
    158, 207, 251, 290, 322, 326, 398, 440,
    471, 477
  ministry, 243
Russia, Emperor of, visit of, 154
  rise of, 302-03
Rymer, James, 124
Rymer, Michael J., 363, 364-65

sabbatarianism, 24, 27, 95, 193-94, 284, 437
Sala, Augustus, 427
Sadler, Michael, 155
Salt Hill murder case, 198
"Sam Hill," ballad of, 426-47
sandwich men, 276
sanitation. See health, public
Sarawak, 295
Sartoris, Mrs. See Kemble, Adelaide
Satirist, The, 110
Savannah (steamship), 231
School for Scandal, The, 303
schools. See education
science, advances in, 236
    See also anesthesia, aviation, germ theory,
    inventions, etc.
Scinde, 153, 209
Scotland, distress in, 291
  royal visit to, 69
Scott, Gilbert, 266
Scott, Sir Walter, 473
sculpture, 261
Scottish Church. See Established Church
    of Scotland
sea bathing, 273-74, 437
sea serpent, 344-46
selection, natural, 189
Self-Help, by Smiles, 132
Senior, Nassau, 85, 158
sentimentalism, 367-68
  in books, 121
sermons, publication of, 23
Seven Lamps of Architecture, by Ruskin,
    266, 380, 381
sewers. See London
Shaftesbury, Earl of. See Ashley, Lord
Shaftesbury, Earl of (father of Lord Ash-
    ley), 176
sewing machines, 247
Shakespeare, William, 59, 314
Shelley, Mary Godwin, 471
Shelley, Percy Bysshe, 46
Sheridan, Richard Brinsley, 74
Sherwood, Mrs. 378
shipping trade, 16
shoe warmer, 16
shooting, 177, 179

Sibthorp, Colonel, *xiii*, 50, 202, 212, 216, 432, 447
Sikh War, first, 247
Silliman, Dr. Benjamin, 145
Simon, Sir John, 337, 392
Simpson, James Young, 289
singing halls, 171
slavery, 25
abolition of, and slavery in the United States, 19
Smiles, Samuel, 132
Smirke, Sir Robert, 263
Smith, Albert, 113, 314
Smith, Sydney, 104, *note;* 210
Smith, W. H., 374
Smithfield, 3
snobbishness, 78, 180
Snobs of England, by Thackeray, 78, 309
social and economic philosophies, 23
social betterment. *See* progress; reform
socialism, 180–81
Socialism, Christian, 23, 336–47
Socialism, Owenite, 181
Societies for the Diffusion of Useful Knowledge, 23, 118, 119, 133
Society for the Propagation of the Gospel in Foreign Parts, 11
Somerville, Alexander, 181
"Song of the Labourer," by Hood, 239
"Song of the Shirt," by Hood, 147, 210
songs, popular, 89, 270, 272–73
"Songs for the People," 89
Southcott, Johanna, 29, 127
Southey, Robert, 138
Soyer, Alexis, 34, 296, 299, 302, *note;* 397, 434, 468
Spain, 326
species, development of, 189
Spectator, The, 107
speculation, 193
See also railways
Spencer, Herbert, 145
Spirit of the Age, by Horne, 211
sports, 21
newspaper; *Bell's Life in London,* 109
stage, the. *See* theatre, the
Stanley, Lord, 46, 208, 471
Stanley, Arthur P., 149, 347
statuary. *See* sculpture
steamships, 231
fares, 293
Step-Mother, The, by James, 249
Stephens, Frederic George, 348
Stephens, Rev. J. R., 88, 89
Stephenson, George, 219, 340
Sterling, John, 32
Stones of Venice, by Ruskin, 266
Strauss (author), 249
Strauss, Johann, 268
Strickland, Agnes, 73

strikes. *See* labor
String of Pearls, The, by Prest, 363–64
Stringfellow, John, 234
Stuart, Lord Dudley, 332
Sturge, Joseph, 88
styles. *See* fashions
suffrage, universal, 87, 88, 331
Summerly, Felix (Henry Cole), 380, 444
Sunday in London, by Cruikshank, 28
Sunday observance. *See* sabbatarianism
Sunday School Union, 25, *note*
Sunday schools, 131
Sunday Times, 109
supper halls, 171
surgery with anesthesia, 286–89
Surtees, 104
Swain, Charles, 369
Sybil, or The Two Nations, by Disraeli, 211
Syria, 9
System of Logic, by Mill, 104

Taglioni, 268, 304, 422
Talbot, Henry Fox, 36, 464
Tancred, or The New Crusade, by Disraeli, 309
tariff, 204, 208, 396
debate on, 35
free trade, 61
protective, on corn, 46
reduction, proposed, 6, 239
taste, public, 6, 22
See also Crystal Palace
tax, income. *See* income tax
tax, window. *See* window tax
Taylor, Tom, 422
Taylor, W. Cooke, 169, 171
Taylor, President Zachary, 327
tea and coffee, 302, *note*
telegraph, electric, 47, 194, 230, 245
telephone, early, 235
telescope, Rosse's, 26
temperance cause, 12
Ten Hours Bill. *See* labor
Ten Thousand a Year, by Warren, 54–56
Tennyson, Alfred, 7, 70, 97, 188, 250, 307, 341, 368–69, 425, 442, 486
poet laureate, 399–400
Testaments. *See* Bibles
Thackeray, William M., 6, 7, 23, 50, 54, 74, 78, 95, 104, 108, 143, 152, 180, 211, 249, 259, 285, 302, 308, 341, 362, 366, 425, 468, 472
Thames Tunnel, 95, 138
theatre, the, 8, 21, 47, 97, 140, 303
actresses, 73
lighting, 60, *note*
patent, 420
prices, 424
provincial, 422–23
See also names of actors, actresses,

theatre (*Cont.*)
    plays, and theatres
Thiers, 9
Thomson, Christopher, 129, *note;* 132, *note*
Times, London, 106
    nostrum advertising in, 284–85
Tite, Sir William, 263
toll roads; revolt in Wales, 140
Tom Burke of Ours, by Lever, 149
Tom Thumb, General, 149, 150, 252
Tories. *See* Conservatives
Tower, the, fire in, 52
Town, The, 111, 428
town planning, 213
Tract 90, by Newman, 23, 29, 32, 33, 361
Tractarianism, 23, 29, 32, 135, 199, 440
tracts, output of, 23, 25
Tracts for the Times, 32, 33, 347
trade. *See* commerce
Travels in North America, by Lyell, 200
Trollope, Anthony, 309, 365
Trollope, Frances, 20, 309, 365
tunnel, Thames, 95
Tupper, Martin, *xiii,* 369, 469
Turks. *See* Ottoman Empire
Turner, J. M. W., 104–05, 152, 260, 480
Tussaud's waxworks, 8, 101, 387
Tyler, President John, 230
Typee, by Melville, 249
typhus, 166, 294, 337

unemployed. *See* labor
Union with Ireland, repeal movement.
    See Ireland
unions, labor. *See* labor
United Irishmen, 332
United States, as seen by Dickens, 81
    books on, 20, 21, 81, 200
    boundary, northeast, dispute over, 21;
        settlement of, 100
    boundary, northwest. *See* Oregon
    criticism of, by Dickens, and others, 104
    exhibits in the Crystal Palace, 463
    immigration to, 292
    Playfair Papers on, 21
    relations with, 19–20
    tension over arrest of British subject, 8
universities, criticism of, 200
Utilitariansim, 85
Utopianism, 23, 32, 181

Vanity Fair, by Thackeray, 308, 341, 366
vans, advertising, 276
Varney the Vampire, or The Feast of Blood, by Rymer, 364–65
Vaughan, Robert, 169
Vauxhall Gardens, 48, 312–13, 428
Vestiges of the Natural History of Creation, by Chambers, 187, 189, 309, 400

criticism of, 190
Vestris, Mme., 8, 47, 97, 304
Victor Emmanuel II, 324
Victoria, Queen, 5, 7, 29, 46, 47, 151, 154, 185, 241, 295, 326, 470
    adulation of, in her later life, 68
    and Melbourne, 342
    and Palmerston, 477
    assassination attempts, 67–68
    at deer shooting, 199
    at the Crystal Palace, 461
    birth of the Prince of Wales, 53
    cheese for, 9
    free trader, 205
    railway journey, first, 217
    visit to France, 146; to Ireland, 385; to Scotland, 69
Victorianism, 5, 23, 486
Vizetelly, Henry, 108
voting. *See* suffrage

Wales, Prince of. *See* Prince of Wales
Wales, revolt in, over toll roads, 140
Walker, G. A., 166
Wallace (composer), 268
Walpole, Horace, sale of Strawberry Hill, 63
Walter, John, 307
Walter, John, III, 106
waltz, denunciation of, 77
Ward, W. G., 31, 199
Ward, Dr. W. Squire, 144
Warren, Samuel, 54–56, 466
wars, little, 17
water closets, 161, 162, 163, 164
water cure, 369
Waterloo Dinner, 140
Way of the World, The, by Congreve, 99
weather, 9, 52, 102, 273, 285
Webster, Professor John W., 442
Weekly Dispatch, 108
weekly magazines, 111
weekly papers, 108
Wellington, Duke of, 4, 18, 46, 52, 53, 74, 140, 154 170, 204, *note;* 240, 251, 318, 328, 447
    on labor, 85, 94
    on the ballot, 87, *note*
    on the poor, 50
    statue, 154, 261
Wells, Horace, 288
Westmacott, R. A., 6, 263
Westminster Abbey, 265
wheat, prices of, 10, 52, 95, 197, 285, 290, 312, 352, 396
    tariff on, 46
Wheatstone, 246
Whigs, 183
whiskers, 80
White Ribbon Movement, 12

Wilberforce, William, 25
Wilkie, Sir David, 35
Williams, Zepahaniah, 10
window tax, 204, *note*, 471
Windsor Castle, by Ainsworth, 104
Wiseman, Nicholas, Cardinal, 439–40, 470–71
Wives of England, by Ellis, 71
woman culprit, defiance by, 14
women, as seen by an American woman, 178
  dress materials, 80
  fashions, 285
  husbands and wives, 70
  labor. *See* labor
  magazines for, 117
  place of, 69
  subjection of, 70, 73
  writers, 73

Women of England, by Ellis, 71
Woolner, Thomas, 348
Wordsworth, William, 108, *note;* 138, 193, 216, 313–14, 368, 369
  death, 399
work. *See* labor
workhouses, 11, 84
Workingmen's Friend and Family Instructor, 116
world, end of, prediction, 14
World of Fashion, 78
writing. *See* books; magazines; newspapers
Wuthering Heights, by Brontë, 311
Wyld, and his model of the globe, 429

yacht race, America's Cup, 464–65
Yeast, by Kingsley, 347
Young, Brigham, 29
Young England, 150, 183, 212